REVOLUTIONARY MOVEMENTS IN WORLD HISTORY

FROM 1750 TO THE PRESENT

REVOLUTIONARY MOVEMENTS IN WORLD HISTORY

FROM 1750 TO THE PRESENT

VOLUME 2: H–P

JAMES V. DEFRONZO

EDITOR

A B C ⬤ C L I O

Santa Barbara, California • Denver, Colorado • Oxford, United Kingdom

Library of Congress Cataloging-in-Publication Data
Revolutionary movements in world history : from 1750 to present / James V. DeFronzo, editor.
    p.   cm.
    Includes bibliographical references and index.
    ISBN 1-85109-793-7 (alk. paper) — ISBN 1-85109-798-8 (ebook)   1. History, Modern.
2. Revolutions.   I. DeFronzo, James.

D295.R49 2006
303.6'4—dc22

2006009532

10   09   08   07   06   05 / 10   9   8   7   6   5   4   3   2   1

Media Editor: Ellen Rasmussen
Media Resources Manager: Caroline Price
Production Editor: Vicki Moran
Editorial Assistant: Alisha Martinez
Production Manager: Don Schmidt
Manufacturing Coordinator: George Smyser

This book is also available on the World Wide Web as an ebook.
Visit abc-clio.com for details.

ABC-CLIO, Inc.
130 Cremona Drive, P.O. Box 1911
Santa Barbara, California 93116–1911

This book is printed on acid-free paper ∞ .
Manufactured in the United States of America

Contents

Entries

VOLUME 3: R–Z

Maps

Contributors

Advisor
Cyrus Ernesto Zirakzadeh
University of Connecticut
Storrs, CT

Contributors
Howard Adelman
Griffith University
Brisbane, Queensland
Australia

David E. Adleman
University of Idaho
Moscow, ID

Ali Abdullatif Ahmida
University of New England
Biddeford, ME

Ayad Al-Qazzaz
California State University
Sacramento, CA

Craig Baxter
Juniata College
Huntingdon, PA

Marc Becker
Truman State University
Kirksville, MO

Angie Beeman
University of Connecticut
Storrs, CT

Leigh Binford
Benemérita Universidad
   Autónoma de Puebla
Puebla
Mexico

P. Richard Bohr
College of Saint Benedict and Saint
   John's University
St. Joseph, MN

Hamit Bozarslan
Ecole des Hautes Etudes en
   Sciences Sociales
Paris
France

Roger Brown
Saitama University
Saitama City, Saitama Prefecture
Japan

Malcolm Byrne
National Security Archive
Washington, DC

Henry F. Carey
Georgia State University
Atlanta, GA

Clayborne Carson
Stanford University
Stanford, CA

Francesco Cavatorta
Dublin City University
Dublin
Ireland

David Chandler
Monash University
Melbourne
Australia

James G. Chastain
Ohio University
Athens, OH

Albert K. Cohen
University of Connecticut
Storrs, CT

James DeFronzo
University of Connecticut
Storrs, CT

Judith Ewell
College of William and Mary
Williamsburg, VA

John Foran
University of California, Santa
   Barbara
Santa Barbara, CA

Will Fowler
University of St. Andrews
St. Andrews
United Kingdom

Andrew S. Fullerton
University of Connecticut
Storrs, CT

Venelin I. Ganev
Miami University of Ohio
Oxford, OH

John D. Garrigus
University of Texas at Arlington
Arlington, TX

Gordon Gauchat
University of Connecticut
Storrs, CT

Paul A. Gilje
University of Oklahoma
Norman, OK

Jungyun Gill
University of Connecticut
Storrs, CT

Roger S. Gocking
Mercy College
Dobbs Ferry, NY

Anthony Gorman
University of London
London
United Kingdom

Alexander Groth
University of California, Davis
Davis, CA

Josef Gugler
University of Connecticut
Storrs, CT

Geoffrey C. Gunn
Nagasaki University
Nagasaki
Japan

Ahmed H. Ibrahim
Missouri State University
Springfield, MO

George Joffe
Cambridge University
Cambridge
United Kingdom

Sanjay Joshi
Northern Arizona University
Flagstaff, AZ

Colin H. Kahl
University of Minnesota
Minneapolis, MN

Stathis N. Kalyvas
Yale University
New Haven, CT

Eran Kaplan
University of Cincinnati
Cincinnati, OH

Mark N. Katz
George Mason University
Fairfax, VA

Damien Kingsbury
Deakin University
Geelong
Australia

Mikolaj Stanislaw Kunicki
Institute for Human Sciences
Vienna
Austria

George Lawson
University of London
London
United Kingdom

J. J. Lee
New York University
New York, NY

Namhee Lee
University of California, Los
    Angeles
Los Angeles, CA

Deanna Lee Levanti
Braintree, MA

Anatol Lieven
New America Foundation
Washington, DC

Richard A. Lobban, Jr.
Rhode Island College
Providence, RI

Jean-Michel Mabeko-Tali
Howard University
Washington, DC

Theresa M. Mackey
Virginia Community College
Annandale, VA

James I. Matray
California State University, Chico
Chico, CA

Brian C. Melton
Liberty University
Lynchburg, VA

Valentine M. Moghadam
UNESCO
Paris
France

Evan Braden Montgomery
University of Virginia
Charlottesville, VA

Michael Mulcahy
University of Connecticut
Stamford, CT

Carlo Nasi
Universidad de los Andes
Bogota
Colombia

Malyn Newitt
King's College London
London
United Kingdom

Michael R. Nusbaumer
Indiana University-Purdue
    University at Fort Wayne
Fort Wayne, IN

Borden Painter
Trinity College
Hartford, CT

Stacie Pettyjohn
University of Virginia
Charlottesville, VA

Roger Price
University of Wales
Aberystwyth
Wales

Jennie Purnell
Boston College
Chestnut Hill, MA

Nathan Gilbert Quimpo
University of Amsterdam
Amsterdam
Netherlands

Kumar Ramakrishna
Nanyang Technological University
Singapore

Mike Rapport
University of Stirling
Stirling
Scotland

James F. Rinehart
Troy University
Troy, AL

Paul A. Rodell
Georgia Southern University
Statesboro, GA

Donald Rothchild
University of California, Davis
Davis, CA

Steven C. Rubert
Oregon State University
Corvallis, OR

Peter Rutland
Wesleyan University
Middletown, CT

L. Sabaratnam
Davidson College
Davidson, NC

Roland Sarti
University of Massachusetts
Amherst, MA

Paul Khalil Saucier
Northeastern University
Boston, MA

Eric Selbin
Southwestern University
Georgetown, TX

Deric M. Shannon
University of Connecticut
Storrs, CT

Julie Shayne
Emory University
Atlanta, GA

Priscilla M. Shilaro
West Virginia University
Morgantown, WV

James Sidbury
University of Texas at Austin
Austin, TX

Paul E. Sigmund
Princeton University
Princeton, NJ

Richard Stahler-Sholk
Eastern Michigan University
Ypsilanti, MI

Lynn Stephen
University of Oregon
Eugene, OR

Jill Stephenson
University of Edinburgh
Edinburgh
Scotland

Stephen M. Streeter
McMaster University
Hamilton, Ontario
Canada

Martin Stuart-Fox
The University of Queensland
Brisbane
Australia

Gebru Tareke
Hobart and William Smith
    Colleges
Geneva, NY

Arlene B. Tickner
Universidad de los Andes and
    Universidad Nacional
Bogotá
Colombia

Thomas Turner
Formerly of the National
    University of Rwanda
Dubuque, IA

Frédéric Volpi
University of St. Andrews
St. Andrews
Scotland

Veljko Vujačić
Oberlin College
Oberlin, OH

Samuel Watson
United States Military Academy
West Point, NY

Kathleen Weekley
University of Wollongong
Wollongong
Australia

Timothy P. Wickham-Crowley
Georgetown University
Washington, DC

Teresa Wright
California State University, Long
    Beach
Long Beach, CA

Cyrus Ernesto Zirakzadeh
University of Connecticut
Storrs, CT

Preface

Revolutionary movements, conflicts, successful revolutions, the transformations they attempt to bring about, and the support or opposition they provoke are all fascinating topics for a wide range of academic fields, including anthropology, economics, history, political science, psychology, and sociology, as well as for people in general. My interest in revolutions stems from several experiences including the U.S. Civil Rights movements and the conflict over U.S. involvement in Vietnam. As undergraduates, Roger Gocking, author of the entry on the Ghana's Independence Revolution, and I founded the Youth Interracial Council at Fairfield University whose participants from several colleges, such as Manhattanville College, and highschools, such as Convent of the Sacred Heart in Noroton, CT, helped run community centers and tutoring programs, discussion panels, and fund raising musical performances in Connecticut and New York. Some of us also participated in in the university's Upward Bound Program for local highschool students (I taught an English grammar and literature course). Roger and I, along with approximately fifty other students, organized what was apparently the first anti-Vietnam War demonstration at the university and participated in the great 1967 New York City anti-war demonstration led by the Reverend Martin Luther King Junior. When we graduated, my younger brother Donald, later mayor of New Britain, CT, and currently state senator and sponsor in 2005 of the state's first public campaign financing election law, carried on in the Youth Interracial Council. Work in the Youth Interracial Council resulted in the award of the university's Saint Ignatius Loyal Medal. Roger headed to Stanford University and eventually became a college professor and expert on West African history. I enrolled at Indiana University. For three years I taught as a lecturer in Sociology at Indiana University's branch campus in Fort Wayne (Indiana University-Purdue University at Fort Wayne), participating in local social movement activity and writing for the city's activist newspaper, the *Fort Wayne Free Press*. As a graduate student at Indiana University, a course on social conflict by Professor Austin T. Turk provided an opportunity for me to write a very long paper on revolution, guerilla warfare, and related topics, which was later published in a book, *Focus on Sociology* (Dubuque, IA: Kendall/Hunt), edited by professors Arnold O. Olson and Sushil K. Usman. Research for this paper and a short volunteer course on revolution which I taught one semester at IU in Fort Wayne, and later study, including work for the political crime section of my criminology course, resulted in the creation of the other large course, which with criminology, I taught every semester at the University of Connecticut for more than twenty years, Revolutionary Social Movements Around the World. This led to my writing a textbook for the course and similar courses, Revolutions and Revolutionary Movements (1991, 1996, 2007 forthcoming, Boulder CO: Westview). Most likely this book led to Mr. Simon Mason of ABC-CLIO asking me to prepare a proposal and to serve as general editor for this project, *Revolutionary Movemens in World History: From 1750 to the Present*. After more than a year of discussing the project with Simon and developing the proposal, the project began at the beginning of 2004. I have been tremendously impressed at the depth of knowledge of our contributors and working on this project was always extremely interesting and educative.

STRUCTURE OF THE ENCYCLOPEDIA

The encyclopedia includes two major types of entries, which appear in alphabetical order: revolution entries and theme or concept entries. The revolution entries—on revolutions and social movements—range in length from about 4,000 to 15,000 words and are divided into six main sections: Chronology; Background; Context and Process of Revolution; Impacts; People and Organizations; and References and

Further Readings. The theme or concept entries deal with topics related to revolution, such as colonialism and neo-colonialism, human rights and revolution, ideology and propaganda,, student movements and revolutions, war and revolution, women and revolution, terrorism, and theories of revolution. These entries generally range in length from about 3,000 to 4,500 words. Two longer theme entries deal respectively with documentaries on revolutions and revolution as the subjects of feature films.

ACKNOWLEDGMENTS

Above all, I am extremely grateful to our authors for the exceptional quality of the entries they wrote.

But many people in addition to the authors contributed directly or indirectly to the production of this encyclopedia. At ABC-CLIO I would particularly like to thank Simon Mason who invited me to develop the proposal for this project and who contributed valuable guidance, information, suggestions, and ideas for the project. Simon's colleagues at ABC-CLIO who also played important roles include, in alphabetical order, Ron Boehm, Valerie Boyajian, Craig Hunt, Alex Mikaberidze, Vicki Moran, Ellen Rasmussen, Wendy Roseth, Vicky Speck, Art Stickney, and Peter Westwick. Others at ABC-CLIO also contributed significantly and deserve appreciation. I would particularly like to thank Wendy, who was my direct contact and project editor for much of time.

Professor Cyrus E. Zirakzadeh of the University of Connecticut's Political Science Department, author of the entry on "The Spanish Revolution and Counter-Revolution," served as my advisor for this project and provided very important guidance and suggestions.

Jack Goldstone of George Mason University, who had edited the earlier *Encyclopedia of Political Revolutions* (Congressional Quarterly) and published a number of important works on revolution, and with whom I worked as an academic consultant on a documentary series on revolutions, provided valuable advice and suggestions from his own experience as an editor. Both Jack and Douglas Goldenberg-Hart of Congressional Quarterly also consented to allow several authors who had written for the earlier encyclopedia to write entries for this project.

My friend and former teaching assistant Jungyun Gill, author of the entry on "Student and Youth Movements, Activism and Revolution," provided valuable assistance, including important insights on Korean history and society, which helped me in the editing of the Korea entries. There are many UCONN students and faculty members to whom I would like to express thanks, in part for encouraging the creation of my revolutions' course, such as then Sociology Department Head Mark Abrahamson, and my book on revolutions that preceded this encyclopedia. In particular, my good friend Professor Al Cohen, the brilliant and well-known criminologist and author of the entry on "Terrorism" for this encyclopedia, provided much encouragement and many useful suggestions in the course of many conversations.

Many family members and other friends also provided important encouragement and assistance. I particularly would like to thank my brother and sister-in-law, Don and Diane DeFronzo, and their children, David and Karen, and my sister, Margaret Pastore, her friend David Timm, and her son, Michael. Thanks also to my parents, Armand and Mary Pavano DeFronzo, my uncle and aunt, Francis and Lenneye DiFronzo, my uncle and aunt, Alexander and Angie Pavano DiFronzo, my aunt Doris Pavano Pitts, and my cousin, Connie Manafort, and all my other cousins for their encouragement. Deanna Levanti (Americorps and graduate of UMASS), who researched and wrote the valuable entry on "Documentaries and Revolution," which lists hundreds of documentaries and the sources from which these may be obtained, provided much encouragement, as did her mother and stepfather, Sue and Tom Ryan, her brothers, Mathew and Evan, and her father, Charles Levanti.

Others who provided important encouragement were my wonderful and long-time friends Professor Jane Prochow, Massey University, New Zealand; and John McVarish of Hull, Massachusetts. John's daughter, Heather, was, to the best of my knowledge, first college student (James Madison University) to read one of the entries for the encyclopedia, the entry on the Iranian Revolution, which was used as a model for all revolution entries. Heather's reaction to it was very positive, enthusiastic, and encouraging. Professor Lance Hannon of Occidental College and Villanova University, another good friend, former teaching assistant, and coauthor on other projects, also provided valuable encouragement as well as suggestions for authors.

I would also like to thank my good friend, Professor Roger Gocking, Mercy College, author, as noted earlier, of the entry on "Ghana's Independence Revolution," for his valuable encouragement and assistance. Other good friends provided encouragement for this project. Thanks to Wendy Kimsey, my former teaching assistant, and her husband, David Fowler, their daughters, Zoe and Hannah, and Steve Merlino, also my former teaching assistant, and his wife, Kathy Mangiafico. Thanks also to Professor Walter Ellis and his wife Becky Ellis of Hillsboro College, Ted Rhodes and Joni Pascal and their children, Jesse and Rachel, and Sue Cook Ringle and Ken Ringle and their sons Dylan and Carter, and John Pearlman, and George Relue, a great friend and the cofounder, along with Ted Rhodes, and editor of the *Fort Wayne Free Press*.

I would also like to express gratitude to Professor William Doyle of the University of Bristol, Professor Josef Gugler of the University of Connecticut, author of the entry on "The Cinema of Revolution," Professor George Lawson of the London School of Economics, author of the entries on "Reform, Rebellion, Civil War, Coup D'état, and Revolution" and "Trends in Revolution," and Professor Roland Sarti of the University of Massachusetts, author of the entry on the "Italian Risorgimento," for their valuable suggestions of several authors.

Introduction

A *social movement* is a collective effort by a relatively large number of people to bring about, resist, or reverse social change. A *revolutionary movement* is a type of social movement whose leaders advocate structural change, the replacement of one or more major social institutions, such as a society's political system or its economic system. Social movements with goals not including structural change are generally called *reform movements* rather than revolutionary movements. *Revolution* is the term for a revolutionary movement that succeeds and accomplishes structural change.

Students of revolution disagree on whether other characteristics should be included in the definition. Some insist that a true revolution must involve participation by the large mass of a society's population. Others assert that only structural change brought about by violence qualifies as revolution. Still others argue that although violence is not a necessary element, only social transformations through illegal means should be labeled revolutions.

The editor of this encyclopedia does not agree with narrowing the conception of revolution by including any of these restrictions. The preference here is for a definition of revolutionary movement based solely on advocacy of institutional change and for revolution as the achievement of institutional change.

The revolutions and revolutionary movements covered in this project include many that were characterized by large-scale popular participation, illegal rebellion against existing governments, and violence, such as the Russian Revolution of 1917 and the Chinese and Vietnamese revolutions, and others that lacked one or more of these aspects. The political revolutions in Eastern Europe in 1989 and later in the Soviet Union, for example, were largely non-violent. And democratic elections brought leftist coalitions, supported in part by movements advocating structural economic change to power legally in Spain in 1936 and Chile in 1970. The resulting governments were crushed by right-wing counter-revo-

lutions spearheaded by the military and permitted or even aided by foreign powers. Efforts of people to structurally change their societies through legal democratic means merit the term *revolutionary*. In fact, it could be argued that the reason for the historic link between past revolutions and violence was precisely that democratic means to accomplish institutional change did not exist in many societies until recently.

WHAT MAKES REVOLUTION POSSIBLE?

Historically revolutionary movements were likely to occur and succeed when five factors were present simultaneously. One key element was the development of a high level of discontent with the existing political or economic systems among a large sector of a society's population. This popular or mass discontent has typically been the result of one of three processes: (1) A decline in living standards due to rapid population growth, economic problems or policies, war, or other factors; (2) a change in the moral acceptability of existing living standards in that people come to believe that their lives could and should be better (such a change in viewpoint can result from messages communicated by recognized moral authorities, such as religious leaders, or contact with people from other societies); (3) a period of general improvement in living standards followed by a significant decline (the period of improvement raises people's expectations for future improvements, which are frustrated by the later deterioration of economic conditions).

In order for the discontent to lead to a revolutionary movement, people must come to believe that their troubles are due not only to the current government leaders, but also to one or more of their society's social institutions. Directing blame in this way is often the result of the efforts of leaders of revolutionary movements and the ideologies they put forth. In the past, revolutionary leadership has often developed from a division within the so-called elite sector of a society. Elites are people with culturally defined characteristics qualifying them for leadership positions in society in general. In many societies these include at minimum high levels of intelligence, education, and talent. Elite members of society can become alienated from existing institutions for a number of reasons. Occasionally young people with elite traits become morally outraged at aspects of the social system or repressive government policies. Others may turn against the pre-revolutionary regime because they feel themselves to be the targets of discrimination or barred from opportunities due to the nature of the political, social, or economic systems.

Whatever the reason, the existence of a division within the elite sector, the second factor in successful revolutionary movements, simultaneous with mass discontent creates the possibility that dissident elite persons may provide leadership and organization for the members of the discontented mass of the population, along with an ideology to motivate, mobilize, and guide them. Such an ideology typically includes a systematic criticism of the existing regime and its policies, an explanation of the need for the revolutionary movement, a plan for overthrowing the governing group, and proposals for revolutionary changes to society. In order for a revolution to succeed, the revolutionary ideology should be characterized by a concept that provides a basis for unifying different groups and social classes in a revolutionary alliance to oust the existing regime.

The unifying motive constitutes a third important factor in successful revolutionary movements. A unifying theme may be hatred for a particular ruler, but nationalism in some form has usually served most effectively as a motive unifying different population groups against either colonial regimes or indigenous rulers or governments perceived as serving foreign interests.

A fourth essential element for the success of a revolutionary movement is the deterioration of the legitimacy and coercive capacity of the state. This may be due to devastating defeat in war blamed on the existing government, as was the case in the Russian Revolution of 1917, a state financial crisis such as that which contributed to the occurrence of the French Revolution in 1789, or loss of faith in a personalized dictatorship such as characterized the Cuban Revolution against the Batista regime in the 1950s. In such situations the pre-revolutionary government lacks the capacity to suppress revolutionary movements.

The fifth crucial factor is whether or not other nations intervene to help suppress a revolutionary movement. If the world is permissive toward a revolutionary movement in a particular society, in that other nations are unwilling or unable to assist an existing government in the repression of rev-

olutionaries, then the revolutionary movement has a chance of success.

Some students of revolution have stressed the importance of one of these factors, for example the breakdown of state authority, over the others. The orientation here is that a successful revolution almost always has involved the simultaneous presence of all five factors: mass discontent; a division among elites with some becoming revolutionary leaders; the development, propagation, and widespread acceptance of an ideology that in the process of defining the problems of the old regime and calling for its overthrow is able to unify different social groups and classes in support of the revolutionary effort; the deterioration of the coercive capacity of the state; and a world context at least temporarily permissive towards the revolutionary movement.

TRENDS IN REVOLUTION

Social conflict over political systems may be as old as civilization. The ancient Greeks experienced forms of democracy, oligarchy, and dictatorship. The Romans at one time abolished monarchy to create a republic. Senators opposed to the establishment of a dictatorship under Caesar killed him and lost a civil war and their own lives in an attempt to preserve the republic. At some point conflict among social elites for control of government came to resemble little more than a circulation of leadership personnel, and Europeans began referring to the revolving of competing elites in and out of control of government as "revolution." But gradually, with the coming of the philosophical concepts of the Enlightenment and the growing belief in the ability of humanity to control nature and alter society, revolution came to mean changing the system of government or other institutions, including the form of a society's economic system.

The American Revolution shifted the type of government in the former colonies from monarchy to republic and attempted to guarantee a wide range of freedoms and rights to citizens, although limited initially to white males. The French Revolution not only changed the form of government, at least temporarily, and abolished privileges of certain groups, such as the aristocracy and the clergy, it also involved proponents of sweeping economic transformations whose aspirations were largely frustrated, although their ideas and efforts inspired later generations of revolutionaries. The French Revolution's "rights of man and the citizen" concepts constituted a type of transnational revolutionary ideology threatening monarchal regimes throughout Europe. The monarchies reacted by forming a grand international counter-revolutionary military coalition to defeat Napoleon and crush the French Revolution. This international anti-revolutionary alliance functioned to some degree in the 1820s, 1830s, and

1840s to repress new multinational revolutionary efforts motivated both by ideals of the French Revolution and aspirations for national liberation.

Marx's historical materialist concept of socialism appealed to a wide range of intellectuals attracted by an ideology that not only supported the creation of what appeared to be a morally superior form of society, but also offered an apparently scientific analysis which seemed to demonstrate that socialism, and eventually communist utopia, were not only achievable but inevitable. The success of the Marxist Russian revolutionaries in seemingly bringing about the first social revolution in which workers and peasants actually seized state power and control of the economy, and destroyed the old ruling class, inspired revolutionaries in many other countries. But the Communists' establishment of one party rule sowed the seeds of Stalin's brutal dictatorship and, ultimately, contributed to discrediting their revolutionary model.

Lenin's theories of revolution and imperialism long held wide appeal for revolutionaries in many developing countries seeking to free themselves from colonial rule. Communist movements in China and Vietnam effectively became the vehicles of their people's national liberation, greatly contributing to their staying power long after the fall of Communist governments in Eastern Europe and the U.S.S.R. Although Marxism-Leninism became a major transnational revolutionary ideology for decades after the Russian Revolution, it eventually lost ground to non-Marxist nationalism, revolutionary democratic ideologies, and Islamic fundamentalism, especially after the 1991 disintegration of the Soviet Union.

FUTURE REVOLUTIONS?

Will the future be characterized by the number of revolutions that occurred in the past? Students of revolution disagree. Goodwin (2001, 273), refers to the period of 1945–1991 as an "age of revolutions" and offers arguments regarding why revolutions should become less frequent. He notes that some claim that growth in the power of multinational corporations and financial institutions has reduced the relative power of the state in many countries, making control of the state less valuable to potential revolutionaries seeking to bring about change. He also discusses what he considered the more plausible explanation, that without the example of the U.S.S.R. as a powerful industrialized alternative to a capitalist system, the attractiveness and feasibility of revolution decrease. However, Goodwin (273) believes that the spread of democracy, in part the result of certain revolutions of the Cold War period that "helped destroy European colonialism, toppled some of the century's most ruthless dictators and humbled the superpowers," is most responsible for the decline of revolution. He argues that democracies offer the opportunity for

voters to punish offensive government officials and to "win concessions from economic and political elites," thus reducing motives for revolution (277). But he qualifies his argument in a telling way by saying that the movements and revolutions least likely to occur are those that "would seriously challenge the capitalist world-system" (274). This assessment clearly points to an external element affecting the frequency of revolutions, not the internal attribute of whether a society's government is democratic or non-democratic.

Many of the "new" democracies of the recent wave of democratization from the late 1980s on, including Chile and Guatemala, had been democracies in the past, but military revolts overthrew the earlier democratic systems, often with great violence and loss of life. Those who had friends or family members killed, imprisoned or abused, or who were themselves the victims of torture, rape, or other mistreatment by members of the armed forces or police (who were virtually never punished) were profoundly affected. Victims of these types of crimes in any society generally avoid engaging in behaviors that they perceive will put them at risk of further victimization. Such is also the case for people who have survived such crimes and suffered repression and the loss of democracy because they favored a particular economic or political policy. If they know that the perpetrators of the crimes against them were not punished—and that these people or others like them are free to commit the same crimes again—they are not likely to even consider repeating the political choices that led to their plight. So in some cases, lack of visible revolutionary aspirations may not have been due to the new democracies, but rather to the lingering fear of state terrorism among their citizens.

Selbin (2001, 290) refers to the wave of democratization of the late twentieth century as "wider," but not necessarily "deeper." Focusing mainly on Latin America, he suggested that poverty and inequality have been increasing and so the motivation for revolutionary change should also be increasing. Selbin (286) stated that neo-liberal economic "globalization…appears strikingly similar to what was once called 'imperialism.'" He also noted (285–286) that "democratic institutions and free markets are not, in any broad historical perspective, natural allies" and as "neo-liberalism fails to deliver on its promise, revolution will become more likely."

In assessing the possible relationship between democracy and revolution, a question that must be asked is whether any revolutionary movement would seek to overthrow a genuinely democratic system, that is, one in which the military is committed to a democratic constitution and obedient to the elected government. If revolutionaries could win popular support, they would most likely not attempt to overthrow the democratic system, but rather use democracy and elections to take power and to carry out their plans for social change without resorting to the dangerous and costly option of violence.

Whether more revolutions will occur in the future cannot be forecast with certainty. The pace of the occurrence of revolutions may have at least temporarily slowed, perhaps not so much due to the wave of democratization as to the maintenance of a generally non-permissive international stance towards revolutionary economic change, particularly on the part of a number of U.S. administrations. The orientation of the United States towards implementing true democracy in other nations and respecting the electoral will of the people in those democracies is essentially the key to determining whether the pace of revolutionary change will accelerate or decline. A major implication is that elections in the United States may determine how permissive or non-permissive the world environment is towards revolutionary change. As has been widely noted, it was no accident that both the Iranian and Nicaraguan revolutions occurred during the human rights–focused U.S. administration of Jimmy Carter. After the reduction of what appeared to be previous near unconditional U.S. support for the pre-revolutionary right-wing regimes in both countries, opponents of these governments were apparently encouraged to mount or escalate major revolutionary efforts.

Real democracy is inherently revolutionary in societies where the majority of the population is impoverished and perceive themselves to be the victims of economic exploitation and/or imperialism. Non-permissive world contexts in the form of the actions of nations opposing radical change have blocked revolutionary movements on numerous occasions. In the twenty-first century, the answer to the question regarding whether revolutionary movements and change re-emerge as a prominent features of world history may be found within the world's wealthiest and most powerful nation.

See Also American Revolution; Chilean Socialist Revolution, Counter-Revolution, and the Restoration of Democracy; Chinese Revolution; Democracy, Dictatorship and Fascism; East European Revolutions of 1989; Elites, intellectuals and Revolutionary Leadership; French Revolution; Iranian Revolution; Nicaraguan Revolution; Reform, Rebellion, Civil War, Coup D'état and Revolution; Russian Revolution of 1917; Russian Revolution of 1991 and the Dissolution of the U.S.S.R.; Spanish Revolution and Counter-Revolution; Student and Youth Movements, Activism and Revolution; Theories of Revolution; Transnational Revolutionary Movements; Trends in Revolution; Vietnamese Revolution

References and Further Readings

Brinton, Crane. 1965. *The Anatomy of Revolution.* New York: Vintage.

DeFronzo, James. 1996. (3rd edition forthcoming in 2007) *Revolutions and Revolutionary Movements.* Boulder, CO: Westview Press.

Foran, John. 2005. *Taking Power: On the Origins of Third World Revolutions.* Cambridge, UK: Cambridge University Press.

———. "Theories of Revolution." Pp. 868–872 in *Revolutionary Movements in World History: From 1750 to the Present* edited by James DeFronzo. Santa Barbara, CA: ABC-CLIO.

Goldfrank, Walter L. 1986. "The Mexican Revolution." Pp. 104–117 in *Revolutions: Theoretical, Comparative, and Historical Studies,* edited by Jack A. Goldstone. San Diego, CA: Harcourt Brace Jovanovich.

Goldstone, Jack A., ed. 1986, 1994. *Revolutions: Theoretical, Comparative, and Historical Studies.* Fort Worth, TX: Harcourt Brace College Publishers.

———. 1998. *The Encyclopedia of Political Revolutions.* Washington DC: Congressional Quarterly.

———. 2001. "An Analytical Framework." Pp. 9-29 in *Revolution: International Dimensions,* edited by Mark N. Katz. Washington DC: Congressional Quarterly Press.

———, Ted Robert Gurr, and Farrokh Moshiri, eds. 1991. *Revolutions of the Late Twentieth Century.* Boulder CO: Westview Press.

Goodwin, Jeff. 2001. "Is the Age of Revolution Over?" Pp. 272—283 in *Revolution: International Dimensions,* edited by Mark N. Katz. Washington DC: Congressional Quarterly Press.

Gurr, Ted Robert. 1970. *Why Men Rebel.* Princeton NJ: Princeton University Press.

Katz, Mark N. 1999. *Revolutions and Revolutionary Waves.* New York: Saint Martin's Press.

———, ed. 2001. *Revolution: International Dimensions.* Washington DC: Congressional Quarterly Press.

———. 2006. "Transnational Revolutionary Movements." Pp. 872–876 in *Revolutionary Movements in World History: From 1750 to the Present* edited by James DeFronzo.

McAdam, Doug, Sidney Tarrow and Charles Tilly. 2001 *Dynamics of Contention.* Cambridge, UK: Cambridge University Press.

Selbin, Eric. 2001. "Same as It Ever Was: The Future of Revolution at the End of the Century." Pp. 284-297 in *Revolution: International Dimensions,* edited by Mark N. Katz. Washington, DC: Congressional Quarterly Press.

Skocpol, Theda. 1979. *States and Revolutions.* Cambridge: Cambridge University Press.

REVOLUTIONARY MOVEMENTS IN WORLD HISTORY

FROM 1750 TO THE PRESENT

H

Haiti's Democratic Revolution

CHRONOLOGY

1986   Popular protest forces Baby Doc from power and a civil-military governing council takes over.

1990   Jean-Bertrand Aristide becomes president after the first democratic elections in Haiti.

1991   A military coup led by Raoul Cédras topples the Aristide government. The Oranization of American States (OAS) imposes sanctions on Haiti after a coup ousts President Aristide.

1993   The UN imposes an oil and arms embargo after failing to negotiate Aristide's return.

1994   The UN Security Council adopts comprehensive sanctions and approves a U.S.-led intervention force which restores Aristide to power. After a December mutiny by army officers, reinstated President Aristide abolishes the army and begins process for establishing a new Haitian National Police (PNH) as the sole legitimate coercive force.

1995   The multinational force led by U.S. commanders hands over peacekeeping duties to the UN Mission in Haiti (UNMIH). Only 5,000 of the original 23,000 troops remain. By April 1, 1995, three rounds of elections are held. Aristide's chosen successor, René Préval, is elected president following contested parliamentary elections. Most parties boycott the December presidential election. The number of UNMIH troops is reduced to under 1,000 by the end of the year.

1996   U.S. troops are withdrawn, except for those engaged in police training and monitoring and civil engineering projects. The UNMIH mandate expires and is replaced by scaled-down UN mission with a mandate to train police and help organize elections.

1997   Haiti holds flawed municipal and parliamentary elections, resulting in a less than 10 percent voter turnout. Prime Minister Rosny Smarth resigns. The opposition blocks the appointment of President René Préval's nominee to succeed Smarth.

Last UN military personnel leave Haiti; only the UN civilian police-training mission remains. The Caribbean Community (CARICOM) conditionally admits Haiti as a member.

1998   Parliament rejects Hervé Denis, another Préval nominee for prime minister. Haiti opens an embassy in Cuba.

1999   President Préval dismisses the parliament after lengthy and unsuccessful efforts to secure approval of his nominee for prime minister, Jacques-Edouard Alexis, who subsequently begins to occupy that position without parliamentary consent. A police intervention following rioting leads Aristide to publicly criticize Minister of Security Bob Manuel and the head of police, Pierre Denize. The United States withdraws all its remaining troops from Haiti, except for embassy personnel and civil engineers.

2000   Popular radio personality Jean Léopolde Dominique and his body guard are assassinated outside his office at Radio Haiti Inter. Dominique had been one of the most famous opponents of the 1957–1986 Duvalier dictatorship and a supporter of Aristide and the Lavalas movement in 1990; however, he dissented from it a decade later, after observing the Aristide-controlled movement's pervasive corruption and human rights violations. After a delay of several months, legislative elections are held. Senate elections are described by the international community as deeply flawed. Loans from international financial institutions remain frozen after the post-election controversy. The opposition boycotts presidential elections in which Aristide is declared winner despite minimal voter turnout.

2001   Aristide takes office, but the opposition refuses to recognize him as president. Nearly 1,000 former soldiers march through Port-au-Prince calling for the reintroduction of the armed forces. In a bid to appease the opposition and the international community, Aristide promises new legislative elections in the controversial seats at the end of the year. Negotiations fail to bring agreement between the government and the opposition over the mandate and composition of a new electoral council to oversee fresh voting. Armed men in army uniforms attack the presidential palace, a prison, a police academy, and a police station, killing five policemen in what the government describes as a coup attempt. The Convergence opposition coalition claims the incidents are simply an excuse for the government to crack down on Aristide's opponents. Aristide government supporters attack opposition headquarters and homes in response, leading respected opposition figure Micha Gaillard to comment that December 17, the date of the alleged coup attempt, changed Haiti like September 11 changed the United States, because the government crackdown represents "an attack against democracy." The UN mission is closed. OAS secretary-general César Gavira visits Haiti to mediate in a stand-off between Aristide and the opposition.

2002   Prime Minister Jean-Marie Chérestal, a boyhood friend of President Aristide who had faced a rising tide of criticism even from within the ruling party, formally resigns. The government had purchased a $1.7-million home to serve as his official residence, drawing widespread criticism. Senate leader and number two figure in the Lavalas Party, Yvone Neptune, is named prime minister. An OAS investigative report concludes that the events of December 17 were not a coup and that the political opposition did not participate. Aristide was not staying in the presidential palace at the time. The report concludes that Aristide party officials armed their followers, who ransacked opposition homes and offices after the attack on the palace.

After a bulldozer crushes a jail wall, a jailbreak on August 2 in Gonaives releases 159 inmates, including Amiot Métayer, a gang leader who was formerly allied to Aristide but had defected after Aristide, under OAS and U.S. pressure, threatened to arrest him for human rights violations.

U.S. ambassador Brian Dean Curran says that democracy in Haiti is threatened and that Haiti will not be invited to participate in a world conference of democratic nations in South Korea in November.

2003   Two police officers are murdered in a drug payment dispute, after they are named by the United States as Haitians known for their trafficking. An OAS delegation arrives to deliver an ultimatum to Aristide to implement OAS Resolution 822 which called for Aristide's government to provide the conditions necessary for democratic elections, including physical security for political opponents and the arrest and punishment of those guilty of violence against anti-Aristide political figures. Aristide responds by appointing corrupt, loyal officials to head the national police. U.S. ambassador to the OAS, Peter de Shazo, criticizes Haiti's failure to form a credible electoral commission and implement other requirements of OAS Resolution 822.

Opposition protests emerge in the latter months of the year, led by the "Group of 184," demanding Aristide's resignation.

2004   In February an uprising by armed rebels takes place in the northern half of the country. In its wake, the United States withdraws its personal security detail from Aristide, and he flees on a U.S.-chartered airplane to Africa on February 29. An interim government is chosen by a group of Haitian leaders organized by U.S., French, and Canadian diplomats. Within a day after Aristide's departure, the UN Security Council sanctions the interim government and establishes initially a three-month, U.S.-led peacekeeping mission to restore political stability. However, terms of engagement for UN peacekeeping troops are vague and they do not engage in policing; Haiti's own police force remains dysfunctional. Occasional joint actions are limited. Police and UN troops sent to subdue pro-Lavalas gunmen in one slum meet fierce resistance and continued violence.

Aristide's paramilitary chimères, while no longer the enforcers for Aristide, have regrouped and started a campaign of armed resistance called Operation Baghdad, which includes the beheading of several PNH officers,

imitating the Islamic radicals in Iraq. Aristide is still believed to control some of their purse strings in order to foment a crisis that would allow him to return from political exile in South Africa. Groups on all sides remain armed, despite UN Security Council mandates to disarm them. Pro-Aristide gunmen control the slums and many small towns.

2006   René Préval elected president.

INTRODUCTION

Haiti is the only country to have been established through a successful slave revolution where everyone was granted full citizenship. Yet even though it has been independent for over two centuries, Haiti has never been able to realize the dreams of its 1804 Revolution. But beginning in 1986, when the country's most successful popular uprising against tyranny led to a military coup and the resignation of Jean Claude Duvalier, the second-generation ruler of the twenty-nine year Duvalier dictatorship, Haiti has been in the process of a "second revolution." Unfortunately, the nation's last two decades have been characterized by frequent changes of government, more violent human rights violations, two sets of UN interventions and peacekeeping missions, and the 2004 demise of the Jean-Bertrand Aristide presidency in which so many hopes for democracy had been placed.

BACKGROUND: CULTURE AND HISTORY

Chronic instability and politically motivated violence have plagued Haiti for two centuries. Haiti is the poorest country in the Americas, and one of the few to have become poorer in last decades of the twentieth century. As a result, its economy is highly dependent on foreign aid, much of which was suspended from 1987 until 2004. Haiti's unemployment rate, by most estimates, has been over one-third, with underemployment (at very low wages or incomes) at another one-third. Haiti's security concerns are largely internal, and the country remained volatile after the departure of most international peacekeepers in 1997 until their return in 2004. The dissolution of the army and the formation of a civilian police force has not improved political stability, as of 2005.

In the mid twentieth century, François "Papa Doc" Duvalier emerged as the leader of a black power movement against the mulattos (mixed race persons of generally higher economic status than most Haitians), who had dominated the Haitian economy for most of its history. Duvalier eventually won election as president in 1957, but the mulattos claimed the election was rigged and refused to recognize him as president. Duvalier quashed their resistance by unleashing a civil militia centered around gangs of youths from the slums. The Volunteers for National Security (VSN), colloquially known as the Tonton Macoutes ("Uncle gunnysack" or "Uncle knapsack," the equivalent to "bogeyman" in Haiti), acted as Duvalier's shock troops, counterbalancing the power of the armed forces and repressing all opposition. Duvalier maintained a mesmerizing power over the people of Haiti through a combination of VSN paramilitary terror, conventional police-state repression, and appeals to Voudou. He declared himself president for life in 1964 and successfully resisted five invasions by Haitian exile insurgents who returned from abroad to try to overthrow the Duvalier government. Duvalier's life was saved by medical treatments provided by the United States after a heart attack in 1963, even though President Kennedy had cut off U.S. aid.

Duvalier eventually died of natural causes in 1971 and was succeeded by his son, Jean Claude "Baby Doc," who also declared himself president for life. But Jean Claude increasingly fell under the influence of the mulattos, alienating his father's poor black power base, and his repression of political opponents became increasingly severe as his popularity evaporated. After a popular uprising in late 1985 that the military refused to suppress and more than a week of mediation by the French and U.S. ambassadors, he fled the country in 1986. He remains in exile in France.

CONTEXT AND PROCESS OF REVOLUTION

In the two centuries since the 1804 Revolution, the only successful slave revolution in history, there have been few signs of traditional armed revolution in Haiti. Four reasons are commonly cited: (1) the very low level of income and bleak prospects for economic improvement (revolutions often occur when times are actually improving, creating rising expectations); (2) the nature of the Voudou religion, which some describe as fatalistic; (3) the control of politics by the elite, which has completely excluded the masses by following the practices of the French slave owners; (4) the counterrevolutionary force exerted by the United States.

Three of these four arguments seem to be borne out by the facts. The argument that the United States subverts democratic movements in the Caribbean and Latin America is not new. In regard to Haiti, that view is epitomized by Paul Farmer's *The Uses of Haiti* (2003). According to Farmer, the "international use of Haiti"—that is, its economic and political exploitation by the United States in particular—

means that Haitians have not been able to control their own destiny.

The argument that Voudou mitigates against revolution is open to question. Since Voudou was so essential in the maroon communities of escaped slaves in the revolutionary struggle of 1791–1803, it is difficult to understand why this religion has had the opposite effect since the revolution. It is a puzzle how a people so exploited, killed, imprisoned, beaten, and otherwise abused by every ruler in Haiti's long history should not have taken up arms more regularly. One factor may have been Voudou. The literature of the Haitian revolution has portrayed the Haitian generals Jean-Jacques Dessalines and Touissant L'Ouverture as enemies of Voudou, regularly punishing anyone caught practicing Voudou. Furthermore, the rural *houngan* (male) priests were mainstays in the Tonton Macoutes militia of the Duvalier dictatorship.

The chief revolutionary force since the end of the Duvalier dictatorship was Jean-Bertrand Aristide and his Lavalas (Flood) movement. Aristide, a Catholic priest, was an opponent of Jean Claude Duvalier and that political system. He was elected in the UN-OAS–supervised elections of 1990. In his book *Dignity*, Aristide made a case for nonviolent resistance, embracing a principled position of nonviolence rooted in Christian scriptures and the models, ideas, and writings of Mohandas Gandhi and Martin Luther King, Jr. But even though Aristide made an impassioned and persuasive case on paper, he was not wedded to total nonviolence in principle. He used violence selectively as a tactic to achieve political goals. In fact, his supporters relied on violence, as soon an attempted coup took place in January 1991 against the interim government of Eartha Pascal Trouillot, a month prior to his inauguration as president in February. His record in office over the next decade, minus the 1,111 days he spent in exile after the September 1991 coup against him, was characterized by violent human rights violations. Immediately following the December 2001 attack on the presidential palace, which the Aristide government alleged was led by disgruntled former police and army officers, not the opposition, Lavalas shock troops called *chimères,* attacked and demolished opposition party headquarters, opposition leaders' homes, Radio Metropole, an independent radio station, and a French cultural center. These militia groups are not necessarily ideological, but their services can be bought with money and/or alcohol, as they have been since at least the time of President Daniel Fignolé in 1957. Ironically, it was the threat of a violent revolution in February 2004 that led to the overthrow of Aristide's "revolutionary" government.

Since the 1986 fall of the Duvalier dictatorship until Aristide's overthrow in February 2004, as Robert Fatton argues convincingly in *Haiti's Predatory Republic* (2002), Haiti has been caught up in a second major revolution. The first ended

Jean-Bertrand Aristide campaigns for president in Haiti in 1990. (Bill Gentile/Corbis)

in 1804, in the transition from slave-centered colony of France to independent nation of free people. The second is the transition from various forms of dictatorship to democracy. Fatton describes this transition as partial at present, stuck in a form of republic he calls "predatory" because government leaders steal property from the state. Rather than attempting to change only the form of government, reformers since 1986 have repeatedly and unsuccessfully attempted to uproot not only the predatory political system, but also the historical patterns of personalized dictatorship. So far, their efforts have failed, but the past two decades represent a sustained effort to create Haiti's second revolution. Fatton describes his own view of Haiti's prospects as a "cautious pessimism."

Duvalierism, a particular form of dictatorship, falls within the typical Haitian style of dictatorship. Fatton describes the key elements of this form of government in terms of class analysis. Historically, there have been only two classes with the cohesion and power to dominate the nation. The possessing class is the group usually referred to as the elites. It owns and controls the means of production, including large portions of the land itself, as well as the other dominant economic institutions. The government class controls government funds and the military might. Government officials, usually not drawn from the possessing class, extract their (sizeable) wealth from the nation's coffers.

The Post-Duvalier Period

After the departure of Jean Claude Duvalier on February 7, 1986, a civil-military transitional junta ruled until 1987, when General Henri Namphy was declared president following elections marred by the unleashing, once more, of the Tonton Macoutes. Barely a year into Namphy's presidency the army decided to rid the country of their own man and, following a coup, installed General Prosper Avril. Avril fled the country in 1990 under international pressure, and fresh elections were organized. Last-minute candidate Jean-Bertrand Aristide, a former Roman Catholic priest and popular anti-Duvalier activist, became president following the first democratic transfer of power in Haitian history. Aristide's rhetoric of class warfare—his slogan was *Lavalas* (Flood)—and the personality cult that grew up around him quickly offended the traditionally powerful elements of Haitian society. He was overthrown in a bloody military coup in September 1991, which installed a civilian government with military backing.

With the help of foreign embassies, Aristide escaped to the United States. The international community refused to recognize the government put in place by General Raoul Cédras in Port-au-Prince. After protracted but unsuccessful negotiations with the OAS, member states imposed an embargo on Haiti in 1992, although oil still reached Haiti from Europe. UN-mediated negotiations initially failed in 1993, and universal sanctions were imposed by the UN Security Council. In July 1993, an agreement for the reinstatement of the Aristide government was negotiated at Governor's Island in New York. However, it was not implemented in October 1993 as planned, due to the U.S. military debacle in Somalia that month. President Clinton did not want U.S. and Canadian peacekeeping troops to disembark amid Haitian protests at the docks by radical right forces, though these forces were actually few in number.

When the Haitian government refused to give up power, the Security Council authorized a blockade (which was never enforced). When that failed to dislodge the regime, the Security Council authorized "all means necessary" in July 1994, if the military-backed regime refused to implement the Governor's Island accords. Led by U.S. troops, a UN force of 23,000 landed on September 19, 1994. They met no opposition, thanks to a successful eleventh-hour negotiation involving the Haitian de facto regime and former U.S. president Jimmy Carter, U.S. senator Sam Nunn, and former chair of the U.S. Joint Chiefs of Staff Colin Powell. They agreed that coup leaders must resign but effectively granted them asylum overseas.

In the decade following their return to power on the back of this U.S.-led intervention in 1994, Aristide and the Lavalas movement managed to tighten their grip on power, though a majority of Aristide's original supporters have since joined the opposition, Convergence. Aristide stood down in the 1995 elections because of a one-term limitation insisted upon by foreign donors. His chosen successor, René Préval, was heavily influenced by Aristide behind the scenes and prepared the way for Aristide's re-election in 2000. In his final year in office, Préval resorted to rule by decree to bypass a confrontational legislature.

Haiti had been without a functioning government since 1997, when controversial legislative elections led to the resignation of the prime minister. Préval's subsequent nominees for prime minister were rejected by parliament, which was in turn disbanded by Préval in January 1999. Fresh elections were initially announced for December of that year but did not take place until May 2000. They were mired in controversy, the opposition correctly claiming that at least seven senate seats had been accorded to Lavalas members when they should have faced a run-off election. The elections were described by the United States, the EU, and the OAS as deeply flawed; as a result, up to $500 million in U.S. assistance was blocked. Aristide was elected to a second term in November 2000 and took office in February 2001.

Aristide's Departure

Without any apparent foresight by the White House, the United States and France induced Haitian president Jean-Bertrand Aristide's resignation on February 29, 2004. The United States admitted only to removing the personal security detail of U.S. Marines that it had provided Aristide for about the previous week, claiming that the United States saved his life by providing a safe exit on a U.S.-chartered airplane to Africa. Aristide maintained that the United States "kidnapped" him, echoing the same after-the-fact complaint of Philippine president Ferdinand Marcos in 1986. The event underscores U.S. secretary of state Colin Powell's "Pottery Barn" dictum, "If you break it, you own it." If the United States is indeed willing this time to "own" this small country of 8 million mostly indigent citizens, it would be a departure from past practices. Haiti is currently a UN protectorate for the second time in less than a decade. Yet, if the United States, through the UN, is unwilling to master the political causes of Haiti's underdevelopment, then the past mistakes of U.S.-inspired UN peacekeeping missions will be repeated. In particular, if the UN is unwilling or unable to effect national reconciliation of its political elites and demobilization of paramilitary forces, then Haiti is likely to continue to explode onto the U.S. radar screen every decade or so as another example of misguided U.S. interference in a neighboring country. Moreover, the problems of the United States and the UN in building peace in Haiti from 1994–2000 should have been a cautionary tale for similar efforts in Afghanistan since 2002 and Iraq since 2003. Now the Haitian example from the 1990s should provide lessons for peacekeeping-redux in Haiti a decade later.

Following a February 29, 2004, overnight UN Security Council resolution, the United States led more than 3,700 soldiers into Haiti to support a provisional government for just over three months, including 1,900 U.S. Marines, 1,000 French, 500 Canadians, and 320 Chileans. The U.S. exit strategy in 2004, to remove its peacekeeping troops after only three months, was of primary importance to the U.S. administration—just as in late 1994, when it planned to remove its large share of the 24,000 foreign troops deployed in Haiti within just six months, by April 1995. The difference in 2005 has been that the number of foreign troops has increased over time, with large contingents of Brazilian, Chilean, Argentinian, and Chinese troops arriving after the United States, French, and Canadian departure in June 2004.

The second UN peacekeeping phase of the second UN peacekeeping mission in Haiti began with the June 2004 hand-over of peacekeeping duties from the UN-authorized, United States-led, multinational force to the Brazilian-commanded UN Stabilization Mission (MINUSTAH, Mission des Nations Unies pour la Stabilisation en Haïti, in French). After some delays in deploying the number of MINUSTAH troops envisioned by the UN Security Council, 6,000 of the 6,700 authorized troops arrived by the end of 2004. The MINUSTAH mission's one-year first Security Council mandate expired in late June 2005 and was reauthorized at least through the summer of 2006.

Without the U.S. troops directly involved, skepticism abounds among the Haitians and the international community, despite the July 2004 donors conference authorizing $1.5 billion in aid and loans to the interim government over the next two years. At the time of writing, July 2005, much of those funds intended to assist in the restoration of order, economic revival, and democratization had not been disbursed. The UN military chief in the first year, Brazilian General Augusto Heleno Ribeiro Pereira, had not been successful at paramilitary demobilization, which his mission claimed was more than just a nominal goal. Many critics found MINUSTAH unwilling to attack both urban gangs and political paramilitaries in the urban slums, or the rightist rebels still at large in the countryside in the northern half of the country. By summer 2005, there were signs of MINUSTAH perhaps engaging more of these violent forces.

Though Haiti no longer struggles under the polarizing influence of President Aristide, whom the international community blamed for so many of Haiti's difficulties, it still needs to develop a working political consensus to build institutions and avoid the reliance on party militia and other ad hoc forces to achieve and maintain political power. Unfortunately, by 2005, the provisional government had made little apparent effort to include the party of exiled President Aristide in the process of planning for the elections. Prime Minister Gérard Latortue seemed unperturbed that Aristide's party is uninvolved, in disarray, and threatened with both physical violence and various criminal investigations and prosecutions. Haiti also needs to begin the process of economic growth, halting the ecological desertification, and building state institutions against overwhelming odds.

Just as the main goal of the Afghanistan and Iraqi provisional governments was to hold elections, the provisional government in Haiti scheduled elections for October and November 2005 respectively. Although Haiti lacks the many armed insurgents opposing the NATO mission in Afghanistan and the U.S./U.K. peace enforcement in Iraq, it has never been able to establish a functional criminal justice system. Facing the worst political and economic problems of the Western hemisphere, Haiti's path to political and economic regenera-

tion seems as difficult to analyze and define as ever. But the current UN mission, MINUSTAH, is much more intrusive, compared to earlier multinational efforts, in trying to establish order with the use of force in the violent slums, especially in Cite Soleil and Belair, both in Port-au-Prince.

IMPACTS

Nineteen years after the end of the Duvalier dictatorship, more than 8 million Haitians still live on 27,000 square miles of eroded land, with less than 5 percent of the national forest left. And because so much of the forest vegetation has been lost, rainwater is not absorbed into the soil but washes it straight downhill. Dams become reservoirs of precious topsoil, and the aquifer that provides fresh water for the island is beginning to salinate.

No plans exist for re-establishing a Haitian army, even though the Haitian National Police (PNH) on its own has failed to maintain security since its formation in 1995, particularly during the violent conflict from late 2003 until Aristide's departure on February 28, 2004, even with the assistance of both UN peacekeeping-mission forces. As in 1994–2000, the international community is focusing economic policy on export promotion and privatization, along with providing food to the hungry, without focusing on a plan where the majority can achieve a minimum standard of living rather than relying on handouts. As in 1994–2000, foreign cooperation requires U.S. Coast Guard penetration of Haitian territorial waters to interdict indiscriminately Haitian boat people, including genuine political refugees, who are returned for more persecution without so much as an inquiry, in violation of the non-return rules of the International Refugee Convention. In addition, U.S. intelligence operations continue in Haiti. One notorious alleged CIA agent, Emanuel Constant, directed a paramilitary organization credited with hundreds, or more likely, thousands of murders during the 1991–1994 coup period. Constant has not been extradited to Haiti on grounds of U.S. national security and has permanent residence in the United States.

PEOPLE AND ORGANIZATIONS

Aristide, Jean-Bertrand (Born 1953)

Jean-Bertrand Aristide first rose to prominence as a Catholic priest whose sermons were openly critical of the Duvalier regime. His populist stance built up a strong following among the poor and made him the obvious candidate to take power. He won a hefty majority in Haiti's first fully democratic elections in 1990. Overthrown in a coup less than a year after taking office, he was returned to power after the U.S./UN invasion and occupation of September 1994. The United States made it clear that he should serve only the remainder of his original mandate, and at the 1995 elections he stepped down. However, he continued as a strong presence in the background throughout the tenure of his chosen successor René Préval. Aristide has remained the figurehead of the Lavalas movement, which has extensive networks throughout Haitian society, particularly among the poor. In November 2000, Aristide won re-election easily, partly because the opposition boycotted the election, protesting severe irregularities in the election process. In office, Aristide's main task was a balancing act between retaining his grip on power and the suppression of opposition, while doing enough to satisfy donor countries that he was in fact a democrat. He increasingly resorted to the repression he so eloquently criticized in Jean Claude Duvalier's dictatorship, particularly in condoning and arming—or at least not suppressing—gangs and paramilitary groups. After his departure from Haiti in 2004, he has been residing in exile in South Africa.

Duvalier, Francois (1907–1971)

Francois Duvalier ("Papa Doc") was president of Haiti from 1957 to 1971. He came to power in a dubious election after a year of political instability. He purged the Haitian army of possible political opponents and established a civil militia, the Volunteers for National Security (VSN), commonly known as the Tonton Macoutes. Both the army and the Macoutes were extremely repressive, murdering political opponents and sending tens of thousands into exile. As a result, many countries reduced or eliminated foreign assistance, though the United States did save Duvalier's life at one point by providing medical treatment after he had a heart attack. Many but by no means all of his victims were mulattos, though there were many arbitrary executions of apolitical people as well. Duvalier made most decisions for his government and was supported by his wife in keeping close control. He died in office.

Duvalier, Jean Claude (Born 1951)

Jean Claude Duvalier ("Baby Doc") assumed the presidency in 1971 after the death of his father, Francois. He was quite young and was not nearly as committed to political control as his father. The United States and other countries re-established foreign assistance, and the United States pushed for liberalization. U.S. aid, conditioned by Congress upon improvement in Haitian human rights during the 1980s, was approved. In 1985, Duvalier was "elected" president-for-life in a dubious plebiscite, claiming 99 percent approval. His regime was softer on opponents than his father's, though he maintained censorship, prevented competitive elections, and incarcerated and tortured political opponents advocating democracy, such as Rev. Silvio Claude. After a political uprising in Gonnaives in the summer of 1985, the army headed by Henri Namphey refused to suppress additional protests. After what may have been a coup, the United States persuaded Duvalier to go into exile in France on February 7, 1986.

Front for National Reconstruction

This organization was led by Secretary General Guy Philippe, who led the armed revolt against Aristide in February 2004. Philippe rode triumphantly into Port-au-Prince in a shiny SUV after his ragtag army helped oust democratically elected President Jean-Bertrand Aristide. A former police official and a political novice, Philippe now is one of a handful of possible presidential candidates in the presidential elections.

Haitian National Police (Police Nationale d'Haiti—PNH)

The PNH numbers between 2,500 and 3,500. It was created to take over from the interim protection force that was established after the 1994 occupation. Originally, the U.S. plan was to modernize the army by taking the police out of it, as both comprised the Armed Forces of Haiti until December 1994, and have the PNH report to the minister of justice. However, after an aborted uprising by cashiered, vetted, or retired military officers in December 1994, President Aristide abolished the army and created a police force based partly on U.S., Canadian, and French plans for its modernization.

KONAKOM (Komité National du Kongrés des Mouvements Démocratiques, National Congress of Democratic Movements)

KONAKOM merged with PANPRA (Parti National Progressiste et Révolutionnaire, Nationalistic Progressive Revolutionary Party of Haiti) and Haiti Can on April 22 and 23, 2005. Professor Micha Gaillard is a spokesman of this merger of Haitian social democratic parties (FPSDH, Fusion). A communiqué signed by Victor Benoit, Secretary General Robert Auguste, and Micha Gaillard expressed concern about the way the Latortue government was leading the country, and especially its inability to guarantee the security of the people and its inability to take action to lower the high cost of living.

Lavalas Movement

Lavalas was a political movement started by Jean-Bertrand Aristide after he announced his unexpected candidacy for the Haitian presidency in late 1989. He had been nominated by the National Front for Democracy and Change, but he soon marginalized these traditional politicians and created the Lavalas movement led by priests and other cronies who would defer to his charismatic and unchallenged leadership. Over the course of the 1990s, many parties that had been part of Lavalas defected, especially the Lavalas Political Organization led by Gerard Pierre Charles. By the time of Aristide's second presidential term beginning in 2001, much of Lavalas was dominated by political thugs using violence, particularly in urban slums, rather than the peasant cooperatives and other mass organizations that originally sought to empower poor Haitians. Violent sectors in Lavalas paralyzed the movement and politics in Haiti. They were dominant through force, but not necessarily in numbers.

Paul, Evans (Born ca. 1955)

Paul, a leading democracy advocate, was one of three dissidents whom President Prosper Avril had tortured in November 1989, which caused an international outcry and contributed to the demise of Avril four months later. Nicknamed "K-plume," his pen name as a writer, he was elected mayor of Port-au-Prince in the 1990 elections, after having been a key manager of the effort to nominate Aristide in the 1990 presidential ticket of the National Front for Change and Democracy (FNCD) party and to dismiss the previously nominated candidate, Victor Benoit. Paul eloquently campaigned for Aristide's election. After fighting for democracy against the coup government of 1991–1994, while Aristide was in comfortable exile, he was unwilling to defer to Aristide after the latter's return. Aristide nominated a popular singer, who defeated Paul for the mayoralty in the 1995 elections, and Paul in turn left Aristide's Lavalas movement. Paul is now one of the leading figures in the Convergence opposition coalition. Paul's offices were destroyed following the December 2001 post-coup attacks. Members of his party have been frequently arrested on trumped-up arms-possession charges. Paul refused to join the Socialist coalition, FPSDH (see KONAKOM), with whom he was allied in 1990 and which will not forgive him for having nominated Aristide in 1990 to replace the original candidate, Victor Benoit.

Henry F. Carey

See Also Documentaries of Revolution; Haitian Independence Revolution

References and Further Readings
Abbot, Elizabeth. 1988. *Haiti: The Duvaliers and Their Legacy*. New York: McGraw-Hill.

Aristide, Jean Bertrand. 1990. *In the Parish of the Poor*. Maryknoll, NY: Orbis.
Arthur, Charles. 1992. *Haiti: A Guide to the People, Politics and Culture*. Brooklyn, NY: Interlink Books.
Carey, Henry F. 1998. "Electoral Observation and Democratization in Haiti." Pp. 143–166 in *Electoral Observation and Democratic Transitions in Latin America*, edited by Kevin Middlebrook. San Diego, CA: Center for US-Mexican Studies. Also available at www.haitipolicy.org/archives/archives/1998/carey.htm
———. 2001. "US Domestic Politics and the Emerging Humanitarian Intervention Policy: Haiti, Bosnia and Kosovo," *World Affairs* 164 (2): 72–82.
———. 2002. "Foreign Aid, Democratization and Haiti's Provisional Electoral Council, 1987-2002," *Wadabagei: a Journal on the Caribbean and its Diaspora*, Vol. 5, no. 2: 1-47.
Dupuy, Alex. 1988. *Haiti in the World Economy: Class, Race and Underdevelopment since 1700*. Boulder, CO: Westview Press.
Farmer, Paul. 2003. *The Uses of Haiti: Updated Edition*. Monroe, ME: Common Courage Press.
Fatton, Robert. 2002. *Haiti's Predatory Republic: The Unending Transition to Democracy*. Boulder, CO: Lynne Rienner.
Harrison, Lawrence. 1993. "Voodoo Politics," *Atlantic* 271 (6): 101–107.
Nicholls, David. 1995. *From Dessalines to Duvalier: Race, Colour and National Independence in Haiti*. New Brunswick, NJ: Rutgers University Press.
Schmidt, Hans. 1995. *US Occupation of Haiti, 1915–1934*. New Brunswick, NJ: Rutgers University Press.
Trouillot, Michel-Rolf. 1990. "The Odd and the Ordinary: Haiti, the Caribbean, and the World," *Cimarrón: New Perspectives on the Caribbean* 2 (3): 3–12.
———. 1994. "Haiti's Nightmare and the Lessons of History," *NACLA Report on the Americas* 7 (4): 46–51. Reprinted in 1995, Pp. 121–132 in *Haiti: Dangerous Crossroads*, edited by Deirdre McFayden and Pierre Larameé. Boston: South End Press.
United Nations. 2004. "MINUSTAH: Overcoming Growing Pains," *UN Peace Operations*, "Year in Review, 2004." http://www.un.org/Depts/dpko/dpko/pub/year_review04/ch2.htm

Haitian Independence Revolution

CHRONOLOGY

1492	Columbus claims the island colony of Santo Domingo for Spain.
1605	Spain evicts its colonists from the island's western coast to discourage smuggling.
1625	France establishes a colony on the island of St. Kitts. Ten years later, it founds new colonies on Martinique and Guadeloupe.

1640	France claims authority over the buccaneers in western Santo Domingo, which it calls Saint-Domingue.
1685	As Caribbean slavery grows, France adopts a comprehensive slave law.
1697	Spain formally recognizes French Saint-Domingue.
1713	Royal census of Saint-Domingue counts 6,831 free people and 24,156 slaves.
1740	Annual slave imports to Saint-Domingue reach approximately 10,000 per year.
1756–1763	Seven Years War puts an enormous strain on the island.
1758	Execution of Makandal, reputed by slaves to be an African sorcerer whose poisons would kill all the whites.
1764–1769	Colonists, free men of color, and poor white immigrants protest and then revolt against a new militia system.
1769–1779	Saint-Domingue's courts draft new discriminatory laws against free people of color.
1779	Five hundred forty-five free colored volunteers and 156 white colonial volunteers sail with a French expedition to fight the British in Savannah, Georgia.
1784	The wealthy free colored planter Julien Raimond leaves Saint-Domingue to seek racial reforms in France.
1787	Over 37,000 enslaved Africans are imported into Saint-Domingue in one year.
1788	In Paris, abolitionists establish the Society of the Friends of the Blacks.
	French census shows close to 28,000 whites and 22,000 free people of color. Saint-Domingue's slave population is greater than 450,000.
1789	Colonists win representation in the French National Assembly; in Paris, Raimond and others argue that free people of color deserve voting rights.
1790	In April, colonial whites elect the radical Assembly of Saint-Marc, which proclaims Saint-Domingue's sovereignty and is forcibly closed in July.
	In October, wealthy free colored merchant Vincent Ogé returns from Paris demanding voting rights; rejected, he assembles several hundred armed free men of color.
1791	In February, the colonial government publicly tortures and kills Ogé and other free colored leaders.
	On May 15, the French National Assembly awards voting rights to qualified free men of color.
	In June and July, colonial whites take up arms to reject the May 15 law.
	Between August 14 and 22, a well-planned slave conspiracy produces a revolt in Saint-Domingue's North Province, which spreads to other regions.
	On September 24, alarmed at the revolt, the French National Assembly reverses itself on free colored civil rights.
1791–1792	Free men of color and whites try and fail to form lasting alliances against the slaves.
1792	On April 4, the French National Assembly decrees that free men of color are legally equal to whites. It sends revolutionary commissioners to enforce the new law.
1793	In February, England and Spain declare war against France. Within months, both invade Saint-Domingue.
	On June 20, Governor Galbaud fails to overthrow the revolutionary commissioner Sonthonax, who saves himself by offering freedom to rebel slaves who defend the revolution.
	From June to September, commissioners extend emancipation across Saint-Domingue.

1794	On February 4, the revolutionary legislature in Paris votes to end slavery.
	In April, Toussaint-Louverture and his men join the French army.
1795	New French constitution outlaws slavery; Spain cedes Santo Domingo to France.
1796	Toussaint-Louverture suppresses a conspiracy and is named lieutenant governor.
1797	Toussaint becomes commander in chief of the French army in Saint-Domingue.
1798	In August, the British withdraw from Saint-Domingue; Toussaint enters into commercial negotiations with United States and Britain.
1799	Napoléon Bonaparte assumes power in Paris, begins to consider colonial options.
1800	Toussaint sends his armies into formerly Spanish territory, defying orders.
1801	Toussaint has a constitution drawn up, naming him governor for life.
1802	In February, a large expedition of French troops commanded by Charles Leclerc arrives in Saint-Domingue.
	In May, Toussaint and his troops capitulate to Leclerc after months of resistance.
	On June 7, Leclerc arrests Toussaint and ships him to France; top mulatto and black officers help the French suppress remaining rebel fighters.
	In October, leading mulatto and black officers begin to join the rebels.
	In November, Leclerc dies; Rochambeau takes command, committing atrocities that unify an "indigenous army" of black and mulatto soldiers across the colony.
1803	On May 18, rebel leaders create the Haitian flag.
1803–1804	As Saint-Domingue news filters back to France, Napoléon sells the Louisiana Territory to the United States.
1804	On January 1, Haiti's independence is declared by Jean-Jacques Dessalines.

INTRODUCTION

The Haitian Revolution of 1791–1804, the sole successful slave revolt in world history, led to the founding of the New World's second independent state. In the third year of the French Revolution, hundreds of thousands of slaves in Saint-Domingue, the largest and most profitable plantation colony of its day, rose against their masters. Their struggle forced France to abolish slavery in 1794. In 1802, Napoléon's attempt to restore the institution turned the colony's black and mulatto soldiers against him. They proclaimed the existence of an independent Haiti on January 1, 1804.

BACKGROUND: CULTURE AND HISTORY

France created Saint-Domingue in the 1640s, when it began to take control of the western coast of Spanish Santo Domingo. Separated from the Spanish by high mountains, this territory attracted an unruly collection of smugglers and pirates. Throughout much of the 1600s, France used these men to attack nearby Spanish colonies. But Caribbean sugar was ultimately more profitable than plundered silver. In the 1690s, France forced buccaneer chiefs to become law-abiding planters. Within a century, Saint-Domingue became a major component of the French economy, producing about 40 percent of Europe's sugar and 60 percent of its coffee (Geggus 1990, 197).

Yet the colony maintained its unique character. True to their buccaneer roots, Dominguan colonists resented French commercial regulations and militia requirements. Plantation slavery generated such immense profits that many colonists believed they were only temporary sojourners who would return to France once they made their fortunes.

The cruel nature of Caribbean plantation society set the stage for the revolution. An eighteenth-century sugar plantation, unlike its counterpart producing cotton or tobacco, was a kind of factory-in-the-field. Plantations did not just grow sugar cane; they manufactured sugar crystals. This complex process of milling, boiling, and draining forced planters to spend huge sums on their sugar-works. They needed as much land and as many workers as possible to recoup those investments. In eighteenth-century Saint-Domingue, an average sugar plantation had over 125 slaves, and the largest had as many as 300 (Geggus 1993, 74). These slaves worked six days a week, fifteen hours a day, and longer yet during harvest season. On average, 5 percent or more of most plantation slave forces died each year from systematic overwork, poor housing, malnutrition, and brutal estate discipline.

Yet sugar and coffee brought such high prices in Europe that planters could replace their workers with newly imported Africans. In the eighteenth century, Saint-Domingue was second only to Jamaica as a destination for slave traders. The volume of slaves imported to Saint-Domingue doubled in the 1740s, again in the 1770s, and again in the 1780s, reaching nearly 48,000 slaves in the record year of 1791 (Eltis, Behrend, Richardson, and Klein 1999, Database on CD-ROM). By 1789, approximately 60 percent of the colony's slave population had been born in Africa (Blackburn 1997, 442). Yet Africans and the creole slaves born on the island (*creole* refers to persons born in Saint-Domingue) did not necessarily speak the same languages or share the same religions, and plantation society was divided in many other ways. On the largest estates, creole slaves were chosen for specialized work, as blacksmiths, sugar refiners, midwives, or servants. Slaves so outnumbered masters that most slave gangs were directed by a "driver" who was himself a slave.

Because rape and concubinage were acknowledged elements of colonial life, Saint-Domingue developed a sizeable population of mixed African and European descent, many of whom were freed from slavery. By 1789, there were about 30,000 "free people of color," almost as many as whites (Geggus 2002, 5). A notable minority of these free coloreds were successful planters and merchants, slave owners who considered themselves French colonists. Though the colony's massive slave population, nearing 500,000, dwarfed both groups, whites believed that free coloreds had to be excluded from proper society.

Causes of Revolution

There were two basic causes of the revolution: the collapse of the colonial system amid the confusion of the French Revolution. and the culture of resistance among Saint-Domingue's slaves.

In 1789 the French Revolution created colonial conflicts on several levels. Saint-Domingue's wealthiest colonists hoped that political reform would allow them to escape the "ministerial despotism" they associated with the commercial monopoly and military governors. Poor whites, disap-

pointed by the difficulty of making a colonial fortune, opposed not only royal officials but wealthy colonists. They were especially aggrieved by the wealth of some well-established free colored families. Some of the colony's wealthiest free coloreds, for their part, were in France when the revolution broke out. By September of 1789 they had come to believe that the Declaration of the Rights of Man guaranteed the civil rights that colonists denied them.

From 1789 to 1791 struggles between these three groups escalated from rhetorical bombast to military action. In May 15, 1791, Paris ruled that wealthy free men of color were entitled to vote in colonial elections. White colonists refused to accept this law, and free men of color took up arms to protect their rights.

During these first few years of the French Revolution, most enslaved men and women in Saint-Domingue stood by and watched. Before 1791 the colony was not known for its slave revolts. While British Jamaica had a dozen such uprisings before 1800, Saint-Domingue had almost none before the revolution. It did have a tradition of marronage, slaves who escaped into the mountains whom planters could not manage to recapture. But these maroons rarely destroyed plantations, as they did in Jamaica and Suriname. Saint-Domingue's most famous rebel was Makandal, an escaped slave who created great panic in the colony's North Province in the 1750s. Rumors circulated that he was a sorcerer using poison to kill all the whites. He was captured and executed in 1758.

Although resistance to slavery produced no massive uprising in the eighteenth century before August of 1791, during that month slaves in the colony's North Province created a massive conspiracy. In at least two meetings on different sugar estates, creole slaves forged a pact with new African arrivals, sealed in a blood oath over the sacrifice of a pig. Despite the traditional story that the Voudou priest Boukman led the conspiracy, his existence has never been confirmed, and scholars debate the centrality of Voudou in the success of the revolt. The rebellion occurred on plantations where creole slaves dominated and was led by slave artisans and drivers, who tended to be creole. They chose to strike during a week when white delegates were gathering in nearby Cap Français for the Colonial Assembly. The first violence came on August 14, and then the full-fledged revolt broke out on the nights of August 21 and 22. Within one week, the uprising had destroyed 184 plantations. Contemporaries guessed there were between 20,000 and 80,000 rebels by late September.

CONTEXT AND PROCESS OF REVOLUTION

The divisions among Saint-Domingue's free population helped the August 1791 rebellion spread. In the North

Province where the uprising began, the free population unified against the rebels, but in Port-au-Prince, white "patriots" (working class whites who identified with the anti-authoritarian politics of revolutionary France) refused to accept free colored equality. Wealthy planters did ally with free mulattos against the slaves, but this alliance collapsed in the fall of 1792, when France declared itself a republic. Paris sent revolutionary commissioners to Saint-Domingue to enforce the civil rights of free men of color. These officials appointed free men of color to key military positions, especially when Spain and Britain invaded the colony in 1793.

Many ex-slave fighters joined the Spanish war against France. One of them was a free black named Toussaint who later took the name "Louverture." Though born in slavery, Toussaint was free by 1776. In the 1780s he leased slaves to harvest his coffee, but by the spring of 1793 he had emerged among the most prominent rebel commanders fighting for Spain.

The revolutionary commissioners and their free colored allies suffered another setback in May 1793, when a conservative military officer from an old colonial family arrived from France to assume the colonial governorship. General François-Thomas Galbaud rallied counter-revolutionary colonists against the commissioners. On June 21, as Galbaud's armed supporters prepared to take control of Cap Français, Commissioner Sonthonax turned to the rebel slaves camped outside the city. If they would defend the revolution, he promised, France would give them freedom. With their help, he defeated Galbaud's forces, provoking a huge exodus of conservative whites from the colony. In June and July the commissioners expanded the freedom decree to other regions of the colony. On August 29, 1793, Sonthonax proclaimed general emancipation in Saint-Domingue. In Paris, the revolutionary government ratified the measure on February 4, 1794, extending it to all territories.

The alliance of ex-slaves and revolutionaries opened a new day in Saint-Domingue. In April 1794, Toussaint and his troops left their Spanish allies to join the French. The following year a French army composed of black, mulatto, and white soldiers expelled the Spanish. Three years later the British invasion force withdrew. André Rigaud, a free mulatto before the revolution, emerged as the dominant commander in the South and West provinces.

Toussaint's military success earned him a series of promotions that in 1797 made him Saint-Domingue's French commander in chief. Cut off from France by a British naval blockade, in 1798 he opened commercial negotiations with the British and the United States. By 1800, his rivalry with André Rigaud had grown so great that he sent his troops into the southern peninsula, accusing Rigaud of "mulatto" racism toward blacks.

Engraving of Toussaint-Louverture. Steward, T. G., *The Haitian Revolution 1791–1804*, 1914)

Meanwhile, the revolution in France had become far more conservative. With Napoléon Bonaparte's rise to power in 1799, colonists who had exiled themselves in 1793 and 1794 began to return to France. A new constitution, promulgated in 1800, signaled a return to colonialism by stipulating "special laws" for overseas territories. That very year, after defeating Rigaud, Toussaint defied orders and sent his army into the eastern half of the island, occupying what had once been Spanish Santo Domingo. In 1801, as Napoléon began to plan how to reassert control over Saint-Domingue, Toussaint convened an island-wide constitutional committee, which named him governor in chief for life.

In 1802, when Britain lifted its blockade of French shipping, Bonaparte sent a large expedition force to Saint-Domingue under the command of his brother-in-law, Charles Leclerc. Although Toussaint and his army initially fought these troops, Toussaint was defeated and in May the black governor agreed to stand down. His army and generals joined Leclerc's forces. Still fearing Toussaint's popularity, Leclerc arrested him several weeks later and shipped him to France, where he died in a mountain prison the following year.

In August 1802 field workers who refused to lay down their guns initiated the revolution's final phase. Leclerc ordered Toussaint's top general, Jean-Jacques Dessalines, and other black and mulatto officers to disarm ex-slave fighters. But their attempts to collect muskets swelled the ranks of anti-French guerrillas. In October the black and mulatto officers assigned to repress these rebels began to turn against the French. In November 1802 Leclerc died of yellow fever, which had already severely weakened his European soldiers. Command passed to Donatien de Rochambeau, the son of the famous veteran of the American Revolution. Rochambeau launched a campaign of racial extermination that further cemented the anti-French coalition. In May 1803 France and Britain began to fight again, delaying reinforcements that Rochambeau badly needed. In November 1803 he surrendered the western one-third of the island to a self-proclaimed "indigenous army" led by Dessalines. France retained control over what had been Spanish Santo Domingo, but on January 1, 1804, Dessalines and his generals proclaimed that what had once been colonial Saint-Domingue was now the independent nation of Haiti.

French Revolution versus Haitian Revolution

The history of the French and Haitian Revolutions cannot be clearly separated. French radicalization between 1792 and 1794 and Bonaparte's authoritarianism from 1799 to 1804 helped steer the course of events in Saint-Domingue. The fact that news took at least three weeks to travel between Saint-Domingue and Paris forced political actors on both sides of the Atlantic to react to unexpected events, such as the 1792 proclamation of the French Republic or Sonthonax's emancipation decrees the following year.

The process of arming groups that had previously not been involved in combat was another important process in the revolution. Before 1791, colonial whites pressed militia and police duties on free men of color and even slaves. Once fighting began, colonial whites armed slaves to fight against free men of color, who resorted to the same tactics. Moreover, all sides in the revolution regularly turned to outside powers for help, allying with Spain, Britain, and even the United States.

Strategies and Tactics

All sides used racism to demonize opponents. Toussaint spoke of "mulatto treachery" to justify his 1799 attack on Rigaud, just as Rochambeau vilified blacks and mulattos in 1803. This rhetoric produced genocidal tactics. After defeating Rigaud in 1800, Dessalines was said to have massacred 10,000 enemy troops. Survivors accused Rochambeau of similar atrocities.

Ideologies

Racism was the dominant ideology of those colonists and French leaders hostile to emancipation and independence. On the other hand, those who advocated expanding civil rights evoked French revolutionary rhetoric of universalism and republicanism. As this vision faded in 1802 and 1803, the intellectuals allied with Dessalines described French inhumanity using images colonists had once applied to black rebels. The former masters were now "blood thirsty monsters."

In various periods a kind of creole nativism also played into revolutionary rhetoric. In the years immediately before the French Revolution, as colonists clamored for more self-government and greater commercial autonomy, one 1788 pamphlet suggested that colonists reclaim the Amerindian name "Haiti" for their homeland. Free men of color voiced a similar nativism in the early years of the revolution and described themselves as best suited to govern the colony. Finally, in the last years of the struggle, a new form of creole identity emerged, as black and mulatto soldiers fought the French, calling themselves the "indigenous army" and disparaging independent guerrilla bands as "Congos," a term suggesting their barbarity. The choice of the name "Haiti" for the new nation-state illustrates that Dessalines and his advisers were familiar with white colonial claims for autonomy.

IMPACTS

The French defeat in Saint-Domingue was one of the major reasons for Napoléon's sale of the Louisiana Territory to the United States in April 1803, ending France's presence as a major power in the hemisphere, even though France retained Guadeloupe, Martinique, Guyane, and smaller possessions.

The end of slavery in 1793 transformed the economy and society of the former colony. Though leaders including Sonthonax, Toussaint, Dessalines, and various nineteenth century presidents tried to force workers back to plantations, none of them fully revived slave-era production. When Haiti signed an 1825 treaty with France, lifting the danger of an invasion, the last of the big plantations faded away. Nevertheless, the Vatican withheld recognition until 1860 and the United States until 1861. As ex-slaves became peasants, coastal cities were left in the hands of administrative, commercial, and military elites. Haitian society in the nineteenth century was effectively divided in two, the world of the port cities and that of the peasants, known as the "outside people," "moun-an-deyò" in the Haitian Creole language.

The Haitian Revolution had a marked impact on the entire hemisphere. The new nation symbolized liberation throughout the Americas. Though historians debate the extent to which Haiti inspired slave rebellions in other societies, the 1790s and early nineteenth century did witness an unprecedented number of uprisings. In Brazil in 1805, mulatto soldiers wore medallions with Dessalines's image. In 1812 Cuban police found pictures of Toussaint, Dessalines, and other Haitian leaders in the home of a suspected free black rebel. In 1806 the Venezuelan independence fighter Francisco Miranda visited Haiti to recruit volunteers, and ten years later Haiti provided Simón Bolívar with muskets, ammunition, and a printing press. In the 1930s and 1940s, the black intellectuals C. L. R. James (Trinidad) and Aimé Césaire (Martinique) published widely read works on the Haitian Revolution, linking it to their own efforts to achieve independence and equality.

Yet the revolution had a negative legacy as well. By driving up sugar and coffee prices, it inadvertently prolonged slavery and the slave trade. In the years after 1800 the African slave trade to Brazil reached new heights. Many of Saint-Domingue's planters fled to Cuba, where they helped build the Cuban sugar industry, which imported over 500,000 enslaved Africans between 1800 and 1867 (Eltis, Behrend, Richardson, and Klein 1999, Database on CD-ROM). The Haitian Revolution brought more repressive slave laws in the United States. For whites, Haiti's dangerous example helped produce Gabriel's Rebellion (Virginia, 1800), the Charles Deslondes Revolt (Louisiana, 1811), and the Denmark Vesey Rebellion (South Carolina, 1822). Even abolitionists were not enthusiastic about events in Haiti. Accounts of the slave revolt confirmed racist stereotypes about African "savagery" of Africans and mulatto "treachery."

PEOPLE AND ORGANIZATIONS

Congos

This name was given to the independent guerrilla bands that continued to fight the French in 1802, after Toussaint and his army had capitulated. Composed mostly of African-born ex-slaves, these guerrilla groups refused to accept the authority of the emerging "indigenous" army, who used the term "Congo" to stigmatize them as African barbarians.

Dessalines, Jean-Jacques (1758–1806)

Toussaint's top lieutenant. A slave when the revolution broke out, Dessalines led the independence struggle after Toussaint's arrest. He proclaimed Haitian independence on January 1, 1804, but was assassinated in 1806 by a coalition of wealthy landowners and military colleagues who felt he had

gone to far in his attempts to maintain state control over plantation agriculture. He was on the verge of nationalizing valuable estates that were claimed by wealthy families.

Friends of the Blacks

The abolitionist society founded in Paris in 1788 by Jacques-Pierre Brissot. Saint-Domingue's planters blamed it for the slave revolt, and it is possible that colonial slaves heard of its members' speeches and pamphlets against the slave trade. The society faded after 1792 but was reborn in 1797 and 1798 with the goal of strengthening French colonialism.

Grégoire, Henri (Abbé Grégoire) (1750–1831)

The most prominent French revolutionary defender of civil rights for colonial men of color. With Julien Raimond, he urged a universal definition of French citizenship achieved in 1794 with the abolition of slavery. Grégoire remained a passionate advocate of racial equality to his death in 1831, publishing his important *De la literature des nègres* in 1808.

Indigenous Army

The name taken by the forces that united to fight against the French expeditionary force in 1802 and 1803. It combined the mostly black ex-slave soldiers who had fought under Toussaint and Dessalines and their former enemies, the mostly mixed-race soldiers who had fought under Rigaud and Leclerc.

Leclerc, Charles (1772–1802)

A successful general who married Napoléon Bonaparte's sister Pauline, Leclerc was chosen by Bonaparte to restore French control of Saint-Domingue in 1802. Though he defeated Toussaint, Leclerc provoked a revolt that ultimately led to Haitian independence. He did not live to see this, however, succumbing to yellow fever in November 1802.

Patriot Movement

In Saint-Domingue's cities in years 1789–1792, "patriots" were the working class whites who identified with the antiauthoritarian politics of revolutionary France. They criticized high royal officials and wealthy planters as well as the free men of color who served in the colonial militias. Their insistence on white superiority caused and sustained the civil war between men of color and whites in 1791 that made slave revolution possible.

Raimond, Julien (1744–1801)

A wealthy mixed-race planter, Raimond was the leading voice of Saint-Domingue's free people of color in revolutionary Paris. Already working in France for racial reforms before the revolution, between 1790 and 1798, he published at least sixteen pamphlets on colonial affairs. He returned to the colony as a revolutionary commissioner in 1796 and 1800, developing a system of forced labor and estate leases that kept the export economy alive after slavery. Although he had long advocated loyalty to France, he joined Toussaint's autonomous government, serving on his constitutional committee before dying in 1801.

Rigaud, André (1761–1811)

A free man of color before the revolution, Rigaud participated in a French expedition to Savannah, Georgia, in 1779. In 1790 he emerged as a military and political leader in Saint-Domingue's southern peninsula, eventually becoming its de facto ruler. He was defeated by Toussaint-Louverture's armies in 1800 and sent into exile in France. He returned to the island briefly in 1802 and 1810 but was unable to re-establish himself politically.

Sonthonax, Leger Felicite (1763–1813)

The man who convinced Saint-Domingue's rebel slaves to join the French Revolution in exchange for official recognition of their freedom arrived in the colony as head of the Second Commission in 1792. Charged with enforcing a controversial decree giving civil rights to free men of color, he defeated counter-revolution by issuing a series of regional emancipation proclamations in 1793. Called back to France, where he was acquitted of treason charges, he returned to Saint-Domingue in 1798. He lost a power struggle with Toussaint, who forced him to leave.

Toussaint-Louverture (ca. 1743–1803)

The future governor of Saint-Domingue was born into slavery, probably in the colony's Northern Province, around 1743. After working as an animal doctor, he either purchased or was given his freedom around 1776. For over a decade he grew and sold coffee, leasing slaves and land. During the revolution, he first emerged as an adviser to rebel leaders but became a leader in his own right in 1793. After joining the French army in 1794, he became the dominant military and political figure in the island by 1798. In 1801 he had himself proclaimed governor for life and was defeated by a French expeditionary force the following year. He died in a prison in the Jura mountains in France in 1803.

John Garrigus

See Also Colonialism, Anti-Colonialism, and Neo-Colonialism; French Revolution; Haiti's Democratic Revolution

References and Further Readings
Blackburn, Robin. 1988. *The Overthrow of Colonial Slavery, 1776–1848*. London: Verso.
———. 1997. *The Making of New World Slavery: From the Baroque to the Modern, 1492–1800*. London: Verso.
Dayan, Joan. 1995. *Haiti, History, and the Gods*. Berkeley: University of California Press.
Dubois, Laurent. 2004a. *A Colony of Citizens: Revolution and Slave Emancipation in the French Caribbean, 1787–1804*. Chapel Hill: University of North Carolina.
———. 2004b. *Avengers of the New World: The Story of the Haitian Revolution*. Cambridge, MA: Harvard University Press.
Dubois, Laurent, and John Garrigus. 2006. *Slave Revolution in the Caribbean*. Boston: Bedford/St. Martin's.
Eltis, David, Stephen D. Behrend, David Richardson, and Herbert S. Klein. 1999. *The Trans Atlantic Slave Trade: A Database on CD-ROM*. Cambridge: Cambridge University Press.
Fick, Carolyn E. 1990. *The Making of Haiti: The Saint Domingue Revolution from Below*. Knoxville: University of Tennessee Press.
Garrigus, John D. 1996. "Redrawing the Colour Line: Gender and the Social Construction of Race in Pre-Revolutionary Haiti," *Journal of Caribbean History* 30, 1-2: 28–50.
———. 2006. *Before Haiti: Race and Citizenship in French Saint-Dominique, 1760–1804*. New York: Palgrave MacMillan.
Geggus, David P. 1990. "Urban Development in 18th Century Saint-Domingue," *Bulletin du Centre d'histoire des espaces atlantique* 5: 197–219.
———. 1993. "Sugar and Coffee Production and the Shaping of Slavery in Saint Domingue." Pp. 73–100 in *Cultivation and Culture: Labor and the Shaping of Slave Life in the Americas*, edited by Ira Berlin and Philip D. Morgan. Charlottesville: University of Virginia Press.
———, ed. 2001. *The Impact of the Haitian Revolution in the Atlantic World*. Columbia, SC: University of South Carolina Press.
———. 2002. *Haitian Revolutionary Studies*. Bloomington: Indiana University Press.
King, Stewart R. 2001. *Blue Coat or Powdered Wig: Free People of Color in Pre-Revolutionary Saint Domingue*. Athens: University of Georgia Press.
Nicholls, David. 1996. *From Dessalines to Duvalier: Race, Colour and National Independence in Haiti*. New Brunswick, NJ: Rutgers University Press.
Trouillot, Michel-Rolph. 1990. *Haiti; State against Nation: The Origins and Legacy of Duvalierism*. New York: Monthly Review Press.

Human Rights, Morality, Social Justice, and Revolution

Questions of morality, social justice, and human rights are deeply intertwined with modern revolutions. In all human societies, people form strong cognitive and emotional commitments to all kinds of ideas about their society, including concepts about *what is*—for example, ideas about categories of people, objects, and other entities, and the relations between them. These concepts are linked in complex ways with concepts about *what should be*—the moral rules that identify certain categories of behavior and action by certain types of people in certain situations as proper or improper, right or wrong, appropriate or inappropriate. These ideas about morality include fundamental perceptions about sets of claims—obligations and entitlements, rights and responsibilities—attached to important institutionalized relationships in a given society, such as the relationships between rulers and the people subjected to their rule, between landlords and tenants, between bosses and workers. These various kinds of claims and expectations govern the exercise of power, the division of labor, and the distribution of goods and services in society. They are the basic elements of *social justice* norms. Institutionalized economic, political, and sociocultural relationships embody and realize specific ideas and beliefs concerning appropriate obligations and entitlements, enforceable rights and responsibilities; social justice norms are the standards brought to bear in evaluating these social institutions. The moral, social justice, and human rights aspects of modern revolutions can be viewed in relation to the emergence of revolutionary movements, the events and actions of the phase of open revolutionary struggle, and the outcomes of revolutionary movements.

There is considerable variation in the extent to which moral codes and ideas of social justice are or are not shared by the diverse members of a society. At any given historical moment, however, it is possible to distinguish between the dominant ideas about morality and social justice, and competing sets of ideas, and to identify the societal actors associated with each. The dominant concepts of rights and responsibilities are usually those embodied in social institutions upheld by law and, ultimately, the coercive power of the state. The dominant institutions may be viewed as just by those who share the concepts embodied in those institutions. Those who hold divergent or opposing conceptions of morality and social justice experience the dominant societal institutions, and the state that enforces them, as unjust. Perceptions of injustice, and the feelings of "moral outrage" (Moore 1978, 5) that accompany the experience of injustice, are not by themselves sufficient to give rise to a revolutionary social movement, but they are a necessary condition for the mass mobilization of opposition that is included in most scholarly definitions of revolution.

INJUSTICE FRAMES, RIGHTS, AND THE EMERGENCE OF REVOLUTIONARY SOCIAL MOVEMENTS

Widespread grievances over perceived economic or political injustices, or both, are particularly important in creating the potential for mass mobilization in support of revolutionary social movements. Peasants may rebel or be willing to participate in revolutionary social movements when the state enforces the capitalist profit-dominated penetration of agricultural production, in violation of the traditional "moral economy" of subsistence, which places the right of the peasant producers to subsistence over the profit motive of landlords or agribusiness interests (Scott 1976, 3; Thompson 1971, 79). Widespread unemployment, declining wages, and inflation can create the potential for mass mobilization among urban workers; this potential can be directed against the state in revolutionary social movements, if the state is perceived as responsible for, or at least ineffective in ameliorating, these threats to workers' economic survival. Urban educated professionals and service workers may also perceive and experience economic injustices such as wage, consumption, and mobility limits, or may experience moral outrage and be mobilized despite relatively secure employment. Peasant injustice grievances were crucial in the majority of twentieth-century revolutions, as well as the English and French revolutions. Urban working classes also played a crucial role in many twentieth-century revolutions, such as the Russian revolutions of 1905 and 1917, the failed German Revolution of 1918/1919, and the Iranian Revolution. The majority of modern revolutionary social movements have also drawn organizational leaders from among the urban educated classes.

In summary, people learn standards of fairness—that is, concepts of social justice that are deeply entwined with their self-understandings and understandings of how the world works and ought to work. When their fundamental standards of fairness are systematically violated, people may feel moral outrage. The state is among the targets of that emotion when state actors are perceived to be the cause or facilitators of the injustice.

Social movement organizations, including revolutionary organizations aiming to force a change in control of power, recruit participants and support using collective action frames, which are interpretative frameworks that social movement organizations use to morally "organize experience and guide action" (Benford and Snow 2000, 614). Collective action frames do this by offering simplified representations of reality that are constructed so as "to mobilize potential adherents and constituents, to garner bystander support, and to demobilize antagonists" (Snow and Benford 1988, 198). To effectively mobilize support for social change goals, collective action frames must include a diagnostic component that identifies the conditions that require change and attributes responsibility for the problems to some set of actors; a prognostic component that outlines alternative arrangements to be established; and a motivational component that exhorts others to participate in the effort to achieve the change. Successful frames resonate with people's experience and interpret their perceptions and emotions in a plausible way. They propose goals and alternative arrangements that are perceived as better expressions of people's sense of justice and as realistic—that is, achievable. Revolutionary social movement organizations generate injustice frames (Gamson, Fireman, and Rytina 1982) that take seriously mass grievances and interpret them as injustices within a diagnostic causal framework that attributes at least partial responsibility to the state, along with other societal and possibly foreign actors. Prognostically, revolutionary injustice frames propose a more just set of social arrangements, to be established after the seizure of state power, and they offer vocabularies of motive emphasizing the severity of the current injustices, the urgency of the need for fundamental change, the efficacy of the revolutionary movement organization, and the justification of the use of extreme means, given the severity of the injustices (Benford and Snow 2000).

Revolutionaries may not find potential adherents in a state of inertia—they may already be involved in spontaneous rebellions or nonrevolutionary forms of collective action, based on alternative interpretations of the situation. In that case, mobilization in support of revolutionary movements requires efforts to bring competing ideologies into some form of alignment with the revolutionary ideology. For example, revolutionaries may attempt to integrate key aspects of competing reformist or religious interpretations of the injustices of the situation, while still insisting on the necessity of popular revolution—as opposed to reform or spiritual preparation for messianic salvation—as the appropriate response.

As noted above, our sense of justice is based on expectations about fair and legitimate claims and obligations. Injustice ideologies have for centuries used the language of rights to express these claims and demand their recognition and enforcement. This sociological concept of rights as legitimate claims includes the political or economic corporate (group) privileges around which pre-modern European societies were organized, the individual natural rights (of white male property owners) with which the early modern revolutionaries in England, France, and the United States justified their violent challenge to corporate privilege, as well as the universal human rights articulated in the United Nations (UN) 1948 Universal Declaration of Human Rights and invoked by revolutionary movements of the late twentieth century (e.g., the Nicaraguan and Iranian revolutions).

Empirically, the claims embodied in legitimate rights, whether to property or privilege, or to civil, political, or economic participation, are established in historical processes of political conflict and bargaining (Sjoberg, Gill and Williams 2001; Tilly 1998). Pre-modern injustice frames grounded claims to land, harvest, or exemption from state or landlord extractions or regulatory intrusions as traditionally guaranteed corporate rights. Corporate rights refer to rights assigned not to individuals but to whole categories of people, such as members of the nobility, the clergy, or people in a particular occupation. European philosophers began to articulate concepts of rights in the sixteenth century, grounding these as granted by God to (adult white male property-owning) persons in an imaginary, pre-social "state of nature"; empirical social scientists emphasize, however, that such philosophical articulations took place in times of revolutionary social change. Lynn Hunt, a historian of the French Revolution, points out that key early formulations of rights doctrines were completed in the context of revolutions—Grotius published his pathbreaking treatise on natural rights in 1625, during the Dutch struggle to free itself from Spanish rule, and the English Levellers invoked their "native rights" in the "Agreement of the People" (1647) during the English Revolution (Hunt 2000, 6).

By the late eighteenth century, American and French challengers of the old social order could draw on over a century of philosophical discourse expounding and justifying the individual natural rights of (primarily adult white male property-owning) man to liberty, property, security, and resistance to oppression, equality before the law, protection against arbitrary exercise of authority or coercive power, freedom of worship, and freedom of the press. Whereas the English Bill of Rights of 1689 justified rights as based in English law, and thus did not assert the equality, universality, and naturalness of these rights, the American Declaration of Independence of 1776 and the French Declaration of the Rights of Man and Citizen of 1789 both asserted the rights of man as natural, equal, and universal (to all adult white male property owners). Both documents also linked legitimacy of the exercise of state power to the guarantee of individual natural rights and asserted the people's right to revolution, should state power fail to protect those rights (Hunt 2000: 7).

Eleanor Roosevelt looking at the Universal Declaration of Human Rights, 1948. (Corel Corporation)

In the nineteenth century, Marx and Engels included the individualism of the Enlightenment rights discourse in their critique of political economy: individualist bourgeois moral philosophy was the ideological justification required for the bourgeois revolutions that ushered in the historical transition to the capitalist mode of production. From a Marxist perspective, individual emancipation would result from the collective struggle to eliminate exploitative social relations and establish economic and political institutions that embodied truly universal human interests, rather than particular interests of the dominant capitalist class. The Marxist-influenced revolutionaries in Russia, Germany, and China, in their struggles to overthrow regimes and transform societal institutions that systematically violated human rights, avoided reference to concepts of injustice based on individual natural rights, to the extent that the latter were in conflict with the language of the collective rights of the working classes, class conflict, and class justice.

The United Nations' adoption of the Universal Declaration of Human Rights in 1948, in reaction to the atrocities of the Nazi regime, changed again the context in which revolutionaries of all kinds could invoke human rights in revolu-

tionary injustice frameworks. The international recognition of basic human political, economic, and social rights created a venue and a language for challenging the legitimacy of existing regimes based on systematic human rights violations. The institutionalization of the universal human rights discourse after World War II also dealt a death blow to the legitimacy of colonial regimes, providing material for anti-colonial revolutionaries' injustice ideologies in Vietnam, Algeria, and elsewhere in Southeast Asia and Africa throughout the middle of the twentieth century. The 1989 popular movements that swept away state Socialist regimes in Poland, Hungary, East Germany, and throughout Eastern Europe invoked the individual political and civil rights guaranteed in the Universal Declaration.

JUSTICE, RIGHTS, AND THE REVOLUTIONARY STRUGGLE

Where revolutionaries are able to mobilize enough resources and popular support to present a serious challenge to the existing regime, and the latter is able and willing to offer resistance, revolutionary struggles can develop into protracted, violent conflicts and internal war. In fact, until the Eastern European revolutions of the late twentieth century, dominant scholarly concepts of revolution explicitly included the use of violent means to overthrow the existing regime. The use of violent means to achieve social change is itself a morally momentous decision, since both insurgent military actions and state counterinsurgency activities are likely to result in destruction and civilian casualties. Furthermore, resources must be secured to supply mobile revolutionary forces and to fund the state's counterinsurgency campaign; they may be extracted from the productive population by force if they are not surrendered willingly.

The Shining Path revolutionary movement in Peru provides an extreme illustration of the moral hazards of revolutionary violence (Iglesias 2000). The initiation of armed struggle by the Marxist-Maoist Shining Path revolutionary movement in 1980 was not preceded by widespread human rights violations on the part of the existing military regime, but it led to a dramatic deterioration of the human rights situation in Peru as a result of the ensuing war. Although a military dictatorship was in power until the 1980 elections, human rights abuses in Peru did not begin to approach the levels of abuse found in other Latin American countries such as El Salvador or Guatemala. The Shining Path revolutionaries, however, explicitly and programmatically rejected the doctrine of universal human rights articulated in the 1948 Universal Declaration as imperialist bourgeois ideology, claiming that the "people's rights"—above all the right to conquer power and transform the existing, oppressive social order into a proletarian state and society—superseded bourgeois, individualistic human rights. Guerrilla tactics were carried out with little regard for civilian casualties and sometimes directly targeted civilians, as in the massacre of more than eighty villagers in the district of Lucanamarca in 1983 (Iglesias 2000, 161, 162f.). The guerrilla strategy provoked equally violent and indiscriminate military and paramilitary responses, resulting in a dramatic increase in the level of grave human rights violations committed by both insurgents and security forces, including thousands of disappearances, countless cases of torture, and numerous massacres, bombings, and extrajudicial executions.

Revolutionary movements engaging in armed struggle thus face the task of continually justifying the use of violence and the sacrifices required of supporters and sympathizers in order to achieve their goals of seizing state power and establishing more just social institutions. Although moral outrage can spill over easily into uncontrolled violence against perceived oppressors, and individuals may seek opportunities to settle old personal grievances amid the turmoil of violent revolutionary conflicts, over the long run people usually will only support revolutionaries' systematic use of violent means, and bear the concomitant sacrifices, when they are convinced that nonviolent methods are futile and that revolutionaries' actions in the course of the struggle are consistent with the social justice concepts they propagate and that most people morally accept. Revolutionaries are particularly morally accountable in territories over which they gain control during the struggle, since they effectively assume state-like powers and functions in those areas. For these reasons, revolutionary leaders like Mao Zedong in China and Ho Chi Minh in Vietnam emphasized the importance of revolutionary ideology, politically committed revolutionary soldiers who would act according to the ideals of the revolution in their treatment of the people, educational efforts, and public self-criticism among revolutionary cadres for gaining and maintaining the support of the civilian population during the protracted violent conflicts those revolutionary struggles entailed. Furthermore, in the second half of the twentieth century, existing regimes confronting armed revolutionary challengers have invoked the language of human rights to undermine the popular legitimacy of revolutionary movement organizations. This has occurred frequently in revolutionary struggles in Latin America, with varying degrees of accuracy and success against the Sandinista revolutionaries in Nicaragua, the Farabundo Marti Front for National Liberation in El Salvador, and the Shining Path movement in Peru.

HUMAN RIGHTS AND SOCIAL JUSTICE NORMS UNDER REVOLUTIONARIES IN POWER

For revolutionary movements that succeed in taking control of the state, the moral dilemmas initially shift from justifying the use of violence against the existing regime to justifying the methods used to defend the revolutionaries' hold on power against counter-revolutionary challenges and internal opposition movements. The vulnerability to moral critique that accompanies the use of violence can be linked to a tendency to moral rigorism in revolutionary social movements and movement organizations. The dictatorship and terror initiated by the French Jacobin revolutionaries and the repression of counter-revolutionaries by the Bolsheviks' secret police during the Russian Civil War are manifestations of this tendency. The German Nazi "revolution from above" of the 1930s, which established a Fascist one-party state modeled in part after that introduced in Italy in the 1920s, also violently repressed opposition. Both German and Italian Fascist revolutionary justice frameworks extolled nationalism and their people's cultural superiority, and condemned the Soviet Union and Communist movements. The Nazis plan for their new society, however, also motivated the removal of inferior groups through sterilization and later physical extermination. It was the many human rights abuses of Fascist nations during the World War II period that constituted, as noted earlier, the primary motivation for the United Nations Declaration of Human Rights.

Revolutionary movements strive to introduce fundamental changes in the organization of society. In post-revolutionary Russia and the Soviet Union, in China, Vietnam, and Cuba, for example, economic inequalities and unemployment were reduced, land redistributed, and medical services and educational opportunities greatly expanded, but under conditions that many people viewed as violating basic political and civil rights. Revolutionary social movements in power have often proven themselves to be as willing to compromise human rights and violate widely held perceptions of social justice as were the regimes that the revolutionary movements struggled to overthrow. In the course of the French Revolution, opponents of the revolution and other "enemies of the state," particularly participants in the Vendée counter-revolutionary movement in the western departments of France, were summarily executed by Jacobin deputies; over 16,000 individuals were put to death during "The Terror" phase of the revolution between late 1793 and the summer of 1794 (Doyle 2002, 253). The Russian revolutionaries, under Stalin's leadership, brutally imposed an ultimately inefficient program of agricultural collectivization on millions of unwilling peasants between 1928 and 1935, arresting and deporting many of the wealthier peasants and opponents of collectivization to forced labor camps. The disorganization of agricultural production caused by forced collectivization resulted in devastating food shortages and starvation for large numbers of peasants. Most of the rights and prerogatives of urban labor organizations were also rescinded, reducing the latter to organizations for the mobilization of workers behind party-determined production goals. During the 1930s, under Stalin's leadership, terror was widely used as a means of controlling the citizenry and political competitors or challengers. The Chinese Communist Party also imposed rapid, forced economic development and social reorganization policies with equally catastrophic results, such as the "Great Leap Forward" of the 1958–1961 years, which resulted in widespread famine leading to the death of between 10 and 40 million people (BBC News 2005). Political rights have also been closely circumscribed and limited in single-party Socialist states such as China, and dissidence has often been met with brutal repression such as that which occurred in response to the Tiananmen Square Democracy Movement protests in Beijing in 1989. Although the Vietnamese revolutionaries, once in power, did not pursue the radical collectivization and in-

dustrialization programs that were the source of so much injustice and human suffering in the Soviet Union and the People's Republic of China, the Vietnamese Communist Party has been equally intolerant of political opposition, prohibiting independent trade unions, responding to political competition with repression, and generally stifling the development of an autonomous civil society. The politically liberal policy of the Sandinista revolutionaries in power in Nicaragua and the Allende government in Chile were exceptions to this pattern among Marxist-influenced revolutionary organizations.

Institutionalist sociologists like John Meyer (et al. 1997) argue that key concepts of Western European individualist rationalism have diffused globally through the world-wide expansion of capitalism, and the activities of states and a growing population of international nongovernmental organizations. Particularly since the formation of the UN, the cultural principles of "universalism, individualism, rational voluntaristic authority, human purposes of rationalizing progress, and world citizenship" (Boli and Thomas 1997, 180) have become institutionalized in a variety of international governance regimes and networks of international governmental and nongovernmental organizations. A Western European model of the national state has become globally legitimized to the exclusion of any alternative legitimate models; according to that model, states are organizations for protecting the individual universal human rights of their citizens and providing for their welfare by fostering rational progress and economic development. With the developing institutionalization of a world culture, the context of action for individuals, organizations, and states has become global. Actors that fail to signal acceptance of these world cultural principles, particularly individual human rights, are viewed in the world community as lacking legitimacy. Both states and organizational actors, including revolutionary social movement organizations, try to employ the rhetoric of human rights strategically to delegitimize their opponents and to portray their own policies and programs as superior manifestations of human rights.

Michael Mulcahy

See Also Chilean Socialist Revolution, Counter-Revolution, and the Restoration of Democracy; Chinese 1989 Democracy Movement; Chinese Revolution; Cinema of Revolution; Democracy, Dictatorship, and Fascism; Documentaries of Revolution; French Revolution; Inequality, Class, and Revolution; Italian Fascist Revolution; Nazi Revolution: Politics and Racial Hierarchy; South African Revolution; Student and Youth Movements, Activism and Revolution; Terrorism

References and Further Readings

Benford, Robert D., and David A. Snow. 2000. "Framing Processes and Social Movements: An Overview and Assessment," *Annual Review of Sociology* 26 : 611–39.

Boli, John, and George M. Thomas. 1997. "World Culture in the World Polity: A Century of International Non-Governmental Organization," *American Sociological Review* 62, 2: 171-190.

Doyle, William. 2002. *The Oxford History of the French Revolution.* 2nd edition. Oxford: Oxford University Press.

Gamson, William A., Bruce Fireman, and Steven Rytina. 1982. *Encounters with Unjust Authority.* Homewood, IL: Dorsey Press.

Hunt, Lynn. 1996. *The French Revolution and Human Rights: A Brief Documentary History.* Boston and New York: Bedford Books of St. Martin's Press.

———. 2000. "The Paradoxical Origins of Human Rights." Pp. 19–42 in *Human Rights and Revolutions,* edited by Jeffrey N. Wasserstrom, Lynn Hunt, and Marilyn B. Young. Lanham, MD: Rowman and Littlefield.

Iglesias, Carlos Basombrió. 2000. "Sendero Luminoso and Human Rights: A Perverse Logic That Captured the Country." Pp. 155–176 in *Human Rights and Revolutions,* edited by Jeffrey N. Wasserstrom, Lynn Hunt, and Marilyn B. Young. Lanham, MD: Rowan and Littlefield.

Meyer, John W., John Boli, George M. Thomas, and Francisco O. Ramirez. 1997. "World Society and the Nation-State," *American Journal of Sociology* 103 (1): 144–181.

Moore, Barrington. 1978. *Injustice: The Social Bases of Obedience and Revolt.* White Plains, NY: M. E. Sharpe.

Morsnick, Johannes. 1999. *The Universal Declaration of Human Rights: Origins, Drafting and Intent.* Philadelphia: University of Pennsylvania Press.

Scott, James C. 1976. *The Moral Economy of the Peasant: Rebellion and Resistance in Southeast Asia.* New Haven, CT: Yale University Press.

Sjoberg, Gideon, Elizabeth A. Gill, and Norma Williams. 2001. "A Sociology of Human Rights," *Social Problems* 48, 1: 11-47.

Snow, David A., and Robert D. Benford. 1988. "Ideology, Frame Resonance, and Participant Mobilization," *International Social Movement Research* 1: 197–217.

Thompson, E. P. 1971. "The Moral Economy of the English Crowd in the Eighteenth Century," *Past and Present* 50, 1: 76–136. Reprinted in E. P. Thompson. 1991. *Customs in Common.* London: Penguin Books.

Tilly, Charles. 1998. "Where Do Rights Come From?" Pp. 55–72 in *Democracy, Revolution, and History,* edited by Theda Skocpol, with the assistance of George Ross, Tony Smith, and Judith Eisenberg Vichniac. Ithaca, NY, and London: Cornell University Press.

Wasserstrom, Jeffrey N., Lynn Hunt, and Marilyn B. Young, eds. 2000. *Human Rights and Revolutions.* Lanham, MD: Rowman and Littlefield.

Wolf, Eric. 1969. *Peasant Wars of the 20th Century.* New York: Harper and Row, Publishers.

Zaret, David. 2000. "Tradition, Human Rights, and the English Revolution." Pp. 43–58 in *Human Rights and Revolutions,* edited by Jeffrey N. Wasserstrom, Lynn Hunt, and Marilyn B. Young. Lanham, MD: Rowman and Littlefield.

BBC News. "Inside China's Ruling Party: Great Leap Forward." http://news.bbc.co.uk/1/ shared/spl/hi/asia_pac/02/china _party_congress/china_ruling_party/key_people_events/ html/great_leap_forward.stm accessed May 18, 2005.

Hungarian Revolution of 1956

CHRONOLOGY

1956   In February, Khrushchev denounces Stalin in a secret speech to the twentieth congress of the Soviet Communist Party.

On July 17, Mátyás Rákosi steps down as party leader. He is replaced by Erno Gero.

On October 6, László Rajk, wrongfully executed for treason in 1949, is formally reburied in Budapest. A crowd of 100,000 attends the funeral.

On October 13, Imre Nagy regains membership in the party.

On October 16, students in the city of Szeged found an independent organization, the first of its kind in the Soviet Bloc.

On October 19, Polish leader Wladyslaw Gomulka persuades the Kremlin not to intervene militarily in Poland, promising to remain within the Soviet Bloc.

On October 22, a student gathering at Budapest Technical University, inspired in part by recent events in Poland, adopts the "16 Points," a set of demands that includes the withdrawal of Soviet troops from Hungary and reinstatement of a multiparty political system.

On October 23, a student-led march begins at 3 p.m. and quickly turns into a full-fledged demonstration involving Hungarians from all parts of society. Other protests take place in university cities around Hungary. At 9 p.m., Nagy delivers a speech from the parliament building but fails to satisfy demonstrators. At 9:37 p.m., in one of many attacks on places and symbols of authority, demonstrators topple a giant statue of Stalin.

On October 24, the first Soviet armored units enter the capital between 3 and 4 a.m. At 8:13 a.m., Hungarian radio announces that Nagy is the new prime minister. Half an hour later, a state of emergency is declared. As groups of rebels form at key locations in Budapest, the first workers' council is formed.

On October 25, at about 11:15 a.m., security forces open fire on a crowd gathered in Kossuth Square. At 12:32 p.m., a radio communiqué announces that Erno Gero has been dismissed and János Kádár has been appointed first secretary of the Hungarian Workers' Party (the Hungarian Communist party).

On October 26, demonstrations and fighting continue to spread around the country. At 4:13 p.m., Hungarian radio announces that a new national government will be formed and Hungarian-Soviet negotiations will be conducted, among other promises. Shortly afterward, the authorities declare an amnesty for all who lay down their arms by 10:00 p.m. The United States, Britain, and France jointly propose that the UN Security Council examine the Hungarian question. Pope Pius XII issues an encyclical on the uprising.

On October 27, the revolution continues to unfold in Hungary. Rebels hold on to their gains while suffering considerable human losses.

On October 28 at 1:20 p.m., Hungarian radio announces a cease-fire. At 2 p.m. the new government is sworn in and signals a basic turn in party policy. That evening the curfew is lifted.

On October 29, Israeli forces attack Egypt in an operation planned with the French and British; its goal is to seize control of the Suez Canal. Although not timed to coincide with the Hungarian uprising, the attack has the effect of amplifying the importance for the Soviets of defeating the insurrection and undermining the West's case against Moscow at the United Nations.

On October 30 at 2:30 p.m., Hungarian radio announces the abolition of the one-party system and the establishment of a coalition government. Previously banned parties begin to reconstitute themselves. The government also recognizes the local self-governing bodies created during the revolution. Rebel forces release the Catholic primate, József Cardinal Mindszenty, from house arrest. After a battle at the local party headquarters in Budapest, several party members are lynched by the crowd. Reflecting support for the revolution in various parts of Eastern Europe, rallies take place in Poland and Romania.

On October 30–31, Soviet forces pull out of Budapest.

On October 31, Nagy, Kádár, and others form the Hungarian Socialist Workers' Party in order to break with the existing Hungarian Workers' Party and the Stalinist practices associated with it. One day after announcing an extraordinary declaration promoting the equal status of East European countries and a peaceful resolution of the Hungarian crisis, the Soviet Presidium reverses its stand and decides to intervene militarily in Hungary. President Dwight D. Eisenhower expresses his admiration for the Hungarian people but also reassures Moscow that Washington will not seek alliances with either the new Polish or Hungarian leaderships.

On November 1, Soviet forces begin to reenter the country without Hungarian approval. Nagy declares Hungary's neutrality and its withdrawal from the Warsaw Pact. He appeals to the United Nations and to other governments in "lands near and far" for help in preventing a Soviet-led takeover.

On November 2, János Kádár arrives secretly in Moscow, where he agrees to form a new Hungarian government.

November 3 at 10 p.m., in the midst of Hungarian-Soviet military negotiations, Soviet secret police arrest the Hungarian delegation.

On November 4 at 4:15 a.m., five divisions of Soviet troops cross the Hungarian border and move on Budapest. Initially, heavy casualties are sustained on both sides. At 5:20 a.m., Nagy broadcasts the news that Soviet forces have entered the country. He then takes refuge in the Yugoslav embassy.

On November 7, Kádár installs the new government, undoing many of Nagy's changes while simultaneously attempting to appease the Hungarian population.

On November 22, Nagy and his associates leave the Yugoslav embassy and are immediately arrested.

1957   In January, the Kádár government institutes numerous harsh measures designed to punish anti-regime activists, limit public political activity, and gear up the economy.

1958   On June 16, Nagy is executed. Several associates suffer a similar fate.

1963   On March 17, after secret Hungarian-U.S. talks over the previous year lead to agreement by the UN General Assembly to drop the Hungarian question, Kádár announces a general amnesty for most of those being punished for revolutionary activities in 1956.

INTRODUCTION

The Hungarian Revolution was a spontaneous, popular uprising by much of a nation against a system imposed on it from the outside. A nation with strong ties to Western history and culture, Hungary fell under Communist rule after World War II much the way other countries of central Europe did. After eight years of often arbitrary repression and centralized control of virtually every aspect of life, the Hungarians struck back. Their cause was hopeless given the huge disparity between their capabilities and those of the Soviet armed forces, but the nature of their aspirations and the bravery with which they carried out their struggle made the Hungarian revolt a symbol for generations to come.

BACKGROUND: CULTURE AND HISTORY

Hungarians trace their national history to the settlement of the Carpathian Basin by the Magyar leader Árpád in the year 896. In 1001, Vajk, a descendent, accepted Christianity, took the name István (Saint Stephen), and subsequently merged the Hungarian tribes of the region into a unified state. The same dynasty reigned until the early fourteenth century, when a succession of non-dynastic rulers held sway. In 1526, the House of Habsburg took power, holding it until 1918. An important event during that period was the revolution of 1848–1849, in which Hungary declared its autonomy from Austria but was ultimately defeated by Austrian forces with the aid of czarist Russia. Hungarians in 1956 would find inspiration in those experiences.

Hungarian culture bridged the two worlds of East and West. For centuries, Hungarian forebears wandered the steppes of Eurasia, finally abandoning that way of life under Árpád in favor of cultivation of the land and animal herding. István's momentous decision to embrace Christianity sealed Hungary's ties to the Western world. The country's most evident link with its Eastern origins remains its language, which belongs to the Ugro-Finnic family and shares both vocabulary and grammar from other languages of the western Urals and northwestern Asian regions. Over the centuries, Hungary developed strong cultural traditions associated with Western civilization, notably the Catholic Church, and chiefly in the areas of architecture and literature. Those traditions survived and at times even flourished under Habsburg rule.

After the collapse of the Austro-Hungarian empire in 1918, an independent republic briefly appeared. It was followed by a short-lived Communist regime under Béla Kun, which received backing from the fledgling Communist government in Moscow but ultimately inadequate local support. In 1919, that regime was overthrown and eventually replaced by an extreme right-wing government under Miklós Horthy, which lasted until 1944. Horthy forged agreements with Adolph Hitler and during the war took further steps to reacquire large parts of the former empire, including portions of Slovakia, Transylvania, Slovenia, and Croatia that had been lost under the Treaty of Trianon of 1920.

Beginning in 1944, the Soviet occupation of Hungary drove Germany's forces out of the country. In Hungary's first post-war elections, in November 1945, the Smallholders Party won 57 percent of the vote while the Soviet-backed Hungarian Workers' Party won 17 percent. But the Communists, supported by the overwhelming Soviet military presence, were able to use "salami tactics"—including threats, alliances, and other means—gradually to divide and weaken other members of the coalition government and simultaneously to place their own party members in several key posts. In manipulated elections in 1947, the Communists emerged as the strongest single party and soon set about wresting full control of the political arena, arresting opposition political leaders or forcing them to flee abroad.

Once in power with Soviet backing, party leader Mátyás Rákosi quickly established a Stalinist regime, featuring a command economy and relying on political terror, including purges, show trials, mass imprisonments, and executions. But the regime soon faced serious problems. A growing crisis in the economy, aggravated by rigid centralized decision making and chronically harsh methods of control, only intensified the pressures for change within society.

After Joseph Stalin died in 1953, the new leaders in the Kremlin began to reverse his most extreme policies. Concerned about the decline in their own economy as well as others in the Socialist bloc, and sensitive to the dangers of social unrest, they stepped away from an emphasis on heavy industry and the military, seeking more balance with the needs of agriculture and the consumer sector. Having faced Stalin's repressive apparatus themselves, they were motivated to relax the most repressive forms of social control, both at home and in their allied countries.

In June 1953, Moscow prevailed on the Hungarian leadership to remove Rákosi as prime minister. In his place, they appointed Imre Nagy, a lifelong Communist who specialized in economics and agriculture. Nagy unfolded a major new program, the New Course, which called for loosening central controls over the economy, redirecting resources away from heavy industry, putting an end to collectivized agriculture, raising living standards, and most significantly, reversing the pattern of official repression of society. These were dramatic measures that ran directly against the previously accepted norms of Socialist development in the Soviet Bloc. Moscow was tolerant at first but soon grew uneasy. Nagy, too, was proving unable to achieve any sort of economic breakthrough. The fault was not entirely his own. The complexity of the problems facing the country was magnified by his hard-line opponents' concerted efforts to undermine his policies.

But the Kremlin was also troubled by the sense that Nagy's approach was creating more turmoil in society, not less. Ironically, the very kinds of reform policies the Soviets had promoted earlier were now causing them to rethink their decision. They realized that loosening political and economic controls to the extent intended by Nagy could end up undercutting the ruling Communist party. By lifting the lid on repression even a little, they had raised expectations among the population for further improvements and freedoms they were unwilling to fulfill. The difficulty for the Soviets was how to strike a balance between allowing greater local autonomy and retaining centralized control.

Caught in this dynamic, Nagy was forced to step down in early 1955. Rákosi regained the ascendancy, but the hard-liners were unable to remove Nagy entirely. He continued to challenge the country's leadership, albeit mainly within official channels. Along the way he gained the support of a growing circle of party members, intellectuals, and journalists who would form a base of growing power for the increasingly popular leader.

A major turning point in the Soviet Bloc came in February 1956 when Khrushchev, now the unconcealed leader of the Kremlin, used the occasion of the twentieth congress of the Soviet Communist Party to deliver an unprecedented speech denouncing Stalin and his crimes. Although he spoke to a closed audience, the contents of the speech soon became widely known. As in other countries of the bloc, Khrushchev's attack on Stalinism had the effect of bolstering proponents of reform in Hungary. This was the case both among the public and within the Communist Party. The officially sanctioned Petofi Circle, for example, grew increasingly strident in its political views, until its activities were suspended in late June 1956.

Also in late June, another significant event occurred. Security forces in Poznan, Poland, crushed a workers' demonstration, taking almost 100 lives and injuring several hundred others. To avert a similar disaster in Hungary, the Soviets stepped in once more, replacing Rákosi and demanding a crackdown on the opposition. But the situation only worsened. Rákosi's successor was ineffectual and the Hungarian leadership, already shaken by the progressive unraveling of party control, concluded that harsh measures would no longer work. Hungarian society was on the verge of revolt.

CONTEXT AND PROCESS OF REVOLUTION

In the fall, events moved rapidly. On October 6, the ceremonial reburial of a prominent Communist official, László Rajk (he had been wrongly accused of various political crimes, including Titoism and spying for the West, and executed after a show trial in 1949), provided the occasion for an unprecedented mass demonstration of popular dissatisfaction with the repressive practices of that era. Ten days later, students at the University of Szeged in the south of the country publicly withdrew from the Communist-controlled Union of Working Youth and established their own independent entity, the first time such a group had been created outside party control. On October 19, in neighboring Poland, a reform-oriented Polish politician, Wladyslaw Gomulka, managed to convince Khrushchev not to intervene to prevent his appointment to head the Polish Communist Party, an accomplishment hailed by the Hungarian students as an act of courage and independence against the Soviet Union. Three days later, students at Budapest Technical University, inspired in part by Gomulka's standoff with Khrushchev, formulated the "16 Points," a list of demands that included the previously unheard-of call for the withdrawal of Soviet troops from Hungary and restoration of a multiparty system. The students also finalized plans for a large protest—without official approval—the following day in the capital.

On October 23, at 3 p.m., the demonstration got under way. Streams of marchers met at symbolic Bem Square, where a monument honored a Polish general who had aided Hungarian freedom fighters in 1848. From there, the demonstrators headed to Budapest's stunning parliament building, to the radio station, and to City Park, site of an enormous statue of Joseph Stalin. Along the way, ordinary citizens, including workers coming off their shifts, spontaneously joined the marchers, swelling their ranks into the tens of thousands. As they marched, their demands grew more extreme, including calls of "Rákosi into the Danube; Imre Nagy into the parliament." At this point, the reform Communist leader still embodied popular hopes for major change.

The Hungarian leadership was taken aback at the size of the protests and soon split over how to handle the new phenomenon. One faction favored harsh action. Another believed accommodation was needed to address the obvious underlying social grievances. As a result, the mixed messages sent to the population over the next several days only complicated the situation. One of the first steps by Prime Minister Erno Gero was to call Moscow for help. A sizeable Red Army contingent was stationed in Hungary, and Khrushchev agreed to send them immediately to Budapest. Moscow also dispatched two Presidium members secretly to Hungary to monitor developments and advise and instruct the Hungarian authorities. At the same time, Gero delivered a speech over the radio denouncing the uprising, but his harsh words only angered the crowds and helped provoke the first violent confrontations that evening.

Others in the Hungarian leadership favored more conciliatory measures. They succeeded in reappointing Nagy to their ranks and prevailed on him to address the crowd gathered at the parliament. But his speech had the opposite of its intended effect. The authorities were caught unawares by how quickly popular expectations had changed. Nagy's call for a return to reform Communist remedies left the crowd deeply dissatisfied and the leadership just as split on how to respond.

That same evening, the uprising turned violent. While Nagy was speaking outside parliament, the crowds at the radio station were fired upon under circumstances that remain unclear. Somehow demonstrators had managed to acquire weapons during the day, and a firefight ensued, producing the first casualties in the capital. Meanwhile, at City Park another large crowd in an act of brazen defiance tore down the statue to Stalin and dragged it through the streets. These developments shocked the leadership but did not yet impart the sense that events were entirely out of hand.

Portrait of Hungarian premier Imre Nagy. (Library of Congress)

Early the next morning, Nagy, newly sworn in as prime minister, declared a state of emergency. Red Army tanks had already arrived and were beginning to stake out positions in the capital. Kremlin envoys Anastas Mikoyan and Mikhail Suslov also arrived, and backed by the Soviet military presence, contributed to a mood of optimism on the part of the Hungarian party leadership. Early on October 25, the government lifted the curfew.

But the revolution was still gathering force, fuelled by long-suppressed public outrage and inept responses by the authorities. A turning point came on the morning of October 25, when soldiers once more opened fire on a large crowd, this time gathered at the parliament. Again, the circumstances are unclear, but it is known that hard-line Hungarian leaders were outraged to discover that local citizens had persuaded some Soviet soldiers not to fight; tanks could actually be seen riding through the city hoisting the Hungarian tricolor flag. Whatever its origins, the violence at Kossuth Square resulted in up to 100 dead and ended any chance of negotiating a quick solution to the crisis.

For the next several days, the revolution unfolded in a variety of ways. Budapest was the scene of widespread street fighting, pitting Soviet heavy armor against ordinary Hungarian citizens. But the resistance was surprisingly effective despite being poorly armed. Using extraordinary ingenuity and taking advantage of their knowledge of the capital as well as their mobility, they were able to disable a number of vehicles, create roadblocks, and make quick getaways. Furthermore, the revolt continued to spread to the rest of the country, where local rebel groups managed to take over municipal centers, factories, and other key facilities. With each victory, the insurrectionists gained confidence in their abilities.

While fighting continued, the rebels began to form new institutions that gave a certain structure to the revolution. The most important were the workers councils, committees established at workplaces to replace party authority with genuine local management. Intellectual groups such as writers, journalists, and university professors, whose activities normally fell under party control, created their own autonomous entities. Independent newspapers sprang up that directly challenged the government and helped to spread information about the revolution around the country. Moreover, the party itself was becoming fractured. The detested Gero, quickly replaced after the Kossuth Square massacre, fled to the Soviet Union while many local leaders went into hiding.

Inside the corridors of power in Budapest and Moscow, the choices available were starker than before: either acquiesce to political demands that included removing all Soviet forces from the country and reinstituting a multiparty system—conditions that were unthinkable just days earlier—or crush the uprising with massive use of force. Nagy, who underwent a remarkable political transformation during the revolution, managed to gain Soviet approval to implement a cease-fire and begin negotiations. He also dissolved the hated security apparatus, agreed to create new institutions with broader participation, and consented to negotiate a Soviet troop withdrawal. Then on October 30, he took the extraordinary step of abolishing the one-party system in Hungary and allowing the immediate re-establishment of banned political parties.

For a time, Moscow went along with Nagy's prescriptions. Khrushchev and his allies in the Kremlin agreed that changes were needed to address deep-seated dissatisfaction. But the Soviet leadership was itself divided and, to complicate matters, was in the midst of an ongoing power struggle between Khrushchev and a more hard-line faction. Ultimately, Khrushchev decided to use force. Reports of increasing chaos in Hungary, including lynchings of Communists, confirmed fears that the situation was spiraling out of control and, furthermore, that the turmoil might spread to neighboring Socialist countries.

At the same time, Moscow was keenly aware of its international position. Radio Free Europe, the U.S.-run broadcasting operation, had been beaming steady reports of the fighting back into Hungary. Some of those broadcasts by the operation's Hungary desk, although not officially authorized, were highly aggressive, feeding suspicions of a Western conspiracy to exploit the emergency (not to mention raising popular hopes of obtaining outside support). Moreover, the unfolding Suez Crisis added further complications. Although Israel's invasion of Egypt on October 29 was not timed to coincide with the revolution—it had been secretly planned with France and Great Britain before the uprising began—its realization at the height of the insurrection had two main effects. By raising the prospect of "losing" both Hungary and Egypt to the West, the attack at least contributed to Khrushchev's decision to crush the revolt or face further damage to the Soviets' world standing. Also, the engagement of French and British forces in an act of aggression against a smaller country, and their subsequent efforts to minimize international sanction, significantly undercut the West's case against Moscow in international forums such as the United Nations.

As a result, on October 31 the Kremlin reversed course and chose the option of invasion in order to crush the revolution. In the early hours of November 4, five Soviet divisions entered the country, this time sweeping through with only initial resistance. Nagy had learned about the possibility of an invasion three days earlier. Hoping to prevent it, he declared his country's neutrality and its intention to pull out of the Warsaw Pact. He also pleaded to the world community to intercede with Moscow. But no help was forthcoming, either from the United Nations or the Western powers. At 5:20 a.m., shortly after Soviet forces crossed the border, Nagy announced over the radio that the invasion had begun. After instructing the population not to put up resistance, he accepted an offer of asylum at the Yugoslav embassy in Budapest.

IMPACTS

Within three days, the Soviets had effectively retaken control of the country and installed a new government. It was headed by János Kádár, a former member of Nagy's government who had secretly flown to Moscow at Soviet behest several days earlier and agreed on a plan to take power at the head of a new Communist regime. While there was little difficulty crushing the armed resistance, the other problems Kádár faced were enormous. For one, Nagy refused to resign as prime minister, presenting the new government with a crisis of legitimacy as long as he remained on Hungarian soil.

Another serious problem was the existence of the workers' councils. In addition to localized groups, which remained in place around the country after major fighting had died down, a new Central Workers' Council of Greater Budapest soon formed. Combining the strength of several smaller entities, it began mounting strikes and espousing broad political demands, positioning itself as a key center of continuing opposition. At first, because of its sheer potential power, the regime had little choice but to negotiate, offering concessions on wages and management issues. But Kádár understood the danger of brooking such a direct challenge to the regime's authority and decided to draw the line at the idea of a national workers' council. At the new organization's opening session, he ordered in tanks and made mass arrests. In subsequent weeks, more harsh actions followed. The regime declared martial law, began making wide-scale arrests, and eventually instituted draconian measures such as imposing the death penalty for those refusing to return to work.

By early 1957, major social resistance in Hungary had ended. But Kádár continued to crack down, launching reprisals that lasted for the next two years. By the summer of 1961, when the last related death sentence was carried out, 229 people had been hanged for their actions during the revolution and some 22,000 had been sentenced to prison. About 100,000 Hungarians were directly affected by the reprisals. In addition, approximately 200,000 more sought refuge in the West.

Of all the acts of oppression following 1956, the most notorious was the execution of Nagy and his closest advisers. Two weeks after the invasion, the Hungarian authorities promised protection for Nagy and his entourage in order to entice them to leave the sanctuary of the Yugoslav embassy, only to arrest them immediately. Nagy was taken to Romania, where he was held incommunicado for several months before being returned to Hungary to await punishment. After many delays, a staged trial took place in June 1958, after which he and two associates were shot and buried in unmarked graves.

In addition to resorting to wide-scale repression, Kádár employed a range of subtler measures aimed at winning acquiescence to, if not acceptance of, the new regime. He targeted for retribution only those segments of the population who participated directly in the revolution or who espoused anti-regime positions. For the rest, he focused on improving living conditions, such as ensuring more goods in shops, granting limited opportunities to travel abroad, and curtailing the degree of state intrusion into citizens' daily lives.

Kádár's operating principle was that most people were not interested in politics as long as their basic needs were met. His approach proved effective in fracturing social opposi-tion, but it also carried a psychological price for the population. For almost three decades, there was a virtual ban against publicly mentioning the revolution or the names of its leaders. As a consequence of this nationwide suppression of memory and hope, a significant if hard-to-quantify degree of social disintegration took place.

The negative impact of 1956 also extended beyond Hungary. Moscow had sent a strong signal of the limits of its tolerance for reform within the Socialist camp, and the populations of other satellite states found themselves existing under a tighter grip. Even during subsequent popular outbreaks in Czechoslovakia in 1968 and Poland in 1980–1981, that lesson would hold firm.

However, the revolution had other effects. The ruthless defeat of the uprising at Soviet hands—hearkening back to Russian aid to the Austrian emperor during the 1848 revolution—planted seeds of determination in the Hungarian population. Soviet brutality also did substantial harm to Moscow's international image, exposing the illegitimacy of its control over the region. The Kremlin understood this might be a consequence of its actions but nevertheless decided that the alternative—potentially losing power in Eastern Europe—was unacceptable. While the invasion succeeded in holding the Socialist camp together temporarily, it exposed the latent power of popular will in the region. That power would eventually wipe out Soviet control in the region and ultimately help bring about the disappearance of the Soviet Union itself.

PEOPLE AND ORGANIZATIONS

Gero, Erno (1898–1980)

Gero replaced Rákosi as first secretary of the Hungarian party in July 1956. A hard-liner, he fled to Moscow during the revolution.

Göncz, Árpád (Born 1922)

A member of the Smallholders' Party and of the Hungarian Democratic Independence Movement during the revolution, Göncz was sentenced to life in prison in 1958 but freed in the general amnesty of 1963. He served as president of the Hungarian Republic from 1990–2000.

Hungarian Workers' Party

The ruling Communist party of Hungary, it was formed through the forced merger of the Social Democratic Party of

Hungary and the Hungarian Communist Party in 1948; it was replaced by the Hungarian Socialist Workers' Party on October 31, 1956.

Kádár, János (1912–1989)

A former minister of the interior, Kádár was imprisoned in the early 1950s but rose to become party first secretary during the revolution. He also served as minister of state in the last Nagy cabinet but accepted Moscow's offer to head a new Soviet-controlled government, which took power on November 4, 1956. He led Hungary until May 1988.

Khrushchev, Nikita S. (1894–1971)

As first secretary of the Soviet Communist Party during the period of the revolution, Khrushchev took the lead in setting Soviet policy toward Hungary, which veered from backing reform to invading the country. Ironically, his secret denunciation of Stalin in February 1956, which soon became public knowledge, encouraged hopes for change throughout Eastern Europe, particularly among Hungarians.

Mindszenty, Cardinal József (1892–1975)

Mindszenty was the Catholic primate of Hungary and a vocal critic of Communist rule. In 1948 he was sentenced to life in prison after a show trial. In 1955 he was placed under house arrest; he was released during the revolution, then given refuge at the U.S. embassy in Budapest from November 4, 1956, until 1971.

Nagy, Imre (1896–1958)

A life-long Communist who spent considerable time in the Soviet Union, Nagy was a leading member of the Hungarian party for periods between 1945 and 1956. A reformist, he also served as prime minister from 1953–1955. After being expelled from the party in late 1955, he was readmitted on October 13, 1956, and renamed prime minister on October 23, serving until the second Soviet invasion on November 4. He remained loyal to Moscow until literally the last days of his tenure, when he broke away and declared his country's neutrality on November 1. He was later arrested and, after a show trial, executed on June 16, 1958.

National Guard

The National Guard was formed on November 1, 1956, to take over the duties of maintaining public order after the ÁVH (State Security Authority) was dissolved.

National Peasant Party (NNP)

The NNP was a radical, populist peasant party formed in 1945 and re-established in October 1956 as the Petofi Party, representing leftist intellectuals.

Petofi Circle

A discussion group in Hungary that initially enjoyed official sanction until it adopted increasingly anti-regime positions and was seen as a focal point for public dissent.

Political Committee (PC)

The PC was the main decision-making body of the Hungarian Communist party.

Presidium

The Presidium was the name given to the Soviet Politburo between 1952 and 1966.

Radio Free Europe (RFE)

A U.S.-government-run radio station broadcasting from Munich into Eastern Europe (with guidance from the CIA), RFE came under attack for aggressive commentary during the revolution.

Rajk, László (1909–1949)

Hungary's interior and foreign minister after World War II, he was feared by Rákosi as a potential political rival. Charged with being a Titoist and an "enemy," he was executed after a show trial in 1949. His rehabilitation in October 1956 helped set the stage for the revolution.

Rákosi, Mátyás (1892–1971)

Rákosi served as leader of the Hungarian Communist party from 1945 to mid 1956 and as prime minister in 1952–1953.

A hard-line Stalinist, he was forced out of power by Moscow in July 1956.

Revolutionary Workers' and Peasants' Government

This was the name of the government headed by János Kádár beginning on November 4, 1956, as he prepared to re-enter Hungary to challenge the Nagy government.

Smallholders' Party

Founded in 1921, the Smallholders became the leading political party in Hungary during the brief period after World War II before the advent of Communist rule. It was re-established temporarily during the revolution.

Stalin, Joseph V. (1879–1953)

As the unchallenged leader of the Soviet Union from 1929 until his death in 1953, Stalin directed the occupation and takeover of political power in Eastern Europe by hard-line Soviet-backed Communists after World War II.

State Security Authority (ÁVH)

The Hungarian security apparatus served as the Rákosi regime's main instrument of popular suppression until Nagy dismantled it on October 28, 1956.

Tito, Josip Broz (1892–1980)

As president of Yugoslavia, Tito, a Communist leader who had defied Stalin and the Soviet Union, granted Nagy asylum in the Yugoslav embassy in Budapest.

Warsaw Treaty Organization

The Soviet Union established the Warsaw Treaty Organization in 1955 as a counter to NATO and used it to mount the invasion of Hungary.

Workers Councils

These local committees were formed by rebels during the revolution to implement worker self-management in facto-ries and other places of employment. The Central Workers Council of Greater Budapest, founded on November 12, 1956, after the cessation of major fighting, combined several smaller entities and became virtually an alternative government for the remaining resistance until the government forced its dissolution in early December 1956.

Malcolm Byrne

See Also Documentaries of Revolution; East European Revolutions of 1989; Nationalism and Revolution

References and Further Readings

Békés, Csaba. 1996. *The 1956 Hungarian Revolution and World Politics.* Cold War International History Project Working Paper No. 16. Washington, DC: Woodrow Wilson International Center for Scholars.

Békés, Csaba, Malcolm Byrne, and János Rainer. 2002. *The 1956 Hungarian Revolution: A History in Documents.* Budapest: Central European University Press.

Borhi, László. 2004. *Hungary in the Cold War, 1945–1956: Between the United States and the Soviet Union.* Budapest: Central European University Press.

Department of State, ed. 1990. *Foreign Relations of the United States, 1955–57.* Vol. 25. Washington, DC: Government Printing Office.

Gati, Charles. 1986. *Hungary and the Soviet Bloc.* Durham, NC: Duke University Press.

Kovrig, Bennett. 1973. *The Myth of Liberation: East Central Europe in U.S. Diplomacy and Politics since 1941.* Baltimore: Johns Hopkins University Press.

———. 1991. *Of Walls and Bridges: The United States and Eastern Europe.* New York: New York University Press.

Kramer, Mark. 1996-1997. "The 'Malin Notes' on the Crises in Hungary and Poland, 1956," *Cold War International History Project Bulletin* 8/9 (Winter): 385–410.

———. 1996-1997. "New Evidence on Soviet Decision-Making and the 1956 Polish and Hungarian Crises," *Cold War International History Project Bulletin* 8/9 (Winter): 358–384.

———. 1998. "The Soviet Union and the 1956 Crises in Hungary and Poland: Reassessments and New Findings," *Journal of Contemporary History* 33 (2) (April): 163–214.

Litván, György, János M. Bak, and Lyman H. Legters, eds. 1996. *The Hungarian Revolution of 1956: Reform, Revolt and Repression, 1953–1963.* New York: Longman.

Marchio, James David. 1993. *Rhetoric and Reality: The Eisenhower Administration and Unrest in Eastern Europe, 1953–1959.* PhD diss. at American University, 1990. Ann Arbor, MI: UMI Dissertation Services.

Zinner, Paul, ed. 1956. *National Communism and Popular Revolt in Eastern Europe: A Selection of Documents on Events in Poland and Hungary, February-November, 1956.* New York: Columbia University Press.

I

Ideology, Propaganda, and Revolution

The various political, social, economic, and religious ideas prevalent in a society and the often extensive efforts to disseminate ideas, ideology, and propaganda play a significant role in all stages of the revolutionary process. The relationship is often an interactive one: ideology informs the content of propaganda, while propaganda seeks to persuade individuals to adopt those ideas that constitute a distinct ideology. This is particularly the case during periods of conflict, such as revolutions, in which adherents to different sets of ideas find themselves in competition. Insofar as ideology plays a role in the struggle between revolutionaries and the Old Regime, or among the revolutionaries themselves, it is often the organizational ability of groups to communicate their ideas to a mass audience that allows them to gain and maintain power.

IDEOLOGY AND ITS HISTORY

A specific ideology can be understood as a relatively consistent set of beliefs that attempt to explain the fundamental nature of society, help individuals understand the world around them, and ultimately provide a basis for social and political action. Like any theory, ideology simplifies and interprets a complex reality, providing both motive and guidance for human behavior. It is these characteristics that distinguish ideology from culture, a broader phenomenon that is generally defined as the taken-for-granted symbols, values, and knowledge expressed by a group through customs and rituals. As a set of ideas that purport not only to explain reality but also to offer an agenda for sociopolitical action, ideology has come to be identified with the great "isms" of the twentieth century: capitalism, Communism, Fascism, liberalism, and Socialism, among others.

Although its origins stretch back to the Enlightenment in France, the term "ideology" first gained currency following the revolutionary upheavals in that country at the end of the eighteenth century. Coined by the scholar Antoine Destutt de Tracy, the word "ideology" was meant to signify the scientific study of ideas, or the theory of ideas (Rudé 1980, 15). This conception of ideology emerged not only from the central tenets of Enlightenment philosophy—namely, the autonomy of reason from dogma, superstition, and other nonrational forms of thought, as well as the belief that the methodology of the natural sciences could be successfully applied to political and social inquiry—but also and more immediately from the Institut de France, created in 1795 to educate individuals in those traditions of the Enlightenment that formed the philosophical guidelines of the revolutionaries.

The notion of ideology as a coherent body of ideas, and its role in both maintaining social stasis and effecting social change, date back to the early works of Karl Marx and his collaborator, Friedrich Engels. In *The German Ideology*, Marx and Engels invoked a distinctly materialistic conception of ideas and ideology. Not only were the political and legal institutions of society the by-products of relations of production; so too were the dominant ideas of a society merely a reflection of class divisions and interests. Because the ruling class controlled both the material and intellectual means of production, its members were able to legitimate their role in society by imposing a false social consciousness on workers who were unable to perceive the reality of their own exploitation. Only when the subjugated classes recognized the nature of this ideology would they have the ability to alter their lives. This view of ideology was qualified in Marx's later and more historical work, which recognized the independent influence that ideas could have on people's beliefs and actions.

IDEOLOGY AND THE REVOLUTIONARY PROCESS

Supporters of a revolution are not only guided by the ideology they hold but often deploy ideology in order to accomplish different goals throughout the revolutionary process. These goals include the unification of groups dissatisfied with the Old Regime, the mobilization of these actors to remove the regime, and shaping the new government that emerges from the revolution. While different ideologies may serve similar purposes, however, individual ideologies are not themselves static; rather, they instead are often modified to fit existing conditions within a particular nation.

Revolutionary ideology first and foremost offers a critique of the Old Regime and a prescription for change. It issues a devastating condemnation of the old order by identifying problems afflicting state and society and presents an alternative political—and often economic—system as the necessary cure. French revolutionaries influenced by Enlightenment philosophy denounced the divine right of kings and dominant hierarchies of privilege while advocating a government founded on the will of the people. Bolshevik revolutionaries similarly used their interpretations of Marxism both to identify the failings of the czarist regime and to guide their implementation of a Communist state. In the pre-revolutionary period especially, criticism of the existing order plays the important role of bridging differences among the regime's opponents and building a coalition capable of challenging that regime. By presenting a well-developed critique and rationale for action, revolutionary ideologies are able to incorporate parochial grievances into a more general framework and thereby unite disparate groups within society that might otherwise share only a sense of frustration with the existing system.

In order to succeed in the period of revolutionary struggle, opposition movements need sufficient participation and support from society to gain the resources necessary to overturn the existing regime. That often requires an ideology capable of mobilizing the masses to action. Convincing people to oppose a regime in power is inherently difficult because the potential costs of individual action are high, while those who choose not to participate may still benefit if the revolution is successful. Ideologies help to overcome this dilemma both by bringing together opponents of the regime and by persuading them to remove the corrupt system so as to improve society. Ideologies offer the promise of a better future, an assurance that promotes group solidarity, encourages individual and group sacrifice for the good of the cause, and serves as a justification for individuals' demands and actions. Ideologies also tap into a preexisting reservoir of cultural symbols that facilitate collective action.

Iran's revolutionary ideology, for example, was built upon the foundation of Shia Islam, which supplied the revolutionaries with a well-known set of symbols and practices that helped to coordinate resistance against the shah's regime. Khomeini and his followers used the Islamic calendar, specifically religious holidays and holy months, as an opportunity to transform religious gatherings into organized protests. Shia Islam's practice of a forty-day period of mourning helped to coordinate and motivate a series of massive protests, one every forty days, for more than a year in response to the Iranian military's violent repression of demonstrations during 1978.

After a revolutionary movement has prevailed against the Old Regime, ideology can act as a guide for those creating the new state and society. Revolutions have produced both radical new states and conservative governments led by fundamentalists. The content of revolutionary ideologies can affect the outcome and therefore the type of regime that emerges. In the post-revolutionary period ideology may also serve as a key mechanism for legitimizing the authority of the new regime. The masses may accept a particular ideology as legitimate because it is presented as the authentic, nationalist identity of the state, or because it calls for the redistribution of material benefits. Both nationalism and redistribution are more general yet important components of most ideologies that often come to dominate political rhetoric after the struggle against the Old Regime has ended.

While different ideologies may play similar roles in the revolutionary process, ideologies themselves may change over time; ideological entrepreneurs often alter distinct sets of ideas to make them more compatible with new circumstances. The evolution of Marxist thought by both Lenin and Mao provides a clear illustration. Marx held that capitalism's collapse would result from its own internal contradictions, and would occur first in the most advanced industrial states (namely, Britain and Germany). Lenin, adapting Marx to the international environment of the early twentieth century and for the benefit of his native Russia, made several critical changes. Lenin argued that most advanced states had entered

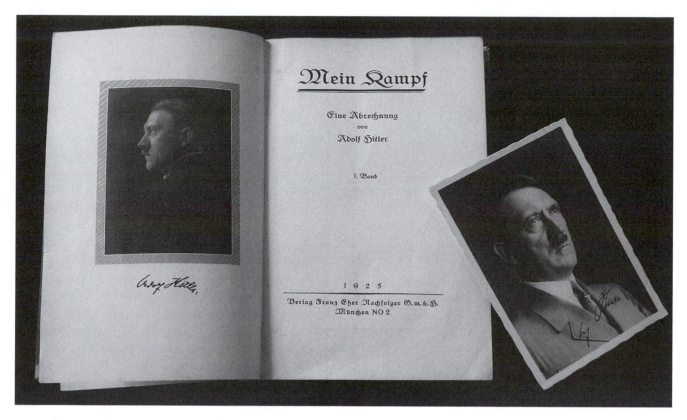

A signed copy of a first edition of Adolf Hitler's book *Mein Kampf* in which he expounded aspects of Nazi ideology and propaganda including placing blame for Germany's problems on Jews, corrupt and traitorous politicians, Communists, and arguing that the Germans needed "lebensraum" or living room to the east in lands occupied by Slavic peoples. The book's widespread appeal among many Germans helped increase mass support for the Nazi Movement. (Carl de Souza/AFP/Getty Images)

the stage of monopoly capitalism: in the absence of domestic investment opportunities, these states had gone abroad searching for colonies to provide cheap labor, raw materials, and new markets. This development had stalled the possibility of revolution in the industrialized states, as workers' standards of living had risen as a result. Nevertheless, the search for colonies by the industrial states would inevitably lead to conflict between them. That, in turn, would provide the opportunity for revolutionary Socialists to seize power in the semi- or nonindustrialized countries that had not, according to Marx, achieved the conditions necessary for Socialism to succeed. A state like Russia that had not fully industrialized would therefore no longer have to wait for Socialism first to arise in Britain or Germany; it would instead be the Socialists in Russia taking power in the hope that doing so would spark a revolt in Germany. Mao further altered these theories to adapt them to China's largely rural, peasant population. He would argue, contra Marx and Lenin, that peasants are sufficient to make a Socialist revolution once they have been instilled with revolutionary ideas and consciousness. According to Mao it was mass struggle, not elite action or economic development, that was the catalyst for social transformation.

PROPAGANDA AND ITS HISTORY

Propaganda includes all sources of information or indoctrination that are intended to spread a set of ideas throughout a given population. More generally, it is the deliberate attempt to alter the way people think and how they behave, in a manner beneficial to the propagandists. Unlike education, which provides individuals with the information and skills necessary to reach their own decisions on an issue, propaganda uses various forms of communication to shape people's attitudes and perceptions in a way that serves the interests of those attempting to influence public opinion. Because the revolutionary process is a struggle to gain and then maintain power, propaganda is a critical alternative to the use of physical coercion and repression. If successful, it can not only mobilize people in support of the revolutionary cause but also inculcate mass acceptance of the revolutionaries' agenda, thus providing the legitimacy necessary to stabilize the new regime.

The negative connotations that accompany the term "propaganda" and its ubiquity in modern society obscure its origins in the Catholic Church. In 1622, Pope Gregory XV issued a papal bull establishing the Congregation for the

Propagation of Faith, an institution that was given the task of organizing various missionary activities in a concerted effort to spread Roman Catholic doctrine and combat the effects of the Protestant Reformation. It was, therefore, an organization designed to use various methods to influence individuals' religious and political beliefs. The use of popular propaganda increased thereafter.

Before and during the French Revolution a growing number of newspapers and pamphlets promoted increasingly radical critiques of the monarchy and government. Forms of dress such as the red, white, and blue tricolor sash, and slogans such as the famous call for Liberty, Equality, and Fraternity, were meant to identify one's political position and influence the position of others. During World War I, Britain created a secret propaganda bureau with the intention of providing the United States with news, pamphlets, and leaflets designed to engage its sympathies and gain its support in the effort against Germany. The effectiveness of British wartime propaganda served as a lesson on the efficacy of persuasion that did not go unnoticed by either the Bolshevik revolutionaries or the Fascist regimes of inter-war Europe.

PROPAGANDA AND THE REVOLUTIONARY PROCESS

During the process of revolution, propaganda is employed to achieve two general goals: agitation and integration. Agitative propaganda is intended to incite an audience to take an active part in bringing about the propagandists' desired outcomes. Integrative propaganda is intended to convince an audience to accept the propagandists' aims voluntarily. The former often appears in the early stages of revolution when opponents of the existing regime work to attract followers to their cause, and later as revolutionaries seek to mobilize their supporters against both the Old Regime and their rivals in the revolutionary movement. Integrative propaganda is prevalent after the revolutionary struggle has been won and the new regime must convince the population of its legitimacy in order to consolidate its rule.

Ayatollah Khomeini's propaganda before, during, and after the 1979 Islamic Revolution in Iran illustrates the effective use of both agitative and integrative propaganda. Living in exile during the years preceding the revolution, Khomeini required a means of communicating his views to the Iranian masses. To do so, he relied on a personal network consisting mostly of former students to spread his denunciations of the shah's regime and his vision of an Islamic state. This network of clerics used the mosques as both a forum for disseminating Khomeini's political ideology and as a platform for organizing opposition activities. Khomeini's supporters would

relate his teachings through their sermons, and distribute copies of his writings and audiocassettes of his lectures. During the annual pilgrimage to Mecca, opponents of the shah's regime obtained these writings and taped lectures, which had been banned in Iran, and secretly introduced them into Iranian society. The contraband tapes were a critical component of Khomeini's agitative propaganda campaign, spreading his ideas to both literate and illiterate members of Iranian society and helping to organize demonstrations and strikes against the regime.

After deposing the old regime and defeating his rivals in the revolutionary movement, Khomeini and his followers focused on solidifying their control of the state through the use of integrative propaganda. To persuade the Iranian public of the appropriateness of Khomeini's vision of an Islamic state—the *vilayat-e faqih* (guardianship of the Islamic jurist [religious law expert])—the Islamic republic transmitted propaganda through education and the pulpit. Khomeini recognized the importance of acquiring the allegiance of the youth, so the state created courses and textbooks that extolled the new regime and denigrated all secular and foreign ideologies. Similar messages were communicated to all Iranians who attended Friday prayers at the mosque, which ultimately played as critical a role in consolidating Khomeini's rule as it had in mobilizing the masses against the shah's regime.

The dissemination of both agitative and integrative propaganda has historically made use of a wide array of mass media, ranging from newspapers, fliers, and oratory, to plays, films, and school texts. As the Iranian example indicates, the media available to revolutionaries are often influenced by the stage of the revolutionary process. In the early stages of revolution, opponents of the Old Regime are likely to rely on speeches, fliers, posters, and underground newspapers to spread agitative propaganda. Acting subversively and sometimes based abroad, revolutionary propagandists often possess a limited organizational apparatus and are forced to rely on informal networks to communicate their views. After revolutionaries seize control of the state, both official news media and the educational system become available as sources of integrative propaganda.

Well before the revolutions of 1917, Lenin and other Social Democrats created the underground newspaper *Iskra* (*The Spark*), which was published in Munich, London, and Geneva and then smuggled into Russia by a network of Social Democrat party agents. After the party split into its better known Menshevik and Bolshevik factions, the latter group went on to establish other newspapers, such as *Pravda* (*Truth*) under the helm of Leon Trotsky. During and after the Russian Civil War (1917–1921), as the Bolsheviks gained control of the apparatus of the state and fought to consolidate their control over Russia's territory, Lenin spearheaded more elaborate propaganda efforts intended to indoctrinate his countrymen into a more collective way of life. Education was viewed as one of the key ways to effect such a transformation. Both formal schools as well as Communist leagues for children and youth (the Pioneers and Komosol) were intended to shape the next generation into a generation of Communists. Because the church was viewed as both a sign of backwardness and a rival to the Bolsheviks' power, the years of the civil war also saw a propaganda campaign intended to reduce the influence of the church. This included official declarations that removed the church's right to own property, the suppression of literature and music deemed religious, and the creation of Soviet festivals that mimicked Christian celebrations but instead venerated the Communist state.

CONCLUSION

Ideology and propaganda play important and interactive roles in the process of social revolution. What is perhaps most notable is that while both the content of revolutionary ideologies and the means by which those ideas are promoted vary considerably, each nevertheless displays strikingly similar functional characteristics when observed in distinct stages of the revolutionary process. Different ideologies serve to unify opposition forces, mobilize collective action against the Old Regime or contending revolutionary groups, and shape the new regime in the pre-revolutionary, revolutionary, and post-revolutionary periods. Whether propaganda is intended primarily to agitate or integrate the masses, and which mass media are used to communicate those ideas, are questions similarly influenced by the social demands and material constraints of the various stages of revolution. Ideology and propaganda are therefore both critical to successful revolutions, and are yet shaped themselves by the course of those revolutions.

Evan Braden Montgomery

Stacie L. Pettyjohn

See Also Anarchism, Communism, and Socialism; Chinese Revolution; Cinema of Revolution; Italian Fascist Revolution; Nazi Revolution: Politics and Racial Hierarchy; Russian Revolution of 1917

References and Further Readings

Arjomand, Said Amir. 1988. *The Turban for the Crown: The Islamic Revolution in Iran.* New York: Oxford University Press.

Figes, Orlando. 1996. *A People's Tragedy: The Russian Revolution: 1891–1924.* New York: Penguin.

Goldstone, Jack A. 1991. "Ideology, Cultural Frameworks, and the Process of Revolution," *Theory and Society* 20 (4): 405–453.

Jowett, Garth S., and Victoria O'Donnell. 1999. *Propaganda and Persuasion.* 3rd edition. London: Sage.

Marx, Karl, and Friedrich Engels. 1978. "The German Ideology." Pp. 146–200 in *The Marx-Engels Reader,* 2nd edition, edited by Robert Tucker. New York: Norton.

Moaddel, Mansour. 1993. *Class, Politics, and Ideology in the Iranian Revolution.* New York: Columbia University Press.

Rudé, George. 1980. *Ideology and Popular Protest.* New York: Pantheon.

Taylor, Philip M. 2003. *Munitions of the Mind: A History of Propaganda from the Ancient World to the Present Era.* 3rd edition. Manchester: Manchester University Press.

Indian Independence Movement

CHRONOLOGY

Historical background

ca. 2500 B.C.	Emergence of an advanced urban civilization based in the valley of the Indus River.
ca. 1500–600 B.C.	The rise of the *Arya*s, a pastoral nomadic people who speak the Sanskrit language and are to have a profound influence in shaping "Indic" cultures and religion.
ca. 600–200 B.C.	The emergence of earliest territorial states, evolving into empires. The Mauryan empire comes close to covering most of India.
ca. 200 B.C.–A.D. 700	The age of empires. The Gupta empire is often spoken of as representing the "Classical" age of Indian history. Classical texts attributed to earlier periods are written up in this period, which also sees the efflorescence of new Sanskrit prose, poetry, and drama.
ca. 600–1200	The era of regional powers. Rajput lineages control the north and Cholas the south. The beginning of an Indo-Islamic world with a Muslim-ruled state is established in Sind ca. 700. Raids by central Asian Muslim invaders begin ca. 1000.
1206 to 1526	Era of the Delhi sultanate. Muslim sultans establish a home base in the Indian subcontinent and make the city of Delhi their capital.

1526 to 1857   Mughal India. Babur defeats the last of the Delhi sultans in 1526 to found the Mughal dynasty. Mughals, who are Muslims, preside over an era of amazing Indo-Islamic synthesis in culture. Mughal political authority declines after 1707, with the death of Emperor Aurangzeb. A titular Mughal emperor survives until 1857.

Coming of the Europeans

1498   Vasco da Gama, a Portuguese explorer, discovers the sea route to India.

1510   Portuguese conquer Goa and establish enclaves along the western coast of India.

1600   East India Company (EIC) is founded in London.

1664–1706   French East India Company is established and makes gains under the leadership of Francois Martin.

1757   Battle of Plassey, armies of the English EIC defeat those of the nawab of Bengal.

1760   Anglo-French Wars in India result in English victory.

1764   Battle of Buxar, English EIC armies defeat the combined forces of the nawab of Awadh, the nawab of Bengal, and the titular Mughal emperor ruling in Delhi.

1765   The English EIC acquires rights of civil administration over Bengal, including the right to levy and collect taxes from agriculture.

1770   Great Bengal Famine. One-third of Bengal's population perishes in a famine that is the direct result of EIC's rapacious tax policies.

1793   The EIC introduces the Permanent Settlement in Bengal—effectively creating private property in land.

1799   The defeat of Tipu Sultan, the ruler of Mysore, by the EIC armies, thus ending the last real military threat to their domination.

1818   British victory over the Marathas, the last of the successor states of the Mughals with the potential to challenge them.

1843–1856   Final phase of consolidation with the conquests of Sind and Punjab and the annexation of Awadh.

Resistance to British rule and the emergence of the Indian national movements

1857   A massive revolt against British authority led by soldiers, peasants, small landlords, and deposed rulers. The revolt is quelled with great brutality. India comes under the direct authority of the British Crown and parliament.

1885   Creation of the Indian National Congress (INC).

1905–1907   *Swadeshi*, or self-sufficiency movement, in Bengal calls for boycott of British goods. Emergence of nationalist terrorist organizations.

1906   Formation of the Muslim League.

1909   Indian Councils Act (Morley-Minto Reforms), limited political reforms granting separate representation to Muslims, landholders, and other special interest groups.

1914–1918   World War I

1915   Home Rule Leagues formed, and Gandhi returns to India.

1917   Gandhi's first satyagrahas.

1919   Government of India Act (the Montague-Chelmsford Reforms) gives limited power to elected assemblies. Rowlatt Act extends martial law. General Dyer massacres a peaceful gathering of Indians protesting the act at Jallianwalla Bagh in Amritsar.

1921   Non-cooperation and Khilafat Movement. The latter takes up Indian Muslims' opposition to the abolition of the Turkish caliphate. Gandhi's first and most successful all-India movement.

1922	Gandhi calls off the Non-cooperation Movement when peasants burn a police station at Chauri-Chaura.
1928–1931	Growth of revolutionary terrorism. Bhagat Singh becomes a folk hero.
1929–1930	The *Purna Swaraj,* or Complete Independence Resolution, is passed by the INC in Lahore.
1930	The Salt Satyagraha, and the First Civil Disobedience Movement.
1932	Communal Award gives separate representation to India's "untouchable" castes. Gandhi threatens a fast unto death.
1935	Government of India Act permits greater power for elected bodies. INC first rejects then participates in elections held under the act.
1937	INC wins handsomely in elections. Muslim League fares disastrously.
1939	INC resigns from provincial legislatures after Britain's unilateral announcement of India's participation in World War II. Muslim League celebrates a "day of deliverance."
1940	The Lahore Declaration of the Muslim League outlines demand for a separate Muslim homeland.
1941	Subhash Chandra Bose escapes to Japan and forms the Indian National Army (INA).
1942	Quit India Movement is launched and repressed. A British mission to negotiate terms between INC and Muslim League fails.
1943–1944	A famine in Bengal kills more than 3.5 million people even as food is exported from India.
1945	Simla Conference. Unsuccessful attempts by Viceroy Wavell to have Muslim League and INC share power in an independent India.
1945–1946	Elections to federal and provincial governments. INC gets all the general seats; the Muslim League wins all Muslim seats.
	Popular uprisings over the trials of the INA soldiers. The Royal Indian Naval sailors revolt in Bombay.
1946	Cabinet Mission proposes a plan for a united India. Muslim League rejects the plan and calls for "Direct Action" to secure Pakistan. Major riots between Hindus and Muslims result.
1947	Partition and independence under the Mountbatten plan. Nehru is India's first prime minister, and Jinnah the leader of Pakistan.

Postscript: India since independence

1948	Gandhi is assassinated by Hindu right-wing extremist. Conflict between India and Pakistan over Kashmir.
1950	Constitution of independent India.
1952	First general elections under the new constitution, which the INC wins.
1962	War with China over border disputes.
1964	Death of Jawaharlal Nehru. Lal Bahadur Shastri becomes prime minister.
1965	War with Pakistan over Kashmir; ends with a cease-fire agreement. Shastri dies; Nehru's daughter, Indira Gandhi, becomes prime minister.
1971	War with Pakistan. East Pakistan secedes to create the new nation of Bangladesh.
1975–1977	Indira Gandhi declares a state of emergency, suspending civil liberties. She calls national elections in 1977 and is defeated, INC's first loss in a national election since independence.
1984	Assassination of Indira Gandhi by extremists demanding a separate state for Sikhs in northern India. Her son, Rajiv, becomes prime minister.
1991	Rajiv Gandhi is assassinated.

1998–2004   A coalition led by the Hindu nationalist Bharatiya Janata Party is elected to lead the country in 1998. India immediately conducts tests of nuclear weapons, and Pakistan retaliates with its own nuclear tests.

INTRODUCTION

The culmination of the Indian Independence Movement marked the end of British rule over India and the creation of two sovereign nation-states in the Indian subcontinent. The loss of this "jewel in the crown" of the British empire began a more global process of de-colonization, inspiring a series of nationalist movements across the colonized world to renew their struggles against imperialism.

BACKGROUND: CULTURE AND HISTORY

British power over India was established in the eighteenth century. States and empires came into being in India from around the sixth to fourth centuries B.C. From about the fifth and sixth centuries A.D., Indian history reveals oscillations between periods of centralized rule and regional autonomy. The Mughal era and its aftermath were one instance of this trend. A rich, prosperous, and relatively centralized state emerged under the Mughal emperors in the sixteenth and seventeenth centuries. The eighteenth century saw the pendulum swing in the opposite direction, with regional powers such as Awadh in the north, Marathas in the west, Bengal in the east, and Mysore and Hyderabad in the south all asserting their independence from declining Mughal power. European traders had been in India since before the Mughals, and as Mughal power grew in the seventeenth century, north Europeans, particularly the English, French, and Dutch came to displace the earlier domination of the Portuguese.

The power of the English East India Company (henceforth referred to as the EIC, or simply the Company) in India, however, was severely circumscribed until the middle of the eighteenth century, first by the powerful Mughals and then by the vibrant regional powers who succeeded Mughal authority. There was also stiff competition from their traditional rivals, the French. As the regional successors to the Mughals fought to establish supremacy over each other, French and English companies allied with one or the other power to provide mercenary troops, training, or equipment. The major commercial benefits from such intervention led to European trading companies building up a significant military presence in In-

dia. The year 1757 marked a watershed that saw the first open conflict, at the battle of Plassey, between the EIC and the ruler of the powerful regional state of Bengal. The Company prevailed by bribing the commander of Bengal's armies to switch loyalties in the midst of the battle. More significant, however, was the next battle, in 1764, in which EIC armies defeated a more powerful combine of native princes and as a result became the virtual rulers of the province of Bengal.

As the revenues collected from Bengal began to pay for its exports from India, the EIC realized the profits of political power. The next seven decades saw the transition of the EIC from being traders to being rulers of large parts of India. By the end of the eighteenth century, the Company had not only bested their French competitors but also defeated the last of the Indian rulers that posed a threat to their military preeminence. Much of the first half of the nineteenth century was spent in consolidation and expansion of their rule over most of India. The empire in India was acquired, not in a "fit of absence of mind," as the prominent British historian J. R. Seeley (1971, 12) suggested, but certainly in a piecemeal fashion. The acquisition was facilitated by outright military conquest, diplomatic maneuvers, and the use of dubious quasi-legal doctrines. Much of the actual work of territorial expansion was carried out by individuals working for the EIC. However, as the British parliament began to regulate more and more of how the EIC ran its proxy empire, these company officials began to function much more as representatives of the British state.

India soon became central to a larger British imperial mission, and in turn the empire had profound transformative impacts on the people it sought to incorporate. Recent revisionist historians have sought to underplay the significance of the change wrought by the British Raj (British rule) in India (Bayly 1998), or indeed to highlight the benefits it brought to the Indians (Ferguson 2004). Yet it is doubtful whether Indians of the eighteenth or nineteenth centuries would have agreed. Indian rulers lost their sovereignty. Company policy of trying to extract the maximum revenue from Bengal's peasants after 1765 directly contributed to a devastating famine in 1770, killing a third of that province's population. Attempts to create private property in land through laws in 1793 only led to further misery for India's peasants. Once Britain emerged as an industrial power, India became a prime captive market for its products, and its artisans bore the loss when they could not compete with machine-made yarn. When British imperial interests expanded, Indian soldiers fought to expand or defend imperial interests across the world. Indian indentured workers were herded into plantations in India and overseas after the empire outlawed the slave trade.

The cultural effects of British rule were equally devastating. Codification of Indian religious texts and laws, often based on incomplete knowledge of Indian society, reinvigo-

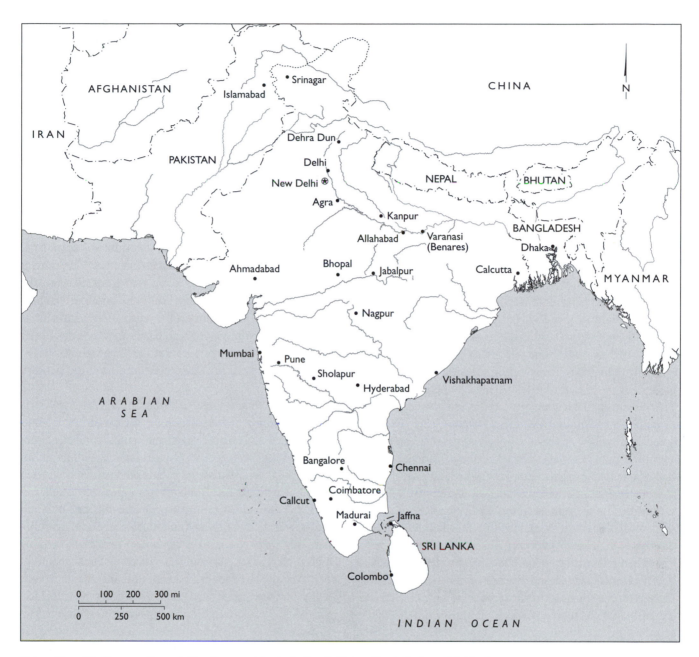

Major cities of India, as well as neighboring countries including Pakistan, Bangladesh, and Sri Lanka.

rated older patriarchal ideas imbedded in some of those texts. Ideas about India, about its people, history, culture, and communities that were generated by British and other Western scholars referred to as the Orientalists, were to have a profound impact on how Indians themselves came to understand their culture, history, and society.

A major revolt against British authority broke out across large parts of north India in 1857, including among its participants a large number of peasants, artisans, smaller landlords, and deposed Indian princes. Although an anti-colonial revolt, its limited geographical base and its aim of restoring deposed Indian monarchs makes it difficult to regard the event as the start of the Indian Independence Movement. The revolt, however, ended the EIC's role in governing India, as well as its policy of territorial expansion. Company territories now came under the direct control of the British parliament, which did not think it appropriate for a private company to exercise such vast political power. The reigning monarch, Queen Victoria, was formally invested with the title of empress of India in 1877.

CONTEXT AND PROCESS
OF REVOLUTION

The late nineteenth century was the high noon of the British empire, with no apparent challenges to British dominance left in India. India's remaining princes had sworn their loyalty to the British in return for being left to run their kingdoms with only indirect British supervision. Vicious public measures were used to put down the revolt of 1857, including mass lynching and the execution of rebels by cannon. Indians were forced to watch these spectacles, ensuring that ordinary folk were unlikely to consider another violent uprising in the near future. The resources of the Indian empire were now being used to balance Britain's global trade deficits. New technologies such as the railways and the telegraph, as well as new techniques of governance relying on close surveillance and monitoring of the ruled, made the British in India appear virtually invincible. Even the scientific discoveries of the age seemed to underscore the superiority and inevitable mastery of the white European races over darker ones. Paradoxically though, this was precisely the time when developments began to undermine British mastery of India.

The British decided to support Western-style education in English over traditional Indian systems. This aimed at "modernizing" the natives and imparting to them "civilized" Western values. They encouraged local associations, debating societies, and newspapers for the same reasons. Yet these came to have unexpected consequences. Indians educated in Western-style institutions found the progressive ideas of equality and liberty they imbibed in schools to be in sharp contrast to their lived experience when dealing with the British. When they tried to point out the sharp disjuncture between colonial racism and Britain's professed liberalism, these Western-educated Indians were derided by their British rulers for parroting Western phrases without understanding their significance.

It is not surprising then, that from this Western-educated middle class came the first spokespersons for Indian nationalism. Faced with colonial racism, they turned colonial ideas and institutions against their rulers. The Indian press and local associations became the main propagators of nationalist ideology in colonial India, and forums in which to express their desire for a greater share in the country's administration. From such beginnings was formed the Indian National Congress (henceforth, the INC) in 1885. Composed for most part of lawyers, journalists, and other professionals, the INC was initially a body devout in its loyalty to the British empire. Its leaders did, however, criticize specific policies of the colonial administration and asked that Indians be allowed a larger role in the administration of their country. Other middle-class Indians "retreated" from the public sphere and focused their attention on religion and the family—which they saw as pure and uncolonized places in which to create or preserve an authentically Indian culture (Chatterjee 1993).

As younger members of the INC came to be increasingly dissatisfied with their more "moderate" seniors, in the early twentieth century they began to use Hindu religious and cultural symbols to try to reach out to a larger audience. In response, and with some help from the colonial state, Muslim aristocrats in 1906 created a rival political party, the All India Muslim League, which aimed at promoting the interests of Indian Muslims. While there were important differences between the INC and the Muslim League, there were great similarities, too. Although they sniped at each other in public forums, that did not prevent them, for instance, from coming together in 1916 when a formal pact of agreement was signed by the two parties. Until the second decade of the twentieth century, moreover, both were largely elitist parties, with little or no mass following. Their fulminations against the administration could be safely ignored by the colonial administration. This was to change with the coming of Mohandas Karamchand Gandhi onto the political scene.

There were many reasons for Gandhi's great success. He became prominent in India around the time of World War I, a war that had created severe hardships for Indians. But by then Gandhi was already famous for successfully agitating against racist injustices in South Africa. There he had developed his political and philosophical philosophy of ahimsa, or nonviolence, and satyagraha, or truth force, and plans for how to use them as political weapons of peaceful, carefully planned civil disobedience. Personal charisma and a minimalist personal way of life meant that India's poor and deprived identified with him at a personal level. Quite unlike earlier generations of leaders, Gandhi also picked up on issues that were significant to India's toiling millions rather than only its urban elites. Yet he took care to choose only issues that united Indian interests against the British. His first major satyagraha in India in 1917, for instance, championed the rights of workers at a British-owned plantation, rather than peasants exploited by an Indian landlord. Even Gandhi's critique of modernity, which directed people's attention to the ills of Western civilization, counterposed it to an idealized vision of traditional Indian civilization. Gandhian emphasis on nonviolence, moreover, made it easier for people to rally to his cause than to that of those calling for more militant, violent action against the British. Finally, of course, Gandhi's success was also a result of his amazing skills as a fund-raiser and an organizational genius. It was Gandhi who spearheaded the drive for mass membership in the INC. In the space of three months in 1921 he was able to recruit more than 5 million members to the party, as well as to set up an effective organizational structure linking village committees to a permanent national-level working committee.

The year 1921 saw Gandhi lead his first carefully planned all-India satyagraha. Gandhi also used issues that united both Hindus and Muslims in nonviolent civil disobedience. He supported Indian Muslims' opposition to the abolishment of the Turkish caliphate. Muslims feared that the victors of World War I would depose the Ottoman sultan, who also held the title of caliph, or *Khalifa*, and was—nominally at least—the temporal head of the world's Muslim community. Through strategic choice of issues and careful planning, the movement brought the British administration to its knees. That his ideology was much more than one of political convenience, however, is evident from the fact that despite its success, Gandhi called off his satyagraha in less than a year because violence had begun to enter the movement.

Gandhi's pivotal role in Indian nationalism, however, cannot blind us to other and different visions of the nation. The most evident was that of the Muslim League. The end of the 1921–1922 satyagraha strained relations between the League and the INC and led to many riots between groups of Hindus and Muslims across northern India during the rest of the decade. Also, peasants and other subordinate groups did not necessarily share his political and philosophical vision. Many peasant movements appropriated Gandhi's message and ideas to their own ends. Using Gandhi's message of moral justice and truth, they began agitations against their immediate oppressors—the upper-caste landlords as well as the colonial state that supported them (Amin 1995).

Similarly, the nationalist mobilization begun by Gandhi led to the politicization of other subordinated groups in Indian society—women, lower-caste groups, industrial workers, and the like. These did not sit well with Gandhi's nondivisive nationalist strategy, however. In some cases, groups and individuals—such as revolutionary terrorists, including the vastly popular Bhagat Singh—broke away from the INC fold altogether. Other, more moderate Socialist leaders and organizations were co-opted back into mainstream INC nationalism. India's earliest feminist leaders, such as Kamaladevi Chattopadhyaya, shared the same fate and had to dilute their feminist agenda for the sake of "national unity." The charismatic leader of India's untouchable castes, Bhimrao Ambedkar, did both: initially compromising with Gandhi and the INC, and later rejecting them.

Perhaps the main reason behind Gandhi's success was that he was able to deliver to the INC a controlled mass movement (Sarkar 1983). As events were to prove, this was to be both the greatest success as well as the most severe limitation of Indian nationalism. With the radical edge taken off the nationalist movement, many leaders in the INC, as well as the Muslim League and other, smaller regional parties, came to forgo Gandhi's principle of complete noncooperation with the colonial state and reveled in the power and patronage they could access through participating in the elections and institutions sponsored by the colonial state. By the middle of the 1930s, different sections of the middle-class nationalist leadership (as well as the colonial authorities, of course) had succeeded in marginalizing Gandhian and popular nationalisms, to define a mainstream of politics concerned primarily with elections, councils, and control over state institutions. From being an opponent of the British Raj, "mainstream" nationalists became more and more like that Raj.

The decision of the INC to participate in elections held under the auspices of the Government of India Act of 1935 proved to have lasting effects on the history of Indian nationalism. The act offered limited franchise to Indians but gave India's middle-class "mainstream" leaders the potential, for the first time, to exercise real political and administrative power. The INC did spectacularly well in these elections, while the Muslim League under the leadership of Mohammed Ali Jinnah fared disastrously. Envisioning themselves now as the new rulers of India, the INC leadership adopted the high moral ground and rhetoric similar to that deployed by British colonial administrators. Claiming that they were the sole representatives of Indian nationalism, the INC sought to relegate the Muslim League to the status of a party that represented "subnational" or "communal" interests. The League and Jinnah in turn replied by insisting that there were not one but two nations in British India—a Hindu nation represented by the INC and a Muslim one, of which they were the "sole spokesmen." A term coined by Muslim undergraduates at Cambridge in 1933, "Pakistan," which was an acronym for the northern and western Muslim-majority provinces in India, now gave its name to that nascent Muslim nation.

The coming of World War II changed the political context considerably. A massive outbreak of popular anti-colonial violence during the Quit India movement of 1942 revealed the depth of people's sentiment against continued British rule. The immense popularity of Subhash Chandra Bose's Indian National Army, aided by the Japanese in Singapore, worried the British considerably, even though it was never a real military threat to the empire. The end of the war saw Britain economically impoverished, militarily exhausted, and under mounting pressure from Indians, the international community, and even large sections of its own population to relinquish control over India. After a few failed attempts at brokering a compromise between the league and the INC, the British and their last viceroy, Lord Louis Mountbatten, decided to divide British India and quit with as much speed as possible.

The two major Indian parties preferred to partition the country rather than share power between themselves. Meanwhile other political and religious leaders, for their own parochial ends, escalated popular anger against rival religious communities. Sovereignty was transferred to India and Pakistan in this milieu. Pakistan was created in two wings, on the eastern and western parts of British India, which housed a majority Muslim population. The transfer of power was very hasty and left little time for people to prepare for the momentous changes with which they were to be confronted. This hasty retreat of the colonial state was, in large measure, responsible for the death of more than a million people in riots between groups of Hindus and Muslims and the forcible displacement of around 10 million. But neither can shortsighted and self-serving nationalist leaderships completely escape the blame for the tragic and forgotten holocaust that accompanied Indian and Pakistani independence.

IMPACTS

For much of the last decade leading up to independence, the man central to making it all happen, Mahatma Gandhi, had been steadily marginalized. Gandhi did not attend the celebrations in Delhi anointing Jawaharlal Nehru as the first prime minister of an independent India on August 15, 1947. Instead he spent the day trying to bring peace to areas torn apart by Hindu-Muslim riots in eastern India. The riots and the angry refugees streaming in from what was now Pakistan created a wave of support for the minuscule extreme right-wing Hindu chauvinist groups in Indian politics. The support was enough for one Hindu extremist, Nathuram Godse, to assassinate the mahatma on January 30, 1948. In an act of ultimate irony, the most famous apostle of nonviolence died by the gun. Despite his death, Gandhi's philosophical and political legacy continued to inform politics in India as well as the larger world. His high-profile international followers have drawn the most attention. Dr. Martin Luther King, Jr., acknowledged his debts to Gandhi as he led a movement for equal rights for African Americans in the United States. More recently it has been Nelson Mandela who revived Gandhi's ideas in the land of their birth to lead South Africa out of apartheid. There are, however, countless other individuals and groups, both within India and overseas, who continue to draw their inspiration from the ideas of Mahatma Gandhi.

Globally, one of the most significant impacts of the Indian Independence Movement was to usher in an era of de-colonization across the colonial world. India's success inspired the many anti-colonial movements to renew their struggles against European imperialism. In the decade following Indian independence, many former colonies in Southeast Asia and North Africa gained their independence. In another decade, there were only a few colonial outposts left in the entire world. While some colonies had to fight bloody wars to gain their independence, others followed the more orderly, peaceful model of transfer of power from European elites to indigenous ones that had first been established in India.

Within India, Nehru, India's prime minister and self-confessed disciple of Gandhi, became the unchallenged titan of Indian politics after the latter's assassination. Philosophically, Nehru did not share Gandhi's disaffection with modernity, and he put most of his efforts toward the modernization of India's industrial infrastructure. In a world coming to be polarized by the Cold War, Nehru sought to guide India's foreign and economic policies between the extremes represented by the Communist world led by the Soviet Union and the Capitalist world championed by the United States. Domestically, Gandhi's assassination shocked most of India out of any nascent sympathies they had with Hindu chauvinist politics, ensuring that Nehru faced no challenges from the Right. A mix of co-optation and systematic low-key repression secured the supremacy of the INC from threats emerging from nascent peasant and Communist movements in India. Nehru died in 1963, but the INC under the leadership of Nehru's successor, Lal Bahadur Shastri, and then Nehru's daughter, Indira Gandhi, remained India's ruling party, winning all national elections convincingly until 1977.

The scars of the colonial legacy and partition, however, have continued to be very evident in relations with India's sibling and neighbor Pakistan. The disputes over Kashmir, which was nominally an independent state under British rule, have contributed to three armed conflicts between India and Pakistan, including one in 1948 that led the Hindu ruler of that Muslim-majority state to join India. In 1971, India sided with Bengali Muslims in East Pakistan who formed a majority of Pakistan's population but were completely marginalized in a state dominated by leaders and institutions from West Pakistan. This led to another war and an Indian victory that resulted in the secession of East Pakistan, now the sovereign state of Bangladesh.

Underlying many of the real and specific problems besetting better relations between India and Pakistan is a colonial legacy. Indian politicians often appear to believe that the Indian state alone succeeded to the British legacy of being the paramount power in the region, and same often aspires to the role of dominant regional power enjoyed by the empire in its heyday. Pakistan's understandable reluctance to accept this has led their leadership to undertake dangerous adventures in overt and covert actions against India. Given that both states are now acknowledged nuclear powers, the region as

Mahatma Gandhi (right), with Jawaharlal Nehru, at a meeting of the India Congress in Bombay, 1946. (Library of Congress)

well as the world has a great deal to benefit from understanding the historical legacy that divides, but also potentially unites, the two countries.

PEOPLE AND ORGANIZATIONS

All India Muslim League

This political party was formed on December 31, 1906, to promote the political interests of Indian Muslims and loyalty to the British. Although initially patronized by a group of aristocratic Muslim landlords, a younger and more radical leadership soon captured the party and led it to a pact with the INC in 1916. The league became marginal in nationalist politics during the agitation to preserve the Turkish caliph in power in the 1920s. However, its fortunes were revived by the

visionary leadership of Muhammad Iqbal and then by Jinnah. Alliances with regional parties facilitated the league's incredible successes in the elections of 1945–1946, and with Jinnah as its leader, the Muslim League became a vocal champion of Pakistan in negotiations with the INC and the British.

Ambedkar, Bhimroa Ramji, also known as "Babasaheb" (1891–1956)

Born an "untouchable," at the very bottom of India's caste hierarchy, Ambedkar struggled to became one of the most significant leaders in India's nationalist movement. He won scholarships to top schools and completed his Ph.D. in economics from Columbia University, New York, before qualifying as barrister (lawyer) in England. Returning to India, Ambedkar became a champion of the rights of India's lower castes. He came into conflict with Gandhi in 1932, when the latter opposed Ambedkar's demands for separate electorates for the untouchables. Faced with Gandhi's threat to fast unto death on the issue, Ambedkar compromised with the INC leadership. However, his relationship with Gandhi and the INC remained ambivalent. Although he chaired the assembly that created India's constitution, he was disappointed with the fate of the lower castes in Hindu society even after independence. Along with thousands of his followers, Ambedkar publicly renounced Hinduism to embrace Buddhism shortly before his death in 1956.

Bose, Subhash Chandra, also known as "Netaji" (1897–1945?)

Subhash Bose's career spanned a stunning variety of occupations—successful candidate for entrance to the Indian civil service, nationalist, labor leader, city mayor, Fascist collaborator, and military general. Twice elected president of the INC, Bose was always reluctant to endorse Gandhi's nonviolent ideology. He had to resign his second term as INC president because of Gandhi's opposition. Bose was a militant nationalist and escaped from British India shortly after the start of World War II and sought help from Nazi Germany. Disappointed with the Germans, Bose went to the Japanese in Singapore and took command of the Indian National Army, recruited from among Indian soldiers taken as prisoners of war; with it he proposed to overthrow colonial rule over India militarily. Despite his failure to do so, Bose remains tremendously popular in Bengal, and some controversy surrounds his death, with many refusing to believe that he died in an air crash over Taiwan in 1945.

Chattopadhyaya, Kamaladevi (1903–1988)

One of India's most prominent radical feminist leaders, Chattopadhyaya worked closely with trade unions in her home district of Mangalore and unsuccessfully contested an election for the Madras legislature in 1926. She joined the INC in 1927, was arrested for her involvement in the civil disobedience movement, and in 1934 became an active member of the leftist Congress Socialist Party. She served four prison sentences for her participation in nationalist agitations. Chattopadhyaya was one of the leading feminist activists from the first wave of the Indian women's movement, and her first book examined the causes of women's enslavement in India. She was very active in the All India Women's Conference and was elected president of the organization in 1944. After independence, Chattopadhyaya focused on her other great passion; she was a strong advocate of folk artists and won many international awards for her work with artists.

Gandhi, Mohandas Karamchand, also known as "Mahatma" (great soul) or "Bapu" (father) (1869–1948)

Gandhi was a unique blend of philosopher, moralist, politician, social worker, revolutionary, and ascetic whose life became synonymous with the Indian Independence Movement. His father was the chief administrator of a small princely state in western India. Mohandas, however, did not appear to be marked for greatness at an early age. For instance, he was a disaster as a practicing lawyer in India. He found his vocation in South Africa, where he was sent to practice law but became a leader of the protest against the racism and discrimination faced by people of color there. Gandhi returned to India permanently in 1915 and became part of the INC, where he soon became the undisputed leader of the party. Gandhi preached complete noncooperation with the colonial state and civil disobedience against unjust laws; his tactics brought the British empire to its knees. Although he distanced himself from politics after the early 1930s, no political action or negotiation even during that period could go forward without the blessings of the mahatma. He could have had the office of his choice after independence but refused any official position. He was assassinated by a Hindu rightwing fanatic in 1948 who saw Gandhi as appeasing Muslims and neglecting the interests of India's Hindus.

Indian National Congress (INC) (1885–present)

India's oldest political party was created in 1885, and an Englishman, Allan Octavian Hume, played an important role in its foundation. From the outset, the INC was an umbrella organization of many different ideologies united by nationalism (or the search for power, if many critics are to be believed). Socialists and capitalists, landlords and peasants, religious leaders and atheists, priests and untouchables—all were accommodated within the INC at different times, and often simultaneously. This eclecticism—unity in diversity by its own credo—has been the traditional strength as well as the weakness of the INC. Under Gandhi's leadership the INC forged a broad nationalist alliance reflecting the aspirations of most sections of Indian society. The lack of a clear ideology, and an exaggerated sense of its own importance, however, allowed the INC to drift toward accepting partition of the country rather than sharing power with the Muslim League in 1946–1947. Its broad social base allowed the party to continue in power after independence, but dependence on many contradictory vested interests did not permit the party to make hard political decisions that could alienate a section of its political base.

Jinnah, Mohammed Ali, also known as Quaid e Azam or Supreme Leader (1876–1948)

Jinnah qualified as a barrister in London and was very successful in his chosen profession. He joined the INC in 1906 and the Muslim League in 1913—there was no contradiction in holding memberships in both parties at the time. Jinnah in fact was one of the major architects of the pact between the League and the INC worked out in 1916. A moderate, a modernist, a strict constitutionalist, and completely secular in his outlook, Jinnah resigned from the INC because he regarded Gandhi's program of civil disobedience as too extremist.

Jinnah briefly left politics to begin a lucrative legal practice in London. He was persuaded to return to India in 1937 and crafted important alliances between the Muslim League and regional parties in Muslim-majority provinces, which led to the resounding success of the League in the elections of 1945–1946. Many scholars insist that Jinnah's demand for a separate Muslim state and even his call to Indian Muslims in 1946 for "direct action" to secure Pakistan were no more than a political gambit for greater political gains (Jalal 1985). In any case, circumstances spiraled out of Jinnah's control, and the demand for a separate Muslim-majority state was realized in 1947. He became *Quaid e Azam,* or supreme leader, of Pakistan in 1947. Jinnah fought his last political battles while also battling tuberculosis, which finally claimed his life a year after Pakistan's independence.

Mountbatten, Louis (1900–1979)

This charismatic aristocrat was chosen to be India's last viceroy in March 1947, after Britain's recently elected Labour Party government had decided to withdraw from India. Mountbatten was selected to supervise the transfer of power. Impatient, and concerned about drawing Britain into a potential civil war between Hindus and Muslims in India, Mountbatten advanced the anticipated date of British withdrawal by almost six months. The decision to transfer power on August 15, 1947, was announced as late as June 3 of that year. Although he maintained excellent relations with the INC leadership, many blame Mountbatten's haste for the scale and extent of the riots that accompanied partition.

Nehru, Jawaharlal (1889–1964)

Jawaharlal trained as a lawyer, and his family expected him to follow the career of his father, Motilal Nehru, as a successful lawyer. However, Jawaharlal, and then his father, fell under the spell of Mahatma Gandhi, and turned their energies to the nationalist movement instead. An idealist visionary, an honest thinker, and a tireless worker, Nehru was personally chosen by Gandhi as his successor as the leader of the INC. Nehru spent more than eleven years in jail for his convictions. Throughout his political life Jawaharlal struggled to reconcile the Socialist beliefs he had embraced while an undergraduate at Cambridge University with Gandhi's very different critique of modern industrial civilization. A committed liberal, he was a firm believer in democracy, equality, diversity, and secularism, which he promoted with zeal as the first prime minister of an independent India. In the international arena he sought to place India at the head of a third block of "non-aligned" nations (many of them former colonies) keeping away from superpower rivalries. While hardly successful in implementing all of his ambitious visions for India and the world, Nehru was hugely successful in creating in India the world's largest democracy.

Rashtriya Swayamsevak Sangh (RSS)

Literally meaning the National Volunteer Corps, the RSS was founded by Keshav B. Hegdewar in 1925 as an organization to promote Hindu revivalism. It has since grown to become the single most important source of extremist Hindu nationalist ideology in India. The RSS blames most of India's troubles on Muslims, Christians, leftists, or westernized intellectuals. However, the RSS's list of potential enemies of the Hindu nation can run wider. Nathuram Godse, the man who assassinated Gandhi, was associated with the RSS too, though the organization was later acquitted of being part of the murder conspiracy. The RSS offers to its largely upper-caste, lower-middle-class male recruits a sense of discipline and order in an uncertain world, as well as a real support system in times of trouble. As a so-called cultural group, the RSS does not participate directly in elections, but over the years it has maintained a variety of front organizations for the purpose. The Bharatiya Janata Party, which ruled India between 1998 and 2004, is one part of what is called the "Sangh Family."

Singh, Bhagat (1907–1931)

Born into a Sikh family in Punjab, Bhagat Singh joined the nationalist movement early in life but soon became a revolutionary Socialist. In 1928, with a group of compatriots, he formed the Hindustan Socialist Republican Army and through revolutionary activities sought to awaken the Indian working class. Their actions popularized the slogan *Inquilab Zindabad* ("Long Live the Revolution") among Indians. Bhagat Singh and his colleagues were arrested while throwing bombs into the British-dominated Central Legislative Assembly in 1929 but were then tried and convicted for an earlier murder of a British police officer. Their bravery won them enormous popularity among ordinary Indians. In 1929–1930, Singh's popularity was said to rival or surpass that of Gandhi himself. Gandhi, in fact, was severely castigated by many of his colleagues for failing to intercede with the British authorities to halt Bhagat Singh's execution in 1931.

Sanjay Joshi

See Also Bangladesh Revolution; Colonialism, Anti-Colonialism, and Neo-Colonialism; Ethnic and Racial Conflict: From Bargaining to Violence; Nationalism and Revolution; Pakistan Independence and the Partition of India

References and Further Readings
Amin, Shahid. 1995. *Event, Metaphor, Memory: Chauri Chaura 1922–92*. Delhi: Oxford University Press.
Bayly, Christopher A. 1998. *Origins of Nationality in South Asia: Patriotism and Ethical Government in the Making of Modern India*. Delhi: Oxford University Press.
Betts, Raymond F. 1998. *Decolonization: The Making of the Contemporary World*. London: Routledge.
Chatterjee, Partha. 1993. *The Nation and Its Fragments: Colonial and Postcolonial Histories*. Princeton, NJ: Princeton University Press.
Cohn, Bernard S. 1996. *Colonialism and Its Forms of Knowledge: The British in India*. Princeton, NJ: Princeton University Press.
Ferguson, Niall. 2004. *Empire: The Rise and Demise of the British World Order*. New York: Basic Books.
Forbes, Geraldine E. 1996. *Women in Modern India*. New Cambridge History of India, IV. vol. 2. Cambridge: Cambridge University Press.
Gandhi, Mohandas Karamchand. 1997. *Hind Swaraj and Other Writings*. Edited by Anthony J. Parel. Cambridge: Cambridge University Press.
Guha Ranajit. 1999. *Elementary Aspects of Peasant Insurgency in Colonial India*. Durham, NC: Duke University Press.
Hardiman, David. 2003. *Gandhi in His Time and Ours*. Delhi: Permanent Black.
Hasan Mushirul, ed. 1993. *India's Partition: Process, Strategy and Mobilization*. Delhi: Oxford University Press.
Jalal, Ayesha. 1985. *The Sole Spokesman: Jinnah, the Muslim League and the Demand for Pakistan*. Cambridge: Cambridge University Press.
Kulke, Hermann, and Dietmar Rothermund. 2002. *A History of India*. 3rd edition. New York: Routledge.
Nehru, Jawaharlal. 1946. *The Discovery of India*. Calcutta: Signet.
Omvedt, Gail. 1994. *Dalits and the Democratic Revolution: Dr. Ambedkar and the Dalit Movement in Colonial India*. Thousand Oaks, CA: Sage.
Sangari, Kumkum, and Sudesh Vaid, eds. 1989. *Recasting Women: Essays in Colonial History*. Delhi: Kali for Women.
Sarkar, Sumit. 1983. *Modern India, 1885–1947*. Madras: Macmillan India.
Seeley, J. R. 1971 (1883). *The Expansion of England*. Chicago: University of Chicago Press.

Indonesian Counter-Revolution

CHRONOLOGY

1965   Indonesian Communist Party (PKI) increases its political influence. Tension grows between PKI and the army as Sukarno's health is seen to falter. The Indonesian economy continues its catastrophic decline, leading to high level of unrest and increasing demands for change. August 17, Sukarno gives his "Year of Living Dangerously" speech concerning the political situation in Indonesia.

September 30, leftist middle-ranking army officers kidnap and kill six senior generals believed to be planning a coup against Sukarno. Sukarno joins kidnappers at Halim Air Force Base in Jakarta, thus implicating himself in the killings and turning remaining generals against him.

October 1, Major General Suharto rallies troops to crush the "30 September Movement," broadened to include members and sympathizers of the Indonesian Communist Party. Between several hundred thousand and more than a million people are murdered over the next several months and hundreds of thousands more jailed, while the government is purged of Communists and left-leaning politicians. Suspicion grows about Suharto's prior knowledge of this alleged "attempted Communist coup." Suharto maneuvers to isolate Sukarno politically.

1966   On March 11, officers loyal to Suharto force Sukarno to sign a letter to "restore order" (*Supersemar*), giving Suharto free reign to eliminate the remnants of the PKI and anyone opposed to his growing power. Purges of government, bureaucracy, and military are completed. Suharto ends "Confrontation" with Malaysia.

1967   Military rule initiated from March of 1966; the election of Suharto as acting president by a purged supreme 'consultative assembly' (MPR) confirms his leadership. Suharto seeks foreign investment, and begins to stabilize the country's shattered economy. "Depoliticization" of Indonesia begins in earnest.

1968   March 27, Suharto elected as president by MPR. The "New Order" government is announced, contrasted with Sukarno's "Old Order."

1970   Sukarno dies while under house arrest.

1971   Parties are formally restricted from campaigning. Government vehicle Golkar ("functional groups") is not formally recognized as a party and hence is not restricted.

1973   Smaller parties merged into two, one representing broad Islamic interests, the other nationalists and Christians, tightly controlled by the government.

1975   Indonesia invades Portuguese Timor, leading to at least 150,000 deaths and twenty-four years of international opposition.

1976   Hasan Di Tiro launches the Aceh-Sumatra National Liberation Front to secure the independence from Indonesia of Aceh Province at the western tip of Sumatra, thus beginning a still unresolved conflict.

1970s   Indonesia's economy is buoyed by exports of oil during oil price boom. Official corruption becomes deeply entrenched up to the highest levels, including the president.

1982   The military's political and defense "dual function" is enacted as law.

1986   Corruption by Suharto, his family, and cronies starts to become a public political issue, leading to alienation of some senior army officers.

Beginning of opening up of Indonesia's economy to greater foreign investment, spurring economic growth into the 1990s.

1988   Suharto's appointment of Sudharmono as vice president further alienates a group of senior officers.

1990s   Suharto moves closer to formal Islam, going on the *hajj* to Mecca, promoting Islamic organizations and Muslim army officers more personally loyal to him. This precipitates a split in the military and fuels destabilizaton of the New Order. Development of a "professional" secular-nationalist ("red and white") faction in the army opposed to explicitly pro-Suharto Muslim ("green") officers.

1996   Attack by soldiers and hired thugs on Indonesian Democratic Party headquarters arranged by supporters of ousted party leader Megawati Sukarnoputri. Jakarta-wide rioting ensues that was seen as a marker in the decline of Suharto's political authority.

1997   The Indonesian rupiah plummets, precipitating financial collapse and economic chaos following falls in the value of Thailand's baht currency, rampant corruption, unregulated borrowing, and capital flight.

1998   Suharto fails to respond adequately to proposed IMF remedies to currency collapse and economic chaos. Rioting and political protests break out across Indonesia, especially Jakarta. More than 1,000 die in rioting and when trapped in burning buildings. Some riots and organized rapes systematically target ethnic Chinese. Amid growing calls even from his appointees, Suharto resigns on May 18, handing power to his hand-picked vice president, B. J. Habibie, who oversees ushering in a process of reform and democratization.

INTRODUCTION

Indonesia's geographic and cultural dispersion has required an internally active army to maintain state cohesion, leading to an active military role in politics. The dominance of the military in Indonesian politics was formally established in

1966, following the alleged "attempted Communist coup" of September 30, 1965, which resulted in the destruction of Indonesia's Communist Party and the removal of leftists from the government, military, and police. The following period was marked by broad economic growth and stable if restrictive political life.

BACKGROUND: CULTURE AND HISTORY

Indonesia includes the cultures of the more than 300 linguistic groups across the 13,000 inhabited islands of the archipelago. The proximity of Indonesia to India and the ancient Middle East meant that Indonesia was exposed to their influences, in particular Hinduism and later Islam. Because of its rice-based economy and position at the trading crossroads, the Indonesian island of Java became the locus of cultural development in the western islands and was the primary site of Dutch colonization, which did not occur in the rest of the archipelago under Dutch control until the early twentieth century. The archipelago was divided between colonial powers, with the British occupying parts of Sumatra and the Malayan Peninsula and controlling a section of Borneo, and the Portuguese occupying half of the island of Timor. The British later exchanged their possessions on Sumatra for Dutch holdings on the peninsula, thus dividing the Malay world along colonial lines and separating the previously close principalities and sultanates of Sumatra from those on the peninsula. What was to become Indonesia therefore reflected the lines of colonial occupation and control, as well as bilateral colonial agreement.

By 1965, Indonesia was still an overwhelmingly rural country in which people lived by subsistence farming and with limited access to the cash economy. Literacy and formal education remained limited. Language and culture were still very largely local affairs, with only the army and to a lesser extent the bureaucracy manifesting an overarching sense of national identity and state cohesion. Those Indonesians educated in Bahasa Indonesia had access to national culture via the mass media and occasionally through inter-island travel. But Indonesia had not cohered as a nation, and there was by 1965 still very little sense of national identity. To the extent that a national identity was beginning to be articulated, it relied heavily on Javanese norms and values of piety, deference, and respect, which tended to be reinvented and reinterpreted in order to suit the emerging nationalist symbolism.

One aspect of Javanese political culture that Sukarno had appropriated, and that Suharto also appropriated in his turn, was the Javanese concept of power. The traditional Javanese notion of power was static, so that an increase in the power of one implied the decrease in the power of another. Sukarno had a type of universal, value-free power (*kesaktian*) in both the symbolic and real sense, right up until the time that it began to ebb from him and accrue as a type of inspiration (*wahyu*) to Suharto. Suharto then increased this power, which he employed in distinctly Javanese refined or overtly demure (*halus*) and distinctly hierarchical ways. Javanese political culture, under Sukarno but more so under Suharto, became fixed in both language and practice, even among those who possessed a more egalitarian or reciprocal understanding of political relations.

As president, Sukarno attempted to spark a sense of Indonesia's national identity (manifesting his *wahyu*) among its people by embarking on grand projects, such as "restoring" Dutch New Guinea to Indonesian sovereignty, by rallying support behind the "Confrontation" with Malaysia, and by proclaiming the revolution as a continuing process.

Domestically, Indonesia's post-independence period had been marked by regional rebellion, unstable government, little and inconsistent economic planning, and consequently, economic decline and more regional rebellion. At the same time, Indonesia was still forming as an idea in the minds of its citizens, and its final shape had not yet been set. The 1955 parliamentary elections had been a genuine if imperfect democratic process. But opposing political camps hardened their positions.

Debate continues as to whether the parliamentary period was a failure or whether it was no more tumultuous than, say, Italian politics of the same period. However, following the nationalization of Dutch industry in 1957, and the military's intervention to both limit that process and to take over nationalized industries, as well as rebellions in the outer islands that were suppressed by the army, parliamentary democracy was ended. In an operation planned by the office of the chief of the army, General Abdul Haris Nasution, President Sukarno in 1959 abolished parliament and established executive presidential leadership, also known as "Guided Democracy."

While Guided Democracy ended the squabbling and inconsistency of parliament, it did nothing to resolve the country's worsening economic problems. Incapable of addressing such issues, Sukarno increasingly turned public attention to what he called completing the revolution that had begun in 1945. The most important element of this was having the Netherlands cede control of Dutch New Guinea to Indonesia. Strapped for cash to pay for the military expansion this required, Sukarno turned to the Soviet Union; during the depths of the Cold War, this step alarmed the United States. Similarly, the increasing size and political role of the Indonesian Communist Party (PKI) also worried the United States, as well as the army leadership.

Into the 1960s, Sukarno balanced the army and the PKI against each other in an increasingly tense and economically desperate environment. The PKI had members from trade unions, peasant organizations, and among writers and artists. It had a wide worker-peasant base and was the world's third largest Communist party by 1965. Indonesia's conservative military leaders were generally veterans of the war of independence, were mostly Javanese, and, for the most part, had been trained during World War II by the Japanese as members of the Japanese-created self-defense army, PETA (Pembele Tanah Air, Volunteer Army to Defend the Fatherland).

In 1963, Indonesia had been successful in gaining control over Dutch New Guinea, but only because the United States had pressured the Dutch to relinquish their control over the disputed territory in a failed bid to win Indonesian support in the Cold War. Sukarno hoped to follow up on this victory by opposing the creation of Malaysia from Malaya and Britain's colonies in north Borneo. With British Commonwealth troops defending Malaysia, Indonesia never posed a meaningful military threat to the new state. The cold War itself had entered a new phase after the Cuban Missile Crisis, and Sukarno's closeness to the Soviet Union and increasingly to China alarmed the United States and other Western powers.

The Confrontation brought Indonesia into direct conflict with British Commonwealth forces (who were allied with the United States), especially on the island of Borneo. The Confrontation was not well supported by the senior military leadership, who worked behind the scenes to broker a settlement. By contrast, it was enthusiastically supported by the PKI (Indonesian Communist Party) as a blow against imperialism. Historically ideologically opposed and at times hostile, the PKI and army leadership jockeyed for position, with the PKI continuing to increase its influence.

By 1965, and with the economy in tatters, Sukarno began to fall ill, raising the specter of his succession. Poverty was rampant, and starvation had become increasingly common. Inflation had reached 500 percent; the price of rice, which was in short supply, had increased 900 percent, and the budget deficit had risen to 300 percent of government revenues. If foreign debt repayments were to have been made, they would have amounted to almost the total of Indonesia's export income.

Political outlets for this buildup of tension had been limited by the banning of some previously popular political parties and censorship of the news media. To ensure the operation of the state, its administration was increasingly run by the army, while the PKI had become a dominant political force, developing numerous front organizations, militating for land redistribution and better working conditions, and increasing its representation in Sukarno's government.

The army, which was politically conservative and in its senior ranks largely pro-Western, became increasingly disenchanted with Sukarno's charismatic but ever more erratic leadership. As Sukarno's health began to fail, the army and the PKI, already wary, began to eye each other with increasing suspicion and hostility. In 1965 Indonesia was at a critical juncture, both in terms of its own development and in terms of international relations.

CONTEXT AND PROCESS OF REVOLUTION

Rumors of an army coup began to focus on the Armed Forces Day parade in Jakarta on October 5, when large numbers of troops loyal to conservative generals would be in the city. In response, a group of middle-ranking officers led by the head of the presidential guard, Lieutenant Colonel Untung, staged a preemptive raid against the six key generals. Three resisted capture and were killed; the three bodies and the three living generals were taken to Halim Air Force Base, where the surviving generals were also killed and their bodies dumped into a well. Untung then went on radio to announce the formation of a pro-Sukarno, anti-U.S. "revolutionary council" (which its named members later denied knowledge of) to replace the government.

It is likely that senior members of the PKI were aware of the plan against the generals and probably endorsed it, but much less likely that they were a part of the affair. General Suharto, who had been thought loyal to Sukarno, rallied troops who stormed the air force base and then hunted down rebellious soldiers in Central Java and sailors at Surabaya. Suharto explicitly targeted the PKI, declaring that the killing of the generals had been an "attempted Communist coup."

Sukarno was at the air force base at the time of the kidnappings, along with PKI leader Aidat, indicating their prior knowledge of at least the kidnappings. However, contrary to its previous practice, the PKI was unprepared for the killings or the announcement of the "revolutionary council," and when the army consolidated under Suharto, the PKI's members were ill prepared for the onslaught that awaited them. Following the events of September 30, 1965, Sukarno's *wahyu* increasingly deserted him and accrued to Suharto. In less mystical terms, Suharto saw an opportunity to seize power and, through a series of well-considered steps, implemented what amounted to a coup, not on September 30 or October 1 (according to Sukarno), 1965, but on March 11, 1966, when legal and practical authority was signed away by the president to the general.

This identification of the PKI as being behind the alleged "attempted coup" was used as a pretext by the army to

Suharto, president of Indonesia (1966–1998). (Embassy of Indonesia)

unleash a wave of terror, in which hundreds of thousands of PKI members and suspected Communists were summarily executed, often by religious vigilante gangs working on behalf of the army. Over the next several months, the state administration was systematically purged of PKI members and then any leftists, as was the government.

Sukarno's presence at Halim Air Force Base, where the kidnapped generals had been taken and killed, seriously weakened his authority, and officers already hostile toward him became increasingly so. The next few months saw him try to maintain authority in a political environment increasingly engineered to delegitimize his presidency. Public protests, often organized by the army, called for his removal, while the army exercised real political control throughout the country.

The key turning point following the murder of the generals was Sukarno's last serious attempt to restore his authority, by announcing a new cabinet on February 21, 1966. Rather than reading the moves against him, Sukarno overestimated his ability to control the situation and appointed a new, large cabinet that included Foreign Minister Subandrio and Air Marshall Omar Dhani, both suspected Communists.

A large student demonstration at the swearing in of the cabinet on February 24 was fired upon by troops, killing two students. Student protests continued, with students breaking into Subandrio's office on March 8, allegedly finding documents showing his links to China. On March 11, in the face of another student protest that made it impossible for him to attend a cabinet meeting, Sukarno flew to Bogor by helicopter, where he was met by officers loyal to Suharto.

With Subandrio and other leftist ministers under direct threat from students and, in an environment in which he had lost effective control, Sukarno capitulated to pressure by the officers and signed a letter that handed over all practical authority to Suharto. Suharto officially banned the PKI on March 12 and arrested Subandrio a week later. From that time, Sukarno was removed from executive authority. In 1967, Sukarno was formally removed from the presidency by a purged national assembly and placed under house arrest, thus smoothing the way for Suharto's own rise to power and marking a shift from what became known as Sukarno's "Old Order" to Suharto's "New Order."

IMPACTS

The effects of Indonesia's 1965–1966 counter-revolution were profound. In the first instance, within months it had left dead hundreds of thousands of Communists and suspected Communists. Estimates vary, but even conservative figures suggest that half a million were summarily executed in that time. Hundreds of thousands more were imprisoned, and when released marked for life as officially untrustworthy. The bloodletting, primarily on Java and Bali, left a deep scar in Indonesia's national psyche and almost four decades later is still too painful and controversial a subject for most Indonesians to revisit in detail.

The second major effect of the events of this period was the bringing to power of a military government that gradually shifted to becoming a military-backed government. This had the effect of making the Indonesian military the preeminent political organization in the state, which has had far-reaching consequences for the process of democratization and how the state functions, even well into the post–New Order era.

The third major effect was the imposition of what amounted to a dictatorship for more than thirty years. Although technically elections were held, the outcome and the representation that chose the president were always a foregone conclusion. The ideological environment was deeply conservative, authoritarian, and occasionally brutal. Power had been established through a wholesale massacre, and now political dissent was not tolerated; any sign of genuine opposition or dissent was met with jailing or quasi-official state violence. Examples included the "mysterious killings" in the early 1980s, when several thousand suspected criminals, former political prisoners, and others were summarily executed; attacks against Muslim protesters in Jakarta in 1984 and South Sumatra in 1987; ongoing repression and the killing of tens of thousands in West Papua and Aceh; and in 1975 the invasion of East Timor, which left at least 150,000 dead.

The fourth and more subtle effect was the effective depoliticization of Indonesia, in which the idea of political participation effectively disappeared and a paternal state assumed total responsibility for policy direction. Civil society, including a free news media, trade unions, and public debate, effectively ceased to exist. This lack of citizen participation in the political process continued to characterize the post–New Order era.

A fifth and extremely debilitating effect was the deepening and widening of official corruption, starting at the top of the state administration with Suharto, his family members, and cronies, and cascading to the lowest levels of bureaucratic administration. Endemic corruption has been widely agreed to be Indonesia's biggest post–New Order problem, and although it existed in the pre–New Order period, it was not on the massive scale that has since seen Indonesia listed among the most corrupt countries in the world.

While the effects of the introduction of the New Order were primarily negative—at least relative to a more balanced and less repressive form of government—there were also other developments. Indonesia drew much closer to the West in the post-Sukarno era and quickly moved to regularize its economic management. Although deeply problematic in many respects, this shift in economic management and in particular Indonesia's windfall profits from oil exports made possible the development of much-needed infrastructure, especially the universalization of primary education.

The late New Order period also saw major steps toward the modernization of parts of Indonesia, in particular the larger cities, and an overall increase in average income, although income inequality was high. Growth and development were unevenly spread, and there were vast accumulations of wealth amid squalid poverty. With much wealth obtained through corrupt practices in a deregulated environment, a final consequence of the Suharto period was economic collapse. The state and its people still very much reflect the fundamental reshaping of Indonesian society that occurred during the Suharto era.

PEOPLE AND ORGANIZATIONS

Military

The Indonesian military (Tentara Republik Indonesia—TNI) was the primary vehicle for Indonesia's assertion of independence from the Dutch, and it has been the primary mechanism for retaining the unity of the state since that time. The TNI has seen itself as a "people's army," in part through its dispersal throughout the Indonesian archipelago, where it engages in local development projects and defends—and, more important, controls—the state. Until 1999 the TNI also had an active administrative function, although with declining representation from serving officers in the cabinet, and until 2004 it had guaranteed representation in the legislature. The TNI's legal and illegal business activities have been reported to make up some two-thirds to three-quarters of its total income, largely from the provinces, much of which is disbursed to senior officers. This means that it has a financial interest in maintaining its regional presence.

Under Suharto, the military was directly loyal to the president and received presidential patronage, while dissenting officers were sidelined. From late 1988, however, concern among some senior officers over Suharto's excessive corruption led to a split between officers loyal to Suharto, increasingly identified as formally Muslim, and "professional" secular-nationalist officers, resulting in tensions that undermined Suharto's presidency.

Parties

Under Suharto, Indonesia was effectively "depoliticized," with some parties banned and remaining parties collected into two new parties; secular parties were united in the Indonesian Democratic Party and Islamic parties in the United Development Party. Leadership and policy platforms had to be approved by the government, while campaigning was not allowed outside narrowly defined times. The party of government, Golkar, was not technically considered a party and thus had no restrictions applied to it, although it could compel government employees to vote for it. The rigging of election outcomes was commonplace.

PKI

The Indonesian Communist Party was the world's largest outside the U.S.S.R. and China at the time of its destruction in 1965. Founded in 1920, the PKI was almost completely destroyed by the Dutch after an abortive uprising in 1926. Various leftist and Communist parties were reformed into a single party in 1948 but again destroyed after an uprising at Madiun in Central Java. The party rebuilt itself throughout the 1950s, becoming the largest single party by the early 1960s. However, its growing influence in national politics was regarded with hostility by the military, and when middle-ranking officers kidnapped and murdered six senior generals in 1965, the army used the opportunity to blame the PKI and destroy it.

Suharto (Born 1921)

Suharto was born in the hamlet of Kemusu Argamulja, Central Java, on June 8, 1921, and after his parents divorced just after his birth, he spent most of his childhood living with relatives, attending local schools in Kemusu and the nearby region. He later remembered his unsettled childhood and youth as a period of suffering. At age seventeen Suharto left school to find work in a nearby bank and then as a laborer, before enlisting in the Royal Netherlands Indies Army (KNIL) in 1940.

After basic military training and a brief posting, Suharto was accepted for training as a sergeant, being promoted to that position just as war broke out in 1942. A week after he took up his new position, in Bandung, the Dutch surrendered to Japan. Suharto returned to Central Java, where, after bouts of malaria, he joined the occupation police force as an assistant inspector. In 1943, Suharto joined the newly Japanese-created self-defense army, PETA (Pembele Tanah Air, Volunteer Army to Defend the Fatherland), in which, soon after taking a commanders' course, he trained as an officer instructed in the equivalent of the Japanese warrior code of *bushido*. In 1944, Suharto was sent to train new PETA recruits. When Japan surrendered in 1945, Suharto helped organize a fighting unit of about company size in Central Java that was quickly incorporated into the newly established republican army.

Suharto led troops against the Dutch in the Central Java area around the republic's provisional capital at Yogyakarta, was promoted to lieutenant colonel, and developed local business connections that helped feed his troops and that gave him his first opportunities at profiteering. Suharto's forces were quite successful in the Central Java area, and troops under his command seized Yogyakarta from the Dutch in early 1949.

At the war's end, Suharto was commander of the Central Java region, where he continued his wartime practice of conducting business, but in 1959 he was charged with corruption and sent to officer training school. His fortunes revived, however, when in 1962 he was appointed by Sukarno to coordinate the operation to seize control of Dutch New Guinea from the Dutch, and then as commander of the newly created Strategic Reserve Command (Kostrad).

Suharto was seen as a Sukarno loyalist and was hence not targeted in the events of September 30, 1965, in which six generals were murdered. However, Suharto rallied his Kostrad troops and remaining senior officers and thwarted what he later claimed was a Communist coup attempt. In the period between the beginning of October 1965 and early 1966, Suharto and officers who recognized his leadership launched a massacre of Communists and their sympathizers, purged the military and bureaucracy, and cleared the legislature of leftist and other unfriendly politicians. On March 11, 1966, President Sukarno effectively handed full authority to Suharto, who ended Indonesia's "Confrontation" with Malaysia. He was appointed acting president in 1967 and formally president in 1968, proclaiming Indonesia's "New Order" government.

Among Suharto's first acts in office were restoring links to Western countries and reorganizing the ailing Indonesian economy, notably through loans and foreign investment. Suharto also sidelined critics and political competitors, restricted the news media and in 1970 banned protests. In 1973, Suharto had the remaining political parties reorganized into two parties effectively controlled by the state, and he won that year's elections at the head of a third group, Golkar (an acronym for "functional groups"), that, while technically not a political party, also stood candidates for election. Under this tightly controlled system, in which a large proportion of the body that elects the president was appointed, Suharto won subsequent "elections" in 1978, 1983, 1988, 1993, and 1998.

There had been public disquiet dating from 1970 about Suharto's corruption and that of his family and cronies, but it became a more public issue in 1986, leading to a division of his support from the army. Suharto, the self-styled "father of development," managed Indonesia's economy by raking off surplus profits during the oil price booms and liberalizing investment rules in lean periods. Such liberalization under the tightly controlled political environment led to a high level of foreign investment and profit making by Indonesia's domestic elites. However, as doubts surfaced about his political longevity, profiteering, speculative investment, and money transferring became rampant.

In mid-1997, Indonesia's economic bubble burst, and Suharto failed to respond adequately. Amid increasing demonstrations and riots, just after being reappointed for a sixth five-year term, Suharto was forced to resign. Although subsequently charged with corruption, he avoided having the cases heard on account of ill health.

Sukarno (See Indonesian Independence Revolution, People and Organizations.)

Damien Kingsbury

See Also Armed Forces, Revolution, and Counter-Revolution; Documentaries of Revolution; Human Rights, Morality, Social Justice and Revolution; Indonesian Independence Revolution; Terrorism

References and Further Readings

Bourchier, D., and J. Legge, eds. 1994. *Democracy in Indonesia: 1950s and 1990s.* Melbourne: Centre for Southeast Asian Studies, Monash University.

Cribb, Robert R., and C. Brown. 1995. *Modern Indonesia: A History since 1945.* London: Longmans.

Elson, R. 2001. *Suharto: A Political Biography.* Cambridge: Cambridge University Press.

Feith, H. 1973. *Decline of Constitutional Democracy in Indonesia.* Ithaca, NY: Cornell University Press.

Geertz, C. 1964. *The Religion of Java.* New York: Free Press of Glencoe.

Holt, C., B. Anderson, and J. Siegel. 1972. *Culture and Politics in Indonesia.* Ithaca, NY: Cornell University Press.

Kingsbury, D. 2005. *The Politics of Indonesia.* 3rd edition. Melbourne: Oxford University Press.

Legge, J. 2003. *Sukarno: A Political Biography.* 3rd edition. Singapore: Archipelago.

Ricklefs, M. 1993. *History of Modern Indonesia since c. 1300,* 2nd edition. London: Macmillan.

Scwatz, A. A. 1994. *Nation in Waiting: Indonesia in the 1990s.* Sydney: Allen and Unwin.

Vatikiotis, M. 1993. *Indonesian Politics under Suharto.* London: Routledge.

Winters, J. 1996. *Power in Motion: Capital Mobility and the Indonesian State.* Ithaca, NY: Cornell University Press.

Indonesian Independence Revolution

CHRONOLOGY

1926   Indies Communist Party revolts, put down by Dutch troops. Sukarno helps found General Study Club in Bandung, West Java. He develops his theory of combining nationalism, Islam, and Communism. This is later known as *Nasakom,* and is a guiding principle of his government between 1958 and 1965.

1927   Sukarno and two others create the forerunner to the Indonesian Nationalist Party (PNI, established the following year), which becomes the main voice of Indonesian secular nationalism.

1928   Second Youth Congress pledges to "one motherland, one nation, and one language," adopting Bahasa Indonesia ("Indonesian language"), a modified form of traders' Malay.

1929   Sukarno's public speaking leads to his being convicted for disturbing public order. He is released in 1931 but rearrested in 1933.

1942   Japan invades Indonesia. Sukarno returns to Batavia (Jakarta) from exile and serves as chairman of the consultative committee to the occupation regime.

1943   Japan forms Volunteer Army to Defend the Fatherland (PETA), which becomes the basis of the Indonesian army.

1945   Japan is defeated. Sukarno declares independence on August 17, precipitating the war of independence. Suharto is appointed as president and Hatta as vice president by the Central Indonesian National Committee, heading a parliamentary government.

Indonesia's short, ambiguous 1945 constitution is enacted, and Pancasila (Five Principles)—belief in one god, just and civilized humanity, the unity of Indonesia, democracy guided by inner wisdom in unanimity arising out of deliberation among representatives, social justice—are adopted as state philosophy.

British and Australian forces accept the surrender of Japanese forces through Indonesia. British refuse to arrest republican leaders. On October 5, Angkatan Darat (Land Force, or army) is founded. Japanese forces operating under British orders push republicans out of Bandung and Semarang. Fighting breaks out between British forces and republicans, including British bombing of Surabaya, which leaves thousands dead. Recognizing capacity for becoming embroiled in a war on behalf of the Dutch, British forces begin to withdraw, passing authority to arriving Dutch forces.

At the end of 1945, a so-called social war breaks out in Aceh, in which former feudal lords who cooperated with the Dutch and Japanese are ousted by Islam-led forces. "Social war" breaks out in Batak area, North Sumatra.

The next four years are marked by fighting by the republic's army throughout the archipelago but predominantly in Java and Sumatra, as well as by negotiations with the Dutch by successive republican governments.

1946   Linggajati Agreement recognizes an Indonesian republic consisting of Java, Madura, and Sumatra, but not other islands of the Netherlands East Indies. In July, British forces officially hand over to the Dutch authority for all of the East Indies except Java and Sumatra, completing their total withdrawal in November.

Battle of Marga, Bali, results in Dutch victory; Dutch create puppet state of East Indonesia.

1947   Dutch continue the creation of puppet states in eastern Indonesia.

First Dutch "police action," resulting in occupation of West Java, East Java, Madura, Semarand, Medan, Palembang, and Padang.

Renville Agreement between the Dutch and nationalist forces leads to cession of territory to the Dutch, abandoning Islamic fighters in West Java. Declaring a "holy struggle" (*jihad*), the Darul Islam (House of Islam) movement fights independently, refusing to recognize the authority of the secular republic.

Dutch initiate a "police action" that, while militarily successful, draws a hostile international response. There are bans on Dutch supply shipping in Australia, and Australia represents the republic in the United Nations. Australia, India, and the U.S.S.R. officially recognize the Republic of Indonesia, supporting it in the United Nations. "Good Offices Commission" established to represent Indonesian claims.

1948   Dutch continue establishment of puppet states in eastern Indonesia.

Leftist parties are welded into a unified Indonesian Communist Party (PKI) with its own armed units. The establishment of a moderate religious-nationalist coalition government panics second-tier Communist

leaders in Madiun, Central Java, who revolt against the government, believing its armed units would be disbanded. The Communist leadership is killed and the Madiun Revolt put down by loyalist troops, marking the beginning of hostility between the army and the PKI.

Second Dutch "Police Action"; republican capital of Yogyakarta falls to the Dutch. All of Indonesia except for Aceh and parts of Sumatra fall under Dutch military control.

1949   Guerrillas under Suharto retake Yogyakarta for six hours. Dutch later announce that they will hand back Yogyakarta if the guerrilla war stops, leading to republican occupation of the city in June.

U.S. pressure on The Netherlands via the Marshall Plan for post-war reconstruction leads to an end to conflict and, on December 30, the formal creation of the federated United States of the Republic of Indonesia (RUSI). RUSI is made up of the Republic (Java and Sumatra) and fifteen smaller states. Darul Islam Rebellion continues, expanding to include South Sulawesi and, from 1953, Aceh, not ended until 1963.

1950   RUSI is claimed as unworkable and the Dutch attempt to continue to exercise authority in some parts of the archipelago, RUSI is abandoned in favor of the Unitary State of the Republic of Indonesia. Former indigenous soldiers of the Dutch army in South Sulawesi rise in rebellion against Indonesian authority, are defeated, and retreat to South Maluku, which also rises in rebellion, declaring the Republic of the South Moluccas (RMS). The RMS is defeated by the end of the year.

1955   Indonesia hosts Asia-Africa Conference in Bandung, forerunner to the Non-Aligned Movement.

1957   Nationalization of Dutch industry.

Anti-Communist, anti-centralist Overall Struggle (Permesta) rebellion in Eastern Indonesia.

1958   Provisional Revolutionary Republic of Indonesia (PRRI), launched in West Sumatra, joins with Permesta rebellion to form PRRI-Permesta. Army defeats rebellion, controls trade union seizures of Dutch industry, which it takes over, and announces its "middle way," incorporating both a civilian and defense function. This is later interpreted as the military's "dual function" and justifies its role in civil politics.

1959   Sukarno ends parliamentary democracy, declares "guided democracy," balancing the PKI against the army.

1963   Dutch relinquish authority in Dutch New Guinea to Indonesia, which it renames Irian Barat and then Irian Jaya (formally incorporated in 1969). Sukarno launches "Confrontation" with the newly created state of Malaysia.

INTRODUCTION

The idea of independence in the Dutch East Indies first stirred in the late 1920s. The Japanese occupation during World War II broke Dutch political control. Although the Dutch returned in 1945, independence had been declared, precipitating a war that lasted four years. Through a mixture of guerrilla strategy and international diplomacy, Indonesia was granted independence as a federation in 1949, and the following year dissolved the federation to form a Unitary State. However, internal struggles—including issues of center-periphery relations, economic management, and Islam—challenged the state, leading to the rise of the military. That was balanced by the rise of the Communist party, amid increasingly personalized power and economic chaos.

BACKGROUND: CULTURE AND HISTORY

Originally comprising various tribal polities, states, and, briefly, local empires, Indonesia did not exist prior to 1945, or even as an idea prior to the 1920s. The most unifying regional empires prior to the arrival of the Dutch in 1602 were the Sri Vijaya empire (ca. 850–ca. 1377), centered near contemporary Palembang in eastern Sumatra, and the Majapahit empire (1309–1400), centered on East Java. Settled by ethnic Malays from as long ago as 2000 B.C., polities be-

gan developing from 300 B.C., the most sophisticated being on Java, and later on Sumatra. Hinduism derived from India became the dominant formal religion in the western islands from this time, later interspersed with Buddhism, while the eastern islands remained largely animist until the arrival of Islam, from the thirteenth century, and Christianity, from the sixteenth century.

The cultures of the more than 300 linguistic groups across the 13,000 inhabited islands of the archipelago can be broadly categorized as belonging to the first and second Malay waves of immigration, and in the east Melanesian. The first Malay wave became more isolated and was characterized by less complex forms of political organization and less permanent architecture (such as the Bataks of North Sumatra and the Dayaks of Kalimantan). The second wave tended to have more complex forms of political administration and architecture. A second broad distinction is between the western islanders, who are very largely of Malay (Austronesian) heritage, and the eastern islanders, who are of mixed Malay and Papuan (Melanesian) heritage, particularly to the farther south and east, and the Melanesians of West Papua. A third method of pre-colonial distinction was (and to some extent remains) between those who practice wet rice agriculture (second wave Malays of the western islands) and those who practice shifting agriculture (first wave Malays and those of the eastern islands).

The proximity of the western islands to India and the ancient Middle East meant that they were first exposed to their influences, in particular Hinduism and later Islam. Sitting astride the sea trade routes between India and China meant that states along the Malacca Straits and the Sunda Straits were at a cultural as well as a trading crossroads. The formal complexity of social organization and the economic capacity afforded by these influences and by the social stability of wet rice agriculture provided significant advantages to the numerically superior Javanese. The inwardly focused Javanese states, although deeply influenced by Hinduism and later by Islam, also retained a strong and complex local cultural identity.

Javanese culture is marked by introspective, demure, and deferential behavior, and is reflected in the Javanese shadow puppet characters of the great Hindu epics, in particular the Mahabarata. However, there is also recognition of a balance of forces in nature, and in human affairs, that contains within it elements of both strength and weakness, or good and bad. Power, which exists in a more complex form than in Western thought, does not imply moral judgment, and it is fixed in its universal quantity. Thus greater power to one necessarily implies lesser power to another. Non-Javanese cultures are often very different, much less reticent or deferential, and sometimes quite blunt.

Because of its rice-based economy and site at the trading crossroads, Java became the locus of cultural development in the western islands and was the primary site of Dutch colonization, which did not occur in the rest of the archipelago under Dutch control until the early twentieth century. The archipelago was divided between colonial powers, with the British occupying parts of Sumatra and the Malayan Peninsula; a British subject privately ruling northwest Borneo and a British-based company in control of northeast Borneo; the Spanish and later United States in the Philippines; and the Portuguese retaining half the island of Timor. The British later exchanged their possessions on Sumatra for Dutch possessions on the peninsula, thus dividing the Malay world along colonial lines—and separating the previously close principalities and sultanates of Sumatra from those on the peninsula. Thus what was to become Indonesia reflected the lines of colonial occupation and control, and bilateral colonial agreement.

Muslims, about 88 percent of Indonesia's population and more than 90 percent Sunni, were generally divided between those who formally accepted the faith (*santri*) and those whose faith was more nominal (*abangan*). In particular on Java, *abangan* Islam melded with preexisting animist and Hindu (briefly Buddhist) beliefs to produce a more mystical version of folk-Islam that later tended to support secular parties and politicians. *Santri* Muslims have tended to support more Islamic parties and politicians, although there were and remain divisions between rural and urban Muslims and over demands for Sharia (Islamic law). Elements of Islamic modernism have also promoted the idea of "holy struggle" (*jihad*) against unbelievers occupying Muslim land and apostates. During the war against the Dutch, Islamic units formed into a "Party of God" (Hizbullah), which refused to recognize the authority of the secular state, leading to the Darul Islam Rebellion of the 1950s and early 1960s, and which provided the genealogy to contemporary militant Islamic groups.

Because Java was generally the most socially complex part of the Dutch colony, the most populous and numerically the best educated, it was largely the Javanese that led the war of independence against the Dutch, which cemented the position of Jakarta as the state's political center. Because of the preponderance of Javanese in the independence movement and later government, and a Javanese tendency toward both centralism and syncretism, Javanese became the dominant cultural influence in the new state—for example, expressed in the use of the Hindu-Javanese language for the state ideology of Pancasila (Five Principles) and the state motto *Bhinneka Tunggal Ika* ("Unity in Diversity") and in the syncretic melding of incompatible ideologies (for example, nationalism, Islam, and Communism).

While the war of independence from The Netherlands was enthusiastically received by many, perhaps most in Java and Sumatra, not all Indonesians supported independence—especially in the eastern islands, which provided most of the

troops for the loyalist Royal Netherlands Indies Army (Koninklijk Nederlands-Indisch Leger KNIL). Following the declaration of the Unitary State in 1950, rebellions broke out in South Sulawesi, South Maluku (Ambon), and Aceh. The imposition of the Unitary State provided organizational cohesion but failed adequately to reflect the considerable diversity of many peoples whose principal common link was the Dutch colonial experience.

CONTEXT AND PROCESS OF REVOLUTION

The Indonesian Revolution occurred at a pivotal time in world history, and was part of a global process that was to continue until the late 1960s, or later. The West's global domination, expressed as colonialism, reached its peak just prior to World War I (1914–1918), during which time The Netherlands consolidated the last of its control across those parts of the archipelago it claimed as its own. Genuine control may not have extended much beyond the towns or coastal areas of some colonial outposts, but there was no other power in the region able to challenge Dutch authority.

However, the inter-war years were marked by the development of nationalist and anti-colonialist movements. Such movements existed in Indonesia at this time, drawing on both modernist Islamic emancipatory ideas and Western ideas of revolution, self-determination, and nationhood.

In the period prior to World War II, however, such ideas were restricted to a small number of intellectuals and activists, whom colonial authorities in the Netherlands East Indies as elsewhere had little trouble in suppressing. Exploitative and often repressive colonial life continued, with surplus resources, such as rubber, coffee, tobacco, and tin, being extracted from the colony's plantations and mines, upon which The Netherlands grew prosperous. Questions that were raised about colonial exploitation in The Netherlands were rare and usually countered with marginal moves toward providing more education and other basic services to at least some of the population.

Colonial dominance may have been ethically unsound and increasingly questioned in Western countries, but it remained powerful. That changed in Southeast Asia in particular with the advent of World War II, and in 1942 Japan's rapid invasion and occupation of effectively all of east and southeast Asia. The European colonial masters who had, to many, seemed invincible were quickly shown both to be capable of suffering defeat and to be defeated by an Asian people.

While Japanese occupation of the East Indies was much less liberation by Asian "brothers" than its rhetoric suggested, there was some co-option of preexisting nationalists into the Japanese cause, under the guise of training for eventual liberation. However, when Japan became more serious about this, through training indigenous troops and establishing rudimentary political structures, it was more as a means of complicating and hence slowing the quickening Allied advance. As a strategy, this failed. However, it did leave in place a local military force and a small but emboldened nationalist elite equipped with some basic political institutions. In the East Indies, this comprised the indigenous Volunteer Army to Defend the Fatherland (Pembele Tanah Air, PETA), a constitutional commission that had drawn up a brief republican constitution, and a basic administrative infrastructure.

At the time of the declaration of independence, in August 1945, Allied troops were already in the East Indies, with British (or Indian) troops in the west and Australian troops in the east. The Allies had orders to accept the Japanese surrender and to secure the colony for the return of the Dutch. However, PETA units and nonenlisted gangs took arms from the Japanese and refused to accept British authority. Australian troops were generally uncooperative in handing authority back to the Dutch. But the British troops followed orders more formally, and fighting quickly broke out, in particular in the large industrial city of Surabaya on Java. Recognizing the possibility of becoming embroiled in a war of independence on behalf of another colonial power, the British withdrew, being replaced by Dutch forces.

The conflict that followed was largely a guerrilla war, with the Dutch occupying the cities and towns and the Indonesian forces the countryside. The recapture of Yogyakarta by Indonesian forces, which had symbolic as well as strategic importance, was one of the few large conventional battles of the war. The period between 1945 and 1949 was marked by periods of negotiation and large-scale Dutch advances when negotiations broke down. Indonesia's regular army was small, poorly equipped, and rarely paid, and consequently its units relied on their own means to survive. Parallel to the regular army were Communist or independent leftist units, which led to some conflict between the two forces, in particular the Madiun Affair of 1948. Another military group was the Hizbullah ("Party of God"), or Islamic militias, which were operative especially in West Java but also elsewhere in the archipelago. These Islamic units did not recognize the authority of the secular republic, especially after the signing of the Renville Agreement in 1947, which withdrew regular Indonesian troops from West to Central Java, abandoning the Islamic units. From that time, Islamic units fought not for the republic but for the creation of an Islamic state (NII—*Negera Islam Indonesia*). A fourth group involved against the Dutch were bandits and gangsters, who took advantage of the turmoil to engage in criminal activities but who also operated against the weakened and distracted Dutch.

The Dutch, however, enjoyed relative military success, and while there were periods of military stalemate and some republican successes, the war could not be won by military means alone. The major problem that The Netherlands faced was that it had been crippled by World War II and was incapable of rebuilding in Europe while also fighting in the colonies. U.S. aid under the Marshall Plan was critical to the rebuilding of The Netherlands, and the U.S. administration was not prepared to sponsor a colonial reconquest, especially one that could encourage a Communist backlash, at a time when it was actively encouraging de-colonization.

Under U.S. pressure, in 1949 the Dutch agreed to Indonesian independence in the form of the United States of the Republic of Indonesia (*Republic Indonesia Serikat*), comprising Java, Madura, and Sumatra, as well as fifteen smaller states in a federal arrangement. While such federalism may have more accurately reflected the desire for relative autonomy of many of the smaller groups in the fifteen states, the arrangement was unrepresentative by population and was deemed by the republic to be a ploy by which The Netherlands could retain significant political influence and economic control. The following year, the republic unilaterally abolished the federal system and proclaimed the Unitary State of the Republic of Indonesia (NKRI—*Negara Kesatuan Republik Indonesia*).

IMPACTS

The Indonesian Revolution had three primary impacts, the first being on the colonial infrastructure, the second domestic, and the third international. The initial impact of the revolution was on the state that was to emerge from four years of conflict: its relatively limited colonial infrastructure was badly damaged; it had lost much of its industry and almost all of its investment; it had a limited skilled workforce; and it was obliged to carry a high level of foreign denominated debt. This had the immediate effect of further impoverishing an already very poor people, and of making attempts to rebuild the economy especially difficult—which in turn created political tensions that undermined the country's political processes.

The second, although equally important, impact of the Indonesian Revolution was on the people of the archipelago themselves. For previously disparate peoples, only sometimes linked by a vague understanding of their common colonial circumstances, and to a very limited extent by the use of traders' Malay (the common language used by regional traders), the creation of the state of Indonesia gave these peoples their first taste of citizenship and, increasingly, of national identity. As well as bringing an increasingly high level of literacy to a very largely illiterate people in the official Indonesian language (Bahasa Indonesia), the development of a common education system, employing both historical fact and myth about the unity of the archipelago and its united struggle against the Dutch, helped to construct an increasingly common political identity.

However, in some regions this specifically defined and nominally secular "national" identity was not accepted. It was opposed by radical Muslims wishing to establish an Islamic state, by separatists in Aceh and the South Moluccas (and later Dutch New Guinea/West Papua and East Timor), and by various other groups whose articulation of the problems of involuntary incorporation into a centralized, Javanese-dominated state was manifested in violent resistance.

Because of the disparate nature of the state and, at least initially, the reliance of the army on surviving more or less independently of government funding, another unifying factor was the location of the army throughout the archipelago and its frequent involvement in local businesses. This helped ensure that the state was maintained intact, despite its being viewed by some as a reconstruction of the Dutch empire under Javanese rule. Without the binding role of the army, the state would not have existed in its original form at all, and it would not have survived in that form at any further point. Thus the active involvement of the military in state affairs was symbiotic with the state itself.

The Indonesian Revolution was also among the very first of the successful anti-colonial movements, and its success put Indonesia at the forefront of such movements. Its achievement of independence in 1949 stood as a model to other regional colonies seeking to throw off the shackles of colonialism, such as Vietnam, Cambodia, and Laos, as well as numerous African colonies.

Indonesia's anti-colonial struggle was often couched by nationalist leaders in Marxist terms, and was paralleled or adopted by many other anti-colonial leaders. This helped to identify anti-colonialism with Communism from the beginning of the Cold War, which after the achievement of independence increasingly had the effect of setting the United States in particular against the leadership of Indonesia, as well as that of other emerging post-colonial states. However, given Sukarno's blended *Nasakom* ideology, the politically conservative influence of Islam, and the spectrum of political views available at that time, Indonesia did not fall neatly into the Communist camp. Indeed, its frequent changes of parliamentary government swung between left and right ideological tendencies, which had the effect of destabilizing the economy and creating anxiety in the potentially more profitable outer islands.

This middle way, between Communism and capitalism, was manifested in Indonesia's hosting of the Asia-Africa Conference in Bandung in 1955, which was the forerunner of the Non-Aligned Movement. Indonesia's well-developed sense of anti-colonialism and anti-Westernism under Sukarno ultimately manifested itself as a rejection of what was perceived as the Western-dominated United Nations, as an attempt to secure Dutch New Guinea (as an original part of the Netherlands East Indies) by military means, and as the so-called Confrontation with Malaysia, which brought Indonesia into conflict with Britain and other British Commonwealth countries.

PEOPLE AND ORGANIZATIONS

Military

From 1945, after the republican government began negotiations with the Dutch, the Indonesian military saw itself as the true embodiment of Indonesia's revolution. Initially styled as a quasi-guerrilla force, in the post-1949 period it was under only nominal civilian control. Putting down the RMS Rebellion in 1950, tackling the Darul Islam Rebellion the same year, and putting down the PRRI-Permesta Rebellion in 1958, the military increasingly saw itself as the republic's savior. As the most organized and geographically dispersed institution of state, the military had its civil function formally enunciated in 1958; in 1959 it became an active partner in government and administration.

Parliament

Indonesia was a parliamentary democracy from 1945 until 1959. Between 1945 and 1949, conservative nationalist-religious and leftist nationalist-religious coalitions took turns in power, each negotiating with the Dutch when in office and being critical of such negotiations when in opposition. After independence the same broad groupings alternated in government, shifting economic policy between protectionism and open trade, leading to high inflation, high foreign debt, and corruption. In 1955 parliamentary elections were held, polarizing the opposing camps. Following a regional rebellion in 1958, which in 1959 was backed by the army, Sukarno ended Indonesia's parliamentary period, instituting executive presidential leadership, known as Guided Democracy.

PKI

The Indonesian Communist Party was the world's largest outside the U.S.S.R. and China at the time of its destruction in 1965. Founded in 1920, the PKI was almost completely destroyed by the Dutch after an abortive uprising in 1926. Var-

Indonesian president Sukarno in 1956. (Library of Congress)

ious leftist and Communist parties were reformed into a single party in 1948 but again destroyed after an uprising at Madiun in Central Java. The party rebuilt itself throughout the 1950s, becoming the largest single party by the early 1960s. However, its growing influence in national politics was regarded with hostility by the military, and when middle-ranking officers kidnapped and murdered six senior generals in 1965, the army used the opportunity to blame the PKI and destroy it completely.

Sukarno (1901–1970)

Indonesia's first president, Sukarno, was born on June 6, 1901, in Surabaya as the only son of a (Muslim) Javanese schoolteacher and his (Hindu) Balinese wife. His parents managed to send the young Sukarno to schools established by the Dutch colonial administration. To attend high school, he stayed with his grandparents for extended periods, exposing him to Javanese animism (*Kejawen*) and mysticism. Another home he stayed in at this time was that of

Tjokroaminoto, a leading nationalist politician. In 1921, Sukarno entered the only Dutch-established tertiary institution open to Indies' "natives," the leftist Bandung Institute of Technology, to study architecture, graduating in 1926. However, while there, he decided that his future lay in politics.

Sukarno married Tjokroaminoto's daughter, Sitti Utari, divorcing her to marry Inggit Garnasih; he subsequently married at least four more times, at one stage four wives simultaneously (permitted under Islamic law).

In 1926, Sukarno (a Muslim) was a founding member of the General Study Club in Bandung, during which time he elaborated his syncretic ideas on nationalism, Islam, and Communism, which became the guiding philosophy for his presidency, particularly after 1958. Sukarno's nationalist aspirations were based on the colony of the Netherlands East Indies, which prior to colonialism had not been united. In 1927, Sukarno founded the Indonesian Nationalist Party (PNI). He quickly became noted as a gifted orator on the subject of Indonesian nationalism, but that led to his being jailed for two years by the Dutch in 1929, and again in 1933. He returned to Batavia (Jakarta) following the Japanese invasion and worked in the occupation government, all the time maintaining his aspiration for an independent state.

Japan had been working toward Indonesia's independence prior to its defeat, largely as a means of delaying the Allied advance. Japan acknowledged defeat on August 15, 1945, and two days later Sukarno and his deputy Hatta declared Indonesia's independence in a small ceremony in the garden of his home. However, other nationalists installed Sutan Sjahrir as executive prime minister, pushing Sukarno to a more ceremonial position. Sukarno, Hatta, and Sjahrir effectively shared power during the first days of the republic, when enthusiasm was high but the territory was still in the hands of Allied troops. Conflicts broke out, and, as the Dutch returned, a war of independence became inevitable.

Sukarno retained his largely ceremonial although publicly inspiring role until the later 1950s. Following a series of governments and a lack of consistent economic policy, Sukarno began talking about "guided democracy." In 1957 he encouraged the nationalization of Dutch-owned industry in response to Dutch reluctance to concede Dutch New Guinea to Indonesia. The PRRI-Permesta rebellion in the outer islands led to implicated political parties being banned and spelled the end of the authority of the parliamentary system. With the support of the army, however, Sukarno declared a return to the 1945 constitution, which placed principal power in the hands of the president and proclaimed Guided Democracy. He then moved closer to the Soviet Union and the Peoples' Republic of China.

With Sukarno's increasing hostility toward the West and an absence of foreign investment or sound economic policy, the Indonesian economy began a downward spiral. In 1962, Sukarno stepped up military pressure on the Dutch to relinquish Dutch New Guinea—which, under U.S. pressure, the Dutch did. Sukarno then turned his attention to the creation of the state of Malaysia from the British colonies and protectorates of the region. He opposed this as colonialism by another form and launched the so-called Confrontation with Malaysia. Meanwhile, he balanced the increasing political power of the PKI against that of the army. As Indonesia's economy plummeted and amid widespread material hardship, senior army officers grew increasingly disenchanted with Sukarno's flamboyant but erratic leadership. Sukarno's health appeared to fail, and tensions between the PKI and the army grew.

An alleged plot to oust Sukarno was thwarted by middle-ranking officers loyal to the president on September 30, 1965, leading to the killing of six generals. However, a less senior general, Suharto, who had been believed to be loyal, turned against the "attempted coup" plotters (the middle-ranking officers who had killed the six generals and were in turn accused by Suharto and other generals of acting on behalf of the Communists to bring about a leftist coup), marginalized

Sukarno, and turned the wrath of the army on the PKI. Sukarno relinquished effective political power on March 11, 1966, and was formally removed from the presidency and placed under house arrest the following year. He died in 1970.

Damien Kingsbury

See Also Colonialism, Anti-Colonialism, and Neo-Colonialism; Indonesian Counter-Revolution; Nationalism and Revolution

References and Further Readings
Bourchier, D., and J. Legge, eds. 1994. *Democracy in Indonesia: 1950s and 1990s.* Melbourne: Centre for Southeast Asian Studies, Monash University.
Cribb, Robert R., and C. Brown. 1995. *Modern Indonesia: A History since 1945.* London: Longmans.
Elson, R. 2001. *Suharto: A Political Biography.* Cambridge: Cambridge University Press.
Feith, H. 1973. *Decline of Constitutional Democracy in Indonesia.* Ithaca, NY: Cornell University Press.
Feith, H., and L. Castels. 1970. *Indonesian Political Thinking 1945–1965.* Ithaca, NY: Cornell University Press.
Geertz, C. 1964. *The Religion of Java.* New York: Free Press of Glencoe.
Holt, C., B. Anderson, and J. Siegel. 1972. *Culture and Politics in Indonesia.* Ithaca, NY: Cornell University Press.
Kahin, G. 1952. *Nationalism and Revolution in Indonesia.* Ithaca, NY: Cornell University Press.
Kingsbury, D. 2005. *The Politics of Indonesia.* 3rd edition. Melbourne: Oxford University Press.
Legge, J. 2003. *Sukarno: A Political Biography.* 3rd edition. Singapore: Archipelago.
Ricklefs, M. 1993. *History of Modern Indonesia since c. 1300,* 2nd edition. London: Macmillan.

Inequality, Class, and Revolution

Inequality and class can each play important roles in social revolutions. Inequality exists to some extent in all societies. But the level of inequality, the dimensions of inequality, and the way people feel about inequalities can vary significantly. Inequality may exist with regard to wealth (income or property), power (the ability to control other people, property, or aspects of the environment), prestige (the level of respect or affection a person receives from other people), access to opportunity, and level of political and civil rights. It can be based on factors such as a person's family lineage, the occupation of parents, race, ethnicity, country of origin, gender, sexual orientation, personal abilities, physical characteristics (such as disabilities), or other factors. Inequality also exists at the international level between whole societies.

INEQUALITY AS AN ENGINE OF REVOLUTION

Economic inequality is often thought to be at the root of revolutionary conflicts. Inequality in society often translates into the economic success of one group (for example, large landowners) at the expense of another (such as peasants or poor farmworkers). The disadvantaged groups in society may develop a sense of "mass frustration," which many scholars see as a necessary condition for revolution (De-Fronzo 1996, 11–12). However, mass frustration often derives from relative rather than absolute economic deprivation. Gurr (1970, 24) defined relative deprivation "as actors' perception of discrepancy between their value expectations and their value capabilities." He further defined "value expectations" as "the goods and conditions of life to which people believe they are rightfully entitled" and "value capabilities" as "the goods and conditions they think they are capable of getting and keeping."

The relationship of inequality to revolution seems to be important primarily in terms of how inequality is perceived in a subjective moral sense. Very high levels of economic inequality, for example, have existed for many generations in societies that did not experience revolutions. Yet in other societies, in which revolutionaries cited inequality as a cause for taking up arms, the level of inequality seems to have been lower than in countries that did not experience civil conflict—or lower or no different from the level of inequality that existed in the past. Inequality appears to play a role in revolution only when the levels or types of inequality have become widely viewed as morally wrong. When the gap between the level of equality that people demand and expect as morally right and the level of inequality that actually exists becomes too great, a situation of "relative deprivation" has developed (many people feel deprived relative to the way things should be, or relative to what other people have). If the sense of relative deprivation is widespread, a state of mass frustration (mass discontent) exists that is one of the essential requirements for the development of a mass-participation revolution.

There appear to be several ways in which a situation of relative deprivation can develop. One possibility is that the level of actual inequality—for example, economic inequality—may rapidly increase to such an extent that it is no longer justified by a society's existing culture (values, norms, religious beliefs). This can be an outcome of what Gurr (1970, 46–50) called "decremental deprivation." For example, defeat in war or introduction of different productive technologies or new patterns of economic activity might suddenly deprive large numbers of people of their land, jobs, or previous income levels, while others in society benefit from the changes. Those whose living standards have been damaged may find little moral justification for their plight in their existing belief system and may respond with anger and be prone to rebellion.

James Davies (1962) proposed a different way in which relative deprivation can develop that has become known as the J-curve theory of revolutions (Gurr 1970, 52–56, referred to this process as "progressive deprivation"). Davies stated that revolutions are likely to occur during a period of economic downturn following a sustained period of economic growth (the graph of such an economic pattern looks like a slanted inverted letter J). People's expectations for continued improvements rise during a period of increasing economic prosperity. But when a subsequent economic downturn occurs, the difference between what people want and what they get eventually becomes intolerable, and they are prone to revolt. Thus, in absolute terms, people may be in a much better economic position than they had been twenty years before, but their rising expectations for living standards and quality of life make decreasing income and employment opportunities seem unbearable. Davies argued that some major revolutions were preceded by such economic trends, including the French Revolution and the Russian Revolution of 1917.

The third form of relative deprivation associated with some revolutionary conflicts is what Gurr (1970, 50–52) labeled "aspirational deprivation." This refers to the form of relative deprivation that results not from the changes in value capabilities, or what people get, but mainly from a change in value aspirations (or what people want). Such a change in aspirations and views regarding acceptable or unacceptable levels of inequality can be brought about by contact with groups or individuals who convey a new view of objective conditions. A modern example was the development of Liberation Theology in Latin America in the late 1960s. This involved a shift in Catholic ideology on the part of some bishops and other clergy to the view that the church should work for social justice in this world, instead of catering only to people's spiritual needs. Inasmuch as the clergy were major educators and sources of moral perception among the poor of Latin America, this somewhat new message—that poverty and great inequality were not the will of God but rather the result of people's greed—raised aspirations and demands among the poor for greater equality. This greatly increased the level of mass discontent in a number of nations, including Nicaragua and El Salvador, contributing to the development of revolutionary struggles in those countries in the 1970s and 1980s.

While the relative deprivation approach has been most often employed in attempts to explain how inequality could contribute to the development of revolution within a society, Skocpol and Trimberger (1978), in their structural theory of revolution, have argued that inequality among nations—or external rather than internal inequality—is the major cause of revolution in less-developed societies. In their formulation, the state exists to serve the function of protecting the welfare of people within a society. When a government is unable to prevent its people from being conquered or economically or otherwise exploited by more powerful nations, movements arise within the exploited society to replace the existing government with one that has the capability of more successfully defending the interests and improving the welfare of the society's population. Thus the twentieth-century Chinese, Vietnamese, and Cuban revolutions, from this point of view, might all be viewed as conflicts in which weak, corrupt, and foreign-dominated regimes were replaced by much stronger and more militarily competent governments.

CLASS AND REVOLUTION

Class can be viewed as a major dimension or constellation of dimensions of inequality. There are several different traditions of class analysis. Karl Marx defined class as one's relation to the means of production, and he focused on two major groups in industrializing society: owners and workers. Neo-Marxists have tried to incorporate the middle classes into class analysis with a focus on how workers are stratified in terms of their ability to exercise authority and skill in the workplace (Wright 1985). Others avoid separate qualitative categories of class and rely instead on gradational measures of class, such as level of income or education. Regardless of the definition, classes exist in one form or another in virtually every society, and the interplay between classes is often an important part of the revolutionary context.

Marxist or neo-Marxist conceptions of class and class conflict have played the most important role so far in conceptualizing how class is related to revolution. Marx, in his theory of historical materialism, argued that the history of social progress is in fact the history of class conflict. According to that view, advances in the forces of production (the means by which to derive life-sustaining resources from the environment) eventually lead to conflict between the class that dominates the economic and political systems at a given time but has become an impediment to further economic progress and an emergent class that, when victorious in conflict with the dominant class, will advance the forces of production and economic development. According to Marx, the urban industrial working class (proletariat) would eventually overcome the capitalist ownership class and create a relatively equalitarian, Socialist economic system that would speed the development of productive forces. That would someday lead to the coming of a Communist utopia characterized by material abundance and the ab-

sence of social classes and major social problems. However, instead of Socialist revolutions occurring first in the most industrialized countries through the efforts of the big urban industrial working classes, as Marx's theory had predicted, they succeeded in lesser-developed, partially industrialized societies—Russia (1917) and China (1949)—in which about 85 percent and 90 percent of the populations, respectively, were rural peasants (DeFronzo 1996, 30, 74).

Lenin's theory of imperialism was an attempt to explain the failure of Marx's theory to predict where Socialist revolutions would first occur, and also to explain how class and inequality domestically and internationally influenced revolution. In Lenin's view, the ruling classes of the more-advanced capitalist nations had, through domination over the resources and labor power of much of the rest of the world, shared the wealth exploited from lesser-developed societies. They had used some of that wealth to improve the well-being of the working classes in the imperialist nations, thus eliminating the economic hardships that Marx had assumed would motivate workers to revolution.

Instead, according to Lenin, Socialist revolution would occur in the poor and exploited nations. As those nations' new governments ended the unfairly profitable exploitation of their societies' resources—this aspect is also suggested by Skocpol's and Trimberger's (1978) structural theory of revolution—class conflict in the advanced nations would intensify, leading to revolutions there as well.

Students of revolutions have repeatedly observed that revolutions are more likely to be successful if they are based on a cross-class coalition, rather than on only a single class. Common opposition to a dictatorial regime or a commitment to a nationalist struggle are two examples of crosscutting motivations for rebellion. Regardless of the validity of Lenin's theory, it was extremely attractive to nationalist intellectuals in many less-developed societies—such as to Mao in China and to Ho Chi Minh of Vietnam—and it inspired them and their associates to organize anti-imperialist Socialist revolutions. The concept of a struggle to free one's people from foreign domination helped create revolutionary cross-class coalitions of workers, peasants, and middle-class people united by nationalism to defeat foreign imperialism and the domestic regimes viewed as serving foreign interests. Mao further modified Marxist theory by arguing that peasants, whom Marx generally considered tradition bound and socially isolated, could become a major revolutionary class.

Revolutions are also often based on cross-class coalitions, in terms of the class origins of their leaders versus that of their popular base of support. While peasants and urban workers often made up the majority of the participants and supporters of the major revolutions, their leadership often came from privileged backgrounds. Mao, for example, came from a relatively wealthy peasant family (most peasant families were very poor), as did Trotsky. Skocpol (1979) demonstrated that divisions within a society's pre-revolution elite were important for the success of revolutions, because they diminished the capacity of the state to suppress rebellion or to offer reforms that might have lessened popular discontent. Lenin also emphasized that revolutionary intellectuals, typically from well-educated families (as was he), would be essential in transforming the working people from what Marx called a "class in itself" (unorganized and not class conscious) to a "class for itself" (aware of its interests and mobilized to change society).

POST-REVOLUTION INEQUALITY AND CLASS

While inequality and class have been important in shaping the course of revolutionary movements, the outcomes of revolutions have important implications for the degree of inequality and class characteristics of the post-revolution society. Socialist revolutions have typically led to a redistribution of land from large landowners to poor peasants and rural laborers. They have often also resulted in great expansion of educational opportunities, medical care, and other services and resources to large numbers of people, and to a reduction in inequality of wages among different occupations. However, certain types of inequality continued to exist, and new forms often developed. Groups with advantages in the pre-revolutionary society often continued to enjoy some advantages after the revolution (such as their previous superior education and skill levels). Additionally, despite attempts to equalize opportunities, personal differences in characteristics, such as capacity or motivation for hard work and intelligence, cause other inequalities, such as differences in income, to persist or develop again. In addition, post-revolution leaders often create new administrative bureaucracies, as happened to perverse proportions in Stalinist Russia, and persons occupying the higher positions can come to exercise much more power than other groups, and enjoy greater privileges for themselves and their children. Economic development programs may also lead to patterns of inequality after Socialist revolutions. People living in new industrializing urban areas often begin to experience a better standard of living and better opportunities than those working in agriculture in the countryside.

Revolutions in the late twentieth century often did little to reduce inequality, and some seemed to increase it. The socioeconomic redistributive aspects of the Nicaraguan Sandinista Revolution of 1979 were limited by the U.S. Reagan administration's destructive economic policies and Contra war, and by the 1990 electoral defeat of the Sandinista Party and the victories thereafter by leaders with more conserva-

tive, neo-liberal economic policies. El Salvadoran revolutionaries made peace in 1992 in return for political democracy with little reduction in the country's level of inequality. The end of apartheid in 1994 brought democracy, opened new opportunities, and provided expanded welfare services for South Africa's non-European population, but the new leaders, constrained by a largely capitalist world economic environment and hoping to prevent the flight of the country's generally well-educated and highly skilled white population, were not able to reduce economic inequality greatly.

The Eastern European revolutions and the Second Russian Revolution to multiparty political democracy in the late 1980s and early 1990s did not primarily aim to reduce inequality, except in terms of ending Communist Party monopoly on governmental and other powers and privileges enjoyed by party members and bureaucrats. Instead, the new market reforms and privatization policies that were introduced seemed to increase inequality. In Russia, some politically connected persons were able to acquire enormously valuable state industries and rapidly become multimillionaires, or even billionaires (Goldman 2003). Although there is some evidence that the transition from Socialist- to market-based economies had little or no effect on inequality, more recent work has found evidence for the re-emergence of inequalities based on inherited rather than achieved characteristics. While Soviet Russia was characterized by a substantial degree of upward social mobility in the late 1980s, post-Soviet Russia exhibits declining levels of mobility and the increasing importance of "social origins," or class background, for determining "social destinations," or current occupational or class standing (Gerber and Hout 2004). The children of workers in the Soviet Union appear to have enjoyed more occupational choices independent of their family background than is the case in post-Soviet society.

INEQUALITY AND CLASS IN FUTURE REVOLUTIONS

The role of inequality and class in future revolutions will likely be much different than in previous revolutions. Inequality based on urban versus rural residence may become decreasingly important as more people come to live in urban areas. Certain other forms of inequality seem to be increasing in significance, however, including educational attainment (having a college degree), technical expertise, and job security (for example, traditional, full-time workers versus part-time or contingent workers).

The salience of class and the degree of class conflict may be fundamentally different in future revolutions. People no longer fit neatly into the categories of proletarians, peasants, capitalists, and landowners. Recent research in class analysis indicates that people today identify more with what they do (that is, their occupations) than some abstract notion of one's relationship to the means of production (Grusky and Sorensen 1998). There are potentially hundreds of different classes, rather than just a handful. Class conflict in the Marxist sense is less likely to occur under the circumstances of the new class systems, in which there is no longer a common source of oppression and target of hostility. While income inequality and inequality of economic security may still be important sources of conflict, other social factors such as gender, race, ethnicity, citizenship, moral concerns, and religion may come to replace class as bases for common beliefs, shared frustrations, and potential sources of revolutionary organization.

Andrew S. Fullerton

See Also African American Freedom Struggle; Anarchism, Communism, and Socialism; Chinese Revolution; Cinema of Revolution; Cuban Revolution; Documentaries of Revolution; East European Revolutions of 1989; French Revolution; Nicaraguan Revolution; Russian Revolution of 1917; Russian Revolution of 1991; Salvadoran Revolution; Slave Rebellions in the United States; South African Revolution; Theories of Revolutions; Vietnamese Revolution; Women's Movement of the United States

References and Further Readings

Chirot, Daniel. 1994. *How Societies Change.* Thousand Oaks, CA: Pine Forge.

Davies, James C. 1962. "Toward a Theory of Revolution," *American Sociological Review* 27 (1): 5–19.

DeFronzo, James. 1996. (3rd edition forthcoming 2007) *Revolutions and Revolutionary Movements,* 2nd edition. Boulder, CO: Westview.

Gerber, Theodore P., and Michael Hout. 2004. "Tightening Up: Declining Class Mobility during Russia's Market Transition," *American Sociological Review* 69 (5): 677–703.

Goldman, Marshall I. 2003. "Render unto Caesar: Putin and the Oligarchs," *Current History,* Volume 102, no. 666 (October): 320–326.

Goldstone, Jack A. 1991. *Revolution and Rebellion in the Early Modern World.* Berkeley: University of California Press.

Grusky, David B., and Jesper B. Sorensen. 1998. "Can Class Analysis be Salvaged?" *American Journal of Sociology* 103 (5): 1187–1234.

Gurr, Ted Robert. 1970. *Why Men Rebel.* Princeton, NJ: Princeton University Press.

Kelley, Jonathan, and Herbert S. Klein. 1977. "Revolution and the Rebirth of Inequality: A Theory of Stratification in Postrevolutionary Society," *American Journal of Sociology* 83 (1): 78–99.

Roberts, B. R. 1990. "Peasants and Proletarians," *Annual Review of Sociology* 16: 353–377.

Skocpol, Theda. 1979. *States and Social Revolutions.* Cambridge: Cambridge University Press.

Skocpol, Theda, and Ellen Kay Trimberger. 1978. "Revolutions and the World Historical Development of Capitalism," *Berkeley Journal of Sociology* 22: 101–113.

Tucker, Robert C. 1978. *The Marx-Engels Reader,* 2nd edition. New York: W. W. Norton.

Wright, Erik Olin. 1985. *Classes.* London: Verso.

Iranian Revolution

CHRONOLOGY

559–529 B.C. Cyrus the Great establishes the Persian empire, the predecessor of modern Iran.

A.D. 642 An Islamic Arab army defeats the Persian (Iranian) army, leading to the conversion of most Iranians from the Zoroastrian religion to Sunni Islam.

1501–1747 The Safavid dynasty rules Iran. The Safavid rulers import Shia clergy from Iraq, Syria, and Lebanon in a largely successful effort to convert the majority of Iran's population from Sunni Islam to Twelver Shiism. This change in the dominant form of Islam in Iran is apparently intended by the Safavids as a way of maintaining the loyalty of Iran's population by religiously isolating most Iranians from the influence of the expanding Sunni Islamic Ottoman empire.

1796–1925 The Qajar dynasty rules Iran. The Qajar shahs (kings) of Iran negotiate agreements with Great Britain and czarist Russia for trade, mineral exploration and exploitation, a telegraph system, and military assistance.

1803–1814, 1828 Czarist Russia defeats Iran in war and as a result obtains territory from Iran and privileged rights to sell Russian goods in Iran. Later, Qajar shahs borrow money from the Russians to finance their luxuriant lifestyles and in return grant Russia the right to collect customs duties in much of Iran, as well as other advantages.

1859–1872 Great Britain builds a telegraph system across Iran to improve communications between Britain and its Asian colonies.

1901 The Qajar monarchy grants Australian businessman William Knox D'Arcy a sixty-year oil concession in Iran that becomes the basis for the Anglo-Persian Oil Company.

1906   The Iranian Constitutional Revolution occurs. Many Iranians, fearing that the Qajar shahs are making agreements with other nations harmful to the welfare of most Iranians, rebel to reduce the power of the monarchy and establish a parliament, or Majlis. The elected parliament is to have the power either to confirm or to veto laws and policies proposed by the shah.

1908   Oil discovered in Iran leads to the creation of the British controlled Anglo-Persian Oil Company (later called the Anglo-Iranian Oil Company).

1921   Reza Khan, an officer in the Iranian army, uses the military to influence the Qajar government and have himself made commander of the army and minister of war.

1923   Reza Khan becomes prime minister of the Iranian government.

1925   The Iranian parliament votes to abolish the Qajar dynasty and establish Reza as the first shah of the new Pahlavi dynasty.

1926   Reza is installed as shah.

1926–1941   Reza Shah Pahlavi begins enacting policies to modernize Iran's educational, social, economic, and military institutions. Reza institutes measures to gain control over Iran's Shia Islamic clergy, in part to reduce their resistance to modernization; German advisors participate in the modernization process. Foreigners and other nations are told by Reza's government to refer to the country in the future as Iran (land of the Aryans), rather than Persia.

1941   Nazi Germany invades the Soviet Union. Germany's enemies, Great Britain and the Soviet Union, desiring the use of Iran's territory and resources for their war effort against the Germans and fearing opposition from Reza, invade and occupy Iran and force Reza to abdicate in favor of his son, Mohammad Pahlavi, who becomes the new shah. After the end of World War II, British and Soviet troops withdraw from Iran.

1951   Mossadeq, leader of the National Front alliance of political parties in the Iranian parliament, becomes prime minister of Iran and begins attempts to limit the power of the monarchy through measures such as placing the military under the control of the prime minister, rather than the shah. Under Mossadeq's leadership, the Iranian parliament nationalizes the formerly British-controlled oil resources of Iran; Great Britain organizes an international boycott of Iran's oil so that, deprived of the ability to sell much of its oil, Iran's economy would begin to deteriorate, undermining support for the Mossadeq government.

1953   Pro-shah Iranian military officers, assisted by U.S. and British intelligence agents, overthrow Mossadeq and the National Front government. The shah establishes a regime widely viewed as a dictatorship serving U.S. and British interests.

1957   SAVAK (Organization of National Security and Intelligence), the shah's secret police agency, is created, reportedly with the assistance of the U.S. Central Intelligence Agency. SAVAK agents function to gather information on and to repress the shah's enemies and are accused of many human rights abuses, including torture and murder.

1963   The shah's regime launches the White Revolution, intended to accomplish a partial redistribution of land toward the poor, facilitate further industrialization and modernization, and reduce popular support for any movement to oust the shah's government. Ayatollah Khomeini criticizes aspects of the White Revolution, including the fact that, in his view, it was organized and carried out without the advice of religious leaders. Khomeini specifically attacks the rule of Mohammad Shah Pahlavi rather than, at this point, the institution of the monarchy itself. Ayatollah Khomeini is temporarily imprisoned, sparking anti-shah protests by Khomeini's followers.

1964   The shah's government grants U.S. citizens working in Iran immunity from prosecution by Iran's courts for crimes they might be accused of committing in Iran. Ayatollah Khomeini vehemently condemns this measure and continues his verbal attacks on the shah's regime. The shah expels Khomeini from Iran. Ayatollah Khomeini takes up temporary residence at Shia holy places in Iraq.

1971 Fedayeen (secular, Marxist-oriented) and Mujahidin (leftist Islamic) anti-shah guerrilla groups are formed, and both launch violent attacks against the shah's regime. Ayatollah Khomeini publicly declares that monarchy is an un-Islamic form of government.

1973 Arab perceptions of U.S. and European intervention to aid Israel in the Fourth Arab-Israeli War result in oil-producing Arab nations temporarily withholding their oil. The shah's government refuses to participate in the Arab oil embargo. Oil prices quadruple, and Iran's earnings from the oil it sells vastly increase. The shah uses much of the oil income to accelerate modernization and expand educational and health care services in Iran, but also to purchase enormous quantities of advanced weapons from the United States, Great Britain, and other nations.

1976 The shah's government attempts to change Iran's calendar from the Islamic calendar to an "imperial" calendar (based on the founding of the Persian empire). This act provokes outrage from many Iranian religious leaders, clerics, and Shia faithful.

1977 Jimmy Carter becomes president of the United States. Carter declares his administration to be a "human rights presidency," making further military aid to Iran dependent on the shah's government improving treatment of opponents of the shah's regime and policies. The shah's government eases repression. Public protest against the shah's regime increases.

In response to deterioration in Iran's economic situation following the end of the Arab oil embargo, the shah's government imposes austerity measures, reducing construction projects and throwing thousands of people out of work.

1978 The shah's government attacks and slanders Ayatollah Khomeini's reputation by means of an article in a major newspaper. Theological students protest in Qom, and some are killed by the shah's armed forces. Throughout the year, public demonstrations against the shah's regime attract thousands and, eventually, hundreds of thousands of participants in major Iranian cities. In some instances, elements of the shah's military open fire and kill protestors. As the year progresses, many soldiers became disillusioned with the shah's regime and refuse to use violence against demonstrators.

1979 The shah permanently leaves Iran on January 16. Ayatollah Khomeini returns to Iran in February. A provisional revolutionary government is formed. In an April referendum, most voters support establishing an "Islamic Republic" in Iran. Khomeini's followers create a separate army for Iran's Shia fundamentalist religious leaders, the Islamic Revolutionary Guard. The seriously ill former shah arrives in New York. In response, hundreds of young Iranian militants storm and occupy the U.S. embassy in Iran's capital, Tehran, taking dozens of embassy employees hostage and demanding, in return for their release, that the shah and the money he had taken out of Iran be sent back. The new Constitution of the Islamic Republic, containing the Vilayat-e Faqih concept that assigns supreme governmental power to a top religious leader selected by the clergy, is enacted.

1980 The death of Mohammad Shah Pahlavi in July removes one of the major obstacles to the return of the U.S. hostages. Iraq invades Iran in September in an apparent attempt to seize contested territory, to discourage Iran's Islamic fundamentalists from assisting or encouraging a revolt against Iraq's secular government by Iraq's Shia majority, and perhaps to topple Iran's clerically dominated regime. In November, President Jimmy Carter, politically weakened by his inability to obtain the release of the U.S. hostages, loses his re-election bid to conservative Republican Ronald Reagan. Inspired by the success of Islamic revolutionaries in Iran, tens of thousands of Islamic men from many nations begin to volunteer to fight the leftist secular government in Afghanistan and the Soviet troops supporting it. Among the volunteers is Osama bin Laden of Saudi Arabia, who, with his associates, will later organize many of the surviving Islamic foreigners that fought against Soviet forces in Afghanistan into al-Qaeda.

1981   In January, the U.S. hostages are finally released.

1988   In the summer, Iran and Iraq agree to a truce, effectively ending the Iran-Iraq War, which had resulted in hundreds of thousands of casualties and cost tens of billions of dollars.

1990   Iraq, heavily in debt to Kuwait for billions it borrowed during the Iran-Iraq War, invades Kuwait and attempts to incorporate it as part of Iraq's national territory. This leads to multinational military action against Iraq in 1991, its forced withdrawal from Kuwait, and its defeat and occupation by U.S., British, and other multinational forces in 2003.

INTRODUCTION

The Iranian Revolution, which succeeded in 1979, not only ousted the Pahlavi family dynasty but also ended some 2,500 years of monarchal rule. The revolution created a new political system for Iran, one that resurrected an ancient tradition of religious domination of government by placing final political authority in the hands of religious leaders. The triumph of Islamic fundamentalism in the Iranian Revolution had major consequences for Iran and the world and helped to inspire Islamic fundamentalist movements in many nations.

BACKGROUND: CULTURE AND HISTORY

Iran, land of the Aryans, has a population that is about 58 percent Persian speaking (including Persian dialects), 26 percent Turkic (mainly Azeri), 9 percent Kurdish, and about 7 percent other language groups including Arab, Balochi, and Luri. Approximately 89 percent of Iranians are Shia Islam, while about 9 percent are Sunni and 2 percent are other religions (Zoroastrian, Jewish, Christian, and Baha'i) (CIA- The World Fact Book–Iran 2005, 3). The division of Islam into the Shia and Sunni branches began around the middle of the seventh century. The Shia were Islamic religious leaders who came to believe that the prophet Muhammad had intended that Ali, who was his cousin and the husband of his daughter, Fatima, was to be his first successor as leader of Islam, and that later leadership of Islam would follow the family line descending from Ali and Fatima. The Shia, or supporters of Ali, also believed that Ali, like Muhammad, was infallible, as were the leaders of Islam descended from Ali's and Fatima's family line. The variety of Shia Islam that became dominant in Iran held that twelve infallible leaders or imams followed Muhammad before the last one disappeared.

In contrast, the Sunni believed that there were no infallible leaders of Islam after Muhammad. Worldwide it is estimated that more than 80 percent of the Islamic faithful are Sunni. Since several early Shia religious leaders were killed while reportedly opposing powerful men who oppressed the faithful (in particular, Imam Hussein, son of Ali), the theme of martyrdom on behalf of the faith and the Islamic community became especially powerful among the Shia.

Three of the major clerical ranks among the Shia are mullah, hojjat al-Islam, and ayatollah. Mullahs are the lower level of the clergy, ministering to the spiritual needs of the people. Mullahs who have demonstrated the ability to memorize the Quran and Islamic law could achieve the title of hojjat al-Islam (proof of Islam). In rare instances, a cleric at the hojjat al-Islam level could rise to the rank of ayatollah (reflection or sign of Allah). To be recognized as an ayatollah by other clergy, a hojjat al-Islam would have to become widely known for his holiness and wise judgments on important religious and social matters. At the time of the modern Iranian Revolution of the 1970s, there were estimated to be at least 23,000 clergy (Milani 1994, 63), of whom about 5,000 were hojjat al-Islam and some 50 were ayatollahs (Abrahamian 1982, 433).

By the 1970s, there were at least three significant variations of Iranian Shia Islam. "Orthodox" Shia clergy tended to advocate a separation of religion and state and the concept that clergy should not attempt to influence politics unless the government took actions that violated Islamic law or endangered the Islamic community. This branch of the clergy tended to express public support for the monarchy. Until the mid-1970s, most top clerical leaders seemed to be orthodox, although fear of the shah's police may have prompted some clergy to behave as orthodox, while hiding their true beliefs.

In contrast to the orthodox clergy, fundamentalists held that religious leaders should play an active role in government and in other areas of social life and that separation of religion and state morally weakened the Iranian people and was a strategy employed by non-Islamic foreign powers to

Major cities of Iran, including Tehran, the capital, the theological center of Qom, and much of neighboring Iraq.

corrupt and control Iran. Fundamentalists had at times during the twentieth century supported the monarchy's efforts to suppress secular and leftist movements such as Iran's Communist Party. But in the 1960s and 1970s the charismatic leader of the fundamentalists, Ayatollah Khomeini, vigorously and courageously attacked the shah's regime as morally corrupt and foreign controlled, and eventually he condemned the monarchy itself as an un-Islamic form of government. Another trend within Iranian Shia Islam by the 1970s was "Modernist Shiism." Modernist Shiism was mainly a movement among lay religious persons who attempted to show that Shiism was compatible with democracy, science, and modern technology. Their desire for democracy led many Modernist Shia to oppose the shah and the monarchy in favor of a more democratic form of government.

The Iranian monarchy had its origins in the creation of the Persian empire by Cyrus the Great in the sixth century B.C. Between 1796 and 1925 the Qajar dynasty ruled Iran. Many Iranians came to view the Qajar shahs as often corrupt and willing to accept what amounted to bribes from foreign powers and businessmen in return for trade rights in Iran, access to Iran's mineral wealth, and other agreements that benefited foreign interests more than the majority of the Iranian people. Outraged Iranians, seeking a way to prevent the monarchy from collaborating with foreigners in ways harmful to Iran, were inspired by the 1905 Revolution in Russia, which led to the creation of a Russian parliament, or Duma, intended to have veto power over laws proposed by the czar.

Many Iranians rebelled against the shah's authority in 1906 and forced him to accept the establishment of an Iranian parliament, or Majlis. That legislature, to be elected by Iranian men, would, in theory, be capable of either confirming or rejecting any law or policy proposed by the shah. The shah, however, remained head of state and commander of the armed forces.

After the 1917 Bolshevik Revolution in Russia, some wealthy Iranians and Shia clergy were concerned that the weak and corrupt Qajar dynasty might not be able to prevent a Bolshevik-type revolution in Iran. On the other hand, many of these relatively powerful men feared that abolishing the monarchy altogether would result in a republic with radical policies that would threaten their interests or even cherished values, as seemed to be happening at that time to the more affluent residents and religious leaders in Russia. The solution was to get rid of the Qajars but preserve the monarchy by establishing a new family dynasty. The British, with major trade, communications, and mineral interests in Iran, such as the Anglo-Persian Oil Company (later renamed the Anglo-Iranian Oil Company), which provided much of the fuel for the British navy as its ships switched from coal to petroleum, also began to favor replacement of the Qajars by a more vigorous and competent ruling family. They preferred to see a ruling family that could strengthen Iran's military and more effectively suppress revolutionary movements. Another British concern was that a successful revolution in Iran could encourage revolutions in other nearby countries in which Britain had interests, in particular their enormous colony of India.

The favored candidate to become the new shah and founder of a new family dynasty was Reza Khan (the term "khan" is not a family name, but rather an expression meaning leader, usually the head of a major clan). Reza was a leading officer of the elite Cossack Brigade of the Iranian armed forces. In 1921 he led a large military force to the capital, Tehran, to help install a new prime minister whom he temporarily supported and to make himself commander of the army. Over the next several years, Reza skillfully manipulated various political factions and interest groups, and he strengthened the military he commanded and used it to suppress leftist rebellions and tribal and minority uprisings, greatly increasing his popularity among most of Iran's Persian-speaking majority. He also worked to reduce the authority and undermine what limited support the Qajars once enjoyed, and to control the elections for members of the Majlis.

In 1925 the Reza-dominated parliament voted by a large majority to end the Qajar dynasty and to designate Reza as the first shah of a new ruling family dynasty. Reza was crowned shah in 1926 and chose "Pahlavi," the expression for an ancient form of the Persian language, as the family name for his new dynasty. Reza further improved Iran's army and launched a modernization program. The modernization effort included building a railroad, the development of industry, an expansion of opportunities for women to be employed outside the home, and the promotion of Western styles of dress. Reza attempted to lessen potential religious opposition to social change—such as the increased freedom for women and change in clothing styles—by providing benefits to powerful religious leaders willing to cooperate with him; he simultaneously moved to bring religious training schools for mullahs and religious funds under state control.

Reza took advantage of his governmental power to acquire great wealth and to become the country's largest landowner. He also attempted to reduce or counterbalance the influence of Great Britain in Iran by inviting German technicians and advisers to come to the country and participate in the modernization process. Reza may have been attracted to the aspect of Nazi German ideology that put forth the concept of Aryan racial superiority. In 1934, he demanded that other nations stop referring to his nation as Persia and in the future refer to it as Iran (the land of the Aryans).

The British eventually became concerned with the possibility of Nazi Germany gaining control of Iran's oil. After Germany invaded the Soviet Union in June 1941, Great Britain and the Soviet Union jointly invaded and occupied Iran for the duration of World War II. Reza was forced to abdicate and to leave Iran. He died in exile in South Africa before the end of the war. The British, however, were concerned with preserving the monarchy, possibly as a way of preventing political instability in Iran after the war or the emergence of a leftist government that might endanger British oil interests.

Therefore, after Reza abdicated, his son Mohammad was installed as the new shah. But during the war Mohammad's power was greatly limited by the occupying nations. After the war, the Iranian parliament, the Majlis, which for years had been essentially controlled by Reza, began to effectively challenge the power of the monarchy.

In the early 1950s, the dominant group in the parliament was the National Front, a coalition of political parties under the leadership of Mohammad Mossadeq. The National Front, with the support of other political groups in the parliament, attempted to place the army under the control of parliament instead of the shah. Mossadeq also tried to reduce the level of state expenditures on the royal family and to use the savings to fund health services. In 1951 the Majlis, unhappy with the share of profits Iran received for its oil from the British, nationalized the Anglo-Iranian Oil Company properties in Iran. In retaliation, Great Britain organized an international boycott of Iran's oil intended to destroy the market for Iran's major export, devastate the country's economy, promote popular dissatisfaction with the National Front government, and restore the monarchy to full power.

Great Britain's intelligence agency apparently convinced the U.S. government that Mossadeq's National Front represented a threat not only to Britain's interests but also to those of the United States. Both British and U.S. intelligence agents reportedly helped set the stage for a pro-shah military takeover by contacting and organizing Iranian military and business leaders to support the shah against Prime Minister Mossadeq and the National Front. In August 1953, the shah tried to remove Mossadeq from office and ordered troops to seize control of the government. The initial attempt failed, and the shah temporarily fled the country. But within a few days, a second pro-shah military coup succeeded.

The shah abolished the National Front and imprisoned Mossadeq, along with many others. Mohammad Pahlavi then proceeded to rule essentially as an absolute monarch until his final flight from Iran in January of 1979. The shah, with the help of the U.S. CIA in addition to his supporters in the armed forces, established a new secret police force to protect his regime, the Organization of National Security and Intelligence, or SAVAK, which would later be accused of the torture and murder of thousands of people thought to be opponents of the shah's regime.

Although Mohammad Pahlavi established an absolute monarchy, his dictatorship accomplished significant improvements for many Iranians. Health facilities and social welfare programs were expanded. High school and college enrollments dramatically increased. Industrial development was accelerated, and hundreds of thousands of poor rural Iranians migrated to urban centers to take advantage of employment opportunities in the many new construction projects. The shah's modernization and development projects were financed by Iran's oil revenue, especially after it grew dramatically in the aftermath of the 1973 Arab-Israeli War; at that time, Arab nations temporarily withheld oil from the United States and other Western nations they accused of militarily aiding Israel during the war. Iran, a non-Arab country, continued to sell its oil, benefiting from the tremendous increase in oil prices.

Successive U.S. and British administrations appeared to support and to arm the shah's brutal, nondemocratic regime, for several reasons. First, the shah, though a dictator, tended to support U.S. and British interests and guaranteed those nations and their allies reliable access to Iran's oil—which a truly democratic Iran might not have been as inclined to do. Second, the shah used much of his country's oil wealth in ways that benefited the U.S. and British economies by buying billions of dollars' worth of technology and military equipment from them. And third, the shah appeared willing to use his armed forces as a surrogate or substitute for U.S. or British military intervention in the Middle East in order to threaten potentially troublesome nations or to militarily suppress undesirable political movements or rebellions in the region.

CONTEXT AND PROCESS OF REVOLUTION IN THE LATE 1970S

The shah, beyond attempting to gain the loyalty or at least the toleration of the masses by measures such as expanding educational opportunities and health services, tried to increase his popular support by creating a new parliament. It had two political parties, although each was controlled by pro-shah leaders and through the reforms of the so-called White Revolution of the early 1960s. The White Revolution was a program imposed by the shah intended, in part, to significantly redistribute lands from large landholders to poor rural workers and to expand rights for women. But many of the landlords from whom land was taken, who had formerly supported the shah, felt betrayed, while the economic situation of many peasants was not significantly improved. Furthermore, certain aspects of the shah's modernization program alienated many religious leaders and appeared to drive a number of formerly orthodox clerics to the fundamentalist position. Among the provocations to religious leaders were the expanded rights for women, including the adoption of more revealing Western styles of dress, perceived immoral practices such as alcohol consumption, the circulation of literature and movies viewed as having pornographic content, and prostitution, partly promoted, in the view of some, by the presence of as many as 60,000 generally highly paid Western technicians and advisers. Many clerics were also outraged when in 1975 the shah's parliament, by then controlled by the shah's Resurgence Party, the result of the fusion of the two earlier pro-shah parties, shifted Iran from the Islamic calendar to one based on the founding of the Persian empire.

The leader of the Shia fundamentalist clergy was Ayatollah Khomeini, whose father and grandfather were also religious scholars. Khomeini criticized the shah in 1963 for carrying out the reforms of the White Revolution dictatorially, without the advice or consent of the Shia clergy, and for leading a corrupt regime that channeled enormous wealth from Iran's oil resource to the royal family and the shah's other associates. Khomeini was arrested and imprisoned, sparking protests by the ayatollah's supporters in several cities in which dozens were killed. In an attempt to calm the religious community, the shah's regime released Khomeini, now the most popular religious leader in the country. But the ayatollah again attacked the shah's regime for enacting a law that made U.S. citizens who were charged with committing crimes in Iran immune from Iranian justice, instead requiring them to be tried by U.S. courts.

In retaliation Khomeini was expelled from Iran, and in 1965 he went to live in the Shia holy city of Najaf in Iraq. The ayatollah's followers smuggled into Iran audio cassettes with continuing attacks on the shah and his regime. Khomeini condemned what he termed the greed and corruption of the shah's government, as well as the increasing secularization of the state and the attempt of the regime to propagate a pro-shah form of Shiism. He accused the shah of fostering the spread of immoral elements of Western culture in Iran and of becoming an instrument of foreign imperialism. By the 1970s, Khomeini was declaring that monarchy was an un-Islamic form of government and advocating revolution to establish a clerically dominated Islamic republic. Khomeini opposed any compromise with the shah's regime and encouraged his followers to believe that, with the aid of God, they could completely destroy the monarchy.

Beyond Khomeini, the other widely recognized author of significant ideological aspects of the revolution was Ali Shariati, prominent Iranian sociologist, theological innovator, and political activist. Shariati's father was a militant Shia Socialist who implanted in his son's mind the view that Shia Islam could inspire a revolutionary transformation to an equalitarian society. Shariati, in contrast to most Marxist-oriented revolutionary writers, felt that in several nations exploited by foreign imperialist powers, such as Iran, local religious traditions could motivate and unite the people in a powerful revolutionary movement. In particular, inspired in part by the life of an early Shia champion of the poor, Abu Zarr, Shariati taught that the prophet Muhammad had sought to create a relatively classless society that would strive toward progress, especially the elimination of social injustice, but that these original goals were later subverted by greedy and false leaders of Islam. According to Ali Shariati, Shia Islam, properly interpreted, was a revolutionary religion inspiring believers to embrace democracy, the pursuit of scientific knowledge, and equality of power, wealth, and opportunity. In these views he differed significantly from Khomeini, who advocated clerical rule and promoted a more conservative version of Shiism, stressing the

People crowd around to try to shake hands with or touch Ayatollah Ruhollah Khomeini in Tehran February 3, 1979. He had returned from exile February 1, 1979, to take control of the revolutionary government. (Bettman/Corbis)

sacredness of private property, at least that acquired through a person's own hard work. Both Shariati and the ayatollah, though, viewed Shiism as a revolutionary religion, and both opposed foreign imperialism and the corruption of the shah's regime. In arguing that Shiism is compatible with and even supportive of the adoption of modern technology, economic socialism, and political democracy, and is in fact a weapon against domestic tyranny and foreign exploitation, Shariati became a major architect of Modernist Shiism and convinced many of the more secular opponents of the monarchy that Shia Islam could be an important component of the anti-shah revolutionary alliance. Shariati's lectures, in both recorded and transcribed versions, inspired hundreds of thousands of young Iranians to support and participate in the revolution against the shah. Shariati was arrested in 1972 and held in prison and then under house arrest until May of 1977, when he was allowed to leave Iran for London. But about a month after his arrival, he suddenly died, many thought as the result of a SAVAK assassination plot, but possibly of natural causes.

In addition to Shia fundamentalism and the existence of Islamic modernist groups such as the Islamic Liberation (Freedom) Movement, whose members advocated a more democratic society, two small but significant armed revolutionary groups, both formed by the end of 1970, initiated violent attacks against members of the shah's government and armed forces in 1971. The Fedayeen-e Khalq (Martyrs of the People) was Marxist oriented and partly inspired by Che Guevara's theory of the *Guerrilla Foco*. Many of its members had parents with careers in modern middle-class professions. The Mujahidin-e Khalq (Islamic Soldiers of the People) was influenced by Modernist Shia thought, advocating an Islamic-oriented society with a far more equalitarian social system than the Iran of the shahs.

By the mid-1970s, these several sectors of Iranian society, characterized by serious disagreements among themselves regarding the future of Iran, were temporarily united by their intense hatred of the shah and the foreign imperialist interests that they jointly felt his regime represented. As internal moral and political opposition to the shah surged, changing economic and international conditions contributed crucial elements to the combination of factors necessary for the development and success of the Iranian Revolution. The key shift in the international environment was the election of Jimmy Carter as president of the United States in the fall of 1976. President Carter indicated that his would be a human rights presidency. Carter put pressure on several authoritarian governments around the world, including the shah's regime, to reduce repression of their citizens as a condition of maintaining good relations with the United States.

The shah responded to Carter administration policy by permitting freer expression of criticism of his government. That resulted in an explosion of public demands by groups such as the National Front and the Islamic Liberation Movement to free political prisoners and to allow the establishment of a more democratic political system. Carter's human rights policy and the shah's response seemed to indicate to many discontented Iranians that the shah's regime no longer enjoyed what in the past had seemed the virtually unconditional support of the most powerful country in the world. They thought that they might finally have a chance to get rid of the shah without fear of U.S. intervention. First thousands and then eventually millions of Iranians were encouraged to participate in the fast-developing anti-shah movement. The shah's later inconsistency in decision making, wavering between restraint and repression during the revolutionary year of 1978, was almost certainly due in part to his fear of Carter's possible reactions to his policies.

Almost simultaneous with the new Carter administration policy and the shah's temporary relaxation of repression, economic conditions in Iran deteriorated significantly for large numbers of Iranians. After Arab nations resumed selling their oil and major oil-consuming nations implemented significant energy conservation measures, Iran's revenues began to fall behind its expenditures, and the size of Iran's foreign debt began to increase. In response the shah's regime slowed or shut down planned construction projects, which threw tens of thousands of often semiskilled and unskilled men out of work. Many of them, often highly religious recent immigrants from rural areas to major cities, would participate in the massive urban anti-shah protests of 1978.

By the end of 1977, Iran was characterized by increasing mass discontent, fueled not only by threat of unemployment but also by the apparent erosion of cherished moral norms and the perception that the shah's dictatorship served foreign rather than Iranian interests. Leaders of distinct rebellious factions began to unite behind the common goal of ousting the shah. All of the anti-shah groups were encouraged by the apparent weakening of U.S. support for the dictatorship. The shah's regime, realizing the increasing danger posed by the growing revolutionary coalition, attempted to disrupt the anti-shah alliance by trying to discredit the reputation of Shia fundamentalist leader Ayatollah Khomeini among both the religious faithful in Iran and the secular groups within the anti-shah alliance. The attack on Khomeini took the form of an article about the ayatollah published in a major shah-controlled newspaper. The article contained what to most Iranians were outrageous and unbelievable accusations against Khomeini, questioning his religious sincerity and claiming that he was an agent of foreign imperialism against the Iranian people.

The attack backfired on the shah in major ways. First, the obvious untruths about Khomeini further tarnished the credibility of the shah's government. Second, by singling out Khomeini for this special attack, the shah's regime indicated that the ayatollah was the revolutionary leader it most feared; in so doing it helped establish Khomeini as the dominant leader of the anti-shah alliance. And third, immediately after the slanderous article was published, students at the theological center of Qom staged a public protest against it. Violence by the shah's forces resulted in the deaths of a dozen protestors. According to religious tradition, forty days after the deaths, processions to mourn and honor the victims as martyrs for Islam were held, which, in some cases, turned into new protests against the shah's regime. More violence resulted in another, new set of martyrs to be commemorated forty days later, at which time still more protestors were killed. Throughout the rest of 1978, participation in commemorations of killed protestors swelled into the hundreds of thousands. Observances of religious holidays also became occasions for protest against the shah's regime.

Ayatollah Khomeini, from his exile first in Shia areas of Iraq and then later in France, instructed the people on how to destroy the shah's regime by undermining the morale and loyalty of the shah's armed forces. Khomeini told his followers not to use violence against the shah's soldiers. Rather, the people should disarm the soldiers psychologically over time through peaceful protest and through demonstrating their willingness to become martyrs. Since most Iranian soldiers shared the same Shia religious culture as the protestors they were told to suppress, the martyrdom of protestors against the shah's dictatorship would destroy the morale of most soldiers and remove the instrument of control and repression from the shah's hands. Khomeini, unlike several other high-ranking religious leaders and anti-shah political figures, refused any compromise with the shah, asserting that resolute resistance could achieve not only the complete removal of the shah but also the total abolishment of the monarchical system and its replacement with a morally superior type of government.

During the second half of 1978 protests against the shah's regime intensified throughout major cities in Iran, and the shah gradually lost the loyalty of the bulk of the armed forces. On January 16, 1979, the shah left Iran never to return. On February 1, Ayatollah Khomeini returned to Iran after fourteen years of exile. More than a million people lined the streets of the capital city, Tehran, to welcome him. To many religious Iranians, Ayatollah Khomeini seemed divinely chosen to free the people from the shah's tyranny and foreign control. Pro-revolution military units, together with armed civilians and Fedayeen and Mujahidin rebels, forced the surrender of the last remaining pro-shah military units.

Ayatollah Khomeini publicly supported the establishment of a temporary provisional revolutionary governing council composed of secular nationalists, Shia Islamic modernists, and Shia fundamentalists. Simultaneously, however, an Islamic Revolutionary Council was organized to act as a shadow government to which much of the population owed its true allegiance (before the formal establishment of the Iranian Islamic Republic). Within the post-shah provisional revolutionary government, the Shia fundamentalists enjoyed distinct advantages over the secularists and the Shia modernists.

First, among the anti-shah groups, only the Shia fundamentalists enjoyed a truly urban and rural nationwide network in the form of thousands of clerics and their congregations and mosques. All of the other revolutionary groups had far more limited support networks and much more limited popular support and were restricted largely to urban areas. Second, the fundamentalists possessed the dominant charismatic leader of the revolution, Ayatollah Khomeini, architect of the strategy that many credited with defeating the shah and his powerful ally, the United States. And third, the fundamentalists organized a new army for Iran, the Is-

lamic Revolutionary Guard (IRG), parallel to the nation's professional army. Thousands of religious young men joined the IRG, which eventually grew to an estimated 200,000. None of the other groups in the revolutionary alliance, if they had armed militias at all, had anywhere near the size of the enormous IRG. The IRG initially appeared to have several primary functions. One was to protect key fundamentalist leaders, such as Khomeini, from any threats, including assassination, posed either by remaining pro-shah elements or by anti-fundamentalist groups within the revolutionary alliance. In particular, the IRG was to prevent any move by the professional army to stage a pro-shah military takeover, as had occurred after the shah temporarily fled Iran in 1953. The IRG also provided important leverage for the fundamentalists to intimidate or even, if necessary, violently suppress revolutionary groups that opposed creation of an Islamic state.

In an apparent effort to accelerate the process of creating a new Islamic political system, Khomeini demanded that a referendum on the political future of Iran be held on April 1 of 1979. Although other anti-shah revolutionary groups objected to the limited choice offered voters in the referendum—voting either yes or no to whether Iran should become an Islamic republic, with no other political options offered—the large majority of voters in the referendum voted yes. About six months later Iranians elected an Assembly of Experts to compose a new constitution. The assembly, dominated by religious fundamentalist delegates, created a Council of Guardians composed of six lay persons and six clerics that, in the new political system, would have the power to approve or disqualify candidates for public office and rule on whether governmental actions violated either the constitution or Islamic law. Most important, the assembly incorporated within the new Constitution of the Islamic Republic of Iran the concept of the Vilayat-e Faqih, the rule of the just Islamic jurist. This principle meant that a member of the Iranian Shia clergy, selected by other Shia clergy, would hold the most powerful position in the political system. This top religious leader would have the authority to block any action of either the elected parliament or the elected president. The Vilayat-e Faqih and related aspects of the Iranian constitution represented the victory of the Shia fundamentalists over the other groups in the anti-shah revolutionary alliance.

IMPACTS

The victory of the Shia Islamic fundamentalists in the Iranian Revolution had enormous consequences not only for Iran but also for other Islamic societies and for major non-Islamic societies, such as the United States and the Soviet Union. In the new Iran, clerics and religious law exercised wide influence. Eligibility for participation in government was generally limited to those judged by clergy to be in good religious standing. Women were required to wear the veil when appearing in public, although they were allowed to work outside the home, hold elected political office, and in fact enjoyed perhaps the greatest level of freedom and opportunity for women in any Islamic society in the Persian Gulf region.

Iran's fundamentalist leaders attempted to encourage Islamic revolutionaries in various parts of the world. These efforts provoked hostile reactions from other nations, such as the United States, whose allies in the Middle East felt endangered by Islamic fundamendalist movements. Iran's much smaller and less populous neighbor Iraq also felt threatened by Ayatollah Khomeini's denunciation of its leader, Saddam Hussein, and Khomeini's call for an Islamic revolution in Iraq (which, like Iran, had a Shia majority in its population of about 60–65 percent [CIA - The World Fact Book - Iraq 2005, 3]) . The United States placed Iran on its list of terrorism-supporting nations and banned U.S. companies from supplying Iran with new military equipment or from selling replacement missiles, engines, electronics, or other components for Iran's U.S.-made military equipment, purchased during the reign of the shah. Partly in reaction to Khomeini's call for fundamentalist revolution in Iraq and the perception that the turmoil of Iran's revolution had disrupted and diminished that country's armed forces, Iraq entered into a devastating eight-year war with Iran in September of 1980. The conflict cost billions of dollars and killed or injured hundreds of thousands in both countries. Iraq came to view itself as the shield against Islamic fundamentalism for much of the Arab world. Many Iraqis later felt betrayed when they perceived that the oil-rich monarchies, whose citizens had done almost none of the fighting and dying, failed to appreciate the sacrifices that Iraqis had made to slow, if at least temporarily, the advance of fundamentalism.

The success of Iran's Islamic fundamentalists in their struggle against the shah, and, in the minds of many Muslims around the world, against the country that the shah really served, the United States, encouraged many Islamic fighters to confront what appeared to be overwhelming odds. When the Soviet Union invaded largely Sunni Islam Afghanistan in 1979 to support a leftist government there, young Islamic men from all over the Islamic world joined with the Islamic Afghan fighters to defeat the world's second greatest military superpower. One of the foreign volunteers, Osama bin Laden, son of a Saudi Arabian billionaire, fought against Soviet forces in Afghanistan for years. He and his associates eventually transformed many of the tens of thousands of foreign volunteers in Afghanistan into the core of al-Qaeda, an international network allied with other Islamic extremist organizations willing to wage war against those whom its members viewed as the enemies of Islam.

In 1990, Iraq, heavily in debt to oil-rich Kuwait, which had loaned the country billions of dollars with which to fight their common enemy, Islamic fundamentalist Iran, during the 1980–1988 Iran-Iraq War, invaded and attempted to annex Kuwait. In response, the United States, Great Britain, and other nations stationed tens of thousands of troops in Saudi Arabia and other locations in the Persian Gulf region. Osama bin Laden and other Islamic fundamentalists, while willing themselves to fight against secular Iraq, were outraged by the presence of non-Islamic troops near the holiest sites of Islam and by what they viewed as the likely perpetual foreign occupation of Saudi Arabia. In response, al-Qaeda began to launch attacks against the United States and its interests around the world, and within the United States itself, including the 1993 truck bomb attack on the New York City World Trade Towers, the 1998 bombings of the U.S. embassies in Kenya and Tanzania, the 2000 bombing of the USS *Cole*, and the 2001 destruction of the World Trade Towers and attack on the Pentagon in Washington, D.C.

Islamic fundamentalists also came to play a role in one of the most persisting and difficult conflicts, that between the modern Zionist movement to establish and maintain a homeland for the Jewish people and the movement to create a homeland for the Arab Palestinian people. When Iraq invaded and attempted to annex Kuwait in 1990, the Palestine Liberation Organization (PLO) supported Iraq's actions. Iraq had long been an opponent of the state of Israel and a supporter of the Palestinian cause. Many Palestinians looked forward to increased aid from Iraq once Iraq added the oil resources of Kuwait to its own. But by taking the side of Iraq, the PLO temporarily lost much of the financial assistance that it had been receiving from oil-rich Arab monarchies such as Saudi Arabia, which opposed the Iraqi ousting of Kuwait's royal family and feared a possible similar fate, either through Iraqi military intervention, internal rebellion, or a combination of the two.

In Kuwait, some residents welcomed the Iraqi invasion. These were often among the several hundred thousand Arab Palestinians who were a large percentage of the hired foreign workers and their families, who actually made up the majority of the residents of Kuwait in 1990. Once the Kuwaiti royal family was back in control, with the aid of the United States and its allies, many Palestinians lost their jobs in Kuwait. The reduction of financial assistance to Palestinians from the Arab monarchies and the decline in financial aid sent by Palestinians working in Kuwait to their relatives in the West Bank and Gaza territories controlled by the Israelis, contributed to the deterioration of what for many Palestinians was an already desperate economic situation. Funds from foreign Islamic fundamentalist sources financed food assistance programs, health care, and schools for poor Palestinians, often organized by members of Hamas, the Islamic Resistance Movement. Many young men affiliated with this organization or related organizations were accused of committing suicide bombing attacks against Israelis.

The revolution in Iran also had a major impact on the U.S. government and politics—and, in so doing, on all the nations and peoples affected by U.S. policies in the years after the Iranian Revolution. In particular, the 1980 U.S. presidential election was influenced by the seizure of U.S. embassy employees by young revolutionary militants in Tehran on November 4 of 1979. The taking of those U.S. hostages occurred shortly after President Carter permitted the former shah of Iran, Mohammad Pahlavi, into the United States in late October, ostensibly to obtain treatment for cancer. His illness had been kept secret until then, apparently because, before the revolution succeeded, the shah's advisers thought that public knowledge of the shah's serious affliction would further weaken his political position in Iran. Those holding the American hostages indicated that they would be released only after the shah was returned to Iran to stand trial for his crimes, along with the money he and his family had taken from Iran and deposited in foreign banks or investments. That money was estimated by the revolutionary government to be somewhere between $10 billion and $30 billion.

The Carter administration refused to return the shah to Iran. But despite the death of the shah from cancer on July 27, 1980, the U.S. hostages were held for a total of 444 days. Carter's inability to obtain the release of the hostages either through negotiations or through military action contributed to his election defeat by the conservative Republican Ronald Reagan. It is possible that if the Iranian Revolution and the subsequent hostage-taking had not occurred, Ronald Reagan might never have been elected president of the United States. The Reagan presidency has been praised by many for its achievements, such as helping to democratize Russia and helping to end the Cold War, but also accused by many others of terrible mistakes, such as supporting right-wing state terrorism on the part of pro-U.S. dictatorships in several countries that resulted in the torture and murder of tens of thousands of civilians. The eight years of the Reagan presidency may also have seriously damaged support for the Democratic Party in the United States. Following the defeat of Carter, only one Democrat, Bill Clinton, served as U.S. president during the period from 1980 to 2008.

PEOPLE AND ORGANIZATIONS

Anglo-Iranian (Anglo-Persian) Oil Company

The Anglo-Persian Oil Company was based originally on the oil exploitation rights granted to Australian businessman William D'Arcy by the Qajar monarchy in 1901. After oil was discovered in Iran in 1908, the Anglo-Persian Oil Company was organized to extract and market this valuable energy resource. Oil soon became more important to Britain as its huge navy switched from coal-burning to petroleum-fueled engines. After the 1930s, the Anglo-Persian Oil Company was known as the Anglo-Iranian Oil Company. In 1951, the National Front–dominated parliament seized the assets of the Anglo-Iranian Oil Company in Iran, provoking a British-organized international boycott of Iran's oil. The resulting deterioration of Iran's economy contributed to a lessening of support for the National Front prime minister, Mohammad Mossadeq, the subsequent overthrow of his government by elements in the Iranian military, and the establishment of Mohammad Shah Pahlavi as the British- and U.S.-supported ruler of Iran until the 1978–1979 revolution forced him to flee the country.

Assembly of Experts

This seventy-two-member assembly was elected in 1979 to write a new constitution for Iran after the revolution. The assembly, controlled by Shia fundamentalists, created a constitution intended to ensure the domination of Iran's religious clergy in the post-revolution government through new institutions, such as the Vilayat-e Faqih and the Council of Guardians.

Carter, Jimmy (Born 1924)

Jimmy Carter was the thirty-ninth president of the United States, serving from January 1977 to January 1981. President Carter pursued a so-called human rights policy, and he indicated that good relations with the United States would depend on other nations' protecting the basic human rights of their own citizens and respecting the human rights of the citizens of other countries. In practical terms, this would typically mean abandoning governmental use of practices such as torture, or imprisoning or executing persons for solely political reasons. Mohammad Shah Pahlavi's regime, heavily dependent on U.S. military assistance and the continued purchase of U.S. military equipment, temporarily reduced the level of internal repression in 1977. The human rights stance of President Carter, coupled with the shah's apparent capitulation to pressure from the United States, was interpreted by some opponents of the shah to mean that his regime no longer enjoyed what in the past had seemed to be the unconditional support of the U.S. government. Many were encouraged to protest openly against the shah's rule. President Carter's policies toward Iran appear to have been among the major reasons for the development and success of the revolution, although Carter's intended purposes were almost certainly to promote changes in Iran that would make a violent and radical revolution less likely. The perception among some Americans that President Carter's policies had helped bring about the Iranian Revolution and the victory of Islamic fundamentalism, and that his administration was unable to cope effectively with the consequences—such as the taking of U.S. embassy employees in Tehran as hostages in November of 1979 by young Iranian radicals—was a major reason for conservative Republican Ronald Reagan's defeat of Carter in the November 1980 presidential election.

Central Intelligence Agency of the United States (CIA)

The CIA was established under the provisions of the National Security Act of 1947 to coordinate the intelligence activities of the United States and to evaluate intelligence that affects national security and disseminate it to appropriate persons and organizations. The CIA was also to carry out other intelligence-related assignments and functions as directed by the U.S. National Security Council, also established by the 1947 National Security Act.

Agents of the CIA were accused of helping to overthrow the National Front prime minister of Iran, Mohammad Mossadeq, in 1954 and establishing Mohammad Shah Pahlavi as a near-absolute monarch. The CIA was also accused of training the shah's dreaded secret police, SAVAK, and otherwise providing assistance to support the Pahlavi monarchy.

Council of Guardians

The Council of Guardians is the court created by the 1979 Constitution of the Islamic Republic of Iran. It is composed of six clerical members chosen by the Shia clergy and six lay persons chosen by the parliament. The Council of Guardians has the authority to approve or disqualify candidates for public office and to rule on whether government actions violate either the constitution or Islamic law.

Fedayeen-e Khalq (Martyrs of the People)

The Fedayeen-e Khalq was a Marxist-inspired, secular, armed revolutionary group founded by the end of 1970 to attack the Iranian shah's regime and encourage increased popular resistance to the shah.

Islamic Liberation (Freedom) Movement

The Islamic Liberation Movement was founded by Mehdi Bazargan and associates, who advocated Modernist Shiism, an ideology whose proponents held that Islam, properly interpreted, supports social goals such as reducing the gap between rich and poor, protecting the people from foreign economic exploitation and cultural subversion, establishing a more democratic political system, and embracing scientific progress. Members of the organization, who advocated an Islamic government controlled by Shia lay persons rather than clergy, joined the struggle against the shah's regime and later participated in the post-revolutionary provisional government in the period leading up to the creation of the Constitution of the Islamic Republic of Iran.

Islamic Revolutionary Council

The Islamic Revolutionary Council was a committee selected by Ayatollah Khomeini to oversee the policies of the post-revolution provisional government. The Islamic Revolutionary Council, supported by the fundamentalist-controlled Islamic Revolutionary Guard, influenced the policies of the provisional government until elections for a new government could be held under the 1979 Constitution of the Islamic Republic of Iran.

Islamic Revolutionary Guard

The Islamic Revolutionary Guard was the huge militia established by Shia Islamic fundamentalist clergy and joined by tens of thousands of young Iranian men. The Islamic Revolutionary Guard functioned to protect fundamentalist leaders, such as Ayatollah Khomeini, from assassination, prevent a possible anti-fundamentalist coup by Iran's professional armed forces, intimidate or defeat the armed supporters of any anti-fundamentalist political groups, and fight the foreign enemies of Iran and its fundamentalist-dominated revolution.

Khomeini, Ayatollah Ruhollah (1902–1989)

Ayatollah Khomeini, the charismatic Shia fundamentalist leader of the Iranian Revolution, was the son and grandson of religious scholars. After joining the ranks of the Shia clergy, Khomeini earned a reputation as an outstanding and inspirational Shia scholar and teacher and eventually acquired the clerical rank of ayatollah. Khomeini taught that religion should influence all areas of life, including government. He advocated the concept that ultimate political authority should reside in the clerical leadership, as the clerics are the representatives of God on earth. This point of view led Khomeini to oppose not only the Pahlavi dynasty but also the monarchical system of government as un-Islamic. Khomeini objected to Reza Shah Pahlavi's modernization program, because it involved limiting the power of the clergy by attempting to make religious leaders subservient to the relatively secular monarchy. Later he expressed outrage at Reza's son, Mohammad Shah Pahlavi, for creating laws and carrying out policies without the consent of clerical leaders, for diverting much of Iran's oil revenue to the benefit of the royal family and its associates, for permitting what Khomeini considered immoral foreign influences to contaminate Iranian culture, and for essentially placing Iran and its resources at the service of the United States, Great Britain, and their allies. Mohammad Shah Pahlavi expelled Khomeini from Iran in 1964 for publicly and defiantly criticizing his behavior and policies. Khomeini continued to attack the shah's regime from exile, however, first from Shia holy places in Iraq and later from France.

Ayatollah Khomeini, who commanded the loyalty of thousands of Shia clergy and millions of Iranians, became widely accepted as the uncompromising leader of the diverse anti-shah revolutionary alliance. Khomeini steadfastly demanded the ouster of the shah, but he instructed his followers to avoid violence and instead participate in peaceful demonstrations against the shah's regime, and even offer themselves in martyrdom before the shah's armed forces. When that strategy succeeded in undermining the morale and loyalty of most of the shah's military personnel, the shah fled Iran and the monarchy was destroyed. Millions of Iranians concluded that Khomeini had been divinely inspired by God to instruct the people in how to rid themselves of the Pahlavi dynasty. Khomeini used his popularity and overwhelming influence to outmaneuver and even repress the more secular and moderate groups in the anti-shah coalition and to ensure that the new Iranian constitution would grant final political power to the top clerical leader—the principle known as the Vilayat-e Faqih. Khomeini held this position in the new Iranian political system until his death in 1989.

Majlis (Majles)

Majlis, or "Assembly," is the term for the Iranian parliament both before and after the 1979 Revolution.

Mossadeq, Mohammad (1882–1967)

Mohammad Mossadeq is generally viewed as a leader who worked for greater democracy in Iran and to reduce foreign control of Iran's resources. He was born into a politically prominent family and was related through his mother to the Qajar dynasty. In 1925, Mossadeq was one of the five members of the Majlis to oppose ousting the Qajar dynasty in favor of establishing the Pahlavi dynasty. Mossadeq helped to organize the National (Popular) Front coalition of parties in 1949, and he worked to increase the power of the elected parliament and reduce that of the monarchy. In 1951, Mossadeq led the successful effort in the Majlis to nationalize British oil holdings in Iran and became prime minister. His government was overthrown by a pro-shah military coup in August 1953.

Mujahidin-e Khalq (Islamic Soldiers of the People)

The Mujahidin-e Khalq was a revolutionary group, inspired by Modernist Shiism, that advocated a far more equalitarian society than the Iran of the shahs. The Mujahideen began violent attacks on the shah's regime in early 1971 and later opposed the establishment of a fundamentalist-dominated political system in Iran.

National Front

The National Front was the coalition of Iranian political parties led by Mohammad Mossadeq that dominated the Iranian parliament in the early 1950s. The National Front–led Majlis nationalized British oil holdings in Iran and attempted to limit the power of the monarchy before its leader, Prime Minister Mossadeq, was overthrown by the August 1953 pro-shah military coup.

Pahlavi, Mohammad (1919–1980)

Mohammad Pahlavi was the son of Reza Pahlavi and the second shah of the Iranian Pahlavi dynasty. After his father abdicated in 1941, Mohammad became the new shah. In August 1953, pro-shah military forces overthrew Prime Minister Mossadeq of the National Front, who had attempted to limit the shah's power, and established the shah as a near-absolute monarch supported by both the British and U.S. governments. Mohammad Shah Pahlavi used his secret police force, the SAVAK, to repress opponents. He used Iran's oil wealth to modernize Iran, expand education and health-care facilities, and purchase huge quantities of U.S. and British military equipment. Mohammad Shah Pahlavi's rule provoked the modern Iranian Revolution led by Islamic fundamentalists. In January 1979, as the revolution was about to triumph, Mohammad Pahlavi left Iran never to return.

Pahlavi, Reza Khan (1878–1944)

Reza Khan, founder of the Pahlavi dynasty, ruled Iran from 1926 to 1944. He rose to prominence as a military commander and eventually gained enough influence over the Iranian parliament to have it vote to oust the previous Qajar dynasty and designate him as the first shah of the new Pahlavi dynasty. He repressed rebellions, enacted policies to accelerate the modernization of Iran, including limiting the power of the religious leadership to resist change, and became enormously wealthy. As World War II began, Great Britain and the Soviet Union viewed Iran under Reza Shah Pahlavi's leadership as a potential ally of Nazi Germany. After Germany attacked the Soviet Union in June of 1941, the armed forces of both Great Britain and the Soviet Union invaded and occupied Iran. Reza abdicated in favor of his son Mohammad Pahlavi and was exiled from Iran to South Africa, where he died in 1944.

Qajar Dynasty

The Qajar dynasty ruled Iran from 1796 to 1926. The Qajar shahs developed a reputation for making agreements for trade or mineral exploitation with foreign nations, such as Great Britain and czarist Russia, that were harmful to the interests of most of the Iranian people. The 1906 Iranian Revolution created a parliament, or Majlis, to limit the monarchy's power to make agreements with other countries. In 1925 the Majlis voted to replace the Qajar dynasty with the Pahlavi dynasty.

SAVAK (Sazman E Amniyat Va Ittilaat E Keshvar, Organization of National Security and Intelligence

SAVAK was Mohammad Shah Pahlavi's secret police, officially established in 1957. SAVAK was accused of the torture and murder of many persons thought to oppose the shah's regime.

Shariati, Ali (1933–1977)

Ali Shariati was a brilliant Iranian sociologist, theological innovator, and political activist who felt that Shia Islam, properly interpreted, was a religious ideology that inspired believers to fight oppression and work for a society characterized by equality of power, wealth, and opportunity, as well as to pursue scientific knowledge and progress. Although Shariati's ideas, a form of Modernist Shiism, differed from those of the more traditionalist leader, Ayatollah Khomeini, both viewed Shia Islam as a revolutionary ideology and both opposed the shah's regime. Shariati's teachings convinced many of the secular and Modernist Shia opponents of the monarchy to ally with the more fundamentalist religious foes of the shah against the regime, and that Shia Islam could be an important unifying element of the anti-shah revolutionary coalition.

Shia Islam

Shia Islam is the form of Islam practiced by approximately 90 percent of Iran's people. The Shia believe that the prophet Muhammad intended that the leadership of Islam should pass directly to Ali, the prophet's cousin and husband of his daughter, Fatima, and that later infallible leaders of Islam were certain male descendants of Ali and Fatima. The expression "Shia" means the partisans or followers of Ali. In contrast, adherents of Sunni Islam believe that there were no infallible leaders of Islam after the prophet. There were also disagreements within Shiism regarding how many infallible leaders of Islam there were after the prophet Muhammad. The type of Shia Islam dominant in Iran is "Twelver Shiism," since its adherents believe that there were twelve such leaders.

There are several major clerical ranks among the Shia clergy, including mullah, hojjat al-Islam, and ayatollah. Mullahs are the lower level of the clergy, who minister to the spiritual needs of the people. Mullahs who demonstrate the ability to memorize the Quran and Islamic law could achieve the title of hojjat al-Islam (proof of Islam). In rare instances, clergy at the rank of hojjat al-Islam could rise to the rank of ayatollah. To be recognized as an ayatollah, a hojjat al-Islam would have to become widely known for his holiness and wise judgments on important religious and social matters. At the time of the modern Iranian Revolution of the 1970s, there were estimated to be at least 23,000 clergy (Milani 1994, 63), of whom about 5,000 were hojjat al-Islam and some 50 were ayatollahs (Abrahamian 1982, 433).

At least three major theological tendencies existed within Iranian Shiism in the years prior to the revolution. Proponents of what some called Orthodox Shiism generally held that the clergy should not play a major political role unless government acted in a way that violated Islamic law or endangered the Islamic community. Advocates of Modernist Shiism sought to show that Shiism was compatible with modern science, democracy, and the struggle to achieve a more equitable society. Shia fundamentalists, such as Ayatollah Khomeini, also attacked the shah's regime, which they viewed as an un-Islamic, repressive government serving to enrich the Pahlavi royal family, morally corrupt the Iranian people, and economically exploit Iran in behalf of foreign interests such as the United States and Great Britain.

Vilayat-e Faqih

Vilayat-e Faqih, the rule of the just Islamic jurist, was the principle included in the 1979 Constitution of the Islamic Republic of Iran which mandated that a member of the Shia clergy, selected by other clergy, would hold the most powerful position in Iranian government. This top religious leader has the authority to block any action of either the elected government or the president. Once the new constitution was enacted, Ayatollah Khomeini held the title of Vilayat-e Faqih until his death in 1989.

James DeFronzo

See Also Afghanistan: Conflict and Civil War; Cinema of Revolution; Colonialism, Anti-Colonialism, and Neo-Colonialism; Democracy, Dictatorship, and Fascism; Documentaries of Revolution; Elites, Intellectuals, and Revolutionary Leadership; Human Rights, Morality, Social Justice, and Revolution; Ideology, Propaganda, and Revolution; Iraq Revolution; Islamic Fundamentalist Revolutionary Movement; Millenarianism, Religion, and Revolution; Nationalism and Revolution; Student and Youth Movements, Activism and Revolution; Terrorism; Transnational Revolutionary Movements; War and Revolution

References and Further Readings

Abrahamian, Ervand. 1982. *Iran: Between Two Revolutions.* Princeton, NJ: Princeton University Press.

———. 1989. *The Iranian Mojahedin.* New Haven, CT: Yale University Press.

Algar, Hamid. 1981. *Islam and Revolution: Writings and Declarations of Imam Khomeini.* Berkeley, CA: Mizan.

Alterman, Jon B. 2001. "Iran: Came the Revolution," *Current History* 100 (642): 27–32.

Ansari, Ali M. 2003. *Modern Iran since 1921: The Pahlavis and After.* London: Pearson Education.

Anthony, John Duke, and John A. Hearty. 1982. "Eastern Arabian States: Kuwait, Bahrain, Qatar, United Arab Emirates, and Oman." Pp. 112–147 in *The Government and Politics of the Middle East and North Africa,* edited by David E. Long and Bernard Reich. Boulder, CO: Westview.

Bakhash, Shaul. 1984. *The Reign of the Ayatollahs.* New York: Basic Books.

DeFronzo, James. 1996. (3rd edition forthcoming 2007) *Revolution and Revolutionary Movements.* Boulder, CO: Westview.

Goodson, Larry P. 2001. *Afghanistan's Endless War: State Failure, Regional Politics, and the Rise of the Taliban.* Seattle: University of Washington Press.

Graham, Robert. 1979. *Iran: The Illusion of Power.* New York: St. Martin's.

Hiro, Dilip. 1987. *Iran under the Ayatollahs.* London: Routledge and Kegan Paul.

Hussain, Asaf. 1985. *Islamic Iran.* New York: St. Martin's.

Katz, Mark N. 1997. *Revolutions and Revolutionary Waves.* New York: St. Martin's.

———. 2002. "Osama bin Laden as Transnational Revolutionary Leader," *Current History* 101 (652): 81–85.

Keddie, Nikki R. 1981. *Roots of Revolution.* New Haven, CT: Yale University Press.

Long, David E. 1986. "Islamic Republic of Iran." Pp. 60–76 in *The Government and Politics of the Middle East and North Africa,* edited by David E. Long and Bernard Reich. Boulder, CO: Westview.

Long, David E., and John A. Hearty. 1986. "Republic of Iraq." Pp. 93–111 in *The Government and Politics of the Middle East and North Africa,* edited by David E. Long and Bernard Reich. Boulder, CO: Westview.

Milani, Moshen M. 1994. *The Making of Iran's Islamic Revolution.* Boulder, CO: Westview.

Miller, Aaron David. 1986. "The Palestinians." Pp. 283–308 in *The Government and Politics of the Middle East and North Africa,* edited by David E. Long and Bernard Reich. Boulder, CO: Westview.

Moshiri, Farrokh. 1991. "Iran: Islamic Revolution against Westernization." Pp. 116–135 in *Revolutions of the Late Twentieth Century,* edited by Jack A. Goldstone, Ted Robert Gurr, and Farrokh Moshiri. Boulder, CO: Westview.

Reich, Bernard. 1986. "State of Israel." Pp. 239–282 in *The Government and Politics of the Middle East and North Africa,* edited by David E. Long and Bernard Reich. Boulder, CO: Westview.

CIA - The World Fact Book – Iran, Iraq. 2005. www.odci.gov/cia/publications/factbook/geos/ir.html (accessed January 4, 2006).

Iraq Revolution

CHRONOLOGY

2334 B.C.	King Sargon I, of the Akkad in southern Iraq, is the first empire builder, sending his troops as far as Egypt and Ethiopia. He creates the first conscripted army.
1792–1750 B.C.	King Hammurabi, the sixth ruler of the Amorites, issues one of the earliest law codes, commonly called the Code of Hammurabi, which deals with land tenure, women's status, marriage, divorce, inheritance, contracts, control of the public order, administration of justice, wages, and labor conditions.
551–331 B.C.	Iran rules Iraq.
331 B.C.	Alexander the Great of Macedon conquers Babylon. He dies in Babylon in 323 B.C. at age thirty-two.
A.D. 634	Islamic forays into Iraq begin.

636	Muslim Arab forces kill Rustum, the king of the Sassanid empire.
661	Ali, the fourth of the Guided Caliphs, is killed in Iraq. He is buried in Najaf in southern Iraq.
680	In October, Husayn, the son of Ali and the grandson of Muhammad, is killed in Karbala, Iraq, where he is buried. His death continues to be observed as a day of mourning for all Shia.
750	The Abbasid dynasty is established in Iraq, lasting to A.D. 1258. Two years later, Baghdad is established, becoming the capital.
786–813	Baghdad becomes an intellectual, trade, and commercial center and experiences high material development.
1258	Hulegu, the grandson of Ghengis Khan, seizes Baghdad and kills the last Abbasid caliph.
1401	Tamerlane sacks Baghdad and massacres many of its inhabitants.
1509	The Safavids of Iran conquer Iraq.
1533	The Ottomans conquer Iraq. Iraq stays under Ottoman rule until World War I, with the exception of a short period in the seventeenth century, when it is reconquered by the Safavid dynasty.
1914–1918	Iraq is occupied by British forces.
1920	An Iraqi revolt takes place against British occupying forces, costly to the British in both manpower and money.
1921	At the Cairo Conference, the British set the parameters for Iraqi political life, establishing a monarchy and an indigenous Iraqi army that are to continue until the 1958 Revolution.
1927	October 15: Oil is discovered in large quantities near Kirkuk in northern Iraq. This discovery is followed by others in south and central Iraq. Iraq becomes important in the international oil market.
1932	October 3: Iraq becomes a sovereign state and is admitted to the League of Nations.
1936	A military coup, the first one in the Arab world, takes place in Iraq under the leadership of General Bakir Siddqi. Subsequently, Iraq experiences more than ten coups. The last one, on July 30, 1968, brings Saddam Hussein to power.
1939	April 4: King Ghazi is killed in an automobile accident that most Iraqis suspect was organized by the British, who do not like the king's policies. He is succeeded by his four-year-old son, Faisal. Abd al-Ilah, Ghazi's first cousin, is made regent.
1941	April 3: A military coup installs an anti-British nationalist government under the leadership of Rashid Ali. The British use the coup to justify their second occupation of Iraq and reimpose Abd al-Ilah as regent.
1948	January: The Wathba (uprising) takes place. It is a massive demonstration against the Portsmouth Treaty of January between Britain and Iraq. The treaty angers nationalists opposed to continued British influence in Iraq.
	May 15: The state of Israel is established, an event that has an enormous impact on Iraqi politics.
1952	November: Economic problems and government refusal to permit direct elections to the parliament lead to the Intifada (uprising), large anti-regime protests, especially in Baghdad. In response, the government declares martial law, bans all political parties, and imposes a curfew.
1955	February 24: Iraq joins a British-sponsored treaty with Iran, Pakistan, and Turkey called the Baghdad Pact, angering many Arab countries including Egypt and Syria.
1956	Egypt nationalizes the Suez Canal, an event that galvanizes the Arab world and makes Nasser, the president of Egypt, very popular throughout the area. Britain and France oppose this and, with Israel, attack Egypt, but the attack fails to achieve its goal.

1958   February 1: Egypt and Syria decide to unite and form one country under the name United Arab Republic.

February 14: In reaction, Iraq and Jordan link together as the Arab Federation of Iraq and Jordan.

July 14: A military coup, organized by the Free Officers' Society under the leadership of General Abdul Karim Qasim, ends the monarchy.

1959   March: An attempted coup led by nationalist officers fails. The coup is in reaction to the rising influence of the Communist party.

October 7: The Baath Party attempts to assassinate General Abdul Karim Qasim. The attempt injured but failed to kill him. Saddam Hussein, who will later control Iraqi politics for thirty-five years, takes part in the assassination attempt and is injured in the process.

1961   December 11: The government passes Public Law 80, which expropriates 99.5 percent of the concession area of the foreign oil companies, leaving only the area currently in production under their control.

1963   February 8: The nationalists, along with the Baath Party, violently remove General Abdel Karim Qasim and replace him with a new government consisting of the Baath Party and other nationalist parties. Abdel Salam Arif becomes the president. He is one of the members of the Free Officers' Society, which brought about the coup of 1958. Unsuccessful unity negotiations with Egypt.

November: Most Baath Party members in the government are ousted in a bloodless coup led by Abdel Salam Arif. Unity talks with Egypt resume but fail.

1965   September 12: Unsuccessful coup takes place under the leadership of Arif Abdel Al Rassaq.

1966   April: Abdel Salam Arif, the president of Iraq, is killed in a helicopter crash. His brother Abdel Rahman is installed as president.

1968   July 17: The Baath Party and the Arab Revolution Movement stage a successful bloodless coup and form a new government.

July 30: The Baath Party ousts non-Baathist elements and takes total control of the government. This coup represents the beginning of the emergence of Saddam Hussein as leader.

1972   Iraq starts the process of nationalizing the oil industry. By 1975, all foreign oil holdings have been nationalized.

1973   July: A civilian faction within the Baath Party led by Nazim Kazzar, the head of the security department, attempts an unsuccessful coup.

1975   March 6: Saddam Hussein signs a pact with the shah of Iran in Algeria that recognizes the thalweg, the middle of the navigable channel, as the boundary in the Shaft Al Arab (Arab River) and drops Iraq's claim to Khuzestan and to the islands at the foot of the gulf. In return, the shah agrees to stop his support of the Kurdish revolt against the central government of Iraq. The Kurdish revolt collapses in a few weeks.

1979   July 16: Saddam Hussein officially becomes the president, the secretary general of the Baath Party Regional Command, chairman of RCC (Revolutionary Command Council), and the commander in chief of the armed forces. A few days later, Saddam eliminates several leading members of the Baath Party, accusing them of conspiring against him.

1980   September 23: The Iran-Iraq War begins. Iraqi troops go deep into Iranian territory. Saddam miscalculates, thinking that the war will lasts for only a few weeks. Instead, the war lasted for eight years, during which the economies of both countries are destroyed and hundreds of thousands in both countries are killed or wounded.

1988   August: The Iran-Iraq War comes to an end, leaving Iraq more than $80 billion in debt to foreign countries including Kuwait, Saudi Arabia, France, and the Soviet Union.

1990	August 2: Saddam invades and annexes Kuwait, resulting in worldwide condemnation. This allows the United States to organize a broad coalition of countries against Iraq. Also, the United Nations imposes economic sanctions against Iraq to pressure it to withdraw from Kuwait.
1991	January 16: The U.S.-led coalition of more than thirty countries bombs Iraq to force the withdrawal of Iraqi armed forces from Kuwait. The war lasts for forty-three days. Economic sanctions are extended for the purpose of disarming Iraq of all weapons of mass destruction. The sanctions are very comprehensive and last for thirteen years, during which more than 1 million Iraqis die. The United States is the main driving force behind the sanctions.
2003	March: The United States, along with Britain, invades Iraq and occupies the country, claiming that Saddam still possesses weapons of mass destruction. The war fails to prove the existence of such weapons. The future of Iraq is not certain. Resistance forces are strong, and the U.S. occupying forces are still unable to eliminate them at the time of this writing.

INTRODUCTION

The successful coup of July 14, 1958, which most Iraqis called a revolution, represented a major and significant change both in Iraq and in the region. While it was not the first military coup in Iraq, it significantly changed both domestic and foreign policies. It ended the Hashemite kingdom, which the British had established and supported since 1921, and ended also the British-inspired Baghdad Pact, which included Iraq, Iran, Turkey, and Pakistan. It began the process of transforming the Iraqi economy into one in which the state was the major actor (Al-Qazzaz 1967, 44–54; Metz 1990, 49–51)

BACKGROUND: CULTURE AND HISTORY

Modern Iraq is a land of about 169,000 square miles, surrounded by six countries—Kuwait, Saudi Arabia, Iran, Turkey, Jordan, and Syria. Almost landlocked, its access to the sea is limited to two ports: Basra (on the confluence of the Tigris and Euphrates rivers) and Um Qasr (on the Persian Gulf). The summer is hot, dry, and often windy, and, except in the north, the rain falls only during the winter.

Approximately 25 million people inhabit the country. The capital city, Baghdad, has more than 5 million residents. Basra, the gateway to the gulf, has more than 1.5 million, and Mosul, in the north, more than 1 million. Kirkuk has more than half a million people. Two especially holy Shia cities, Al-Najaf and Karbala, are both on the Euphrates, southwest of Baghdad.

About 95 percent of all Iraqis are Muslim (around 60 percent of them following the Shia tradition, 40 percent Sunni), while 4 percent are Christian. Small numbers adhere to other faiths.

Sunni and the Shia (the word "Shia" is spelled differently by different writers) are two major sects within the Islamic faith. The split involved the question of who was to lead the Muslim community after the death of Muhammad in A.D. 632. Some insisted that the elders of the community should choose the leader (this view led to the Sunni sect), and the others insisted that Muhammad's cousin Ali should be the leader. The supporters of the latter view were called Shii. "Shia" is an Arabic word that means the follower or the supporter of Ali. Over the years the Shia developed their own theological interpretation. A main difference between the Shia and the Sunni Muslims is their meaning for the word "imam." From a Sunni perspective an imam is an ordinary person who leads the Muslims in Friday prayer. He may officiate over marriages and give a sermon on Friday. From a Shia perspective, an imam has three important characteristics: he must be a descendant of Ali; he has special ability to understand the Quran on a deeper level than ordinary Muslims; and he is infallible when he acts in his capacity as an imam. The majority of the Shia believe that there were twelve imams and that the last one went into hiding around A.D. 870, for fear of being assassinated by the government of the day. The Shia believe that the last imam will return one day to bring an end to injustice and oppression; he will bring the true Muslim society to earth, which is based on justice and fairness. The Shia believe that today there is no imam. In place of the imam there are a very few imam's deputies. The grand Ayatollah Sistany in Iraq is in 2004 considered to be one of the few imam's deputies who may act on the behalf of the imam.

Ethnically, about 76 percent of the population are Arab and 18 percent are Kurds (chiefly Sunni). In addition, there are a few smaller ethnic communities, such as the Turkomans, Assyrians, Yazidis, and Armenians. Arabic is the official language and is universally understood, but in the Kurdish area (mostly in the mountains of the north and east) one can also hear two distinct dialects of Kurdish: Sornji and Karamanji.

Understanding the modern political history of Iraq requires some discussion of the roles of both the Shia and the Kurds. Their inadequate representation in the Iraqi government has caused major difficulties. The Shia live mainly in southern Iraq. Since the 1940s, many Shia have migrated to Baghdad to improve their standard of living. Today about half or more of the city's population is Shia. Approximately 1 to 2 percent of the Shia are of Iranian origin; they came mainly to visit major Iraqi Shia shrines in Najaf, Karbala, Qadimaya, and Samarra. Most of the Iraqi Arab Shias of the south are descendants of the Arab tribes that migrated from the Arabian Peninsula to the river valley of southern Iraq in the seventeenth and eighteenth centuries looking for water and food. These tribes were originally Muslim Sunni, but they were converted to Shia Islam by Shia religious leaders who were active among them (Marr 2004, 14).

During the Sunni Ottoman rule of Iraq, which began in the sixteenth century and lasted for more than four centuries, Shias were excluded from administration positions and from the military. In the late nineteenth century, the Ottoman governor Madaht Pasha and his successors established a few modern secular schools, mainly for the children of wealthy Sunni Muslims.

Upon the establishment of Iraq as a separate country by the British in 1921, the overwhelming majority of the Iraqi population were illiterate. There were, however, a handful of literate people, mainly from wealthy Sunni families. As a result, the British relied heavily on the Sunni Muslims for filling positions in institutions and departments of government ministries. With the passage of time, the Shia community benefited greatly from steady improvement in modern education and other aspects of development. Thus their representation at all levels inside and outside the government improved significantly. Yet those improvements were not sufficient to stem their frustration with the various governments of the twentieth century, because the major political positions were still in Sunni hands. This dissatisfaction manifested itself in various developments, including in the formation of opposition political parties such as the Daawah, and demonstrations in the holy cities. The most obvious example was the uprising in the south in the aftermath of the 1991 Gulf War, which Saddam put down very brutally.

The Kurds live in the mountains of northeastern Iraq and along the borders of Iran and Turkey; approximately 1 million Kurds live in Baghdad. In the aftermath of World War I, the victorious Allied countries promised the Kurdish community self-determination, but they did not fulfill that promise. Instead, the Kurdish population was divided among four countries: Iraq, Turkey, Iran, and Syria. The Kurds in Iraq never accepted the authority of the Iraqi government. Since the establishment of Iraq under the British in 1921, the Kurds on various occasions have rebelled against the central government. Outside powers, such as Iran, Israel, and the United States, have at times encouraged or supported the Kurds to revolt, in order to destabilize Iraq, which they viewed as a threat to their own national interests. The last revolt was in the aftermath of the 1991 Gulf War; it ultimately ended (with help of the United States, Britain, and France) in the establishment of a semi-independent Kurdish area in the northern part of Iraq.

The British occupied Iraq during World War I. In 1920, the Iraqis revolted against the British occupying forces. The Iraqis refer to this revolt as the Great Iraqi Revolution (the British called it a rebellion). It is considered by the Iraqis to be one of the seminal events in the modern history of Iraq. Shia as well as Sunni, the tribes, and the city people all worked together in common cause against the British occupation. The revolution was costly to the British, both in money and personnel (Metz 1990, 35). In 1921 the Treaty of Sevres officially placed Iraq under British rule, and the British established a constitutional monarchy with Faisal Ibn Hussein as head of state. Faisal was a member of the Hashemite dynasty of Arabia and had been one of the leaders of the anti-Turk Arab Revolt of 1915. On October 13, 1932, Iraq became independent and joined the League of Nations. Between 1932 and 1941, Iraq's political situation was unstable and marked by tribal rebellion, ethnic revolts, military coups, and countercoups. In 1941 a military coup installed a nationalist government under the leadership of Rashid Ali, who was unfriendly toward the British. The British used the coup to justify their second occupation of Iraq. The British employed the Transjordan Arab Legion against the Iraqis and reinstalled Abd al-Ilah as regent.

CONTEXT AND PROCESS OF REVOLUTION OF THE 1950S

After World War II, Iraq, like many other Third World countries, experienced a rise in anti-imperialist sentiment, demanding the elimination of British influence and the introduction of social and economic reforms. Several factors contributed greatly to the growth of anti-imperialist feelings in Iraq.

First, the Portsmouth Treaty of 1948, between Britain and Iraq, provoked outrage among most Iraqis and led to the January 1948 anti-treaty Wathbah (literally "leap"; a better translation is "uprising"). The Wathbah was a mass demonstration organized by opposition political parties such as the National Democratic Party (NDP), the Istiglal Party (IP), and the Iraqi Communist Party(ICP) involving people from all walks of life that continued for several days in the streets of Baghdad. Scores of people died. Still angered by the second

British occupation, begun in 1941, most Iraqis thought that the purpose of the treaty was to perpetuate British control over Iraqi affairs. Rampant discontent over rising prices, scarcity of bread, and regime failure to liberalize the political system also motivated the demonstrators (Metz 1990, 47). The treaty was canceled. Another outcome was that the opposition discovered the value of street demonstrations in discrediting the government and its policies. The opposition used this tactic in the following decades to defame the monarchy (Marr 2004, 65).

On May 15, 1948, the state of Israel was established. This event had an enormous impact on the politics of Iraq and the Arab world. It generated a great deal of resentment among the Arab people against their governments' failure to cope with the Zionist movement and against the West for supporting the creation of Israel. Many Iraqis viewed Israel as an instrument for continuing the influence of imperialist forces in the Arab world. The Iraqi government was blamed for sending poorly equipped and undertrained Iraqi troops to Palestine to fight the Israelis. The condition of Iraqi forces was the product of drastic reductions in the defense budget in the preceding years. As a result, the army fared very poorly and returned to Iraq more alienated from the regime (Metz 1990, 48). Many Iraqis accused the government of scheming with Britain and other Western powers to establish the state of Israel.

By 1952 the economic situation had deteriorated, and the government refusal to change the election of the parliament from indirect to direct elections led to large anti-regime protests organized by the opposition parties. A strike by students of the college of pharmacy in late October mushroomed into mass protests against the government in the middle of November. Iraqis refer to this as the Intifada ("Uprising"). In response, the regent asked General Nur al Din Mahmoud, chief of staff of the Iraqi armed forces, to form a new government to deal with the crisis facing the monarchy. The new government declared martial law, banned all political parties, imposed a curfew, suspended seventeen newspapers, and arrested more than 300 leaders of the opposition parties (Khadduri 1960, 283).

In 1955, Iraq joined a British-sponsored treaty with Iran, Pakistan, and Turkey called the Baghdad Pact. The pact was extremely unpopular among most Iraqis because it was widely viewed as a means for Western powers to control Iraq and to protect Western interests in the area. Furthermore, the pact angered many Arab countries, and it isolated Iraq from its Arab neighbors including Egypt and Syria.

In 1956, Gamal Abdel Nasser, the president of Egypt, successfully challenged Britain and France by nationalizing the Suez Canal Company, despite aggressions against Egypt by England, France, and Israel in October. The attack on Egypt led to large-scale demonstrations in the streets of Baghdad,

Mosul, Najaf, and many other Iraqi cities in support of Egypt. The Syrians sabotaged the pipeline that carries Iraqi oil to Western markets.

The aggression put the Iraqi government into a difficult position. It was obliged to make a face-saving statement protesting the attack, but in the meantime declared martial law, clamping down on the opposition and arresting hundreds of people. The Suez Crisis further isolated the government of Iraq both from its own people and from the Arab world, and it hastened the government's downfall (Sluglet and Sluglet 2001, 44). It spurred the growth of opposition, particularly among discontented young officers in the armed forces. Many of these officers became part of the Free Officers' Society, which toppled the monarchy on July 14, 1958. Nasser's success had momentous effects among the Arab masses, including the Iraqis.

In February 1957, the United National Front was established. The front consisted of the National Democratic Party, the Iraqi Communist Party, the Baath Party, and the Istiglal Party. The front's purpose was to coordinate the efforts of these parties in effectively challenging the regime, which was becoming more and more autocratic and repressive. While the front did not have a large membership, it did have a lot of support among professionals in urban areas, among students, and among critical workers in certain industries such as the oil industry. The front advocated democracy, abolition of martial law, withdrawal of Iraq from the Baghdad Pact, and the pursuit of positive neutralism (Tripp 2000, 143). Many people in the front cultivated links with members of the armed forces. This later played a crucial role in the coup of July 14, 1958.

The Arab nationalist movement against Western imperialism, led by Gamal Abdel Nasser of Egypt, was on the rise in the 1950s. Nasser challenged the West through his leadership at the Bandung Conference of Non-Allied Countries in 1955, his successful nationalization of the Suez Canal in 1956, unity with Syria in 1958, his buying of weapons from the Soviet Bloc, and his social reform in Egypt. Nasser's efforts generated a great deal of sympathy among the majority of discontented Iraqis, including the armed forces.

In February of 1958, Syria and Egypt united under the leadership of Nasser and adopted the name United Arab Republic. While this unification was popular among people throughout the Arab world, the Iraqi monarchy felt threatened. In response, it decided to federate with the Kingdom of Jordan. This federation of monarchies was interpreted as another Western effort to counter Nasser's Arab nationalism. Nasser's success in establishing unity with Syria inspired many of the officers who carried out the 1958 military coup in Iraq (Khadduri 1969, 13–14).

During the 1950s, modern secular education became accessible in a limited way to the Iraqi public. Overall, economic

Vice Premier Abdel Salam Arif addresses a crowd in Najaf, Iraq, explaining the objectives and reforms of the new government, August 9, 1958. Colonel Arif and General Abdel Karim Qasim overthrew the ruling monarchy and took control of the new Iraqi republic. (Bettman/Corbis)

development was slow, and its benefits did not reach most Iraqis. In 1958 only 1,000 students graduated from institutions of higher learning, and more than 80 percent of the people were still illiterate. Land ownership was highly concentrated. Only 3 percent of landholders controlled about 70 percent of the land. Health services were poor. Only 40 percent of municipalities had safe water supplies, most had no electricity, and sewage was basically neglected, even in Baghdad (Marr 2004, 69–70).

These issues and, in particular, the Suez Crisis of 1956, gave birth to many secret cells within the armed forces for the purpose of overthrowing the pro-British monarchy. In 1957 many of these cells united to form the Free Officers' Society, which had an executive committee of fourteen persons headed by Brigadier General Abdel Karim Qasim. He was chosen because of his seniority in military service. The members came mainly from the middle or lower-middle classes. Most were Arab Sunni Muslims with a few Shia Muslims, all 1930s graduates of the Iraqi Military Academy. They were associated with different political parties, including the Liberal National Democratic Party, the Istiglal Party, the Communist Party, and the Baath Party. However, the majority tended to

be Pan-Arab nationalists (Khadduri 1969, 17–19; Tripp 2000, 144). The 1958 revolt in Lebanon against President Sham'un, who was trying to change Lebanon's constitution in order to extend his presidency for six more years, provided a golden opportunity to two members of the Free Officers' Society (Abdel Salam Arif, henceforth Arif, and Abdel Karim Qasim, henceforth Qasim) to execute the coup of July 14, 1958.

The Iraqi government, fearing that the Lebanese revolt might extend to Jordan, with which it was federated, ordered the Twentieth Brigade of the army to move to Jordan to buttress the unpopular King Hussein's security forces. Arif headed one of the three battalions in the Twentieth Brigade. Arif and Qasim, who headed the Ninetieth Brigade, decided to act. Arif was to execute the coup as he passed through Baghdad on his way to Jordan, while Qasim was to stay in Jalaula as a backup force in case resistance was encountered. As the Twentieth Brigade moved to Baghdad, Arif managed to take charge of the entire brigade and executed the coup by occupying all strategic buildings in Baghdad, including the broadcast station. From that station, Arif made the first announcement of the revolution, declaring the end of the monarchy and the establishment of a sovereignty council of three members to lead the country. Furthermore, Arif encouraged the Iraqi people to show their support for the revolution and to get rid of the agents of the monarchy (Marr 2004, 85; Tripp 2000, 146). In response, thousands of people marched in the streets of Baghdad celebrating the death of Nuri al as Said and Abd al-Ilah , the two most hated symbols of the monarchy. The revolution encountered virtually no opposition.

IMPACTS

The revolution of 1958 brought significant changes in both domestic and foreign policy in Iraq, and it had effects on the region and on world politics as well.

The new regime ended the British-supported Hashemite kingdom, seceded from the federation with Jordan, and withdrew from the Baghdad Pact. The pact's headquarters was moved from Baghdad to Turkey, where it was renamed the Central Treaty Organization. Iraq pursued a foreign policy of nonalliance and established diplomatic relations with the Soviet Union and China (Peretz 1978, 421)

Two months after the revolution, the new government initiated the radical Agrarian Reform Law, which limited land ownership to only 1,000 dunams (approximately 250 acres) of irrigated land or 2,000 dunams of rain-fed land per person. The confiscated excess land would be distributed to peasants in lots of 30 to 60 dunams of irrigated or 60 to 120 dunams of rain-fed land. (Marr 2004, 99). The intention of the law was to undermine the power of the landed sheikhs and absentee landlords, while enhancing the position of the peasants and bringing about greater equality among Iraqis (Metz 1990, 50).

In December of 1959 the government issued a new decree, extensively revising the personal status code that defined family relations traditionally shaped by Islamic law. The new law limited men's right to practice polygamous marriage. It protected women against arbitrary divorce, required a minimum age of eighteen for marriage, and gave women equal rights with men in matters of inheritance. The new code applied to both Sunni and Shia Iraqis. This decree brought, for the first time, all Muslim Iraqis under one statute (Marr 2004, 100).

The new government expanded all levels of education and made it more accessible to all people. The revolutionary government also challenged the existing profit-sharing arrangement with oil companies, and on December 11, 1961, it enacted Public Law No. 80. This law resulted in the expropriation of 99.5 percent of the IPC group's concession land, leaving those companies to operate only on the areas currently in production. The law also established the Iraqi National Oil Company, to be in charge of developing the expropriated areas (Marr 2004, 102).

The revolution, however, plunged Iraq into a series of political struggles that hindered the fulfillment of many of the intended social and economic reforms. The revolution failed to create permanent political institutions that could govern the country and mobilize effective popular support. Basically, power was vested in one person, Qasim, who acted as prime minister, defense minister, and head of the armed forces. He was labeled Al-Zaim Al-Awhad ("sole leader"). Furthermore, the revolution reopened the door for direct intervention by armed forces in Iraqi politics in subsequent decades (Marr 2004, 112).

The first signs of trouble emerged within the group that organized and executed the coup, as well as within the National Front. The Free Officers' Society included officers with different political views. The new government consisted of both military and civilians, drawn from various parties of the National Front. While united in removing the monarchy, they were unable to agree on a number of issues that split them apart in the first weeks of the revolution. The first disagreement, regarding the relations of Iraq with the United Arab Republic of Nasser, emerged almost immediately. Some members advocated immediate unity with the UAR. Others believed that domestic social reform and the building of an Iraqi national community should precede any serious engagement with the Arab world. Qasim, the head of the government, preferred the latter approach, and he was supported by the Communist Party and National Democratic Party. Arif, his deputy, advocated the first alternative, and he was supported by the Baath Party and the Istiglal Party.

The Communists and National Democratic Party and their supporters proved to be more powerful at the time. This in turn led to the resignations of pro-unification members from the cabinet. In March of 1959, a group from the Free Officers' Society, who had become increasingly disappointed with Qasim, his increasing links to the Communists, and his opposition to unity with the UAR, attempted a coup in Mosal. The failure of the coup provided the Communist Party and its supporters with unprecedented power inside and outside the government. That in turn alarmed the Baath Party, which decided to assassinate Qasim. Saddam Hussein, the future leader of Iraq, participated in the assassination attempt, which injured Qasim but did not kill him. The failed assassination increased the influence of the Communists in running Iraq and led to more suppression of the nationalist parties.

But Qasim himself became alarmed at the growing power of the Communists and started to curb their activities. By 1961, Qasim's domestic power base had become very limited. He had alienated both Communist and nationalist forces. His aloof, detached manner and his monopoly on power only added to his isolation. Then, in September of 1961, full-scale fighting broke out between the army and the Kurdish guerrillas led by Mulla Mustafa Barzani. By 1962, the Qasim government was unable to check the Kurdish insurrection, which further eroded his support (Metz 1990, 53). Qasim's problems were further compounded by foreign policy issues. One was the growing conflict with Iran regarding the border as Iran became more alarmed with the increasing influence of the Communist Party in Iraq. The second was Qasim's attempt to annex Kuwait in 1961, which alienated him from his Arab neighbors as well as from other countries (Metz 1990, 52). By late 1962, Qasim was isolated both domestically and internationally. On February 8, 1963, he was overthrown and killed along with his closest associates as well as thousands of Iraqis in a bloody military coup organized by a coalition of the Baath Party and other nationalist forces. The succeeding regime was characterized by conflicts within the Baath Party itself as well as between the Baath Party and the other members of the government. Nine months later several Baath Party members and their sympathizers were expelled from the government by a coup led by Arif.

But on July 17, 1968, following the 1966 death of Arif in a helicopter crash, the Baath Party came back to power through a bloodless coup. This marked the ascendance to power of Saddam Hussein, which lasted until the U.S. invasion of Iraq in March 2003. From 1968 to 2003, Saddam dominated the political scene, even while he was vice president, between 1968 and 1979. He ruled Iraq with an iron fist through multiple security forces eliminating opposition by imprisonment and killings. For all practical purposes, all political activity outside the Baath Party was outlawed.

In the early 1970s, Iraq nationalized its oil industry, and in the 1970s the price for crude oil went up. As a result, the government invested a large amount of money in improving the country's infrastructure and its educational system and social services. The Kurdish revolt reached its peak in the mid 1970s as the result of the support it received from Iran, Israel, and the United States, which viewed Iraq as a threat to their interests and wanted to destabilize the regime. The Kurdish rebellion continued, which led Saddam, in 1975, to conclude a treaty with the shah of Iran in which Iraq conceded to share Shatt Al-Arab (the river waterway to the Persian Gulf) with Iran in return for Iran's ending support for the Kurds. Within a few weeks of the agreement, the Kurdish revolt ended. For more than a decade, the Kurdish region was relatively quiet. On July 16, 1979, Saddam formally assumed the presidency. In addition, he became secretary general of the Baath Party Regional Command, chairman of the Revolutionary Command Council, and the commander of the armed forces. He began his presidency by eliminating a number of high-ranking members of the Baath Party accused of plotting against him.

Relations with Iran began to worsen in the aftermath of the Iranian Revolution. Border skirmishes between the two

Iraqi soldiers patrol Baghdad following a coup by the Arab Baath Socialist Party in 1963. Abdel Karim Qasim, the deposed prime minister, was executed. (AFP/Getty Images)

countries were used by Saddam as an excuse to invade Iran on September 22, 1980. Saddam, however, thought that the war would last only a few weeks. He believed that the debilitated and demoralized Iranian army, in the aftermath of the Islamic Revolution, would put up little resistance, and that the Arab population in the southern part of Iran would rise in his support. Both assumptions were wrong.

The war dragged on for eight years. It was one of Saddam's biggest miscalculations and had tragic consequences for Iraq and its neighbors. Hundreds of thousands were killed or wounded. The war drastically damaged Iraq's economy, including its bombed oil industry. In addition, it shifted spending from development projects to the military to meet the requirements of war. The Kurds resumed their revolt, with the support of the Iranian government. Finally, by the time the war ended on July 18, 1988, Iraq was more than $80 billion in debt to several countries, including Kuwait, Saudi Arabia, France, and the U.S.S.R.

Between 1988 and 1990, Saddam's government was struggling to rebuild the country. He attacked the Kurds for siding with the Iranians during the war. Many were forced to leave the mountains for detention centers located in the flatlands.

Then a drop in international oil prices led to serious tension between Iraq and Kuwait. Saddam accused both Kuwait and the United Arab Emirates of conducting economic war against Iraq by keeping the prices low through intentionally flooding the oil market and exceeding their OPEC quotas. This resulted in big reductions in Iraqi oil revenue, which was sorely needed to rebuild the country. That issue—along with Kuwaiti government stubbornness, the U.S. ambassador to Iraq's ambiguous message that any dispute between Arab countries was not a U.S. matter, and U.S. and British encouragement to Kuwait not to be flexible in its dealings with Iraq—led to Saddam's decision to invade Kuwait on August 2, 1990. The invasion ultimately brought about the First Gulf War, led and executed by the United States on January 17, 1991. This war, code-named "Operation Desert Storm," lasted forty-three days. The United States and its allies dropped a total of 99,000 to 140,000 tons of explosives on Iraqi targets, the equivalent of five to seven Hiroshima nuclear bombs. The war destroyed the country's infrastructure, knocking out its electricity grids, roads, bridges, sewage and water purification systems, factories, and communication systems. A UN report written shortly after the war indicated that the destruction had returned the country to a preindustrial stage. In the aftermath of the war, both the Kurdish ethnic community in the north and the Shia Muslim community of the south revolted against Saddam's regime. The Kurds were hoping to establish an independent state, while the Shia were hoping to topple Saddam's regime and replace it with a more sympathetic government. Despite the fact that Saddam's armed forces had been badly beaten by the United States and its allies, he was able to muster enough power to crush both rebellions, killing thousands of people and wounding many more. Hundreds of thousands of Kurds fled Iraq to Turkey and Iran, causing the United States, England, and France to impose a zone in the north of the country in which no Iraqi aircraft were allowed to fly, and an area banned to Iraqi forces in which Kurds could rule themselves. This made it possible for hundreds of thousands of refugees to return to their homes. The Kurdish zone had, for all practical purposes, become independent. It has its own currency, taxes, and educational system. In addition, Kurdish is the primary language.

On August 6, four days after Iraq invaded Kuwait, the UN Security Council passed Resolution 661, imposing on Iraq the most comprehensive economic sanctions and trade embargo in UN history. As the war ended, the UN Security Council passed several new resolutions. These included Resolution 687, on April 3, 1991, to continue the sanctions on Iraq until it dismantled its weapons program, including all long- and medium-range missiles, and its chemical, biological, and nuclear facilities. This was to be implemented in part by the newly established UN Special Commission (UNSCOM).

Resolution 713 was to establish a permanent UN monitoring system for all Iraqi missile test sites and nuclear installations. Resolution 986, passed in 1992, allowed Iraq to sell $1.6 billion worth of oil every six months to purchase food and medicine. Of the money raised through oil sales, about one-third was to go for reparations to Kuwait and for UN operations in Iraq. Iraq agreed in principle to the first two resolutions, but it temporarily rejected the third on the grounds that it did not allow Iraq to control the funds realized from the sales.

Iraq was unhappy with UNSCOM's intrusive inspections, which, on a number of occasions, led to confrontations between Iraqis and the inspection teams. The United States, the driving force behind the inspections, used these confrontations to bomb Iraq in 1993, 1996, and 1998. Before the last bombardment began, Richard Butler, head of UNSCOM, withdrew the inspectors without UN authorization. The inspectors did not return to Iraq until 2002. By the time of the 1998 confrontation, the United Nations had destroyed more than 95 percent of Iraq's weapons systems of mass destruction (MD). Iraq claimed that it destroyed the other 5 percent but could not adequately account for it. The inspectors faced difficulties because of Iraq's concern with the inspections violating its sovereignty, and with its fear that some inspectors were U.S. spies.

The sanctions and the embargo had a terrible impact on Iraqi society. They further devastated the sanitation and health systems. They also led to the breakdown of the electrical system, resulting in chronic problems with sewage and water treatment. The sanctions also contributed to inadequate diets, causing malnutrition, the proliferation of disease, and a high mortality rate among children. Many other social ills followed, including street children, increasing crime rates, a high divorce rate, and a decline in the marriage rate. The educational system was devastated, and thousands of schools were left in a state of disrepair. Last, but not least, the sanctions weakened the oil industry, the mainstay of Iraq's economy, for lack of spare parts and lack of investment to update oil facilities. The thirteen years of sanctions led to the death of more than a million persons, many of them children and the elderly. Two UN chief relief coordinators, Denis Halliday in 1998 and Han von Sponeck in 2000, resigned their jobs in protest over the devastation caused by continuation of the sanctions. As its people approached destitution, the Iraqi government was forced in 1996 to accept the terms of Resolution 986, selling $1.6 billion worth of oil every six months. This was raised in 1998 to $5.52 billion in oil every six months, and in October 1999 to $8.3 billion.

September 11, 2001, was a turning point regarding U.S. policy toward Iraq. It came at a time when Republicans had assumed power in the White House. The foreign policy of the new administration was controlled by neo-conservatives who advocated a regime change in Iraq. Some planners of the new policy were behind the passage of the Iraq Liberation Act of 1998, in which the U.S. Congress allocated $100 million to help Iraqi opposition groups in their quest to remove Saddam from power. Immediately after September 11, neo-conservatives used the incident to push for the removal of Saddam by military means. Because of worldwide pressure, the United States first went to the United Nations, pushing for a new, strong resolution calling for the return of weapons inspectors. The United Nations adopted Resolution 1441, demanding that Iraq allow inspection teams to return. There were two teams. One, headed by Muhammad Baradei of Egypt, was from the International Atomic Energy Agency. The second was the UN Monitoring, Verification, and Inspection Commission (UN-MVI), headed by Hans Blix from Sweden. Iraq agreed to the resolution and emphatically denied having any weapons of mass destruction, stating that it had destroyed them all. However, it did not give a full account of missing items. The heads of both inspection teams wanted more time to finish the job. The United States, along with Britain, refused to wait, although almost all of the rest of the world wanted to give more time for inspections. The United States claimed that Saddam had weapons of mass destruction, and that he was a threat to the United States and world security.

On March 17, the United States and Britain initiated their invasion of Iraq, defying overwhelming world opinion, and, in the view of most nations, violating international law. On April 9, 2003, Baghdad fell, and the occupation of Iraq began. The claims that Iraq possessed weapons of mass destruction—biological, chemical, or nuclear—turned out to be false, appearing to many to have been a deception manufactured by the neo-conservatives to sell the war to the American public. In May, the UN Security Council, under U.S. pressure, adopted Resolution 1483, which in effect legalized the result of the invasion that most of its members had considered illegal. On October 16, 2003, the United Nations adopted Resolution 1511 to authorize a multinational force under U.S. leadership to replace and reduce the burden on the U.S. occupying forces. At this moment, the future of Iraq is uncertain. Resistance to the occupation is strong in various parts of the country.

PEOPLE AND ORGANIZATIONS

Abd al-Ilah (1913–1958)

Regent of Iraq (1939–1953). Born in Hijaz, Saudi Arabia, he moved to Iraq in 1926. He was educated at Victoria College, Alexandria, Egypt. He acted as regent for King Faisal II, who inherited the throne at age four. Abd al-Ilah became crown prince (1953–1958). Iraqis always identified him as al Wasi, the regent, even after he relinquished the regency in 1953. Most Iraqis considered him the pro-British manifestation of all the evils and shortcomings of the monarchy. He was assassinated along with other members of the Iraqi royal family during the revolution of July 14, 1958.

Arif, Abdel Salam (1921–1966)

Arif was born into a modest family in Al-Karkh, a suburb of Baghdad. He began military college in 1938 and was commissioned an officer in 1941. He sympathized with Rashid Ali's anti-British nationalistic revolt. In 1948 he participated in the Palestine War, which left him embittered and disappointed with the leadership of Arab governments. He was a member of the Free Officers' Society and carried out the July 14, 1958, revolution, becoming deputy prime minister, minister of the interior, and deputy commander of the armed forces. Because he favored unity with the United Arab Republic, he was dismissed from all his posts shortly after the revolution. He participated in the coup against Qasim in 1963 and then became president. Arif was killed in a helicopter crash near Basra City on April 13, 1966.

Baath Party (Renaissance or Rebirth)

The Baath Party was created in Syria in the 1940s by Michel Aflaq and Salah al-Bitar. It had three objectives: nationalism, unity, and Socialism. It emerged in Iraq in the early 1950s. In 1957, the party joined the United National Front and participated in the revolution of 1958. Its participation in the new government ended following the tension between Arab nationalists and leftists who supported Abdel Karim Qasim, the head of the government. The party attempted to assassinate Qasim in 1959. It assumed power in Iraq in 1968 and held it until it was overthrown by the U.S. invasion in March 2003.

Baghdad Pact

A British-inspired pact, the Baghdad Pact was formed in 1955 and consisted of Iraq, Turkey, Iran, and Pakistan. The United States did not formally join the pact, but it provided most of the financial support and served on its numerous committees. Many Arab countries, particularly Egypt and Syria, denounced the pact as a tool of the imperialist West. In 1959, Iraq formally withdrew from the pact, which then was renamed the Central Treaty Organization, or Cento.

Bakr, Ahmad Hassan (1912–1982)

Born in Tikrit, Bakr enrolled in the military academy in 1938. He joined the Baath Party in 1956 and later became a member of the Free Officers' Society, which staged the revolution of 1958. He played a significant role in the coup of 1963 that ousted Qasim. He became prime minister for a few months. In mid 1968, Bakr headed the coup ousting Abdal Rahman Arif. He became president from 1968 to 1979. He was under house arrest until he died in 1982.

Faisal I (Faisal Ibn Hussein; 1885–1933)

Born in Taif, Saudi Arabia, and educated in Constantinople, he was one of the Arab leaders who led the revolt against the Ottoman empire during War World I. He was installed by the British as king of Iraq from 1921 to 1933. During his regime Iraq achieved formal independence.

Faisal II (Faisal Ibn Ghazi; 1935–1958)

Faisal II, grandson of Faisal I, inherited the throne at the age of four , when his father, King Ghazi, died in a car accident in 1939. He was educated in England. A regent (Abd al-Ilah, his uncle) ruled for him until he assumed power on May 2, 1953, when he became eighteen years of age. He became the head of the short-lived Arab Federation between Iraq and Jordan in 1958. He was killed along with other members of the royal family on July 14, 1958.

Free Officers' Society

The group of officers who planned and carried out the July 14 revolution in 1958.

Ghazi (Ghazi Ibn Faisal I; 1913–1939)

Born Hijaz in 1913, Ghazi became king of Iraq in 1933 at the age of twenty-one. He was educated partly in Britain, but mostly in Iraq, including at the military college in Baghdad. He was popular for his Arab nationalism and his dislike of British policy in the area. He was killed on April 4, 1939, in a horrible car accident. Most Iraqis believed that it was planned by the British, who disliked his Arab nationalism and had difficulty influencing his policies.

Hussein, Saddam (Born 1937)

Hussein was the former Baath Party leader and president of Iraq, 1979–2003, ousted by the March 2003 U.S.-led invasion. He was born to a poor farming family living close to Tikrit, a town to the north of Baghdad, and joined the Arab nationalist Baath Party in 1957. He was wounded in the 1959 assassination attempt against Iraqi leader General Qasim, who was criticized for being too favorable toward the Iraqi Communist Party. After the Baath Party took power in 1968, Hussein was charged by the new Iraqi leader, General al-Bakr, with attempting to solve some of the country's difficult problems, including nationalizing the oil industry and negotiating a treaty with Iran in 1975. After Bakr retired, Hussein assumed the presidency. Apparently fearing the spread of Islamic fundamentalist revolution from Iran to Iraq's Shia population, Hussein went to war with Iran in September 1980. The war lasted for eight years, resulting in enormous loss of life and devastation. After the war, Iraq was approximately $80 billion in debt, part of that being owed to Kuwait. Hussein accused Kuwait of collaborating with the United States to lower Iraq's desperately needed oil revenue. He claimed that this was accomplished through reducing the price for oil by Kuwaiti overproduction. In response, Hussein occupied and attempted unsuccessfully to annex Kuwait to Iraq in 1990. Accused of brutal policies against political opponents and Shia and Kurdish rebels inside Iraq, Hussein was finally overthrown by the U.S.-led invasion in March 2003 and captured in December of that year.

Intifada (Uprising)

A mass demonstration against the Iraqi government in 1952, protesting the bad economic situation and demanding direct election of parliament.

Iraqi Communist Party

First appearing in the early 1930s, the Communist Party gained strength in the 1940s. The party played important roles in the Wathba of 1948 and the uprising of 1952. The party in 1957 joined the United National Front, which cooperated with the Free Officers' Society to bring down the monarchy in 1958. The Communist Party gained great power during the first two years of the Qasim regime, both inside and outside the government. But after the February 1963 military coup, many of its members were jailed, killed, or forced to leave Iraq. The party lost most of its importance during the Baathist regime of 1968–2003.

Iraqi Petroleum Company (IPC)

Before the collapse of the Ottoman empire, the British-controlled Turkish Petroleum Company obtained an oil concession in the Mosul area of Iraq. In 1925, the Turkish Petroleum Company obtained a new oil concession from the Iraqi government. In October 1927, oil was discovered in large quantities in the Kirkuk area. In 1928, the shareholders of the company signed a formal agreement dividing the Iraqi oil concession in the following fashion: the Anglo-Persian Oil Company, 23.7 percent; the Dutch Shell Group 23.7 percent; the French Petroleum Company 23.7 percent; five American companies 23.7 percent; and 5 percent to Mr. Gulbenkian. In June of 1929, the name of the company was changed to the Iraqi Petroleum Company. The company formed two subsidiaries to explore for oil in other parts of Iraq. Iraq started to export for oil in 1936. After the overthrow of the monarchy, the Iraqi government enacted law No. 80 in 1961, which expropriated the 99.5 percent of the IPC concession areas that were not in production. The Iraqi National Oil Company was established in 1964 to develop oil in the expropriated areas. Between 1972 and 1975, Iraq nationalized the remainder of IPC holdings in Iraq.

Istiglal (Independence) Party

Formed in 1946, this party advocated a strong Arab nationalist policy and moderate social reform. Some of its members had participated in the 1941 revolt against the second British occupation. The party joined the United National Front in 1957 and participated in the 1958 Revolution.

National Democratic Party (Al Watani al-Demoqrati)

This left-of-center party, which advocated moderate socialistic principles, was formed in 1946. It participated in the uprisings against the government in 1948, 1952, and 1956. It joined the United National Front in 1957 and supported the 1958 Revolution. The party eventually split into two parties over disagreements regarding the regime of Qasim.

Qasim, General Abdel Karim (1914–1963)

Qasim was born in 1914 in Baghdad. His father was a Sunni Muslim carpenter, while his mother was a Shia Muslim of Kurdish (Faili) background. After finishing high school, he taught for a year in a primary school. Then he joined the military college and was commissioned an officer in 1938. He participated in the 1948 Palestine War, which left him embittered over the defeat of the Arab armies. He attributed this to the corruption of the Iraqi and other Arab governments. He led the Free Officers' Society and with Arif carried out the coup of 1958. He was the leader of Iraq between July 14, 1958, and February 8, 1963, in effect being a dictator. He was overthrown by a military coup organized by Arab nationalist forces and the Baath Party on February 8, 1963, in which he was killed.

Said, Nuri al as (1888–1958)

An Iraqi military officer and an influential politician, Said was born in Baghdad into a middle-class Sunni family and educated in an Ottoman military school, where he graduated as an officer in 1906. He participated in the Arab Revolt against the Ottoman empire. During the monarchy he was appointed prime minister eight times and appointed many times as defense minister or foreign minister. Most Iraqis considered him the pro-British embodiment of the evils and corruption of the monarchy. He was assassinated during the revolution of July 14, 1958.

United Arab Republic (UAR)

This was the name for the 1958 political union between Egypt and Syria that lasted until 1961.

Wathba (Leap or Uprising)

Wathba refers to the mass demonstrations that took place in Iraq in 1948 to protest the Portsmouth treaty.

Ayad Al-Qazzaz

See Also Arab Revolt 1916–1918; Armed Forces, Revolution, and Counter-Revolution; Colonialism, Anti-Colonialism, and Neo-Colonialism; Democracy, Dictatorship, and Fascism; Documentaries of Revolution; Human Rights, Morality, Social Justice, and Revolution; Islamic Fundamentalist Revolutionary Movement; Transnational Revolutionary Movements; War and Revolution

Note Part of "Impacts" section from "Iraq" by Ayad Al-Qazzaz. Pages 1129–1136 in the *Encyclopedia of Modern Middle East and North Africa*, Philip Mattar et al. eds., Macmillan Reference USA, ©2004. Reprinted by permission of the Gale Group.

References and Further Readings

Al-Qazzaz, Ayad 1967. "Military Regimes and Political Stability in Iraq, Syria and Egypt," *Berkeley Journal of Sociology* 12 (summer): 44–54.

———. 1969. "The Story of the July Fourteen 1958 Revolution," *Middle East Forum* 45 (4): 63–71.

———. 1971. "The Changing Patterns of Politics of the Iraqi Army." Pp. 335–361 in *On Military Interventions,* edited by Morris Janowitz and Jacques Van Doorn. Rotterdam: Rotterdam University Press.

———. 1976. "The Iraqi British War of 1941: A Review Article," *International Journal of Middle East Studies* 7: 591–596.

———. 1996. "Ahali Group." Pp. 60–61 in *The Encyclopedia of the Modern Middle East*. Vol.1, edited by Reeva S. Simon, Philip Mattar, and Richard W. Bulliet. New York: Macmillan Reference USA.

Khadduri, Majid. 1960. *Independent Iraq 1932–1958: A Study in Iraqi Politics*. Oxford: Oxford University Press.

———. 1969. *Republican Iraq: A Study in Iraqi Politics since the Revolution of 1958*. Oxford: Oxford University Press.

Marr, Phebe. 2004. *The Modern History of Iraq*, 2nd edition. Boulder, CO: Westview.

Mattar, Philip, et al., eds. 2004. *Encyclopedia of the Modern Middle East and North Africa*. New York: Macmillan Library Reference.

Metz, Helen Chapin. 1990. *Iraq: A Country Study*. Washington, DC: Government Printing Office.

Peretz, Don. 1978. *The Middle East Today*, 3rd edition. New York: Holt, Rinehart and Winston.

Sluglet, Marion, and Peter Sluglet. 2001. *Iraq since 1958: From Revolution to Dictatorship*. London: I. B. Tauris.

Tripp, Charles. 2000. *A History of Iraq*. Cambridge: Cambridge University Press.

Irish Revolution

CHRONOLOGY

432	Traditional date for the coming of St. Patrick to Christianize the country.
795	Viking raids on Ireland begin, which damage flourishing culture of "the island of saints and scholars" but also establish trading centers, including Dublin.
1014	Defeat of Vikings at Battle of Clontarf by Brian Boru.
1169	English invasion of Ireland in the reign of Henry II. English control some parts of Ireland from that time.
1367	Statutes of Kilkenny prohibit (unavailingly) contamination of English settlers by native Gaelic culture.
1536	"Reformation Parliament" in Dublin enacts Henrician Reformation.
1541	Henry VIII of England proclaimed also king of Ireland.
1601	Battle of Kinsale; decisive defeat of leading Gaelic chiefs effectively ends the most dangerous rebellion against encroaching English authority. The defeat is followed by a savage campaign of destruction against the Ulster strongholds of Irish chiefs, their flight to Europe in 1607, and the plantation of Ulster with Scottish and English settlers from 1609 on the conquered lands, sowing the seeds of the religious and racial conflict in Ulster that has continued in varying forms until the present day.
1641–1650	Native rebellion against planters in Ulster initiates protracted and complex conflict. English Protestant forces under Cromwell 1649–1650 defeat the rebels in a campaign whose ferocity becomes notorious in Irish memory. Many of the forfeited lands of the defeated are allotted to officers and soldiers in the Cromwellian Plantation.
1689–1691	William III defeats James II, at the Boyne, 1690, celebrated by Protestant parades on July 12 that have often proved a flashpoint in Northern Ireland for violent confrontation with Catholics. Williamite victories ensure the Protestant succession against the Catholic threat posed by James, the conflict ending with the Treaty of Limerick, 1691, allowing the Jacobite Army to sail for France and promising Catholics a degree of religious liberty.
1695	Beginning of Penal Laws against Catholics, creating the potent image of the Broken Treaty of Limerick.
1782	Establishment of "Grattan's Parliament," representing the "colonial nationalism" of the Protestant Ascendancy in a semi-autonomous assembly under the king of England as king of Ireland.
1791	Establishment of Society of United Irishmen, associated with Theobald Wolfe Tone, the founding father of republicanism in Ireland.
1795	Establishment of Orange Order to protect Protestant supremacy after a sectarian conflict, the Battle of the Diamond.

1796–1800	A large French fleet, with Wolfe Tone on board, is unable to land the army in 1796 because of adverse winds. Fearful of invasion and rebellion, the government provokes a rising in 1798 that it crushes in savage conflict. Wolfe Tone and other rebel leaders are captured or killed, and the threat of Ireland's being used as a backdoor for a French invasion of England impels Pitt, the British prime minister, to induce "Grattan's Parliament" to vote for its own abolition in an Act of Union in 1800 that incorporates Ireland into the United Kingdom.
1803	An attempted rebellion by Robert Emmet is easily crushed, but leaves a powerful memory of defiance of British rule in the public imagination.
1829–1843	Catholic Emancipation, allowing Catholics to sit in parliament, is granted in 1829 after a campaign of mass mobilization led by Daniel O'Connell, the first great popular tribune of the Irish masses. O'Connell's campaign for Repeal of the Union defeated when the prime minister, Sir Robert Peel, threatens to crush the movement by military force in 1843.
1842	Launch of *The Nation* as the newspaper of the Young Ireland Movement, preaching a vigorous version of romantic nationalism.
1845–1852	The Great Famine. At least 1 million people out of more than 8 million die, and another 2 million emigrate, mainly to the United States and Britain. A Young Ireland rebellion is easily crushed in 1848, but the memory of the suffering, and the belief in British genocidal intent, fosters hatred for Britain in the diaspora, especially in the United States, which proves a major source of support for anti-British movements down to the Northern Ireland conflict.
1858	Founding of the Irish Republican Brotherhood, later the Fenians, dedicated to establishing an Irish republic. But the Fenian Rising in Ireland in 1867 is easily crushed.
1870	Isaac Butt begins a campaign for devolved government—"Home Rule"—for Ireland, while remaining loyal to the English monarchy.
1879	In response to a threat of starvation following poor harvests, the Land League is established under the leadership of the Fenian Michael Davitt and Charles Stewart Parnell, the rising star of Home Rule politics, agitating for security for tenant farmers.
1881	Gladstone's major Land Act.
1884	Gaelic Athletic Association is founded.
1885	In general election, Nationalist Party under Parnell wins 85 of 103 seats in Ireland.
	Gladstone converts to Home Rule.
1886	Lord Randolph Churchill visits Belfast to rouse the support of the Orange Order and Ulster Protestants against Home Rule.
	Gladstone's first Home Rule bill is defeated in House of Commons.
1890	Parnell's Nationalist Party splits when Gladstone warns that he cannot guarantee continuing Liberal support for Home Rule if Parnell, following his exposure as an adulterer, remains leader of the Nationalist Party. The majority of the Nationalist Party deposes Parnell, who dies during the bitter party struggle in 1891.
1893	Gladstone's second Home Rule bill is rejected by the Lords after passing Commons.
	Foundation of Gaelic League.
1894	Foundation of Irish Trades' Union Congress.
1896	James Connolly establishes the Irish Socialist Republican Party.
1898	The Irish Local Government Act establishes local councils by election.
1900	The "Parnell Split" ends.
1905	Arthur Griffith establishes Sinn Féin.
1908	National University of Ireland and Queens University of Belfast are established under the Irish Universities Act.

1910   Sir Edward Carson is elected leader of Irish Unionists.

Irish Nationalist Party holds balance of power in British parliament after general elections.

1911   Irish Women's Suffrage Federation is established.

1912   Conservative leader Andrew Bonar Law pledges unconditional support for Ulster Unionist resistance to Home Rule.

Prime Minister Asquith introduces third Home Rule bill.

1913   Home Rule bill passed in Commons, but rejected by Lords.

Ulster Volunteer Force founded to resist Home Rule.

James Larkin and James Connolly establish Citizen Army in Dublin to protect workers locked out, or on strike, from police.

Irish Volunteers founded to support Home Rule.

1914   "Curragh Mutiny" by British officers.

Ulster Volunteer Force undertakes major importation of guns and ammunition.

Small-scale importation of arms by the Irish Volunteers.

Following outbreak of World War I, Home Rule is passed in parliament but suspended until end of war.

Redmond urges Irish Volunteers to join British army.

Split between Irish Volunteers rejecting Redmond and his new National Volunteers.

1916   Easter Rising is crushed. Public opinion is profoundly influenced by execution of leaders.

1917   Eamon de Valera is elected president of Sinn Féin.

1918   Sinn Féin wins 73 of 105 seats in the general election.

1919   Dáil Éireann, an independent Irish parliament, meets but is attended only by Sinn Féin deputies.

Sinn Féin is refused admission to Peace Conference in Paris.

War of Independence begins.

1920   The War of Independence escalates, exacerbated partly by sectarian conflict between Ulster Unionist Protestants and Irish nationalist Catholics.

British establish Northern Ireland in Government of Ireland Act.

1921   Edward Carson resigns as Ulster Unionist leader and is succeeded by his deputy, Sir James Craig, as first prime minister of Northern Ireland.

British and Sinn Féin agree to a truce in July.

December 6, the Anglo-Irish Treaty.

1922   De Valera rejects Anglo-Irish Treaty, but the Dáil approves it by 64–57.

The Dáil elects Arthur Griffith as president of the Dáil in place of de Valera by 60 to 58, and Michael Collins becomes chairman of the Provisional Government.

Special Powers Act in Northern Ireland.

Civil war breaks out in South in June 1922, lasting until May 1923.

Constitution in conformity with the Anglo-Irish Treaty is introduced.

Griffith dies, Collins is killed, and W. T. Cosgrave becomes president of the executive council (prime minister).

1932	De Valera's Fianna Fail (Soldiers of Destiny) Party triumphs in general election.
1937	De Valera's new constitution.
1939–1945	Ireland remains neutral in World War II.
1949	Ireland is declared a republic.
1968–1970	Outbreak of "Troubles" in Northern Ireland.
1972	After a "Bloody Sunday" in the city of Derry, in which British paratroopers fire on demonstrators, killing thirteen, the British government invokes the Government of Ireland Act of 1920 to suspend the Northern Ireland parliament and impose direct rule from London.
1998	The Good Friday Agreement, involving the British and Irish governments, and the unionist and nationalist sides in Northern Ireland, although neither is fully represented in the signatures to the agreement, establishes a Northern Ireland Assembly based on a commitment to equality of civil rights within Northern Ireland and a united Ireland only with the consent of the electorates of both Northern Ireland and the Irish Republic.

INTRODUCTION

Ever since the first invasion of Ireland by English forces in 1169, English/British military power has been central to Irish history. While military fortunes fluctuated until the whole country was brought under complete English control in the seventeenth century, and while the immediate issues were often more complex than simple direct confrontation between English power and Irish resistance, nevertheless English power determined the framework within which Irish history would play out over the centuries. The events of the Irish Revolution cannot be understood unless located in this historical context.

BACKGROUND: CULTURE AND HISTORY

Controversy still swirls around the issue of whether the events that culminated in the establishment of the Irish Free State in 1922 can be termed a revolution. Was the Irish War of Independence, 1919–1921, which succeeded in persuading the British to abandon their military control of about three-quarters of the island, the territory covered by the new Irish Free State, a revolution? It might seem that the revocation of the Act of Union of 1800, which declared Ireland an integral part of the United Kingdom "in perpetuity," abolishing the Irish parliament, was of sufficient importance to merit the designation. Yet many reject the term, particularly those claiming that all that happened was that an Irish bourgeois regime superseded a British one. If approached purely on the basis of class, that was largely true, even if there were significant differences between the old and new ruling classes even in class terms. From that perspective, Ireland during the War of Independence experienced, in a celebrated phrase, "the social revolution that never was" (Lynch 1966, 41), mainly because the urban working class failed to gain immediate concrete advantages from the creation of the new state.

This, however, is to adopt too dogmatic a definition of revolution in colonial circumstances. Since 1800, Irish politics had come to revolve around the issue of the union, with public opposition crystallizing into a mass political movement by the 1840s. In general, Catholics, constituting about 75 percent of the population, and mostly descended from the Gaelic people conquered by the English during the long struggle between the English invasion in 1169 and the crushing Gaelic defeat at Kinsale in 1601, now opposed the union, while the big majority of Protestants, predominantly descended from the conquering Protestant armies and the plantation of English and Scottish settlers in the sixteenth and seventeenth centuries, now strongly supported it. In a colonial situation, in which foreign conquest determines the parameters within which public life is conducted, the fundamental criterion of revolution is the degree of the undoing of conquest, in both physical and psychological terms. By that criterion the Irish achievement, for all its incomplete nature, was quite extraordinary.

Fundamental though the British military withdrawal in 1922 was, its full significance can be appreciated only if it is placed in the context of the forty-year period from 1881 to 1921. Over that period, Ireland experienced a threefold revolution: social, cultural, and political.

CONTEXT AND PROCESS OF REVOLUTION

The idea of a social revolution may appear strange, given the fact that the urban working class did not achieve an enhanced status in the Irish Free State. But the urban working class constituted no more than 15 percent of the earning population of the new Irish Free State. The real social revolution was the destruction of landlord power and the creation of a peasant proprietorship that began with Gladstone's major Land Act of 1881. That act constituted the essence of a true social revolution in the sense of shifting the balance of fundamental socioeconomic power from about 10,000 landlords to about 500,00 tenant farmers, who constituted nearly 50 percent of the earning population. The process imposed by the 1881 Land Act transferred the authority to set rents from the landlords to an independent Land Commission, and revoked the power of landlords to evict tenants except for failure to pay those officially determined rents, generally set well below the previous ones.

The "Land Question" would be finally settled only through a sequence of acts that bought out the landlords, mainly before 1921, ultimately through compulsory sale. Although the purchase terms were generous, the land legislation meant the death of a ruling class in the countryside, a revolutionary change in power and status relations. That social revolution did not preclude occasional bitter social conflict within the agricultural population, involving landless laborers, small farmers, and strong farmers (big tillage farmers, big dairy farmers, and graziers), which would continue to smolder in the Free State. Nevertheless, the destruction of landlord power marked a huge real and psychological shift in a social power structure that was based ultimately on conquest. Given that the bulk of the landlord class, and of its dependent social and economic clientele, was Protestant and unionist, the fall of landlordism involved a significant undermining of the political standing of the unionist population, except in the northeast, where Protestants were in a majority.

Gladstone's Land Act of 1881 came as a response to the Land War waged by the Land League established in 1879 to combat the threat of rising evictions in the face of an agricultural crisis that activated the memory of the Great Famine of 1845–1852. This was the vein into which Charles Stewart Parnell (1846–1891), the rising leader of the Nationalist Party, campaigning for Home Rule, tapped when exhorting tenants in 1879 to "keep a firm grip of your homesteads and lands. Do not allow yourselves to be dispossessed as you were dispossessed in 1847" (Lyons 1977, 92). The Land War of 1879–1881, a remarkably extensive and well-organized campaign, combined public meetings, local and national election campaigns, rent strikes, boycotts, and assaults, sometimes fatal, on landlords and their agents. Although Britain ultimately ruled Ireland through her military power, a succession of British governments came to the conclusion that popular hostility toward the landlord class made it more in Britain's interest to buy out the landlords than to shore them up through repeated military and/or armed police actions.

The cultural strand in the Irish Revolution included the founding of a national sports organization, the Gaelic Athletic Association, in 1884; a literary revival associated in particular with W. B. Yeats and Lady Gregory, and the Abbey Theatre they founded as an explicitly national theater in 1904; and above all a language revival organization, the Gaelic League, established in 1893. The intimacy of the relationship between the cultural and political revolutions is reflected in the fact that the most important leaders of the 1916 Easter Rising, and the subsequent War of Independence, had "gone to school in the Gaelic League." The leader of the 1916 Rising, Patrick Pearse, had edited the Gaelic League newspaper, and the key leaders during the War of Independence, Eamon de Valera and Michael Collins, Arthur Griffith and Richard Mulcahy, were also Gaelic Leaguers. It was Pearse himself who wrote in 1913 that "when the seven men met in O'Connell Street to found the Gaelic League they were commencing not a revolt . . . but a revolution" (Pearse 1952 [1913], 94–95).

The essence of that cultural revolution was a recovery of pride in native culture. The Irish language, the vernacular of about 4 million people in 1845, declined dramatically during and after the Great Famine of 1845–1852, which took a terrible toll among the poor, who were disproportionately Irish speakers. Subsequently the teaching of English and the suppression of Irish in the state system of national schools led to the rapid decline of Irish, with the general approbation of parents induced to consider Irish as inferior or useless. The intellectuals who drove the Gaelic League, Dr. Douglas Hyde, later professor of Irish at University College Dublin, part of the new National University, and Eoin MacNeill, later renowned as a historian of Celtic Ireland and also a professor of history at UCD, sought first to halt the decline of Irish as a spoken language and then to revive it sufficiently to make Ireland at least a bilingual country.

Language was the cutting edge of cultural revival, which also embraced music, place names, personal names—everything that sought to inculcate pride in a distinctive Gaelic identity. The Gaelic League launched a cultural revolution by striving to overcome the self-image of inferiority that the dominance of English cultural power had inculcated in much of the population. As the conquerors projected their culture as superior, and as large numbers of the conquered internalized this image of inferiority, the Gaelic League was engaged in a conflict about the very essence of Irish identity. The issue was whether it was the destiny of Ireland to become an imitation culture, or whether it would be able to build a distinctive cultural identity, partly on the remnants of the old Gaelic culture, rapidly disappearing in the face of the apparently remorseless progress of Anglicization.

Appealing partly to the resentment felt by the growing lower-middle-class Catholic population—increasingly educated and increasingly frustrated by the disdain of English cultural supremacists, represented most volubly by professors of Trinity College Dublin, the intellectual bastion of unionism—the league achieved a major victory in making Irish a required subject for entry to the new National University in 1908.

The same sense of self-worth, and spirit of self-reliance, that inspired the Gaelic League led to the founding of Sinn Féin by Arthur Griffith, an indefatigable nationalist journalist, himself a Gaelic Leaguer, in 1905. The translation history of Sinn Féin itself provides a revealing insight into the battle of two civilizations, as it came to be called. The term literally translates as "ourselves." As its detractors sought to depict Sinn Féin's self-reliant nationalism as obscurantist, ignorantly turning its back on the wider world, they chose to translate Sinn Féin not as "ourselves" but as "ourselves alone," to conjure up an image of insular isolationism. There were certainly insular isolationists in Sinn Féin. But many Sinn Féin leaders had a more intense interest in European affairs than had their unionist counterparts, who could rarely see beyond Britain, saturated with the assumption that Britain was the world. As Patrick Pearse himself put it, the more European Ireland became, the better. What Pearse meant by "European" was essentially pride in a distinctive culture of one's own, capable of contributing to the diversity of European culture.

Drawing on European precedents, Sinn Féin sought economic regeneration through the application of Friedrich List's protection for infant industries theory. It sought political regeneration through establishing an independent Irish parliament in a dual monarchy arrangement similar to that between Austria and Hungary. But if Sinn Féin was fertile in theory, it was weak in application. How were the ideas to be implemented? All Griffith could propose was that Irish members of parliament should withdraw from the British parliament and establish their own assembly in Dublin. Given that this would scarcely induce the British to withdraw their army, or disarm the police, Griffith could only advocate "passive resistance." As the main losers from passive resistance in the face of massive military force would be the passive resisters, it is hardly surprising that, for all its intellectual energy, Sinn Féin remained in electoral terms in a small minority compared with the Nationalist Party, much the biggest political movement in the country, still seeking Home Rule since 1900 under the leadership of John Redmond.

As the Nationalist Party never defined Home Rule precisely, this allowed it to secure the support of a wide spectrum of public opinion, which took it to mean, essentially, the greatest degree of independence that Ireland could achieve in the face of the overwhelming firepower of the British army: "In the popular perception . . . Home Rule transcended specific legal and political categories and denoted, quite simply, Irish control and Irish power. Home Rule was freely interpreted as the ending of the Union, the undoing of the con-

quest and the panacea for Irish problems" (John A. Murphy, quoted in Ward 1994, 87). The British command of firepower made the idea of rebellion so ludicrous that the handful of Irish nationalists in a small secret society, the Irish Republican Brotherhood (IRB), could be derisorily dismissed as impossibilists. Objectively, they were. The Irish rebellions of 1803, 1848, and 1867 had all failed, hopelessly, in military terms, however stirring a rebel tradition they bequeathed to later generations.

It was not until 1886, when Parnell's Nationalists took 85 out of 103 Irish seats and held the balance in the House of Commons, that a British party leader, Gladstone, accepted the right of Ireland to Home Rule. But even Gladstone could not carry the full Liberal Party with him, a section defecting to the Conservatives to defeat his proposal. Although Gladstone's second Home Rule bill did pass the House of Commons, it foundered in the House of Lords, controlled by the Conservatives, in 1893. In 1911, however, the power of the Lords to veto Commons legislation was restricted to a three-year period. Asquith, the Liberal prime minister, introduced a third Home Rule bill in 1912 that would now inevitably become law in 1914, with Redmond's nationalists holding the balance of power in the Commons—or so it appeared. What the assumption failed to anticipate was that Irish unionists would threaten revolt against Home Rule, and against any British government that sought to introduce it. These unionists acquired immensely powerful reinforcements from within Britain itself, when Andrew Bonar Law, leader of the Conservative Party, promised to support Ulster Unionists to any lengths they chose to go in resisting Home Rule, and supported the formation of an Ulster Volunteer Force (UVF) of about 100,000 men in 1913. This threat acquired real force when British officers in Ireland effectively preemptively refused to move against Ulster Unionists in the Curragh Mutiny of March 1914, and in April when the UVF landed 25,000 guns and 3,000,000 rounds of ammunition to make good their threat to defy any attempt to impose a Home Rule parliament (Alvin Jackson, in Connolly 1998, 363).

In reality, the powers of that parliament would be severely limited. The fundamental issue was the military one, and under the bill the British army would remain in Ireland, which could have no army of its own, and no foreign policy. Having in addition very limited economic autonomy, a Home Rule parliament would be little more than a glorified local government assembly.

Yet it roused intense unionist resentment. But however bitterly the 250,000 Irish unionists scattered through the south and west detested it, they could not effectively oppose it. But there was a substantial unionist population of nearly 900,000 in the nine counties of the northern province of Ulster, most of it clustered in the four northeastern counties, about one-eighth of the country (Lee 1989, 1–2). The mass signature by Ulster Unionists of a Solemn League and Covenant in September 1912, rejecting Home Rule by "all means that may be found necessary," demonstrated the widespread support among unionists for resistance.

Confident after the Curragh Mutiny that they were safe from the British army, Ulster Unionists were able to organize effective military resistance through the UVF. It might not have seemed that the Home Rule bill was worth opposing, so anemic were its provisions. But they were terrified that this would be the thin edge of the wedge of a drive toward a sovereign Irish state, which would in their minds, however elaborate the safeguards for their religion and property included in the bill, subject them to the tyrannical rule of the Catholic Church. Their fear was reflected in their favorite slogan, "Home Rule is Rome Rule," and also in the idea that Home Rule would destroy the flourishing industrial city of Belfast and the economy of Ulster, either through specific policies or simply the axiomatic incapacity of the Catholic Irish to manage anything economic.

Under the leadership of a commanding personality, the saturnine Dubliner Sir Edward Carson—a leading parliamentarian and outstanding public performer, strongly supported by the local Ulster Unionist organizations under the effective Sir James Craig, a prominent Presbyterian whiskey distiller, and backed by Bonar Law—Ulster Unionists resolved to resist Home Rule at all costs. Their own armed strength ensured that they could be compelled to come into a Home Rule Ireland only by the British army, which would not, or by a militarily superior Irish nationalist force, which could not—because there was no such force, though an Irish Volunteer movement was established in November 1913 as a response to the Ulster Volunteer Force. Even this did not derive from Redmond, but rather from an initiative of the Irish Republican Brotherhood, now resurrected through the work of Tom Clarke, a veteran Fenian revolutionary, and the younger Seán MacDermott. Under the public leadership of Eoin MacNeill, a founder of the Gaelic League twenty years earlier, the Irish Volunteers seized the opportunity offered by the arming of the UVF to establish a movement at least nominally in support of Home Rule. Without weapons, however, they were mainly aspirational, and had succeeded in bringing only about 1,500 guns ashore before World War I broke out (Connolly 1998, 251).

The war placed Redmond in a cruel dilemma. Home Rule was enacted in September 1914, but with its application immediately suspended until the end of the war and provision still to be made for Ulster, which in effect meant some form of partition. If Redmond didn't support the British, he would have no bargaining power whatever over partition at the end of the war, widely expected within a year, thus handing Carson, who was supporting the war, an impregnable negotiating position to demand partition not simply for the four

counties in which unionists had a majority but also for as much extra territory as they could militarily control.

Redmond's decision to support Britain split the Irish Volunteers. A big majority joined his new National Volunteers, but only about 20 percent of those actually joined the British army. The small minority, probably no more than 5 percent, who opposed him, formed the nucleus of the Irish Volunteer Movement, whose most active members, using Eoin MacNeill as a front, would plan for a rising on Easter Sunday in 1916.

The Easter Rising became a blood sacrifice. But the rising that actually broke out on Easter Monday of 1916 was not the intended rising. The rebels had envisaged a much more ambitious affair, relying on a substantial supply of weapons from Germany in time for a rising on Easter Sunday. When the aid from Germany—which fell far short in any case of their expectations—was intercepted by the British navy, and Eoin MacNeill, still the titular leader of the volunteers, issued a countermanding order for the mobilization announced for Easter Sunday, the rebel leaders hastily decided on a rising on Easter Monday. But the Easter Monday Rising, the organization in disarray, now with no hope of any effective action throughout the country in the absence of the intercepted weapons, was not the rising planned for Easter Sunday. That explains why the Proclamation of the Irish Republic read on that day declared that the rebels rose "in full confidence of victory." Those words were already a mockery at the time they were declaimed by Patrick Pearse on Easter Monday. But they hadn't been written for Easter Monday, but for the previous day. "Full confidence of victory" was still distinctly ambitious, under the circumstances. But it would have been less unrealistic on Easter Sunday than on Easter Monday.

The rising on Easter Monday had no chance whatever of success. The confusion about mobilization meant that only some 1,000 volunteers, and about 200 members of James Connolly's working-class Citizen Army, rose in hopeless rebellion, to be crushed within a week. Fifteen leaders were executed. It has been customary to claim that the rising was strongly denounced by public opinion, which regarded it as a stab in the back for Redmond. The real historical record is much more complex. The rising was indeed denounced by news media loyal to Redmond immediately following the surrender. It was naturally also denounced by unionists, who constituted a disproportionate section of the articulate Dublin press and the Dublin middle class. The evidence concerning the Dublin working class suggests that many of those with relatives fighting in France and drawing separation money were hostile to what they thought of as a German-supported rising, while many others were sympathetic. But it would be a mistake to see the rising in mainly class rather than national liberation terms. Even as committed a social revolutionary as James Connolly regarded national revolution as a prerequisite for social revolution.

It is impossible to be certain about real public opinion during the rising, because so little information was actually available to the public during the rising itself. As long as it could be presented as German inspired, it roused a good deal of resentment. Once more information began to filter through, however, public opinion appears to have been far more sympathetic. This sympathy is normally attributed, and clearly rightly, up to a point, to the revulsion at the executions. But it may have been also partly due simply to more accurate information, and to the realization that British propaganda about the rising as "made in Germany" was false.

The fundamental fact of Irish political life was the presence of overwhelming British military power. So habituated had the public become to this that they had come to accept it as normal. The executions tore aside the fictional facade that British rule in Ireland was, somehow, based on principles of democratic consent. After the rising it was no longer possible to sustain that fiction.

The Proclamation of the Irish Republic insisted on the right of the Irish people to determine their own government on the basis of a democratic franchise with full adult female as well as male suffrage—itself a revolutionary gesture at a time when no women had the vote.

The executions, together with the internment in Britain of more than 2,000 suspects, drove public opinion in the direction of Sinn Féin, even though Arthur Griffith's Sinn Féin organization had not been involved in the rising. But the British labeled the rising a Sinn Féin rising, and the name came to be attached to the growing republican movement after 1916. This new Sinn Féin began to make significant inroads into the Home Rule electoral base in by-elections, most spectacularly in a handsome victory for the East Clare parliamentary seat in July 1917 by Eamon de Valera, the senior surviving commandant of the rising, whose death sentence had been commuted. In October 1917, de Valera was elected president of Sinn Féin, Griffith being relegated to the vice presidency of his own party—although in reality it was no longer his party. Talented a journalist as Griffith was, however, his electoral appeal fell far short of that of de Valera, now wrapped and packaged in the colors of the Easter Rising.

The ability of the Home Rule Party to resist the rise of Sinn Féin was seriously damaged by Redmond's gullibility in agreeing to the proposal of David Lloyd George, dispatched by Asquith to Ireland in May 1916 to pick up the pieces after the rising: Redmond agreed to partition for a six-year period, as a quid pro quo for the granting of immediate Home Rule. When it emerged that Carson had also agreed to this proposal, but on the written assurance that partition was to be permanent, Redmond was exposed as a dupe in accepting a fraudulent British promise.

As Redmond's star waned, so that of de Valera waxed. In an ironic twist, Redmond would die in March 1918, the same month that a British move to impose conscription on Ireland further alienated Irish public opinion and drove more potential voters in the direction of Sinn Féin as the only effective defense of Irish interests against British policy. The following month the British compounded their political ineptitude by arresting several Sinn Féin leaders whom they falsely accused of involvement in a "German plot."

The electoral rise of Sinn Féin was consolidated in a dramatic general election victory in December 1918, when it won 73 of 105 Irish seats, compared with 26 Unionist and 6 Home Rule. Sinn Féin campaigned as the inheritor of the legacy of the Easter Rising, proclaiming itself the Republican Party and asserting its intention of renewing the struggle for a republic by establishing an Irish parliament (the Dáil) in Dublin and refusing to attend the British parliament, whose right to rule Ireland it utterly rejected. While it approved of all means to expel the British army, it argued that a further rebellion would not be necessary. Instead it proposed to present Ireland's claim for independence before the Peace Conference in Paris, on the grounds that the application of President Wilson's principle of the right to national self-determination would guarantee a sovereign Irish state. What it could not explain was how a victor in the war, Britain, could be compelled to observe this principle. When Sinn Féin was inevitably refused admittance to the Peace Conference, the leaders found themselves increasingly dependent on the volunteers, gradually coming to be known as the Irish Republican Army (IRA), to challenge British firepower.

Recognizing the importance of securing weapons, IRA activity during 1919 consisted mainly of raids on police to capture their arms. Indeed, it remains one of the extraordinary achievements of the IRA that a few thousand badly armed men were able in 1921 to hold down more than 40,000 British soldiers, in addition to more than 10,000 armed police and about 10,000 specially recruited terror squads, the Black and Tans and the Auxiliaries (Elizabeth Malcolm, in Connolly 1998, 32, 47). Not all of the British military were operationally active at any given time, but the IRA had no more than 3,300 operational guns at their peak. Yet if the IRA achievement was extraordinary in purely military terms, it nevertheless depended heavily on three further factors.

First was widespread public support. The IRA could not have survived as fish in the water if the currents did not run deep.

Secondly, the counter intelligence squads of the IRA, particularly under the control of Michael Collins, succeeded in killing enough spies to keep the British in the dark about many IRA activities. Previous Irish rebellions had been rendered ineffectual by infiltration of rebel movements. That happened to a much lesser extent in 1919–1921. Although British intelligence improved in 1921, the degree of success did not suffice to achieve military victory by the summer.

Michael Collins, military leader of Sinn Féin and director of intelligence in the Irish Republican Army (IRA) during the early twentieth century. (Library of Congress)

Nevertheless, military victory could have been achieved if the British had applied their full potential force. The third factor therefore in permitting relative IRA success was that the British didn't punch their full military weight. Why not? There were two main reasons.

Firstly, Sinn Féin propaganda achieved outstanding success in exploiting British brutality, exerting an enormous influence on liberal opinion in Britain, which took the view that if Ireland could not be held by civilized means, it was contrary to British values that it should be held at all. Furthermore, de Valera spent eighteen months, from June 1919 to December 1920, in the United States in an attempt to persuade the administration to recognize the Irish Republic. Although he failed, the attention devoted to Irish affairs influenced the British government to seek a solution in Ireland at a time when relations with the United States were highly sensitive.

Secondly, for the first time since the sixteenth century, the English did not have to fear that Ireland could be used as a backdoor by a hostile Continental power. The Irish nationalist slogan "England's danger is Ireland's opportunity" was politically uncomprehending. An England in mortal danger could not afford to risk losing Ireland at any cost.

Nevertheless, despite the growing revulsion in sectors of public opinion in Britain, the dominions, and the United States, British military power remained crucial. It was this power that enabled the British to partition Ireland under the Government of Ireland Act of 1920. That not only established Northern Ireland but also accepted the opinion of Ulster Unionist leaders in opting for a Northern Ireland of six northeastern counties, instead of the four with unionist majorities. Unionists had a 65 percent majority in the entire area, because of their heavy majority in the four counties. But they were in a minority over roughly half the land area of the new Northern Ireland. It was not percentages, however, but calculations of military power that decided both the principle of partition and the line of the actual border. By insisting on incorporating so large a nationalist minority, unionists stored up for themselves problems that would surface with a vengeance fifty years later.

The British government imposed the line of partition at the urging of Ulster Unionists. Even without the support of the British army, the firepower of the Ulster Volunteer Force, reconstituted after World War I and far superior to that of the IRA, would have allowed it to determine where the border would be drawn.

It was only when they had Ireland safely partitioned that the British turned toward disengaging from the rest of the island. Within a month of the opening of the Northern Ireland parliament in June 1921, a truce was arranged with the IRA from July 11. Following months of negotiation in London, a treaty was signed on December 6, 1921.

That should have been, despite partition, the beginning of a new chapter in Anglo-Irish relations. But the Irish delegation—led by Griffith and including Collins, but not de Valera, who remained in Ireland on the grounds that he could best preserve the unity of Sinn Féin if he were not directly involved—signed the treaty under Lloyd George's threat of immediate and terrible war. The treaty was in effect a diktat. The decisive issue was the oath of fidelity to the king that the British required from all members elected to the Irish parliament. This would oblige Dáil members to renege on their basic political loyalty and engage in an act of fealty to British power. After agonizing over the threat, the delegates concluded that they had no alternative but to sign. Decisive, in the view of the immensely reluctant Collins, was British military superiority.

The oath led to civil war. Partition was not directly an issue, but this was not because it wasn't deemed highly important. It was rather because the British negotiators, by including a clause that a Boundary Commission would be established to revise the boundary, led the Irish representatives to persuade themselves that partition was simply a temporary arrangement.

De Valera opposed the treaty. His alternative, Document No. 2, jettisoned the oath, searching for a middle ground between the ideological purity of monarchy on the one hand and republic on the other. It kept the king but not as king of Ireland: only as head of the Commonwealth, which Ireland would join voluntarily, while retaining veto powers over Commonwealth decisions. In deference to English susceptibilities, however, de Valera did not employ the term "republic" but proposed instead that the new state would simply be called "Ireland." This was far too subtle for both doctrinaire monarchists and doctrinaire republicans. Although Collins grasped it, he was committed to the treaty, in the belief that the alternative was the unleashing of a campaign of British terror. The Dáil carried the treaty by 64 to 57 and elected Griffith president of the Dáil, if only by a 60 to 58 majority, over de Valera. The crucial post, however, was chairman of the Provisional Government, which was charged with implementing the treaty; it was Collins who filled that post.

Collins, who remained at heart a republican, sought in effect to smuggle Document No. 2 into the proposed Constitution of the Free State, but this was blocked by the British, who would claim veto rights over the Irish constitution until de Valera, having come into government in 1932, successfully submitted his own constitution for adoption by referendum in 1937. Much of de Valera's thinking would become accepted in the Commonwealth a generation later, but in 1922 it was too sophisticated for imperial mindsets. All that de Valera had was words. His enemies, Ulster Unionists, protreaty Irish, and British, had one thing in common. They all had guns.

Although de Valera took the anti-treaty side in the civil war that broke out in June 1922, he was effectively marginalized until the main anti-treaty military commanders were killed by May 1923, when he induced the survivors to dump arms. Fought essentially over the oath, the civil war was therefore less a civil war in the Finnish, Russian, or Spanish sense of a social conflict than a continuation of the Anglo-Irish war under another name. There was nevertheless some social element in the civil war, in that the poorer sections of the population, particularly among the small farmers and agricultural laborers, were somewhat more likely to oppose the treaty than the better off, who had far more to lose from a resumption of the conflict than the poor. But it would be a mistake to regard the social dimension as remotely as important as the political.

IMPACTS

By the summer of 1923, the pro-treaty government under W. T. Cosgrave was firmly in control of the Irish Free State. In Northern Ireland the Unionist government had crushed attempts by Irish nationalists to destabilize the new state and enjoyed complete military control. But the civil war left a legacy of bitterness that poisoned Irish politics for half a century. Even today, the two biggest parties, Fianna Fail, founded by de Valera in 1926, and Fine Gael, long led by Cosgrave, owe their origins to the civil war split. And in Northern Ireland, politics is still dominated by the partition issue.

The victory of the pro-treaty forces in the civil war, particularly given the emergence of the more conservative elements following the sudden death of Griffith at the age of fifty-two, and the killing of Collins in an ambush at the age of thirty-one, both in August 1922, led to the institution of a more conservative regime than had appeared likely a year earlier. At that time, de Valera, and to some extent Collins, had represented a socioeconomic policy more sympathetic to the people of small or no property, and Griffith had a strong commitment to economic growth. The introduction of policies sympathetic to the plight of the rural poor and the urban working class had to await the arrival of de Valera in power in 1932.

By 1923, then, the contours of the consequences of the three strands of the Irish Revolution could begin to be seen, though various futures were still possible. English/British physical control of Ireland, which had begun in the twelfth century and which had been complete for more than 300 years, had been broken. True, partition would remain a festering sore, and British cultural influence would prove more difficult to escape. But whatever criticism may be made of the Cosgrave government from 1922 to 1932, it cannot be said that it could not rule. Socially modestly reactionary, economically modestly conservative, politically it proved highly successful in sustaining stability in often challenging circumstances, and rendered a final service in handing over power peacefully to its civil war enemies when de Valera and his new party, Fianna Fail (Soldiers of Destiny), won the general election of 1932. De Valera adopted a policy more sympathetic to the poorer sectors of society, if in evolutionary rather than revolutionary terms. He implemented the essence of Document No. 2, consolidated in a new constitution, legitimized through referendum in 1937, and maintained formal neutrality in World War II, though it was not until 1949 that a republic was officially proclaimed. Ultimately, the political revolution was for the right of the Irish people to rule themselves according to their own freely given consent. With the British army gone, independent Ireland became one of the most peaceful states in the modern world.

In Northern Ireland the Unionist Party remained in power from 1921, with Irish nationalists effectively excluded from positions of state authority. Their resistance to the new state was decisively crushed by the Special Powers Act in April 1922, which would be made permanent in 1933.

Only with growing Catholic/Irish nationalist resistance in the 1960s, increasingly dominated from 1970 by the Provisional IRA's demand for a united Ireland, leading to the collapse of the Northern Ireland parliament in 1972 and the reversion to direct rule from London, did the settlement of 1920–1921 unravel. The Good Friday Agreement of 1998 sought to restore a Northern Ireland parliament, but now on the basis of "parity of esteem" between the roughly 55–60 percent unionists and the 40–45 percent Irish nationalists, rather than one-party rule—although insisting on partition until a majority in both North and South agreed to a united Ireland.

The international impact of the Irish Revolution was indirect. As the pioneer of successful anti-colonial struggles, the Irish experience was closely studied in several other countries. Both Bose and Nehru drew lessons for India from the Irish case, and more recently the Northern Ireland experience of conflict resolution has been examined closely in conflict areas around the world. The struggle for the protection and revival of the Irish language is still ongoing. The Gaelic League did not make Ireland Irish-speaking again. But it did halt the decline of Irish and helped to expand the base of Irish speakers in urban Ireland, where it had almost entirely died out. Although Ireland is an English-speaking country, the Irish language is more widely known than a century ago. Instead of being now dead, in 2005 it was declared an official working language of the European Union. Moreover, the Irish experience is becoming increasingly relevant to a world in which more and more languages are coming under threat from the homogenizing power of English, and in which issues of cultural identity promise to significantly influence the nature of global society in the twenty-first century.

The Irish Revolution was in many respects incomplete. But it was nonetheless a revolution. The scale of a revolution has to be measured in terms of the forces it confronted. The British empire was the greatest in the world. How then does one take the measure of the men and women who were the first to break the physical and loosen the mental grip of that empire on a small people, defying overwhelming odds? In assessing revolution in small countries striving to escape from conquest by incomparably more powerful ones, one must look at what the change prevented as well as what it achieved. One must take the most plausible alternatives into account in the sense of projecting what would have happened—the effective disappearance of any distinctive Irish national identity—but for the revolutionary movements. A twenty-year-old who had prophesied in 1880 that he or she expected to live to see landlord power smashed, the Irish language still vibrant, and the British army gone, bullet and bayonet, out of an Irish Free State, would have been deemed crazy. But it all came to pass.

PEOPLE AND ORGANIZATIONS

Collins, Michael (1890–1922)

Born onto a medium-size farm, he fought in the 1916 Rising. The main organizer of Sinn Féin in the 1918 general election, and of the IRA in the War of Independence, 1919–1921, he reluctantly signed the treaty with Britain in 1921 and became the dominant figure in political as well as military life as chairman of the Provisional Government to implement the treaty that he hated. Sought desperately and unavailingly to avoid civil war with former comrades, and was killed in an ambush.

Parnell

Cosgrave, William T. (1880–1965)

Fought in the 1916 Rising and served in de Valera's cabinet after 1919. Generally careful and managerial rather than adventurous, he supported the treaty with Britain and became prime minister—technically president of the Executive Council, 1922–1932—following the deaths of Collins and Griffith. His most important service was to resist pressure for a military coup to forestall de Valera's assumption of power following his election victory in 1932.

De Valera, Eamon (1882–1975)

De Valera was born in New York and sent home to Ireland at the age of two by his mother after his father's death to be reared in an agricultural laborer's cottage. He rose through scholarships and was active in the Gaelic League and the Irish Volunteers; he was sentenced to death in 1916 but his sentence was commuted, and he became president of Sinn Féin in 1917 and of the republic proclaimed by the Dáil in 1919. De Valera opposed the treaty with Britain but had little control over anti-treaty forces. He founded his own party, Fianna Fail, in 1926, which since 1932 has remained the largest political party. He was prime minister (taoiseach) 1932–1948, 1951–1954, 1957–1959, and president 1959–1973, a strong advocate of a distinctive Irish identity, widely regarded as the most consummate Irish politician of the century.

Griffith, Arthur (1871–1922)

A printer and newspaper editor, Griffith founded Sinn Féin in 1905. Vice president and foreign minister of the republic in 1921, he led the delegation that signed the treaty with Britain, which he vigorously defended. Elected president of the Dáil in January 1922, he was less central than Collins to subsequent decision making. Died from a cerebral hemorrhage in August 1922.

Irish Republican Army (IRA)

This is the name gradually acquired by the Irish Volunteers during the War of Independence, 1919–1921. The IRA split on the treaty with Britain, forming the bulk of the anti-treaty forces in the civil war. It subsequently had a checkered existence, small groups mounting bombing campaigns in Britain in 1940 and in Northern Ireland in 1956–1957, before enjoying a dramatic revival during the Northern Ireland struggle since 1970.

Irish Republican Brotherhood (IRB)

The IRB was a secret society established in conjunction with the Fenian revolutionary organization from 1858 in both Ireland and the United States. U.S. support played a key role, not least in the planning of the 1916 Rising. Michael Collins became its president during the War of Independence. It dissolved in 1924.

Parnell, Charles Stewart (1846–1891)

Although himself a Protestant landlord, Parnell achieved remarkable success in turning the Nationalist Party into a formidable mass movement for Home Rule after accomplishing major land reforms in 1881–1882. Having converted British prime minister Gladstone to Home Rule in 1885–1886, he appeared poised for success with the imminent return of Gladstone to power when he split his party in 1890 through a divorce case that led to Gladstone's threatening to abandon Home Rule as long as Parnell was leader.

Pearse, Patrick (1879–1916)

Patrick Pearse was the son of an English artisan and an Irish mother; he became a passionate cultural nationalist, editing the Gaelic League newspaper 1903–1909. Pearse established his own school, in which he applied progressive educational techniques. He became a powerful literary polemicist, advocating a spiritual rather than a material sense of nationality. Initially supporting Redmond, he became disenchanted and moved to a strong republican position, joining the IRB and becoming convinced of the need for a rising during World War I, however hopeless the prospects; nevertheless, he worked hard to import weapons. He was a leader of the rising and was virtually deified in republican tradition after his execution.

Redmond, John (1856–1918)

A middle-class leader of the reunited Nationalist Party after 1900, Redmond persuaded Asquith to steer Home Rule through parliament. But the act remained stillborn during World War I, in which Redmond strongly supported Britain, with the Ulster Question remaining unsettled. He gradually lost his authority after the Easter Rising of 1916.

Sinn Féin (Ourselves)

This movement was established by Arthur Griffith in 1905 to foster self-reliance. It has experienced many metamorphoses since the first in 1917 when it was commandeered by survivors of the 1916 Rising, then led by de Valera. Subsequently it was used as a political shell by various IRA activists. It has emerged as the largest Irish nationalist party in Northern Ireland, and in the republic it has established a foothold in the Dáil, leaving it now the only all-Ireland party.

Ulster Volunteer Force (UVF)

The Ulster Volunteer Force was established in 1913 to organize Ulster Unionist military resistance to Home Rule. Outstandingly successful after importing a substantial supply of weapons in 1914, it constituted a major part of the 36th Ulster Division, which fought bravely in World War I, suffering heavily at the Somme. It was largely reconstituted in 1920 to continue pre-war defense of Ulster Unionist interests during the War of Independence, and then as an Ulster special constabulary in 1921 to suppress Catholic dissidents. An organization of the same name emerged from 1969 to resist Catholic demands, especially through sectarian assassination.

J. J. Lee

See Also Colonialism, Anti-Colonialism, and Neo-Colonialism; Documentaries of Revolution; Elites, Intellectuals, and Revolutionary Leadership; Ethnic and Racial Conflict: From Bargaining to Violence; Literature and Modern Revolution; Nationalism and Revolution; Terrorism; War and Revolution

References and Further Readings
Boyce, D. G. 1972. *Englishmen and Irish Troubles: British Public Opinion and the Making of Irish Policy 1918–22.* London: Jonathan Cape.
Connolly, S. J., ed. 1998. *Oxford Companion to Irish History.* Oxford: Oxford University Press.
Coogan, Tim Pat. 1990. *Michael Collins.* London: Hutchinson.
Farrell, Brian, ed. 1994. *The Creation of the Dáil.* Dublin: Gill and Macmillan.
Fitzpatrick, David. 1998. *Politics and Irish life, 1913–1921: Provincial Experience of War and Revolution.* Cork: Cork University Press.
Hennessey, Thomas. 1998. *Dividing Ireland: World War I and Partition.* New York: Routledge.
Hopkinson, Michael. 1988. *Green against Green: The Irish Civil War.* Dublin: Gill and Macmillan.
———. 2002. *The Irish War of Independence.* Dublin: Gill and Macmillan.
Hoppen, Theo. 1998. *Ireland since 1800: Conflict and Conformity.* New York: Longmans.
Jackson, Alvin. 1999. *Ireland 1798–1998: Politics and War.* Oxford: Oxford University Press.
Keogh, Dermot. 1994. *Twentieth Century Ireland: Nation and State.* Dublin: Gill and Macmillan.
Laffan, Michael. 1999. *The Resurrection of Ireland: The Sinn Féin Party 1916–1923.* Cambridge: Cambridge University Press.
Lee, J. J. 1973. *The Modernisation of Irish Society, 1848–1918.* Dublin: Gill and Macmillan.
———. 1989. *Ireland 1912–1985: Politics and Society.* Cambridge: Cambridge University Press.
Lynch, Patrick. 1966. "The Social Revolution that Never Was." Pp. 41–54 in *The Years of the Great Struggle, 1916–26,* edited by Desmond Williams. Dublin: Gill and Macmillan.
Lyons, F. S. L. 1971. *Ireland since the Famine.* London: Hutchinson.
———. 1977. *Parnell.* London: Collins.
Mansergh, Nicholas. 1975. *The Irish Question 1840–1921.* London: Allen and Unwin.
Maume, Patrick. 1999. *The Long Gestation: Irish Nationalist Life 1891–1918.* Dublin: Gill and Macmillan.
Murphy, John A. 1975. *Ireland in the Twentieth Century.* Dublin: Gill and Macmillan.
Pearse, Patrick H. 1952. "The Coming Revolution." Pp. 94–95 in *Political Writings and Speeches.* Dublin: Talbot.
Ward, Alan J. 1994. *The Irish Constitutional Tradition.* Dublin: Irish Academic Press.

Islamic Fundamentalist Revolutionary Movement

CHRONOLOGY

632–661   The period of the Rashidun, or "rightly guided," caliphs, the first four leaders of the new Islamic world who had had direct personal contact with the prophet Muhammad, who died in 632. The Rashidun period ends in 661 with the death of Ali, the fourth caliph, who is the prophet's cousin and son-in-law.

680   The killing of Ali's son, Hussein, near Karbala begins the lasting division within Islam between the Sunni and the Shia. The Shia ("Shi'at Ali," or "Partisans of Ali") believe that the legitimate leaders of Islam after the prophet Muhammad are first Ali, and then later certain male descendants of Ali and his wife, the prophet's daughter Fatima.

1258   The Mongols capture the Islamic city of Baghdad. Despite the fact that some Mongol leaders convert to Islam, Islamic jurist Ibn Taymiyya (1263–1328) argues that Mongols must abandon their *yasa* code of honor and accept the teachings of Islam, particularly Islamic law, in their entirety or they cannot be true Muslims. This view becomes a justification for leaders of the *neo-salafi*, or *salafi-*

jihadi, movement within Islam (which begins in the 1980s) to criticize Muslims who fail, in their view, to fully manifest the original values of Islam.

1501   The first Safavid shah, Abbas, decides to make Shia Islam the official religion of Persia (Iran).

1744   An alliance is formed between the al-Saud family and the Islamic revivalist religious leader Muhammad ibn Abd al-Wahhab that leads to the Saudi conquest of Saudi Arabia and the establishment of the conservative Wahhabi version of Islam there.

1798   Napoléon's forces conquer Egypt and modern Europe occupies Islamic Arab territories for the first time. This shocks many Islamic leaders into a realization of European technological superiority compared with most Islamic societies at the time.

1860s   Jamal al-Din al-Afghani's argument that Islamic societies could find the inspiration to develop the institutions necessary to compete with European nations by returning to the Islamic vision current in the Rashidun period creates the *salafiyya* movement. The movement advocates learning from the *salaf* (the ancestors) of the Rashidun period in order to confront modernity.

1917   The British government announces support for the Zionist Movement, which seeks a homeland for the Jewish people. The new homeland, it declares, will be located in Palestine, which is then overwhelmingly populated by Arabs.

1928   The Ikhwan Muslimin, the Muslim Brotherhood, is created in Ismailiyya in Egypt by Hassan al-Banna as the first Islamic political movement.

1948   The state of Israel is created by UN fiat against Arab and Muslim protest.

1966   Execution of Sayyid Qutb in Egypt, who had criticized the legitimacy of governments in Islamic societies for failing to embody Islamic values and ideals properly.

1967   Israeli victory over Egypt, Syria, and Jordan in the "Six-Day War" results in the occupation of the West Bank and the Gaza Strip, weakening the appeal of Arab nationalism and increasing support for revivified Islamist movements.

1970s   Ayatollah Khomeini gives a series of lectures in Najaf, Iraq, in which he argues that the political process requires the guidance of a religious leader, the jurisconsult.

1979   The Islamic Revolution succeeds in Iran.

1979–1989   Tens of thousands of Islamic volunteers from the Muslim world, predominantly from the Middle East and including Osama bin Laden of Saudi Arabia, combat Soviet forces in Afghanistan and, together with Afghani fighters, eventually force them to withdraw. Many of the surviving volunteers form an international network, al-Qaeda, to fight the perceived enemies of Islam.

1981   President Sadat of Egypt is assassinated by Islamic extremists.

1990–1991   Following the expulsion of Iraqi forces from Kuwait, the United States establishes an expanded military presence in Saudi Arabia, which is violently opposed by Osama bin Laden and other al-Qaeda members.

1993   The New York World Trade Center towers are attacked by a truck bomb constructed and detonated by Islamic extremists.

1997   Members of extremist Egyptian Islamist groups provide al-Qaeda with new leaders.

1998   Al-Qaeda associates bomb the U.S. embassies in Kenya and Tanzania.

2001   On September 11, al-Qaeda associates use passenger aircraft to attack the United States, destroying the two New York World Trade Center towers.

2004   March 11: Islamic extremists bomb trains in Madrid, contributing to the electoral victory of the Spanish Socialist Party. The new

Spanish government decides to withdraw Spanish soldiers from the U.S.-led alliance occupying Iraq.

2005   July 7: Islamic extremist suicide bombers attack the London public transport system.

INTRODUCTION

In the wake of the events of September 11, 2001, there has been a growing concern in Europe and the United States that a new phenomenon, intrinsically opposed to the secular values of democratic society, has emerged in the Islamic world. There is also a widespread conviction, despite disclaimers by politicians, that such opposition and the violence that accompanies it is in some way inherent in Islam. This has lent massive support to the concept of the "clash of civilizations" proposed by Samuel Huntington in a famous article in *Foreign Affairs* in 1993. These views have been given specific intellectual content in the publications of a leading Orientalist, Bernard Lewis, who has argued that, in terms of historical experience, the Islamic world has failed to provide a fertile ground for the construction of democratic values and political processes. Indeed, revolutionary Islamic fundamentalism, according to Bernard Lewis, is the inevitable response to pressure toward such ends.

BACKGROUND: CULTURE AND HISTORY

The term "fundamentalism" arose in the early twentieth century in the United States to describe a specific form of Christian Protestantism that was committed to a literalist interpretation of the Bible and the inerrancy of scripture. In the Islamic context, it has been used to refer to the universal Muslim conviction that the invariant core of Islamic doctrine lies within the beliefs and practices of the Islamic world when its members had personal and direct experience of the prophet Muhammad: the period of the so-called Rashidun, or "rightly guided," caliphs. This period covered the reigns of the first four caliphs after the death of the prophet in A.D. 632, ending in the death of Ali, the prophet's cousin and son-in-law. But in many respects, "fundamentalist Islam" is a misnomer and a term that is not used in the Islamic world itself. Instead, those who reify the values of the Rashidun period are probably better defined by a neutral term, such as "Islamist," which is the term that will be used here.

The views of Samuel Huntington and Bernard Lewis, which suggest that the confrontation with the West is in some way inherent within the doctrinal and cultural content of Islam, as a result of profound ideological distinction and an inability to handle the challenge of modernity, overlook the historical context in which such a confrontation—if confrontation there be—is taking place. Instead, it could be argued, the crisis implicit in the concept of a revolutionary Islamist vision reflects a series of responses to specific political challenges, in which the ways that Muslims react may be culturally determined. Political and ideological confrontation between the developed and developing world, after all, is nothing new, and it reflects the profound asymmetries that emerge in such relationships, in which developing societies may respond to what they perceive as threats. Inflamed nationalism in which indigenous social and cultural norms are reinforced has often been such a response. The manipulation of Islamic doctrine and culture for such political ends, as has widely occurred in the Middle East and North Africa, especially since 1967, is no different. As Fouad Ajami (1981) points out, the phenomenon became a dominant political theme in the region because of the perceived bankruptcy of Arab nationalism in the wake of the Arab defeat in the Six-Day War in that year.

"Islamic fundamentalist revolution" is often a culturally determined political response to perceived external threat. It appears to be revolutionary because one of its objectives is a domestic transformation of the political scene on the grounds that only in that way can the external threat be effectively countered: it had been a domestic political failure that had allowed the threat to develop in the first place. Indeed, this, too, is nothing new. One of the justifications for extreme nationalism and Fascism in Europe was that this was the only way in which the resources of the nation could be mobilized to counter internationalist cultural and political threats, whether from Communism or other foreign conspiracies.

In short, there is nothing unique in the practice of "Islamic fundamentalist revolution" except the specific medium through which it justifies its practices. It is, in effect, a political response to perceived threat, characterized by the further perception that such a response needs to be legitimized in culturally and politically appropriate terms. This certainly applies to the modern phenomenon of "Islamic terrorism," insofar as such a phenomenon exists at all, for there is little difference between so-called Islamic terrorism and other forms of terrorism in terms of technique and objective—only in the justification used for it. If that is the case, then the sole feature that requires detailed consideration is the means by which such legitimization is achieved and the degree to which—if any—it may condition the nature of the response. To appreciate this requires an excursion into the sociopolitical implications of Islam and the way in which Islamic doctrine developed.

Politics and Islam

The links between Islamic doctrine and collective life have always been intimate and inextricably intertwined, certainly from the moment when the prophet Muhammad moved from Mecca to Medina at the request of the population there, to organize the life of the community and its environs. The relationship between the various groups involved was regulated by the Constitution of Medina (*Misaq al-Madinah*). The relationship that was ultimately to be more significant from a constitutional point of view, however, evolved after the prophet Muhammad's death ten years later, in A.D. 632. This was the concept that, since sovereignty over the Islamic community, the *umma,* was a divine attribute and since the ideal life was to be lived in accordance with the revelations of the Quran, Muslim society should be ordered for that primary purpose by those taking responsibility for it after the prophet's death.

Thus, those who ruled over the new Islamic world as the "deputies" (*khalifa*) of the deceased prophet had, as a primary duty, to preserve and facilitate that social order, so that faith (*din*) and society (*dunya*—the temporal world) were indissolubly linked. Inherent in this concept was the subsidiary concept that rulers who did not properly discharge such duties could and should be removed by the Islamic community, so that rule and obedience were contractually linked. Later additions emphasized other aspects of the relationship; thus *fitna* (discord) and *ridda* (apostasy) were not tolerated, for they disrupted the essential unity (*tawhid*) of the *umma.* This later hardened, under Persian influence as Islam conquered the non-Arab world to its east, into a vision of the caliph as the "shadow of God upon earth"—a view that stood very much at odds with the original political vision but that mirrored the overtly political view that unity could be more important than injustice.

Clearly, over time the original pure vision, derived from the time of the prophet himself, underwent change as the Muslim world expanded and adapted to the new challenges it met. Political theory had to evolve as well but was always to be judged against the original vision—hence the importance of the "rightly guided caliphs" as the touchstone of the orthodox golden age. As time went by, political dissatisfaction was articulated by reference back, not only to the original sources of Islam—the Quran and the sunna (the practices of the prophet Muhammad, including his sayings, the *hadith,* as well as the four schools of Sharia law, the Malaki, Hanafi, Shafi, and Hanbali *madhhabs*—but also by reference to the Rashidun period.

Thus political dissidence often expressed itself as a form of religious revisionism, seeking to re-create the lost perfection of the Rashidun period. On the other hand, rulers sought to dominate the religious sphere politically by controlling those recognized as embodying legitimate religious orthodoxy, the *ulama* and *faqihs*—individuals learned in *fiqh* (jurisprudence and theology)—to ensure that they should not be condemned as having failed in their declared political purpose. Their opponents often sought support from other scholars or scholarly movements—hence, for example, the alliance between the al-Saud family and the Wahhabi movement in the early eighteenth century that eventually led to the creation of the modern Saudi state two centuries later. The Wahhabi movement was created by Muhammad ibn Abd al-Wahhab (1703–1791), who decreed that no doctrine or practice originating after the end of the third Islamic century would be acceptable.

These revivalist movements, therefore, represent a recognized political tradition in Islamic history and were bound to find an echo once the Arab Islamic world, in particular, came into confrontation with the aggressive expansionism of nineteenth-century Europe. The key event in modern times that provided this challenge was the advent of colonialism in the Middle East, an experience that conventionally begins with the Napoleonic conquest of Egypt in 1798.

CONTEXT AND PROCESS OF REVOLUTION

The Colonial and Post-Colonial Confrontation

The French conquest was a profound cultural shock for Muslims, as it raised serious questions about their geopolitical assumptions, particularly about the innate supremacy of Muslim society, given European technological domination. Throughout the nineteenth century, Muslims sought to analyze and respond to this, basing their arguments on the need to find inside Islamic society itself the dynamism to respond to European occupation.

Salafiyyism

The most important response was generated in the 1860s by Jamal al-Din al-Afghani, who argued that Islam did indeed contain the elements of an effective response to apparent European superiority; it too could generate the institutions that Europe had exploited to achieve its predominance. The route to success lay in a revaluation of the past, to a search for the moral and doctrinal core from which the institutions of a modern state and society could be constructed. In other words, by understanding the true meaning of the *salaf,* those who preceded the modern world—a term usually confined to those who had had direct experience of the original world of Islam, in the Rashidun period—contemporary success and modernization could be achieved that would be consonant with Islamic values.

The ideas he put forward were enshrined in a movement known as the *salafiyya,* a modernist movement that inspired the early attempts to come to terms with the reality of European colonialism. Colonial powers, however, were loath to end their control or to compromise with it. Even more important, Britain began, after it acquired the Palestine mandate in 1921, to encourage the development of the Jewish community in Palestine as promised in the Balfour Declaration of 1917. This was widely seen as a direct challenge to the integrity of the Islamic *umma,* or community.

By the 1930s, little of the early optimism of the *salafiyya* movement remained, and, instead, Muslims began to consider how they could escape the colonial yoke. One answer, since European military power—at least until World War II—seemed impregnable, was to turn inward and re-Islamize society by example, demonstrating to a dispirited population the innate potential of Islam to revive their lives. This gave rise to the Ikhwan Muslimin, the Muslim Brotherhood, as an experiment in Islamic reformism, using the old traditions of revivalism to respond to the consequences of the colonial experience. Another, which developed particularly in the 1940s and was directed specifically at the corruption of governments and their acquiescence to European and—after 1945—increasingly U.S. demands, was urban guerrilla warfare and terrorism, a revolutionary response. On occasion the two went hand in hand, and behind both lay the shared fundamental conviction that the *salafiyya* would provide the path to success. Salafiyyism thus acquired a violent extremist fringe alongside the quietist search for self-improvement and revival.

The Muslim Brotherhood

The Ikhwan Muslimin, which was created in Ismailiyya, Egypt, in 1928 by Hassan al-Banna, was to become the model for all subsequent Islamist movements, whether quietist or violent, in the Sunni Muslim world. The Ikhwan sought a revival of the political and social role of Islam, as manifested in the early Islamic state, as the best means to confront the growth of secular Western influences and as the means through which modernization of the Islamic world could be achieved.

Although the movement initially sought to operate as a political party—and that was its innovative aspect—official antagonism in Egypt soon stimulated the growth of a clandestine faction, the Jihaz al-Khazz, which, in the late 1940s, engaged in attacks and assassinations of government officials, provoking official repression of the Ikhwan and the assassination of its leader. Although relations between the movement and the authorities improved after 1952 in the initial years of the Nasser regime, the movement was soon repressed again. This culminated in the execution, in 1966, of

Sayyid Qutb, who was one of the theoreticians of modern political Islam. He argued that the Muslim world was in a state of *jahiliyya* (ignorance) comparable to that which had existed before the advent of Islam, except that, in the modern world, such ignorance was culpable, since Islamic revelation to guide individual and collective life had already occurred. Governments that tolerated such behavior had, therefore, forfeited their legitimacy and should be replaced by true Islamic governance—*hukumiyya.*

Under the influence of such principles, the Egyptian Islamic movement split between those who renounced violence and sought influence through established government and those who rejected all such government, seeking instead its overthrow. The Ikhwan Muslimin, as an organized movement, always chose the former path of moderate reformism and has sought, as part of this process, a significant role within the al-Azhar mosque-university in Cairo, the center of orthodox Sunni Islam and a close collaborator with the Egyptian government. It has, since World War II, spread to many other countries, where it has often sought a recognized political role and, at times, when allowed, has actually participated in formal political life. It influenced other Islamist initiatives, such as those in Algeria, both political and violent, in the 1990s.

Other Islamist movements

The Ikhwan Muslimin's rejection of violence, despite official repression, meant that the activist arena was seized by other, more extreme Islamist movements from the end of the 1960s onward. Their appearance had been ushered in by the execution of Sayyid Qutb and by Egypt's defeat in the Six Days War in 1967. A group of populist Islamic preachers, such as Abdelhamid Kishk, began to popularize an Islamic political message in contradistinction to Arab nationalism, and clandestine Islamist groups seeking a violent alternative to existing government began to appear. Although their original motivation sprang from the Ikhwan tradition, these groups, which were not the result of a concerted campaign by a centralized organization and were not linked by any formal structure, maintained a loose network of contacts with radical theologians. One such was Sheikh Umar Abd ar-Rahman at the theological faculty in Assiyut and formerly of al-Azhar University, whose pronouncements (*fatwas*) were used to justify violent action. It was one such group, led by Khalid as-Stambouli, that assassinated President Sadat in 1981.

Alongside such groups, more organized clandestine movements began to form. One, the Hizb at-Tahrir al-Islami, created in 1951 in Beirut, sought specifically to restore the social and political order of the Rashidun caliphate and operated by seeking to build networks within military and security forces. Two others, however, were more linked to the Egyptian experience and were derived from the extremist branch of the Ikhwan Muslimin.

One strand of this opposition sought mass action to alter the formal political arena and was particularly important in universities; this was the Gam'iyat Islamiyya (Islamic Groups). The Gam'iyat did not have a complex leadership structure and relied heavily on its espousal by radical clerical figures who would legitimize its activities through *fatwas*. The other, which sought a more clandestine violent approach involving armed attack on government, was the Jihad Islamiyya (Islamic Holy War). It was cohesive, organized on a cell system, and had a secret leadership. Small, autonomous groups associated with such movements began a campaign of violence after 1974 in Egypt.

It is important to note, however, that, like the Ikhwan Muslimin, the Gam'iyat Islamiyya was not initially involved in violence. Ikhwan Muslimin has never, as a movement, been formally linked to violent action, whatever individual members may have done. The Gam'iyat Islamiyya, on the other hand, was, ironically enough, used by the CIA to recruit young Muslims for the war against the Soviet Union in Afghanistan during the 1980s, an initiative that ultimately led to its religious leader, Sheikh Umar ar-Rahman, being allowed into the United States as an immigrant—where later he was imprisoned for involvement in the 1993 New York World Trade Center bombing.

The movement turned to violent opposition only in 1992, two years after tensions between it and the Egyptian government dramatically worsened when a leading Gam'iyat activist was killed, apparently by security forces, in Giza. By this time the movement had spread out of the universities into the vast slums around Cairo, particularly Imbaba and Ain Shams, where it began to provide the rudimentary administration and social services that the authorities should have provided but apparently could not. It also became active for the same purposes in the *ashwai'at*—unplanned and uncontrolled shantytowns around all the major towns and cities in the country that had proliferated in the 1960s and 1970s.

The 1992 campaign, which seemed at times likely to threaten the stability of the Egyptian state, was eventually crushed four years later, with its leadership splitting between those, mainly in prison by then, who sought accommodation with the Egyptian state and those who had not been captured and had fled abroad seeking new arenas for action. Led by Ayman al-Zawahiri, they eventually joined forces with a quite new phenomenon, al-Qaeda. That movement sought a far more unforgiving and austere vision for the Muslim world, including the rejection of Western paradigms and practices.

In essence, the al-Qaeda movement, in its confrontation with the West, also seeks an ideal Islamic community, in the terms it considers the prophet Muhammad defined for the original Islamic community created in Medina in the early seventh century. Were this to be done, its adherents believe, it would be possible for every Muslim to live a life to ensure salvation, and Muslim society would achieve its own perfection. It is implicit and integral to this view that Muslim society must be controlled by Muslims qualified to do so, through their emulation of the qualities of the prophet.

Thus the idea of non-Muslim control is morally and doctrinally unacceptable, and Western influence is pernicious and to be eradicated. That is not, in itself, a particularly unusual view, although the particular variant espoused by al-Qaeda, with its violence and exclusiveness, alongside its holistic intolerance and rigidity, is shared by very few Muslims. Yet it is a response to a perception of Western imposition, either directly through globalization or support for Israel or indirectly through its support for corrupt regimes inside the Islamic world, against which al-Qaeda mobilizes a modern version of *jihad*.

The violent alternative—jihad

The continued presence of neo-colonial influence, particularly over governments, and the failure of alternative paradigms, such as Arab nationalism, led back to the Salafiyyist ideal. As described above, by 1967 a major revival of Salafiyyist influence appeared to be under way. By now, however, its more activist fringe was informed by new ideas and objectives so that the original doctrine, which had emphasized parallel development toward modernity, was replaced by exclusion. In Egypt, Sayyid Qutb had laid out a new agenda to revitalize the original political vision and combat corrupt government through the concepts of *hukumiyya* and *jahiliyya*, while, earlier in Pakistan in the 1940s, Maulana Maududi had revived the old Islamic tradition of *jihad* to combat colonialism and its modern counterpart, neo-colonialism.

The concept of *jihad* has become key to any understanding of the nature of the modern radical movements in the contemporary world, for modern *neo-salafis* have become even more intolerant of extraneous doctrine than the highly austere Wahhabi movement in Saudi Arabia. Not only do they look to the first four Rashidun Islamic caliphates, the so-called rightly guided caliphs; they also reject any specific school of Islamic law, turning instead in an eclectic manner to those statements in original sources that best accord with the basic criteria of the early Islamic world as the guide to the creation of a new Islamic order. It is an order, furthermore, that is now to be achieved through *jihad*, the sole means available to counter the corrupting effects of the continued neo-colonial Western presence in the Muslim world.

Jihad for most Islamic theologians is a process of internal strife designed to achieve personal purification and betterment. Originally, however, it also meant warfare sanctioned by Islam. Initially it was warfare to expand the Islamic world, but for the past five hundred years at least, if not longer, it has meant a defensive war to protect the *umma* and region it occupies. This is the vision of the extremist fringe of the *salafi* movement today. It is a vision that was given particular definition by the war in Afghanistan, largely because it was the intellectual instrument whereby up to 40,000 Arabs were persuaded to take part.

During the conflict, the concept of *jihad* was given particular significance by Abdallah Azzam, a Palestinian educated in the al-Azhar mosque-university in Cairo and collaborator with Osama bin Laden. He defined two types of *jihad*: *jihad* to harass the enemy in order to discourage attack upon the Islamic world, and *jihad* actually to defend it against attack. The first kind of *jihad* was a collective responsibility, in that any Muslim group could undertake it and thereby relieve other Muslims from doing so. But the second kind was an individual responsibility, as important as the observance of the five pillars of faith. The war in Afghanistan was of the second kind, thus obliging Muslims to ensure that the Soviet invasion should not succeed.

With the end of the war in Afghanistan, those who had been engaged soon found other arenas where Muslims were threatened: Bosnia, Chechnya, and Kosovo, to mention but the three most important. This Wiktorowicz (2001, 25–26) terms the "nomadic *jihad*," for those involved in it began to enter a world of unbounded perpetual conflict to protect the Islamic *umma*. However, most important for our purposes, is the *jihad* that is to be pursued within the Islamic world, because, as Sayyid Qutb had made clear, Islamic states themselves fell far short of the Islamic ideal, particularly in view of their compromises with the West. Here the *neo-salafis* had recourse to the teachings of a fourteenth-century jurist, Ibn Taymiyya (1263–1328), who argued, in the context of the Mongols, that a Muslim had to accept all the principles of Islam to be considered a true member of the Muslim community.

The Mongols did not fully endorse Islamic law, even though some of them had converted to Islam after their thirteenth- and fourteenth-century conquests. Since they persisted in applying the Mongol *yasa* code of dignity, honor, and excellence, rather than simply Islamic Sharia law in its entirety, Ibn Taymiyya condemned them as being in a state of *jahiliyya* and thus apostate. The Mongols had also ended the Abbasid caliphate, the emblem of Arab civilization, in 1258 with their conquest of Baghdad and, in so doing, gave an enduring symbol to the Arab and Muslim world, for Baghdad became the embodiment of the achievements of that Arab-Islamic civilization; its capture and occupation by the United States has been a very unpleasant historical reminder of humiliation by infidels to the contemporary Arab and Is-

lamic world. At the same time, such *neo-salafi* or *salafi-jihadi* doctrines, as they became known, made unpleasant reading for governments in the Muslim world as well.

The relevance of these principles to modern Muslim regimes is immediately obvious, for they all claim some kind of legitimization through religion, even if they are basically repressive and corrupt. Virtually none of them could live up to such standards as set—or, indeed, would want to. Even those that claim strict adherence to Islamic law in their legal codes and practices, such as Saudi Arabia, fail the test in terms of the personal behavior of their rulers. Even worse, any evidence of involvement with Western powers is clearly a breach of these strict conditions, so that *jihad* against them becomes an obligation incumbent, in the extremist *salafi-jihadi* vision, on every Muslim; those who do not agree are *kuffar,* apostates.

For the *salafi-jihadi* extremists, such as those involved in al-Qaeda and similar networks elsewhere, as in Algeria during the 1990s, the circle is now complete. A defensive *jihad* against Western influence and intrusion is a moral duty. An inner-directed *jihad* against corrupt Muslim governments that connive with Western influence is an imperative to protect the Muslim world, and Muslims themselves must be purged of their own apostasy if they do not accept these obligations. Unless they do, the Muslim world itself will be in sin—and, of course, the traditional sentence for apostasy is death in Sharia law. This, in essence, is the ideological imperative for the Islamic extremists who make up movements such as al-Qaeda and its associates, and who form the core of "Islamic fundamentalist revolution" today.

The Shia alternative

Shia Islam arose from the martyrdom of the fourth Rashidun caliph, Ali, and from the subsequent martyrdoms of his sons: Hasan, who was allegedly poisoned, and Husayn, who was killed in battle at Karbala. It became a doctrine of the downtrodden and suppressed, in which legitimacy of rule was incarnated in the lineal descendents of Ali, who were themselves constantly repressed by the dominant Sunni caliphate. As a result, they became the embodiment of immaculate moral virtue against the corruption of temporal power, even though they lacked power themselves. Eventually, the twelfth imam, as he became known, Muhammad al-Mahdi, disappeared around A.D. 878 and was believed by the Shia to have gone into occultation, hidden from human view until he would return, to lead the Shia to an era of justice and salvation.

Shia Islam, given these millenarian characteristics, paradoxically became a creed of toleration, quietism, and submission, but with the potential for revolutionary change, should the occulted imam return. The situation began to change only when, for political reasons, the first Safavid shah, Abbas, decided to make Shia Islam into the official religion of Persia in A.D. 1501. Toward the end of the nineteenth century, as European and Russian pressure on Persia intensified, coercing the weak and corrupt Qajar dynasty, Shia divines began to acquire political significance as the guardians of this politico-religious culture, despite their quietist traditions.

It was this tradition that Ayatollah Ruhollah Khomeini exploited when, in the 1960s, he began to oppose the developing relationship between Iran and the United States. His initial objections reflected the threat that he perceived to the Iranian Islamic world arising from U.S. involvement there. However, after his exile to Najaf in Iraq in 1963, he began to reconsider the relationship between Shia Islam and political power, arguing, in ways that began to reflect many of the assumptions of Sunni Islam, that Shia divines had responsibility for ensuring that political systems in the Islamic world conformed to appropriate doctrinal principle. In his famous series of lectures, "Hukumat-i Islami," given in Najaf in the 1970s, he argued that the political process required guidance from a jurisconsult, a figure distinguished by his knowledge of *fiqh* to be able to perform the role of guidance that would otherwise have been occupied by the occulted imam, were he to have returned to earth.

These views were certainly revolutionary in the context of Shia philosophy as it had developed over the centuries, for most Shia divines believed in avoidance of direct political involvement in favor of moral guidance. The new ideas, however, were given massive added force by the Iranian Revolution, in which Ayatollah Khomeini was able to play a decisive role as the embodiment of an alternative vision to that of the shah. However, they were not revolutionary in the same sense as the challenges developing in the Sunni Muslim world that sought to overturn completely the existing assumptions of Islamic society. Instead, in Iran, the revolution would eventually impose the authority of an existing clerical class upon society.

There were, of course, radical alternatives available, perhaps the most important being that created by Ali Shariati, an Iranian sociologist who died in Britain in 1977 just before the Islamic Revolution occurred. Ali Shariati, one of the most important ideologues of the Islamic Revolution, argued an Islamic-Marxist agenda in which the world was divided into oppressors (*mustakbarin*) and oppressed (*mustadafin*) and that the duty of the true Muslim was to struggle against the oppressors to restore justice to the oppressed. Not only did this neatly align Iranian Shia against the shah's repressive regime but it also reflected Marxist doctrine of proletarian revolution and the Shia vision of millenarian justice transposed from the metaphysical world into the contemporary arena.

It was a vision that was, in effect, adopted by the Ayatollah Khomeini when he argued that true Islamic government, dedicated to social justice—and thus the interests of the oppressed—should be monitored and guided by a jurisconsult who reflected the perfection of the Shia imam—otherwise occulted until the Day of Judgment. He did not, however, endorse the political implications of Ali Shariati's arguments, for his political vision was intensely conservative and linked to the primacy of the established divines, the *mullahs,* within organized political life.

Thus, even though at the time, at the end of the 1970s and in the first half of the 1980s, the Iranian Revolution had tremendous demonstrative force and excited emulation throughout the Islamic world, it was not philosophically related to the dramatic intellectual changes taking place within Sunni Islam; in that sense it does not form part of an investigation of "Islamic fundamentalist revolution."

al-Qaeda: a Network of Networks

These intellectual developments came to express themselves in the Sunni world, primarily in al-Qaeda's eyes, as a challenge to the West, particularly the United States, given its preeminence in the crises over Palestine, Iraq, and Saudi Arabia, and its allies. Included were perceived corrupt governments in the Middle East and elsewhere that had abandoned the true Islamic path. The historical role of the events in Afghanistan was crucial; it was there that the ideology of al-Qaeda was forged, and it was there that the organization itself began.

al-Qaeda and Afghanistan

Al-Qaeda was a direct consequence of the Soviet invasion of Afghanistan in 1979 and the subsequent U.S. reaction. U.S. and Western policy involved an indirect response, itself the product of Saudi reactions to the invasion. The Saudi government, with U.S. encouragement, began supporting the religious Afghani factions opposed to the Soviet presence with money, weapons, and manpower. It also encouraged private individuals and organizations to support this new *jihad.* The manpower was recruited from the Middle East—and here the *neo-salafis* played a key role—and, to a lesser extent, from Muslim minority communities in Europe and elsewhere. An organization was created for that purpose, *al-Maktab al-Khidmat* (the Recruiting Office). This was organized by Abdallah Azzam, who was already in Peshawar, Pakistan, leading the Islamic Coordination Council.

Shortly after the conflict started, he was joined by a Saudi national, a member of one of the richest families in the kingdom, the bin Laden family, which originates from Yemen. Osama bin Laden was actually recruited by the then-director of Saudi national intelligence, Prince Faisal bin Turki, for the purpose. From 1984 onward, the CIA provided additional funding and weaponry, as well as logistical and training support. In 1988, as the struggle wound down, Osama bin Laden created a support organization, al-Qaeda (the Base), that was to provide a means of contact among the thousands of non-Afghani Muslims—mainly Arabs—who had participated in the struggle. By this time, Abdallah Azzam had been killed under mysterious circumstances.

Between 1991 and 1994, most of the foreign nationals involved in the Afghani struggle were forced to leave Pakistan, where they were based, along with many staff from Muslim humanitarian organizations that had been providing essential relief work in the refugee camps in Pakistan. The Pakistani decision to force them out was apparently taken at U.S. insistence and was, in retrospect, an extremely unwise move. Although Osama bin Laden himself returned to Saudi Arabia at the start of the 1990s, this scattering of highly trained and radicalized fighters made the role of al-Qaeda even more important, for it now became the only means by which its members could remain in touch. At this time, that is essentially all it was. But it was about to change into something far more dangerous.

Up to 1996, Osama bin Laden had supported protest in Saudi Arabia about the failings of the government and had been involved in such initiatives as the Committee for the Defence of Legitimate Rights (CDLR) and the Arab Reform Committee (ARC), both resolutely nonviolent organizations that enjoyed support from within the core institutions of Saudi society, even though they were condemned by the government. Yet bin Laden was forced out of Saudi Arabia in 1991 and his citizenship was revoked in 1994 because of that support and because of his opposition to the U.S. presence in the country. It is said that his expulsion occurred in response to the Saudi realization that he could mobilize up to 35,000 men, when he offered them as shock troops against the Iraqi presence in Kuwait. In 1996, however, Osama bin Laden returned to Afghanistan, after he had been forced out of Sudan, again as the result of U.S. pressure, because of suspicions over his involvement in the 1993 attack on the World Trade Center and the 1996 attack on the al-Khobar military housing complex in Saudi Arabia itself.

IMPACTS

Global Terrorism

Osama bin Laden, now radicalized by the way in which he had been treated, began to contemplate using the al-Qaeda organization as a means of confronting corruption in the Middle East and countering the role there of the United States. By

the latter part of the 1990s, the al-Qaeda leadership had also been altered significantly by the introduction of Egyptian militants, particularly leaders of the Gam'iyat Islamiyya and Jihad Islami who were forced out of Egypt in 1995 and 1996. Its analysis of the crisis in the Middle East targeted corrupt Middle East regimes and those responsible for maintaining them in power, primarily the United States. The issue of a permanent U.S. presence in Saudi Arabia in the wake of the war against Iraq in 1990–1991 was also high on the list of its grievances.

This was quite unlike nationally based movements, such as Hizbullah in Lebanon, Hamas in the Occupied Territories, or the Algerian movements such as the Groupes Islamiques Armés (Jama'at Islamiyya Musalaha—GIA) or the Armée Islamique du Salut (Jaysh Islamiyyia li'l-Inqadh). They continued to address specifically domestic agendas and, where spillover into Europe occurred, it was still primarily connected with those domestic events. This was true even of the Egyptian terrorist crisis initially provoked by the signing of the peace treaty with Israel and involving the subsequent assassination of President Sadat. The tensions there later erupted into violence for powerful domestic reasons in 1992, and these continued to predominate until the movements were effectively defeated in 1997, without there being any significant spillover effects in Europe or the United States. However, at the same time, the groups in Egypt had developed a political analysis of the Middle Eastern situation in which the United States was seen as playing a crucial role in supporting and abetting corrupt regimes. This their leaderships took with them when they fled to Afghanistan after their defeat in Egypt.

Thus, toward the end of the 1990s, there was a clear link between the influence of these Egyptian groups on the al-Qaeda leadership and the growing radicalization of the group itself, with its objectives widening from the question of U.S. influence in Saudi Arabia to identifying the United States itself as the primary target and thus becoming truly international in its scope and objectives. In 1995 the first direct evidence of an al-Qaeda action was its involvement in the Gam'iyat Islamiyya attempt to assassinate President Husni Mubarak in Addis Ababa. That was followed by al-Qaeda endorsement of the Riyadh and al-Khobar bombings in 1995 and 1996. Its first *fatwa* attacking the United States was issued in August of that year.

Two years later came the "Declaration of the World Islamic Front for Jihad against the Jews and the Crusaders," in which the movement joined forces with five other groups, two of them Egyptian and the others Asian. The first document clearly envisaged direct threats against Americans—not others—and the second clearly identified new al-Qaeda targets. These were to be the United States and its allies (clearly including Israel), "until the Aqsa mosque and the

Osama bin Laden (left) sits with his adviser Ayman al-Zawahiri, an Egyptian linked to the al-Qaeda network, during an interview with Pakistani journalist Hamid Mir (not pictured) in an image supplied by the respected Dawn newspaper November 10, 2001. (Reuters/Corbis)

Haram mosque were freed from their grip"—in other words, until Jerusalem and Mecca were liberated from a U.S. and Israeli presence.

The subsequent attacks on U.S. embassies in East Africa (August 1998) and the USS *Cole* in Aden harbor (September 2000) demonstrated that the al-Qaeda movement had now become global in its scope and was directed against the United States as well as against corrupt Arab regimes, particularly Saudi Arabia. Egyptian influence continued to make itself felt, for the attacks on the U.S. embassies in East Africa were preceded by a U.S.-inspired repatriation to Egypt of a leading Egyptian Islamist from Albania who had been condemned to death. Some time after the repatriation had taken place, the Gam'iyat Islamiyya issued a warning that it would retaliate. Shortly afterward, the East African embassy bombings took place.

The addition of the leaderships of the Egyptian groups to al-Qaeda gave it a professionalism in organization and operation that it had not before had. It was that factor, more than any other, that transformed it from being a *jihadist* organization, dedicated to the collective struggle against alien influences in the Middle East and to the protection of the Islamic *umma*, into an organization prepared to use terror as its major technique against corruption inside the Islamic world and against Western intervention. It has developed its own policy of preemption, for its operations have become increasingly aggressive and global in scope.

Globalism and Localism

This global agenda could not easily be handled by a single organization. Instead al-Qaeda seems to operate in a much more decentralized fashion, in which the core makes strategic decisions but leaves the actual execution to quite separate groups with which it is in contact. Such contact derives from its previous role in recruiting for the Afghani war in the 1980s and from acting as an information center in the early 1990s.

Beyond the nomadic *jihad* described by Wiktorowicz (2001), there are also a series of groups concerned with the social and political struggle within national borders and, most important, within immigrant communities, especially in Europe. They may well be linked to al-Qaeda, if only by the common thread of the experience of the Afghani war and the subsequent training offered by al-Qaeda to Mujahidin (those who fight *jihad*). They may also be prepared to take part in operations either suggested by the core movement or that might fit within its overall strategy. But they have domestic agendas to deal with as well. They form a kind of dispersed *jihad,* as a third stage in the evolution of the *salafi-jihadi* threat—a series of disparate, autonomous movements with access to a shared ideology in a world of global communications. Such groups may have been responsible for the Casablanca massacres in May 2003 and the Madrid bombings in March 2004. The threat that the West faces has become far more complex since clear, traceable links no longer exist, only shared objectives, means, and doctrines.

Migration and *Jihad*

The final piece in this increasingly complex jigsaw of groups and movements also reflects al-Qaeda's nature as a network of networks and is directly relevant to the events of September 11, 2001. This is that the groups that have been most involved in the actual commission of actions such as the attacks in the United States have been recruited especially for the specific task involved. Thus the September 11 hijackers were identified and recruited in Hamburg; Ahmad Rezzam, the unsuccessful Los Angeles airport bomber, was recruited in Montreal; and Robert Reid and Zacarias Moustafaoui, the "shoe bomber" and the "twentieth hijacker" for September 11, respectively, were recruited in Britain. They were, in short, part of the massive wave of migration into Europe, and their involvement was a statement about alienation in the European context as much as about commitment to *salafi-jihadi* ideals.

There was no evidence, apart from assertion, that the modus operandi of these groups in Europe changed after September 11, 2001, so that migrant involvement in the activities of al-Qaeda had been a question of opportunism building on long-standing social and political alienation arising from the migration experience itself, even if there were direct links to organizations such as al-Qaeda. If migrants were so easily persuaded into terrorism, then the probable explanation has far more to do with the problems of handling the transformation of Europe into a complex heterogeneous society than it does with the arcane issue of protecting the Islamic *umma,* even though this has become the rhetoric in which the problems of failed integration are voiced. It is highly questionable whether the logic of the "War on Terror" has much to say about solving what is essentially a European problem but that links back into the core problems of the Middle Eastern region.

The Outcome

Terrorism linked to the al-Qaeda movement was a statement about quite specific problems in the Middle Eastern region, and to that extent it formed part of "Islamic fundamentalist revolution." These related to developmental failure there, for which Arab governments are at least as culpable as their Western counterparts. In part, however, they were the consequence of decades of arrogance and neglect of the key issues in the region: of governance, corruption, and of Israeli intransigence. They also reflected a massive insensitivity to the values and specificities of Muslim society and an unawareness of historical memory. Given this indifference, was the al-Qaeda phenomenon so surprising, and could a "war on terror" that ignored these issues succeed?

Far better would be an approach that constructively engaged the regional problems in which the West is implicated, alongside the rejection of violence. That alone might create the climate in which popular attitudes in the Middle Eastern and North African regions might no longer sympathize with the wider aims of the *salafi-jihadi* movement and decry the brutality of its more extreme adherents. This would, of course, mean that, alongside the very necessary task of intelligence and control, designed to eliminate a terrorist threat, the political issues that lie behind such terrorism would have to be taken seriously and resolved, no matter how difficult such a task might be.

Yet, in the end, the greatest weakness of al-Qaeda and the hydra-headed movements that share its ideals is its intolerance and victimization of those who do not necessarily actively agree with its objectives or methods. Despite its obsessive concern about legal justification, enshrined in its attention to *fatwas* to justify its actions, the movement fits squarely within the category of totalitarianism, defined by Hannah Arendt (1951) as a system characterized by charismatic leadership of a repressive regime based on a holistic ideology but operating with arbitrary power. Her arguments were formulated in the context of European Fascism, but they apply equally well to repressive regimes elsewhere, whether in charge of countries, such as the Taliban, or arrogating to themselves the supposedly moral imperatives of global terrorism. It is the authoritarian and arbitrary nature of al-

Qaeda and similar movements that is their real weakness and the measure of the degree to which "Islamic fundamentalist revolution" has betrayed its Islamic origins.

PEOPLE AND ORGANIZATIONS

al-Afghani, Jamal al-Din (1839–1897)

One of the key figures in the Islamic modernist movement, the *salafiyya* movement. He sought to demonstrate that the key European political concepts that lay behind its technological achievements were inherent in Islam, particularly within the pure Islamic doctrines of the Rashidun period, and would allow Muslims to derive parallel institutions from their own religious and philosophical inheritance.

bin Laden, Osama (Born 1957)

Saudi Arabian born into a wealthy family who volunteered to fight the Soviets in Afghanistan. He and his associates organized a network of tens of thousands of Islamic volunteers for the Afghani war, later called al-Qaeda, elements of which were mobilized to engage in violent attacks against perceived enemies of Islam, such as the United States.

Gam'iyat Islamiyya (Islamic Groups)

Egyptian Islamist movement that emerged in the 1970s, coming to prominence in the wake of the assassination of President Sadat. Initially committed to radicalizing university students, it moved into violent confrontation with the Egyptian state in 1992, organizing many atrocities. In 1996 its leadership split, with imprisoned leaders seeking an accommodation with the state and others moving abroad to join al-Qaeda in Afghanistan.

Hamas (Islamic Resistance Movement)

A Palestinian Islamist movement derived from the Ikhwan Muslimin in Palestine, which was involved in providing education, health care, and welfare assistance to Palestinians under occupation. Hamas was created as an offshoot in 1989 to participate in the first Palestinian *intifada*. Since 1991 its clandestine wing, the Izzedine Qassim Brigades, has engaged in terrorist attacks against Israelis. In January of 2006, Hamas won the majority of the seats in the election for the Palestinean parliament.

Hizbullah

A Lebanese Islamist movement created in the late 1970s with Syrian and Iranian support to challenge the Israeli invasions of Lebanon in 1978 and 1982, as well as the subsequent Franco-U.S. intervention in Beirut. It took Western hostages in the 1980s in Beirut to force Western influences out of the country and led the violent opposition to Israel's continued presence in the "Security Zone" until the unilateral Israeli withdrawal in June 2000. It continues to challenge the Israeli presence in the Shab'a Farms area and to support Palestinian resistance to the Israeli occupation of the West Bank.

Ikhwan Muslimin (Islamic Brotherhood)

Created in 1929 in Ismailiyya in Egypt by Hassan al-Banna, the Ikhwan Muslimin was the first Islamist political movement. During the 1940s and 1950s it spread throughout the Arab world; although it sought peaceful change of Islamic society, more radical factions split off to form most of the violent movements in existence today.

Jihad Islami (Islamic Holy War)

This movement arose from the Ikhwan Muslimin after the execution of Sayyid Qutb, coming to prominence after the assassination of President Sadat in 1981. It was notable for its secretive vanguard party structure and later collaborated with the Gam'iyat Islamiyya. After 1996 its leadership moved to Afghanistan and collaborated with al-Qaeda. There are similarly named movements in Palestine and Jordan. The Palestinian Islamic movement collaborates with Hamas.

Jihaz al-Khazz (1940s)

A violent and clandestine movement derived from the Ikhwan Muslimin in the late 1930s and responsible for attacks on leading Egyptian politicians, including the assassination of the prime minister in 1948. It disappeared after the Egyptian security services assassinated the founder of the Ikhwan Muslimin, Hassan al-Banna, in 1949.

Khomeini, Ayatollah (1902–1989)

Leader of Iran's Shia Islamic Fundamentalist Revolution.

The Prophet Muhammad (571–632)

Founder of Islam.

al-Qaeda (The Base)

Originally this was the organization created by Osama bin Laden and his associates for the thousands of largely foreign Islamic volunteers who came to Afghanistan during the 1980s to fight against Soviet troops and their leftist Afghan allies. Later this network was turned against other perceived threats to the Islamic community internationally and is thought to be responsible for a series of terrorist attacks, including the September 11, 2001, destruction of the two New York World Trade Center towers and the attack on the Pentagon in Washington.

Qutb, Sayyid (1906–1966)

An Islamic leader who argued that Islamic societies should adopt the ideals of the very early Islamic community. He also considered that Islamic governments which were corrupt should not be tolerated and should be overthrown.

Rashidun (632–661)

The reigns of the four "rightly guided" caliphs who had personally known the prophet. Sunni Islamic fundamentalist leaders advocated the development of modern Islamic societies based on the religious standards and practices of this period.

Shia Islam

Less than 20 percent of Muslims are Shia. They believe that the leadership of Islam followed the line of descent from the prophet's daughter Fatima and her husband, the prophet's cousin Ali. "Shia" means followers or supporters of Ali (the original name was Shi'at Ali). They also believed that these imams, of whom there were no more than twelve, were infallible, as the prophet had been.

Sunni Islam

About 80 percent of Muslims are Sunnis. They believe that no person after the prophet Muhammad was infallible and that people should base their lives on the Koran and other elements of the tradition, or "Sunna," of Islam.

al-Wahhab, Muhammad ibn Abd (1703–1791)

Sunni Islamic religious leader who advocated a form of Islam that returned to the fundamentalist doctrine and practices of early Islam. He and his followers formed an alliance with the Saudi family that gave the Saudis a religious legitimization to justify and rally support for their conquest and unification of Saudi Arabia. In the process, the Saudis established al-Wahhab's conservative form of Islam throughout Saudi Arabia.

George Joffé

See Also Afghanistan: Conflict and Civil War; Algerian Islamic Revolt; Chechen Revolt against Russia; Cinema of Revolution; Documentaries of Revolution; Iranian Revolution; Iraq Revolution; Student and Youth Movements, Activism and Revolution; Terrorism; Transnational Revolutionary Movements

References and Further Readings

Ajami, F. 1981. *The Arab Predicament: Arab Political Thought and Practice since 1967.* Cambridge: Cambridge University Press.

Arendt, H. 1951. *The Origins of Totalitarianism.* New York: Harcourt.

Benedict, R. 1934. *Patterns of Culture.* Boston: Houghton Mifflin.

Burke J. 2003. *Al-Qaeda: Casting a Shadow of Terror.* London: I. B. Tauris.

Eatwell, R. 1995. *Fascism: A History.* London: Chatto and Windus.

Gunaratna, R. 2002. *Inside al-Qaeda: Global Network of Terror.* London: Hurst.

Halliday, F. 1995. *Islam and the Myth of Confrontation: Religion and Politics in the Middle East.* London: I. B. Tauris.

Halper, S., and J. Clarke. 2004. *America Alone: The Neo-Conservatives and the Global Order.* Cambridge: Cambridge University Press.

Huntington, S. P. 1993. "The Clash of Civilizations," *Foreign Affairs* 72: 28–50.

Joffé, E. G. H. 2000. *International Implications of Domestic Security.* Lisbon: EuroMeSCo Paper 9, IEEI.

———. 2004. *Global Terrorism.* Lisbon: EuroMeSCo Paper No. 30, IEEI.

Lewis, B. 2002. *What Went Wrong? Western Impact and Middle Eastern Response.* London: Weidenfeld and Nicholson.

———. 2003. *The Crisis of Islam: Holy War and Unholy Terror.* London: Weidenfeld and Nicholson.

Malley, W. 1998. *Fundamentalism Reborn? Afghanistan and the Taliban.* London: Hurst.

Rashid, A. 2000. *Taliban: Militant Islam, Oil, and the New Great Game in Central Asia.* New Haven, CT: Yale University Press.

Wiktorowicz, Q. 2001. "The New Global Threat: Transnational Salafis and Jihad," *Middle East Policy Council,* 8 (4): 18-38. www.MEPC.org.

Italian Fascist Revolution

CHRONOLOGY

27 B.C.–
A.D. 14   Augustus reigns as the first Roman emperor.

306–337   Emperor Constantine recognizes Christianity and moves his capital to the new city of Constantinople.

476   Last Roman emperor in the west is deposed.

590–604   Pope Gregory the Great assumes political as well as spiritual role in the city of Rome.

756   Frankish leader Pepin gives land to the papacy, the Donation of Pepin, which is the foundation of the papal states.

800   Charlemagne is crowned emperor in Rome by Pope Leo III.

1056–1303   The popes and the holy Roman emperors compete for political control of Italy.

1325–1525   Italy remains divided politically, and separate territorial states emerge during the Renaissance period. The five major states are Venice, Milan, Florence, the Papal States, and the Kingdom of Naples.

1559–1797   The Italian states are dominated by foreign powers, principally Spain and then Austria. Napoléon conquers Venice, 1797, the last independent Italian state.

1805–1814   Napoléon establishes the Kingdom of Italy, which disappears following Napoléon's defeat and exile.

1820–1860   The period of the Risorgimento, the national revival, marked by revolutions in various cities and calls for establishing an Italian state.

1860–1861   The charismatic soldier and adventurer Giuseppe Garibaldi leads a group of volunteers, the Mille, or Thousand, who conquer Sicily and southern Italy, thus toppling the Kingdom of Naples. Count Camillo Cavour of the Kingdom of Savoy-Piedmont sends troops south, led by King Victor Emmanuel II. Garibaldi meets the king and defers to him. The Italian kingdom is proclaimed with Victor Emmanuel as the king of a constitutional monarchy. Pope Pius IX maintains his rule of the city of Rome, protected by French troops.

1870   France withdraws troops from Rome during the Franco-Prussian War. Italian troops capture the city, and Rome becomes Italy's capital in 1871. Pope Pius IX refuses to recognize the Italian state and imposes excommunication on Catholics who serve in politics.

1871–1915   Italy is governed by a constitutional monarchy and representative parliament. The right to vote is restricted to a small number, based on literacy and payment of taxes, until the extension of the franchise to most adult males in 1913. Political leadership comes from an elite group of politicians divided between a conservative Right and a progressive Left. The first challenge to the political elite comes from the organization of a Socialist party in 1892 and a Nationalist Association in 1910. To counter the growing influence of Socialism, the papacy encourages Catholic participation in national politics.

1912   Benito Mussolini, a leader of the radical wing of the Socialist Party, becomes editor of the Socialist newspaper *Avanti!*

1914–1915   General war erupts in Europe in 1914 between the Entente powers—Great Britain, France, and Russia—and Germany and the Austro-Hungarian empire. Italy remains neutral. A growing movement campaigns for Italian intervention in the war. Mussolini joins the interventionists and is expelled from the Socialist Party and the post of editor of *Avanti!*

1915–1918   The Italian army fights the Austrians in the mountainous border area in northeastern Italy. The Italians suffer a devastating defeat at Caporetto in 1917 but recover sufficiently to counterattack and defeat the Austrians by the conclusion of the war in November 1918. The Italians lose more than 600,000 dead.

1919   Mussolini founds the Fascist movement. The first Catholic political party is organized as the Popular Party. In the first post-war national elections, the Fascists fail to gain a seat in parliament. The Socialist and Popular parties win the largest number of seats, but no one party has a parliamentary majority.

1920–1922   As unrest and unemployment spread in Italy, the Fascist movement forms squads that use violence to attack political opponents and protect landowners. The government appears weak and unable to govern effectively. In 1921, Mussolini is among the thirty-five Fascists elected to parliament.

1922   A general strike fails, with the Fascists playing a leading role in breaking it. The Fascists threaten to march on Rome and seize power. On October 28, 1922, King Victor Emmanuel III seeks to resolve the crisis by inviting Mussolini to become prime minister and form a coalition government.

1924   Elections give the Fascist Party a majority in parliament. The murder of anti-Fascist parliamentary deputy Giacomo Matteotti by Fascists threatens to topple Mussolini's government, but Mussolini takes measures to consolidate his control.

1925–1926   New laws give Mussolini special powers as head of government. All political parties except the Fascist Party are abolished and made illegal. The Fascist government controls the press.

1927   The Charter of Labor establishes Fascist control of labor relations and the dominance of the Fascist labor unions.

1929   The papacy and the government sign the Lateran Treaty. The pope recognizes the Italian state in return for a financial settlement and the establishment of Vatican City as a sovereign state.

1931   University professors and schoolteachers are required to take an oath of loyalty. Achille Starace becomes Fascist Party secretary. In the following years party membership increases markedly as a requirement for work and other benefits.

1932–1934   The Exhibition of the Fascist Revolution in Rome draws nearly 4 million visitors in two years.

1933   Adolf Hitler becomes chancellor of Germany.

1934   Mussolini establishes corporations that will provide the cooperation of employers, workers, and the government in economic and political affairs.

1935–1936   Italy invades and conquers Ethiopia. Mussolini declares that Italy has a new Italian empire.

1936–1939   Mussolini and Hitler form the Rome-Berlin Axis. They send armed forces to support General Francisco Franco in the Spanish Civil War.

1937   A Ministry of Popular Culture is established to control the news media and communications. Youth groups are reorganized in the Gioventù Italiano del Littorio (GIL), the Italian Youth of the Littorio. (Littorio refers to the Fascist symbol.)

1938   Hitler visits Mussolini in Rome. The Fascist government enacts racial laws against the Jews. Mussolini plays a major role in the Munich Conference to resolve the crisis over Czechoslovakia.

1939   A Chamber of Fasci and Corporations replaces the existing Chamber of Deputies. Italy occupies Albania. Italy signs a Pact of Steel with Germany but remains neutral when Britain and France declare war on Germany following the German invasion of Poland.

1940   As the German army begins to overrun France, Mussolini declares war and invades

France. Italy invades Greece, but Italian troops get bogged down and require German intervention to attain victory.

1941   Germany invades Russia, and Italy sends troops. Following the Japanese attack on Pearl Harbor, Germany and Italy declare war on the United States.

1943   Italian and German forces surrender to the Allies in North Africa. The Fascist Grand Council passes a vote of no confidence in Mussolini. The king removes Mussolini from office and places him under arrest. Italy signs an armistice with the Allies. The Germans occupy Italy, rescue Mussolini, and establish a puppet government in northern Italy.

1943–1945   Mussolini heads the Italian Social Republic that seeks to revivify radical elements of the Fascist Revolution. The Allies defeat German and Fascist forces in Italy by April 1945. Partisans capture Mussolini and execute him.

1946   Italians vote in a referendum to abolish the monarchy.

1948   The new Italian constitution takes effect and establishes the Italian Republic.

INTRODUCTION

The Italian Fascist Revolution promised to transform Italian society through the creation of a new national community that would unite Italians of all classes and make Italy a major international power. The revolution rejected Socialism and liberalism in favor of a totalitarian state directed by Benito Mussolini as the leader, or Duce, of the Italian people. Mussolini promised to institute new economic and political structures while educating and training a new generation of Italian youth to carry out the revolution. The revolution would produce a powerful and unified Italy in which individuals found fulfillment through dedication to the national community.

BACKGROUND: CULTURE AND HISTORY

Italy is well-defined geographically as a peninsula surrounded by water on three sides and the Alps to the north.

More than 90 percent of Italians are Roman Catholic, and the pope, the bishop of Rome, is the leader of worldwide Catholicism. These marks of unity are, however, offset by a history of cultural and political fragmentation.

Ancient Rome achieved political dominance of the peninsula and went on to conquer the Mediterranean world. The Roman empire reached its height in power and size between the first and fourth centuries. In the fourth century, the center of power shifted to the east as a consequence of the Emperor Constantine's founding of the city of Constantinople. Germanic tribes occupied much of the western portion of the empire, including Rome itself after 476. The attempt to reconquer Italy by the eastern emperor Justinian in the sixth century led to a series of devastating wars. Historians estimate that the city of Rome's population fell from an estimated 1 million in the fourth century to probably less than 50,000 by the end of the sixth century.

During the Middle Ages the pope, as bishop of Rome and successor of St. Peter, exercised both spiritual and political authority. The medieval popes succeeded in asserting their spiritual and moral authority over the Western church after the rupture with the Eastern Orthodox Church in 1054 and until the challenge of the Protestant movements of the sixteenth century.

The popes had a more difficult time in asserting political authority. They did establish papal control over the central portion of Italy, which became the Papal States which lasted until the nineteenth century. They were less successful when they attempted to exercise ultimate, God-given authority over princes and kings.

The Holy Roman emperors ruled over a large portion of central and eastern Europe in what is today Germany and Austria. They made repeated attempts to conquer Italy. The popes led in resisting the incursions of the emperors. By the fourteenth century, the result was a standoff. The Holy Roman emperors gave up the conquest of the Italian peninsula, and the papacy moved to Avignon, in what is now southern France, for seventy years (1309–1378) and then suffered a split, the Great Schism, with rival popes in Rome and Avignon (1378–1414).

The political vacuum in Italy made possible the formation of independent territorial states by the fifteenth century. The five major states were Venice, Milan, Florence, the Papal States, and the Kingdom of Naples. In the sixteenth century, these states were no match for the revived Holy Roman empire and the emerging national monarchies of Spain and France. These major powers fought for control of Italy. After the peace settlement of 1559, Spain played a dominant political role until displaced by Austria in the early eighteenth century.

The idea of a politically unified Italy emerged in the early nineteenth century when Napoléon conquered and established a Kingdom of Italy north of the papal territories. Napoleonic rule ended in 1814. The next year, the Congress of Vienna restored Austrian control of the northern regions of Lombardy and Venice and effectively put an end to thoughts of unification.

The legacy of the French Revolution and the Napoleonic period, however, included a new sense of nationalism and calls for political reforms. In Italy the movement to create a unified nation took the name Risorgimento, meaning rebirth or resurrection. Giuseppe Mazzini (1815–1872) gained wide recognition for his theories of nationalism. He founded the Young Italy movement, which advocated reform and revolution. In the revolutionary upheavals of 1848, Mazzini worked to establish a republic in Rome after the pope had been ousted by the heroic military leader Giuseppe Garibaldi. Austrian intervention ended the Roman Republic, as well as similar experiments in other cities. Italy remained divided.

In the 1850s the Kingdom of Piedmont-Sardinia in northwestern Italy took the lead in efforts to create an Italian state. The kingdom's leading minister and diplomat, Count Camillo Benso Cavour (1810–1861), sought to establish Piedmont's authority over northern Italy. He wanted to challenge Austrian control of the north through diplomatic maneuvers and a military alliance with France. A series of dramatic events between 1859 and 1861 transformed the situation. Garibaldi's expedition of volunteers toppled the Kingdom of Naples by conquering Sicily and southern Italy. King Victor Emmanuel II of Piedmont led troops into the Papal States to link up with Garibaldi's forces. Garibaldi deferred to the Piedmontese. In 1861, Victor Emmanuel became king of the newly declared Kingdom of Italy.

The pope still controlled Rome, however, protected by French troops. When France went to war with Prussia, it withdrew from Rome. The Italian army assaulted Rome on September 20, 1870, and took the city after token resistance from the papal army. The next year, Rome became the capital of Italy. Pope Pius IX (1848–1878) protested the loss of his political authority in Rome and refused to recognize the Italian state. He claimed to be a "prisoner in the Vatican" and warned Catholics not to participate in politics under threat of excommunication.

Italy had attained political unification, but it faced the daunting task of creating national institutions and national identity. A sense of nationhood and nationalism was foreign to most Italians. The political and cultural history had developed sharp differences among the regions. Most Italians spoke dialects, and it was only in the nineteenth century that Italian was defined as a national language. Most Italians identified with their city or region, and so thought of themselves as Sicilians, Florentines, Venetians, and so forth. Northern Italy had a more developed economy than the poorer south. Voting was restricted to less than 10 percent of the adult population. Few people thought of themselves as Italians or believed that they had a stake in national politics.

Italy was a constitutional monarchy that accorded the king considerable authority. The king appointed the prime minister, who presided over a governing council or cabinet. The king could issue decrees that had the force of law. The king called and dissolved parliament. The members of the Chamber of Deputies were elected by the small number of men who were eligible to vote, but the king appointed the members of the Senate. The king had a major role in foreign policy and was commander of the armed forces.

Count Cavour's skill as a politician enhanced the prime minister's role, but Cavour died suddenly in 1861, shortly after unification. Nevertheless, the elite political class furnished Italy with able political leaders. Initially northerners were in the majority, but by the end of the century southerners, including prime ministers, emerged. The conservative Right dominated governments from 1861 to 1876, when the progressive Left came to power. The tendency, however, was to form coalition governments that included both the Left and Right.

Prime ministers "transformed" members of the opposition by inviting them to join the government. The practice of forming such coalitions became known as *trasformismo*. While it facilitated the formation of moderate and centrist governments, it also played down the importance of political programs and principles.

Between unification in 1861 and entrance into World War I in 1915, Italy did make considerable progress in forming a unified nation. Government legislation and programs expanded education in an effort to overcome the high rate of illiteracy. Roads, railways, and ships provided the infrastructure that improved communications and transportation. Industry and commerce grew, especially in the northern triangle of Milan, Turin, and Genoa.

In the same period Italy also took its place in Europe's diplomatic world as one of the acknowledged great powers, along with Great Britain, France, Germany, Austria-Hungary, and Russia. In 1881, Italy joined Germany and Austria-Hungary in the Triple Alliance, balanced by the Triple Entente of Britain, France, and Russia. Italy also acquired the colonies of Eritrea and Somaliland in East Africa. In 1911–1912, Italy conquered Libya in North Africa, wresting it from the disintegrating Ottoman empire.

The achievements of Italy were offset by three persisting problems. The first was a relatively weak economy compared especially with those of the more advanced economies of Britain, Germany, and France. Those countries had larger populations and more natural resources, such as coal and iron. Germany, for example, had attained political unification only in 1871, yet by 1914 its economy had developed much more rapidly than Italy's.

The second problem was Italy's relative military weakness. Its economy could not sustain the military forces of the other great powers. Italy was in the unenviable position of being the "least of the great powers." Finally, despite the growth of Italian nationalism and national institutions, there persisted a gap between large portions of the Italian population and the Italian government, between the "real" Italy and the "legal" Italy.

Italy's first Sicilian prime minister, Francesco Crispi (1887–1891, 1893–1896), pursued an aggressive foreign policy to assert Italy's place among the other powers. He sought to expand Italy's colonies in East Africa by conquering Ethiopia. A native army defeated an Italian force at Adowa in 1896, forcing Crispi to resign and leaving many Italians with a feeling of national humiliation. Avenging this defeat became part of the Fascist program in the 1930s.

The dominant politician and frequent prime minister in the decade before World War I was Giovanni Giolitti, a traditional-style politician from the north. Giolitti, however, understood the problems facing Italy and attempted to address them. He pursued a cautious foreign policy in keeping with Italy's limited economic and military resources. He sought to bring more Italians into the political process, including Socialists, nationalists, and Catholics. In 1913 he supported successful legislation that gave the vote to nearly all adult males.

Whether Giolitti's reforms would have succeeded in overcoming Italy's problems in the longer run will never be known, because of the advent of World War I. When war began in 1914, Giolitti opposed Italian participation. The Italian government decided to remain neutral, claiming that the terms of the Triple Alliance did not obligate it to enter the war on the side of Germany and Austria-Hungary. In reaction, a movement began that called for Italy to intervene in the war, although most of the interventionists wanted to ally with Britain and France. The interventionist crisis of 1914–1915 set the stage for the emergence of the Fascist movement.

CONTEXT AND PROCESS OF THE FASCIST REVOLUTION, 1915–1945

The interventionists came from a variety of political backgrounds. Nationalists saw an opportunity to assert Italy's great power status and to win from Austria the South Tyrol— the area on the southern side of the Alps—and complete Italy's "natural" frontiers. Socialists opposed the war on the grounds that the only real war for the workers was class warfare. Benito Mussolini, a leader of the radical Socialists and editor of the party newspaper *Avanti!*, decided to support intervention; he was promptly expelled from the party and the newspaper. When millions of men marched off to war, however, it was clear that nationalism had a greater appeal than Socialism.

By early 1915, both the prime minister, Antonio Salandra, and his foreign minister, Sidney Soninino, were convinced that Italy would have to declare for one side or the other. Both sides made offers to attract Italy into the war. In the meantime, Mussolini and other interventionist leaders organized mass demonstrations in favor of war against Austria. For the first time, Italy experienced politics brought to the people, the "politics of the piazza." Mussolini established his own newspaper, *Il Popolo d'Italia,* and used its pages to champion intervention. Although out of office, Giolitti continued to oppose the war, but parliament seemed weak and indecisive in the face of the initiatives of the Salandra government and the growing popularity of intervention. Giolitti, fearing civil strife, refused the king's offer to form a new government. Salandra continued and declared war on Austria on May 23, 1915.

The Italian army engaged the Austrians on the northeastern border area of the two countries. During the three and a half years of fighting, Italy lost more than 600,000 dead. The Italians suffered a disastrous defeat at Caporetto in October 1917, but the army recovered sufficiently to defeat the Austrians in the closing campaign of the war in 1918. Mussolini served in the army and was wounded.

The Italians did gain the South Tyrol as a result of the peace treaties of 1919. Nevertheless, there was a widespread belief among Italians that Italy had not received all the territory it should have from the breakup of the Austrian empire—particularly areas along the eastern shore of the Adriatic Sea, which were given to the new state of Yugoslavia. Italians complained of the "mutilated victory" that failed to recognize Italy's historical claims to territory and the great sacrifice Italy had made during the war.

The port city of Fiume provided a particular point of tension. Italy claimed but did not get the city, with its large Italian population, in 1919. When occupying Italian troops withdrew, the writer and war veteran Gabriele D'Annunzio led a group of volunteers who took over the city and set up the Regency of Carnaro in September 1919. A year later Italy and Yugoslavia agreed to make Fiume a free city, and Italian troops cleared D'Annunzio from the city. D'Annunzio's one-year experiment in Fiume, with its dramatic political rallies and speeches, provided Mussolini with examples of techniques for mass politics that he would use subsequently with his Fascist movement. For example, the Italian shock troops of the war, the Arditi, in their black uniforms, played a prominent role in Fiume and subsequently in the Fascist movement, thus providing the black shirts that became a Fascist trademark.

Italy faced serious political and economic problems after the war. Inflation and unemployment rose. Veterans found it difficult to find jobs, and many of them had difficulty adjusting to civilian life after three years of war. Industrial workers began to occupy factories in late 1920. Peasants attempted to seize land. Industrialists and landowners sought ways to defend their interests and property. The Bolshevik Revolution in Russia raised fears of a similar upheaval in Italy.

Benito Mussolini founded the Fascist movement, the Fasci di Combattimento, Combat Groups, on March 23, 1919, at a rally of several hundred supporters in Milan. Mussolini initially sought to bring together and to reconcile nationalism and Socialism. Its original program called for a peace that would reward Italy for its sacrifices while also supporting traditionally left-wing goals such as an eight-hour workday, voting rights for eighteen-year-olds and women, a republic to replace the monarchy, and worker participation in management. Fascists argued that they were at war, not with Socialism but with Socialists who had betrayed the nation by not supporting the war. In the 1919 elections, however, not a single Fascist won election to parliament.

The two major parties that emerged from the 1919 elections were the Socialist Party (PSI) and the Popular Party (PPI). The latter was Italy's first Catholic party. No single party had a majority, and the PSI and PPI refused to cooperate. In January 1921, radical Socialists who wished to follow the lead of the Bolshevik Revolution formed the Communist Party (PCI), thus dividing the left-wing forces. Given these divisions, it was difficult to form a stable national government. Giovanni Giolitti, the grand old man of Italian politics, served one more time as prime minister in 1920–1921. By 1922 the national government appeared unable to govern effectively in addressing the problems facing the country.

The Fascist movement began a dramatic growth by 1921. Fascist armed squads appeared in agricultural regions of central and northern Italy. They used violence to attack Socialists and Communists. In response to worker occupation of factories and peasant seizures of land, the squads defended the property rights of landowners, who increasingly supported the Fascists. The Fascists claimed that they were providing the law and order that the national government was not.

The Fascist movement reorganized itself as a political party, the Italian National Fascist Party (PNF), in 1921. It had several hundred thousand members and was growing. Mussolini led the party, but the squad leaders in each region had considerable influence and power. Giolitti, in the tradition of *trasformismo,* sought to include the Fascists in a coalition for the elections of May 1921. The Fascists gained thirty-five seats, only a fraction of the 535 members of the Chamber of Deputies, but this gave them a voice and a place in national politics.

Mussolini chose to make his bid for national office in October 1922. The national government under a succession of weak prime ministers seemed incapable of ruling the country. Fascists had taken control of local governments in a number of cities. Using these cities as bases, they began a "march on Rome" with thousands of black-shirted Fascists converging on Rome. King Victor Emmanuel III decided against using the army to stop them. Instead, on October 28, 1922, he invited Mussolini to form a coalition government. Mussolini agreed and became prime minister, with a cabinet that included Fascists, *popolari* (members of the Popular Party), liberals, and social democrats. Events would reveal whether this was the latest version of Italian *trasformismo* or the beginning of a Fascist revolution.

In his first two years as prime minister, Mussolini faced a dilemma. On the one hand, his most ardent Fascist followers called for the implementation of a Fascist revolution. They wanted to "Fascistize" government ministries, the armed forces, schools, universities, newspapers, and cultural organizations. On the other hand , Mussolini had reached accommodations with a variety of more conservative forces, such as the church, the army, the monarchy, and the industrialists, in order to gain office. He promised them law and order, and a measure of calm after the upheavals of 1919–1922.

There were also divisions among the Fascists. Some were Catholics, while others were anti-clerical; some were monarchists, while others were republicans; some wanted more rights and benefits for workers, while others favored employers. In 1923 the nationalist political party, Italian Nationalist Association, merged with the PNF. This move further strengthened the conservatives within the PNF and Mussolini's government.

The most outspoken critic in parliament of the Fascist-led government was a social democrat, Giacomo Matteotti. On June 10, 1924, two weeks after he made a major speech criticizing the government for violence and corruption, he was kidnapped and murdered by Fascists close to Mussolini. The Matteotti murder ignited a firestorm of criticism and calls for Mussolini's resignation. The more radical Fascists pressured Mussolini to take charge of the situation, which he eventually did in a speech to parliament on January 3, 1925. He appointed the Fascist boss of Cremona, Roberto Farinacci, as secretary of the PNF and began a crackdown on critics.

Mussolini used his considerable skill as a political tactician to put the other political parties on the defensive. He charged the Socialists and Communists with being subversives. He exploited the differences between Pope Pius XI and the Popular Party. He used the majority that the PNF had won in parliament in the April 1924 elections to pass legislation that step by step created a dictatorship by 1926. The PNF was now the only legal party, the government controlled the press, and the Fascist labor union was the only legal union.

It now remained for Mussolini to lead a Fascist government that continued to promise the Fascist Revolution while reassuring conservative forces in society that this revolution would not displace them. To keep his own Fascist Party under his control, he increased the power of the state at the expense of the party. The various factions in the Fascist Party did have one belief in common: Mussolini was their Duce. The subsequent history of the Fascist regime is the history of how Mussolini sought to keep alive the hope and expectation for the revolution of the Fascist movement while bringing stability to Italy through the Fascist regime.

Mussolini promised the Italian people that he would bring them unity as a national community. He would fulfill the hopes of the Risorgimento. He also promised that Italy would finally be a great power. Italy would no longer be the least of the great powers. Fascist Italy would revive the grandeur of the Roman empire and a true sense of "Romanness," or *Romanità.*

In economic and social policy, the Fascist Revolution claimed to offer a "third way" between capitalism and Socialism. It created corporations based on spheres of economic activity. In each corporation the employers and workers were represented, along with government members. By 1934, twenty-two such corporations became part of the National Council of Corporations. In 1939 a Chamber of Fasci and Corporations replaced the traditional Chamber of Deputies. The corporative system was supposed to resolve employment and production issues within each industry in the national interest. The system in fact was weighted in favor of employers and government policies. Strikes were illegal. The large bureaucracy required to administer the system provided jobs awarded to people on the basis of loyalty to the government and the party.

The creation of a new national community required the training of a new generation dedicated to the ideals of the Fascist Revolution. The Fascist "new man" would emerge from a combination of the educational system, youth programs, and the vigorous inculcation of physical training for sports and the military. Programs for girls and women were included, but the essential virtues and skills were male and military. War was to men what motherhood was to women, and "war alone brings all human energies to their highest state of tension and stamps with the seal of nobility the nations which dare to face it" (Mack Smith 1997, 355).

Youth organizations existed for boys and girls from elementary school through university. The most important were the Balilla, for boys eight to fourteen, and the Avanguardisti, from fourteen to eighteen. They participated prominently in the rallies and parades that were an integral part of public life in Fascist Italy.

The Fascist Revolution sought to win over the people through the development of a Fascist mass culture. The National Organization for Afterwork, the Dopolavoro, sponsored sports contests, excursions, vacation trips, and entertainment such as plays, movies, and listening to the radio. The government controlled the mass media: newspapers, radio, and movies. The Luce organization produced the newsreels shown in all movie houses. The creation of a Ministry of Culture and Propaganda in 1937 further enhanced the ability of the regime to "go to the people."

The military style of Fascism also revealed itself in the "battles" waged by the government to achieve "autarchy," economic self-sufficiency, for Italy. Mussolini led a very public "battle for grain" to make Italy self-sufficient in wheat. Although the program produced dramatic increases in wheat production, it was economically inefficient and meant using often marginal land for wheat instead of more productive exports such as fruits, vegetables, and wine. There was also a "battle for the lira" to strengthen the currency, although it artificially overvalued the lira. This meant higher prices at home and fewer exports. The goals of autarchy were political and showed Mussolini's concern for politics over economics.

Mussolini also waged the "battle of births" to increase the Italian population. There were financial incentives to have large families. The Ministry for Maternity and Childhood (OMNI) provided medical and other benefits. Despite these efforts, however, there was not a marked increase in the population.

The Fascist Revolution included ambitious public works programs to provide employment and to demonstrate the vigor and modernity of the new Italy. Government buildings, housing projects, sports facilities, railroad stations, roads, and highways appeared all over the country. Architects and artists designed such projects in a variety of styles, some strikingly modern. An example was the Exhibition of the Fascist Revolution in Rome in 1932, which attracted nearly 4 million visitors over two years. Fascism sought to portray itself as modern and dynamic, as an alternative system to decadent liberal capitalism and subversive Socialism and Communism, which would undermine national unity by fomenting class warfare.

The Fascist government accomplished the long-desired goal of draining the Pontine Marshes south of Rome. That vast project of land redemption provided new farm land and space for five new towns. The regime used the project as a demonstration of its ability to get jobs done that previous governments had only talked about. The concept of land redemption, *bonifica,* also became a metaphor for the redemption of the nation by the Fascist Revolution.

Fascism, unlike Nazism, had no racial doctrines or anti-Semitism, and many Jews supported the Fascist regime. Mussolini, however, hoping to give new life to the Fascist Revolution, introduced racial laws in 1938 barring Jews from the party, the government, the professions, and schools. Generally, Italians were not enthusiastic about this move, and some saw it as simply imitating Germany.

Mussolini believed that ultimately war would demonstrate the power of the new Italy and fulfill the Fascist Revolution. The conquest of Ethiopia in 1935–1936 avenged the humiliating defeat at Adowa in 1896 and showed the world that Italy was a power to reckon with. Mussolini responded to condemnation by the League of Nations by withdrawing from the League and accepting diplomatic support from Nazi Germany.

In 1936, Mussolini declared that a new Rome-Berlin Axis was emerging in Europe. Although he had fears about Germany's economic and military power, he saw Hitler as a potential ally, ideologically compatible with Fascism. Hitler had admired Mussolini in the decade before he came to power in Germany in 1933. The two demonstrated the new relationship by giving military assistance to General Francisco Franco's forces in the Spanish Civil War from 1936 to 1939.

Mussolini hoped that as Hitler's partner he could develop Italy's power in the Balkans and the Mediterranean. Italy signed a formal alliance with Germany in early 1939 under the leadership of Mussolini's foreign minister and son-in-law, Count Galeazzo Ciano. When Germany invaded Poland on September 1, 1939, Britain and France responded by declaring war on Germany. Mussolini, realizing Italy's lack of military readiness, remained neutral. In June 1940, however, as the German blitzkrieg overran France, he declared war as Hitler's ally and invaded France.

The war that should have fulfilled and demonstrated the strength of the Fascist Revolution led instead to its defeat. Italian forces invaded Greece in October 1940 but met sharp Greek resistance and required German support to win. After Hitler invaded Russia in 1941, Mussolini sent an army to the Russian front that met defeat and disintegration in the winter of 1942–1943. Italian and German forces in North Africa surrendered to the Allies in May 1943. The United States and Britain invaded and conquered Sicily in July. These military failures and the imminent Allied invasion of the Italian peninsula led to Mussolini's downfall.

The Fascist Grand Council, meeting for the first time in years, gave Mussolini a vote of no confidence at an all-night meeting on July 24–25. The king exercised his constitutional authority to dismiss Mussolini, place him under arrest, and appoint a career army leader, Marshal Pietro Badoglio, the new prime minister. The Germans managed to rescue Mussolini and set him up in northern Italy in a puppet regime called the Italian Social Republic. As the Allied armies fought their way up the Italian peninsula, they liberated Rome on June 4, 1944. German armies in Italy surrendered on April 25, 1945. Three days later Mussolini was shot by armed Italian partisans. His body, along with that of his mistress and a group of his closest Fascist followers, was strung up in a gas station in Milan. The Fascist Revolution was over.

IMPACTS

The armed resistance to German and Italian Fascist forces from 1943 to 1945 had brought together a broad spectrum of groups and parties: liberal, republican, Communist, Socialist, and Catholic. They were willing to set aside their differences to fight the common enemy. Immediately after the war their shared anti-Fascism formed the basis of the new political order.

The referendum in 1946 rejected the monarchy that had compromised itself through its association with Fascism. The new constitution of 1948 banned the Fascist Party and provided for a weak prime minister as a reaction to the dictatorship of Mussolini. Anti-Fascism permeated cultural life as well. The historical appraisals of the Fascist period, for example, concentrated on opposition elements during the 1930s and the armed resistance during the war.

Despite these measures, a neo-Fascist party did emerge: the Italian Social Movement, the Movimento Sociale Italiano. The party initials, MSI, suggested Mussolini's name. Most of the leaders of the party had been active in the Italian Social Republic, which Mussolini led after his rescue by the Germans in September 1943 until his death in April 1945. This so-called Salò Republic, named for the town in northern Italy where Mussolini had his headquarters, had revived the rhetoric of the initial Fascist movement, calling for a program that would favor labor over the "parasitic plutocracies." Mussolini charged the king with treason for going over to the Allies. Now his new Fascist republic would be free to implement a more radical program, calling for the nationalization of industries and more rights for workers, reminiscent of the original Fascist program in 1919. Given the war and Salò's subordination to the Germans, there was no opportunity to carry out such a program.

The MSI party normally received less than 10 percent of the vote in national and local elections, but it occasionally had some influence because Italy's multiparty system gave no one party a clear majority. The Christian Democratic party dominated the national coalition governments during the Cold War (1948–1990) and refused to admit the Communist Party (PCI) into its coalitions. The MSI was not taken into coalitions either, but occasionally it had some influence by delivering votes to the government coalition.

In the 1990s, after the Cold War, the political situation in Italy underwent a dramatic transformation. The absence of Cold War issues and the public outcry against the re-established parties as a result of revelations of systematic corruption undermined the strength of the leading parties: the Christian Democrats, the Communists, and the Socialists. The Communist Party changed its name to the Democratic Party of the Left (PDS), and the neo-Fascist MSI changed its

Italian dictator Benito Mussolini (left) and German chancellor Adolf Hitler in Munich, Germany, ca. June 1940. (National Archives)

name to the National Alliance (AN). The leader of the AN, Gianfranco Fini, disavowed the party's Fascist origins and worked to establish the party as a broad-based conservative party.

On the international level, Italian Fascism gave its name to the broad political concept of "Fascism" in the 1930s. The term became generic for a host of revolutionary nationalist movements in Europe, although only the German National Socialist Party under Adolph Hitler came to power. Historians continue to debate the relationship of these two movements, but by the mid 1930s the term "Fascism" had become popular in referring to Italian Fascists, German Nazis, and movements that resembled them. The Spanish Civil War (1936–1939) served as a catalyst in the emerging definition and understanding of Fascism.

General Francisco Franco led a revolt against the leftist Spanish Republic in 1936. In the bitter civil war that followed,

Mussolini and Hitler sent military support to Franco. The republican side received aid from the Soviet Union. Volunteers from a number of countries including the United States fought in international brigades for the republic. The struggle quickly became defined as a struggle between Fascism and anti-Fascism. The Italian term "Fascism" now took on a broader meaning as part of an international struggle. Franco won the civil war, although he never defined his government as Fascist and refused Mussolini's and Hitler's invitations to ally with them during World War II.

World War II itself became a war to defeat Fascism. The term was even extended to the Japanese regime allied with Italy and Germany. The alliance of Britain, the United States, and the Soviet Union found common cause in combating Fascism. The Soviet Union's major role in defeating Germany temporarily silenced the British and U.S. fears of international Communism controlled by the Soviet Union.

After World War II the Soviet Union continued to use its anti-Fascism to legitimize international Communism. Fascism thus continued to find use in referring generally to right-wing or conservative movements opposed by Communist, left-wing, and "progressive" forces. Increasingly the term "Fascism" became a term used in the polemics of the Cold War. The end of the Cold War did not bring an end to the use of the term. It is still heard in partisan political debates when one side demonizes opponents as "Fascists."

Since World War II historians have studied and debated the meaning of Fascism. The most common view sees a connection between many of the movements in the 1930s that mixed nationalism with new forms of mass politics that promised some sort of national rebirth. Mussolini's movement and regime emerged in the early 1920s and thus furnished an example to Hitler and others—as well as the term "Fascism," which became widely used in the 1930s. Italian Fascism and German National Socialism have come under particular scrutiny as the only two of these movements to take control of national governments.

Some scholars believe that Fascism was strictly a European phenomenon between the two world wars, spawned by the conditions of the time, while others argue that the essential elements of Fascism could reappear in other times and places, such as Juan Peron's movement in Argentina. The continuing study of Fascism and the debate about its meaning is the most obvious legacy of the Italian Fascist Revolution.

PEOPLE AND ORGANIZATIONS

Balbo, Italo (1896–1940)

Italo Balbo was a Fascist leader and aviator. After serving in World War I, he joined the Fascist movement in 1921, quickly establishing himself as the *ras,* or boss, of Ferrara. He organized the armed squads that came to dominate the Po Valley and took part in the March on Rome. Balbo served as minister of aviation and gained international fame for his transatlantic flights, including one to New York and Chicago in 1933. Mussolini sent him to Libya as governor-general in 1934. Balbo remained loyal to Mussolini, although he opposed the alliance with Nazi Germany and the anti-Semitic racial laws. He died early in the war when Italian gunners mistakenly shot down his fighter plane.

Bottai, Giuseppe

Giuseppe Bottai (1895–1959) was one of the principal intellectuals in the Fascist regime. He served in the Italian shock troops, the Arditi, during World War I. Bottai believed that the Fascist Revolution should be carried out by a new governing elite based on merit. He served as minister of corporations 1929–1932, as governor of Rome 1935–1936, and as minister of education 1936–1943. He edited a literary journal, *Primato,* 1940–1943, that appealed to intellectuals who had grown skeptical of the Fascist regime. As a member of the Fascist Grand Council, Bottai voted against Mussolini at the meeting of July 24–25, 1943. The next year he escaped from Italy and joined the French foreign legion.

Ciano, Galeazzo

Count Galeazzo Ciano (1903–1944) married Mussolini's daughter Edda in 1930. Mussolini appointed him foreign minister in 1936. Ciano quickly centralized control of the foreign ministry and played a central role in key areas such as intervention in the Spanish Civil War and the alliance with Nazi Germany. Although he had some doubts about the latter, he represented Italy at the signing of the Pact of Steel in May 1939. He sought to counterbalance Germany's growing domination of central Europe by Italy's takeover of Albania in 1939. Ciano's influence waned following the failed Italian invasion of Greece that required German intervention to achieve victory. He voted against Mussolini at the Fascist Grand Council meeting of July 24–25, 1943, and was subsequently imprisoned. Ciano and several others who had voted against Mussolini went on trial in Verona in January 1944. Ciano was condemned and executed by firing squad.

Corporations

Fascism created a system of corporations that represented various sectors of industry and the arts. Each corporation contained representatives of employers, workers, and the government with jurisdiction over policy matters, working conditions, and wages. In theory, corporativism provided a new and better way to govern economic, social, and political relationships than traditional parliamentary systems. By 1934, twenty-two corporations were established, and the large Ministry of Corporations, opened in 1932, housed the bureaucracy entrusted with administering the system. In fact, the corporate structure favored employers over employees and failed to bring about major changes in Italian social and economic life. A Chamber of Fasci and Corporations replaced the Chamber of Deputies in 1939, but parliament had already become a rubber stamp for the dictatorship.

D'Annunzio, Gabriele

Gabriele D'Annunzio (1863–1938) was a well-known literary figure when he led a force of volunteers who occupied the disputed city of Fiume in 1919. His Republic of Canaro lasted only a year, but his theatrical style of politics influenced the subsequent development of Fascism. Mussolini saw D'Annunzio as a potential rival but managed to confer enough honors on him to keep his support. D'Annunzio died in 1938 shortly after Mussolini had appointed him president of the Royal Academy.

Dopolavoro

The Opera Nazionale Dopolavoro (OND) was the after-work, leisure-time organization of the Fascist regime. It sponsored a wide variety of programs for peasants and white- and blue-collar workers that included sports, excursions, plays, movies, and vacation trips. The ONB was a major attempt to win the adherence of Italians through a program of mass culture.

Farinacci, Roberto

Roberto Farinacci (1892–1945) was one of the leading Fascist radicals; he served as the *ras,* or boss, of Cremona in 1921–1922. In 1924, following the murder of Giacomo Matteotti, Farinacci and other Fascist intransigents pressured Mussolini to take action and impose dictatorial powers. Mussolini appointed Farinacci secretary of the Fascist Party in 1925 but dismissed him after a year in order to maintain his own control of the party. Despite marginalization, Farinacci continued to be loyal to Mussolini while advocating implementation of revolutionary Fascism. Farinacci supported the racial laws of 1938 and became pro-Nazi in sympathy. When the Germans occupied Italy in 1943, Farinacci returned to Cremona during the German occupation. He was executed by a partisan firing squad in April 1945.

Fascist Grand Council

The Fascist Grand Council began as an advisory committee in the Fascist Party but later became part of the Fascist state. In 1928 a law established the grand council as parallel to the cabinet. It met only when Mussolini called it, and its members included leading Fascist Party members and ministers of state. In theory it had a wide range of power, but in fact it functioned as an extension of Mussolini's dictatorship. Mussolini did not call it into session after 1939 until July 24, 1943, when a vote of no confidence by the grand council led to Mussolini's dismissal by the king.

Gentile, Giovanni

Giovanni Gentile (1875–1944) was the most important philosopher to support Fascism. He became the leading ideological figure during the Fascist regime. He served as minister of education from 1922 to 1924 and wrote the educational reforms of 1924. Gentile was the editor of the *Italian Encyclopedia,* which appeared in 1932. It is believed that he wrote the entry on "Fascism" attributed to Mussolini. The article defined Fascism in terms of an all-powerful totalitarian state. The radical Fascists criticized Gentile as too conservative, and conservative clerical Fascists denounced him for his opposition to the Lateran Treaty of 1929. He remained loyal to Mussolini and supported the Salò Republic. Partisans executed him in 1944.

Grandi, Dino

Dino Grandi (1895–1988) was an early and prominent member of the Fascist movement in Bologna. He played an important role in the March on Rome, but his political maneuvering made Mussolini suspicious of him. Grandi remained sufficiently loyal to Mussolini to emerge in the 1920s as a diplomat for the regime. As minister of foreign affairs, 1929–1932, he sought to implement a moderate policy that would strengthen Italy's European status without recourse to war. Grandi's moderation led to his dismissal by Mussolini in 1932, but he subsequently became ambassador to England, where he served until 1939. Grandi's quiet diplomacy and anti-German stance after 1936 earned the enmity of foreign minister Galeazzo Ciano, although later he worked with Ciano to keep Italy out of war in 1939. It was Grandi who introduced a motion of no confidence in Mussolini at the meeting of the Fascist Grand Council on the night of July 24–25, 1943. The vote carried, and the king dismissed Mussolini from office. The new government under Marshal Pietro Badoglio sent Grandi to Portugal, where he remained until after the war, returning to Italy in the 1950s.

Italian Fascist Party

Mussolini founded the first Fasci di Combattimento, Combat Group, at a rally in Milan on March 23, 1919. Fasci referred to loosely organized political groups, not political parties. The movement adopted the symbol of the fasces, a bundle of rods held together to show unity, with an ax protruding from the center, that the lectors had carried in ancient Rome as a symbol of authority. The successful organization of local fasci in central and northern Italy in 1920–1921 led to the formal organization of the National Fascist Party (PNF) in November 1921. Following the March on Rome, the Italian Nationalist Association merged with the PNF, further encouraging Mussolini to impose state control over the Fascist Party. By 1926, the PNF was the only legal party as Mussolini established his dictatorship. The party's initial appeal was to war veterans, youth, and segments of the urban and rural middle classes fearful of a Socialist- or Bolshevik-style revolution. Its ideology was firmly nationalist, with the promise of a Fascist revolution to create a new national community based on class collaboration, although it promised action to bring stability, law, and order as more important than ideological abstractions. In the 1930s, when Achille Starace served as party secretary, membership in the PNF became open, and thousands applied for the party card that increasingly was required for jobs and political favors. The PNF had a number of factions, but they all agreed on Mussolini's leadership. This led to the cult of the Duce. Thus Mussolini became the embodiment of the Fascist Party and the Fascist Revolution.

Italian Nationalist Association

Founded in 1910, the Italian Nationalist Association functioned as a political party and pressure group favoring a strong state, protectionist economic policies, and an aggressive colonial policy. It never attained a mass base or large numbers of deputies elected to parliament, but its program and firm anti-Socialist stance gained adherents among conservative industrialists and landowners. It merged with the Fascist Party, the PNF, in March 1923, further strengthening Mussolini's standing among conservative interests and his subsequent creation of a strong Fascist state, a strong foreign policy, and state domination of workers' organizations and unions.

Ministry of Popular Culture

The Fascist regime sought a totalitarian control of culture and society through control of the mass media. It transformed its press office in 1937 into a new ministry of popular culture, patterned after Josef Goebbels's ministry in Nazi Germany, supervising the press, radio, film, and cultural policies generally. The ministry never attained its goal of creating a Fascist revolutionary culture for the mass of Italians.

Mussolini, Benito

Benito Mussolini (1883–1945) was the creator of the Fascist movement and leader, or Duce, of the Fascist regime from 1922 to 1945. Initially Mussolini was a leader of the radical wing of the Socialist Party (PSI) and editor of the party newspaper *Avanti!* He opposed the Italian conquest of Libya in 1911–1912 as an imperialist war that was irrelevant for the struggles of the working class. When Italy remained neutral in 1914, Mussolini changed to an interventionist position and campaigned for Italy's entrance into the war. Italy did go to war against Austria in May 1915. Mussolini served in the army until wounded in a grenade accident. In 1919 he founded the Fasci di Combattimento, the movement that quickly became known as Fascism. The movement became a political party, the Partito Nazionale Fascista, or PNF, in 1921. Fascist agitation and the use of violence to attack Socialists and defend landowners in central and northern Italy gained wide support in 1921–1922. Fascism presented itself as a true national revolution that would save Italy from a bloody Bolshevik-style revolution. The Fascist March on Rome in October 1922 led to King Victor Emmanuel III's invitation to Mussolini to form a coalition government. Mussolini accepted and transformed the constitutional government into a dictatorship by 1926. He ruled Italy until 1943, attempting to carry out a revolution to create a new national community to unify Italians and make Italy a great power. As Italy's Duce he allied with Germany's Führer, Adolf Hitler, in the Rome-Berlin Axis. He took Italy into war against France and Britain in 1940 when the German army overran France. Mussolini had failed, however, to produce the modern armed forces that he had promised. Italy suffered major military defeats that led to Mussolini's dismissal by the king with the support of dissident Fascist leaders in July 1943. The Germans rescued Mussolini and set him up in northern Italy as head of a new Fascist government. Partisans executed Mussolini after capturing him as he tried to escape to Switzerland in April 1945.

MVSN, The Militia

The Fascist movement gained its initial momentum beginning in late 1920 from its armed squads, or *squadristi,* which defended landowners from Socialists and land-occupying peasants. The squads justified their violence as necessary to save Italy from a bloody, class-based revolution in the face of a weak and indecisive national government. After Mussolini became prime minister, he sought to control the squads through creation of the Militia, the Milizia Volontaria per la Sicurezza Nazionale, or MVSN. Militia members had certain privileges and militia units performed various civic and military duties, but the more militant members were frustrated that Mussolini did not carry out a more thorough Fascist Revolution.

OVRA

OVRA was the name of the secret police organization during the Fascist regime, under the direction of Arturo Bocchini until his death in 1940. Bocchini was a professional police officer and not a Fascist. OVRA functioned primarily to strengthen the Fascist state, not to further the goals of Fascism.

Special Tribunal for the Defense of the State

Mussolini established the Special Tribunal in 1927 as a new mechanism outside the established legal system to prosecute anti-Fascist activities. More than 5,000 political opponents of the regime were sentenced between 1927 and 1943. The majority received prison sentences, and twenty-nine were condemned to death.

Youth Organizations

The Fascist regime promised to produce a new generation of Italians dedicated to the Fascist Revolution through the educational system and an elaborate set of youth organizations. Primary emphasis was on the groups for boys, who were trained for sports, gymnastics, and the military, but there were also parallel organizations for girls. The reorganization in 1937 put all the youth groups under the umbrella of the Gioventù Italiana del Littorio (GIL). The best known of the groups was the Balilla, named for a heroic boy who had opposed the Austrians; it enrolled boys from ages eight to fourteen.

Borden Painter

See Also Democracy, Dictatorship, and Fascism; Documentaries of Revolution; Human Rights, Morality, Social Justice, and Revolution; Ideology, Propaganda, and Revolution; Italian Risorgimento; Japanese New Order Movement; Literature and Modern Revolution; Nationalism and Revolution; Nazi Revolution: Politics of Racial Hierarchy; Terrorism; War and Revolution

References and Further Readings
Bosworth, R. J. B. 2002. *Mussolini*. London: Arnold.
Cannistraro, Philip V., ed. 1982. *Historical Dictionary of Fascist Italy*. Westport, CT: Greenwood.
De Felice, Renzo. 1976. *Fascism: An Informal Introduction to Its Theory and Practice*. New Brunswick, NJ: Transaction.
———.1977. *Interpretations of Fascism*. Cambridge, MA: Harvard University Press.
De Grand, Alexander. 2000. *Italian Fascism*. 3rd edition. Lincoln: University of Nebraska Press.
De Grazia, Victoria. 1981. *The Culture of Consent: Mass Organization of Leisure in Fascist Italy*. Cambridge: Cambridge University Press.
———. 1992. *How Fascism Ruled Women: Italy, 1922–1945*. Berkeley: University of California Press.
Delzell, Charles, ed. 1970. *Mediterranean Fascism, 1919–1945*. New York: Walker.
Eatwell, Roger. 1997. *Fascism: A History*. New York: Penguin.
Gentile, Emilio. 1996. *The Sacralization of Politics in Fascist Italy*. Translated by Keith Botsford. Cambridge, MA: Harvard University Press.
Griffin, Roger. 1993. *The Nature of Fascism*. London: Routledge.
Knox, MacGregor. 1982. *Mussolini Unleashed, 1939–1941: Politics and Strategy in Fascist Italy's Last War*. London: Cambridge University Press.
Koon, Tracy H. 1985. *Believe, Obey, Fight: Political Socialization of Youth in Fascist Italy, 1922–1943*. Chapel Hill: University of North Carolina Press.
Lyttelton, Adrian. 1987. *The Seizure of Power: Fascism in Italy, 1919–1929*. 2nd edition. Princeton, NJ: Princeton University Press.
Mack Smith, Denis. 1982. *Mussolini*. New York: Knopf.
———.1997. *Modern Italy*. Ann Arbor: University of Michigan.
Paxton, Robert O. 2004. *The Anatomy of Fascism*. New York: Knopf.
Payne, Stanley G. 1995. *A History of Fascism, 1914–1945*. Madison: University of Wisconsin Press.
Pollard, John F. 1985. *The Vatican and Italian Fascism, 1929–1932*. Cambridge: Cambridge University Press.
Stille, Alexander. 1991. *Benevolence and Betrayal: Five Jewish Families under Fascism*. New York: Summit.
Stone, Marla Susan. 1998. *The Patron State: Culture & Politics in Fascist Italy*. Princeton, NJ: Princeton University Press.
Whittam, John. 1995. *Fascist Italy*. Manchester: Manchester University Press.

Italian Risorgimento

CHRONOLOGY

1494	French invasion of Italy shows that the Italian states cannot defend the peninsula. France and Spain vie for control in the "Wars of Italy" (1494–1529).
1559	Treaty of Cateau-Cambrésis confirms Spanish hegemony in Italy.
1714	Treaty of Rastatt ends War of the Spanish Succession (1702–1714) and gives Austria the dominant role in the Italian peninsula.
1789	Outbreak of the French Revolution encourages expectations of change in Italy.
1796	General Napoléon Bonaparte (later Emperor Napoléon I) invades Italy, establishes "Jacobin republics" in northern Italy.

1797	France and Austria sign Treaty of Campoformio, which liquidates the Venetian Republic and cedes its territory to Austria.
1798	The Roman Republic extends French influence to central Italy.
1799	French establish Parthenopean Republic in Naples. Peasant revolts topple its government. Austro-Russian armies drive French out of northern Italy while Napoléon is away on his Egyptian campaign.
1800	Napoléon returns, defeats Austrians at the Battle of Marengo.
1801	Treaty of Luneville confirms French control of Italy. The Italian Republic formed in northern Italy.
1802	France annexes Piedmont and parts of Tuscany. Napoléon assumes title of president of the Italian Republic.
1805	The Italian Republic becomes the Kingdom of Italy, with Napoléon as its king and Napoléon's stepson, Eugene de Beauharnais, as viceroy. France annexes Liguria. Austria cedes Venetia to the Kingdom of Italy after losing the battle of Austerlitz. Giuseppe Mazzini is born in Genoa.
1806	French occupy the Kingdom of Naples and install Napoléon's brother, Joseph Bonaparte, as king.
1807	Giuseppe Garibaldi is born in Nice.
1808	French occupy Rome. Napoléon's general and brother-in-law Joachim Murat succeeds Joseph as king of Naples.
1809	France annexes the Papal States, imprisons Pope Pius VII.
1810	Camillo Benso, Count of Cavour, is born in Turin.
1814	Napoléon is defeated by a coalition of conservative powers. Kingdom of Italy collapses. Austria annexes Lombardy and Venetia.
1815	Congress of Vienna (1814–1815) restores the Bourbons to Naples, House of Savoy to an enlarged Kingdom of Sardinia, the pope to the Papal States, House of Habsburg-Lorraine to Tuscany; consolidates Austrian control of Italy.
1817	First uprisings in central Italy led by Carboneria and other secret societies.
1820	A military revolt inspired by a similar one in Spain breaks out in Naples. Neapolitan troops put down a Sicilian insurgency demanding constitutional government and autonomy from Naples.
1821	Insurgents in Piedmont demand a constitution. Austrian troops put down uprisings in Naples; Austrian and Piedmontese troops do likewise in Piedmont-Sardinia.
1827	Alessandro Manzoni publishes the first version of his novel *I promessi Sposi* (*The Betrothed*), which becomes a patriotic text.
1831	Revolt in France triggers uprisings in Bologna, Modena, and Parma; Austria suppresses the revolts. Charles Albert becomes king of Piedmont-Sardinia. Giuseppe Mazzini founds Young Italy in Marseilles.
1834	Mazzinian insurrections fail in Genoa and Savoy.
1843	Vincenzo Gioberti's book *On the Moral and Civil Primacy of the Italians* stirs patriotic sentiment in Italy and launches the Neo-Guelph movement, which calls on the pope to lead the movement for Italian independence.
1844	Cesare Balbo's *Delle speranze d'Italia* (On the Hopes of Italy) sees the House of Savoy as leading the national movement.
1846	Pius IX (Pio Nono) is elected pope; his reputation as a liberal encourages the Neo-Guelph movement and expectations of peaceful change.
1848	Revolts break out in Sicily, Naples, Tuscany, Milan, and Venice; constitutions are promul-

gated in Naples, Rome, Tuscany, and Piedmont-Sardinia. Charles Albert of Piedmont-Sardinia declares war on Austria (First War of National Independence); Austrian counterattack drives Charles Albert's army back into Piedmont.

1849   Proclamation of the Roman Republic led by Mazzini; France, Austria, and Spain send troops to suppress the Roman Republic; Piedmont-Sardinia, Rome, and Venice capitulate. Charles Albert abdicates in favor of his son Victor Emmanuel II. Piedmont-Sardinia retains its constitution.

1850   Piedmont parliament adopts anticlerical laws to curb power of clergy and welcomes anti-Austrian political exiles from other Italian states.

1852   Cavour becomes prime minister of Piedmont-Sardinia.

1855   Piedmont-Sardinia allies with England and France; sends 15,000 troops to fight Russia in the Crimean War, leaving neutral Austria diplomatically isolated.

1857   The Italian National Society calls on all patriots to unite behind Piedmont-Sardinia and King Victor Emmanuel II.

1858   Cavour and Napoléon III negotiate the secret agreement of Plombières to wage war on Austria.

1859   Cavour provokes war with Austria (Second War of National Independence). Piedmont-Sardinia annexes Lombardy. Anti-Austrian revolts calling for union with Piedmont-Sardinia break out in Tuscany, Parma, and Modena.

1860   Garibaldi leads the successful Expedition of the Thousand that topples the Bourbon dynasty in Sicily and Naples. Piedmontese forces invade the Papal States and seize the regions of Marches, Umbria, and part of Latium, leaving Rome to the pope.

1861   Kingdom of Italy proclaimed (March 17). Rome and Venice remain under papal and Austrian rule, respectively.

1862   Troops of the newly formed Kingdom of Italy prevent Garibaldi from marching on Rome (Battle of Aspromonte). Brigandage and peasant uprisings spread in the south.

1866   Italy joins Prussia in war against Austria (Third War of National Independence); Austria yields Venice and the Venetia region to Italy.

1867   French troops stop Garibaldi's second attempt to take Rome (Battle of Mentana).

1869   Italy takes its first step toward colonialism in Africa with the establishment of a settlement in Eritrea.

1870   Italian army occupies Rome, which becomes the national capital, a major goal of the Risorgimento. The provinces of Trent and Trieste remain within the Austrian empire until the end of World War I (dubbed the Fourth War of National Independence by Italian irredentists).

INTRODUCTION

Various interpretations of the origins of the Risorgimento have one thing in common: they all suggest that the movement aimed at more than political independence, that it was an effort to restore Italy to a place of prominence in European and world affairs. Risorgimento ("resurgence, renewal") meant recapturing some glorious aspect of the past. The legal traditions and power of ancient Rome, the republican spirit and commercial dynamism of medieval communes, the cultural achievements of Renaissance city-states, even the universalism of the Roman Catholic Church—all were plausible points of reference for nineteenth-century Italian patriots. Perhaps not surprisingly, it was the "myth" of ancient Rome that appealed to the young. Goffredo Mameli (1827–1849), the poet who became one of the Risorgimento's young martyrs, expressed the Risorgimento's passion for the military glory of ancient Rome in the lyrics of Italy's national anthem:

> *Fratelli d'Italia, l'Italia s'è desta,*
> *Dell'elmo di Scipio s'è cinta la testa.*
> *(Italian brothers, Italy has risen,*
> *Scipio's helmet adorns its head.)*

BACKGROUND: CULTURE AND HISTORY

Italian aspirations for independence and unity found brief but significant encouragement in the Napoleonic invasion of Italy in 1796. But hopes for independence were soon dashed. In the years of full Napoleonic control (1800–1814), Italy became part of the French empire, and Italians had to be satisfied with mostly symbolic concessions to the spirit of independence, such as the adoption by the Kingdom of Italy, one of Napoléon's satellite states, of the green-white-red tricolor, modeled after the blue-white-red flag of post-revolutionary France. The more substantial Napoleonic contributions to the movement for national unification were unintentional. Thousands of unemployed Italian officers trained to fight Napoléon's wars rallied to the national cause after Napoléon's defeat. The Carboneria, one of several secret societies born in opposition to Napoleonic rule, served as incubator of the movement for national independence. Secret societies would flourish in the climate of conservative restoration that prevailed after 1815, this time in opposition to Austrian dominance.

The Congress of Vienna (1814–1815) set the stage on which the Risorgimento played out. Its guiding figures redrew the map of Italy so that it would fit into their scheme of restoring monarchs to their thrones, while simultaneously creating a balance of power that would hem in France, the country held responsible for the outbreak of revolution and war. Austria regained its dominant position and role of policeman in the Italian peninsula. The regions of Lombardy and Venetia were incorporated into the Austrian empire, and the rest of the peninsula was divided into satellite states that relied on Austrian protection. Among these states, the Kingdom of Sardinia, comprising the island of Sardinia and the mainland regions of Savoy, Piedmont, and Liguria, and generally referred to as the Kingdom of Piedmont-Sardinia, was the most independent-minded.

The Carboneria proved the most troublesome, for it appealed to the educated and included lawyers, doctors, and journalists, flanked by smaller numbers of educated urban workers and mariners. Carbonari insurgencies occurred in Naples, Piedmont, and Lombardy in 1820–1821, and in the Papal States and the Duchies of Modena and Parma in 1831. Insurgents demanded constitutions and elected parliaments to limit the power of absolute monarchs. Demands for independence reflected anti-Austrian feelings rather than any widespread desire for national unity. *Libertà* was the other great watchword of nineteenth-century revolutions. It meant constitutional guarantees, civil rights, parliamentary government, and limited voting rights for property holders and the educated. But in the minds of some revolutionists, such as Filippo Michele Buonarroti (1761–1837), the concept was stretched to mean that there could be no liberty without economic equality. His secret Society of the Sublime and Perfect Masters plotted first against Napoléon, then against Austria. In the 1820s he took over the Carboneria. His book *Babeuf's Conspiracy for Equality* (1828) was obligatory reading for all radicals of his generation.

It was Austria's role to repress these movements, which alarmed not only governments but also conservatives and moderates who feared a repetition of the bloody events of the French Revolution and Napoleonic Wars. Under the guidance of Prince Clemens von Metternich (1773–1859), Austrian policy banked most on setting an example of fairness and correctness in matters of public administration. Thus he encouraged Italian rulers to pursue administrative reforms, to rely on competent civil servants, and to include members of the Napoleonic administration who were loyal to the new order.

CONTEXT AND PROCESS OF REVOLUTION

Opposition to Austrian rule took a radical turn after 1831. In that year, Giuseppe Mazzini founded Young Italy (Giovine Italia) in Marseilles, where he had expatriated after his arrest as a carbonaro. Young Italy supplemented the conspiratorial methods of the secret societies with open proselytizing. It used the political press to spread its message. Young Italy was uncompromisingly republican and the enemy of monarchy in any form. It called for national unity rather than the more nebulous concept of national independence, which had left the door open to loose forms of association that Mazzini deemed incompatible with the kind of strong leadership he expected of a national government. Mazzini rejected all social philosophies based on materialism, and later on would explicitly condemn Socialism for precisely that reason. But in the 1830s Socialism was in the process of being defined. Mazzini made his contribution to that effort by stressing the urgency and legitimacy of the social question, but insisting also on the dangers of any ideology that ignored spiritual needs, divided the social classes, and undermined national unity. Young Italy insisted that the national question and the social question could not be separated, and that the national state democratically run was an essential link on the continuum that tied individuals to humanity through the intermediate institutions of family and nation.

Young Italy wanted to speak for the people, defined as the aggregate of men and women who were politically sentient. Mazzini's problem was that he found too few of those. Young Italy's attempts to stir up revolution failed spectacularly in 1833–1834, but its commitment to action, its broad network of cells, and its appeal to the people spoke to its revolutionary nature. Metternich called Mazzini the most dangerous man in Europe.

Italy and the rest of Europe remained outwardly calm until the mid 1840s. Disaffection found an outlet in the arts and literature of Romanticism. Literature, theater, and music played a special role in Italy. Censorship could not silence the cry of *Viva la libertà* that was lodged in novels, plays, and operas. Manzoni's *I promessi sposi* (1827) was read as a tale of divine retribution against the arrogant oppressors of the humble and powerless. Gioacchino Rossini (1792–1868) understood the theatrical appeal of patriotism, and used it to good effect in *William Tell* (1829). Alessandro Silvio Pellico's popular *Le mie prigioni* (1832) was a religious meditation on his experiences as a political prisoner. Its several translations popularized the Italian cause, particularly in the Anglo-Saxon world, where the religious note evoked a sympathetic response. Others struck warlike poses. Massimo d'Azeglio's novel *Ettore Fieramosca* (1833) reminded Italians of their former military valor, supposedly lost under foreign domination. Historical novels, plays, and operas, especially those of Giuseppe Verdi (1813–1901), stirred patriotic sentiments. Mazzini's writings were smuggled into Italy. Vincenzo Gioberti published his *On the Moral and Civil Primacy of the Italians* (1843) in Brussels. The popularity of Gioberti's book was largely the result of the author's faith that the papacy would lead the crusade for Italian independence, thus avoiding conflict with the church and the dire prospect of revolution.

A growing number of political exiles took advantage of the relative freedom that they enjoyed in places such as Belgium, England, and France to keep the idea of revolution alive in Italy, where by the mid 1840s a new generation of young activists, who had not experienced the failures and disillusionments of the "generation of 1820," was ready to act. The surprise election of Cardinal Giovanni Maria Mastai-Ferretti as Pope Pius IX in 1846 electrified Italian patriots, who thought that they had found a champion in the young, handsome, likable, and reputedly liberal prelate. The political demonstrations that followed the papal election coalesced with developments elsewhere to create the revolutionary climate of 1848. The Year of Revolution began with the Sicilian uprising of January, directed primarily against Bourbon rule. Europe took notice when revolution broke out in Paris in February and the Parisians proclaimed the republic. In March, insurgents forced the Austrians to evacuate the Lombard capital of Milan after five days of street fighting. Venice, Florence, Naples, and Rome joined the fray.

On March 23, 1848, King Charles Albert of Piedmont-Sardinia (1831–1849) declared war on Austria (First War of National Independence) and led his army into Lombardy, promising to bring help to the Lombard insurgents. Like his fellow monarchs in Italy, he granted a constitution (*Statuto*).

Piedmontese policy wanted the quick annexation of Lombardy and the nearby region of Venetia in order to prevent the spread of republican revolution. But the Austrians recovered and defeated the Piedmontese army, providing republicans with new opportunities elsewhere. A radical government came to power in Tuscany. Republicans took control of the revolution in Rome, invited the firebrands Mazzini and Garibaldi to come to the city, held elections to the republican parliament, and proclaimed an end to the temporal power of the pope. The Roman Republic of 1849 succumbed to an international coalition headed by the French, but not before giving the Risorgimento an impressive list of martyrs and consolidating Garibaldi's reputation as a fighter.

By the end of the summer of 1849, Italy seemed to be at peace once again. Republicans had fought well, but republicanism would never recover fully from the setbacks of that year. The Piedmontese monarchists were in better shape, for although they were latecomers to the cause of national independence, they salvaged something of value from the losses of 1848. Alone among the Italian states, Piedmont-Sardinia retained its constitution, and with it parliamentary government, civil liberties, and voting rights. There was also a new asset in the person of Charles Albert's son, King Victor Emmanuel II (1849–1878), who succeeded to the throne when his father abdicated. Ambitious, shrewder and luckier than his father, and perhaps also more of an Italian patriot, the young king worked with liberals in parliament, accepting anti-clerical laws that offended his Catholic conscience, welcoming political exiles from other Italian states, and waiting for another chance to loosen Austria's hold on Italy.

The accession of the Count of Cavour to the prime ministry of Piedmont-Sardinia in 1852 further strengthened the liberals' hand. His program of constitutional monarchy, parliamentary government, and economic progress won the support of Italians who wanted independence and unity without revolution. He favored free trade, but also protected fledgling industries from foreign competition. A landlord who had amassed a considerable fortune, he wanted a balanced economy and stimulated agriculture, commerce, and manufacturing. By connecting Italy to the rest of Europe with railroads, tunnels, and steamships, he hoped to restore Italy to the position of economic prominence it had lost when trade routes shifted from the Mediterranean Sea to the oceans. The review that he founded to propagate his ideas he called *Il Risorgimento*. A formidable opponent of republicans who believed in popular revolution, Cavour preferred the traditional governmental tactics of diplomacy and war. But he was willing to work with moderate republicans who were prepared to sacrifice their personal convictions for the sake of Italian independence. National unity was not his immediate goal. Still, he and the king supported the Italian National

Society founded in 1857. Its slogan was "Italy and Victor Emmanuel."

Cavour's work came to fruition in July 1858, when he concluded a secret agreement with Emperor Napoléon III of France. The so-called agreement of Plombières promised France the territories of Nice and Savoy in return for the military muscle needed to defeat Austria. Piedmont would gain Lombardy and Venetia, and Austria would be expelled from the peninsula. The resulting Second War of National Independence was fought in April–July 1859. Cavour was enraged when his French partner pulled out prematurely, and Piedmont had to settle for the acquisition of Lombardy alone. Events took an unexpected turn in his favor, however, when patriots in the duchies of Tuscany, Modena, Parma, and the papal Romagna seized power and promptly asked for union with Piedmont. An even greater windfall came Cavour's way when Giuseppe Garibaldi launched the famed Expedition of the Thousand in May 1860. To general surprise, that daredevil enterprise toppled Bourbon government in southern Italy. Fear that Garibaldi's republican followers might seize control of the south and that the French might intervene to protect the pope if Garibaldi went on to attack Rome prompted Cavour to dispatch the Piedmontese army to Naples with the tacit consent of governments that shared Cavour's dislike of revolution. On their way south the Piedmontese army defeated the papal army that stood in its way and occupied most of the Papal States.

The Kingdom of Italy was proclaimed on March 17, 1861, minus the city of Rome, which was still papal territory, and the region of Venetia, still in Austrian hands. The Italians acquired Venetia in 1866 after fighting another war against Austria (Third War of National Independence), this time as the ally of Prussia. Rome became Italy's capital in September 1870 when the Italian government decided to take advantage of the Franco-Prussian War to take the city from the pope. Pius IX proclaimed himself the "Prisoner in the Vatican" and continued his ideological war against the Italian state. The conflict of church and state would bedevil Italian political life until 1929, when Benito Mussolini and Pope Pius XI formally closed the rift.

IMPACTS

In its time, the Risorgimento was an inspiration to movements of national independence in the Balkans, Central and eastern Europe, and the Middle East. Its achievements were all the more impressive considering their rapidity and relatively low cost in human lives. It ended Austrian domination, unified Italy, extended Piedmontese laws to the rest of Italy, centralized the administration, broadened access to government, abolished the temporal power of the papacy, and challenged the cultural dominance of the Catholic Church. National unification extended constitutional protections and civil rights to all Italians, Jews being the principal beneficiaries. Cavour's policies appealed to liberal governments. Mazzini's principles inspired democrats everywhere. Gandhi was inspired by Mazzini's faith and perseverance. Garibaldi was a model to Zionists who believed that Jews should fight for an independent state of Israel. Domestically and internationally, the Risorgimento had the hallmark of revolution.

The Risorgimento lost its revolutionary aura in the anticlimactic aftermath of national unification when the "era of poetry" gave way to the "era of prose," and governments had to address urgent questions of taxation, spending, budgets, and security. Mazzini condemned the monarchy, parliamentary corruption, and indifference to spiritual values. Another republican, Carlo Cattaneo (1801–1869), argued that because of its pronounced regional diversity, Italy should be organized as a loose federation of states. Carlo Pisacane (1818–1857) had warned that the national movement would fail if it did not offer material incentives to the masses, particularly to the impoverished and land-hungry southern peasantry. His warning sounded like prophecy after 1860, when regional and class animosities threatened the survival of the newly born Kingdom of Italy.

While the Risorgimento was a national movement in the sense that its supporters came from all regions, there were pronounced imbalances. The north was dominant: Piedmont with its army, and Lombardy and Liguria with large numbers of volunteers. Peasants, the largest social class, were indifferent or hostile. When they did join the movement in Sicily in 1860, they did so expecting land for their efforts. The forcible repression of peasant land seizures in Sicily by Garibaldi's lieutenants put a tragic end to this brief episode of popular involvement. Peasant insurgencies against the national state, officially dubbed "brigandage," created a state of virtual civil war in parts of the south in the 1860s.

The phenomenon of brigandage attests to the alienation felt by many southerners after national unification. From a southern perspective, the Risorgimento resembled another conquest of the south by an outside power. The administration and laws of the Kingdom of Sardinia that were extended to the whole of Italy after national unification were as foreign to the south as those of any other occupying power. The abolition of trade barriers left struggling southern manufacturers vulnerable to more efficient northern competitors. Northerners also complained that the south was an economic deadweight and a drain on state finances.

Republicans were defeated, peasants received no land, expectations of quick national resurgence were frustrated:

Soldiers from Piedmont-Sardinia and French troops under Napoléon III defeat the Austrians in 1859 during the Battle of Solferino in Lombardy (part of present-day Italy). The resulting annexation of most of Lombardy by Piedmont-Sardinia helped usher in the unification of disparate Italian states. By 1861, Victor Emmanuel II of Piedmont-Sardinia was crowned Victor Emmanuel I, king of a united Italy. (Library of Congress)

these failures tainted the Risorgimento in the eyes of its critics. Yet the Risorgimento's legacy of radical change can be appreciated in context. The liberal leadership of the national state promoted secular education, science, and philosophical positivism. Anti-clericalism became a strong component of Italian culture that fed into anarchism and Socialism. The Risorgimento was the necessary premise to the formation of a national market and the process of regional integration. Fascism carried the quest for national glory to a tragic conclusion. Thus the Risorgimento bred the Left and Right revolutions of the twentieth century.

PEOPLE AND ORGANIZATIONS

Carboneria

This secret society played a major role in the revolutions of 1820–1821 and 1830–1831. Translated as "charcoal-burners," the origins of the name are uncertain, referring possibly to obscure Masonic rituals (see Freemasonry, below) or to nightly meetings held by the light of charcoal fires. Military officers opposed to Napoleonic rule and favoring constitutional monarchy formed it in Naples in 1807–1810. It was a rival of Giuseppe Mazzini's Young Italy in the 1830s. It played a minor role in the revolutions of 1848.

Cattaneo, Carlo (1801–1869)

Economist, historian, and republican political reformer, Cattaneo was born in Milan, studied law, and graduated from the University of Pavia in 1824. A moderate Italian patriot, Cattaneo supported the revolution of 1848 and headed the revolutionary council that took charge in Lombardy. Instead of a unified republic, Cattaneo favored a national federation of autonomous republics as more compatible with the regional and historical diversity of the Italian peninsula. Cattaneo supported Giuseppe Garibaldi's liberation of the south in 1860 but opposed the resulting centralized monarchy.

Cavour (1810–1861)

Camillo Benso, Count of Cavour, was the chief architect of Italian political unification and served as first prime minister of the Kingdom of Italy. He was born to a family of the Piedmontese aristocracy and attended military school. After 1831 he pursued business ventures in farming and agricultural management. Cavour turned his attention to public affairs after attaining financial independence. He was a spokesman for childhood education, agricultural improvements, free trade, civil liberties, and constitutional monarchy. In 1847 he founded *Il Risorgimento,* the newspaper that gave its name to the movement for national unification. He welcomed the constitution (see *Statuto*) that King Charles Albert granted in March 1848 and in that year was elected to the first parliament of the Kingdom of Sardinia. He emerged as the leader of the liberal center against the clericals and supporters of absolute monarchy on the Right and the democrats and republicans of the Left. A Catholic believer, in the 1850s, Cavour pushed through parliament anti-clerical measures that curbed the power of the church. He held the post of prime minister with only one brief interruption from November 1852 until his death in June 1861, the last three months as prime minister of the recently unified Kingdom of Italy. Cavour promoted railway construction, naval expansion, and industrialization. He encouraged the growth of the Italian National Society, courted Giuseppe Garibaldi, and opposed republicans, particularly Giuseppe Mazzini. The French alliance, the war of 1859 against Austria, and the acquisition of Lombardy, the Central Duchies, and Romagna were results of Cavour's personal diplomacy with Napoléon III. He did not encourage Garibaldi's Expedition of the Thousand but did not prevent it. Garibaldi's unexpected success in the south and fear of revolution prompted Cavour to launch a Piedmontese invasion of the Papal States and incorporate Sicily and the south, to form the Kingdom of Italy on March 17, 1861.

Charles Albert (1798–1849)

King of Sardinia from 1831 to 1849. Charles Albert's father had sympathized with the French Revolution and served in Napoléon's army. The son, educated in France and Switzerland, patronized by Napoléon I, also served in the French army. Charles Albert apparently schemed with Piedmontese insurgents calling for a constitution in 1821. He atoned for that youthful indiscretion by leading troops against Spanish liberals in 1823 and taking an oath never to grant a constitution. He ruled as an absolute monarch, repressed Mazzinian uprisings to destabilize the monarchy, and cultivated friendly relations with Austria. He introduced uniform laws for the entire kingdom, created an advisory council of state, negotiated commercial treaties, encouraged maritime trade, expanded the navy, and helped to police the Mediterranean Sea against Muslim raiders. Charles Albert may have expressed secret encouragements to liberals and hints that he would be ready to fight for Italian independence at the right moment. That moment came in March 1848, when he granted a constitution (*Statuto*), declared war on Austria, and led his army into Lombardy. Insurgents had already forced the Austrian army to evacuate the Lombard capital of Milan. Metternich faced an uprising in Vienna and fled from the city. But the Austrian army recovered, regained Milan, and went on to defeat the Piedmontese. Charles Albert abdicated in favor of his son, Victor Emmanuel II, who a decade later reaped the benefits of his father's initiatives to become the first king of united Italy.

Crispi, Francesco (1808–1901)

This Risorgimento patriot was born in Sicily to a family of grain merchants of Albanian origin, graduated from the University of Palermo with a law degree (1837), pursued a career in journalism, was appointed to a judicial post in Naples (1845), and returned to Sicily to take part in the unsuccessful revolution of 1848 as a Sicilian separatist. Later, in London, Crispi was a tenacious follower of Giuseppe Mazzini, sharing a commitment to republicanism and Italian national unity. But in 1859 he supported Cavour's alliance with Napoléon III and the war against Austria, notwithstanding Mazzini's objection. Crispi abandoned his republican convictions and argued that the monarchy united the country, while a republic would divide it. In 1860 he helped persuade a hesitant Garibaldi to launch the Expedition of the Thousand that unified Italy, and he played a decisive role in preparing the Sicilian uprising. In 1861 he was elected to the first Italian parliament and to all successive legislatures until the end of his life. But his colonial ambitions led to the defeat of Italian troops at Adowa, Ethiopia, in March 1896 with great loss of life.

Freemasonry

Secret Masonic lodges spread from England to France and Italy in the 1720s. The secret organization fostered faith in the progressive role of reason and education and opposed forces of "obscurantism," principally Roman Catholicism and popular superstition. Condemned by the papacy in 1738, Masonic lodges continued to proliferate into the 1780s with the support of secular-minded aristocrats, government officials, and monarchs. Italian Masonic lodges attracted sympathizers of the French Revolution. Freemasonry survived the hostility of conservative governments after 1815 and was a breeding ground for secret societies, particularly the Carboneria. Its secular philosophy and anti-clericalism attracted prominent Risorgimento figures, including Giuseppe Garibaldi. After national unification, Freemasonry opposed clericalism on the Right and Socialism on the Left, promoting secular, middle-class liberal ideologies.

Garibaldi, Giuseppe (1807–1882)

Giuseppe Garibaldi is generally regarded as modern Italy's most popular political figure. The qualities of selflessness, courage, and integrity have a solid foundation in his character and his adventurous life. Born to a seafaring family in Nice when that city was part of the Kingdom of Sardinia, at the age of sixteen he shipped out as a merchant seaman and traveled widely in the eastern Mediterranean. Influenced by the ideas of the French radical thinker Henri de Saint-Simon, he gravitated toward the republican movement. His involvement in the Mazzinian conspiracies of 1833–1834 forced him to leave the country. In South America he led a legion of Italian volunteers fighting for the independence of Uruguay. Garibaldi returned to Italy in 1848 to fight for Italian independence and distinguished himself in the defense of the short-lived Roman Republic (1849) against French, Austrian, Neapolitan, and Spanish troops. Forced again into exile, he worked on Staten Island (New York), traveled in Central America, and sailed the Pacific Ocean as a trader. In 1855 he built his own house on the island of Caprera off the coast of Sardinia and farmed the land. With the outbreak of the Second War of Independence in 1859, he effectively led troops against the Austrians. Then, in 1860, he successfully led the Expedition of the Thousand against the armies of the Kingdom of the Two Sicilies. That venture was the principal cause of the unification of Italy and made Garibaldi a national hero. Without professional military training, he had exceptional skills as a guerrilla fighter and in conventional warfare. His example inspired many, reconciled monarchist and republican patriots, and created the coalition that unified the country.

Gioberti, Vincenzo (1801–1852)

Gioberti was ordained a priest in 1825. In 1831 he was appointed to teach theology at the University of Turin and as court chaplain to King Charles Albert. He lost both positions for suspected political ties to Giuseppe Mazzini. His *Del primato morale e civile degli italiani* [*On the Moral and Civil Primacy of the Italian People*, 1843] was his most influential work. In it he developed the view that Catholicism was the es-

sential ingredient of the Italian national identity and that national independence could be attained under papal leadership without recourse to war or revolution.

Italian National Society

The Italian National Society (Società Nazionale Italiana) was founded in 1857 to promote the cause of Italian independence and unity. Its principal figures were the Venetian Daniele Manin and the Lombard aristocrat Giorgio Trivulzio Pallavicino (1796–1878), who served as its president. Manin, a republican, and Pallavicino, a monarchist, joined forces to promote independence and unification under King Victor Emmanuel II of Piedmont-Sardinia and to oppose the republicanism and revolutionary tactics of Giuseppe Mazzini. Endorsed also by Giuseppe Garibaldi, who served as its vice president, the Italian National Society became a rallying point for republican and monarchist patriots willing to set aside their differences. Its strategy of collaboration made a decisive contribution to the cause of national unity.

Manin, Daniele (1804–1857)

Manin, born in Venice to a family of Jewish extraction that had converted to Christianity in the eighteenth century, practiced law. He came to politics by way of economics, arguing that only closer ties with the rest of Italy could reverse Venice's economic decline. He supported the revolution of 1848, during which Venice challenged Austrian rule and proclaimed its independence as the Republic of Saint Mark, the city's patron saint. As the republic's president, Manin led the unsuccessful defense against Austrian troops in August 1849. In the 1850s he was the most outspoken critic of Giuseppe Mazzini's tactics of revolution, which he described as "the theory of the dagger." He was a founder of the Italian National Society, which endorsed the eventually successful program of national unity under the Piedmontese monarchy.

Mazzini, Giuseppe (1805–1872)

Mazzini's creed rested on the concepts of patriotism, republicanism, and democracy, tied in with a religious view summed up in his slogan "God and the People." Born in Genoa to a family of the upper-middle class (his father was a prominent physician and university professor), Mazzini briefly practiced law. In 1827 he joined the Carboneria, which he found ineffective. Arrested for political subversion in 1830, he chose to expatriate to France. In Marseilles he founded Young Italy (1831) to spread the message of national unity and independence. Hounded by the French police, in 1833 Mazzini shifted his base of operations to the Swiss canton of Geneva. But Mazzinian conspiracies and insurrections failed in 1833–1834. In London, where he moved in 1837, he reorganized Young Italy, opened a school for Italian immigrant workers and children, and won recognition as the voice of the movement for Italian independence and unity. An opponent of monarchy in any form, he acknowledged the popularity and good intentions of King Victor Emmanuel II, whom he would have accepted as president of an Italian republic. Giuseppe Garibaldi he regarded with mixed feelings, admiring his bravery and military talents while deploring his willingness to work for the monarchy. Mazzini was aware of his own limitations as a field commander and usually relied on others, including Garibaldi and Carlo Pisacane, to carry out his plans. In his later years he fought against Socialism, which he rejected because of its materialist philosophy and encouragement of class warfare, and as incompatible with the ideal of national unity. Democratic republics, in which the voice of the people could be freely expressed, he regarded as essentially peace loving.

Metternich, Prince Clemens von (1773–1859)

The Austrian chancellor Clemens von Metternich, who steered Austrian policy and influenced conservative governments from the Congress of Vienna (1814–1815) to his forced resignation at the time of the revolutions of 1848, was a stubborn opponent of the Risorgimento. At the Congress of Vienna he secured Austrian dominance in the Italian peninsula and cast Austria in the role of principal guardian against revolution in Europe, including the establishment of an independent Italy. Metternich's "Concert of Europe" was a system of international government cooperation designed to prevent the recurrence of war or revolution. Metternich's success in repressing revolution in Naples and Piedmont in 1820–1821 led to his advancement from foreign minister to chancellor (prime minister). Under his guidance, Austria suppressed the revolution of 1831 and the conspiracies of Giuseppe Mazzini. Metternich believed in gradual change controlled from above. He encouraged administrative and economic reforms that would not imperil absolute monarchy. Democracy he equated with instability and war. The cautious reform favored by Metternich prevailed in Lombardy and Venetia, which were part of the Austrian empire, and in the Grand Duchy of Tuscany, ruled by Habsburg princes. In the Papal States and Kingdom of the Two Sicilies, opponents of reform prevailed. The Kingdom of Sardinia under Charles Albert and his son Victor Emmanuel II combined reform with territorial ambitions that could be satis-

fied only at Austria's expense. The election of Pope Pius IX in 1846 dealt the first blow to Metternich's system because the new pope's liberal reputation encouraged expectations of change everywhere in Italy. The revolutions of 1848 were the final blow, forcing Metternich from power.

Napoléon I (1769–1821)

Born Napoléone Buonaparte in Corsica to a family of Tuscan origin the year after the Republic of Genoa ceded the island to France, the young Napoléon attended a French military academy and was commissioned as an artillery officer in 1785. The wars of the French Revolution gave him ample opportunities to display his military talents, and he advanced rapidly. He commanded the army that in the spring of 1796 defeated the Piedmontese, Austrian, and papal armies in rapid succession, and established French dominance in Italy. He was crowned emperor of the French (1804) and king of Italy (1805). He ruled Italy directly by incorporating Piedmont, Liguria, Tuscany, and Latium, including Rome, into the French empire (the pope was exiled to France), and indirectly through members of his family such as his brother Joseph Bonaparte (1768–1844), who ruled as king of Naples from 1806 to 1808. French dominion brought to Italy the French system of centralized administration, military conscription, and uniform laws; it introduced uniform weights and measures, provided new career opportunities in the military, government, and public administration, encouraged secular schooling, and promoted land reform. Military conscription and heavy taxation were resented especially by the peasantry, which went into open revolt in the south in 1798–1799 and in 1805–1806. Napoléon's Continental System favored French at the expense of Italian manufacturers. Military officers formed secret societies that called for constitutional government and Italian independence. Whether for or against, reactions to Napoleonic rule were a stimulus for national independence during 1815–1848.

Napoléon III (1808–1873)

The nephew of Napoléon I had a special attachment to Italy, where he had spent part of his youth, joined secret societies, and participated in the 1830–1831 revolts. On the strength of his family name, he was elected president of France in 1848 and was declared Emperor Napoléon III in 1852. He looked to Italy as a place where he could challenge Austria and regain French ascendancy. Cavour played upon his ambition, and the two worked out the agreement of Plombières (July 1858), which promised France the district of Nice and the region of Savoy in return for French military intervention against Austria. The resulting Second War of National Independence (1859) gave Piedmont-Sardinia the region of Lombardy and set in motion the events that led to Italian unification in 1860–1861.

Pisacane, Carlo (1818–1857)

Carlo Pisacane combined the roles of military captain, political figure, and social theorist. Born to a prominent Neapolitan family, he studied at the Naples military academy. His military career in the Neapolitan army was cut short by his radical sentiments and the scandal of a love affair with the wife of a fellow officer. In the revolutions of 1848, he fought against Austria in Lombardy and then was given a command in the army of the short-lived Roman Republic. In Rome he established the close rapport with Giuseppe Mazzini that lasted for the rest of his life. In his reflections on the failure of the revolutions of 1848, he argued that to be successful, revolutions must offer material incentives to the masses, which the revolutionists of 1848 had failed to do. He looked upon the land-hungry peasantry of southern Italy as a potentially revolutionary class, if enticed by the prospect of land redistribution. He mounted an expedition that came to a quick and bloody end in the mountains of Calabria, where the very peasants that Pisacane hoped to arouse against the Bourbon Neapolitan regime turned against him and his few followers. Pisacane committed suicide to avoid capture. A martyr of the Risorgimento, his posthumously published writings brought him fame as a social theoretician. These writings deplored the purely political character of the Risorgimento and its failure to reach out to the masses. Anarchists found inspiration in Pisacane's writings for his faith in the effectiveness of the individual deed, and Socialists for his materialist analysis of the phenomenon of revolution.

Pius IX (1792–1878)

The election of Cardinal Giovanni Maria Mastai Ferretti as Pope Pius IX (*Pio Nono* to Italians) in 1846 did not please conservatives, for the new pope was reputed to be a political liberal and anti-Austrian. But while Pius IX may have sympathized with the idea of Italian independence, he could not sanction national war or revolution against Catholic Austria. In November 1848 he fled Rome after insurgents assassinated his prime minister. Pius IX, always theologically conservative, became a declared enemy of liberalism, revolution, and Italian unification. Cavour and Victor Emmanuel II, excommunicated by the pope, received last rites from dissenting priests. After the Italians seized Rome in September 1870, Pius IX declared himself a "prisoner in the Vatican" and re-

fused to acknowledge the legitimacy of the Italian state, plunging Italy and the church into the long conflict that lasted until 1929.

Sardinia, Kingdom of

This name entered history in 1720, when the House of Savoy, which ruled over Piedmont, Savoy, and Nice, ceded the island of Sicily to Austria in return for the island of Sardinia and the coveted royal title. The kingdom was often referred to as Piedmont-Sardinia. Its monarchs Charles Albert and Victor Emmanuel II both encouraged the aspirations of Italian independence, but it was the policies of Prime Minister Cavour that gave Piedmont-Sardinia the uncontested lead in the movement for national unification and independence. Victor Emmanuel II became the first king of Italy in March 1861, and the House of Savoy became the ruling dynasty, until 1946 when Italians voted the monarchy out of existence.

Statuto

This was the name of the constitution granted by King Charles Albert of Piedmont-Sardinia in February 1848, the only Italian constitution granted in the revolutionary euphoria of 1848 to survive the failure of revolution. It became the constitution of the Kingdom of Italy when the country was unified in 1861. It remained in force until 1946, when Italians voted the monarchy out and later substituted the constitution of the Italian Republic. The *Statuto* protected civil freedoms, provided for an elected lower house of parliament, and gave parliament powers over legislation, budgets, and taxation. Less liberal clauses gave the king command of the armed forces and control of foreign policy. Original suffrage was based on high property and educational qualifications. The franchise in national elections was broadened progressively in 1882, 1912, and 1919. Italian women voted for the first time in the elections of 1946.

Victor Emmanuel II (1820–1878)

Victor Emmanuel II came to the throne of Piedmont-Sardinia in 1849 following the resignation of his father, Charles Albert. The young king retained the *Statuto* granted by his father. The decision to govern as a constitutional monarch set Victor Emmanuel apart from other Italian rulers and endeared him to liberals. Victor Emmanuel took full advantage of the provisions that permitted the throne to conduct foreign policy independently of parliament, but he usually respected parliament in internal matters, even when parliamentary measures conflicted with his personal beliefs, as they did in the case of anti-clerical legislation. His personal popularity reconciled many former republicans to the monarchy and defused the more radical impulses of the Risorgimento.

Roland Sarti

See Also European Revolutions of 1848; French Revolution; Italian Fascist Revolution; Literature and Modern Revolution; Nationalism and Revolution; War and Revolution

References and Further Readings

Abba, Giuseppe. 1962. *The Diary of One of Garibaldi's Thousand.* London: Oxford University Press.

Beales, Derek. 1971. *The Risorgimento and the Unification of Italy.* London: Allen and Unwin.

Coppa, Frank J. 1992. *The Origins of the Italian Wars of Independence.* London: Longmans.

Garibaldi, Giuseppe. 1889. *Autobiography.* 3 vols. London: Walter Smith and Innes.

Ginsborg, Paul. 1979. *Daniele Manin and the Venetian Revolution of 1848–49.* Cambridge: Cambridge University Press.

Greenfield, Kent Roberts. 1965. *Economics and Liberalism in the Risorgimento: A Study of Nationalism in Lombardy, 1814–1848.* Rev. ed. Baltimore: Johns Hopkins University Press.

Grew, Raymond A. 1963. *A Sterner Plan for Italian Unity: The Italian National Society in the Risorgimento.* Princeton, NJ: Princeton University Press.

Hearder, Harry. 1983. *Italy in the Age of the Risorgimento, 1790–1870.* London: Longmans.

Hibbert, Christopher. 1965. *Garibaldi and His Enemies.* Boston: Little, Brown.

Laven, David. 2002. *Venice and Venetia under the Habsburgs, 1815–1835.* Oxford: Oxford University Press.

Lovett, Clara M. 1982. *The Democratic Movement in Italy, 1830–1876.* Cambridge, MA: Harvard University Press.

Mack Smith, Denis. 1954. *Cavour and Garibaldi, 1860: A Study in Political Conflict.* Cambridge: Cambridge University Press.

———. 1972. *Victor Emmanuel, Cavour, and the Risorgimento.* New York: Oxford University Press.

Mazzini, Giuseppe. 1945. *Selected Writings.* Edited by N. Gangulee. London: Drummond.

Pellico, Silvio. 1963. *My Prisons.* London: Oxford University Press.

Riall, Lucy. 1998. *Sicily and the Unification of Italy: Liberal Policy and Local Power.* Oxford: Clarendon.

Sarti, Roland. 1997. *Mazzini: A Life for the Religion of Politics.* Westport, CT: Praeger.

Whyte, Arthur J. 1930. *The Political Life and Letters of Cavour, 1848–1861.* London: Oxford University Press.

J

Japanese New Order Movement

CHRONOLOGY

1920s   Although Japan experiences the pre-war apex of parliamentary government and participates fully in the post–World War I agreements governing international relations, these same years also witness the emergence of various reformist factions critical of the status quo both at home and abroad.

1930   Against a backdrop of economic depression, Japan signs the London Naval Treaty extending the regime of naval arms limitations begun at Washington in 1922; however, the agreement energizes military and political leaders who oppose "cooperative diplomacy" and the party-led governments they associate with this approach to foreign relations. A right-wing youth shoots and mortally wounds Prime Minister Hamaguchi Osachi, whose cabinet had concluded the London Naval Treaty limiting Japanese naval tonnage to less than that of the United States and Great Britain.

1931   On September 18, Japanese army officers secretly set off a bomb along the railway out-side Mukden and succeed in precipitating the military occupation of Manchuria. The Manchurian incident elicits popular support within Japan and poses a direct challenge to the status quo in East Asian relations. The incident also contributes to the sense of Japan having entered a "period of crisis" requiring new departures in foreign and domestic policy. Meanwhile, behind the scenes, abortive coups d'état by army officers and civilian nationalists in March and October signal a radicalization of domestic politics.

1932   The first half of the year sees the murder of business and government leaders by members of the Ketsumeidan (Blood Pledge Brotherhood) and the assassination of Prime Minister Inukai Tsuyoshi by young naval officers. Inukai's death marks the end of party-led cabinets until after the Second World War. While party politicians continue to compete with other elite groups for preeminence in policy making, the two "national unity cabinets" established in the wake of Inukai's death reflect the rising power of civilian and military technocrats dedicated to reforming the domestic political order and embarking on a foreign policy designed to bolster Japanese power in East Asia. The latter development is visible in March with the establishment of the puppet state of Manchukuo.

1933   The emerging shift in Japan's approach to foreign relations is underscored further when, in protest of a League of Nations report calling for a return to the status quo in Manchuria, Japanese diplomatic representatives stage a dramatic walkout symbolizing their nation's withdrawal from the league. Meanwhile, efforts to reorient Japan's foreign policy are linked increasingly to domestic political struggles.

1936   On February 26, junior army officers lead an attempted coup d'état. While directing soldiers under their command to occupy key government buildings, the plot's leaders proceed to assassinate three high-ranking officials and make attempts on the lives of several others. Although the coup ends in failure and the eclipse of the army faction involved, the army in general, and military bureaucrats in particular, emerge with their position strengthened vis-à-vis other political elites. Together with allies in the civil bureaucracy and the political parties, the army continues to push for reforms that will facilitate the creation of a national defense state.

1937   On July 7, Japanese and Chinese ground forces clash near the Marco Polo Bridge outside Beijing, with the fighting soon escalating into a general Sino-Japanese War that lasts until August 1945. Domestically the war ultimately facilitates the passage of national mobilization legislation and strengthens the political position of those seeking to further centralize political authority and economic planning.

1938   In November, as the conflict with China drags on, the government of Prime Minister Konoe Fumimaro redefines the war as part of a larger "holy war" to break Anglo-American power in the region and thereby facilitate the creation of a "New Order for East Asia."

1940–1941   In September, the second Konoe cabinet concludes the Axis Pact with Nazi Germany and Fascist Italy, and expands the definition of the New Order to encompass a Greater East Asia Co-Prosperity Sphere. Meanwhile, in August the New Order Movement officially gets under way. In October, the Konoe government oversees the creation of the Imperial Rule Assistance Association. Supporters hope the IRAA will provide the totalitarian "new structure" through which to mobilize the political energies of the masses and reorganize Japanese political and economic activity. However, conservative and bureaucratic opponents—aided by Konoe's last minute defection from the movement—eviscerate the organization as a political force, and the IRAA ends up supplementing already existing mechanisms for mobilizing popular morale behind the policies of the state.

1942   April sees the first and only parliamentary elections held during the existence of the IRAA. Although government-endorsed candidates comprise a majority of those who win election, the role of party politicians in determining the roster of recommended candidates and the success of candidates lacking official approval underscore the limited authority of the New Order.

1945   On June 13, as Japan enters the final desperate summer of the Asia-Pacific War, the IRAA is abolished.

INTRODUCTION

The Japanese New Order Movement (*shin taisei undo*) refers specifically to the constellation of political and military factions that in 1940 gathered around Prime Minister Konoe Fumimaro to establish a new political structure under the umbrella of the Imperial Rule Assistance Association, or IRAA(*Taisei Yokusankai*). The intended purpose of the movement was to centralize power under military and civilian administrators who would reform Japan domestically by ending the perceived depredations associated with party rule and secure Japanese dominion over an East Asia freed from Western military forces and colonial enterprises. Although the drive to create the New Order occurred in the context of the late 1930s and early 1940s, the movement is understood best when conceptualized within a broader chronological and historical context stretching back to the 1920s. Although that period is remembered for the pre-war apex of party-led government and "Taisho democracy," the decade also contained the seeds for a subsequent era of political reformism and military expansionism. The resulting challenge to the status quo derived momentum from the changed domestic and international context of the 1930s and propagated the rejection of liberalism, individualism, and capitalism. These developments were accompanied by the spread of revolutionary violence, the relative weakening of party political power, and the steady strengthening of military and bureaucratic authority. Although posing a potentially radical threat to the political status quo, the New Order Movement ultimately did not result in a revolution. Whether it represented the realization of a Fascist regime or not remains a subject of scholarly debate. What is clear is that the consequences for Japan and the world were profound, both in the immediate context of the 1930s and in the decades following the end of the Asia-Pacific War in 1945.

BACKGROUND: CULTURE AND HISTORY

In July 1853, the arrival of American warships in Japan set in motion a foreign crisis that, together with latent domestic difficulties, led to the collapse of the Tokugawa shogunate (*bakufu*) that had ruled the country since 1603. The resulting Meiji Restoration of 1868 produced long-term consequences that were ultimately revolutionary in facilitating the creation of Japan as a modern nation-state. Besides preserving their own newly won authority, the leaders of the new government sought to secure their country's sovereignty and create a prosperous, strong nation capable of joining the Great Powers as an equal. Toward these ends they instituted far-reaching reforms that included replacing the old warrior estates with a system of prefectures, establishing a conscript army to take over from the abolished samurai class, and instituting a stable revenue base in the form of a land tax that supplanted the traditional village-assessed grain levy. Having lost tariff autonomy under the commercial treaties of the 1850s, government officials worked to foster an industrial economy through import substitution and support for domestic industries deemed of strategic importance. By 1885 a cabinet system was in operation, and in 1889 the Meiji emperor promulgated a new German-influenced constitution.

Along with erecting the first constitutional polity and industrial economy in East Asia, Japanese leaders expanded their definition of security to include dominion over the Korean Peninsula. Wars waged against Qing China in 1894–1895 and czarist Russia in 1904–1905 established Japan as a colonial state and confirmed the nation's place as a regional power increasingly involved in imperialist competition for advantage in China. Further recognition for the completion of Japan's transition from potential colony to colonial overlord came through repeal of the last of the unequal treaties with foreign powers by 1911, formal alliance with Great Britain from 1902 to 1922, and full participation in the Paris Peace Conference of 1919 to 1920 and the Washington Conference of 1921 to 1922. These conferences produced treaties predicated on the principles of multilateral diplomacy, naval arms limitations, support for free trade, and respect for the territorial integrity of China. Participation in this system of "cooperative diplomacy," an approach often referred to as the Washington Order, served as the centerpiece of Japanese foreign policy for the remainder of the 1920s.

Meanwhile, as the elder statesmen (*genro*) who created and ruled the Meiji state passed away, their personalized style of governance gave way to a competition for political power among newly institutionalized elites. During the 1920s party politicians assumed a central role in mediating intra-elite conflicts and thereby making the Meiji constitutional system work. Along with members of the mainstream political parties, participants in Japan's pluralistic elite included the leaders of powerful family-centered business combines (*zaibatsu*), a military officer corps drawn from the army and navy academies, and a newly professionalized civil bureaucracy staffed by graduates of the imperial universities. Factional competition among—and within—these elite groups came to constitute a central characteristic of inter-war politics and, consequently, of the movement to create a New Order.

By the early 1920s, Japanese had recreated their country as a modern nation-state resting atop an increasingly industrial economy and boasting a full-fledged colonial empire. In many respects, the objectives of the Meiji leadership had been met. Nonetheless, the changes wrought by modernization also fueled discontent with the status quo and convinced some Japanese of the need for reform. The decade thus witnessed the emergence of various factions seeking their own version of reform for the country's bureaucratic state and capitalist economy. Such dissatisfaction was not entirely new, for as early as the turn of the twentieth century the first generation of Socialists was holding the bureaucratic state responsible for corrupt politics and overall moral decline. However, conditions following the end of the Great War in 1918 facilitated the spread of more diverse and radical critiques. In tandem with the post-war enthusiasm for Wilsonian idealism, theorists of liberalism heralded democracy as the wave of the future, yet found themselves struggling to reconcile democratic thought with the reality of a constitution that located sovereignty in the emperor rather than the people. Meanwhile, invigorated by the Russian Revolution and labor unrest within Japan, a revived and more radical Socialist movement rejected the gradual, limited reform promised by liberalism in favor of rapid, fundamental political reorganization. In 1922, the establishment of the Japanese Communist Party marked the arrival of an explicitly revolutionary agenda. Although the party was promptly banned and the repression of left-wing political movements soon intensified, the impact of Marxist theory within intellectual circles and among political activists is difficult to overestimate.

This influence even extended to self-professed enemies of such "dangerous ideas" (*kiken shiso*) as Marxism. While nationalist organizations such as Gen'yosha (Black Ocean Society) and Kokuryukai (Amur River Society) had for years been involved in Japanese politics and in promoting continental expansion, during the 1920s the activities of a younger generation of nationalists both perpetuated these legacies and incorporated new theoretical insights by which to determine the failings of contemporary society. Influential leaders of the new right-wing movement, most notably Kita Ikki, started out embracing Socialism and, while rejecting revolution that would topple the emperor-centered state, remained enamored of the Marxist critique of capitalism and the goal of radically restructuring the status quo. Similar thinking shaped the outlook of a younger generation of technocrats with ties to the nationalist movement, a phenomenon exemplified by Kishi Nobusuke, who in the 1930s emerged as an important reformist bureaucrat and rose to positions of political authority in wartime—and post-war—Japan. Consequently, in the years leading up to the New Order Movement of 1940–1941, anti-capitalist sentiment remained an important motivation for many of the radical nationalists and other reformists who sought to renovate the Meiji order, regardless of whether their tactic of choice was political assassination or bureaucratic planning.

If the anti-capitalist critique of the status quo constituted a new development in the right-wing movement, the desire to enhance Japan's position in East Asia marked an area of continuity with the agenda of Meiji nationalists. Pan-Asianism, or the vision of a rejuvenated Asian civilization liberated from the bane of Western imperialism, constituted a constant theme in right-wing circles during the 1920s. Invariably linked to the goal of domestic renovation, belief that Asian liberation required Japanese leadership became a ubiquitous component of the reformist movement. As the influence of this style of nationalism grew, the goal of creating a new political structure inside Japan came to be virtually synonymous with overseeing a new departure in the nation's foreign relations. Indeed, members of the nationalist movement and their reformist allies were among the earliest and most strident critics of Japanese participation in the post-war system of cooperative diplomacy, a policy they scorned as merely a recipe for perpetuating an international status quo dominated by the Anglo-American powers. A minority view in the early 1920s, by the late 1930s those championing the creation of a new political structure had helped make rejection of the Washington Order a fundamental and widely held component of public discourse.

Along with distaste for radical left-wing thought, suspicion of the Washington Order and belief in Japanese leadership of Asia were ideas shared by numerous conservative nationalists. Reform from this perspective centered on a "restoration" of cultural and moral values supposedly being eroded under the weight of modern Western materialism. Rather than rejecting the Meiji order as hopelessly corrupt, however, proponents of this view sought a revival of fundamental mores that would reverse the corrosive impact of modernity and ameliorate the attendant phenomenon of mass political participation. This restoration was to be fostered through the leadership of a moral elite of talented officials imbued with the ethic of imperial loyalism and working within—rather than attempting to overthrow—the Meiji constitutional order. This ideal of gradual, top-down reform appealed to more moderate officials interested in reforming the status quo while also preserving and indeed bolstering their own prerogatives.

For a period of time in the early 1920s, radical and conservative styles of nationalist reformism overlapped, as many of the same individuals cooperated together in both right-wing organizations like the Yuzonsha ("Society of Those Who Yet Remain") and conservative institutions such as Takushoku Daigaku ("Colonial University"). Ultimately, however, the tension between proponents of radical right-wing "reform" (*kakushin*) and conservative "restoration" (*fukko*) resulted in an ideological fissure that would continue to run through the political terrain of the 1930s and 1940s. Meanwhile, those advocating avowedly left-wing radical agendas faced increasingly stiff repression by government authorities. However, for those leftists willing to renounce Marxism and proclaim loyalty to the emperor-centered state, the concept of *kakushin* presented an alternative path toward radical reorganization of the capitalist status quo.

CONTEXT AND PROCESS OF REVOLUTION

Although the 1920s witnessed the appearance of various visions of reform and restoration, it took a confluence of domestic and international developments to facilitate the emergence of these concepts as major political forces. Some of these dynamics, such as worldwide economic depression and the rise of a more unified and nationalist China, lay largely beyond the control of Japanese. Other factors, however, including terrorist violence by military officers and political opportunism on the part of reformist bureaucrats and politicians, reflected conscious efforts to heighten the sense of crisis in the service of particular political and ideological agendas. By the late 1930s, with domestic terrorism in support of totalitarian revolution in decline following the failed coup d'état of early 1936, military and civilian technocrats took the lead in guiding the nation toward a centrally planned national defense state (*kokubo kokka*). In October 1940, the establishment of the Imperial Rule Assistance Association seemed to herald the realization in Japan of a totalitarian or fascist political order. However, the domestic agenda of the reformists worried conservatives and others invested in the status quo, who responded with increasing hostility and moved to tame the radical potential of the IRAA.

By 1928 the potential reunification of China under Chiang Kai Shek's Nationalist Party and the prospective return of Russian power to the region in the form of the Soviet Union left some members of the Japanese army worried about the future of their nation's self-proclaimed "special position" in Manchuria. On September 18, 1931, conspirators within Japan's Kwantung Army acted to solve what they viewed as the "Manchurian-Mongolian problem" by setting off a bomb along the railroad outside the capital city of Mukden and using this act by "bandits" as a pretext for occupying Manchuria. Their fait accompli, enormously popular with the Japanese public, was acceded to by officials in Tokyo and, on March 1, 1932, resulted in the establishment of the puppet state of Manchukuo. In February 1933, Japan withdrew from the League of Nations after rejecting the international organization's call for a return to the territorial status quo in northeast China.

Facilitating the decision for Japan's dramatic walkout of the league was an atmosphere of domestic political uncertainty said to constitute evidence that the country had entered a "period of crisis" (*hijoji*). By the start of the 1930s, the Great Depression was exacerbating a decade of uneven economic growth, with suffering in the rural regions being particularly intensified by the subsequent collapse of the export markets for such vital commodities as silk. As the depression worsened, the free trade element of the Washington Order crumbled. Likewise, in 1930, naval officers, opposition politicians, and right-wing nationalists pilloried the government of Prime Minister Hamaguchi Osachi for signing the London Naval Treaty. Opponents of the treaty viewed the lower tonnage for warship construction allowed Japan in comparison to the United States and Great Britain as a threat to national security and further evidence of how the post-war order failed to secure Japan's interests. Although successful conclusion of the agreement meant the "treaty faction" achieved victory in the short-term, hard-liners of the navy's "fleet faction" gained influence. In 1934, Japan declined to attend the next conference scheduled for the following year, thereby guaranteeing the lapse of the naval arms limitations component of the Washington Order.

Meanwhile, in November 1930 a right-wing youth shot and mortally wounded Hamaguchi at Tokyo Station, initiating a period of political violence by radical nationalists. In March and October of the following year, army officers of the Sakurakai (Cherry Blossom Society) joined hands with radical civilian nationalists in plotting to overthrow the government. Although amateurish and undone once higher-ranking officers failed to provide hoped-for support, these plots signaled the spread of revolutionary nationalism within elements of the officer corps. Seeking a vaguely defined "Showa Restoration" ("Showa" designates the reign of Emperor Hirohito from 1926–1989), young officers of the Imperial Way faction (*Kodo-ha*) and their civilian allies viewed themselves as embodying the same loyalist spirit as the young samurai who used political terror to help bring about the Meiji Restoration of 1868.

In early 1932, the radical nationalists of the Ketsumeidan (Blood Pledge Brotherhood), inspired by the agrarian utopianism of a Buddhist priest, embarked on a policy of *ichinin-issatsu* (one man, one murder), whereby each member would kill one person from a list of individuals viewed as pillars of a corrupt capitalist and bureaucratic status quo indifferent to the suffering of rural Japanese and the larger interests of the nation. Although arrests prevented the group's members from murdering more than two of the targeted individuals from their list, on May 15 naval officers associated with the Ketsumeidan plot forced their way into the official residence of the prime minister and murdered Premier Inukai Tsuyoshi.

Rapid realization of a Showa Restoration through assassination was not the only approach to reform unsettling the political terrain during the "period of crisis." In contrast to the vague spiritual nationalism of their Imperial Way counterparts, army officers of the so-called Control faction (*Tosei-ha*) devoted themselves to realizing national reorganization through centralized bureaucratic planning. During the 1920s, rising stars within the army such as Nagata Tetsuzan and Tojo Hideki became enamored of the idea that victory in Japan's next war would necessitate mobilizing all of the nation's material and human resources to wage "total war." While sharing their counterparts' militarism, imperial loyalism, and belief in Japan's right to further expansion on the Asian continent, officers of the Control faction focused on the imperative of proper material mobilization and sought to reorder the polity in support of that objective. Moreover, rather than rely on assassination, these officers were willing to work together with other members of the political elite to accomplish their long-range goals.

Among the strongest allies of these army bureaucrats were their counterparts within Japan's powerful civil bureaucracy. In particular, the goals of army officers like Nagata coincided with the agenda of a rising generation of bureaucrats seeking to enhance their own administrative autonomy. Since the early 1920s, the first group of reform-minded officials, later known as "new bureaucrats" (*shin kanryo*), had been working to control the spread of democratic values and limit the political power of party politicians. Particularly worrisome was the manner in which party influence had spread into the higher reaches of the civil service and into local administration. Rather than seeking revolutionary change, however, powerful members of organizations such as the Kokuikai (National Mainstay Society) sought a controlled renovation of the political order that would at once integrate the masses smoothly beneath their own administrative control while reducing the policy-making power of the political parties. Numerous "new bureaucrats" staffed the non-party-led "national unity cabinets" erected in the wake of Inukai's assassination and cooperated with army bureaucrats through a series of cabinet planning agencies meant to overcome the "sectionalism" of ministerial turf battles. Although above all concerned with domestic politics, these officials also linked their internal agenda to a rejection of the party-tainted "cooperative diplomacy" of the 1920s.

In early 1936, the pursuit of a Showa Restoration by radical young officers of the Imperial Way faction, abetted by factional tensions within the army, produced the pre-war period's major incident of political violence. On the morning of February 26, these officers ordered their troops to occupy important government buildings in the capital of Tokyo while the leaders themselves initiated a series of assassinations. However, although seeking to erect a military dictatorship in the name of Emperor Hirohito, the young officers found themselves thwarted by the young sovereign, who demanded that senior officers—some of whom secretly sympathized with the plotters—put down the insurrection. This was soon accomplished and, in contrast to the very public yet comparatively lenient punishment meted out in earlier cases of right-wing terrorism, the insubordinate officers and two civilian associates (including Kita Ikki) were tried in a closed court and executed.

The February 26 Incident marked the apex of terrorism by young army officers and, at the same time, signaled the decline of Imperial Way faction officers as a significant force in domestic politics. Nonetheless, the army as a whole exerted increased influence as military technocrats allied with reformist bureaucrats and sympathetic party politicians to push forward plans for national mobilization. Out to challenge the political and economic status quo, these members of the elite increasingly pinned their hopes for radical change on the prestigious and popular Prince Konoe Fumimaro. Along with being a member of one of Japan's oldest aristocratic families, Konoe was an early critic of the Washington Order, with close ties to some of the leading advocates for

thorough reform of the Meiji constitutional order, an objective he gradually came to share.

On June 4, 1937, Konoe established the first of three cabinets he would head in the years leading up to the outbreak of the Pacific war in 1941, a period that witnessed the height of the New Order Movement and the establishment of the IRAA. Although initially spurning entreaties that he lead a new political party, Konoe did begin advocating passage of legislation to enhance the authority of the central government. Likewise, following the outbreak of fighting with China on July 7, 1937, the prince helped connect the objective of domestic reform to successful prosecution of the war. A proposed national mobilization law allowed for the stockpiling of strategic goods and, in time of war, provided for sweeping government powers to include overseeing business and labor, controlling wages and profits, and managing transportation and production. This agenda encountered stiff resistance from the lower house of the legislature, passing only after the creation of a party-dominated committee, the approval of which would be required to actually implement the wartime measures. Likewise, it was agreed that these powers would not be invoked during the current Sino-Japanese War. As the fighting in China dragged on, however, some wartime measures were indeed implemented, and with the expansion of the war to the Pacific in 1941, the mobilization law was revised and strengthened.

Meanwhile, in November 1938, the Konoe government sought to redefine the war in China by proclaiming that the conflict was part of a national mission to create a Japan-led New Order for East Asia (*Toa Shinchitsujo*). Along with endeavoring to more effectively mobilize material resources, government officials put increased effort into promoting a "national spiritual mobilization" that would convince the general populace of the need to bear ever-greater sacrifices in support of the nation's wartime objectives. Reform at home and new policy objectives abroad thus became increasingly bound together. Detailed articulation of the supposed link between domestic reform and a global destiny to liberate Asia fell to reformist intellectuals and bureaucrats participating in policy research organizations like the Showa Kenkyukai (Showa Research Society).

As the New Order Movement gained momentum in 1940, proponents of radical change sought to use the creation of a new political structure to wrest power from the existing political and economic elites. Army technocrats and reformist bureaucrats (*kakushin kanryo*) joined together with members of the reformist right wing (*kakushin uyoku*) and political outsiders from the established parties in seeking to create a totalitarian political organization that would mobilize the populace in a fashion similar to the Nazi and Fascist parties of Japan's new German and Italian allies. Such a mass political party would supplant the mechanisms of control already in place under the Meiji constitutional order and, consequently, undermine the authority of conservative elites. At the same time, reflecting the anti-capitalist sentiment long a constituent part of the radical *kakushin* perspective, the new structure would exert greater central control over the economy and reduce the independence and political power of private industry.

Not surprisingly, status quo elites threatened by this agenda responded sharply. Business leaders, while willing to cooperate in the profitable pursuit of national mobilization, began to resist as those very profits and the prerogatives of management came under attack from reformists. Further opposition came from mainstream politicians out to protect their legislative authority and local bases of power. Likewise, the political infighting over the IRAA brought into clear relief the schism between the national Socialism of the reformist right wing and the conservatism of members of the idealist right wing (*kannen uyoku*). Those of the latter inclination attacked supporters of the New Order for being closet Communists or Fascists out to create a new *bakufu*, a reference to the authoritarian shogunate that had restricted the imperial court to the realm of cultural pursuits during the Tokugawa period (1603–1867). Finally, members of the civil bureaucracy viewed with suspicion any political reorganization that might impinge on their own administrative prerogatives. Officials in the powerful Home Ministry, in particular, some of whom had themselves earlier advocated reform in their struggle to reverse the inroads made by party politicians in the 1920s, now moved to blunt the challenge posed to their authority by the IRAA.

The battle over the New Order reached a climax in late 1940 and early 1941. In June 1940, just prior to forming his second cabinet, Konoe announced his interest in establishing a new political structure, and in August his government created the New Order Preparatory Committee. By the end of the summer, a combination of defections from party ranks by New Order supporters and a general desire by other party members to secure a place within the new political structure hastened the self-dissolution of the established political parties. Then, on October 12, 1940, Prime Minister Konoe gave a speech formally launching the IRAA. Under the leadership of Konoe two mass hierarchical organizations were created: the first was to oversee a network of guilds linking the IRAA to the nation's economic activities, and the second a system of youth, educational, and cultural associations for mobilizing the political energies of the populace.

Seemingly, the New Order was at hand. However, at roughly the same time, Konoe's enthusiasm for the IRAA as a tool for political reorganization declined precipitously. The reasons for Konoe's change of heart remain a matter of debate, with intimidation by the idealist right wing and weak personal character often cited as explanations. But Konoe's experience at maneuvering in the face of political opposition and ability to garner the support of various political factions suggest a more deliberate calculation on the part of the prince. Specifically, the concurrent collapse of peace negotiations with China apparently convinced Konoe of the inadvisability of pushing for truly far-reaching political reorganization and thereby heightening already intense intra-elite conflict while engaged in the seemingly endless war on the continent. Whatever the final reason, by November Konoe was distancing himself from the IRAA, content to see the new organization integrated into existing methods for mobilizing popular morale behind the state. During the first half of 1941, radical reformist officers of the IRAA were replaced with more moderate individuals, while officials in the Home Ministry moved to utilize the new organization to supplement the spiritual mobilization campaigns over which their ministry had held sway since 1937.

Ultimately, the New Order Movement failed to accomplish the radical political reorganization sought by its most fervent supporters. The IRAA, intended to serve as the centerpiece of the new political structure, instead experienced incorporation into already existing institutions under the control of status-quo elites. Later efforts by the wartime government of Prime Minister Tojo Hideki to breathe new life into the IRAA by divorcing it from the control of the Home Ministry similarly ended in failure. Likewise, the effort to enhance central authority by further weakening the position of politicians in the lower house through the "IRAA elections" of 1942—this time with army officers and Home Ministry officials cooperating—proved futile. Indeed, by 1943 former party politicians had returned to the cabinet. Finally, on June 13, 1945, the IRAA was officially abolished. Japanese elites thus faced military defeat and foreign occupation operating within the same form of "limited pluralism" that had characterized pre-war and wartime politics, and that was so visible in the struggle over the New Order Movement.

IMPACTS

Despite the failure of the New Order Movement to accomplish a revolutionary transformation of the Meiji political and economic institutions, the effects of the drive for renovation and mobilization for war produced far-reaching consequences in both the near and long term. Attempts to realize political and economic reform through centralized planning by military and civilian bureaucrats resulted in unprecedented government involvement in the lives of the populace. Pursuing the construction of a national defense state meant not only intervening more directly in the daily lives of the Japanese people, this objective also heightened the desire to achieve control over external material resources. Fueled

Prince Konoe Fumimaro (left), outgoing premier, and General Tojo Hideki, the new premier, pose for the camera following a transfer of state affair in 1941. (Bettmann/Corbis)

further by the ideological linking of domestic reform to a Pan-Asian mission to lead Asia, the pursuit of the New Order helped make the war in China more intractable, facilitated the decision to join the Axis Pact, and helped place Japan on the road to conflict with the Allied powers and, ultimately, to defeat in the Second World War.

But the consequences of the New Order Movement did not end with the loss of the war and the results of subsequent occupation-era reforms. Although much that attended the battle over the IRAA was gone—notably the army and the objective of constructing a totalitarian national defense state—the drive to realize a new political structure nonetheless bequeathed significant legacies to post-war Japan, influencing the reconstruction of the nation and, consequently, affecting its relations with other countries. More specifically, the mobilizing of human and material resources at the direction of centralized bureaucratic authority, while ultimately insufficient to bring about wartime victory, produced a wealth of expertise available for the task of post-war economic reconstruction. The application of this knowledge was facilitated by the continuing power of the civil bureaucracy, an institution that largely escaped political purge by American

occupation authorities. Indeed, some of the same bureaucrats who devoted their early professional lives to the renovation of Japan's pre-war political and economic order used the skills thus acquired to embark on post-war careers fostering their nation's revival as a major economic power. Moreover, some of these men, via their personal rebirth as party politicians, became stalwarts of the post-war party system and, as in the case of Kishi Nobusuke, even served as prime minister. Consequently, the influence of the pre-war bureaucracy and the values it embodied extended not only to the drafting of economic strategy, but also helped shape the conduct of politics well into the second half of the twentieth century.

PEOPLE AND ORGANIZATIONS

Ketsumeidan (Blood Pledge Brotherhood)

Radical nationalist group organized by the Buddhist monk Inoue Nissho (1886–1967). Preaching a form of agrarian nationalism and advocating violent action to destroy the status quo and facilitate national renovation, Inoue attracted idealistic young university graduates and military officers to his plot to assassinate leading figures in the worlds of business and government. In February 1932, members of the group embarked on a campaign to kill individuals they viewed as representative of the corrupt political and economic status quo. Although these individuals were soon arrested by Home Ministry police, participants in a related plot assassinated Prime Minister Inukai Tsuyoshi on May 15, who turned out to be the last party premier until after the Second World War. Subsequent cabinets were increasingly influenced by right-wing reformists from within the military and civil bureaucracy.

Kikakuin (Cabinet Planning Board)

Centralized planning organ created in 1937 with the intent of integrating the policies of the bureaucratic ministries and facilitating national mobilization. Originating in the Cabinet Research Bureau created in 1935, the board opened a new path through which military personnel could participate in civil administration. In March 1941, seventeen of the bureau's members found themselves detained and interrogated as possible Communist agents. This "Kikakuin Incident," coming amidst a reaction by big business to the increasingly anti-capitalist objectives of the bureau's reformist bureaucrats, underscores the intensified intra-elite struggles that accompanied the New Order Movement. The bureau itself survived until 1943, when it was absorbed into the newly created Munitions Ministry.

Kishi Nobusuke (1896–1987)

Leading reformist bureaucrat who promoted a controlled economy in the puppet state of Manchukuo and served as minister of commerce and industry in the cabinet of Prime Minister Tojo Hideki. Arrested after the war as a suspected war criminal, Kishi was eventually released without trial. He soon became a key politician within the conservative Liberal Democratic Party and served as prime minister from 1957 to 1960.

Kita Ikki (1883–1937)

Radical nationalist whose ideas influenced young army officers. A subject of much research by students of pre-war nationalism, Kita is often viewed as Japan's prototypical Fascist or national Socialist. Initially a Socialist, Kita exemplifies the influence of anti-capitalist radicalism in the right-wing movement following the First World War. By the 1930s, Kita was largely inactive and living off money extorted from large businesses; however, his ties to the young army officers who led the February 26 Incident landed him before a firing squad in 1937.

Kodo-ha (Imperial Way faction)

Term used to refer to those army officers devoted to a vague vision of direct imperial rule to be realized through revolutionary violence directed against the capitalists and government officials they held responsible for political corruption, economic distress, and weak-kneed diplomacy. The failure of the February 1936 coup by Imperial Way faction officers precipitated the decline of the group as a force in domestic politics.

Kokuikai (National Mainstay Society)

Organization formed in January 1932 and centered on reformist "new bureaucrats" and their allies among other non-party elites. The society served as a forum for criticizing the failures of the political parties, highlighting their supposed inability to effectively lead Japan through its "period of crisis," and airing various ideas for reforming the status quo. This agenda was directed toward enhancing their own administrative autonomy at the expense of the mainstream parties and reflected the bureaucratic idealism and top-down moral reformism propagated by the society's leader, the Confucian nationalist Yasuoka Masahiro (1898–1983). Although less radical than other reformist bureaucrats, numerous "new bureaucrats" wielded considerable power prior to the February 26 Incident and facilitated the expansion of technocratic authority.

Konoe Fumimaro (1891–1945)

Member of one of Japan's most prestigious aristocratic lineages, three-time prime minister, and the key political figure of the New Order Movement. Although groomed by the last of the Meiji "elder statesmen" to take over the role of helping mediate intra-elite competition within the Meiji constitutional order, Konoe instead emerged as a critic of that order and the man various reformist groups hoped would lead them to a radical reorganization of the status quo. His last-minute defection from the IRAA ensured the undermining of the organization by political opponents. Subsequently, he came to share the perspective of those who viewed radical reformists as closet Communists out to foster revolution. In December 1945, Konoe committed suicide rather than stand trial as a war criminal.

Nagata Tetsuzan (1884–1935)

Army officer who was associated with the future prime minister Tojo Hideki and other officers advocating national mobilization to prepare for total war. Nagata emerged as the leading officer of the army's Control faction, inspired an important pamphlet in 1934 laying out a case for national mobilization, and allied with reformist bureaucrats in an effort to prepare the way for a national defense state. In 1935, a disgruntled member of the Imperial Way faction murdered Nagata, who was then serving as head of the Military Affairs Bureau. The future, however, lay with technocrats of Nagata's perspective.

Naimusho (Home Ministry)

Established in 1873, the ministry became the dominant civil force in domestic administration and, by the 1920s, was run by officials imbued with an elite sense of being "shepherds of the people." However, the same period witnessed higher-level positions in the ministry become plum jobs in a spoils system whereby the political party in power removed and appointed officials based on their party affiliation. By the early 1930s, a rising generation of reformist bureaucrats responded with a largely successful effort to roll back party power by defending and then enhancing their own prerogatives as "officials of the emperor." In 1941, ministry officials concerned over the potential threat posed by the IRAA to their administrative prerogatives successfully moved to co-opt the new organization.

Sakurakai (Cherry Blossom Society)

Nationalist society comprised of middle-ranking army officers. Together with civilian nationalists such as Okawa Shumei (1886–1957), members of this group plotted the abortive coups of March and October 1931. Subsequently banned by army authorities, participants nonetheless escaped with minor punishment, reflecting a breakdown of military discipline and the sympathy of some higher-ranking officers. The plots themselves reflect the radicalization of some portions of the officer corps, particularly the "young officers" who were enamored of the idea of toppling the Meiji bureaucratic and capitalist order in order to achieve a Showa Restoration.

Showa Kenkyukai (Showa Research Association)

Study group comprised of academics, public intellectuals, army officers, and reformist bureaucrats that served in an advisory role to Konoe Fumimaro. Society members emphasized the need to utilize the leadership of intellectuals and technocratic experts in order to reorganize the capitalist order. In seeking to give philosophical meaning to the war in China, recasting it as a "holy war" to create a New Order for East Asia, society members helped link the drive for renovation at home to a belief in a national mission abroad.

Taisei Yokusankai (Imperial Rule Assistance Association, IRAA)

Established on October 12, 1940, the IRAA was to be the institutionalization of the New Order; however, undermined by the last-minute withdrawal of support by Konoe and under concerted attack by conservative opponents, the new structure ended up assimilated into existing government institutions. The IRAA was disbanded on June 13, 1945.

Tojo Hideki (1884–1948)

Army general and military bureaucrat who was associated closely with "total war" officers of the Control faction and served as prime minister from October 1941 to July 1944. As prime minister, he accrued an unprecedented amount of

power and attempted to use the IRAA to further enhance central authority. Ultimately, Tojo's efforts to strengthen totalitarian control, together with his failure to successfully prosecute the war in the Pacific, sparked an opposition movement from within the ruling elite. Forced to resign following the fall of Saipan to U.S. forces in July 1944, Tojo was subsequently tried by the Allies as a war criminal and hanged on December 23, 1948.

Tosei-ha (Control faction)

Referring to what was less of a true faction than the Imperial Way group, the term—originally one of derision applied by factional opponents—is nonetheless useful in designating those army officers devoted to realizing national mobilization through bureaucratic planning and in cooperation with like-minded political allies. Although these officers shared the Imperial Way belief in the need for control over Manchuria, the enhancement of Japanese power in East Asia, and the imperative to mobilize the nation for war, they shied away from the terrorist tactics of the young officers and were less inclined to view the Soviet Union as a mortal enemy requiring immediate destruction. The collapse of the Imperial Way faction in the wake of the failed coup attempt of February 26, 1936, cleared the way for these military bureaucrats and their political allies to play a key role in the New Order Movement.

Roger H. Brown

See Also Armed Forces, Revolution, and Counter-Revolution; Chinese Revolution; Democracy, Dictatorship, and Fascism; Documentaries of Revolution; Human Rights, Morality, Social Justice, and Revolution; Italian Fascist Revolution; Nationalism and Revolution; Nazi Revolution: Politics and Racial Hierarchy

References and Further Readings

Berger, Gordon M. 1977. *Parties Out of Power in Japan, 1931–1941.* Princeton, NJ, Princeton University Press.

Crowley, James B. 1962. "Japanese Army Factionalism in the Early 1930s," *Journal of Asian Studies* 21 (3) (May 1962): 309–336.

———. 1966. *Japan's Quest for Autonomy: National Security and Foreign Policy, 1930–1938.* Princeton, NJ: Princeton University Press.

Duus, Peter, and Daniel I. Okimoto. 1976. "Fascism and the History of Prewar Japan: The Failure of a Concept," *Journal of Asian Studies* 39 (1) (November): 65–76.

Fletcher III, William Miles. 1982. *The Search for a New Order: Intellectuals and Fascism in Prewar Japan.* Chapel Hill: University of North Carolina Press.

Gordon, Andrew. 1991. *Labor and Imperial Democracy in Prewar Japan.* Berkeley: University of California Press.

Ito, Takashi. 1973. "The Role of Right-Wing Organizations in Japan." Pp. 487–509 in *Pearl Harbor as History: Japanese-American Relations, 1931–1941,* edited by Dorothy Borg and Shumpei Okamoto. New York: Columbia University Press.

Johnson, Chalmers. 1985. *MITI and the Japanese Miracle: The Growth of Industrial Policy, 1925–1975*. Stanford, CA: Stanford University Press.

Kasza, Gregory J. 1984. "Fascism from Below? A Comparative Perspective on the Japanese Right, 1931–1936," *Journal of Comparative History* 19 (4) (October 1984): 607–629.

Maruyama, Masao. 1969. *Thought and Behavior in Modern Japanese Politics*. Ivan Morris, ed. New York: Oxford University Press.

Morley, James W., ed. 1971. *Dilemmas of Growth in Prewar Japan*. Princeton, NJ: Princeton University Press.

Reynolds, R. Bruce, ed. 2004. *Japan in the Fascist Era*. New York: Palgrave.

Silberman, Bernard S., and H. D. Harootunian, eds. 1974. *Japan in Crisis: Essays on Taisho Democracy*. Princeton, NJ: Princeton University Press.

K

Kenyan Mau Mau Rebellion

CHRONOLOGY

1886   On November 1, an Anglo-German agreement is signed dividing a portion of the East African mainland between Great Britain and Germany. Most of the territory that becomes Kenya falls within the British sphere.

1896   On August 5, construction of the Kenya-Uganda railway begins.

1901   On December 20, the Uganda railway reaches Port Florence (now Kisumu) on Lake Victoria.

1905   On April 1, the protectorate is transferred from the Foreign Office to the Colonial Office.

1906   On April 4, the Report of the Land Commission affirms that the highlands are reserved exclusively for Europeans.

1907   On August 17, the Legislative Council (LegCo) holds its first meeting.

1908   On March 19, Lord Elgin, secretary of state for the colonies, pledges that land grants in the highlands will not be made to Indians.

1919   On November 1, the registration of African males begins in Nairobi with the issuing of the *Kipande* (identity card).

1920   On June 11, the East Africa Protectorate is renamed Kenya Colony. Until independence, the territory is officially known as the Colony and the Protectorate of Kenya.

1934   On May 14, the report of the Kenya Land Commission is made public.

1937   Resident Native Laborers Ordinance adopted, implemented in 1940.

1940   On May 30, the colonial government bans the Kikuyu Central Association (KCA).

1944   On October 1, the Kenya African Union (KAU) is formed.

1946–1950   The Mau Mau movement develops, and members begin a campaign of violent opposition to British rule.

1947   On June 1, Jomo Kenyatta is elected president of KAU.

1949   Colonial government passes and adopts the Vagrancy Bill.

1950   Voluntarily Unemployed Persons Ordinance empowered government to remove unemployed Africans from Nairobi.

On August 12, colonial government proscribes Mau Mau.

1952   On October 7, Chief Waruhiu wa Kung'u, a prominent Kikuyu pro-government chief is assassinated.

On October 20, Governor Sir Evelyn Baring declares a state of emergency and orders the arrest of Kenyatta and other KAU leaders.

On December 3, the Kapenguria trial for Kenyatta and his associates begins.

1953   On March 26, Mau Mau fighters successfully raid the Naivasha police station and kill ninety-seven Kikuyu loyalists at Lari.

On April 8, Judge R. S. Thacker sentences Jomo Kenyatta to seven years' imprisonment with hard labor for "managing" and "assisting in the managing" of Mau Mau and three years for belonging to Mau Mau.

On June 8, the colonial authorities proscribe KAU.

1959   On March 3, eleven "hardcore" Mau Mau detainees perish at Hola detention camp.

1960   On January 12, Governor Sir Patrick Renison signs a proclamation officially ending the state of emergency.

On January 18, the first Lancaster House constitutional conference opens in London.

1961   On August 14, Kenyatta is released after serving his term followed by a period of restriction.

On October 8, Kenyatta becomes president of the Kenya African National Union (KANU).

1962   On April 6, the second Lancaster House constitutional conference concludes in London.

1963   On May 26, Kenya's first universal suffrage general election ends.

On June 1, Kenya achieves internal self-government, with Kenyatta as first prime minister.

On December 12, Kenya achieves independence.

INTRODUCTION

Scholarship on Kenya's Mau Mau Rebellion continues to evoke significant controversial debates. Initial studies on the rebellion focused on defining the movement and discerning its goals with respect to the end of British rule in Kenya. In the official account, the Corfield Report (1960), Mau Mau was a rejection of civilization, a return to primitive barbarism, and a mass mental breakdown of its followers. Some scholars consider Mau Mau a manifestation of a unified Kikuyu cultural nationalism, while others view it as a Marxist-inspired insurgency, or a peasant revolt, or a civil war among the Kikuyu of Central Province (Elkins 2003, 193; Ogot 2003, 134–148). Recent Mau Mau studies have discerned the movement's ideology and membership, the nature of the Land Freedom Army (LFA), the relationship between the rebellion and nationalism in Kenya, and the government's rehabilitation programs for former Mau Mau participants. Mau Mau had far reaching implications for Great Britain, Kenya colony, and the world. The violence and brutality that characterized the rebellion forced the British government to move fast toward dismantling the empire. Ultimately, the guerrillas suffered a military defeat but won the psychological war against the British. This result would influence other liberation struggles around the world.

BACKGROUND: CULTURE AND HISTORY

In much of British Africa, the transfer of power to independence was smooth, with the exception of Kenya, where African freedom fighters waged a bloody war of liberation. In 1999, Kenya's population was placed at 28,686,805 people, comprising forty-two different ethnic groups (Republic of Kenya. Central Bureau of Statistics 2002, 237). In the disputed 2001 population census, the population was estimated to be over 30 million. The majority of Kenyans are black Africans, but other races include Arabs, Asians, and both Kenya and non-Kenya Europeans. Of the forty-two recognized African ethnic groups, the largest in numerical order are the Kikuyu of Central Province, the Luyia of Western Kenya, the Luo of Nyanza Province, the Kamba in Northeastern Province, and the Kalenjin who occupy most of the Rift Valley (Fay 1998–2000, 1). While Kiswahili and English are Kenya's national languages, each ethnic group speaks a specific vernacular, making for considerable linguistic variety within the nation. With regard to religious affiliation, about 70 percent of Kenya's African population is Christian, with Protestants outnumbering Roman Catholics. Muslims make up about 7 percent and the rest adhere to largely indigenous African religions. Kenya has a small number of Hindus and Sikhs (Fay 1998–2000, 1).

British interests in East Africa were initially centered on the control of Egypt and the river Nile. Seeing that the Nile originated in Lake Victoria, the British moved quickly to take over Uganda, the Sudan, and Egypt in the closing decades of the nineteenth century. To ease transport costs and open up the interior to British commerce, the Kenya-Uganda railway was constructed between 1896 and 1901. The British government, in order to make the railway a viable paying project, encouraged European settlers from Britain and South Africa to settle in the highlands of Kenya, later known as the "White Highlands." Indigenous populations including the Kikuyu and the Maasai in the Rift Valley were forcibly removed to pave the way for European settlement (Maxon and Ofcansky 2000, 6). This explains why Mau Mau followers were primarily Kikuyu and their closely related Embu and Meru neighbors (Rosberg and Nottingham 1966, 296).

The advent of colonial rule inaugurated new classes of leaders who lacked traditional legitimacy. Colonial functionaries, including chiefs and headmen, came to wield unprecedented power and authority over their subjects. Often, chiefs used their positions to accumulate wealth, including land and cash (Maloba 1993). Apart from the oppressive and arbitrary power of chiefs, the advent of western schooling pioneered by missionaries produced a new group of African educated elites, whose salaried employment in the colonial hierarchy transformed them into a wealthy social category. Like the colonial chiefs, these educated elites sought to invest in land and other economic enterprises. The individualization of land (shifting previously communally held land into private ownership) created new tensions and fissures between the Kikuyu *ahoi* (landless peasants) and individual landowners. Such *ahoi* drifted to the white highlands as squatters (Throup 1988, 8–11; Maloba 1993, 27–28).

The emerging capitalists or petty bourgeoisie looked forward to becoming successful traders, shopkeepers, and investing in road transport and construction work. However, they faced stiff competition from Asian traders who dominated both retail and wholesale trade, and they struggled against government resistance and lack of assistance in their attempt to thrive. The colonial government had no credit provisions for African entrepreneurs. In most cases, the pro-settler colonial economic policies sought to limit competition from emerging wealthy Africans. Most of the capitalists were farmers who were adopting new agricultural technologies and desired to cultivate cash crops such as coffee. Their hopes were crushed when European settlers managed to ban Africans from cash crop production (Maxon 1994, 233).

Africans resented their exclusion from political participation. In the period between the two world wars, various provincial African political associations began to emerge. The Kikuyu Central Association (KCA), founded in 1924, was the most active political association among the Kikuyu. KCA membership comprised young mission-educated Kikuyu, who demanded the return of Kikuyu stolen lands, resented the growing power of colonial chiefs, and desired more education for Africans.

In the social sphere, the mission encounter with the Kikuyu was characterized by intense conflict over Kikuyu customs, especially female circumcision. As pioneers of western formal education in Africa, mission stations served interchangeably as church and school. Here, mission adherents, both church members and students, were forbidden to undergo this rite. Kikuyu cultural guardians including Jomo Kenyatta, the general secretary of KCA from 1928, left mission churches to start Kikuyu independent churches and the Karinga school movement, which tolerated female circumcision (Kanogo 1987, 79–80). Kenyatta rallied the Kikuyu against the Church of Scotland Mission's attack on Kikuyu culture. In 1929 and later in 1931, KCA sent Kenyatta to England to champion Kikuyu grievances. Kenyatta would stay in England until 1946. His book, *Facing Mount Kenya,* published in 1938, represented Kikuyu cultural nationalism at its best (Maloba 1993, 48). During World War II, the colonial government banned all African political associations, including KCA, which re-emerged later as the Kenya African Union (KAU).

CONTEXT AND PROCESS OF REVOLUTION

The Mau Mau Rebellion occurred against a backdrop of a depressed African economy, a settler-dominated political and economic terrain, land hunger, increasing social differentiation, and a suffocating, racially segregated society in Kenya. While the name Mau Mau has no meaning among the Kikuyu or in any other language spoken in Kenya, it became the catch phrase used by the colonial government to describe anti-

European activity (Maxon 1986, 231). Kenyans had earlier coined the Swahili phrase, "*Mzungu Arudi Ulaya, Mwafrika Apate Uhuru* (MAU MAU)," which loosely translates to "Europeans return to Europe, so that Africans can get freedom."

Although the seeds of the rebellion were sown early in the 1900s, it was not until 1950 that the colonial government recognized the existence of a movement aimed at uniting the Kikuyu in order to rid Kenya of European settlers (Throup 1988, 113). The organizing ideological tools for Mau Mau leaders and followers constituted *ithaka* (land) and *wiathi* (Kikuyu term meaning freedom) (Kanogo, 1987, 127; Elkins 2003, 193).

Land scarcity in Kikuyuland was a result of land alienation (depriving indigenous Kenyan peoples of their land), population pressure, and the closing of the Kikuyu expansion frontier by the establishment of the white highlands and African reserves (Maloba 1993, 27). Landless Kikuyu and those displaced in the Kikuyu reserves managed a decent living as squatters on settler farms for quite a while. The adoption and strict enforcement of the Resident Native Laborers Ordinance (RNLO) of 1937 and the implementation of the Kenya Land Commission's (KLC) (1932–1934) recommendations in 1939 fundamentally curtailed squatter existence. The RNLO gave European settlers power to limit squatter cultivation and livestock, and to increase the number of working days per year. Squatters who rejected these conditions or refused to sign work contracts were evicted or declared voluntarily unemployed. Such "undesirable" squatters were forcibly removed and placed in overcrowded reserves where they were not welcome. The growing Kikuyu militancy and the post–World War II colonial agricultural improvement and soil conservation programs served to intensify disquiet and exacerbate the situation.

Although the KLC acknowledged the scarcity of land in Kikuyu reserves, it endorsed the policy of reserving the white highlands for Europeans. The commissioners also proposed that Kikuyu landowners at Tigoni, a Kikuyu reserve in the middle of settler farms, be moved to Lari, near Nairobi, to give way to European settlers. While most Tigoni Kikuyu rejected the proposal, ex-chief Luka Wakahangara did agree to move (Rosberg and Nottingham 1966, 286–292). When the government commenced the forcible removal of Tigoni Kikuyu in May 1940, many became either *ahoi* in the Kikuyu reserves or squatters in the Rift Valley. Some settled in Lari but saw Wakahangara as a traitor.

In 1939, the colonial government had purchased 34,700 acres of land south of Mau plateau to settle Africans displaced by the RNLO (Kanogo 1987, 107, 112). The settlement, Olenguruone, became a hotbed of squatter resistance to colonial agricultural impositions. Enforced limits on squatter cultivation and livestock, and varied forms of anti-soil-erosion measures, including terracing and crop rotation, made squatter existence difficult. The Olenguruone experiment destroyed Kikuyu agricultural practices and the social fabric that held the community together. It transformed indigenous Kikuyu inheritance laws and eliminated possibilities for access to land by sale, rent, mortgage, or other forms of disposal (Kanogo 1987, 107–121). Olenguruone residents began to organize and seek support from antagonized squatters in the white highlands and from Kikuyu reserves (Kanogo 1987, 105–106).

Rising discontent and despondency, both among squatters in the white highlands and in the reserves, was followed by mass oathing. In most African societies, an oath is a sacred symbol of loyalty or trust. It may involve blood, spoken words, or sacrifice of a spotless animal. The Kikuyu traditional oath was administered selectively as a tool for enhancing ethnic unity. However, in the mid 1950s, it was transformed into a symbol of loyalty to the Mau Mau, and an instrument for mass obedience, encompassing open defiance of colonial authority.

By 1946, most people relocated to Olenguruone had taken this oath in which they committed themselves to violence and personal sacrifice for a just nationalist cause (Rosberg and Nottingham 1966, 248, 255). The new oath, called *batuni* (platoon), created the discipline, the will, and the unity required of revolutionaries (Rosberg and Nottingham 1966, 243). This fuelled political radicalism and subversive activities, such as maiming white settler livestock and acts of arson against settler property. By 1947, squatter resistance to government regulations included strikes, violence, and sabotage. Time was almost ripe for the Mau Mau Rebellion (Kanogo 1987, 97, 104). And by 1948, colonial chiefs, other agents, and symbols of colonial oppression became targets of violent attacks (Maxon 1986; Maloba 1993, 33–34). The Kikuyu oath was now an apparatus of mass mobilization and politicization.

Apart from squatter discontent, Kikuyu militancy increased when the Kenya African Union (KAU) emerged in 1946. Founded in 1944 by Nairobi-based African elites and former members of KCA as a national African political party, KAU was pressured by the colonial government to adopt the name Kenya African Study Union (KASU). In 1946, it reverted to its original name. In June 1946, Kenyatta returned to Kenya, and assumed KAU's presidency in 1947 (Kanogo 1987, 126). KAU embraced trade union leaders and the African masses in Nairobi and Central Province.

Discontented groups provided a fertile recruiting ground for political and trade union activists. In January 1947, under the leadership of Chege Kabachia, the African Workers Federation (AWF) led a successful dockworkers strike in Mombasa (Maloba 1993, 39–40). In August, Kabachia organized a general strike in Nairobi, but he was arrested and deported. AWF disintegrated, but trade union leaders thrived within the KAU (Maloba 1993, 39–40; Ogot 2003, 29–31).

KAU's demands included the return of Kikuyu alienated lands, provision of land for the landless, increased educational opportunities, African representation in the Legislative Council (LegCo), and an end to racial discrimination, forced labor, low wages, and increased taxation. KAU also called for more economic opportunities for Africans, and self-government and full independence for Kenya (Maloba 1993; Maxon and Ofcansky 2000, 6, 116).

While Kenyatta and other moderates in KAU preferred the gradualist constitutional approach involving appeals for social, political, and economic reforms, the politics of memoranda and petitions failed to achieve any changes. On June 10, 1951, Fred Kubai and Bildad Kaggia, both radical trade unionists, were elected to office in the Nairobi branch of KAU. This shifted KAU's leadership from Kenyatta and the moderates to the young radicals who had immense acceptance among discontented unemployed African migrants in Nairobi (Kanogo 1987, 128; Maloba 1993, 59). Many in KAU turned to militancy and supported the violence that characterized the Mau Mau Rebellion.

In the meantime, the colonial government thought the unemployed and landless would be absorbed in industrial employment in Kenya's emerging colonial urban centers, principally Nairobi. Yet, the colonial government did little to industrialize the economy or provide skills for most urban migrants (Maloba 1993, 32).

Located in the vicinity of Kikuyu territory, Nairobi was flooded by migrants from Kikuyu and the Rift Valley who viewed the city as the last survival option. These included landless Kikuyu who were pushed out by the individualization of title to land in Central Province, squatters evicted from the Rift Valley, or those marginalized by restricted squatter cultivation on settler farms. Statistics show that between 1948 and 1952, Nairobi received large numbers of African immigrants. It is estimated that in 1948, Nairobi's total African male workforce stood at 30,000, of whom 17,000 (56 percent) were Kikuyu. By 1952, the total had doubled to 60,000, of whom 45,000 (75 percent) were Kikuyu. By 1954, Nairobi's segregated areas set aside for Africans were home to many displaced Kikuyu, including women and children (Anderson 2003, 159). Demobilized WWII African ex-servicemen with no land, technical skills, or capital to establish businesses joined them. Their efforts at establishing viable retail businesses in urban and rural market centers failed dismally, creating another group of angry, embittered urban unemployed (Maloba 1993, 35–36).

Migrants to Nairobi settled in areas designated for Africans. These areas were characterized by inadequate sanitary facilities, overcrowded hazardous existence, poverty, and low wages for those employed (Maloba 1993, 36–39; Anderson 2003, 159). The harsh economic realities in Nairobi's African neighborhoods offered limited options besides the informal sector and crime. Criminal activities became an important part of the livelihood in these areas. With racial discrimination evident in employment, residential areas, social amenities, and a host of other areas, Nairobi was becoming the hub of Mau Mau operatives. The adoption of the Vagrancy Bill in 1949 and the Voluntarily Unemployed Persons Ordinance in 1950 gave the colonial government power to move all unemployed Africans from Nairobi to reserves (Maloba 1993, 43).

Sir Philip Mitchell retired as governor of Kenya in June 1952, but his successor, Sir Evelyn Baring, did not arrive in Kenya until the end of September. The long interregnum significantly impacted the administration's handling of the Mau Mau crisis. After a brief tour of Central Province, Baring returned to Nairobi convinced that KAU and Kenyatta, its president, were behind Mau Mau (Berman 1992, 252; Maloba 1993, 74–75). The assassination, on October 7, of senior chief Waruhiu, a Christian and strong supporter of the colonial government, on his way home from a meeting with the governor in Nairobi provoked a harsh reaction from colonial authorities. Waruhiu's murder provided an opportunity for European settlers to put pressure on Governor Baring to deal with the rebellion.

On October 20, 1952, with approval from the Colonial Office, Baring declared a state of emergency. Under emergency rules, the colonial state commenced Operation Jock Scott, in which between 145 and 181 "known" leaders of the Mau Mau—including Kenyatta, its alleged mastermind, and his close associates in KAU, Achieng' Oneko, Paul Ngei, and Kungu wa Karumba and trade unionists Fred Kubai and Bildad Kaggia—were arrested and detained in Kapenguria (Berman 1992, 252; Elkins 2003, 193).

Kenyatta and his associates were arraigned in the famous Kapenguria trial on December 3, 1952, where Kenyatta was charged with managing an unlawful and secret criminal society called Mau Mau. Since the trial aimed at justifying the state of emergency, it was important that the state obtain a guilty verdict. The government schooled and bribed witnesses as well as the trial judge, Ransley Thacker, who was paid £20,000 (Maloba 1993, 98–99; Maxon & Ofcansky 2000, 106). On April 8, 1953, Thacker found the defendants guilty and sentenced them to seven years hard labor. On June 8, KAU was proscribed as an unlawful society.

But Mau Mau could not be defeated by outside forces alone, so the colonial government turned to Africans, mostly Kikuyu, and a few Embu and Meru loyalists and home guards. Loyalists were landed and wealthy Kikuyu, including chiefs, government servants, some businessmen, teachers, and Christian converts. Most were older men who sought to guard against lawlessness and the attack on private property, cherished Kikuyu traditions and customs, and their faith. They were committed to using the constitutional approach to reform the colonial system (Ogot 1972, 140–143). Comprising about 8,000 in 1953, the number of home guards had reached approximately 25,000 by 1954. After the Lari massacre, the government began to equip home guards with rifles and shotguns and incorporate them into the armed forces. Representing African opposition to Mau Mau, the home guards gathered intelligence and helped to control the civilian population. While some used their power with impunity against civilians, others remained sympathetic to the movement (Maloba 1993, 93)

Between October 1952 and June 1953, Mau Mau fighters successfully launched numerous attacks upon settler farms and African allies of the security forces (Anderson 2003, 150). On March 26, 1953, Mau Mau rebels raided Naivasha prison in the Rift Valley, released 150 prisoners, and captured several rifles and automatic weapons and substantial ammunition. On the same night, ex-chief Wakahangara, twenty-six members of his family, and seventy other loyalists perished in the Lari massacre (Ogot 2003, 28). The massacre was part of a long, drawn-out land feud between Kikuyu "haves" and "have-nots." The movement had become a civil war among the Kikuyu.

The Lari massacre boosted government counter-insurgency. The destruction of civilian lives in the massacre significantly undermined the credibility of the movement and alienated sympathy outside Kenya for the African cause. The colonial government seized this opportunity to depict Mau Mau as a bestial and pagan oathing movement (Rosberg and Nottingham 1966, 291–292).

The colonial government also sought to contain Mau Mau by closing off Central Province to visitors and the outside world. Using villagization (concentration of the rural population into large government-guarded and -policed villages) as a punitive measure against known core Mau Mau–supporting areas, Kikuyu, Embu, and Meru regions came under siege. Thousands of the civilian population were resettled in these large villages. Residents were ordered to construct long, deep trenches around the guarded villages, ostensibly to protect civilians from Mau Mau. Surrounded by barbed wire, the villages constituted an effective military tactic aimed at cutting off contact, supplies, logistics, and other forms of services to the forest fighters (Maloba 1993, 90). This strategy significantly checked the spread of Mau Mau to other parts of the colony.

Having secured the Mau Mau hotbed, the British government appointed Sir George Erskine as commander in chief of the colony's armed forces in May 1953 (Maloba 1993, 83; Anderson 2003, 160). Erskine's military stratagem included increased intelligence using spies, interrogation, home guards, and captured guerrillas (Maloba 1993, 84). Despite the imposition of curfew, segregation of suspected pro–Mau Mau areas of Nairobi, regulation of movement in and out of these locations, and a visible police and home guard presence, Mau Mau operatives continued to make advances.

From the middle of 1953, however, the government increased surveillance, heightened security around potential Mau Mau targets, and improved intelligence on Mau Mau activities. This restricted the guerrillas to the forests.

After significantly curtailing Mau Mau activities, the government focus shifted to Nairobi. It had become the base for Mau Mau operatives and organizations that provided supplies and logistical information to the forest fighters. To isolate the fighters, the government launched Operation Anvil, a codename for a three-week joint military and police operation to break up Mau Mau command structures and networks within Nairobi (Anderson 2003, 160). This operation was the most extensive and brutal offensive against Mau Mau in Nairobi. Commencing April 23, 1954, security forces cordoned off Nairobi and mounted searches aimed at ridding Nairobi of all Kikuyu, Embu, and Meru ethnicities. Over the next three weeks, about 50,000 were subjected to interrogation and 30,000 were placed in detention camps (Maloba 1993, 860; Anderson 2003, 159). By the middle of May 1954, when Operation Anvil officially ended, over 24,000 Kikuyu, Embu, and Meru had been arrested. Two thousand women and 4,000 children had been repatriated to the reserves of Central Province. Of those arrested, 10,000 were sent to detention camps reserved for hardcore Mau Mau supporters (Anderson 2003, 160–161).

Operation Anvil dealt a major blow to the Mau Mau movement. It dramatically reduced the recruiting ground by detaining Kikuyu, Embu, and Meru workers in Nairobi, cut off the forest fighters from essential supplies, and crippled the passive wing of the movement (Anderson 2003, 161). By October 1954, forest gangs were falling apart due to lack of basic supplies, weapons, and new recruits (Anderson 2003, 162).

The growing desperation of the isolated forest fighters is illustrated in the September 25, 1954, raid on Lukenya prison, in which twenty fighters raided the prison housing about 300 detainees. Although the raiders sought to free the detainees, the underlying impetus was to capture arms from the prison's armory. Indeed, 296 detainees were released, a guard killed, and several others wounded. But the raiders were disheartened with the limited arms they found: three rifles, two shotguns, a revolver, and about 300 rounds of am-

Kikuyu women, who previously were Mau Mau adherents, renouncing their Mau Mau oath during a cleansing ceremony in Nyeri. (Library of Congress)

munitions. By January 1955, the Mau Mau movement seemed to have adopted coercion and entrapment to recruit younger fighters (Anderson 2003, 162, 172). By 1956, Mau Mau had lost the military battle. It was time for the government to rehabilitate the Kikuyu.

The British rehabilitation program was guided by the government's belief that the Kikuyu had been indoctrinated with terrorist ideologies and that they had to be made to renounce terrorism and the basic tenets of the Mau Mau movement. Detention, communal punishments, and confessions began to weaken the peasants' resolve to support Mau Mau (Maloba 1993, 137). The government also sought to replace Mau Mau ideology with Christianity. Through a program called "Pipeline," the colonial administration disposed of Africans who were involved in the Mau Mau movement or systematized the rehabilitation of those perceived by colonial authorities to be capable of being reformed through religious indoctrination. Detainees were first sent to a screening camp where those viewed as capable of rehabilitation were later sent to a work camp. Eventually, many were allowed to go to open

camps in their villages (Maloba, 1993, 138; Elkins 2003, 199–200). Detainees were categorized as "black" (hardcore), "grey" (capable of renouncing Mau, Mau) and "white" (the innocent). Mackinnon and Manyani, Mageta Islands, and Hola were the main "hardcore" holding camps (Maloba 1993, 138–140).

Conditions in detention camps were rough and brutal. On March 3, 1959, eleven hardcore detainees were clubbed to death. The government's attempt to cover up failed when an official investigation pointed to physical force. The Hola incident shook Kenya, Britain, and the world, and marked a turning point in Kenya's history. Internal and international pressure pushed the British toward disengagement, and the emerging African politicians seized this opportunity to demand the end of the state of emergency and ultimately, independence (Maxon 1986, 234–235; Maloba 1993, 150). In three successive Lancaster House Conferences held in London between 1960 and 1963, Kenya moved to African majority rule, internal self-government, and independence by December 1963.

IMPACTS

There is no consensus among Mau Mau scholars on the impact of the rebellion in Kenya's history. While some scholars argue that Mau Mau delayed Kenya's independence, some regard it as a nationalist movement aimed at freeing Kenya from British control. Others view Mau Mau as purely a Kikuyu affair: a civil war among the Kikuyu. Recently, Bethwell Ogot has authoritatively concluded that Mau Mau was an expression of militant nationalism and a peasant war emerging out of the growing class struggle among the Kikuyu. The militants fought a war of liberation that had nationwide support (Ogot 2003, 9).

Mau Mau emanated from deeply seated political, economic, and social problems. The cost of defeating Mau Mau convinced the imperial government that British taxpayers would not continue to subsidize the settler economy and political dominance. The British government was willing to embark on social, economic, and political reforms in Kenya (Maxon 1986, 233).

While initial British government intervention was limited to stabilizing the situation through incremental constitutional changes and financing counter-insurgency, by the late 1950s, metropolitan policy formulation had begun reversing some of the pre-war policies. Priority was given to African cash crop production and the provision of higher education and other social amenities, better working conditions, increased opportunity in the civil service, and more African participation in government. The 1959 Hola affair convinced the newly appointed secretary of state for the colonies, Ian Macleod, that change was inevitable (Maxon 1986, 235). Kenya's governor, Sir Patrick Renison, who succeeded Baring in 1959 and had described Kenyatta as a leader to "darkness and death," was forced to release Kenyatta in August 1961 (Maxon 1986, 236). Assuming the presidency of the newly formed Kenya African National Union (KANU), Kenyatta and other Kenyan nationalists pushed forward to end British rule in Kenya.

Economic reforms focused on rural areas. In 1954, the colonial government unveiled the Swynnerton plan. It aimed at transforming African agriculture through land consolidation and issuance of individual title to land, introduction of cash crops, improved extension service, provision of credit, and the formation of African farmers' cooperatives. Holdings belonging to forest fighters were confiscated and claimed by loyalists. These agrarian changes thus benefited traditional Kikuyu conservatives, including chiefs, businessmen, and farmers who employed more modern farming techniques (Maxon 1986, 233). The independent Kenya government agreed to the British offer of loans to buy farms owned by European farmers who chose to leave Kenya at independence.

In January 1960, about 7.5 million acres were in European possession. An initial loan of £12 million was granted to purchase 1.2 million acres (Huxley, 1967, ix). More loans were disbursed as Europeans scrambled to leave an African-ruled Kenya. As the first president of independent Kenya, Kenyatta adopted the principle of "willing seller–willing buyer" in the post-colonial land settlement. Ex-squatters and former guerrillas who outlived the rebellion returned to destitute lives. To this day, the land question causes both inter-ethnic and intra-ethnic clashes in Kenya.

PEOPLE AND ORGANIZATIONS

Kenyatta, Jomo (ca. 1889 to 1898–1978)

Kenya's first prime minister and first president. Secretary general of KCA in 1928, he lived in England from 1929 to 1946, then returned to Kenya. He became president of KAU. In October 1952, he was arrested and convicted for "managing" Mau Mau. He was released in 1961 and became president of Kenya in 1963.

Kikuyu Central Association (KCA)—After 1944, Kenya African Union, KAU

Formed in 1924 by Kikuyu elites to articulate Kikuyu grievances including land alienation. KCA sent Kenyatta to England to petition the British government on the issue of white confiscation of Kikuyu ancestral land, the Kipande (identity card), taxation, forced labor, and unpaid communal soil conservation measures. The KCA was proscribed in 1940, but it re-emerged in 1944 as KAU (Kenya African Union).

Kubai, Fred (1915–1996)

Founder of the African Workers Federation in 1947. In 1949, he and Asian trade unionist Makhan Singh founded the East African Trade Union Congress. President of the Nairobi branch of Kenya KAU in 1951, he was among KAU leaders arrested with Kenyatta and charged with managing Mau Mau in 1952.

Land Freedom Army (LFA)

Hardcore Mau Mau fighters who waged a guerrilla war against British forces in Kenya from the forests of Mt. Kenya and Nyandarwa ranges during the Mau Mau Rebellion.

Mitchell, Sir Philip (1890–1964)

Governor of Kenya from 1944 to 1952. Mitchell's tenure coincided with African nationalism in Kenya and the serious economic and social discontent that flared up in the Mau Mau Rebellion.

Renison, Sir Patrick (1911–1965)

Governor of Kenya from 1959 to 1962. Due to his inability to work with the imperial government and Kenyan nationalists to accelerate de-colonization, he was forced to resign in November 1962.

Priscilla Shilaro

See Also Colonialism, Anti-Colonialism, and Neo-Colonialism; Documentaries of Revolution; Ethnic and Racial Conflict: From Bargaining to Violence; Literature and Modern Revolution; Terrorism

References and Further Readings
Anderson, David M. 2003. "The Battle of Dandora Swamp: Reconstructing the Mau Mau Land Freedom Army, October 1954." Pp. 155–175 in *Mau Mau and Nationhood: Arms, Authority and Narration,* edited by E. S. Atieno Odhiambo and John Lonsdale. Athens: Ohio University Press.
Berman, Bruce. 1992. "Bureaucracy and Incumbent Violence: Colonial Administration and the Origins of the 'Mau Mau' Emergency." Pp. 227–264 in *Unhappy Valley: Book Two: Violence and Ethnicity,* edited by Bruce Berman and John Lonsdale. Athens: Ohio University Press.
Elkins, Caroline. 2003. "Detention, Rehabilitation, and the Destruction of the Kikuyu Society." Pp.191–226 in *Mau Mau and Nationhood: Arms, Authority and Narratives,* edited by E. S. Atieno Odhiambo and John Londsale. Athens: Ohio University Press.
Fay, Robert. 1998–2000. "Kenya" in *Microsoft Encarta*: 1–3.
Huxley, Elspeth. 1967. *White Man's Country.* Vol. 1. New York: Frederick A. Praeger.
Kanogo, Tabitha. 1987. *Squatters and the Roots of Mau Mau, 1905–1963.* Athens: Ohio University Press.
Lonsdale, John. 1992. "The Moral Economy of Mau Mau: The Problem." Pp. 265–314 in *Unhappy Valley: Book Two: Violence and Ethnicity,* edited by Bruce Berman and John Lonsdale. Athens: Ohio University Press.
Maloba, Wunyabari O. 1993. *Mau Mau and Kenya: An Analysis of a Peasant Revolt.* Bloomington and Indianapolis: Indiana University Press.
Maxon, Robert M. 1986. *East Africa: An Introductory History.* Morgantown, WV: West Virginia University Press.
———. 1994. *East Africa: An Introductory History,* 2nd rev. ed. Morgantown: West Virginia University Press.
Maxon, Robert M., and Thomas P. Ofcansky. 2000. *Historical Dictionary of Kenya,* 2nd ed. Lanham, MD and London: Scarecrow Press.
Ochieng', W. R., ed. 1989. *A Modern History of Kenya 1895–1980.* London, Nairobi: Evans Brothers (Kenya).
Odhiambo, E. S. Atieno. 1995. "The Formative Years 1945–55." Pp. 25–47 in *Decolonization and Independence in Kenya, 1940–93,* edited by B. A. Ogot and W. R. Ochieng'. Athens: Ohio University Press.
Odhiambo, E. S. Atieno., and John Lonsdale, eds. 2003. *Mau Mau and Nationhood.* Athens: Ohio University Press.
Ogot, Bethwell. A. 1972. "Revolt of the Elders." Pp. 134–148 in *Politics and Nationalism in Colonial Kenya. Hadith 4.* Edited by Bethwell A. Ogot. Nairobi: EAP
———. 2003. "Mau Mau & Nationhood." Pp. 8–36 in *Mau Mau and Nationhood,* edited by E. S. Atieno Odhiambo and John Lonsdale. Athens: Ohio University Press.
Ogot, Bethwell, and W. R. Ochieng', eds. 1995. *Decolonization and Independence in Kenya 1940–93.* Athens: Ohio University Press.
Republic of Kenya. 2002. *Central Bureau of Statistics, Economic Survey 2002.* Nairobi: Government Printer.
Rosberg, C. G., Jr., and John Nottingham. 1966. *The Myth of "Mau Mau": Nationalism in Kenya.* New York: Frederick A. Praeger.
Throup, David. W. 1988. *Economic and Social Origins of Mau Mau: 1945–1953.* Athens: Ohio University Press.

Korean Civil War

CHRONOLOGY

1392   Yi Song-gye establishes the Choson dynasty (also known as the Yi dynasty), Korea's last monarchy. Under Yi's successors, Korea's political, economic, and social system emulates China. During the nineteenth century, internal weakness leaves the Yi government unable to protect itself against imperialist domination.

1637   Korea declares allegiance to the new Qing dynasty in China. The Yi government then issues edicts to achieve a self-imposed isolation, closing tightly the northern border, prohibiting outside travel and visitors, and allowing trade only with China and Japan.

1783   First Koreans convert to Christianity, reflecting the increasing introduction of Western ideas into Choson Korea.

1786   Yi government prohibits Christianity because the foreign creed threatens state control. Vigorous persecution begins after 1800, with the banning of Christian books as subversive.

1839   Yi government begins a campaign to suppress Christianity, executing three French

Catholic missionaries and arresting, imprisoning, and killing converts. Fears of European retribution repeating events in China after the first Opium War ends the campaign, resulting in an estimated 20,000 Koreans converting to Catholicism over the next two decades.

1866   Renewed persecution of Christians results in the arrest and execution of foreign priests. France sends a punitive expedition of seven ships and 600 soldiers against Korea that loots and burns a west-coast town on Kanghwa Island.

1875   Japanese warships destroy the fort on Kanghwa Island after Koreans fire on a Japanese survey expedition. Tokyo then compels the Yi government to sign a treaty removing barriers to access in Korea and recognizes Korea's independence, ending its tributary status with China.

1884   Korean faction favoring modernization following the Japanese model stages a failed attempt to seize control of the Yi government, breaking into the palace, burning buildings, capturing King Kojong, and murdering his pro-China advisers.

1894   Tonghak (Eastern Learning) Rebellion ignites the Sino-Japanese War, resulting in the Japanese easily defeating Chinese forces on land and at sea. A treaty ends the conflict the next year, with China recognizing Japan's dominance over Korea.

1896   Russia presses for total control in Korea after signing a joint protectorate agreement with Japan. Russia's advisers supervise military reorganization and control the military in time of war. In response, So Chae-pil forms the Independence Club, Korea's first political party, to protest against any limits on national sovereignty.

1904   Japanese naval forces attack the Russian fleet at Port Arthur in China, starting the Russo-Japanese War. The Treaty of Portsmouth ends the conflict the next year and recognizes Japan's dominance over Korea. Japan imposes a protectorate on Korea.

1910   Japan's formal annexation of Korea begins the systematic political and economic incorporation of the peninsula into the Japanese empire.

1919   Massive March First Rebellion demanding Korea's independence is met with brutal Japanese repression. Fleeing Korean leaders meet in Shanghai, China, and form the Korean Provisional Government (KPG).

1921   Leftist Koreans form the Koryo Communist Party in Shanghai, China, advocating a Bolshevik-inspired program to end poverty and oppression in Korea after liberation from Japanese rule. In 1928, the Soviet Union, after providing limited financial help, withdraws its support because of factional disputes within the party.

1943   During World War II, President Franklin D. Roosevelt, Prime Minister Winston Churchill, and Generalissimo Jiang Jieshi (Chiang Kai Shek) issue the Cairo Declaration, promising independence for Korea "in due course." Korean exile leaders denounce plans to delay restored sovereignty, but at the Yalta Conference in February 1945, Roosevelt and Soviet premier Joseph Stalin agree to a post-war trusteeship for Korea.

1945   Soviet-American military occupation divides Korea at the thirty-eighth parallel. Yo Un-hyong creates the Korean People's Republic as Korea's post-war government.

1946   Peasants and workers participate in Autumn Harvest Uprisings in southern Korea to protest political repression and economic hardship.

1948   North-South conference in Pyongyang during April fails to end Korea's division, leading to the establishment of the Republic of Korea (ROK) in August and the Democratic People's Republic of Korea (DPRK) in September. Soviet occupation forces withdraw from the DPRK in December.

Leftists and Communists stage Yosu-Sunchon Rebellion in October following the uprising on Cheju Island the prior summer, demonstrating widespread opposition to an ROK government opposed to sweeping political, social, and economic reforms.

1949   Violent border clashes between DPRK and ROK military units occur at the thirty-eighth parallel. U.S. occupation forces withdraw from South Korea in June.

1950   North Korea attacks South Korea, igniting the Korean War. DPRK officials assert political control over most of South Korea until September, when U.S. forces land at Inchon and force the retreat of North Korean forces above the thirty-eighth parallel. ROK government then establishes political control over most of North Korea until Chinese military intervention pushes U.S. and ROK forces back into South Korea.

1953   An armistice agreement ends the fighting in Korea. A state of war continues, but the ROK and the DPRK abandon serious efforts to resume the Korean Civil War.

INTRODUCTION

By 1800, Korea was experiencing revolutionary changes after four centuries of political, economic, and social stability. Imperialist encroachments culminating in Japanese annexation in 1910 postponed and then altered the character of the Korean Civil War, which was a clash between divergent visions of the nation's future following monarchial rule. Soviet-American division of the peninsula in August 1945 and military occupation led to creation of two Korean governments and, in June 1950, to a conventional conflict. U.S. and Chinese military intervention ended the Korean Civil War without reunification, but with the impact of intensifying and militarizing the Cold War.

BACKGROUND: CULTURE AND HISTORY

Debate persists about whether the North Korean attack of June 25, 1950, on South Korea was an act of Soviet-inspired external aggression or the next stage in an ongoing Korean civil war. For the next three decades, few disagreed with President Harry S. Truman's unequivocal endorsement of the former interpretation when he announced in a press release on June 27, 1950, that "communism has passed beyond the use of subversion to conquer independent nations and will now use armed invasion and war." Bruce Cumings eventually challenged conventional wisdom in the first volume of his *The Origins of the Korean War* (Cumings 1981, xxi). He asserted that "the conflict was civil and revolutionary in character, beginning just after 1945 and proceeding through a dialectic of revolution and reaction. The opening of conventional battles in June 1950 only continued this war by other means." This characterization dominated thinking about the war until the release of Soviet documents during the early 1990s undermined the Cumings interpretation. Historian William Stueck argued that this new information reaffirmed the primacy of international involvement, insisting that describing the conflict as "The Korean Civil War" is a "clear-cut distortion of reality" (Stueck 2002, 83). But he accepts as accurate the consensus that there were domestic origins of the Korean War dating from at least World War II.

Japan bears a preponderance of the responsibility for the civil strife in Korea after 1945, because four decades earlier it had silenced an existing internal debate about the nation's political future. Japanese domination and annexation of Korea after 1905 resulted not only in brutal oppression and unrestrained exploitation, but set the stage following liberation for political division and a destructive war. Korea suffered these unhappy events because it was unable to defend itself during the late nineteenth century, when initial imperialist apathy toward the Hermit Kingdom (the nickname other countries gave to Korea because Korean rulers tried to prevent the opening of the country to foreign trade by closing the borders) ended. By 1800, the Choson dynasty, having ruled Korea since 1392, had entered a period of rapid decline, because a system that had maintained stability was crumbling everywhere. Domestic disruption accelerated as social stratification broke down. Royal artisans became private craftsmen. Rich peasants obtained more land and wealth, allowing them and wealthy merchants to purchase *yangban* (aristocratic) status and escape taxation. At the same time, many *yangban* now were impoverished. These and younger *yangban* denied government office joined in a revolt among intellectuals who rejected the rituals and empty formalism of Confucianism. They embraced *sirhak* or "practical learning" from the West, demanding government reorganization, land reform, and equal rights. A civil conflict was already percolating in late seventeenth-century Korea.

Popular unrest in rural Korea added intensity to dynastic instability. Destitution stalked the countryside. Beginning in the seventeenth century, droughts, floods, and other natural disasters ignited frequent famines that resulted in widespread hunger, disease, and disorders. One famine in 1784 alone caused the deaths of a half million people from starvation. Thousands of beggars and vagrants joined unorganized mobs that engaged in rampant banditry and lawlessness, and during 1811 and 1812, organized peasant uprisings protested taxation and corrupt officials. Abject misery boosted the appeal of Christianity among the people, and by 1860 an estimated 20,000 Koreans had converted to Catholicism, motivating an anti-foreign reaction in the Yi government. In 1866, renewed persecution of Christians resulted in arrest and execution of foreign priests and the massacre of 18,000 Korean converts. (Matray 2004, 34). In response, France launched a punitive expedition, looting and burning a coastal town. When Koreans destroyed an American vessel and killed its crew that same year, the United States staged a retaliatory assault as well. But both nations then retreated. The Yi government reaffirmed its policy of refusing to negotiate with Western nations and continued a policy of seclusion and religious repression. It reiterated this position in 1872 when Japan asked for representation in Seoul.

Japan was determined, however, to dominate Korea. In 1876, Tokyo compelled the Choson dynasty to sign a treaty that recognized Korea as an independent state and ended its tributary status with China. A faction in the Yi government now began pressing for modernization following the Japanese model. In 1882, opponents of change staged a failed attempt to seize power, providing a reason for China to impose a new treaty on Korea giving it broad advisory, military, and economic power. The Yi government's refusal to enact meaningful reforms allowed popular misery to grow, increasing the appeal among the oppressed of a religious cult known as the Tonghak or "Eastern Learning." In 1894, leaders associated with the Tonghak movement led a rebellion against corrupt and inefficient local administrators. Japan then maneuvered China into deploying troops to provide a pretext for sending its own soldiers, who then occupied the palace in Seoul and captured King Kojong. This event ignited the Sino-Japanese War, in which Japan scored quick and easy victories at sea and on land in Korea and Manchuria. In April 1895, the treaty ending the fighting forced China to pay an indemnity, transfer Taiwan to Japan, and abandon all claims to authority over Korea.

No sooner had Japan begun to enact measures for modernization and dominance in Korea than Russia accelerated its existing plans for economic and political penetration of the peninsular nation. Late in 1895, the Japanese administrator allowed disaffected Koreans to storm the palace and murder Kojong's mother, an ardent traditionalist who was working with Russia to oust Japan. Russia immediately deployed 200 soldiers in Seoul to restore law and order, as well as providing King Kojong with asylum in its legation. Russia now was the dominant force in Korea, a dramatic reversal that Japan patiently waited to rectify, expanding its military capabilities in preparation for war. Meanwhile, imperialist impositions on Korea discredited the Yi government and

gave birth to internal political dissent. In 1896, So Chae-pil (Philip Jaison) returned from studying in the United States and formed the Independence Club (Tongnip Hyophoe). An embryonic political party, the first issue of its newspaper proclaimed a platform of "Korea for the Koreans, clean politics, the cementing of foreign friendships." The Independence Club initiated a mass campaign for reform aimed at ending corruption and poor administration. It also condemned any limits on sovereignty, criticizing Kojong for granting economic privileges to Russia and staying in its legation. Popular protests forced Russia to foreswear a large concession, close a bank controlling government funds, and withdraw troops. But the Yi government rejected the Independence Club's demand for reform, imprisoning dissidents and forcing them underground in 1898. So Chae-pil might have led a mass rebellion to topple the monarchy, had he acted to mobilize a peasantry ready to join a revolution.

Russia exploited success in suppressing Korean dissent to impose new controls on Korea's military. Japan responded in 1903 with an offer to Russia proposing recognition of its hegemony in Manchuria in return for Japanese dominance over Korea. Russia's categorical rejection reflected its confident expectation of victory in the Russo-Japanese War that began with Japan's surprise sea attack on the Russian naval base at Port Arthur in Manchuria. To the world's surprise, Japanese forces easily destroyed Russia's military units on land and at sea. The Treaty of Portsmouth in 1905 required Russia to recognize "Japan's predominant political, military, and economic interests in Korea" and agree not to interfere with "any measure of direction, protection, and supervisions which the Imperial Government of Japan may deem necessary to adopt in Korea."

CONTEXT AND PROCESS OF REVOLUTION

Forty years of Japanese colonial rule dramatically altered the political, economic, and social context in Korea, but without the input and consent of the Korean people. Certainly there was near unanimous popular agreement on the need for a revolution, but one that would end imperialism and restore national sovereignty. Under a protectorate agreement that Japan forced the Choson dynasty to accept, a resident general supervised economic exploitation of the peninsula. King Kojong sought international help to restore Korea's sovereignty, appealing to the Hague Tribunal in 1907, but it refused to hear the case. His effort infuriated Tokyo, resulting in Kojong's forced abdication and the imposition of a new agreement giving dictatorial powers to the resident general. A nationwide network emerged to stage armed attacks and

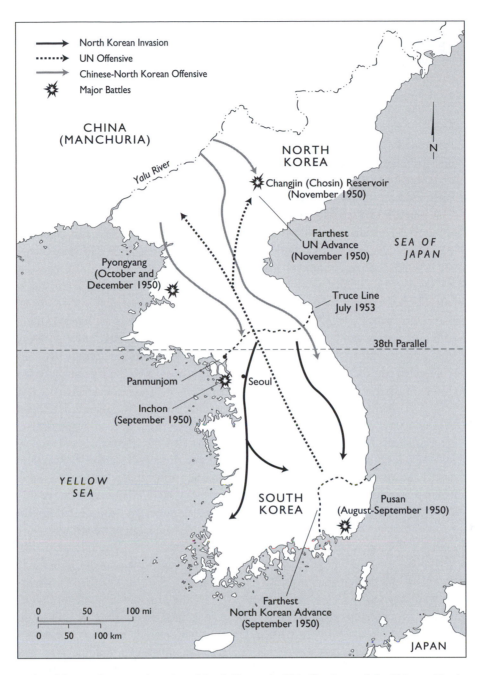

Paths of the North Korean invasion of South Korea, the UN offensive, and the Chinese–North Korean offensive.

wage guerrilla warfare against Japanese installations. Japan reacted with brutal repression, burning many villages and killing 12,000 Koreans. Failure of pacification and assassination of the resident general led to formal Japanese annexation of Korea in 1910.

Mass resistance to Japanese colonial rule persisted. Operating from sanctuaries in China and Russia, Korean rebels fought fierce engagements with Japan's imperial army. More dramatic in its impact was the March First Rebellion in 1919, a mass movement for liberation from Japanese rule during

the Versailles Conference after World War I. Japan's police force quickly crushed the uprising, killing hundreds of demonstrators and imprisoning thousands, as well as burning villages and torturing civilians. Violent repression succeeded in eliminating all nationalist opposition inside Korea, compelling Koreans to work for outside assistance to achieve independence. Rebel leaders fled to China, the Soviet Union, and the United States, leading to the unusual dominance of exiles in the liberation movement. In the autumn of 1919, a diverse group of Korean politicians met in Shanghai, China, and created the Korean Provisional Government (KPG). Leftist Koreans opposed the KPG, not only because it emphasized diplomacy and propaganda instead of direct action to end Japanese rule, but also because it defended the interests of the landowning and wealthy class. Western indifference at Versailles to Korea's plight caused many to seek aid from Russia's new Bolshevik government.

Cumings has described the revolutionary impact that imperial Japan's governance had on Korea from 1920 to 1945. The Japanese modernized the peninsula, constructing roads, railways, and harbor facilities, managing land reclamation, and providing electric, telegraph, and modern banking services. Along with major industrial installations in the north, Japan also built hospitals and schools, while improving sanitation and public health. Imperial policies encouraged the rise of a Korean working class but discouraged development of native entrepreneurship. These changes assaulted the traditional Korean social structure, causing *yangban* to withdraw to personal education or private contemplations and peasants to rebel against new absentee tenancy arrangements. Other Koreans conducted guerrilla raids against Japanese garrisons from bases in Siberia and Manchuria. To control Korean resistance and channel internal economic and social change to serve imperial goals, Japan created a highly intrusive governing structure that contradicted traditional Korean ideas about the role of the state. Peasants participated in sweeping social and economic mobilization efforts that would transform a sedentary society into a revolutionary one with a large majority of the populace ready to fight for change.

Koreans expected a quick restoration of sovereignty after Japan's defeat in World War II. But at the Cairo Conference late in 1943, the Allies promised only "that in due course Korea shall become free and independent." Korean exiles denounced plans for a post-war trusteeship, insisting on instant self-government, but their administrative inexperience and a history of great power rivalry for control over the peninsula were arguments for a period of tutelage until Korea could ensure its own independence. Divisions within Korea's liberation movement were another compelling reason for not recognizing a post-war government. The KPG urged U.S. military assistance for the Korean Restoration Army operating with Nationalist forces in China. Another suitor was the Sino-Korean Peoples' League located in Manchuria. The Soviet Union was providing training and equipment to Korean guerrillas in Siberia. None of these groups had measurable popular support inside Korea, but U.S. president Harry S. Truman's decision not to finalize a trusteeship plan prevented the Korean people from having the time to reach a consensus on the right path for Korea's future.

Japan's sudden surrender in August 1945 resulted in an eleventh-hour Soviet-American agreement to partition Korea into two zones of military occupation at the thirty-eighth parallel. In Seoul, Japan's governor, fearing a popular uprising and acts of retribution, asked leftist leader Yo Un-hyong to form a provisional government. Yo organized the Committee for the Preparation of Korean Independence and immediately set about creating local "people's committees" to assume administrative responsibilities in liberated Korea. Most Koreans accepted Yo's authority, including landlords, intellectuals, students, and professional people. By September, Yo was the unchallenged de facto leader of all Korea. Soviet forces recognized his authority after occupying northern Korea during August, prompting Yo to establish the Korean People's Republic (KPR) as a new national government. When U.S. forces arrived in September, however, Lieutenant General John R. Hodge, the U.S. occupation commander, instantly rejected the KPR's legitimacy because Communists held leadership positions in Yo's government and he viewed them as surrogates of the Soviet Union.

Two years of Soviet-American negotiations failed to reunite Korea, institutionalizing a civil conflict on the peninsula. During this period, both occupying powers encouraged creation of two Koreas, each following their respective models for political, social, and economic development. In the north, Koreans elected local people's committees, but the Soviets put selected leaders in positions of national authority, most notably wartime guerrilla leader Kim Il Sung. A major reform program expropriated land belonging to Japanese collaborators, large landlords, and the church. In addition to nationalizing all industry, transportation, communications, and banking, it mandated an eight-hour workday and proclaimed sexual equality. These measures had a dramatic impact on the U.S. zone, as members of the propertied classes fled south. By contrast, U.S. officials worked with right-wing politicians and delayed reform, awaiting the formation of a government to rule a united nation. The U.S. Military Government did create a South Korean Interim Government to share administrative responsibilities, and fraudulent elections produced a South Korean Interim Legislative Assembly.

During 1948, Koreans established the Republic of Korea (ROK) south of the thirty-eighth parallel and the Democratic People's Republic of Korea (DPRK) to the north. President Syngman Rhee built a repressive, authoritarian, anti-Communist regime in the ROK, and Premier Kim Il Sung replicated the Soviet system in the DPRK. U.S. troops withdrew in June 1949, six months after the Soviets departed, leaving behind two governments obsessed with achieving reunification. The focus of this new phase of the Korean Civil War was first inside South Korea, where bloody rebellions in 1948 on Cheju Island and in the town of Yosu reflected widespread mass support for adopting the DPRK model of development. After the ROK army restored order with ruthless brutality, it began instigating border clashes with DPRK units along the

Kim Il Sung, president of the Democratic People's Republic of Korea and general secretary of the Committee of the Korean Workers' Party. (Xinhua News Agency)

The new Republic of Korea, with Syngman Rhee as president, is inaugurated at a ceremony in Seoul on August 15, 1948. The U.S. supported the Rhee administration, and by June 1949 had withdrawn all forces in South Korea that had remained after World War II. (Bettmann/Corbis)

thirty-eighth parallel that escalated into major warfare in the summer of 1949. Rhee and Kim Il Sung pressed their patrons for help in launching an offensive, but both the Soviet Union and the United States would not risk igniting another world war. In the spring of 1950, Kim finally secured Soviet and Chinese approval for an invasion with assurances that South Koreans would join his forces in quickly destroying the ROK.

IMPACTS

On June 25, 1950, the Korean Civil War ignited the first conventional conflict of the Cold War. Rhee would have acted on his persistent pledge to "march north" if the United States had not limited the ROK's military capabilities. Beating Rhee to the punch, the Korean People's Army (KPA) offensive sent smaller and weaker ROK units into a helter-skelter retreat. With the approval of the United Nations, the United States sent ground troops and internationalized the

war but could not halt the KPA advance until August, when a defensible front stabilized around the southeastern city of Pusan. By then, the DPRK had exercised administrative control over most of South Korea for nearly two months. While the KPA assaulted the Pusan perimeter, thousands of northern and southern Korean Communists worked to reshape the political, social, and economic structure. The first objective was to re-establish the people's committees. Many southerners greeted the KPA as an army of liberation. A large majority of the workers and half the students in Seoul rallied behind the DPRK, and many voluntarily enlisted in the KPA. Nearly fifty members of the ROK National Assembly remained in Seoul and held a meeting to declare their allegiance to the DPRK.

South Korean Communists exploited popular support to form a Seoul people's committee that quickly confiscated property belonging to the ROK government, its officials, and "monopoly capitalists." The KPA distributed surplus rice to the poor, and Communist cadres prepared for radical land redistribution. Elsewhere in the ROK, reemergence of local people's committees was less spontaneous, and northern cadres had to ensure conformity with DRPK practice and discipline. Expectations of widespread uprisings in support of the invaders created overconfidence but contributed to delays in the KPA's advance when they were not fulfilled. Pyongyang sent two of its best divisions into the southwestern Cholla provinces, where Communist support was strongest, to recruit troops. Soon the United States was superior in numbers and equipment, and held air control. During September, the KPA could not exploit battlefield successes because of shortages of food, ammunition, and fuel, as well as reliance on young and inexperienced conscripts. After the amphibious landing of U.S. forces at Inchon, the North Koreans retreated above the parallel. Outside military intervention had prevented Kim Il Sung from securing a leftist triumph in the Korean Civil War.

Rhee now ordered ROK forces to invade the north. For nearly two months, his government worked to achieve a rightist victory in the Korean Civil War. Thousands of National Police quickly entered North Korea and by early October controlled nine towns. Recruitment was under way for a special force of 30,000 for occupation duty. In Pyongyang, Kim Chong-won, nicknamed "the Tiger" for his brutal treatment of suspected Communists, was in charge and rightist youth groups held political indoctrination sessions. Reportedly, the ROK, as a matter of official policy, sought to locate and eliminate Communists and collaborators as part of a right-wing counter-revolution. Later, the DPRK charged that Rhee's agents had executed "hundreds of thousands" of North Koreans. There were many other atrocities. During DPRK occupation of the ROK, freed political prisoners gained retribution from their former oppressors. Rhee had ordered the execution of 50,000 political prisoners, and in July the KPA uncovered mass graves at Taejon. During late September, retreating northerners committed large-scale massacres before ROK officials regained control and initiated a new round of violent and bloody retribution against collaborators with North Korea.

China's military offensive late in November forced ROK officials and soldiers to evacuate the north. This not only eliminated expectations for reunification, but ended the Korean Civil War. Once battle lines stabilized near the pre-war boundary, the United States and China worked for the armistice achieved in July 1953 that presumed the coexistence of two Koreas for the foreseeable future. Thereafter, Korean leaders on both sides of the demilitarized zone exploited memories of a destructive three-year conflict to forge domestic political unity. In the ROK, Rhee, Pak Chong-hui, and Chun Doo-hwan relied on the threat of North Korea to punish anyone even suspected of Communist sympathies and justify forty years of dictatorial rule. In the DPRK, Kim Il Sung executed his rivals after making them scapegoats for wartime failures. Hatred and fear of the United States buttressed his ideology of *juche,* which called for achieving national self-reliance under his absolute supreme rule. Turning inward, the DPRK constructed an almost completely closed society, making possible massive fabrications of history to reinforce obedience to governmental authority.

Debate about whether there was a Korean Civil War contrasts with agreement about the international impact of the Korean War that began in June 1950. A watershed event, the conflict militarized in the Cold War. Reacting to North Korea's attack, the United States vastly increased defense spending, strengthened the North Atlantic Treaty Organization militarily, and pressed for a rearmed West Germany. In Asia, it greatly expanded its commitments to prevent more Communist seizures of power. Despite U.S. references to collective security, the Korean War in fact severely strained relations between the United States and its allies. U.S. relations with China were poisoned for twenty years. Most significant, the Korean Civil War caused the United States to adopt a policy of global intervention emphasizing a reliance on military means to block revolutionary change. Had it not been for the Korean War, the Cold War might have ended much earlier and at far less cost in both human lives and material resources.

PEOPLE AND ORGANIZATIONS

Hodge, John R. (1893–1963)

Lieutenant General John Reed Hodge was the commander of U.S. occupation forces in Korea from September 9, 1945, until August 15, 1948. His priority was preserving law and order. Lacking administrative training, political experience, or familiarity with Korean history and culture, he committed many errors. Hodge infuriated Koreans when he reportedly commented that they were "the same breed of cats" as the Japanese. An even more significant error was Hodge's reliance on wealthy and conservative Korean landlords and businessmen, including some who had collaborated with the Japanese. He neither understood nor dealt effectively with Korean political factionalism. After first assisting the return of Syngman Rhee, Kim Gu, and other conservative exile leaders to Korea, Hodge ignored Rhee's demand to hold quick elections for a separate government in the south. He then worked with Kim Kyu-sik to create a moderate political coalition in 1946 but abandoned this effort without placating the conservatives. Rhee never forgave Hodge and forced his recall.

Kim Il Sung (1912–1994)

Founder of the Democratic People's Republic of Korea (DPRK), Kim Il Sung ordered the attack on South Korea in June 1950 that initiated the conventional phase of the Korean Civil War. After the armistice in July 1953, he sought to destabilize the Republic of Korea (ROK), anticipating that its collapse would bring reunification. His strategy led to military clashes along the demilitarized zone and harassment and capture of southern fishing boats. In 1968, North Korean commandos raided the ROK presidential residence in a failed attempt to murder Pak Chong-hui. Discovery of tunnels in 1981 dug under the demilitarized zone signaled plans for a future invasion. In 1983, North Korean operatives exploded a bomb in Rangoon killing nineteen people, including four ROK cabinet members. Four years later, North Korean agents were responsible for the bombing of Korean Airlines flight 858. By then, however, economic development in South Korea meant that the DPRK's hostile behavior only strengthened popular support for the ROK.

Korean Communist Party (KCP)

In 1921, Yi Tonghwi organized the Koryo Communist Party, which advocated a Bolshevik-inspired program to end poverty and oppression. Cho Pong-am and Pak Hon-yong acted to strengthen the movement with formation of the Korean Communist Party (KCP) in 1925. Later that year, Japanese authorities almost destroyed its leadership, necessitating reorganization, only to face collapse again in 1926 with the arrest of most members. From 1928 to 1930, the Japanese disrupted attempts at reorganization, arresting Pak and forcing other members to leave Korea. Communism did not gain popular support inside Korea until after liberation. Korean Communists returned from abroad in 1945 to join those already there, among them Pak Hon-yong, who quickly asserted leadership. Factional disputes weakened the KCP. It was active in promoting the Korean People's Republic, but also suppressed nationalist rivals. During 1946, U.S. authorities arrested party members for forging currency and punished many more after they instigated the Autumn Harvest Uprising. The KCP then divided into the North and South Korean Workers' parties.

Korean Democratic Party (KDP)

Korean conservatives formed this party in September 1945 to contest the legitimacy of the Korean People's Republic (KPR). Dominating membership of the Korean Democratic Party (KDP) were intellectuals, landowners, businessmen, and industrialists. The KDP was committed to support for Kim Gu's Korean Provisional Government (KPG) still in China and its swift return to Seoul. The KDP manifesto called for land reform, freedom of speech, and improved standards of industrial management, education, and health care. The party anticipated a gradual transition to democracy. The American Military Government worked closely with KDP members, especially Kim Song-su, to discredit the KPR, but refused to recognize the KPG.

Korean People's Republic (KPR)

Yo Un-hyong's Committee for the Preparation of Korean Independence formed this body in Seoul on September 6, 1945, to assume governmental authority after Japan's unexpected surrender. Seeking to create a united front, 600 delegates met to choose a cabinet and draft a constitution. They selected Syngman Rhee as president of the Korean People's Republic (KPR), with Yo as vice president and Ho Hun as premier minister. Among the cabinet members were Kim Gu (interior), Kim Kyu-sik (foreign affairs), Cho Man-sik (finance), and Kim Song-su (education), even though none were present or had agreed to serve. Its manifesto anticipated land reform and nationalization of large companies. The Soviet Union recognized the KPR in the north, where the KPR's people's committees provided the structural foundation for the Democratic People's Republic of Korea. In the south, the American Military Government rejected the KPR's legitimacy and, reacting to criticism of the U.S. occupation, outlawed it late in 1945.

Mao Zedong (1893–1976)

As president of the People's Republic of China (PRC) and chairman of the Chinese Communist Party (CCP), Mao Zedong made decisions that influenced the course of the Korean Civil War. His triumph in the Chinese Civil War placed pressure on Soviet premier Joseph Stalin to approve North Korea's plan to attack South Korea to demonstrate his commitment to the expansion of Communism in East Asia and confirm his leadership of the Communist movement. Mao was not enthusiastic about an invasion; economic recovery had just begun after years of war, the CCP had not yet consolidated its power, and seizing Taiwan was his main priority. He advised against haste, although he did send two divisions of Korean troops that had fought in China back to North Korea. In April 1950, Stalin approved an invasion if Mao also agreed. Kim Il Sung then met with Mao, who could not fail to support his comrade's quest for reunification and so had little choice but to consent. But Mao expected U.S. military intervention and occupation of North Korea. When Stalin refused to save Kim Il Sung and suggested locating a government in exile in Manchuria, Mao ordered massive Chinese intervention in the Korean War.

Rhee, Syngman (1875–1965)

Syngman Rhee was a conservative nationalist leader and first president of the Republic of Korea (ROK). A disciple of So Chae-pil, a famous reformer and independence fighter, he worked in his youth for anti-government newspapers. Rhee led an anti-Japanese demonstration in 1897 that resulted in his arrest and a sentence of life imprisonment. In 1904, a year before Japan seized Korea, a royal amnesty brought his release. Rhee then fled to the United States and earned a doctorate at Princeton University.In 1919, the Korean Provisional Government (KPG) elected Rhee as its first president. Accused of misusing funds, he was impeached by the KPG in 1932. He then established the Korean Commission in Washington, D.C., to lobby for Korean independence. During World War II, Rhee delivered Voice of America broadcasts to Korea to incite uprisings against Japan. In 1945, he publicly predicted that Soviets would attempt to repeat dominance over East Europe in Asia. The U.S. State Department tried, but failed to prevent his return to Korea because of his intense hostility to Communism. Rhee's reputation caused both the leftist Korean People's Republic and rightwing Korean Democratic Party to elect him as their leader, but he refused. His determined and ruthless political maneuvering pushed the United States into a position where it had to comply with Rhee's demands for a separate government in South Korea, but it did so for its own reasons.

Stalin, Joseph (1879–1953)

Joseph Stalin became general secretary of the Soviet Union's Communist Party in 1922 and Soviet premier in 1941. His priority during World War II was to prevent the emergence of hostile governments on the borders of the Soviet Union. Stalin had good reason to believe that Soviet-trained Koreans, as well as domestic Communists and those returning from exile in China, would exert strong influence on any post-war Korean government. He therefore endorsed a trusteeship in Korea and then agreed to divide the peninsula into two zones of military occupation. Stalin also cooperated in negotiations for a united Korea until the

Cold War intensified, resulting in creation of a separate northern government in 1948. Stalin then ordered military withdrawal but let Soviet advisers remain and continued arms shipments. He finally approved an invasion because he thought a reunited Korea under Communist rule could help neutralize the U.S. military presence in Japan and spread Communism without the danger of direct Soviet involvement. But the typically cautious Stalin pulled back Soviet advisers to prevent their capture and reduce the risks of igniting a larger war. Four days after the attack, he issued a statement describing the struggle as a civil war in which the great powers (especially the United States) had no business. Achievement of an armistice in Korea came only after Stalin's death in March 1953 ended the deadlock in negotiations.

Truman, Harry S. (1884–1972)

As president of the United States from 1945 to 1953, Harry S. Truman made a series of decisions that dramatically altered the course of the Korean Civil War. Perhaps most important, he abandoned pursuit of a post-war trusteeship agreement for Korea in April 1945. He gambled that dropping the atomic bomb on Japan would end World War II quickly, removing the need to share occupation of the peninsula with the Soviet Union. With the Red Army poised to enter Korea in August, Truman persuaded Soviet premier Joseph Stalin to divide the country into two zones of military occupation. When Cold War tensions blocked reunification, Truman applied containment, creating a separate government in the south and working to provide it with the ability to defend itself. Then, in response to North Korea's attack in June 1950, Truman committed U.S. military power to prevent a Communist victory in the Korean Civil War. Caring little about Korea, and certain that the North Koreans had attacked on Stalin's orders, his overriding purpose was to deter Communist expansion elsewhere in the world. Before U.S. troops landed at Inchon, Truman approved an offensive to destroy Kim Il Sung's regime that led to Chinese military intervention.

Yo Un-Hyong (1885–1947)

In September 1945, Yo Un-hyong organized the Korean People's Republic (KPR) as a new national government. He had served in the Korean Provisional Government and established the Korean Nationalist Youth Association. Yo reportedly joined the Koryo Communist Party, although others deny that he was ever a Communist. In 1921, he did attend the Congress of Far Eastern Laborers in Moscow. As a moderate nationalist leader, he collaborated in convening a major meeting of international representatives from Korean anti-Japanese organizations in Shanghai in 1923, but political views were too diverse to achieve significant results. Returning to Korea, Yo was imprisoned for his political activities from 1929 to 1932. Upon his release, he was newspaper editor for the *Chungang Ilbo.* As a leader of the leftist Korean Workers' Party, he was positioned to establish Korea's new government after liberation. But after the Communists gained control, Yo withdrew from the KPR in November 1945 and founded the Korean People's Party. In 1946, he worked for accommodation across the political spectrum. This included his partnership with Kim Kyu-sik as leaders of the moderate Coalition Committee. Yo was assassinated in July 1947.

James I. Matray

See Also Chinese Revolution; Documentaries of Revolution; South Korean Democracy Movement; War and Revolution

References and Further Readings

Armstrong, Charles K. 2003. *The North Korean Revolution, 1945–1950.* Ithaca, NY: Cornell University Press.

Cho, Soon Sung. 1957. *Korea in World Politics, 1940–1950: An Evaluation of American Responsibility.* Berkeley: University of California Press.

Cumings, Bruce. 1981, 1990. *The Origins of the Korean War.* 2 Vols. Princeton, NJ: Princeton University Press.

Goncharov, Sergei, John W. Lewis, and Xue Litai. 1993. *Uncertain Partners: Stalin, Mao, and the Korean War.* Stanford, CA: Stanford University Press.

Henderson, Gregory. 1968. *Korea: The Politics of the Vortex.* Cambridge, MA: Harvard University Press.

Kim, Joungwon. 1976. *Divided Korea: The Politics of Development, 1945–1973.* Cambridge, MA: Harvard University Press.

Lee, Chong-sik. 1963. *The Politics of Korean Nationalism.* Berkeley: University of California Press.

McCune, George M., and Arthur L. Grey, Jr. 1950. *Korea Today.* Cambridge, MA: Harvard University Press.

Matray, James I. 1985. *The Reluctant Crusade: American Foreign Policy in Korea, 1941–1950.* Honolulu: University of Hawaii Press.

———. 2004. *Korea Divided: The Thirty-Eighth Parallel and the Demilitarized Zone.* Philadelphia, PA: Chelsea House.

Merrill, John. 1989. *Korea: The Peninsular Origins of the War.* Newark: University of Delaware Press.

Pratt, Keith, and Richard Rutt, eds. 1999. *Korea: A Historical and Cultural Dictionary.* Surrey, UK: Curzon Press.

Scalapino, Robert A., and Lee Chong-sik, eds. 1972. *Communism in Korea: The Movement.* Berkeley: University of California Press.

Stueck, William. 2002. *Rethinking the Korean War: A New Diplomatic and Strategic History.* Princeton, NJ: Princeton University Press.

Suh, Dae-sook. 1988. *Kim Il Sung: The North Korean Leader.* New York: Columbia University Press.

Kurdish Movements

CHRONOLOGY

1514	Following the Ottoman-Persian Wars, the Ottoman empire recognizes the autonomy of sixteen Kurdish emirates. The autonomy of some Kurdish entities is also accepted in the Persian empire.
1808–1880	Ottoman policy of centralization aims at the destruction of the Kurdish emirates. Kurdish regions enter a period of revolts, which ends in 1880 with the suppression of the Cheikh Ubeydullah Revolt.
1890	The Kurdish Hamidiye Cavalries are formed.
1909–1914	Following the dethronement of Sultan Abdul Hamid II, new Kurdish revolts take place, some with nationalist goals.
1914–1922	Alliance of the Ottoman state and the former Hamidiye Cavalries, which play an important role in the extermination of Armenians.
1920	Treaty of Sèvres proposes local autonomy for Kurdish areas of Turkey and provides for future consideration of the creation of an independent Kurdish nation.
1919–1926	The *vilaya* (Ottoman province) of Mosul is occupied and progressively annexed to Iraq. Some Kurds become Syrian subjects.
1923	The Lausanne Treaty, which replaces the 1920 Sèvres Treaty and gives birth to today's Turkey, destroys the hopes of the Kurdish nationalists to form an independent Kurdistan.
1919–1938	A long series of Kurdish revolts takes place in Iran, Iraq, and Turkey.
1946	The proclamation and fall of an autonomous Kurdish republic in the Mahabad region in Iran. The leader of the republic, Qadi Muhammad, is executed in 1947.

1961   The Barzani Revolt begins in Iraq.

1970   Following Iraqi-Kurdish negotiation, a moratorium on fighting of four years, intended to lead to a settlement of the Kurdish issue, is declared by the two parties. Baghdad accepts the principle of Kurdish autonomy as well as the organization of a population census in the oil city of Kirkuk.

1971   Coup d'état in Turkey. Repression of the Kurdish nationalists (as well as the Turkish Left).

1974–1975   The second phase of the Barzani Revolt. But following the Algiers Agreement between Iraq and Iran, which ends any Iranian assistance to the Kurds, Barzani stops the revolt.

1977–1978   Abdullah Öcalan founds the Kurdistan Workers' Party (Partiya Karkeren, PKK).

1979   In the wake of the Iranian Revolution, Kurdish political organizations take control of the major Kurdish cities. Following heavy fights with the newly established Islamic regime, they abandon the cities and start guerrilla warfare.

1980   Coup d'état in Turkey. Repression of Kurdish and left-wing Turkish organizations.

1980–1988   The Iran-Iraq War. While Baghdad assists militarily the Iranian Kurdish organizations, Tehran supports the Iraqi Kurdish ones.

1984   The beginning of the PKK's guerrilla war against the Turkish state.

1988   Chemical weapons are used in Halabdja (Iraqi Kurdistan) and followed by the Anfal Campaigns, which cost the lives of more than 180,000 civilians.

1989   Abdulrahman Ghassemlou, head of the PDK-Iran, is assassinated while negotiating with Tehran's envoys.

1991   The First Iraq War. Following the repression of a popular Kurdish revolt, the United Nations Security Council declares northern Iraq a Kurdish "safe haven" (Resolution 688).

1992   Sadiq Sharafkandi, new leader of the PDK-Iran, is assassinated by Iranian agents.

1994–1997   The beginning of Kurdish self-rule, with a period of internal violence.

1999   Abdullah Öcalan, head of PKK, is captured in Kenya. He is delivered to Turkey. PKK's guerrilla warfare ends.

2003   Second Iraq War. Kurdish forces enter Kirkuk.

2004   New battles between PKK members and Turkish military.

INTRODUCTION

From the 1960s to the end of the 1990s, many Kurdish organizations throughout the Middle East described themselves as "revolutionary movements." The concept *chorech,* which derives from Persian, has been widely used by these groups to define social and political "revolution" and national "liberation." Throughout these decades, the Kurdish movements projected themselves both as a part of the Kurdish national struggle and as a component of Turkish, Iranian, Iraqi, and Syrian revolutionary movements. Many Kurds were members of the left-wing parties of these countries, and a certain fluidity was accepted both by the Kurdish political organizations and by left-wing organizations (to a lesser extent, this is still the case in Turkey). These double affiliations oblige scholars to avoid a rigid typology and pay specific attention to the subjective aspects of these movements.

In general, armed struggles for Kurdish independence were not successful, and the ideologies of Kurdish movements tended to shift from the 1960s to the present from relatively radical aspirations for independence and social revolution to more moderate goals. In the 1990s, the Iraqi Kurdish movements, with the assistance of the United States, established an autonomous self-governing region.

BACKGROUND: CULTURE AND HISTORY

Most Kurds are Sunni Muslims. By the early twenty-first century, there were more than 25 million Kurds, living mainly in Turkey (about 14 million, or 20 percent of Turkey's population), Iran (about 8 million or 10 percent of Iran's popula-

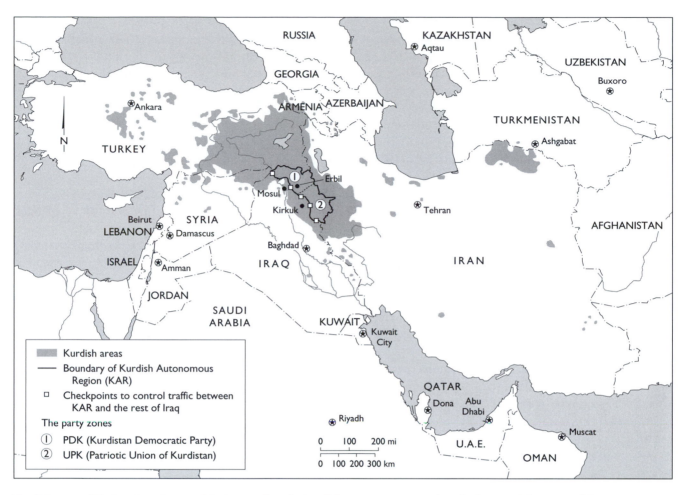

Kurdish areas of Turkey, Iraq, Iran, and Syria, as well as the Kurdish Autonomous Area (KAR) of Iraq and the zones of the KAR dominated by the Kurdistan Democratic Party (PDK) and the Patriotic Union of Kurdistan (UPK).

tion), and Iraq (around 5 million or about 20 percent of Iraq's population).

From the Nineteenth Century to the Formation of the Modern States

From the beginning of the nineteenth century, and particularly after the Tanzimat Reforms (1839–1876) in the Ottoman empire, the Kurdish regions entered a period of constant rebellions. The reforms were intended to improve and centralize administrative systems within the empire, following the French model. But they replaced the negotiations between the central government and the Kurds with massive state coercion and provoked widespread resistance. From 1808 to 1880, a series of revolts took place, aiming either at the preservation of autonomy or the establishment of an independent state. The last revolt of the nineteenth century, led by Ubeydullah, a religious dignitary, developed a quasi-nationalist discourse, describing the Kurds as a different nation

with the right to govern themselves. Ubeydullah's project was to "liberate" Persian Kurdistan first, before dealing with the issue of Ottoman Kurdistan.

State coercion was successful in suppressing these revolts and destroying the emirates from the 1840s to 1880. The destruction of the emirates produced two unintended consequences. First, a political vacuum, along with the enormous security problems linked to the presence of a massive, ill-paid, and starved imperial army, pushed the Kurds to seek protection through tribal networks. Instead of the dozens of autonomous emirates that governed Kurdistan earlier in the nineteenth century, almost 1,000 tribes now held de facto power. Second, unlike the former emirates, these tribes refused to identify themselves with an exclusive territory. Many of them were active in the border area between Russia, Persia, and the Ottoman empire. They could challenge these states, yet change alliances when necessary.

The Ottoman state's answer to this unexpected evolution was to integrate the Kurdish tribes into the state's coercive policy. In 1890, Sultan Abdul Hamid II accepted the creation of the so-called Hamidiye Cavalries, in which some fifty tribes were transformed into Ottoman auxiliary forces. Largely autonomous in their actions, these tribes received salaries and weapons from the state. The Ottoman palace intended to use their military potential in a triple strategy: first, to prevent unification of the Kurdish tribes by favoring some over others; second, to prevent transborder affiliations and to deploy a cavalry force comparable to the Cossacks of the Russian empire to protect the Ottoman-Russian border; and third, to "Islamize" the peripheral regions of the empire. The cavalries were used against the Christian Armenians during the massacres of 1894–1896.

The fall of Abdul Hamid II in 1909 and the ambition of the newly established Committee of Union and Progress to resolve the Armenian agrarian question pushed the Kurdish "allies" into rebellion. This new stage of revolts continued until 1914 and was marked by the slide of the tribes (and some religious dignitaries) toward nationalist aspirations, which included regional autonomy and use of Kurdish as an official language.

World War I radically changed the situation, namely in the Kurdish-inhabited areas of the Turkish Republic. The Union and Progress government decided during this war to exterminate the Armenian population (according to Ottoman figures dating from 1919, 800,000 were killed; more recent estimates put the number killed at more than one million (Kieser and Schaller 2002). It also sought a new alliance with the Kurdish tribes, mainly the former Hamidiye Cavalries, which were renamed "Tribal Light Cavalries." The cavalries participated in the extermination, linking their fate (and that of the Kurds) to the alliance with the Ottoman state.

After the end of World War I, many parts of the Ottoman empire were occupied by Allied troops. While small sections of the Kurdish-inhabited areas were included in French-occupied Syria, Southern Kurdistan was occupied by the British. The Sèvres Treaty of 1920 offered the other Kurds the possibility of having an autonomous state near an Armenian state. It also affirmed that this autonomy could lead to the formation of an independent Kurdish nation.

Some Kurdish nationalist movements, such as the Kurdish Clubs and the Society for Kurdish Elevation, were quite sympathetic to this project. However, the majority of Kurdish leaders rejected this solution for four reasons: (1) they were reluctant to accept the creation of an Armenian state. Some of them had participated in the extermination of Armenians and they feared reprisals by the survivors; (2) Mustafa Kemal, the general leading the Turkish War of Independence after the collapse of the Ottoman empire during the end of World War I had promised the Kurdish leaders a new entity based on the equality and fraternity of the Turkish and Kurdish peoples and suggested the possibility of Kurdish autonomy within this new political framework; (3) according to the

Turkish National Pact of March 1920, Mustafa Kemal affirmed his determination to liberate Iraqi Kurdistan and unify the Kurds; (4) Kemal assured the Kurds that the Turkish Khalifa—the universal religious authority of Sunni Islam that was the main link between the Kurds and the Turks—would be protected.

Revolts of 1919–1946

By the end of the Turkish War of Independence in 1922, it was obvious that the division of the Kurdish populations among Iran, Iraq, Syria, and Turkey was a reality.

In this situation, the Kurds faced some common circumstances, but also different local situations. The first common feature was political. All four governments criminalized political, sectarian, and ethnic differences and aspirations. Turkey was the most radical case, governed by an authoritarian single-party regime. Although less rigid, the other states also had nationalist programs that refused to accept the Kurds as a distinct group and Kurdish culture as a legitimate component of society. The second common factor was that compared to the former Ottoman-Persian border, the new borders were militarized. Crossing the borders meant, in the states' perspective, abandoning national allegiance and the national economy. Kurdish cross-border activities, including family gatherings, were militarily repressed, which provoked a spontaneous non-political but armed resistance. The later Kurdish rebellions were either transborder conflicts or exerted heavy impacts on Kurdish populations across borders. Except for three periods—1927–1929, 1961–1974, 1980–1998—cross-border movement was repressed by the states.

The 1920s and 1940s were decades of harshly repressed rebellions and uprisings, giving birth to both a traumatic collective memory and dreams of collective vengeance. Often, these revolts brought together two different, to some extent socially antagonistic, forces: the nationalist and widely westernized intelligentsia, which opposed the states because they were not Kurdish, and rural forces, mainly tribes and religious brotherhoods, which opposed the states because they were coercive entities that tried to impose taxes and intervene in what they viewed as non-state domains. Kurdish nationalism became the dominant political response.

In Iran, the main rebellious force was that of Ismail Agha Simko, influential leader of the Shikak tribe. Simko's revolt, which mobilized mainly tribal forces at the end of the 1910s and the beginning of the 1920s, was suppressed in 1930 (Simko was killed by the state's representatives while he was attending negotiations). In Iraq, where the Kurds did not accept their attachment to the newly founded state, the alliance between the westernized nationalist elite and the rural forces made possible a few revolts, dominated by the figure of Cheikh Mahmoud Berzendji (1919, 1922–1923, 1931) or members of the Barzani family (1943). Finally, in Turkey, where the Kurdish leaders had the impression that the Kemalist regime had betrayed them (the new government declared Turkish nationalism as its official ideology, abolished the khalifa, adopted a forced policy of westernization, and did not honor its promises to liberate Iraqi Kurdistan), no less than sixteen revolts took place between 1924 and 1938. The most important, the 1925 Cheikh Said Rebellion, the 1927–1930 Ararat Rebellion, and the 1936–1938 Dersim Revolt, had clearly nationalist agendas. Repression killed tens of thousands of civilians.

The last in this series of rebellions was that of Qadi Muhammad in Iranian Kurdistan, who, in the aftermath of the Second World War, and while the Russian troops were still occupying Iran, proclaimed an autonomous republic (the so-called Mahabad Republic). Although based on a massive mobilization of the Kurdish tribes and Iraqi Kurdish fighters, the republic's survival was contingent on the presence of Soviet troops. It was crushed after the Soviet withdrawal. Qadi Muhammad was executed in 1947. The fall of the Mahabad Republic marked the beginning of what is called the "period of silence" in the Kurdish nationalist struggle.

CONTEXT AND PROCESS OF REBELLION

The 1961 Barzani Rebellion

By 1961, when the Barzani Rebellion started, the situation in the entire Middle East was radically different from that of the 1940s. First of all, the Cold War created an unprecedented polarization and the conditions for new social and political mobilizations. Second, urban intelligentsia adopted leftist views such as the dream of national independence and ideas of progress and social change. Third, the cities replaced the countryside as the centers of social and political activity. The new urban intelligentsia included military officers along with university students and, more and more, high school students. Though living outside the realities of the working class and the peasantry, the intelligentsia viewed itself the agent of the social revolution leading to their emancipation. Fourth, thanks to transistor radios, popular magazines, and harshly repressed left-wing literature, this intelligentsia was aware of the realities of the outside world. The situation was similar in Kurdistan and, broadly speaking, among the Kurdish communities in the big cities of Tehran, Baghdad, and Istanbul. Leftist goals for Kurdish youth included social emancipation and national liberation.

The renewal of the Kurdish movement took place as an outcome of this process of radicalization. In the aftermath of the 1958 military coup in Iraq, Mustafa Barzani, who had participated in the formation of the autonomous Kurdish republic in Iran, returned to Iraq from the Soviet Union. He assumed leadership of the Kurdistan Democratic Party (PDK). Although he had spent almost fifteen years in exile in the Soviet Union and was nicknamed the "red Mollah," Barzani remained a conservative figure. But for many party leaders and members, among them the well-known Kurdish writer Ibrahim Ahmad (1914–2000) and leftist Kurdish leader Jalal Talabani, *chorech* meant a revolutionary experience that included sacrifice, social and political change, and national liberation. Through the *chorech,* the fate of the Kurdish nation was linked to that of all exploited classes in Iraq and to that of "humanity."

According to some Kurdish sources, when the negotiations between the Iraqi central government and the PDK failed, the "revolutionary" branch of the Kurdish party decided to start a new revolt. This rebellion was one of the most important guerrilla struggles of the 1960s and the early 1970s. It continued until March 11, 1970, partly thanks to Iranian, American, and Israeli aid. Then the newly established Iraqi Baath regime accepted the principle of regional autonomy and the organization of a general census in Kirkuk city to determine whether the Kurds constituted its majority. But following the policy of the forced Arabization of the city and the proclamation of a unilateral law of autonomy, which excluded Kirkuk, the uprising resumed. In March 1975, Iran and Iraq signed a treaty of reconciliation in Algiers, and, with the blessing of the United States, Iran stopped aiding (namely offering shelter for the fighters) the rebellion. Barzani then ended the Kurds' armed struggle.

Compared to past Kurdish movements, the Barzani uprising, which did have important rural components, also enjoyed the support of urban populations, namely the youth, who participated massively in the rebellion. The urban intelligentsia accepted the leadership of Mustafa Barzani, but it was much more radical. The *peshmarga* ("those who face death") were the Kurdish guerrilla soldiers of the revolt for an independent Kurdish nation and became world famous; but a new type of participant, called *militant,* who shared many common features with other left-wing activists in the Middle East also emerged in the armed struggle.

Thanks to its durability (almost fifteen years) and the technical means at its disposal (including a radio station), the Barzani Rebellion became the main inspirational example of the Kurdish movement well beyond Iraqi Kurdistan. Its collapse in 1975 was a major trauma for the Kurds, resulting in three radicalizing effects. First, the loss of what seemed to be the Kurdish activists' most successful liberation movement created a vacuum that led to the formation of many new Kurdish groups, namely PUK (Patriotic Union of Kurdistan) in Iraq and PKK (Kurdistan Workers' Party) in Turkey. Second, the American "betrayal" in supporting

Armed with Kalashnikov automatic rifles, a group of Iraqi Kurdish *peshmergas* who sent their families to the mountain villages for safety man the Zavita checkpoint March 18, 2003, outside the northern Iraqi town of Dohuk, in the Kurdish-administered zone which broke from Baghdad rule in the 1991 Gulf War. Thousands of Iraqi Kurds packed their belongings and headed for the mountains fearing war could bring chemical attacks from President Saddam Hussein's forces stationed nearby. (Reuters/Corbis)

Iran's 1975 withdrawal of support for the insurgent Iraqi Kurds undermining the Barzani revolt pushed the entire Kurdish movement toward anti-Americanism and far-left positions. Some Kurdish organizations in Turkey, such as Kemal Burkay's PSK (Socialist Party of Kurdistan), chose the pro-Soviet camp, while the Iraqi PUK of Jalal Talabani, hostile to the Soviet Union because it supported the Baath regime in Iraq, became Maoists. Others, among them the PKK, adopted an independent "revolutionary strategy." Third, Kurdish nationalists redefined Kurdistan as a colonized country. The new kind of colonialism of the states that divided Kurdistan, they argued, was not solely an economic one; it aimed also at the destruction of Kurdishness. The domination of the Kurds by the Turkish, Persian, and Iraqi states was part of a wider "imperialist" domination over the world, in the sense that these states were either dependant on or supported by the United States. The liberation of Kurdistan was thus portrayed as a means for the emancipation of the colonized Iranian, Arab, and Turkish populations.

1975–1991: Years of "Revolutionary Commitment"

Other major events shook the Kurds: the Iranian Revolution (February 1979), the Iran-Iraq War (September 1980), and a military coup d'état in Turkey (1980) whose leaders openly aimed at destroying left-wing activities and viewed Kurdishness as a pathological illness to be cured. In Iraq, the Kurds had begun a new guerrilla war immediately after the end of the Barzani Rebellion in 1975. With the start of the Iran-Iraq War in 1980, it gained momentum, and with Iranian support, Kurds were able to gain control of wide sections of the Iraqi Kurdish countryside. Both the PDK and the PUK had strong support, mainly among the urban populations, but their political options were limited. They were dependent on the war. Moreover, while the war forced the Iraqi Baath regime to withdraw from sections of Kurdistan, it also provoked more coercive force, including the use of chemical weapons against the Kurds on March 16, 1988, at Halabdja, a city of 50,000 people, causing the death of some 5,000 people (Human Rights Watch 1995). Also, the abandonment of Maoism in China and the crisis of the Soviet system obliged the Kurds to develop social-democratic or even purely nationalist programs.

In Iran, Kurdish cities had participated in the Iranian Revolution, which, in its initial stage, had a left-wing orientation. Although many Kurds were members of Iranian left-wing organizations, Kurdish political life passed rapidly under the control of two Kurdish parties, the radical leftist Komeleh of A. Ilkhanzade and the more social-democratic PDK-Iran, headed by Abdulrahman Ghassemlou. Iran's new Islamic regime, however, was opposed to Kurdish national autonomy. Following heavy fighting, which probably cost tens of thousands of lives, and many death sentences pronounced by Iranian revolutionary tribunals, the Iranian Kurdish organizations abandoned urban centers and turned to rural guerrilla warfare. During the Iran-Iraq War, they received military support from Iraq. After the war, the PDK-Iran accepted the central government's proposal to negotiate, but Ghassemlou and his delegation were assassinated in Vienna by Tehran's "envoys."

In Turkey, after military repression that lead to the death of many of its members, the PKK decided to start a guerrilla war in 1984. The PKK won massive popular support among Kurdish youth. By the end of the 1980s, the guerrilla war had resulted in some 3,000 deaths (*See* Randal 1997, 256–257; White 2000, 166–167).

Post 1991

By 1990, the Kurdish movement was once again facing an *ashbetal* (capitulation). The Iranian Kurdish movement had been "beheaded," weakening possibilities for further military resistance; in Iraq, the physical destruction of rural areas made a new phase of resistance impossible to envision.

This situation changed radically after the defeat of Iraq in the First Iraqi War of 1991. President George Bush's appeal to resist the Baath regime inspired a popular uprising. But when the United States refused to intervene, the Iraqi Re-

Iraqi president Jalal Talabani, an Iraqi Kurdish leader, responds to a reporter's question during a joint press conference with Secretary of Defense Donald H. Rumsfeld following their meeting in the Pentagon on September 9, 2005. (Department of Defense)

publican Guards crushed the rebels. Fearing a renewal of chemical warfare, almost two millions Kurds decided to flee Iraq to Turkey and Iran (Randal 1997, 58–59). On the insistent demands of François Mitterrand and Turgut Özal, the French and Turkish presidents respectively, the UN Security Council declared the northern part of Iraq a "safe haven," where the Iraqi army was not allowed to operate. But a civil war broke out among the Iraqi Kurds during 1994–1997, resulting in the division of Iraqi Kurdistan between Jalal Talabani's PUK and Mesud Barzani's PDK. Later the situation improved considerably and a form of self-rule was established, mainly under the direction of the PDK. After the Second Iraq War of 2003, Kurdish forces entered into the largely Arabized city of Kirkuk, where tensions between the Turkoman, Kurdish, and Arab communities continued. While leaving aside the issue of the future status of Kirkuk, the Provisional Iraqi

Constitution of 2004 accepted the principle of a federal solution to the Kurdish question in Iraq.

In Iran, the Komeleh lost popular support, and a new generation of PDK leaders, among them Dr. Sharafkandi, was assassinated by Iranian agents. Kurdish armed struggle has largely ended, replaced by civil forms of resistance within Iran itself. The demand of regional autonomy within the framework of a democratized Iran still constitutes the Kurdish nationalists' main political goal.

In Turkey, guerrilla warfare intensified in the 1990s (White 2000). During these years, PKK was simultaneously expressing its desire to be recognized by the United States and the European Union as the legitimate representative of the Kurds while pursuing its goal of leading a Socialist revolution throughout the Middle East in order to "hunt out imperialist forces" (Çalislar 1993, 18–19). When Abdullah Öcalan was captured in Kenya and delivered to Turkey in 1999, many militants reacted with self-sacrificial forms of violence (suicide-bombings, self-immolation). Only the appeals of Öcalan himself and other party leaders brought such actions to stop.

After his arrest, Öcalan ordered the end of the armed struggle, which was generally accepted by his followers. But the organization did not disarm; it preserved its squadrons as the "people's defense forces." And after June 1, 2004, in reaction to what its leaders claimed were repeated Turkish attacks on their forces and the non-satisfaction of the PKK's minimal demands, it started a new phase of limited guerrilla war.

IMPACTS

The PKK of the 1990s was the last example of what one can call a revolutionary Kurdish organization. Its history illustrated how reaction to state coercion, as well as the practice and romanticism of its revolutionary armed struggle, can lead to extreme forms of violence, including self-sacrifice.

Currently, Kurdish political activity is generally linked to Kurdish nationalist goals dissociated from any kind of class struggle. Some forms of cross-ethnic revolutionary radicalism have emerged, particularly among poorer members of Kurdish society. Common religious beliefs have united members of different ethnic groups in the Hizbullahî organization in Turkey, which has been widely armed and used by Turkish security forces against PKK militants, or in Ansar al-Islam, which is seemingly a part of the al-Qaeda networks. These organizations were originally purely Kurdish but later became mixed Kurdish-Turkish and Kurdish-Arabic, respectively.

Decades of Kurdish struggle for self-rule, which has repeatedly provoked brutal repression, has also been greatly affected by international conflicts and developments. Finally, partly as a result of Iraq's defeat in wars in 1991 and 2003, the Iraqi Kurds achieved the creation of an autonomous homeland, which likely will encourage the aspirations of Kurds in Turkey, Iran, and Syria.

PEOPLE AND ORGANIZATIONS

Barzani, Mesud (Born 1946)

Son of Mustafa Barzani and current leader of the Democratic Party of Kurdistan. After decades of exile and guerrilla struggle, he became the president of the Kurdish government established in Erbil, Iraq in 1997.

Barzani, Mustafa (1903–1979)

Leader of the Democratic Party of Kurdistan and of the 1961–1975 revolt. After leading a series of uprisings in Iraq in the 1930s and 1940s, Barzani participated in the formation of the autonomous Kurdish Republic in Iran in 1946 and lived in exile in the Soviet Union from 1946 to 1958. He returned to Iraq following the overthrow of the monarchy in 1958 and started a new revolt. After the failure of the revolt in 1975, he lived in exile in the United States until his death.

Ghassemlou, Abdulrahman (1930–1989)

A Prague-educated economist, lecturer of Kurdish in Paris, and leader of the Kurdistan Democratic Party of Iran, Ghassemlou had adopted a social-democratic program by the 1970s and commanded the Iranian Kurdish guerrillas in the war that started in 1979. After the Iran-Iraq War, he was convinced that the Kurdish issue in Iran could not be resolved by military means but called for a political solution achieved through negotiations. He was assassinated in Vienna during negotiations with an Iranian delegation.

Khomeini, Ayatollah Ruhollah (1902–1989)

Militant cleric and leader of the Iranian Revolution. After some promises and concessions to the Kurdish movement in 1979, he declared the incompatibility of regional autonomy with Islamic premises and declared a war against the urban centers that were controlled by the Kurdish organizations. According to his doctrine, the very concept of "minority" was invented by those opposed to unity among Islamic peoples and could lead to the internal discord within the *umma* (Islamic community).

Mahabad Republic (January–December 1946)

An autonomous Kurdish republic founded by a religious judge, Qadi Muhammad. Although indirectly supported by the Soviet troops that were then occupying Iran, Qadi Muhammad rejected the accusation that he was a Communist and separatist, and advocated regional autonomy. The republic was crushed by the Iranian army after the withdrawal of Soviet troops, and Qadi Muhammad was executed. Despite its short-lived existence, it plays a highly symbolic role in Kurdish nationalism.

Öcalan, Abdullah (Born 1949)

Leader of the PKK (which he founded sometime between 1977 and 1978). After a period of sympathy for the Islamist movement, he joined Turkish leftist organizations in the 1960s and later the Kurdish movement. Rejecting any pro-Soviet or pro-Chinese affiliation, his initial aim was to transform Turkish Kurdistan into the starting point of a Middle Eastern Socialist revolution. He commanded, from Syria and Lebanon, the PKK's guerrilla war. He was arrested in Kenya, delivered to Turkey in 1991, and condemned to death (this sentence was commuted to life imprisonment). In prison, he decided to stop the armed struggle and advocated the cause of the Kurdish cultural rights within a "democratic Republic."

PDK-Iran (Parti Dimuqrati Kurdistan, Kurdistan Democratic Party)

Founded in 1946, the Iranian PDK was, for many decades, the most important political party of Iranian Kurdistan. During the Cold War period, it adopted an essentially Marxist discourse, but during the 1980s switched to a social-democratic program. After the assassination of its leaders in 1989 and 1992, the party decided to develop mainly civil and political forms of resistance.

PDK-Iraq (Parti Dimuqrati Kurdistan, Kurdistan Democratic Party)

Founded in 1946, the Iraqi PDK was for few decades the most important Kurdish organization. Under the leadership of Mustafa Barzani, it constituted the hard core of the Barzani Revolt. During the 1975–1980 period, it adopted a radical "anti-imperialist" discourse but later became a liberal nationalist party. It is one of the two most important political forces in Iraqi Kurdistan and controls both the Behdinan and Erbil regions.

PKK-Turkey (Partiya Karkeren, Kurdistan Workers' Party)

Founded in 1977–1978 by Abdullah Öcalan, the PKK maintained its Marxist-Leninist program until the end of the 1990s and conducted a guerrilla war. After 2000, without abandoning its Socialist program, it advocated the proclamation of a democratic republic in Turkey and the recognition of Kurdish cultural rights. It also changed its name, becoming first KADEK (Kurdistan Congress' of Liberty and Democracy) and then Kongra-Gel (People's Congress). On June 1, 2004, its leaders decided to start a second stage of armed struggle.

PUK (Yekiti Nishtimanî Kurdistan, Patriotic Union of Kurdistan)

Founded in 1975 by Jalal Talabani following the failure of the Barzani Revolt. Pro-Maoist during its first years, it adopted a social-democratic and more-and-more-Kurdish nationalist program later on. It was a decisive component of the guerrilla warfare that took place between 1975 and 1991, and of Iraqi Kurdish self-rule begun in 1991. Engaged in the civil war against the PDK-Iraq from 1994 to 1997, the PUK today controls the Suleymaniyeh region.

Sharafkandi, Sadiq (1938–1992)

Dr. Sharafkandi, a physicist, replaced A. Ghassemlou as the leader of the PDK-Iran. This social-democratic politician was killed in Berlin by Iranian agents. His assassination provoked a crisis between Germany and Iran.

Talabani, Jalal (Born 1933)

A jurist by training, Talabani participated in the Kurdish movement in the 1950s and was one of the leading figures of the left-wing branch of the Democratic Party of Kurdistan. After many conflicts with Mustafa Barzani, he founded the PUK. During the 1980s he switched to a social-democratic position. He played an important role in Iraqi Kurdish self-rule after 1991.

Zana, Leyla (Born 1961)

Wife of Mehdi Zana, former Kurdish mayor of Diyarbekir, who was arrested and tortured during the 1980 military regime. She was elected in 1991 to the Turkish Assembly and promoted brotherhood between the Turkish and Kurdish peoples and the open use of the Kurdish language. As she continued to work for Kurdish rights her parliamentary immunity (and that of some other Kurdish deputies) was lifted in 1994 and she was condemned to fifteen years in prison for alleged membership in the illegal Kurdistan Workers' Party. While in prison, she was awarded the Sakharov Human Rights Prize. She was released in 2004.

Hamit Bozarslan

See Also Documentaries of Revolution; Ethnic and Racial Conflict: From Bargaining to Violence; Iranian Revolution; Iraq Revolution; Nationalism and Revolution; Turkish Revolutions of 1908 and 1919–1923

References and Further Readings

Barkey, H. J., and G. E. Fuller. 1998. *Turkey's Kurdish Question.* Boulder, CO, and New York: Rowman and Littlefield.

Bruinessen, M. M. van. 2000. *Kurdish Ethno-Nationalism versus Nation-Building States.* Istanbul: ISIS.

Çalislar, O. 1993. *Öcalan ve Burkay'la Kürt Sorunu.* Istanbul: Pencere.

Chaliand, G., ed. 1982. *People without a Country.* London: Zed Press.

Human Rights Watch. 1995. *Iraq's Crime of Genocide: The Anfal Campaign against the Kurds.* London: Yale University Press.

Kieser, H. L., and D. J. Schaller, eds. 2002. *Der Völkermord an der Armeniern und die Shoah.* Basel, Switzerland: Chronos Verlag.

McDowell, D. 1995. *A Modern History of the Kurds.* London and New York: I.B. Tauris.

Randal, J. C. 1997. *After Such Knowledge What Forgiveness? My Encounters with Kurdistan.* New York: Farrar, Strauss and Giroux.

White, P. 2000. *Primitive Rebels or Revolutionary Modernizers? The Kurdish National Movement in Turkey.* London: Zed.

L

Lao Communist Revolution

CHRONOLOGY

1353	King Fa Ngum founds the kingdom of Lan Xang (Million Elephants), forerunner of the modern Lao state.
1560	Capital of Lan Xang is moved from Luang Prabang to Vientiane (Viang Chan) during wars with Burma.
1633–1690	Lan Xang is at its zenith. First Europeans visit Vientiane (1641–1647).
1707–1713	Lan Xang is divided into three kingdoms, all of which soon fall under Siamese (Thai) domination.
1826–1828	Lao war of independence to throw off Siamese suzerainty results in Lao defeat and sacking of Vientiane.
1893	France seizes control of Lao territories east of the Mekong River.
1901–1908	Ethnic minority groups in southern Laos revolt against French.
1907	Franco-Siamese treaty establishes borders of modern Laos.
1914–1922	Revolts against French rule by ethnic minority groups in northern Laos.
1945	On April 8, independence of Laos is proclaimed under duress from Japanese.
	In September, following Japanese surrender, Lao Issara (Free Lao) government seizes power.
1946	French reoccupy Laos; Lao Issara leaders flee to Thailand.
1947	First elections for National Assembly are held under French direction; Lao Issara conducts guerrilla operations against the French.
1949	Lao Issara government-in-exile is dissolved. Moderates accept amnesty and return to Vientiane; radicals form Pathet Lao (PL), the Lao Communist-led revolutionary movement allied to the Viet Minh in Vietnam. First unit of the revolutionary Lao People's Liberation Army (LPLA) is formed.

1950   The United States and United Kingdom recognize Royal Lao government (RLG) of independent Lao state. Pathet Lao forms rebel resistance government.

1953   Viet Minh twice invades Laos, establishes "liberated area" for Lao revolutionaries.

On October 22, France grants Laos independence.

1954   Geneva Agreements on Indochina leave Pathet Lao in control of two provinces adjoining North Vietnam. Talks begin with Royal Lao government on administrative reunification.

1955   Pathet Lao Congress establishes Lao Patriotic Front; Marxist leadership forms secret Lao People's Party following dissolution of Indochinese Communist Party in 1951. Kaison Phomvihan named first secretary general.

1957   Agreement between Royal Lao government and Pathet Lao creates First Coalition government under leadership of neutralist prime minister Souvanna Phouma, against strong opposition from the United States.

1958   Following electoral success of the Left, United States engineers replacement of Souvanna Phouma by right-wing government, which arrests Pathet Lao National Assembly deputies (July 1959) and declares state of emergency. Renewed insurgency.

1960   Rigged election returns right-wing government; all Pathet Lao deputies escape with their guards. Crack military unit carries out neutralist coup d'état; rightists, with U.S. support, respond by marching on Vientiane. Battle of Vientiane results in withdrawal of neutralists to join forces with Pathet Lao on the Plain of Jars.

1961   The incoming U.S. administration of President John F. Kennedy changes policy toward Laos, favors neutralization.

On May 16, new Geneva Conference on Laos opens.

1962   Second Coalition government formed, again under Souvanna Phouma. Neutralists subsequently divide into pro– and anti–Pathet Lao factions.

1964   As Laos is drawn increasingly into the Second Indochina (Vietnam) War, the Second Coalition government collapses. Pathet Lao drives anti-PL neutralists from the Plain of Jars. Souvanna Phouma survives right-wing military coup, thanks to international support. U.S. jets begin secret bombing of targets in Laos; CIA recruits Hmong minority to form "secret army" to fight Pathet Lao in northern Laos.

1965–1971   Second Indochina War rages; Ho Chi Minh Trail through eastern Laos used to infiltrate troops from north to south Vietnam; United States subjects Lao territory to devastating secret bombing campaign. Ground fighting involving Vietnamese Communists increases area under Pathet Lao control.

1972   Second Congress of Lao People's Party changes its name to Lao People's Revolutionary Party (LPRP), calls for negotiated settlement.

1973   Cease-fire is declared; negotiations on formation of Third Coalition government.

1974   Third Coalition government takes office. All U.S. military personnel leave Laos.

1975   Political unrest follows Communist military victories in Cambodia and South Vietnam. Senior rightists flee. RLG officials and military officers are sent to camps for "political re-education." Cities across Laos are "liberated" by the LPLA, culminating in the liberation of Vientiane in August. Congress of People's Representatives meets to dissolve Third Coalition government, accept the forced abdication of the king, and proclaim formation of the Lao People's Democratic Republic on December 2.

1976–1977   Withdrawal of U.S. aid and poor harvests lead to collapse of the Lao economy. Vietnam and the Soviet Union prop up new regime. Laos and Vietnam sign 25-year Treaty of Friendship and Cooperation in July 1977.

1979–1982   LPRP relaxes tight economic and political controls to improve economic conditions. First five-year plan is announced (1981–1986). Buddhist worship is allowed. Tensions with China following Third Indochina War, in which Laos sided with Vietnam against China.

1986   Fourth Party Congress endorses New Economic Mechanism paving the way for economic reforms leading to a market economy.

1989   First elections for Supreme People's (later National) Assembly.

1991   Constitution promulgated.

1992   Kaison Phomvihan dies; replaced as president of LPRP by General Khamtai Siphandone.

1996   Sixth Party Congress elects politburo dominated by the military (seven out of nine members).

1997   Laos joins the Association of Southeast Asian Nations (ASEAN).

2001   Seventh Party Congress expands politburo to eleven members, but military dominance is maintained.

INTRODUCTION

The Lao Revolution of 1975 brought an end to the six-century-old Lao monarchy and replaced it with a Communist "people's democracy" modeled on similar regimes in the Soviet Union, China, and Vietnam. The triumph of the Lao Revolution owed much to political and military support from Vietnam throughout the First and Second Indochina wars. By contrast with Cambodia and Vietnam, however, the final seizure of power in Laos by the Lao revolutionary movement (the Pathet Lao) was semi-constitutional and without violence. In this it continued a revolutionary trajectory that was peculiarly Lao.

BACKGROUND: CULTURE AND HISTORY

The borders of the modern Lao state include less than half the area of settlement of ethnic Lao in the middle Mekong basin included in the kingdom of Lan Xang at its greatest extent in the seventeenth century. In the eighteenth century, Lan Xang broke into three separate kingdoms—Luang Prabang in the north, Vientiane (Viang Chan) in the center, and Champasak in the south—all of which fell eventually under the political domination of Bangkok. When France expanded its Indochinese empire in the 1890s, it seized only part of the former territory of Lan Xang. The rest was incorporated into the modern state of Thailand. As a result, many more ethnic Lao live today in the northeastern provinces of Thailand than in the Lao People's Democratic Republic (LPDR).

According to the most recent (1995) census, ethnic Lao account for 52.5 percent of the estimated population of Laos: estimated in 2005 at 6.2 million (CIA 2006). Closely related groups speaking Tai languages bring the figure up to 66.2 percent. Hilltribe minorities speaking Austroasiatic languages make up a further 22.7 percent, the largest being the Khamu with 11 percent. Hmong and Mien (Yao) scattered through the mountains of northern Laos make up 7.4 percent, while speakers of Tibeto-Burman languages in the far north account for the remaining 2.9 percent. In all, the government officially recognizes 47 ethnolinguistic groups, though other counts, using different defining criteria, put the number as high as 130. Laos is thus the most ethnically diverse country in Southeast Asia.

By far the majority of ethnic Lao are Theravada Buddhists. Among other Tai-speakers, most are Buddhist, though some upland Tai are animists. All cultivate wet-field rice, mostly of the glutinous variety, whether in upland valleys or on the riverine plains of Mekong basin. Together they are referred to as Lao Loum, or Lao of the plains. The Austroasiatic-speaking minorities are animists, though some have been converted to Buddhism and a few Khamu are Christians. Known collectively as the Lao Theung, or Lao of the hill slopes, they practice moving slash-and-burn agriculture, growing vegetables and dry-field rice. So too do the Hmong, Mien, and the Tibeto-Burman minorities, collectively known as the Lao Soung, or Lao of the mountain heights. Because of their geographic location, these minorities played a significant role in the Lao Revolution.

Buddhism provided not only a system of social morality for the Lao, but also legitimized the structure of political power. According to the notion of karma, the king ruled by moral right because of the meritorious deeds he had performed in numerous previous existences. He was expected further to demonstrate his karma by performing more meritorious deeds, notably by giving generously to the Sangha, the Buddhist monastic order. Karma, the accumulated moral effect of thought and action, explained for the Lao the vicissitudes of fortune, and still does. People are reborn, the Lao believe, in the social class they deserve. In this way Buddhism religiously reinforces the social order, and so is essentially anti-revolutionary.

Traditional Lao political culture centered on the *meuang*. This was a territory of variable extent, ruled by a *chao meuang,* or lord of the *meuang.* He was assisted by three deputies in descending rank, all drawn from a small aristocracy defined by birth. The *meuang* comprised a center of power surrounded by dependent villages whose peasant farmers owed the ruling aristocracy their personal loyalty: goods and services were given in exchange for social order and protection. A number of smaller *meuang* would be nested within a larger one, their rulers owing allegiance to the greater lord. Larger *meuang* in turn comprised Meuang Lao, the kingdom of Lan Xang.

This loose political structure depended on loyalty and due recognition of hierarchical status. No centrally appointed bureaucracy was dispatched to administer distant *meuang.* Meuang Lao was strong when the center was strong—that is, when the king was able to concentrate social power (political, military, economic, and ideological). It was weak when the center was weak, especially when power there was divided during a disputed succession. At such times distant *meuang* might transfer their allegiance to a rival kingdom, so the extent of Meuang Lao varied.

This system was common to all the Buddhist states of mainland Southeast Asia. After Lan Xang split into three, the Lao rulers were coerced into recognizing the superior power of Bangkok. It was always possible, however, karma permitting, that a Lao ruler would reconstitute Meuang Lao. An attempt by Vientiane to do just that in 1827–1828 led to defeat and the elimination of the Vientiane royal house.

In the end it was the French who reconstituted a truncated Lao kingdom over the period 1893 to 1907. The Mekong River, instead of being the central artery of the Lao kingdom, marked most of the western frontier with Thailand. The Laos that remained was reduced to a minor territory of French Indochina. For half a century France did little to develop either the economic or human resources of Laos, which it administered in two parts—a protectorate over the kingdom of Luang Prabang and direct colonial rule elsewhere—a division that not only perpetuated disunity and regionalism, but left intact traditional dependence on political patronage derived from the *meuang.*

Early opposition to French rule came not from the lowland ethnic Lao, but from the upland minorities in both the south and the north of Laos. Rebellions were suppressed by the French, who thenceforth treated the minorities with suspicion. Only when faced with a resurgence of Thai nationalism and war in Europe did French authorities encourage a sense of Lao national identity in preference to loyalty to the French construct of Indochina.

France continued to administer Indochina during World War II under agreement with Japan, until the Japanese seized power in March 1945. Under Japanese pressure the king of Luang Prabang declared Lao independence. In the power vacuum following the Japanese surrender, the Lao Issara (Free Lao) movement confirmed Lao independence and formed a government. The Lao Issara were mostly young nationalists from the tiny Lao educated elite, led by Prince Phetsarat Rattanavongsa, scion of a collateral branch of the royal family of Luang Prabang. When the French reoccupied Laos in 1946, the Lao Issara were forced into exile in Thailand. After three years, the movement divided into moderates who returned to help prepare Laos for full independence and radicals who entered into alliance with the Vietnamese Communist movement, the Viet Minh. The radicals called themselves the Pathet Lao (PL) (literally Land of the Lao).

Four years of fighting followed before the Geneva Agreements of 1954 brought an end to the First Indochina War. This left Laos fully independent (October 1953) but divided, with two provinces in the hands of the Pathet Lao. It took three years of negotiations before the country was reunified through formation of the First Coalition government. The inclusion of two Communist ministers was vigorously opposed by the United States, which maneuvered to force the government from office. Civil war then followed, provoking a neutralist military coup. When right-wing forces retook the capital, the neutralists made common cause with the Pathet Lao, and Laos seemed about to fall to the Communists.

In 1961 the incoming administration of U.S. president John F. Kennedy decided to back the neutralization of Laos. A new Geneva Conference was convened and a Second Coalition government formed. But already Laos was being drawn into the Second Indochina War. The government collapsed in all but name, and a decade of war followed, during which Laos was heavily bombed. When the United States and Vietnam signed a cease-fire in 1973, the Pathet Lao quickly followed suit. A Third Coalition government was formed, equally divided between Left and Right to reflect the much stronger strategic position of the Pathet Lao, who by then controlled four-fifths of the country, though still well under half the population.

CONTEXT AND PROCESS OF REVOLUTION

The Lao Communist movement was directed, from its foundation in 1955 by the secret, avowedly Marxist, Lao People's

Pathet Lao troops during military exercises in Laos, 1959. (Library of Congress)

Party (from 1972 the Lao People's Revolutionary Party—LPRP). As in Vietnam, the party operated behind the facade of a broad popular front, known as the Lao Patriotic Front (LPF). The party secretary general was a shadowy figure by the name of Kaison Phomvihan, whose mother was Lao but whose father was Vietnamese. Far more prominent was Prince Souphanouvong, half-brother of the long-serving neutralist prime minister Prince Souvanna Phouma. It was Souphanouvong who negotiated on behalf of the Pathet Lao in establishing all three coalition governments, and who was the most prominent Pathet Lao representative in those governments.

The Pathet Lao subsequently justified its readiness to form and take part in these coalition governments as a deliberate Leninist strategy designed to strengthen the movement to the point where it could seize power in its own right. In reality, Pathet Lao leaders had little alternative. The movement had, of political necessity, to hide its heavy dependence on the Viet Minh leading up to the First Coalition, and it had to broaden its support base. The two northeastern provinces under its administrative control after 1954 were mountainous and backward, inhabited primarily by tribal minorities on whom the Pathet Lao relied for military recruitment. Coalition government allowed the LPF to communicate its

message to the lowland Lao population through political campaigning as a legal political organization (the existence of the Lao People's Party remained secret) and through the activities of younger and more radical Buddhist monks (ironically, one of the portfolios allotted to the Pathet Lao was the Ministry of Religion).

With the collapse of the First Coalition, the Pathet Lao reverted to armed opposition—and to complete dependence for training and weapons on North Vietnam— while all the time calling for a peaceful resolution of the conflict and formation of a new coalition government. The 1960 neutralist military coup and the uncompromising right-wing response played into the hands of the Pathet Lao, and for a while it seemed that the country might fall to the Communists.

At this point the incoming administration of President John F. Kennedy changed tack and backed a new international attempt to install a neutralist government. For a while, with the formation of the Second Coalition, the neutralists were politically influential in that they held the balance of power. But intense pressure from both Right and Left split the neutralists into pro- and anti-PL factions. Once again political positions polarized.

The Second Coalition really broke down, however, because neither the United States nor North Vietnam was prepared to accept the neutrality of Laos in anything but name. The North Vietnamese continued to use Lao territory to infiltrate troops to the south, down the famous Ho Chi Minh Trail, while the United States embarked on intensive secret bombing of these infiltration routes. Souvanna Phouma's government continued as a facade behind which civil conflict continued. Each side blamed the other for the breakdown of the coalition, but it was the Pathet Lao who profited most by extending their control of rural areas—with help from their Vietnamese allies. The revolutionary movement expanded, particularly through recruitment of minority cadres, to whom the Pathet Lao appealed through promises of improved living conditions, especially health and education.

By the early 1970s the LPRP was in a position to demand equal representation in the Third Coalition government. One of the conditions was that the administrative and royal capitals (Vientiane and Luang Prabang) were neutralized, patrolled by equal numbers of PL and rightist troops. This gave the Pathet Lao a strong foothold in the heart of the Royal Lao government zone, while conceding no equivalent right of access to the zone under their control. Pathet Lao agents and sympathizers were thus able to organize among lowland Lao trade unionists and students. Their appeal was to Lao nationalist sentiment and to those tired of the war and its corrosive effect on Lao culture, the symbol of which was the substantial U.S. presence in Laos.

The Pathet Lao also took the lead in policy formulation, drawing up an "eighteen-point political program" to achieve political reconciliation. This guaranteed preservation of the monarchy, support for Buddhism, rights to democratic freedoms, and a neutral foreign policy—none of which were honored once the Pathet Lao eventually seized power. The "eighteen points" were widely disseminated and gained widespread political support.

The Third Coalition government took office in 1974. By the beginning of 1975 the military situation in Vietnam and Cambodia looked ominous. Pathet Lao forces also moved closer to Vientiane. Prime Minister Souvanna Phouma ordered rightist forces under Hmong general Vang Pao not to retaliate. In April, first Phnom Penh, then Saigon fell to Communist forces. In both countries Communist regimes took power.

This completely changed the political dynamics in Laos. Organized demonstrations forced several prominent rightist politicians and generals to flee the country and the United States to close down its aid mission. Other soldiers and officials, believing a Pathet Lao victory inevitable, agreed to undergo political re-education in remote camps where they expected to remain for a few months. Most were not permitted to return for several years. One after another provincial capitals were "liberated" by the peaceful arrival of Pathet Lao

forces, to which rightist military units surrendered. In August a People's Revolutionary Committee took control of Luang Prabang, while a contingent of Pathet Lao women soldiers were flown in to symbolically "liberate" Vientiane.

The Lao Revolution was all but complete, but even then there seems to have been some discussion within the party on the wisdom of immediately abolishing the Third Coalition and the monarchy. At any rate, the party moved slowly, making sure that most of its opponents were confined to re-education camps and that its actions conformed to the "semi-legalism" that had marked its strategy throughout the "thirty-year struggle" (1945–1975). Local elections turned power over to revolutionary cadres throughout the country; a "representative" Supreme People's Assembly was appointed by the party to take the place of the defunct, popularly elected Royal Lao National Assembly until the new constitution was created; the king was prevailed upon to abdicate; and the Lao People's Democratic Republic (LPDR) was proclaimed on December 2, 1975.

IMPACTS

The impact of the Lao Revolution was immediate, both internally and externally. Internally, the artificial wartime economy, which had been heavily dependent on U.S. aid, virtually collapsed, while the value of the Lao currency (the *kip*) plummeted. Heavy-handed controls imposed on the movement of goods created unnecessary shortages in towns, which could no longer import commodities from Thailand since Bangkok had closed the border. To make matters worse, over the next two years flood and drought severely reduced the rice crop. Restrictions were also placed on personal movement and Buddhist worship, particularly the donation of food to monks, which was discouraged on the grounds that this was a wasteful practice and monks should grow their own food.

The strict administrative controls were partly to compensate for the weakness of the regime. The educational level of cadres who had been fighting in the mountains for more than two decades was abysmally low, but the party did not trust former Royal Lao bureaucrats. It also greatly feared organized opposition to the new regime supported from Thailand. For that reason it kept thousands of former civil servants and military officers in re-education camps, despite promising their imminent return. By so doing, and through dispensing with the "eighteen-point program," the new regime lost the trust of the educated class that had been prepared to work with it. Thousands of educated Lao, followed by most of the Chinese and Vietnamese communities, Hmong tribesmen, and eventually even many peasants, crossed the Mekong River to Thailand. In the end, ten percent of the then population of 3 million fled the country, including an estimated 90 percent of the small Lao educated class. Almost all were resettled in third countries, notably in the United States, France, Australia, and Canada, where they now form a substantial Lao diaspora. The effect of this exodus was to retard the country's development for at least a generation.

For ideological reasons, the LPRP leadership was determined not only to nationalize all industry, but also to cooperativize agriculture. As the few landlords had fled and peasant land holdings were not too unequal, no land reform took place. Villagers first formed work teams, then were encouraged to pool land and implements. This policy was much resented. Some peasants killed their draft animals rather than turn them over to the cooperative. Others burned crops. Some fled to Thailand. In mid 1979 a halt was called to the program, and although cooperative agriculture remained government policy, it was not pursued. In the late 1980s, peasants were given "land use rights" that were exchangeable and heritable, thus restoring private property in land in all but name.

The failure of Socialist economics forced the LPDR government in 1986 to embark on a set of policies known as the New Economic Mechanism (NEM). This consisted in opening up the Lao economy to market forces and foreign investment, a change in direction given impetus by the collapse of Communism in Eastern Europe and the Soviet Union (until then the LPDR's principal source of foreign aid). Laos welcomed aid both from Western countries (Australia, Sweden, France) and Japan and from international aid donors (notably United Nations Development Programme, the World Bank, and the Asian Development Bank).

Economic liberalization did not bring with it more open politics, however. The LPRP maintained its monopoly of political power by suppressing every hint of dissent. Though the party remained unified, powerful political leaders reverted to traditional forms of political culture to build up networks of political support and patronage based not on ideological differences, but on personal and family interests that were often linked to business ventures. In this way a political-economic elite developed, which used its political influence for economic ends. The result was to encourage massive and ingrained corruption and disinclination by party members to abide by the rule of law.

Externally the Lao Revolution increased the nervousness of non-Communist Thailand, especially when Laos signed a twenty-five-year Treaty of Friendship and Cooperation with Vietnam, thus cementing the close relationship of the two countries during war. The treaty also angered China, though at the time criticism was muted. When Vietnam invaded Cambodia at the end of 1978, Laos threw its support, with some hesitation, behind Hanoi. Vientiane denounced China's retaliatory attack on Vietnam and ordered Chinese officials out of northern Laos. Relations with Beijing reached a nadir with Chinese support (briefly) for a rival Lao Socialist Party and armed anti-government insurgency. By the mid 1980s, however, relations had returned to normal, and Laos today is careful to maintain warm and close relations with both Hanoi and Beijing (which together provide the principal international support for the Lao regime.)

Lao relations with Thailand remained strained throughout the 1980s, with Laos accusing Thailand of supporting anti-government insurgents recruited from sprawling Lao refugee camps, and Thailand accusing Laos of training Thai guerrillas. Relations improved after Laos announced its New Economic Mechanism and Thai investment began flowing into Laos. Trade picked up, Thai tourists followed in the footsteps of Princess Sirindhorn, daughter of the king of Thailand, and a commission was established to demarcate the Thai-Lao border. Improved relations in the 1990s culminated in Lao membership in the Association of Southeast Asian Nations (ASEAN) in 1997. Relations with other ASEAN states also warmed. The treaty with Vietnam was not renewed in 2002, though relations between Vientiane and Hanoi remained close.

Relations with the United States have been more prickly than with other Western powers. The United States was furious at the humiliating way it was forced to close its aid mission in 1975. Although Washington did not break diplomatic relations, for years the United States was represented only by a chargé d'affaires. The United States provided very little aid, even after Laos agreed to joint missions to find the remains of Americans missing in action from the Second Indochina War and launched its NEM. In particular, the United States provided minimal support to remove, and has never accepted responsibility for, the unexploded ordnance left over from the war, which continues to inflict casualties. The large expatriate Lao community in the United States has been instrumental in preventing improved Lao-U.S. relations.

PEOPLE AND ORGANIZATIONS

Bounyang Vorachit (Born 1937)

Named prime minister in 2001 following the Seventh Party Congress, Bounyang joined the Pathet Lao in 1954 and served in the Lao People's Army, reaching the rank of colonel. He was appointed to the LPRP central committee at its Second Congress in 1972. A protégé of Nouhak Phoumsavan, he was governor of Savannakhet Province from 1982 to 1992, when he became mayor of Vientiane. At the Sixth Party Congress in 1996, Bounyang was elected to the political bureau and brought into the government as minister of finance.

Choummaly Sayasone (Born 1936)

Appointed state vice president in 2001 following the Seventh Party Congress, General Choummaly joined the Pathet Lao in 1954 and served in the LPLA throughout the "thirty-year struggle." After 1975 he continued his military career, rising in both the army and party hierarchy. He was elected to the LPRP central committee in 1982, and as a full member of the political bureau in 1991, when he succeeded his fellow southerner Khamtai Siphandone, both as army commander and as minister of defense.

Hmong

The last significant minority to migrate to Laos in the nineteenth century, the Hmong settled in the mountains of northern Laos, where their principal cash crop was opium. During the 1930s a bitter personal feud divided two of the principal clans. This was perpetuated by the decision to support opposing sides during the First and Second Indochina wars. While some Hmong joined the Pathet Lao, others fought for the Royal Lao government. In the early 1960s the U.S. Central Intelligence Agency (CIA) recruited many of these to form a "secret army" under the command of Hmong general Vang Pao. The Hmong suffered heavy casualties fighting for the Plain of Jars. After 1975, fearing retaliation, many fled the country. Some who remained kept up their resistance to the new Communist regime, mounting occasional attacks on military and civilian targets. These attacks were continuing as late as 2003, as Lao army forces attempted to track down remaining Hmong guerrillas in the high mountains south of the Plain of Jars.

Kaison Phomvihan (1920–1992)

The founding secretary general of the Lao People's Revolutionary Party, Kaison was born in Savannakhet Province, the son of a Vietnamese father and a Lao mother. After school in Laos he studied law in Hanoi, where he joined the Indochinese Communist Party in 1949. Kaison was entrusted with forming the first Lao Communist guerrilla unit in 1950 and was named minister of defense in the Pathet Lao resistance government. When the Lao People's Party was formed in 1955, Kaison became its first secretary general. From that point on he led the Pathet Lao, in close collaboration with the Vietnamese Communist leadership. Kaison directed the Pathet Lao strategy of joining successive coalition governments, though he was never himself a member of these. In 1975, Kaison emerged from the shadows when he became prime minister of the government of the LPDR. He was the principal figure responsible for the change in economic policy known as the New Economic Mechanism. In 1991, Kaison strengthened his position further when he succeeded Souphanouvong as state president as well as being president of the LPRP. He died on November 21, 1992. Since his death, the party has encouraged a personality cult focusing on his life and work, to which a museum has been dedicated in Vientiane.

Khamtai Siphandone (Born 1924)

The second president of the Lao People's Revolutionary Party, Khamtai was born in Champasak Province, where he joined the anti-French resistance forces in 1946. When the Free Lao movement split in 1949, Khamtai joined the radical wing in coalition with the Viet Minh and fought in the southern Lao theater. He was a founding member of the Lao People's Party in 1955 and in 1960 was appointed commander in chief of the Pathet Lao armed forces. He was elected to the political bureau of the LPRP at its Second Congress in 1972 and was minister of defense and deputy prime minister in the first government of the LPDR. When Kaison Phomvihan died in 1992, Khamtai became party president, and when Nouhak Phoumsavan relinquished the state presidency in 1998, Khamtai added that office as well, marking the dominance of the military within the Party. He was expected to retire at the Eighth Party Congress in 2006.

Lao Front for National Construction (LFNC)

This took the place of the Lao Patriotic Front following the founding of the LPDR and held its First Congress in 1979. Like the LPF, the LFNC is tightly controlled by the LPRP. Though non-party members can join, all its principal officeholders are members of the party. Representatives of all approved organizations are also members, including the Lao United Buddhists Association. The front has branches throughout the country and meets in national congress every five years. The purpose of the front is to unify all ethnic groups, raise political consciousness, and mobilize support for the government's policies and programs to build and develop the country. One of its tasks is to vet all potential candidates for elections for the National Assembly. As political power has become increasingly concentrated in the politburo of the party, the front has lost much of its political influence.

Lao Issara

Literally "Free Laos," the name taken by the movement for Lao independence from France in 1945. The French re-conquest of Laos forced the Lao Issara government to flee to Thailand. In 1949 the movement split into moderates who accepted an amnesty and returned to Laos and radicals who joined the Viet Minh.

Lao Patriotic Front (LPF)

This was established in 1956 to act as a broad political front for the Pathet Lao. At all times it was directed by the Lao People's Party, which formed its political core. Throughout its existence the president of the front was Prince Souphanouvong, the public face of the Pathet Lao. When the Pathet Lao was in coalition government, the LPF was constituted as a political party. It was superseded by the Lao Front for National Construction in 1979.

Lao People's Party (LPP)

Secretly formed in 1955 following dissolution of the Indochinese Communist Party four years earlier, the Marxist-Leninist LPP changed its name to the Lao People's Revolutionary Party (LPRP) at its Second Congress in 1972.

Lao United Buddhists Association

Officially sponsored organization to which all Buddhist monks in the LPDR must belong. It is a member organization of the Lao Front for National Construction. In the 1990s, as Marxism-Leninism lost its ideological appeal, Buddhism became encouraged in the LPDR for nationalist reasons. Party members from the politburo on down habitually attend Buddhist ceremonies, where they show their respect to senior monks.

Lao Women's Union

Officially sponsored organization run by and for Lao women. It is a member organization of the Lao Front for National Construction but exerts additional political influence.

New Economic Mechanism (NEM)

Name given to the set of policies passed at the Fourth Party Congress in 1986 designed to move from a Socialist to a free market economy and to encourage foreign direct investment.

Nouhak Phoumsavan (Born 1916)

Second in power only to Kaison throughout the "thirty-year struggle" (1945–1975) of the Lao revolutionary movement, Nouhak too came from Savannakhet. Tough and resilient, he drove trucks from Laos to Vietnam, where he was recruited by the Viet Minh and joined the Indochinese Communist Party in 1950. He was a founding politburo member of the Lao People's Party and was deputy prime minister and minister of finance in successive governments of the LPDR. In 1992, Nouhak succeeded Kaison as state president, a post he held until his retirement in 1998.

Pathet Lao

Literally "land of the Lao," the name given to the Lao revolutionary movement by the Western press through the "thirty-year struggle" from 1945 to 1975.

Souphanouvong (1909–1995)

The first president of the Lao People's Democratic Republic, Prince Souphanouvong was born into a collateral branch of the royal family of Luang Prabang. He was educated in France and worked as a civil engineer in Vietnam before returning to Laos in 1945 to join the Lao Issara. The following year Souphanouvong was wounded while commanding Lao forces opposing the French re-conquest of Laos. When the Lao Issara split in 1949, Souphanouvong sided with the Viet Minh. From 1955 he was secretly a member of the politburo of the Lao People's Party. Throughout the First and Second Indochina wars, Souphanouvong's public position was as president of the Lao Patriotic Front. He was a prominent member of all three coalition governments. In 1975, Souphanouvong became president of the LPDR, a position he retained until his death in 1995.

Souvanna Phouma (1901–1984)

The neutralist prime minister in all three coalition governments, Souvanna was born into the same collateral branch of the royal family of Luang Prabang as his nationalist elder brother Prince Phetsarat and his younger half-brother Souphanouvong. Souvanna was educated in France as an engineer and was a member of the Lao Issara government of 1945. In 1949 he accepted an amnesty and returned to Laos, where he entered politics and became prime minister for the first time in 1951. Souvanna negotiated the formation of, and became neutralist prime minister in, all three coalition governments. After 1975 he remained in Laos, where he died in 1984.

Viet Minh

The abbreviated title of the League for the Independence of Vietnam, established as a broad political front for the Indochinese Communist Party in 1941. It became the name by which the Vietnamese Communist movement was known.

Martin Stuart-Fox

See Also Colonialism, Anti-Colonialism and Neo-Colonialism; Cambodian Revolution; Documentaries of Revolution; Vietnamese Revolution; War and Revolution

References and Further Readings

Bourdet, Yves. 2000. *The Economics of Transition in Laos: From Socialism to ASEAN Integration.* Cheltenham UK: Edward Elgar.

Brown, MacAlister. 1991. "Communists in Coalition: Lessons from Laos." Pp. 41–63 in *Laos: Beyond the Revolution,* edited by Joseph J. Zasloff and Leonard Unger. Basingstoke, England: Macmillan.

Brown, MacAlister, and Joseph J. Zasloff. 1986. *Apprentice Revolutionaries: The Communist Movement in Laos, 1930–1985.* Stanford, CA: Hoover Institution Press.

Butler-Diaz, Jacqueline. 1998. *New Laos, New Challenges.* Tempe: Arizona State University Program for Southeast Asian Studies.

CIA. 2006. The World Factbook–Laos. http://www.odci.gov/cia/publications/factbook/geos/la.html (accessed March 16, 2006).

Evans, Grant. 1995. *Lao Peasants under Socialism and Post-Socialism.* Chiang Mai, Thailand: Silkworm Press.

———. 1998. *The Politics of Ritual and Remembrance: Laos since 1975.* Chiang Mai, Thailand: Silkworm Press.

Gunn, Geoffrey. 1998. *Theravadins, Colonialists and Commissars in Laos.* Bangkok: White Lotus.

Kremmer, Christopher. 2003. *Bamboo Palace: Discovering the Lost Dynasty of Laos.* Sydney: Flamingo.

Stuart-Fox, Martin. 1997. *A History of Laos.* Cambridge: Cambridge University Press.

———. 1999. "Laos: From Buddhist Kingdom to Marxist State." Pp. 153–172 in *Buddhism and Politics in Twentieth Century Asia,* edited by Ian Harris. London: Continuum.

———. 2001. *Historical Dictionary of Laos.* 2nd edition. Lanham, MD: Scarecrow Press.

———. 2002. *Buddhist Kingdom, Marxist State: The Making of Modern Laos.* 2nd edition. Bangkok: White Lotus.

Libyan Revolution

CHRONOLOGY

1650–1911	Libya, known as Tarabulus al-Gharb, is a peripheral province of the Ottoman empire.
1911	Italy invades Libya.
1911–1932	Libyans resist Italian occupation and colonialism. As many as 500,000 Libyans—half the population—perish in the conflict, and about 60,000 are forced into exile, mostly to nearby countries.
1918–1920	Libyan resistance forces establish the first republic in the region, the short-lived Tripolitanian Republic.
1931	Umar al-Mukhtar, leader of the heroic Libyan Sanusi resistance movement against Italian Fascist forces is executed by the Italians.
1932	Italian military completes the conquest of Libya.
1951	After defeating Italy in World War II, Britain and France establish an independent Libya under the leadership of Amir Muhammad Idriss al-Sanusi, the pro-British leader of the regionally based Sanusiyya movement, who is crowned King Idriss I of the United Libyan Kingdom.
1961	Oil is discovered in Libya. Libyan monarchy launches modernization programs in the areas of health, education, transportation, and housing.
1969	The Revolutionary Command Council (RCC) of the Libyan Free Unionist Officers' Movement, led by a twenty-seven-year-old charismatic officer, Mu'ammar Abu-Minyar al-Qadhafi, and composed mainly of educated

military officers from lower-middle-class background, overthrows the monarchy in a bloodless coup.

1971   Libya establishes a one-party state, the Arab Socialist Union.

1973   After the Arab Socialist Union political system fails to inspire or mobilize the majority of the Libyan people, Qadhafi declares a popular revolution against the country's ineffective bureaucracies.

1975   An attempted coup by some technocratic members of the RCC, including Minister of Planning Umar al-Muhashi, fails.

1977   The Libyan People's General Congress renames the country the Libyan Arab Popular and Socialist Jamahiriyya.

1981   The administration of U.S. president Ronald Reagan considers the Qadhafi regime of Libya a sponsor of terrorist groups opposing the United States and its allies. Libya's armed forces are defeated in a war with Chad.

1986   Blaming Libya for a bombing attack on U.S. soldiers in Berlin (which later investigation indicates Libya was not responsible for), the United States launches an air strike on Libya killing fifty people, including Qadhafi's young adopted daughter.

1988   Qadhafi blames Libyan Revolutionary Committees for committing abuses. He releases political prisoners and ends some of his economic experiments in collective markets and bartering.

In late December, a U.S. Pan American airliner, flight 103, is destroyed over Lockerbie, Scotland, by a bomb planted in luggage.

1992   The United States accuses two Libyan agents of planting the bomb that destroyed the Pan American airliner over Lockerbie. The United Nations imposes economic sanctions on Libya.

2000   Libya allows the trial of two of its citizens for the Lockerbie airliner bombing by a Scottish court in Holland.

2001   One Libyan is convicted of the airliner bombing and one is acquitted.

2004   Libya renounces terrorism and agrees to eliminate its weapons of mass destruction program. Most sanctions against Libya are lifted.

INTRODUCTION

The Libyan Arab Popular and Socialist Jamahiriyya, the official name of the state of Libya, is a self-declared revolutionary state governed by an organization of popular committees and congresses with a rich oil-based economy. This regime is the creation of what most Libyans call the First of September Revolution. It originated on September 1, 1969, when a group of young Pan-Arab, Nasserite officers in the Libyan Royal Army, led by a twenty-seven-year-old charismatic officer named Mu'ammar Abu-Minyar al-Qadhafi, overthrew the monarchy of King Muhammad Idriss al-Sanusi in a bloodless coup d'etat. The twelve junior officers were the central committee of a secret organization within the Libyan army called the Libyan Free Unionist Officers' Movement. Renaming itself the Revolutionary Command Council (RCC), the committee of twelve officers declared the creation of the Libyan Arab Republic.

The RCC assumed all executive, legislative, and judicial powers and began to refer to its political and social policies as a "revolution." Although advocating anti-colonialism, anti-Communism, Arab nationalism, Islam, and anti-corruption, the RCC did not have a clearly delineated program and looked for guidance to the 1952 Egyptian Revolution, at least in the early years. Libyan society did experience major social, political, and economic transformations after 1969. The new government initially enacted its social, economic, and political policies from above without significant popular participation from below. After consolidating his power in 1975, Qadhafi began to experiment with creating a "precapitalist socialist society" using the luxury of oil revenues and employing many non-Libyan workers.

BACKGROUND: CULTURE AND HISTORY

The Libyan Revolution with its radical and nationalist ideology was a reaction to the crisis of the Sanusi monarchy, and regional and international politics since the 1960s. Libya between 1650 and 1911, known as Tarabulus al-Gharb, was a poor and peripheral province of the Ottoman empire. In 1911 Italy invaded the country but could not control the interior until 1932. Italy waged one of the most brutal colonial wars in modern Africa, aside from the French in Algeria and the Belgian armed forces in the Congo. Libyan anti-colonial resistance was based in kinship organizations and on the reformed Sunni Islamic ideology of the Sanusi brotherhood. The resistance movements formed the first republic in the region, the Tripolitanian Republic (1918–1920) in Western Libya. The heroic Sanusi resistance in Barqa, led by Umar al-Mukhtar, fought the Fascist armies of Italy until 1931, when al-Mukhtar was captured and executed. The following year the Italian Fascist government managed to conquer the entire country after destroying half the population—at least a half million people (Anderson 1986, 38) including the educated elite—and forcing some 60,000 Libyans into exile in Tunisia, Egypt, Chad, Niger, Palestine, and Turkey. This devastating colonial experience made most Libyans very suspicious of European powers and the West; they assumed that since most European powers did not acknowledge their tragedy, the rest of Europe was Fascist like Italy. Members of the RCC, and particularly Qadhafi, portrayed themselves to the Libyan people as heirs to the anti-colonial resistance of the Tripolitanian Republic and Umar al-Mukhtar.

After the defeat of Italy in World War II, Libyan Independence in 1951 was brought about by victorious Britain and France in alliance with the exiled Sanusi and some Tripolitanian leaders in Egypt. The British wanted to use Libya as a key asset to safeguard Britain's security in the Middle East and to protect its interests from the waves of Arab nationalism by supporting the Sanusiyya in Eastern Libya over the Tripolitanian urban nationalist movement. The exiled leader of the Sanusiyya, Amir Muhammad Idriss al-Sanusi, grandson of the founder of Sanusiyya order, agreed to support British interests in return for political independence. On December 24, 1951, Amir Idriss was crowned King Idriss I of the United Libyan Kingdom, a constitutional federal monarchy with two capitals and three provincial governments in the country's main regions of Tripolitanian, Barqa, and Fezzan. Upper-class urban families and tribal leaders, mainly from Barqa, the home base for King Idriss and the Sanusiyya, dominated the government. The new state was extremely poor, with annual per capita income of $35 (Gunther 1955, 175), and desperately needed revenues for its budget. It rented military base rights to Britain and the United States and also received economic aid as payment. Young Libyan activists, and Qadhafi later on in the late 1960s, criticized the monarchy and the old elite for betraying Libya's long anti-colonial national struggle for independence by giving Western countries military bases.

CONTEXT AND PROCESS OF REVOLUTION

After the discovery and the exportation of oil in 1961, the monarchy initiated modernization programs in education, health, transportation, and housing. A new Libyan university with two campuses in Benghazi and Tripoli provided expanded educational opportunities. New educational policies led to the rise of a salaried middle class, a student movement, a small working class, trade unions, and modern intellectuals by the late 1960s. Yet the Sanusi monarchy and its British advisers could not isolate Libyan society from the currents of radical nationalist movements in the region, especially from Egypt, since most of the first generation of higher education graduates attended Egyptian universities and the monarchy relied mostly on Egyptian teachers in Libyan schools. However, despite the social and economic modernization programs, the monarchy continued the ban on all political parties, initially imposed after the 1953 elections. Bashir al-Si'dawi, the leader of the most popular party, the Tripolitanian Congress Party, was stripped of his Libyan citizenship and forced into exile in Saudi Arabia.

Many young Libyans became involved in the Nasserite or Baathist branches of Arab nationalist politics. The crisis of the monarchy was aggravated because the king was a very socially detached man and lived in Tubruq near the main British military base at al-'Adam, making it appear that he preferred the company and protection of the British. Worsening the situation for the king's regime, corruption was widespread among the elite. Despite the nation's oil revenues, many ordinary Libyans remained poor in rural areas. The monarchy became the victim of its own modernization programs when it did not also modernize the government by providing political participation to its growing middle class. Many young educated but marginalized middle- and lower-middle-class Libyans found themselves outside the political patronage of the old tribal leaders and the influential notable families. The military faction of this emerging middle class was the most organized of all the anti-monarchy groups and, in the absence of political parties, the only force able to effectively challenge the old elite.

The social base of the Libyan Free Unionist Officers' Movement's Revolutionary Command Council (RCC) was mainly the lower middle class created by the monarchy's modernization programs after 1951. Of the twelve members of the RCC, the majority came from poor and minor tribes of the interior, or poor social strata in the coastal towns. Only two members came from majority tribes, the Magharba and the Awagir, and one came from a prominent coastal family. It could be argued that the revolution was led by the lower middle class from the interior and the oases against the dominant tribal leaders and the prominent families of the large towns. The monarchy had relied on the police force for its security rather than the army. The members of the police force were recruited from loyal tribes and were well equipped. In contrast, the small Libyan army was open to non-elite students, from which came many members of the clandestine Free Unionist Officers' Movement and its central committee. On September 1, 1969, the Free Officers' Union, led by Qadhafi, used the Libyan army to overthrow the monarchy. The king was outside the country, and the top police officers were caught by surprise and arrested.

The ideology of the central committee of the Free Officers' Union, which renamed itself the Revolutionary Command Council or RCC, stressed Arab nationalism, Islam, self-determination, social justice, and denounced the corruption of the old regime. The officers were also anti-Communist, which brought them international recognition from the U.S. Nixon administration. The new regime continued the modernization policies of the monarchy. The RCC developed the country's infrastructure on a larger scale, building new hospitals, roads, and schools. Most Libyans began to benefit from the expanded welfare state, thanks to increased oil revenues and the policies of the RCC, and popular support for the regime increased after it successfully negotiated the departure of British and U.S. forces from Libya. Asserting Libyan control over its oil resources, the revolutionary government raised oil prices and achieved state participation in oil production in 1973. This policy differed from that of the old regime, which had left the entire oil sector under the control of multinational corporations.

In 1970, the RCC banned political parties and independent trade unions, as had the monarchy before, and the council adopted the Egyptian one-party system in 1971. This was called the Arab Socialist Union. But this form of government was abandoned two years later because it failed to inspire and mobilize the majority of the Libyan people. Faced with opposition from the traditional elite and the failure of the Arab Socialist Union, Qadhafi declared his own popular revolution against the old bureaucracy in a famous speech in Zuwara on July 15, 1973. He asked the people to replace the ineffective bureaucracy with popular committees of employees in places of work. Qadhafi's innovation led to a division within the RCC over the role and authority of the new popular committees. The split over these issues reflected major ideological differences inside the RCC between two factions over the direction of the revolution. A technocratic group led by Umar al-Muhashi, the minister of planning, argued that priority be given to expertise and professional competence. In contrast, Qadhafi insisted on ideological mobilization and political loyalty. The inability to resolve this internal conflict led to a coup attempt against Qadhafi in 1975 by some members of the RCC led by al-Muhashi. When Abdulsalam Jalud, a key member of the RCC, sided with Qadhafi, the coup failed.

Libyan leader Colonel Mu'ammar Abu-Minyar al-Qadhafi at a news conference in 1984. (Bettmann/Corbis)

Umar al-Muhashi escaped to exile in Tunisia and later Egypt. Qadhafi then consolidated his power. Only a few RCC members remained in power with him, and the RCC was dissolved.

Qadhafi began to apply his ideas, which were presented in his "green book" of political and social theory. He advocated what he called the Third Universal Theory, a third way between capitalism and Marxism based on direct democracy through popular participation in congresses and committees. This involved an effort to undermine other social and political organizations, including independent trade unions, student organizations, and even the army itself. In March 1977, the People's General Congress met in the southern city of Sabha and, proclaiming people's power, renamed the nation The Libyan Arab Popular and Socialist Jamahiriyya. Qadhafi became impatient with opposition within the popular committees and the People's General Congress and called for the formation of a new organization, the Revolutionary Committees (a single organization with local branches or committees), that would instruct and mobilize the popular committees. In reality, the new committees were made of Qadhafi loyalists indoctrinated to protect the security of the regime. Still, most Libyans continued to enjoy the benefits of the welfare state and supported the government during most of the 1970s; however, at this stage an estimated 100,000 of the best-educated Libyans lived outside the country (Vandewalle 1998, 184). In 1988, Qadhafi blamed the Revolutionary Committees for being too zealous and for abusing their power. He released political prisoners and abandoned many of his experiments with collective markets and bartering. This change signified the decline of Jamahiriyya populist experiment. Instead, Libya became an authoritarian national security state.

By the early 1980s, the regime faced a hostile regional and international environment and new challenges. It severed relations with the government of President Sadat in Egypt over that country's agreements with Israel and the United States, and it faced a series of confrontations in the Gulf of Syrte with the Reagan administration, which accused Qadhafi of supporting terrorist groups. Worst of all the challenges was the big Libyan military disaster in the war with Chad in 1981: the Libyan army was defeated and many soldiers captured; many weapons and military bases were lost. The regime became isolated in the Arab world and was targeted for overthrow by the U.S. government. A number of opposition groups were formed in exile. Then in 1986 oil prices drastically declined, significantly reducing Libya's international export earnings. Also in 1986, the United States, mistakenly blaming Libya for a bombing attack on U.S. soldiers in Berlin, launched an air raid on Libya in which a number of people were killed. In 1992, the United States blamed Libyan agents for planting the bomb that destroyed a Pan American airliner in December 1988 over Lockerbie, Scotland, and in response, the United Nations placed new economic sanctions on Libya. In January 2001, one Libyan agent was convicted by a Scottish court for the airliner bombing. Libya agreed to pay reparations to families of the victims, and most sanctions were lifted in 2004.

IMPACTS

Since the September Revolution of 1969 led by the charismatic Colonel Mu'ammar Qadhafi, Libya has played an influential role in African politics. An objective assessment of this topic requires a departure from the Western media's and mainstream scholarship's demonizing view of Qadhafi and portrayal of Libyan policies as the product of an irrational and unpredictable leader. This skewed ideological view reduces Libya's culture, history, and society to its leader and vice versa. Also, such an interpretation of history assumes,

as in the colonial period, that the Sahara is an empty space and a divide between the Maghrib and sub-Saharan Africa, and that Libya's role in the rest of Africa is a temporary aberration.

The alternative approach is to focus on the social forces and historical factors that linked Libya to the Sahara and the Sudan through the local states, the trans-Sahara trade, and the heritage of the Sanusiyya movement deeply rooted in the Sahara and Libya in the nineteenth and early twentieth centuries. Furthermore, Qadhafi's September Revolution manifested strong opposition to colonial regimes and to white minority governments in Africa. Finally, the policies of the revolutionary regime in Tripoli were motivated by personal and national interests, especially in playing balance-of-power politics against its rivals in Egypt, Israel, Tunisia, Sudan, Algeria, and Morocco. The changes in Libyan policies from one stage to another resulted from the shifting power relations in the region and from the confrontations with the United States and France in Africa. These factors also pressured the regime to have alliances or unity agreements with various North African or Saharan states. In short, Libyan behavior toward other African nations has shifted in response to changing domestic, regional, and international conditions and politics.

Between 1969 and the present, Libyan policies in Africa went through three stages: a period from 1969–1980 of defiance against colonialism and Israeli influence, coupled with support for liberation movements; a second period, 1980–1994, characterized by isolation and confrontation with the United States, which led to internal struggle in Libya and the disastrous defeat in Chad, along with American and UN sanctions in 1986 and 1992, respectively. In this period Libyan policies were reactive and supported repressive regimes in Uganda, Liberia, and the Central African Republic.

The third stage of Libyan policy, 1994 to the present, is more realistic and positive. The regime, which received African support during the sanction years, accepted the International Court of Justice's ruling on the Aouzo strip dispute with Chad despite the fact it lost the case in 1994. It also managed to accept responsibility for the Lockerbie crisis. Furthermore, Libya led the effort to revitalize the Organization of African Unity (OAU) and to create the African Union in 2001, mediated many African disputes, and has invested millions in other African states—more than any other country with the exception of South Africa. In short, Libya's mature Pan-African policies today qualify the state to play a constructive and positive role in African conflicts, especially if the new realism and reconciliation with the West result in changes in domestic politics such as enhancing the rule of law, state building, and the empowering of civil society.

The Libyan revolutionary process brought many benefits to ordinary Libyans, such as free medical care, major development of the country's infrastructure, and free education far beyond the achievements of the monarchy, especially for Libyan women. At the same time the Libyan economy is more dependent on oil for its revenues than under the old regime, and agriculture continues to decline despite all the large and expensive projects. In 1990, Libyan agriculture contributed only 2 percent to the national budget (Vandewalle 1998, 77), and most Libyans are still employed in the state service sector. The active civil associations that made Libyan society seem more democratic than many Gulf states in the 1970s were either weakened or eliminated. Despite its diverse consequences, however, the Libyan Revolution is a turning event in the emergence of modern Libya.

PEOPLE AND ORGANIZATIONS

Free Officers' Union Movement (1959–1977)

A clandestine anti-monarchy political organization founded by Mu'ammar al-Qadhafi when he was a student activist in the city of Sabha, the capital of the southern region of Libya, in 1959. Many members of the organization decided to attend the Libyan military academy in Benghazi. Qadhafi headed both the civilian and the military wing of the organization. On September 1, 1969, the Free Officers toppled the Sanusi monarchy in a bloodless coup and declared a republic. The military leaders of the organization that took power called themselves the Revolutionary Command Council, which was headed by Qadhafi and included other officers such as Abdullsalam Jalud, Umar al-Muhashi, Bashir Hawadi, Abubakar Yunis Jabir, Muhammad Najim, Awad Hamza, Ahmad al-Gurwi, Khwaildi al-Hmaidi, Mihammad al-Mugariyaf, Abdal Mi'im al-Huni, and Mustafa al-Kharubi. They became the collective leadership of the country, but after a power struggle some were put under house arrest, stepped down, or fled into exile. Only three of Qadhafi's comrades—Jabir, al-Hmaidi, and al-Kharubi stayed in power.

Jalud, Abdullsalam (?)

Born in the town of Brak of the southern region Fezzan, he met Qadhafi in school in Sabha and has been his close friend since that time. He joined the military academy with Qadhafi and after the 1975 coup was the second man in the Libyan leadership until 1988. He was close to the U.S.S.R. and as prime minister of Libya, engineered most of the arms sales for the country.

al-Muhashi, Umar (?–1981?)

He was the only member of the RCC who came from a prosperous middle-class family in the western Tripolitanian city of Misurata. He became known in the early years of the revolution as a fiery prosecutor in the Peoples Court who tried the officials of the old regime. He became minister of planning and research, and in 1975 clashed with Qadhafi and led a coup attempt that failed. He managed to escape into exile in Egypt, where he led an opposition group. In 1981 his plane was forced to land in Libya, and unconfirmed rumors indicate that he was executed immediately.

al-Mukhtar, Umar (1863–1932)

He was the legendary charismatic leader of the anti-Italian colonial resistance in eastern Libya. He was educated in the Sanusi schools and became a Shayhk of one of the Sanusi religious order's main lodges. In 1902, when France invaded Chad, he defended the Sanusi lodges there, and after the 1911 Italian invasion of Libya, al-Mukhtar emerged as the undisputed leader of the resistance. He was captured and hanged in front of 20,000 people in the town of Slug in 1931. His leadership and uncompromising view made him a legend, not only in Libya but throughout the Muslim world. An American filmmaker, Mustafa Aqqad, made a movie called *Lion of the Desert* about his life, and Anthony Quinn played the role of the aged leader.

al-Qadhafi, Mu'ammar Abu-Minyar (ca. 1942–)

His real birthdate is still unclear, but he has said he was born in 1942 to a poor shepherd family in a Bedouin camp outside the city of Syrt in the central region of Libya. He did not go to school until after studying the Quran, then studied in the southern city of Sabha, in Fezzan. He became a Pan-Arab and Nasserite student activist, which led to his expulsion from the region to the coastal city of Misurata. He led the Free Officers' opposition movement and encouraged its members to attend the military academy to topple the monarchy. He has been the leader of Libya since 1969. He has five sons, Muhammad, Saif al-Islam, al-Sa'di, Hannibal, Khamis, and two daughters, 'Aisha, and an adopted baby girl, Hana, who was killed during the American raids on Tripoli in 1986.

Revolutionary Command Council (RCC) (1969–1977)

The committee of the military officers headed by Qadhafi that ruled the country from 1969 until 1977.

al-Sanusi, Amir Muhammad Idriss (1889–1983)

The grandson of the founder of the Sanusi order, Sayyid Muhammad B. Ali al-Sanusi. He became the fourth leader of the order, and after the Italian Fascists took over power in Rome in 1922 and abrogated all agreements with the Sanusi order, he fled into exile in Egypt. He allied with the British and recruited thousands of Libyans to fight against Italy during World War II. In 1951 he became king. When the revolution took place in 1969, he was outside the country in Greece. He went into exile in Egypt, where he died in 1983.

Sanusiyya Movement (1837–1932)

The Sanusiyya Movement was founded by Sayyid Muhammad B. Ali al-Sanusi, known as the grand Sanusi, an Algerian-born scholar who studied and was educated in Fez, Cairo, and Mecca by his teacher, Ahmad B. Idriss al-Fasi. In 1837 the grand Sanusi founded his first lodge in Hijjaz, and in 1842 he founded his first lodge in Barqa in the eastern region of Libya. The movement became one of the most successful modernist Islamic social movements in North Africa due to its focus on education and trade. It built over one hundred lodges in Libya, Chad, western Egypt, and Tunis.

Tripolitanian Republic (1918–1920)

The Tripolitanian Republic was created in 1918 by the leaders of the Tripolitanian anti-colonial resistance movement in western Libya during the Italian colonial period. A compromise between the leaders led to the acceptance of the collective leadership of the four leaders of the region: Sulayman al-Baruni, Ramadan al-Suwayhli, Abdnabi Belkhair, and Ahmad al-Mariyyid. They formed a parliament, an army, and a police force. They sent letters to President Woodrow Wilson and the other Western leaders asking them for recognition and support. But conflict among the leaders and lack of outside support led to the downfall of this pioneering republic in 1920.

Ali Abdullatif Ahmida

See Also Armed Forces, Revolution, and Counter-Revolution; Colonialism, Anti-Colonialism, and Neo-Colonialism; Documentaries of Revolution; Literature and Modern Revolution; Student and Youth Movement, Activism and Revolution; Terrorism

References and Further Readings
Ahmida, Ali Abdullatif. 1994. *The Making of Modern Libya: State Formation,Colonialization, and Resistance, 1830–1932.* Albany: State University of New York Press.
Anderson, Lisa S. 1986. *The State and Social Transformation in Tunisia and Libya, 1830–1980.* Princeton, NJ: Princeton University Press.
Ansell, M. O., and I. M. Al Arif. 1972. *The Libyan Revolution: A Source Book of Legal and Historical Documents.* Harrow, UK: Oleander Press.
Davis, John. 1987. *Libyan Politics: Tribe and Revolution.* Berkeley: University of California Press.
El Fathaly, Omar, and Monte Palmer. 1980. *Political Development and Social Change in Libya.* Lexington, MA: Lexington Books.
First, Ruth. 1974. *Libya: The Elusive Revolution.* Harmondsworth, England: Penguin.
Gunther, John. 1955. *Inside Africa.* New York: Harper Pros.
Obeidi, Amal. 2001. *Political Culture in Libya.* London: Curzon Press.
Vandewalle, Dirk, ed. 1995. *Qadhafi's Libya, 1969 to 1994.* New York: St. Martin's.
———. 1998.*Libya since Independence.* Ithaca, NY: Cornell University Press.

Literature and Modern Revolution

Throughout the world, writers of creative literature have been influenced by the political and social realities that surround them. Writers have described, justified, and criticized these realities, and they have envisioned ways in which societies might change, both positively and negatively. Literature's role in revolution has never been limited to the descriptive, however. To varying degrees, literature has helped to incite, support, or suppress revolution.

PRE-MODERN LITERATURES OF REVOLUTION

Pre-modern literatures were primarily descriptive. Writers described events they witnessed or heard about, recounted history and legend, and embellished existing tales about deities and heroes. Unlike historians, literary writers rarely seek comprehensive coverage of wars or revolutions. Instead, creative writers provide insights into historical characters and historical moments. At its best, creative literature offers a more complete understanding of certain figures and occurrences. Though Homer's *Iliad* (ca. 850–800 B.C.) describes only a few weeks in the ten-year Trojan War, it presents historical figures as completely three-dimensional humans and provides insights into the motivations of gods. Literary writings offer the reader a chance to experience a given world, to hear important figures discuss concepts and ponder their own motivations.

Because readers tend to identify with at least one character in a fictional work, literatures about political events or ideas offer more than just an understanding of revolution. Readers may be inspired to imitate a character or further his/her goals. This power was realized as early as the sixth century B.C. In *The Republic* (ca. 360 B.C.), Socrates warns of literature's dangers: certain stories, particularly those told with greater poetical skill, might encourage listeners (or readers) to imitate undesirable characters, sympathize with weakness or illegal action, or become too fearful of death to defend a state. Socrates therefore recommended strict censorship of literary works to ensure political stability and moral soundness.

In the most classic sense, the ancient epics and dramas did not support revolution. Heroes did not create their own values; they supported values already established by society, even if the current monarch did not abide by those values. Where rebellion occurred, it was to preserve established values and structures, not to establish a radically new way of life. In *Antigone* (442 B.C.), for example, the title character opposes Creon, the king, in order to uphold a way of life supported by tradition, not to establish a radically new order.

In many ways, the literature and philosophy of the European Renaissance set the foundation for politically revolutionary thought. Unlike the literatures of the Middle Ages and medieval period, which emphasized the divine, Renaissance literature emphasized human accomplishment. Because a belief in human potential is a precondition for any attempt to change political realities, the revival of ancient human-centered texts was an important precondition to forging new political realities in Europe.

Though fictional/philosophical conceptions of radically new political states had been considered by ancient writers, these were not precursors to modern revolution. By contrast, Thomas Moore's *Utopia* (1516) introduced ideas central to modern revolution. *Utopia* is permeated by a strong spirit of democratic republicanism: it argues that the true function of government is to serve the people and promote their well-being. This text also anticipated Socialism by describing a society in which private property was forbidden.

Revolutionary sentiments are also found in Shakespeare's plays. Shakespeare portrayed the nobility as fallible, a radical thought for the time, and argued that individuals must be true to themselves. These sentiments were counterbalanced, however, by his portrayal of the firmness of sociopolitical structures and the high cost of opposing such traditional or legal standards. This can be seen in *Macbeth* (1623*), King Lear* (1608*),* and *Romeo and Juliet* (1597). Spain's Felix Lope de Vega went yet further. His play *Fuenteovejuna* (1613) not only portrayed a fallible nobility but suggested that people were entitled to rebel when the aristocracy went against established law. This is not yet revolutionary literature, however, since Lope de Vega affirmed the rightness of previously established power structures and law.

THE MODERN LITERATURES OF REVOLUTION

Most scholars see the eighteenth century as beginning an age of revolution politically and socially. As the interest in individual potential grew, literary works came to reflect individual perceptions rather than objective accounts or retellings of history or myth. The demand for human-centered literature grew with the development of the middle class. In France, the *philosophes,* or philosopher-writers, questioned political authority more directly, inspiring many later revolutionists. England's John Locke had already argued that humans are born free (*Two Treatises of Government,* 1690), but philosophe Jean-Jacques Rousseau added the rousing "yet we see him everywhere in chains" at the start of his *The Social Contract* (1762: Cranston translation 1968, 49) In his fictional as well as his philosophical works, Rousseau contributed several other ideas essential to later revolutions: the notions that the will of the people must be heard and respected; that the majority is generally right, though sometimes the minority position actually benefits the majority; and that freedom must sometimes be imposed on a population (accustomed to authoritarian control). In part, both the French and American revolutions were inspired by his writings and those of others, such as Francois Voltaire. In Germany, Friedrich Schiller's play *The Conspiracy of Genoa* (1783) criticizes political injustice and supports republicanism. In Italy, the poet Guiseppe Parini satirized the abuses of the nobility.

More powerful revolutionary works were produced in the nineteenth century, an age of literary nationalism. Because nationalist revolution requires not only a sense of nation but pride in that nation, literatures celebrating national identity can have a powerful effect. Whether or not the writer intended nationalism is not important, particularly where a dominating foreign power seeks to suppress nationalist pride. Revolutionary sentiments need not be overt. A work that does little more than argue for the beauty and majesty of a country or people can be revolutionary when political conditions are ripe, particularly where the work is in a national language that has been suppressed by the hegemonic power. Recognizing this, many colonial powers sought to suppress any literary expression of indigenous languages.

The Irish cultural renaissance, which began in the nineteenth century, helped set the stage for the 1916 Easter Rebellion by supporting Irish language and culture. Patrick

Pearse (Padraig Pearse), a leader of the Easter Rising of 1916, was also a poet and storywriter. During the 1919–1921 war of independence that followed, such works as William Butler Yeats's *Caitlin ni Houlihan* (1903*)*, a play in which the title character represents Mother Ireland, were essential to motivating revolutionary participation. Today, the Irish Republican Army continues to support Irish language and literature as a means of fostering revolutionary sentiment.

In most of Eastern Europe, writers have also been important to revolutions. Much of Russian literature grew from opposition to political or social realities, from the liberal nobility in Pushkin's time to the writers who helped fell the Soviet Union. Biographers of Lenin stress the impact of Nikolai Chernyshevski's novel *What Is To Be Done* (1863) on Lenin and on the development of his revolutionary strategy. Lenin borrowed the title of his major political treatise, *What Is To Be Done* (1902), from the novel. After the October Revolution, when literature was required to support the new order, many writers continued the tradition of protest, openly when possible, covertly or in exile when not. Trotsky believed that artists who are created by the revolution would necessarily write about the revolution, and he was correct. With good reason, Soviet authorities took writers seriously. Writers known for their political writings include Vladimir Maiakovsky, Osip Mandelstam, and Alexandr Solzehitzyn.

Later in the century, literary writers contributed to the fall of the Soviet Union, though the frequency and effect of political literature varied with the political situation. Receptivity to revolutionary literature tends to be low where an otherwise unpopular regime has effected substantive economic or other improvements, and to a lesser extent, where neighboring governments are even more repressive. In 1988–1989 Eastern Europe, political revolutionary writings were particularly well received in the Ukraine and Poland, somewhat less so in Hungary and Czechoslovakia, much less so in Yugoslavia, far less so in Romania and Bulgaria, extremely less so in Albania. One writer who was particularly effective was the playwright Vaclav Havel, who was later elected president of Czechoslovakia.

In the Spanish Civil War, literature and literary figures were very involved in the revolution against the old economic and social systems. This conflict inspired literary writers throughout the world to participate. Most writers opposed General Franco, including Stephen Spender, W. H. Auden, John Cornford, and C. Day Lewis. Federico García-Lorca's poetry and politics so incensed Franco's government that he was murdered. Others, however, supported Franco, including Hilaire Beloc and Roy Campbell. Yet others were motivated to describe the revolution, including George Orwell, who held that every line he wrote after that time was written against totalitarianism and for democratic Socialism.

Nikolai Chernyshevski, Russian radical activist who wrote the classic revolutionary novel *What Is to Be Done?* (Mary Evans Picture Library/The Image Works)

In some ways, post-colonial Latin American revolutions were sparked by a poem: Jose Hernandez's *Martín Fierro* (published in two parts, 1872 and 1879). This nineteenth-century gaucho epic poem was widely read and recited, first in Hernandez's native Argentina, then throughout the continent. It was the first work to glorify a common Latin American, the gaucho (an Argentinian cowboy), and to criticize the Europeanization of America.

Throughout the twentieth century, Latin American literary works continued to promote or describe Socialist revolution. In *Canto General* (Verse Song, 1950), an epic verse-history of Latin America, the Chilean poet and politician Pablo Neruda describes the problem of dictators, the need for class struggle, and the evolution of Socialist consciousness. In his play *Pedro y el capitán* (*Pedro and the Captain*, 1979), Mario Benedetti described the horrors of the Uruguayan penal system and the potential for revolutionaries to triumph.

Though most Latin American writers have supported Socialist revolution, not all do. Herberto Padilla and Reinaldo Arenas have written poems that present a scathing indictment of Castro's government. Others have chosen to describe and critique revolutions. Carlos Fuentes's *The Death of Artemio Cruz* (1962) is an example of the latter. This innovative novel offers an exploration of the Mexican Revolution, telling the story from three perspectives. Another such novel is *Rebellion in the Backland* (1902), by Euclides da Cunha, which is both a military history of a rebellion and a critical exploration of Brazilian nationality.

The degree to which politics and literature are intertwined in Spain and Latin America is evidenced by the high number of politicians and revolutionaries who are also writers. Nicaraguan poet Ernesto Cardenal was first a revolutionary, then a minister in the Sandinista government. Ernesto "Che" Guevara, possibly the most famous Latin American revolutionary, was a poet as well as a physician. He was greatly influenced by creative literature, including works by Neruda and García-Lorca. In Peru, Mario Vargas-Llosa was a presidential candidate as well as an innovative novelist; his creative literature represents a wide range of political thought, because the author moved from leftism to rightism.

Political literature also had an important role in much of the Middle East during the twentieth century through the present, in contrast to previous epochs, when most of that area's literature was apolitical. The revolutionary founder of modern Turkey, Ataturk, understood the importance of both separating Turkish identity from Ottoman identity and reaching a wide audience; he replaced Ottoman with the Turkish vernacular. The Turkish populist literary movement, which began in 1911, supported these reforms in the name of nationalism. In the 1908–1923 nationalist revolution against the Ottomans, Turkish poets reached a wide audience.

Among Arabic countries, the word for commitment, *iltizam,* became essential in literary criticism after 1950. In Egypt, the success of the 1952 army revolution and the rise of Nasser inspired Arabic pride that encouraged Arab theater and cultural forms. Most nationalist revolutions in the Middle East were supported by literary writers who have been heavily involved in both social and political revolutions. Exceptions were in countries with low literacy rates, such as Libya, and where non-religious creative writing was devalued.

Within literature, the Palestinian situation has been a central theme for many Arab writers, including those outside Palestine. For Palestinian writers, revolutionary themes are almost essential. In the 1920s–1930s, Ibrahim Tuqan's poetry argued for a Palestinian identity. After the founding of Israel, nationalist Palestinian writings became more strident. The poetry of Mahmoud Darwish has inspired many Palestinians to revolt against the Israeli government. Another poet, Fadwa Tuqan, raged not only against Israel but against the sexism within her society; she observed the frustration of politically committed Palestinian women who are unable to participate at the same level as Palestinian men. Understanding that cultural pride is essential to national pride, the Palestinian Liberation Organization supports many cultural institutions and programs, including literary production.

In Vietnam, too, literature has been important to revolutionists. Ho Chi Minh was a poet as well as a political figure. In part, he was motivated to lead the rebellion to free Vietnam (then Indochina) by reading literary works, including Shakespeare, Tolstoy, and Zola. Whereas Ho's father expressed nationalism by refusing to learn French, Ho learned the French language and was inspired by some of France's greatest writers.

In other parts of the economic Third World, a history of devaluing national, ethnic, or other cultural traditions has worked powerfully against literature's revolutionary function. Many colonial powers have used this knowledge to great effect. Thus, nobelist Wole Soyinka notes that the traditional African artist was the conscience of his society, and that the cultural domination of Africa by France, Portugal, and England minimized writers' efforts by marginalizing their expression. Use of a new language and literary forms led almost necessarily to imitation of colonial models and to the loss of the authenticity that gave indigenous art so much power. For this reason, the Kenyan novelist Ngugi wa Thiong'o argues that African literatures must be written in African languages. Other writers, such as Chinua Achebe, disagree, seeing the use of English as inevitable as well as important in reaching the world outside Africa, thus making the international community more aware of the struggle. In his novel *Things Fall Apart* (1958), Achebe communicates pride in Ibo traditions to his own community at the same time he shows the international community the high price that colonialism has exacted.

FACTORS AFFECTING LITERATURE'S ROLE IN REVOLUTION

The ability of literature to incite or suppress political revolution differs widely throughout the world. Certain preconditions or precipitants are essential for any revolution to transpire; otherwise the most eloquent revolutionary messages will be ineffective. In essence, there must be cause and constituency. There must be a perception that wrongness has been done to some self-recognized group, and there must be a discrediting or degeneration of an established order or elite. Where popular sentiment upholds the established powers, where a reform movement offers hope, where an unpopular regime has effected substantive economic or other improvements, or, to a lesser extent, where the governments of neighboring countries are perceived as more repressive, revolutionary literature has less effect.

There must also be a collective identity, as defined by culture, ethnicity, language, religion, and/or history. In colonial or neo-colonial situations, this identity must differ from that of the dominating foreign power. Where writers are respected by the society at large, they wield considerable power, particularly in societies in which literature is recognized as a valid (if not necessarily traditional) means of conveying historical, sociological, and/or political truths. Where artistic production is seen as less valuable—as elitist, decadent, unmasculine, or simply unimportant—writings have little effect. Thus in Algeria, literary production virtually ceased from 1954 to 1962 during the anti-colonial revolution, while many of those Algerians who continued to write expressed guilt at writing poetry while their nation suffered. In such situations, literature may still affect the revolutionary elites, but it will not have a substantive effect on motivating the rank and file.

In advanced technological societies, occupational specialization normally separates literature from other forms of production. Where writers in such countries involve themselves in revolution, their involvement tends to be essayistic rather than literary (novels or poetry), or they concentrate on social or political reform rather than actual revolution. Excepted here are writers who involve themselves in the causes of less industrialized countries. It is difficult to generalize about industrialized societies, however, since they usually tend to be more stable and less ripe for revolution than other types of societies.

EFFECTS OF REVOLUTION ON LITERATURE

In most of the world, revolutionary struggle has increased the importance of creative literature. People are more likely to read serious literature and to attend the theater during times of revolution. Sometimes this is a reaction against censorship. After political revolutionary periods pass, not only interest in political literature passes; interest in literature in general diminishes. In Eastern Europe, fewer people now attend plays or read serious novels, whereas before the 1989 revolution's success, even Shakespearean productions drew strong audiences.

Where strict censorship policies exist but can be circumvented, writing is strongly empowered. The same is true where strict censorship policies are relaxed, however briefly. When censorship was relaxed in Hungary in the 1950s, the production of revolutionary literature increased dramatically. Illegal presses can reach a large number of people. The

Polish Solidarity movement's paper had a wide circulation, and underground presses published literary and other works.

Not all censorship is so direct or simple as banning potentially problematic works, of course. Censorship varies greatly in focus and intensity, and indirect censorship (such as mandating certain styles or rewarding writers who conform) can be more difficult to circumvent. Whereas nineteenth-century dictators simply banned certain books and writers, later censors were often more thorough. The architects of Socialist realism in Stalin's Soviet Union not only required the presentation of Socialist ideals; they also mandated the content and style of literary works. Such censorship is rarely sustained effectively. Where censorship is strong and effective, however, and where no tradition of subverting censorship exists, literary writings have very little effect, as in Qadhafi's Libya. At the other extreme, where freedoms of the press exist, as in most liberal democracies, revolutionary writings also have little effect. Literature with revolutionary themes is most effective in societies characterized by inconsistent or mid-range censorship.

Fascist regimes proved especially talented at disempowering or dismotivating revolutionary literature by purporting to support literary culture. By nature a perversion of nationalism, Fascism appropriates the most powerful nationalist themes. Where a government supports some national literary culture, such as that with a folkloric basis, dissident writers face powerful opposition: government-supported cultural expression popular with the masses. Revolution also affects literature's styles and forms. Changes are not always conscious; instability motivates a return to traditional styles and forms, whereas stability encourages innovation.

Literature and revolution, then, have a symbiotic relationship. Each affects the other. Literature can offer powerful descriptions of political, social, and military events. When conditions are right, it can also be a powerful motivator or suppressor of political revolution.

Theresa M. Mackey

See Also Chilean Socialist Revolution, Counter-Revolution, and the Restoration of Democracy; Documentaries of Revolution; East European Revolutions of 1989; Egyptian Revolution of 1952; French Revolution; Irish Revolution; Italian Fascist Revolution; Kenyan Mau Mau Rebellion; Libyan Revolution; Literature and Modern Revolutions; Mexican Revolution; Nicaraguan Revolution; Palestinian Movement; Polish Solidarity Movement; Russian Revolution of 1917; Spanish American Revolutions of Independence; Spanish Revolution and Counter-Revolution; Turkish Revolutions of 1908 and 1919–1923; Vietnamese Revolution

References and Further Readings
Harlow, Barbara. 1987. *Resistance Literature.* New York: Methuen.
Hauser, Arnold. 1985. *The Social History of Art.* Vol. IV. New York: Vintage Books.
Hernandez, Jose. 1996. *Martín Fíerro.* Madrid: Alianza Editorial, S.A.

Lenin, Vladimir I. 1902 (1961). "What Is To Be Done." Pp. 347–530 in *Lenin Collected Works.* Vol. 5. Moscow: Foreign Language Publishing House.

Mackey, Theresa. 1996. "Literature and Revolution in the Mediterranean World." Pp. 41–52 in *Mediterranean Perspectives: Literature, Social Studies and Philosophy,* edited by James E. Caraway. New York: Dowling College Press.

———. 1997. "Giving a Damn: An Interdisciplinary Reconsideration of English Writers' Involvement in the Spanish Civil War," *Clio* 27 (1): 89–108.

Nagorski, Andrew. 1993. *The Birth of Freedom: Shaping Lives and Societies in the New Eastern Europe.* New York: Simon and Schuster.

Parkhurst, Priscilla. 1987. *The Making of a Culture.* Berkeley: University of California Press.

Rousseau, Jean-Jacques. 1968 (1762). *The Social Contract.* Translated by Martin William Cranston. New York: Penguin.

Ruhle, Jurgen. 1969. *A Critical Study of the Writer and Communism in the Twentieth Century.* Translated and edited by Jean Steinberg. London: Frederick A. Praeger.

Trotsky, Leon. 1992. *Art and Revolution: Writings in Literature, Politics, and Culture.* Edited by Paul N. Siegel. New York: Pathfinder Press.

Wilkinson, James D., 1981. *The Intellectual Resistance in Europe.* Cambridge, MA: Harvard University Press.

M

Malayan Rebellion

CHRONOLOGY

1826   British East India Company consolidates Penang, Malacca, and Singapore as the Straits Settlements.

1850s–1890s   European demand for Straits tin and rubber leads the British to encourage extensive immigration of labor from southern China and southern India.

1867   Straits Settlements pass to Colonial Office control.

1896   Federated Malay States of Perak, Selangor, Negri Sembilan, and Pahang formed.

1909–1914   The four northern Malay States of Kedah, Perlis, Kelantan, and Trengganu pass into British control from Siam. Control of southernmost state of Johore established later. These are called the Unfederated Malay States.

1930   The Communist Party of Malaya (CPM) is inaugurated.

1930s   Chinese and Indian immigrant population in Malaya becomes more settled, and the CPM gradually increases influence among Malayan Chinese, especially after Japanese invasion of China in 1937.

1941–1945   Japanese invasion and occupation of Malaya. CPM forms Malayan People's Anti-Japanese Army (MPAJA) and wages guerrilla war in Malayan jungle; forges strategic partnership with British guerrillas. CPM builds close ties with rural Chinese in this period.

1945–1946   British Military Administration reoccupies the country after Japanese surrender; fails to deal with social and economic dislocation of post-war Malaya; hands over power to the controversial Malayan Union Government in April 1946. United Malays National Organization (UMNO) formed in protest against Malayan Union.

1946–1948   CPM conducts "open and legal" struggle in post-war Malaya, seeking to dominate social organizations, labor unions, and left-leaning political parties. Chin Peng becomes CPM secretary-general in 1947. Federation of Malaya government replaces moribund Malayan Union in February 1948. Henry Gurney appointed high commissioner. Kuala Lumpur begins crackdown on CPM activists; CPM launches armed struggle, and the Emergency is declared in June 1948. Communist movements take up call to arms elsewhere in Southeast Asia.

1949   CPM officially designates its guerrilla forces the Malayan Races Liberation Army (MRLA). Dato Tan Cheng Lock sets up the Malayan Chinese Association. Police and military treatment of the rural Chinese alienates many, compelling some to join the CPM fold. Gurney's amnesty for MRLA guerrillas is inaugurated. It proves ultimately ineffective.

1950   Lieutenant General Harold Briggs arrives in March to become the first director of emergency operations. He announces the "Briggs Plan," the aim of which is to snap the organic links between the MRLA and its rural Chinese base of support along the Malayan jungle fringe. Large-scale resettlement of Chinese into Resettlement Areas begins.

1951   MRLA activity is at its peak. Gurney is assassinated in October, and Briggs resigns at the end of the year. CPM releases its so-called October Directives toward the end of the year, admitting errors in the insurgency campaign, and calls for less reliance on violence and more on political education, especially of the rural Chinese masses. Tunku Abdul Rahman becomes president of UMNO.

1952   Lieutenant General Sir Gerald Templer arrives in Malaya as both high commissioner and director of emergency operations. He energizes the implementation of the Briggs Plan, especially resettlement. The Resettlement Areas are renamed "New Villages." The UMNO-MCA (Malayan Chinese Association) electoral alliance is successful in the Kuala Lumpur municipal elections.

1953–1954   The MRLA is gradually put under increasing military pressure. Focused Security Force operations employing food control procedures, aimed at starving the guerrillas into submission, begin to have an effect. Many guerrillas withdraw from the war, leaving a harder core behind in the jungle. Templer continues to call for a "propaganda-minded" approach by the government at all levels in dealings with ordinary Malayans. Templer hands over to Donald MacGillivray in June 1954.

1955   Tunku-led Alliance Party wins the July federal elections. Tunku becomes chief minister and preparations for *Merdeka* (independence) from Britain accelerate. The Indochina cease-fire suggests that the southward expansion of international Communism has been checked, and this has an impact on MRLA morale. Tunku announces an amnesty for MRLA guerrillas in September 1955. Chin Peng seeks peace talks with Tunku that fail at Baling, Kedah, in December. Good Citizens' Committees (GCCs) spring up and are extended throughout Malaya, demonstrating that ordinary Chinese are gradually lining up behind Kuala Lumpur against the Communists.

1956–1957   Centralized cooking of rice is introduced in 1956, and the pressure on starving MRLA guerrillas is greatly increased. The CPM-government political endgame to decide the terms under which MRLA guerrillas exit the jungle intensifies. Malaya achieves independence on August 31, 1957, and Tunku, now prime minister, declares the *Merdeka* Amnesty, the most liberal on record.

1958–1960   MRLA mass surrenders occur. Tunku extends the *Merdeka* Amnesty till July 1958. The CPM is forced to demobilize by the end of 1958. Because of the vastly improved internal security situation, Tunku formally declares the end of the Malayan Emergency on July 31, 1960.

INTRODUCTION

The Malayan Rebellion, more commonly known as the Malayan Emergency, lasted from June 1948 to July 1960. In an era of almost continuous Communist successes in so-called national liberation wars in the Far East, Malaya stood out as the one counter-insurgency contest in which the Free World stood its ground and outlasted Communist totalitarianism. The success of the British and later independent Malayan governments in defeating the insurgency of the Chinese-dominated Communist Party of Malaya (CPM) proved to have strategic longer-term consequences. At a time, up to the 1980s, of Communist expansion in mainland Southeast Asia, independent Malaya (later Malaysia), along with its partners in the staunchly anti-Communist Association of Southeast Asian Nations (ASEAN), played a role in ensuring that the Free World held the line in the heart of maritime Southeast Asia.

BACKGROUND: CULTURE AND HISTORY

Modern Malaya assumed special significance in the eyes of British imperial strategists. The British East India Company, eager to defend the eastern flank of colonial India on the one hand and the security of the China trade route on the other, understood that control of the Strait of Malacca, the slender waterway running between the western coast of peninsular Malaya and eastern Java, was essential. By 1826, therefore, the company had formally established the Straits Settlements of Penang, Singapore, and Malacca, three Malayan ports that facilitated trade as well as naval control of the Malacca Strait. From 1867, the Colonial Office assumed direct administrative control of the Settlements. Subsequently, recognizing the economic potential of the Malayan interior, the British gradually expanded their control inward from the Straits Settlements. Starting in 1874, the Malay States of Perak, Selangor, Negri Sembilan, and Pahang came under British influence. In these states, Malay rulers agreed to permit British "residents" to assume administrative powers over all matters except those pertaining to Malay customs and Islam, a religion that had arrived in the Malay archipelago several centuries earlier. In 1896, the administration of these Federated Malay States was unified under a high commissioner who was concurrently governor of the Straits Settlements. British expansion continued apace. By 1914 the four northern states of Kedah, Perlis, Trengganu, and Kelantan had been secured from Siam, and finally, in 1914, the southernmost state of Johore was added. These five states were known collectively as the Unfederated Malay States, and they accepted British "advisers."

British political, administrative, and economic consolidation generated significant demographic change. The indigenous Malays and ethnically similar migrants from the surrounding archipelago who assimilated with them tended to reside in villages located near coasts and river estuaries, and they much preferred farming and fishing at leisure to being supervised wage workers in the mushrooming tin and rubber industries. To plug the ensuing labor gap, the British stepped up Chinese and Indian immigration into Malaya. Madrasi Tamil immigration from south India proceeded more or less in tandem with the expansion of the Malayan rubber industry. By 1931 the Indian

population, only 30,000 in 1870, had reached 625,000. Malaya was to become the leading producer of natural rubber in the world by the late 1930s.

Far more important to the Emergency in Malaya, however, was Chinese immigration. The earliest Chinese immigrants had been from Fukien in southern China who settled in Malacca in the 1500s. Many of them intermarried with the Malays, producing the progeny that became known as the Straits Chinese, or *Babas*. Subsequently, from the 1850s, increased European and British demand for Straits tin led to a massive increase in Chinese coolie immigration into tin-rich states such as Perak, Selangor, and Negri Sembilan. The demographic impact was dramatic. By the end of the Japanese Occupation, while the Malays formed 44 percent of the population of approximately 5 million, the Chinese formed a hugely significant 38.5 percent (Ramakrishna 2002, 4–7).

CONTEXT AND PROCESS OF REVOLUTION

Especially crucial in the context of the Emergency were the rural Chinese tappers, miners, and agriculturalists. In the inter-war years, during times of food shortages and economic slumps, the government in Kuala Lumpur established food production reserves and issued Temporary Occupation Licenses (TOLs) to the rural Chinese to encourage them to grow food and cash crops. Although the tin and rubber industries, once recovered from the effects of the worldwide depression that had forced layoffs, re-employed these Chinese, and the government withdrew the TOLs, many Chinese continued cash cropping, as they found it more stable and profitable than working on estates or mines. Hence, by the time the Japanese army invaded Malaya in December 1941, 150,000 rural Chinese were squatting illegally in rural areas. That number had doubled by the end of the Japanese Occupation in September 1945. Three factors contributed to this increase: Japanese persecution of Chinese in the urban areas; urban food shortages; and, finally, the Japanese policy, similar to that of the inter-war government, of seeking to alleviate food shortages by resettling urban Chinese in the rural hinterland. Furthermore, immediately after the war, because wages in the rubber and tin industries were insufficient to support families, many Chinese, even if working on estates and mines, continued to squat illegally and engage in food cultivation to supplement their incomes. It was these rural, squatter Chinese who ultimately constituted the chief source of material, money, and manpower for the CPM during the Emergency.

The British sought consciously to preserve a "Malaya for the Malays," building up a Malay elite capable of assisting them in administering and maintaining the Malay identity of the country. Racial divisions were exacerbated further during the Japanese Occupation. While Malay rulers, civil servants, and ordinary people collaborated with the Japanese, 40,000 Chinese perished as part of the notorious *sook ching* campaign mounted by the Japanese army. It was during the occupation that the CPM developed into a major political and military force in Malaya. Formed in 1925 by mainland Chinese Communists, the clandestine CPM was revamped on Moscow's instructions in 1930 so as to establish more multiracial credentials. Throughout the 1930s, however, repeated disruptions of its communications with the Soviet Communists, internal power plays, and police repression took their toll. Nevertheless, following the Japanese invasion of China in July 1937, the CPM succeeded in mobilizing Malayan Chinese in decrying Japanese aggression. During the occupation, the CPM—assuming battle-dress as the Malayan People's Anti-Japanese Army (MPAJA)—built very close ties with the squatter Chinese. As those Chinese generally bore the brunt of Japanese brutality, they welcomed the MPAJA's attempts to strike back in their behalf and joined MPAJA fighting and support units in droves. So significant did the MPAJA become that by 1943 the British were supplying the organization with instructors and arms. By the end of the war, the MPAJA boasted 7,000 to 8,000 men under arms, with thousands more in support cells. Significantly, before the return of British forces, the MPAJA emerged from the jungle to dispense summary justice to collaborators with the Japanese. This resulted in large-scale Sino-Malay clashes in Johore. These and later clashes greatly ingrained the perception that the CPM remained very much a militant chauvinistic Chinese party—an image that sharply undermined the party's multiracial appeals during the Emergency. The Japanese Occupation had another far-reaching effect: on September 1, 1942, senior CPM leaders were ambushed by Japanese forces, thanks to the treachery of the CPM secretary-general at the time, Lai Tek. This paved the way for the rapid promotion of relatively young and inexperienced, more militant leaders, such as Chin Peng, who became secretary-general in 1947, after Lai Tek had run away with party funds.

The end of the occupation saw British moves to effect a fundamental transformation in the political landscape of Malaya. Wartime British planners had recognized that change was overdue for several reasons: first, the politically disparate Straits Settlements and Malay States were unwieldy administratively. It was felt that a unitary Malayan state was desirable if the country's natural resources were to be efficiently marshaled to assist in Britain's economic rehabilitation after the war. Second, a common citizenship embracing not only Malays but also the immigrants, especially the Chinese, was seen as necessary to reward the latter for helping defend British interests in Malaya during the war. Moreover,

such a scheme needed direct British sovereignty over Malaya—bypassing the traditional royal Malay rulers—in order to succeed. Finally, direct rule of Malaya, leading to the imposition of a uniform political framework on the country, as well as common citizenship for all Malayan races, was regarded as a necessary prerequisite to the long-term goal of self-government, an outcome calculated to appease Britain's American ally.

Accordingly, the Malayan Union was promulgated on April 1, 1946, unifying the Settlements of Malacca and Penang (but not Singapore) and all nine Malay states under a governor representing the British king, and depriving the traditional Malay rulers of their sovereignty. In response, Malay opposition coalesced around Dato Onn bin Jaafar, the *Mentri Besar* (chief minister) of Johore; the United Malays National Organization (UMNO) was formed in May 1946 to protest against the union. The British, caught flat-footed, balked and, after several months of negotiations and despite opposition from the educated non-Malays, agreed to replace the union on February 1, 1948, with the Federation Agreement. That represented a closer balance between elite Malay ideals of sovereignty of the rulers and state autonomy on the one hand, and British concerns for strong central government and common citizenship on the other.

Post-war Malaya was also racked by serious social and economic unrest. The British Military Administration (BMA), which administered the country from September 1945 to March 1946, as well as the civil administration, which took over from April, were utterly unable to meet basic needs. Rice was in short supply and prohibitively expensive. The cost of living in November 1945 was estimated to be a few hundred percent higher than in pre-war days, and yet basic wages were still paid according to pre-war scales. Little wonder that labor unrest broke out in urban areas in the peninsula from the very month that the BMA was set up. Meanwhile the CPM, which had demobilized the MPAJA in December 1945, but in the new politically liberal climate was no longer proscribed, fully exploited the situation. From about March 1946 until June 1948, the CPM focused its energies at three levels: first, it intensified its labor agitation through its cadres in the unions, a strategy so successful that by March 1947, the CPM-dominated Pan-Malayan Federation of Trade Unions (PMFTU) had branches in every industry in Malaya. Second, the Communists set up front organizations to penetrate all sectors of the public. Finally, the CPM participated in the Malayan political arena by infiltrating the left-leaning Malayan Democratic Union (MDU), as well as the pro-Indonesia Malay Nationalist Party.

Nevertheless, despite its success in extending its influence through its "open and legal struggle," in mid-June 1948 the CPM switched strategy: its members left the urban areas of Malaya, reactivated the wartime rural support organization among the squatters, and, from the recesses of the Malayan jungle, launched an insurrection against the government. The origins of this revolt have been controversial. One perspective posits that international factors were crucial in determining the timing of the Malayan uprising. Proponents of this view argue that in September 1947 in Poland, the Soviet leader Andrei Zhdanov formally declared that wartime cooperation was at an end and that the world was divided into two irreconcilably opposed camps, imperialism and anti-imperialism. The Zhdanov line was repeated in February–March 1948 in Calcutta, at the Second Congress of the Communist Party of India and the Southeast Asian Youth Conference. According to this argument, therefore, it was no coincidence that revolts broke out in Malaya, Indonesia, and Burma in 1948. Another argument suggests that the change of CPM tack came about because of factors internal to Malaya. Those included the assumption of the party secretary-generalship by the capable but relatively inexperienced Chin Peng, who was more militant than his predecessor, the traitorous Lai Tek; the restlessness of CPM members who had been unhappy with the earlier decision to demobilize the MPAJA; the erosion of the party's ability to influence the masses because of the recovering economy; and the failure of the CPM to secure power through constitutional means. A further view holds that labor unrest on estates between 1946 and 1948 prompted a growing pattern of government repression of labor, culminating in the designation of the PMFTU as illegal at the end of May 1948. Taken aback by the rapidity and ferocity of government action, the CPM was forced to the jungle prematurely, as a defensive reaction to government measures (ibid., 10). In his recent memoirs, Chin Peng gives the impression that the decision to wage an armed revolt was the result of the CPM's interpretation of both internal Malayan circumstances and the direction of the international Communist movement (Chin Peng 2003, 203–206).

The government's counter-insurgency campaign against the CPM, which referred to its armed units, from February 1, 1949, as the Malayan Races Liberation Army (MRLA), more or less proceeded in three phases (Ramakrishna 2003, 161–179). The first stage, roughly between the declaration of the Emergency in June 1948 and December 1951, could be characterized as a period of strategic stalemate. During this time MRLA activity was at its peak. Throughout 1950 and 1951 the Communists, numbering at this point about 8,000 guerrillas, perpetrated 10,400 incidents, many of which were calculatedly brutal. The Communists belatedly realized, however, the counterproductive nature of their ill-considered campaign of intimidation and terror (Hack 1999, 143). This led to the promulgation of the October 1951 directives calling for less reliance on terror and more political education in winning over the rural Chinese masses. The CPM, however, was not alone in making mistakes. Because most

MRLA guerrillas were Chinese, the security forces tended to regard ordinary Chinese villagers as "hostile." Hence the latter were often treated roughly, regardless of innocence or guilt. This anti-Chinese mentality was reflected in the application of harsh Emergency measures that fell largely on the rural Chinese. These included individual and mass detentions, deportations, communal fines, and curfews on entire Chinese villages. By February of 1951, 2,800 Chinese had been deported to China; by the end of that year, of the 25,641 Malayans detained more than twenty-eight days under the Emergency regulations, 22,667 were Chinese (Ramakrishna 1999, 247). English-educated Malayan Chinese community leaders, such as Tan Cheng Lock, president of the Malayan Chinese Association (MCA), implored the government not to alienate the rural Chinese through indiscriminate and counterproductive application of such harsh measures.

The slow and painful second phase of the counter-insurgency campaign, that of improving government-rural Chinese relations, began in earnest only with the arrival in February 1952 of the new high commissioner and concurrently director of emergency operations, Lieutenant General Sir Gerald Templer. Templer quickly grasped the complex situation in Malaya and understood the importance of winning over the rural Chinese in particular. Under Templer, therefore, the security forces and other government officials in daily contact with the population—and in particular the rural Chinese—were ordered to be "propaganda-minded." In other words, all in government, regardless of position or function, had to ensure that they treated ordinary Malayans with dignity and respect. Templer's call was critically necessary to compensate for the gross errors committed by the agents of government between June 1948 and the end of 1951.

Templer saw to it that "propaganda-minded" adjustments were made to the government's policies as well. In 1953, Templer did away with harsh Emergency measures such as mass detention and deportation, as well as collective punishment. In September 1953, moreover, the first "White Area"—in which all irksome Emergency restrictions were removed and the public could live normally once more—was inaugurated in Malacca, to considerable public acclaim. Finally, Templer also greatly sped up the resettlement of the rural Chinese into better-defended and -equipped New Villages, an important policy that had been started by his predecessor as director of operations, Lieutenant General Harold Briggs.

Templer's determination, to project through words and deeds that the government in Kuala Lumpur was a "friend" of the ordinary people, was maintained by first High Commissioner Donald MacGillivray and later Prime Minister Tunku Abdul Rahman. Thus the figures for detentions and deportations continued to drop drastically. In addition, in mid 1956, the stringent rice rationing that had been introduced by Briggs in June 1951 in order to stem the flow of surplus rice to MRLA guerrillas was modified by the introduction of centralized cooking of rice. Cooked rice—in contrast to the uncooked variety—was bulky, spoiled quickly, and could not be readily smuggled out by Communist supporters. Thus while the already-starving MRLA guerrillas were rendered even worse off, the public could now eat as much cooked rice as they wanted to, instead of being limited to the previously austere operational rice ration. Furthermore, the Police Special Branch by mid 1955, thanks to a better information flow from an increasingly appreciative public, was able to perfect the technique of the surgical swoop upon New Villages so as to detain Communist supporters without inconveniencing the mass of innocent villagers.

The cumulative impact of government efforts to improve relations with the rural Chinese gradually bore fruit. After a Special Branch swoop had eliminated the Communist support network in the town of Banting in Selangor, in March 1955 the grateful Banting Chinese formed a Good Citizens' Committee (GCC). The basic task of the GCC was to rally public support behind the government through public rallies and demonstrations. The GCC movement proved very successful, and it was extended throughout Malaya by the end of 1955.

By 1954 the MRLA ranks were filled largely by militarily weaker but psychologically harder-core guerrillas. However, even those men, including ranking cadres, were defecting the following year, citing loss of hope in final victory as the key reason. There were good reasons for this loss of confidence. It was increasingly clear that an independent multiracial Malayan government, formed by the UMNO-led Alliance Party, would soon become a reality, thereby robbing the CPM of a major political justification for its rebellion: to eliminate colonial rule in Malaya. In addition, the unfavorable geopolitical environment, strategic retreat within Malaya itself, and the emergence of the GCC movement in April 1955 clearly suggested to the remaining guerrillas that they were no longer backing the winning horse. The Communist leadership decided, therefore, that if the armed struggle was no longer tenable, the party would emerge from the jungle—but on its own terms, rather than Kuala Lumpur's. Hence, the CPM launched the so-called political offensive in June 1955, offering to lay down arms in return for legal recognition of the party. CPM secretary-general Chin Peng sought to snatch a political/psychological victory from the jaws of military defeat.

It was at this point that the counter-insurgency campaign transitioned into the climactic final phase: the government-CPM endgame for the allegiance of the remaining MRLA guerrillas. Because Tunku Abdul Rahman agreed to meet Chin Peng at Baling in Kedah at the end of 1955, the CPM was able to tell its rank and file to ignore Tunku's September 1955 amnesty, because at Baling the party would be able to secure better exit terms. This maneuver in fact nullified the effect of the amnesty. At Baling, moreover, Chin Peng rejected the amnesty outright and demanded that in return for a cease-fire there should be legal "recognition of the M.C.P., no detention, no investigation and no restriction of movement" of surrendered enemy personnel (SEP). Tunku disagreed, insisting on the CPM's dissolution, and the talks broke down.

The years 1956 and 1957 witnessed the intensification of the tussle between the CPM and the government for MRLA hearts and minds. Finally, following the independence of Malaya on August 31, the *Merdeka* Amnesty was inaugurated on September 3, intended to last until the end of the year. It promised nonprosecution for all SEP, regardless of what they had done under Communist direction and every opportunity for regaining their place in society if they were sincere in professing loyalty to Malaya. It was the *Merdeka* Amnesty that proved to be the proverbial straw that broke the camel's back: after it was announced, the surrender rate between October and December of 1957 shot up to about forty a month, five times more than the monthly average for that year. Chin Peng wrote to Tunku on October 12, suggesting a second round of peace talks to obtain "a just and fair agreement to end the war." Tunku replied on November 8, agreeing to a preparatory meeting and asking for more details. It was obvious by early December, however, that Chin Peng, as he had done two years earlier, had suggested fresh peace talks in order to ensure his weary rank and file that he would be able to get better exit terms than those of the *Merdeka* Amnesty. When Tunku realized that Chin Peng was once again stonewalling, he dismissed any possibility of peace talks and extended the *Merdeka* Amnesty by another four months.

By early 1958, the remaining guerrillas recognized that the liberal *Merdeka* terms were going to be the only ones on offer. That year the remaining CPM strongholds in the last "black" states of Johore and Perak crumbled completely, in Special Branch operations. Some 118 guerrillas gave up in south Perak between October 1957 and July 1958, while in Johore, the CPM Southern Bureau collapsed, producing 160 SEP. These mass surrenders were utterly disastrous to the CPM, which by the end of 1958 had only 868 guerrillas left, with 485 on Thai territory (ibid., 252–262). By the end of the year, in Chin Peng's own words, the MRLA was "hard up" and "finished" (Ramakrishna 2002, 202). The CPM felt compelled to introduce the demobilization policy, permitting MRLA men to give up party membership and leave the jungle with severance pay (Chin 1995, 50–51).

IMPACTS

By the time Tunku formally declared the Emergency over, on July 31, 1960, almost 2,000 Security Force personnel had been

Chin Peng, leader of the Malay guerrilla group MPAJA, in Baling for peace talks, December 1955. (Bettmann/Corbis)

killed; 3,000 civilians had been killed or abducted; and the tin and rubber industries had suffered losses running into millions of dollars. In addition, almost 6,000 CPM guerrillas had been killed, 1,173 had been captured, and 1,752 had surrendered (Asprey 1994, 573).

The Emergency also had lasting effects on the political and constitutional development of Malaya. The counter-insurgency campaign accelerated progress toward Malayan independence, which was eventually attained on August 31, 1957. The resettlement of hundreds of thousands of rural Chinese into New Villages helped bring this strategic community within the mainstream body politic. At a regional level, the successful Malayan counter-insurgency campaign ensured that the country became an anti-Communist bastion in maritime Southeast Asia and provided a tonic effect on anti-Communist forces within the region at a time when Com-

munism appeared to sweep all before it on the mainland in the 1970s and 1980s.

Finally, the Malayan Emergency threw up the so-called hearts-and-minds counter-insurgency model (Thompson 1966; Clutterbuck 1967). The British Army later applied elements of the model during Malaysia's so-called Confrontation with the left-leaning Sukarno regime in Indonesia and elsewhere. A major controversy ensued over the applicability of the hearts-and-minds model to the U.S. war in South Vietnam (Thompson 1969). In the current war against radical Islamist terror, the negative impact on the moderate Muslim world of an over-militarized counter-terrorism approach, exemplified by the unpopular U.S. invasions of Afghanistan and Iraq, have prompted some analysts to call on Washington to employ softer, "indirect" approaches derived from the Malayan Emergency to win

Muslim hearts and minds worldwide. That, it is argued, would help deprive globally active radical Islamist terror networks like al-Qaeda of material and moral support (Desker and Ramakrishna 2002, 173–174).

PEOPLE AND ORGANIZATIONS

Abdul Rahman Putra al Haj, Tunku (1903–1990)

A British-educated lawyer of royal Malay stock from Kedah, Tunku became president of UMNO in August 1951 and subsequently leader of the multiracial Alliance Party. He became Malaya's first chief minister in August 1955, following the victory of the Alliance Party in the first federal elections a month earlier. Tunku became prime minister when Malaya achieved independence, on August 31, 1957.

Alliance Party

The British made it clear that a precondition for the transfer of power to Malaya was the establishment of a popular, multiracial political party capable of running the country. That prompted Tunku Abdul Rahman and Dato Tan Cheng Lock, the leaders of the two most important communal political parties in Malaya, UMNO and the MCA, respectively, to cooperate in local elections. This eventually resulted in the formalization of the UMNO-MCA Alliance in March 1953. The smaller Malayan Indian Congress joined in 1954, and the Alliance went on to triumph at the first federal polls, in July 1955.

Briggs, Lieutenant General Harold Rawdon (1894–1952)

An experienced senior officer, Briggs was appointed the first director of emergency operations in Malaya in March 1950. He served in that capacity until the end of 1951. During his tenure in Malaya, Briggs devised the so-called Briggs Plan, the heart of which called for massive resettlement of half a million rural Chinese from the exposed jungle fringe to better defended and equipped Resettlement Areas (later renamed New Villages).

Chin Peng (Born 1924)

Nom de guerre for Ong Boon Hwa, a Malayan Chinese born in Sitiawan in Perak, who rose to prominence during the Japanese Occupation of Malaya as a guerrilla leader of the MPAJA. He became secretary-general of the CPM in 1947, leading the party through the Emergency, and negotiated with Tunku Abdul Rahman at the abortive December 1955 Baling Talks.

Communist Party of Malaya (CPM)

Sometimes also referred to as the Malayan Communist Party (MCP), the CPM was set up originally by mainland Chinese Communists in 1925. It was revamped under Moscow's direction in 1930 in order to project a more multiracial image. Throughout the Emergency, however, the CPM never succeeded in divesting itself of its image as a party dominated by Chinese chauvinists. The CPM was unsuccessful in its quest to win power in Malaya by force of arms and was forced to demobilize by the end of the 1950s. The CPM in fact relaunched its armed struggle in 1969, but it suffered from serious internal fissures and remained unsuccessful. It finally abandoned the armed struggle officially in 1989.

Good Citizens' Committees

The first GCC was set up in the town of Banting, Selangor, in March 1955, after a successful Special Branch operation had wiped out Communist influences there. The basic task of the GCC was to rally public support behind the government through mass rallies and demonstrations. The GCC movement proved very successful, and it was extended throughout Malaya by the end of 1955.

Gurney, Henry Lovell Goldsworthy (1898–1951)

An experienced colonial administrator, Gurney was appointed high commissioner in Malaya in 1948. He felt that a major solution to the Communist insurrection required political reforms increasing the stake of the Malayan Chinese in the country. He was thus instrumental in setting up the Malayan Chinese Association in February 1949, hoping that the MCA would be a political counterweight to the CPM. He was assassinated in October 1951.

Lai Tek

This mysterious Vietnamese became secretary-general of the CPM in April 1938. He was in fact an agent for the British and during the occupation was responsible for the September 1, 1942, massacre of senior CPM leaders at Batu Caves, near Kuala Lumpur, by Japanese forces. This incident had far-reaching effects on the CPM, resulting in the rapid promotion of relatively inexperienced Communist leaders, such as future secretary-general Chin Peng.

MacGillivray, Sir Donald Charles (1906–1966)

MacGillivray took over as high commissioner when Templer left in June 1954. He oversaw with great competence Malaya's transition to independence in August 1957.

Malayan Chinese Association (MCA)

The MCA was formed by wealthy English-educated Malayan Chinese businessmen in February 1949. Most rural Chinese during the Emergency tended to see the MCA as a "rich man's party" not attuned to the real needs of the ordinary Chinese squatter, miner, or tapper. Nevertheless, the MCA appealed to the politically active English-educated Chinese business and professional class, and that political base enabled it to formalize the successful multiracial Alliance Party with UMNO in March 1953.

Onn bin Jaafar, Dato (1895–1962)

Onn was an English-educated state government official and later *Mentri Besar* (chief minister) of Johore who formed UMNO in 1946 in protest against the British-imposed Malayan Union.

Special Branch

The Special Branch of the Federation of Malaya Police played a strategic role in the counter-insurgency campaign against the CPM. It was originally a part of the Criminal Investigation Division (CID), but when Templer arrived, he reorganized the intelligence setup in the government. Apart from centralizing all intelligence assets under the Federal Intelligence Committee under a director of intelligence, Templer also split Special Branch from CID. Henceforth, while CID dealt with ordinary crime, Special Branch focused on Emergency intelligence collection.

Tan Cheng Lock, Dato

A wealthy, English-educated Malayan Chinese businessman who set up the MCA in February 1949, Tan later worked closely with Tunku Abdul Rahman of UMNO to form the pro-British, anti-Communist, multiracial Alliance Party, which went on to secure victory in the July 1955 federal elections. Those elections paved the way for *Merdeka* (independence) in August 1957.

Templer, Lieutenant General Sir Gerald Walter Robert (1898–1979)

Templer was appointed both high commissioner and director of emergency operations in Malaya in February 1952. He contributed a great deal to energizing all aspects of the successful counter-insurgency campaign.

United Malays National Organization (UMNO)

UMNO was formed in May 1946 by the charismatic Johore *Mentri Besar* (chief minister) Dato Onn bin Jaafar to agitate against the creation of the unitary Malayan Union. UMNO successfully derailed the Malayan Union scheme in favor of the less controversial federation arrangement that came into effect on February 1, 1948. UMNO acted then, as now, as the main vehicle for the articulation of Malay rights and privileges. In the context of the Emergency, no political scheme for the transfer of power from the British Crown to Malaya would have been possible without UMNO playing the central role in any post-colonial ruling coalition of multiracial parties.

Kumar Ramakrishna

See Also Chinese Revolution; Colonialism, Anti-Colonialism, and Neo-Colonialism; Documentaries of Revolution; Guerrilla Warfare and Revolution

References and Further Readings

Asprey, Robert B. 1994. *War in the Shadows.* Rev. ed. London: Little, Brown.

Chin, Aloysius. 1995. *The Communist Party of Malaya: The Inside Story.* Kuala Lumpur: Vinpress.

Chin Peng, as told to Ian Ward and Norma Miraflor. 2003. *My Side of History.* Singapore: Media Masters.

Clutterbuck, Richard. 1967. *The Long, Long War: The Emergency in Malaya 1948–1960.* London: Cassell.

Desker, Barry, and Kumar Ramakrishna. 2002. "Forging an Indirect Strategy in Southeast Asia," *Washington Quarterly* 25 (2): 161–176.

Hack, Karl A. 1999. "British Intelligence and Counter-Insurgency in the Era of Decolonisation: The Example of Malaya," *Intelligence and National Security* 14 (2): 124–155.

Ramakrishna, Kumar. 1999. "Content, Credibility and Context: Propaganda, Government Surrender Policy and the Malayan Communist Terrorist Mass Surrenders of 1958," *Intelligence and National Security* 14 (4): 242–266.

———. 2001. "'Transmogrifying' Malaya: The Impact of Sir Gerald Templer (1952–1954)," *Journal of Southeast Asian Studies* 32 (1): 79–92.

———. 2002. *Emergency Propaganda: The Winning of Malayan Hearts and Minds 1948–1958.* Richmond, Surrey, UK: Curzon.

———. 2003. "Making Malaya Safe for Decolonization: The Rural Chinese Factor in the Counterinsurgency Campaign." Pp. 161–179 in *Transformation of Southeast Asia: International Perspectives on Decolonization,* edited by Marc Frey, Ronald Pruessen, and Tan Tai Yong. Armonk, NY: M. E. Sharpe.

Short, Anthony. 2000. *In Search of Mountain Rats: The Communist Insurrection in Malaya 1948–60.* Singapore: Cultured Lotus.

Stockwell, A. J. 1993. "'A Widespread and Long-concocted Plot to Overthrow the Government in Malaya'? The Origins of the Malayan Emergency," *Journal of Imperial and Commonwealth History* 21 (3): 66–88.

Stubbs, Richard. 1989. *Hearts and Minds in Guerrilla Warfare: The Malayan Emergency 1948–1960.* Singapore: Oxford University Press.

Thompson, Robert. 1966. *Defeating Communist Insurgency: Experiences from Malaya and Vietnam.* London: Chatto and Windus.

———. 1969. *No Exit from Vietnam.* London: Chatto and Windus.

Mexican Revolution

CHRONOLOGY

1810–1821	Independence wars.
1821	Mexico achieves independence from Spain.
1846–1848	U.S.-Mexican War.
1854–1855	Revolution of Ayutla ushers in period of liberal rule (1855–1876) known as La Reforma.
1856	Lerdo Law requires all civil and ecclesiastical corporations, including the Catholic Church, Indian villages, and municipalities, to divide and privatize most of their property.
1857	Liberal constitution is passed, providing for a democratic and federal republic and civil and political liberties, and reducing the powers and prerogatives of the Catholic Church.
1858–1861	War of the Reform (or Three Years War).
1862–1867	French Intervention and installation of Austrian archduke Maximilian as Mexican emperor.
1867–1876	Period of liberal rule after the defeat of the imperial armies, known as the Restored Republic.
1872	General Porfirio Díaz, liberal hero of the French Intervention, attempts to overthrow President Benito Juárez in the failed Rebellion of La Noria.
1876	Díaz successfully overthrows President Sebastián Lerdo de Tejada in the Rebellion of Tuxtepec and assumes office as president.
1876–1911	Period known as the Porfiriato, during which Porfirio Díaz held the presidency for all but four years (1880–1884).
1906	Mexican Liberal Party (PLM) founded as a source of radical opposition to Díaz regime. Federal army opens fire on striking workers at U.S.-owned Cananea copper mine, killing dozens.
1907	Federal army kills between 100 and 200 striking workers and their family members at French-owned Rio Blanco textile mills.
1908	Díaz suggests to U.S. journalist James Creelman that he will not seek re-election in 1910, setting off political struggle over the presidential succession. Díaz did run for an eighth term.
1910	After campaigning against Díaz for the presidency, Francisco Madero is briefly imprisoned and then placed under house arrest in the city of San Luis Potosí. After the re-election of Díaz is announced, Madero leaves Mexico for the United States and issues the Plan of San Luis Potosí, calling on all Mexicans to rise up in armed rebellion against Díaz on November 20.
1910–1911	From November through May, armed movements spread across northern and central Mexico, under the leadership of Pascual Orozco of Chihuahua and Emiliano Zapata of Morelos, forcing Díaz out of office and into exile.
1911	From May through November, interim presidency of Porfirian minister Francisco León de

la Barra. Madero calls for the demobilization of the revolutionary armies. General Victoriano Huerta sent to Morelos in largely unsuccessful attempt to demobilize Zapatistas.

1911   In November, Madero assumes presidency with José María Pino Suárez as his vice president. Zapata issues the Plan of Ayala, denouncing Madero and calling for the redistribution of land to peasant villagers.

In December, General Bernardo Reyes, a Porfirian general, rebels against Madero in Coahuila, followed by Emilio Vásquez Gómez, a former prominent Maderista.

1912   In March, Pascual Orozco, former Maderista general, rebels against Madero in Chihuahua.

In October, Félix Díaz, nephew of Porfirio Díaz, leads federal garrison in Veracruz in rebellion against Madero.

1913   In February, Victoriano Huerta and Félix Díaz conspire to overthrow Madero's government, aided and abetted by U.S. ambassador Henry Lane Wilson, during the period known as the Decena Trágica (Ten Tragic Days). Madero and Pino Suárez are arrested and assassinated, and Huerta assumes presidency.

1913–1914   Venustiano Carranza of Coahuila issues the Plan of Guadalupe in March 1913, denouncing Huerta's government as unconstitutional, and declaring himself the first chief of the Constitutionalist Army. Alvaro Obregón and Pancho Villa lead the northern armies against Huerta, aided by the Zapatistas of central Mexico. U.S. troops occupy the port city of Veracruz in April 1914.

1914–1915   After the ouster of Huerta in the summer of 1914, Villa's faction of the Constitutionalist Army joins forces with Zapata, while Obregón and his troops remain loyal to Carranza. Civil war breaks out between the Villistas and Zapatistas, on the one side, and the Carrancistas on the other.

1915   Carranza issues the first revolutionary agrarian reform law in an effort to draw popular

support away from Villa and Zapata. He also forms an alliance with the Casa del Obrero Mundial and deploys 5,000 urban workers in Red Brigades against the rural Villistas and Zapatistas. Obregón secures a military victory in Carranza's behalf, and Carranza assumes provisional presidency.

1916–1917   Villa crosses the border and attacks Columbus, New Mexico. U.S. government responds by sending punitive expedition of John J. Pershing into Mexico with 10,000 troops.

1917   Promulgation of 1917 Constitution, which provides for extensive economic, social, and political rights, and attacks the powers and prerogatives of the Catholic Church. Carranza is elected president.

1919   Agents of Carranza assassinate Zapata in Morelos.

1920   In the Plan of Agua Prieta, Sonorans Alvaro Obregón, Adolfo de la Huerta, and Plutarco Elías Calles rebel against Carranza's efforts to install a successor. Carranza is assassinated, de la Huerta serves briefly as interim president, and Obregón wins presidential elections.

1920–1924   Presidency of Alvaro Obregón, who carries out educational and land reforms. The Mexican government begins to sponsor the great muralists Diego Rivera, José Clemente Orozco, and David Siqueiros.

1923   Assassination of Pancho Villa.

1923–1924   Unsuccessful rebellion of de la Huerta against Obregón and Calles.

1924–1928   Presidency of Plutarco Elías Calles, most notable for government's implementation of anti-clerical provisions of 1917 Constitution. The church hierarchy orders all Mexican churches closed in response.

1926–1929   *Cristiada*, or *Cristero*, Rebellion, during which tens of thousands of Mexicans, primarily country people in the center-west, rebel against the government's anti-clericalism. In 1929 the church agrees to reopen church buildings, and rebellion comes to an end.

1928   Obregón is elected to second term as president but is assassinated before assuming office.

1928–1934   Period known as the "Maximato," during which Calles, as "Jefe Máximo," rules behind the scenes during the presidencies of Emilio Portes Gil (1928–1930), Pascual Ortiz Rubio (1930–1932), and Abelardo Rodríguez (1932–1934).

1929   Calles founds National Revolutionary Party (PNR).

1934–1940   Presidency of Lázaro Cárdenas. Cárdenas carries out massive redistribution of land, nationalizes foreign petroleum companies, and reorganizes the PNR to include confederations of workers and peasants. The party is renamed the Mexican Revolutionary Party (PRM) in 1938.

1939   Foundation of the National Action Party (PAN) by opponents of the revolutionary government.

1940   Manuel Avila Camacho, a moderate, is handpicked by Cárdenas as his successor in presidency.

1946   The PRM is renamed Institutional Revolutionary Party (PRI).

INTRODUCTION

The Mexican Revolution was the first of the major social revolutions of the twentieth century. While the great majority of participants were poor working people from the countryside, the revolutionary armies included Mexicans from all social classes, ethnic groups, and regions, motivated by quite varied grievances and aspirations. The military phase of the revolution lasted from 1910 until 1920, and it was followed by two decades of reconstruction, revolutionary state formation, and, in the 1930s, radical reform.

BACKGROUND: CULTURE AND HISTORY

Throughout the summer of 1910, Mexicans prepared for an elaborate month-long celebration of the centennial anniversary of the wars of independence in September. President Porfirio Díaz was elected to his eighth term in office, having already served for a thirty-year period characterized by unprecedented political stability and economic prosperity. Díaz had faced, for the first time, a formidable challenge from an opposition candidate, Francisco Madero, but Madero's arrest and the usual electoral fraud produced an overwhelming victory for the eighty-year-old president. Few observers could have predicted that Díaz would be swept from office the following May by tens of thousands of armed Mexicans who responded to Madero's call for "effective suffrage and no reelection." How did such an apparently stable and long-standing regime fall so quickly?

For decades after achieving independence from Spain in 1821, Mexico suffered from chronic political instability, economic stagnation, civil wars, and foreign interventions. In the absence of a central state capable of exercising sovereign political authority throughout the territory of Mexico, regional military strongmen, or caudillos, seized and lost power through military coups. Between 1821 and 1855, Mexicans witnessed fifty-five different presidencies, each lasting an average of less than one year, thirty-five of them held by military men. The most notable of the nineteenth-century caudillos, General Antonio López de Santa Anna, seized the presidency himself on nine different occasions.

Throughout this period, liberals and conservatives—the two main political factions in nineteenth-century Mexico, as elsewhere in Latin America—struggled to establish a central state capable of providing for political stability and economic development. The crux of the difference between the two groups was whether the state would be secular, limited in its powers, and federal in organization, as the liberals would have it, or centralized, powerful, and closely linked to the Catholic Church, as advocated by the conservatives. The liberals gained ascendancy in the Revolution of Ayutla (1854–1855), after ousting Santa Anna from the presidency for the final time, in the wake of Mexico's disastrous loss of half of its national territory to its northern neighbor in the U.S.-Mexican War (1846–1848).

Beginning in 1855, the liberal government issued a series of far-reaching reforms designed to spark economic growth, radically curtail the power and activities of the Catholic Church, and foster a common national identity rooted in liberal citizenship. The most notable of these reforms was the 1856 Lerdo Law, which mandated that almost all of the property owned by civil and ecclesiastical corporations—including the Catholic Church, Indian villages, and municipalities—be privatized through sales to occupants and tenants. The church's extensive properties were ultimately nationalized and sold off in the context of the civil war generated by the liberal reforms. The privatization of municipal and village lands was a much longer, contested, and incomplete process. Liberals intended this property to remain in the hands of its mainly peasant cultivators, but in many regions and villages, wealthier residents and outsiders were able to acquire municipal and village lands through various types of sales, procedural irregularities, and frauds, giving rise to one of the central grievances that would later fuel the revolution.

The promulgation of the liberal Constitution of 1857 set off a civil war between liberals and conservatives known as the War of the Reform (1858–1861). Just as the liberals, under the leadership of President Benito Juárez, defeated their conservative opponents, they faced the French Intervention (1862–1867) and the installation of Austrian archduke Ferdinand Maximilian as emperor of Mexico by Napoléon III. With the defeat and ouster of the imperial armies and the execution of Maximilian in 1867, leading liberal leaders then began to fight among themselves. Porfirio Díaz, a popular liberal general and hero in the war against the French, attempted to oust the increasingly autocratic Juárez from the presidency in the failed Rebellion of La Noria in 1872. Four years later, he successfully unseated Juárez's successor, President Sebastián Lerdo de Tejada, in the 1876 Rebellion of Tuxtepec, and assumed the presidency himself, ushering in a period of unprecedented political stability and economic development.

The period from 1876 to 1911 is known as the Porfiriato in Mexico. Apart from a four-year period (1880–1884), Porfirio Díaz held the presidency throughout. The famed "political peace" of the Porfiriato (*pax porfiriana*) was achieved and maintained through a combination of coercion and patronage politics. The national police force (*rurales*), established by Juárez but greatly expanded by Díaz as a counterweight to the federal army, was charged with maintaining order in the countryside through the suppression of both banditry and unruly peasants. Well aware of the dangers posed to his own rule by a large and politicized military, Díaz quickly brought the federal army under his control, through a sweeping reorganization of the command structure and significant reductions in the numbers of both soldiers and officers. While this much smaller army was well trained and supplied during the Porfiriato, it proved incapable of defeating the revolutionary armies of 1910–1913 (Buffington and French 2000, 409–410).

The Porfiriato was a period of both constitutional and authoritarian rule. Díaz simply had the 1857 Constitution amended by a compliant legislature whenever it suited his purposes to do so. Elections were held regularly for all levels of government, but in reality it was Díaz who appointed governors, members of the national legislature, and judges. Governors, meanwhile, controlled the state legislatures and appointed the all-important *jefes políticos,* local political bosses charged with implementing laws and maintaining order at the district and municipal level. Díaz thus ruled through complex patron-client networks held together by patronage, pragmatism, and personal loyalties. As Buffington and French (ibid., 412) put it: "Díaz's remarkable ability to manipulate the traditional social relations of patronage, clientage, and even god-parentage was the keystone in the arch of order." This order could not be maintained indefinitely, however. Toward the end of the Porfiriato, Díaz became much less adroit in his handling of these personalistic networks, imposing unpopular, abusive, and corrupt authorities on an increasingly resentful population. Furthermore, these networks were exclusionary, leaving large numbers of provincial elites and a growing rural and urban middle class with no means of competing for political power and few channels for expressing their grievances and demands.

Political stability, together with a massive influx of foreign capital, made possible a remarkable period of rapid economic growth in Mexico. Foreign companies, attracted by the very generous concessions offered to them by the Díaz government, invested heavily in railroads, mines, and textile mills. Mexican investors, meanwhile, took advantage of Porfirian land laws, and the liberal Lerdo Law of 1856, to acquire vast new holdings, often at the expense of peasant villagers. On their new properties, they expanded production of agricultural export crops such as cotton, sugar, henequen, coffee, and beef. Both foreign and Mexican companies invested in the development of new industries producing for domestic and international markets, including textiles, shoes, cement, and glass. The Porfirian economic boom brought great prosperity to many Mexicans (and foreigners), but it left the majority of the population—working country people—in precarious straits, landless or land poor, increasingly reliant on insecure wage labor, and unable to provide for their own subsistence in the face of declining food production and rising prices for basic goods. Furthermore, the model of export-oriented development adopted by the Díaz government rendered Mexico quite vulnerable to the vicissitudes of the international economy, as became readily apparent after 1907: an economic downturn in the United States, corn and cotton crop failures in northern Mexico, falling international silver prices, and a reduction in the U.S. import quota for Mexican sugar all contributed to a deep economic crisis (Hart 2000, 436).

This economic crisis contributed to a political crisis, which in turn generated a revolution. Political opposition to

Díaz had been growing for some time on the part of provincial landowners and middle-class groups that were excluded from political power and that resented the intrusions of the Porfirian state into local and regional affairs. One of the more radical sources of opposition was the Mexican Liberal Party (PLM), founded by Ricardo Flores Magón in 1906 and home to numerous anarchists and socialists as well as anti-Díaz liberals. The PLM called for armed resistance to the Díaz government and encouraged labor militancy; PLM-backed strikes in the Cananea copper mines and Rio Blanco textile mills in 1906 and 1907 resulted in the deaths of hundreds of workers, shot by the federal army. However, it was the (initially) far more moderate anti-re-electionist movement of Francisco Madero, a wealthy landowner and industrialist from the northern state of Coahuila, that would spearhead the first phase of the Mexican Revolution.

Running against Díaz in the presidential elections of 1910, Madero drew widespread support from Mexicans across social classes and regions. Recognizing the threat posed by his opponent, Díaz had Madero arrested in the summer of 1910 on the charge that he was fomenting rebellion; subsequently, he declared himself to be the overwhelming winner of blatantly fraudulent elections. In response, Madero fled to the United States, where he issued the Plan of San Luis Potosí, declaring the recent elections void, designating himself as interim president, making a passing reference to the need for social reforms, and calling on all Mexicans to rise up in arms against the government on November 20, 1910. A little more than five months later, Díaz was ousted from the office he had held for more than thirty years by the tens of thousands of Mexicans, mainly poor and mainly rural, who responded to Madero's call to revolution. Upon leaving for exile in Paris, Díaz was reported to have said: "Francisco Madero has unleashed a tiger; now let's see if he can tame it." As would soon be apparent, Madero could not.

CONTEXT AND PROCESS OF REVOLUTION

Most of the Mexicans who responded to Madero's call to revolution came from two quite distinct regions of the country: Chihuahua and its neighboring states in the north, and Morelos and its neighboring states in central Mexico. Northern Mexico was the region most dramatically affected by the rapid expansion of mining, cattle ranching, and export agriculture during the boom years of the Porfiriato. Its residents also suffered greatly from the economic crises that began in 1907. The revolutionary armies of the north were particularly heterogeneous in terms of social class and, to a lesser extent, ethnicity, including provincial landowners such as Madero himself, miners, ranch hands, small and medium-size farmers, peasant villagers, hacienda workers, artisans, merchants, dispossessed Yaqui Indians, and a relatively small number of urban workers, most notably from the textile sector. The grievances of these revolutionaries were equally varied, including rising unemployment and food prices, the usurpation of municipal and village lands, the preferential treatment granted by Díaz to foreign investors, the imposition of corrupt and abusive local authorities, and the monopolization of state-level political power by Díaz's allies and cronies. Throughout the course of the military phase of the revolution (1910–1920), the northern armies were most important in military terms, under the leadership of such men as Pascual Orozco, Francisco (Pancho) Villa, and future president, Alvaro Obregón.

Morelos, in contrast, produced an almost purely peasant revolution, its participants and leaders being drawn from the many Indian villages that had lost their communal landholdings to expanding sugar plantations and other commercial estates producing for export. Under the leadership of Emiliano Zapata (and called Zapatistas), these peasants fought an unrelenting war for *Tierra y Libertad* (Land and Liberty)—meaning the restoration of village lands and local self-government. Centered in Morelos during the Maderista phase of the revolution (1910–1911), the Zapatista movement later spread throughout much of central Mexico. Although the Zapatistas were ultimately defeated, revolutionary state builders would find it necessary to meet at least some of their demands in order to bring about an enduring social peace.

In the north, the Maderista revolution was led by Pascual Orozco, an enterprising muleteer with long-standing grievances against the reigning Terrazas-Creel family, which, in the latter years of the Porfiriato, used its monopoly on state-level political power in Chihuahua to create an economic empire that included millions of acres of the state's best farmland, mines, banks, breweries, textile factories, and flour mills. After a few early and easy victories against the federal army in late 1910, Orozco's forces expanded rapidly, as other revolutionary leaders, including Pancho Villa, placed themselves and their recruits under his command. The Zapatista peasants of Morelos rose up in the spring of 1911, forcing the federal army to fight on two fronts and rendering it incapable of meeting the growing military challenge posed by Orozco in the north. After Orozco achieved the decisive defeat of the federal garrison in Ciudad Juárez in May 1911, Madero reached a peace agreement with representatives of Díaz, providing for the resignation and exile of the old president, an interim presidency under Porfirian minister Francisco de la Barra, and new presidential elections. Madero won those elections and assumed office in November 1911, but he immediately faced armed opposition from the very same armies that ousted Díaz in his name.

Mexican revolutionary Emiliano Zapata fought the injustice of wealthy landowners who gained territory at the expense of the nation's peasant class during the late nineteenth and early twentieth centuries. (Library of Congress)

Even before he assumed the presidency, Madero was far more concerned with the restoration of social order than he was with the implementation of radical reforms. In what might have been his most disastrous move, he ordered the revolutionary armies to demobilize and disarm after Díaz was ousted, recognizing the Porfirian federal army as the only legitimate armed force in the country. Madero then proceeded to exclude important revolutionary leaders from power, and, with little understanding of the grievances and aspirations of his poor, rural supporters, adopted a very slow and legalistic approach to reform. Just weeks after Madero took office, Zapata issued the Plan of Ayala, denouncing the president and calling for the immediate restoration of village lands dispossessed during the nineteenth century, as well as the expropriation and redistribution of one-third of Mexico's large estates. Zapata's rebellion quickly spread throughout the neighboring states of Guerrero, Tlaxcala, Mexico, and

Puebla, as thousands of other villagers mobilized under the banner of Zapatismo and in support of the Plan of Ayala. Soon the Zapatistas began to confiscate landed estates and divide them up among themselves and their families, disrupt telegraph and railroad service, seize small towns, and hold Madero's federal army at bay.

Shortly thereafter Madero faced two smaller rebellions in the north, one led by General Bernardo Reyes, the popular Porfirian governor of Coahuila, and the other by Emilio Vásquez Gómez, previously a prominent Maderista supporter. These were quickly suppressed, but then Pascual Orozco initiated a more serious rebellion in March 1912, condemning the Madero government as corrupt and ineffective and calling for a wide range of labor rights, agrarian reforms, and the nationalization of the railroads. The president relied on Victoriano Huerta, a Porfirian general known for his skill at counter-insurgency, to defeat Orozco and his followers. Shortly after Orozco's defeat, Félix Díaz, nephew of Porfirio, led the federal garrison in Veracruz in rebellion against Madero.

None of these rebellions were strong enough to topple Madero, and all but the Zapatistas were defeated. But they did weaken his government and made it more vulnerable to being overthrown by a military coup in February 1913, orchestrated by General Huerta and Félix Díaz, acting with the complicity of the U.S. ambassador Henry Lane Wilson. Huerta had Madero and his vice president, José María Pino Suárez, arrested, and a few days later they were assassinated, presumably by the general's agents. Huerta then assumed the presidency himself, unleashing a second and much longer—and more devastating—round of warfare (LaFrance 1990).

Venustiano Carranza, the Maderista governor of Coahuila, issued the Plan of Guadalupe in March 1913, denouncing Huerta's government, calling for the re-establishment of the constitutional order, and designating himself as first chief of the Constitutional Army and future provisional president. Carranza was joined by Alvaro Obregón and Pancho Villa, the former commanding 18,000 soldiers from Sonora and the latter 20,000 from Chihuahua. In their battle against Huerta, the northerners were aided by the Zapatistas of central Mexico, who shared a common enemy but never incorporated themselves formally into the ranks of the Constitutionalist movement or recognized the leadership of Carranza. Huerta, forced to fight on two fronts with an army augmented by reluctant and untrained forced recruits, and deprived of revenues by the U.S. occupation of Veracruz and its customhouse, was ousted in the summer of 1914, allowing the Constitutionalists and Zapatistas to seize control of Mexico City.

Divisions, however, were already growing in the anti-Huerta ranks. Throughout the war against Huerta, both Villa and Zapata seized large estates, Villa maintaining them intact and using the proceeds to fund the war effort and pay his soldiers, Zapata distributing them to peasant villagers. Carranza, a wealthy landowner himself, opposed such measures and had very little interest in social reforms generally. In October 1914, representatives of the different anti-Huerta factions met in the Convention of Aguascalientes in an effort to promote reconciliation; instead, Villa and Zapata broke with Carranza and designated Eulalio Gutiérrez as provisional president. Carranza ordered his delegates to leave the convention, and he established a parallel government in Veracruz, leading to a second round of civil war, this one pitting the forces of Zapata and Villa against the Constitutionalists loyal to Carranza (and henceforth referred to as Carrancistas), under the command of Obregón. Concerned about the radicalism of the Villistas and the Zapatistas, the U.S. government decided to support the Carrancistas; prior to the withdrawal of U.S. ships from the port of Veracruz in November 1913, a huge stockpile of arms was unloaded and left for Carranza's army (Hart 2000, 453).

Obregón convinced Carranza that some support for social reform was necessary to draw popular support away from Villa and Zapata; Carranza subsequently issued the first of the revolutionary agrarian reform laws in January 1915, mandating the return of village lands that had been illegally seized since the promulgation of the Lerdo Law in 1856. Carranza also courted the support of urban workers organized in the anarcho-syndicalist Casa del Obrero Mundial (House of the World Worker); some 5,000 workers battled the mainly rural Villistas and Zapatistas in the Red Brigades in exchange for Carranza's promise to support the Casa's labor militancy at the war's end (Gonzales 2002, 147). It was Obregón's army that inflicted the major defeats on Zapata and, especially, Villa, reducing both armies to much smaller guerrilla organizations capable of operating only in their home states of Morelos and Chihuahua by the summer of 1915. Fighting would continue throughout the decade, but the Carrancistas had won the war and set about establishing a government.

Obregón convinced Carranza to convene a constitutional convention in order to legitimize his presidency and create the institutions of a new revolutionary state. Carranza limited participation in the convention to his most loyal followers, but the delegates still produced a far more radical document than he would have liked. The 1917 Constitution was, in fact, one of the most progressive in the world, providing for far-reaching economic, social, and political rights and reforms, and a democratic, federal, and presidential political system. Obregón and Francisco Múgica, future governor of Michoacán and presidential aspirant in 1940, were largely responsible for three of the constitution's most innovative articles: Article 3, which provided for universal, free, and secular education; Article 27, which required the government to redistribute land to peasants who could demonstrate need of it, and declared all subsoil wealth, including petroleum and

industrial and precious metals, to be the property of the nation; and Article 123, which recognized the right of workers to unionize, engage in collective bargaining, and strike, established a minimum wage, an eight-hour day, and a six-day workweek, and mandated that women receive equal pay for equal work. The constitution also contained a number of anti-clerical provisions, reflecting the revolutionaries' belief, which they shared with the liberals of the nineteenth century, that the Catholic Church constituted a major threat to economic and social progress in Mexico.

Carranza accepted the constitution but simply ignored most of its provisions. Rather, he focused much of his attention on suppressing organized labor, most notably his former allies in the Casa del Obrero Mundial, restoring large estates seized by Zapata and Villa to their former owners, and extending the reach of his government into regions of Mexico heretofore largely unaffected by the revolution—most notably in western, southern, and southeastern Mexico. By 1919, the year in which he had Zapata assassinated, Carranza had lost the support of many of his former allies, including three prominent leaders from Sonora: Obregón, Plutarco Elías Calles, and Adolfo de la Huerta. When Carranza attempted to impose his own unknown candidate as president in 1920, the Sonorans ousted and assassinated him in the Rebellion of Agua Prieta.

After the brief interim presidency of de la Huerta, Obregón was elected president. He made peace with a number of local and regional rebel leaders and then initiated a long process of reconstruction, reform, and state formation that would continue under the leadership of Calles (1924–1934) and culminate in the radical presidential administration of Lázaro Cárdenas. Although there were sporadic uprisings and one significant popular rebellion in the 1920s (the *Cristiada* of 1926–1929), the military phase of the Mexican Revolution is considered to have come to a close with Obregón's election in 1920.

IMPACTS

The basic institutions of the post-revolutionary state were thus established between 1920 and 1940, and important aspects of Mexican society were transformed through the partial implementation of the 1917 Constitution—most notably its provisions regarding land redistribution, subsoil wealth, and the Catholic Church.

Some scholars point to continuities between the Porfirian and post-revolutionary states and argue that Mexico did not really experience a genuine revolution. Both states were highly centralized and interventionist, with powerful presidencies and compliant legislatures and courts. Both took an active role in promoting economic development:

the Porfirian state directed foreign investment toward the agricultural and mining sectors; the post-revolutionary state provided generous incentives for Mexican industrialists to produce for domestic markets and engaged in significant economic production itself in key sectors of the economy. (Carlos Salinas, president between 1988 and 1994, radically changed the role of the state in the economy when he adopted economic liberalism.) Like the Porfirian state, the post-revolutionary state was, until quite recently, authoritarian, but it was authoritarian in a different way. The PRI monopolized political power at all levels and in all branches of government until the 1980s; it did not lose the presidency until the 2000 victory of Vicente Fox of the National Action Party (PAN), making it the longest-ruling party of the twentieth century. But since the Cárdenas administration (when it was called the PRM), the PRI has been a very inclusive and pragmatic organization; while it has certainly served to control the demands of workers and peasants, it has also afforded them minimal representation and a fair amount of patronage. Co-optation through inclusion and patronage, rather than repression, has been the norm in dealing with opposition movements in post-revolutionary Mexico.

Mexican presidents since the revolution have wielded great powers, both constitutional and otherwise, but since 1934 they have wielded it for a limited period of time. Every six years the presidency has changed hands (re-election remains prohibited), bringing about wholesale changes in government personnel and thus providing many opportunities for elites who hanker after political power. Civilians have exercised firm control over the military since the 1940s, precluding the pattern of military coups and brutal, large-scale repression so common elsewhere in Latin America.

The most dramatic reforms of the revolutionary period occurred during the presidency of Lázaro Cárdenas. Cárdenas, like Calles before him, implemented the many anti-clerical policies of the 1917 Constitution, drastically reducing the church's role in education and preventing clergy, as individuals and as representatives of the church, from participating in politics. Most Mexicans continue to identify themselves as practicing Catholics, but the church has played only a minor role in Mexican politics since the revolution, in striking contrast to its importance in other Latin American countries.

In 1938, Cárdenas expropriated all foreign oil companies in Mexico, following a two-year dispute between oil workers and their U.S. and British employers, and created a state-owned oil company called Petróleos Mexicanos, or Pemex. The move was wildly popular in Mexico and was applauded throughout Latin America, although it caused considerable tension between Mexico and the United States until the matter of compensation was resolved. Public ownership of oil wealth remains a vital symbol of Mexican nationalism and sovereignty, even as Mexico has opened up some aspects of the petroleum industry to foreign investment and ownership.

Finally, Cárdenas carried out a sweeping redistribution of land that transformed property rights in the Mexican countryside; the political capital accrued through this reform helped to sustain the PRI through the 1980s. Over the course of his six years in office, Cárdenas distributed some 50 million acres of land to 11,000 agrarian reform communities, or *ejidos*. In contrast to his predecessors and successors, Cárdenas expropriated some of the richest and most productive land in the country, including vast cotton estates in the northern region of La Laguna, coffee plantations in Chiapas, and henequen plantations in Yucatán. The National Ejido Credit Bank was created to provide the new peasant beneficiaries (*ejidatarios*) with financing. By the time Cárdenas left office, in 1940, almost half of the cultivated land in Mexico was held by 20,000 *ejidos* with more than 1.6 million peasant members (Benjamin 2000b, 492).

Since 1940, most Mexican presidents have ignored the reformist provisions of the 1917 Constitution (not to mention the democratic ones), but the very existence of the constitution, together with the PRI's adherence to a revolutionary discourse and its glorification of Mexico's revolutionary past, has always served to legitimate claims for redistributive justice and democratization. Repression has been real, but limited; elections have been fraudulent, but held on a regular basis and sometimes genuinely contested. With the emergence of a wide variety of social movements and opposition parties in the 1980s and 1990s (joining the much older PAN), Mexico has gradually undergone a profound, if still partial, process of democratization, even as many of the important redistributive provisions of the constitution have been eliminated.

PEOPLE AND ORGANIZATIONS

In Mexico, political groups and organizations tend to be named after their leaders. Hence the Maderistas (Francisco Madero), Orozquistas (Pascual Orozco), Villistas (Francisco "Pancho" Villa), Zapatistas (Emiliano Zapata), Carrancistas (Venustiano Carranza), Huertistas (Victoriano Huerta), Felicistas (Félix Díaz), Obregonistas (Alvaro Obregón), delahuertistas (Adolfo de la Huerta), Callistas (Plutarco Elías Calles), and Cardenistas (Lázaro Cárdenas).

Calles, Plutarco Elías (1875–1945)

Plutarco Elías Calles led the Constitutionalist troops of northeastern Sonora against Huerta. He broke with Carranza in 1919 over the president's repression of organized workers,

Mexican president Lázaro Cárdenas (seated center) meeting with oil labor leaders in the Tamaulipas State, Mexico, 1938. (Library of Congress)

and participated in the Rebellion of Agua Prieta, through which Carranza was ousted. Calles was elected president for the term 1924–1928, and he remained Mexico's de facto ruler throughout the period from 1928 to 1934, known as the *Maximato*. Calles is best remembered for his extreme anti-clericalism, which sparked a Catholic rebellion (the *Cristiada*) between 1926 and 1929.

more than 50 million acres of land, supported labor militancy, nationalized foreign petroleum companies, and reorganized the ruling party to include organized workers and peasants, renaming it the Mexican Revolutionary Party (PRM). Cárdenas served in a number of government positions after his presidency, including a stint as minister of defense.

Cárdenas, Lázaro (1895–1970)

Lázaro Cárdenas joined the Constitutionalist Army in 1913, fighting under Obregón and Calles. Prior to his election as president in 1934, Cárdenas served as secretary of the interior, secretary of national defense, governor of Michoacán, and president of the PNR. As president, Cárdenas mobilized and even armed workers and peasants, distributed

Carranza, Venustiano (1859–1920)

The Maderista governor of Coahuila, Venustiano Carranza, led the Constitutionalist Army against Huerta. After the split in the anti-Huerta forces at the Convention of Aguascalientes, Carranza's army defeated the rival Villistas and Zapatistas, and Carranza assumed the presidency in 1915, an office he held until his ouster and assassination in 1920.

Casa del Obrero Mundial (House of the World Worker)

Founded in 1912, this anarcho-syndicalist workers' organization with 5,000 workers in the Red Brigades, helped Carranza defeat the rural Villistas and Zapatistas.

de la Huerta, Adolfo (1881–1955)

Adolfo de la Huerta joined forces with the Constitutionalists in opposition to Huerta. Together with Obregón and Calles, he ousted Carranza in the 1920 Rebellion of Agua Prieta and briefly held the interim presidency. With presidential aspirations of his own, de la Huerta broke with Obregón in 1923–1924 over the president's support of Calles as his successor.

Díaz, Félix (1868–1945)

Félix Díaz was best known for being the nephew of Porfirio Díaz. He developed a popular following in his home state of Oaxaca, but his uncle never allowed him to become governor. Díaz led the federal garrison of Veracruz in a rebellion against Madero in October 1912. Imprisoned in Mexico City, he conspired with Huerta and U.S. ambassador Henry Lane Wilson to overthrow Madero's government. Conservative opponents of the Constitutionalists and Carrancistas often called themselves Felicistas, but Díaz never led a coherent counterrevolutionary movement.

Díaz, Porfirio (1830–1915)

Porfirio Díaz was born in the city of Oaxaca. He gained national fame as a liberal general during the French Intervention, particularly after his defeat of the French on May 5, 1862 (Cinco de Mayo), in Puebla. Díaz served seven complete terms as president (1876–1880, 1884–1910) and was elected to an eighth term in 1910, an event that precipitated the Mexican Revolution. During the period known as the Porfiriato (1876–1911), Díaz brought unprecedented political stability and economic development to Mexico. After his defeat by the Maderistas, Díaz left Mexico for exile in Paris on May 31, 1911.

Huerta, Victoriano (1854–1916)

Victoriano Huerta joined the Porfirian army as a youth and was commissioned as an officer in 1877. Madero appointed Huerta to command the federal army against the rebels led by Félix Díaz and Bernardo Reyes in February 1913. Instead, Huerta and Díaz combined forces to overthrow Madero, and Huerta subsequently assumed the presidency. He was ousted by the Constitutionalist and Zapatista armies in 1914.

Madero, Francisco (1873–1913)

The family of Francisco Madero was one of the wealthiest in Coahuila, its holdings including large agricultural estates, cattle ranches, mines, and industrial enterprises. Madero founded the anti-re-electionist movement in 1909 and campaigned against Porfirio Díaz for the presidency in 1910. After Díaz was elected for his eighth term in office, Madero issued the Plan of San Luis Potosí, calling on all Mexicans to rise up in arms to oust Díaz and defend the principles of "effective suffrage and no re-election." Madero's government was weakened by numerous rebellions and overthrown in a military coup orchestrated by Huerta and Félix Díaz.

National Revolutionary Party (PNR, Partido Revolucionario Nacional)

Founded by Calles in 1929, the PNR was intended to consolidate the power of the revolutionary leadership and to provide a means for resolving conflicts over the presidential succession without resorting to armed rebellion. Cárdenas reorganized the party in 1938 to incorporate the Mexican Workers Confederation and the National Peasant Confederation, renaming it the Mexican Revolutionary Party (PRM, Partido Revolucionario Mexicano). The party's name was changed once more in 1946, to the Institutional Revolutionary Party (PRI, Partido Revolucionario Institucional).

Obregón, Alvaro (1880–1928)

A brilliant military commander, Alvaro Obregón of Sonora was largely responsible for the Carrancistas' defeat of the Zapatistas and Villistas, as well as Carranza's assumption of the presidency in 1915. Together with Calles and de la Huerta, Obregón overthrew Carranza in 1920 and was himself elected president later that year, serving until 1924. Obregón was elected to a second term as president in 1928, but he was assassinated before he could take office.

Orozco, Pascual (1882–1915)

Pascual Orozco of Chihuahua led the Maderista armies of the north against Díaz, inflicting the final blow on the Porfiriato through the defeat of the federal garrison of Ciudad Juárez in May 1911. Orozco subsequently rebelled against Madero in March 1912.

Villa, Francisco (Pancho) (ca. 1877–1923)

Born in Durango as Doroteo Arango, Francisco (Pancho) Villa adopted his well-known name when he formed his own bandit gang as a young man. Prior to joining the Maderista revolution, he also worked as a muleteer, butcher, bricklayer, milkman, and railroad foreman. Villa led the Division of the North, part of Carranza's Constitutionalist Army, in the war against Huerta and then broke with Carranza at the Convention of Aguascalientes over the issue of Villa's expropriation of large landed estates. After his defeat by Obregón in 1915, Villa turned to guerrilla warfare; on March 9, 1916, he attacked Columbus, New Mexico, with 480 men. In response, General John J. Pershing led a punitive expedition of 10,000 troops into Mexico. After Carranza's ouster, Villa reached a peace agreement with Obregón, and he and his troops were awarded four haciendas in northern Mexico. Villa was assassinated by unknown assailants in 1923.

Zapata, Emiliano (1879–1919)

Born and raised in the Morelos village of Anencuilco, Emiliano Zapata witnessed the expansion of sugar plantations onto the lands of the villages throughout his youth. A village leader prior to the revolution, Zapata organized a small guerrilla army in March 1911, nominally under the leadership of Madero but primarily concerned—as the Zapatistas always were—with the restoration of village lands and local self-government. After Zapata issued the Plan of Ayala in November 1911, denouncing Madero and calling for both land and liberty (*tierra y libertad*) for the Mexican peasantry, his movement spread throughout much of central Mexico. His followers carried out their own agrarian reform by seizing and redistributing landed estates. Excelling at defensive guerrilla warfare, the Zapatistas were not as effective as an offensive army. Zapata was assassinated by agents of Carranza in 1919. His name remains a potent symbol of agrarian activism and social justice in Mexico, as evidenced by the creation of the Zapatista Army of National Liberation by Mayan rebels in Chiapas in 1994.

Jennie Purnell

See Also Cinema of Revolution; Documentaries of Revolution; Inequality, Class, and Revolution; Literature and Modern Revolution; Millenrianism, Religion, and Revolution; Spanish American Revolutions of Independence; Zapista Movement

References and Further Readings

Benjamin, Thomas. 2000a. *La Revolución: Mexico's Great Revolution as Memory, Myth and History.* Austin: University of Texas Press.

———. 2000b. "Rebuilding the Nation." Pp. 467–502 in *The Oxford History of Mexico*, edited by Michael C. Meyer and William H. Beezley. Oxford: Oxford University Press.

Brading, David, ed. 1980. *Caudillo and Peasant in the Mexican Revolution.* Cambridge: Cambridge University Press.

Buffington, Robert M., and William E. French. 2000. "The Culture of Modernity." Pp. 397–432 in *The Oxford History of Mexico*, edited by Michael C. Meyer and William H. Beezley. Oxford: Oxford University Press.

Fallaw, Ben. 2001. *Cárdenas Compromised: The Failure of Reform in Postrevolutionary Yucatán.* Durham, NC: Duke University Press.

Gonzales, Michael J. 2002. *The Mexican Revolution, 1910–1940.* Albuquerque: University of New Mexico Press.

Hart, John Mason. 2000. "The Mexican Revolution, 1910–1920." Pp. 435–465 in *The Oxford History of Mexico*, edited by Michael C. Meyer and William H. Beezley. Oxford: Oxford University Press.

Joseph, Gilbert M., and Daniel Nugent, eds. 1994. *Everyday Forms of State Formation: Revolution and the Negotiation of Rule in Mexico.* Durham, NC: Duke University Press.

Katz, Friedrich. 1981. *The Secret War in Mexico: Europe, the United States, and the Mexican Revolution.* Chicago: Chicago University Press.

Knight, Alan. 1986. *The Mexican Revolution.* 2 vols. Lincoln: University of Nebraska Press.

LaFrance, David. 1990. "The Regional Nature of Maderismo." Pp. 17–40 in *Provinces of the Revolution: Essays on Regional Mexican History, 1910–1929*, edited by Thomas Benjamin and Mark Wasserman. Albuquerque: University of New Mexico Press.

Purnell, Jennie. 1999. *Popular Movements and State Formation in Revolutionary Mexico: The Agraristas and Cristeros of Michoacán.* Durham, NC: Duke University Press.

Tutino, John. 1986. *From Insurrection to Revolution in Mexico: Social Bases of Agrarian Violence, 1750–1940.* Princeton, NJ: Princeton University Press.

Wasserman, Mark. 2000. *Everyday Life and Politics in Nineteenth Century Mexico: Women, Men, and War.* Albuquerque: University of New Mexico Press.

Womack, John, Jr. 1968. *Zapata and the Mexican Revolution.* New York: Vintage.

Millenarianism, Religion, and Revolution

The idea of a messiah, or savior, who will suddenly and miraculously someday return to earth to usher in a utopian world of justice and harmony, is an underlying principle of Judeo-Christian teaching. Its origin may be traced to Christ's prophesied reign in person on earth, which will last for a thousand years before the final judgment, biblically foretold in the twentieth chapter of *Revelation*. This concept, called millenarianism, has also been used to characterize the Shia Islamic prophecy of the return of the imam, which exhibits distinct similarities to Christian apocalyptic beliefs.

In addition, millenarianism has been identified as an underlying component of many traditional religions in Asia, Africa, the South Pacific, and the pre-conquest Americas (Rinehart 1997, 3). Indeed, most cultures in the world possess a belief in a messianic figure, of some form, who will return to save society in times of crisis.

Three important patterns may be identified that link millenarianism and revolution across both time and space. First, millenarianism has been an ingredient in most modern European revolutions, and important similarities exist between some of these Western upheavals and revolutionary events in the non-Western world. Second, through the processes of exploration and colonization, Western millenarian ideas and doctrines have been exported to non-Western regions and have frequently had a profound impact on the development of millenarian movements among local populations (Rinehart 1997). Finally, Communism and Fascism have both been characterized as secular religions and, thus, modern millenarianism (Cohn 1970).

Since ancient times millenarianism has appeared as a sporadic yet identifiable response by a community to a specific set of conditions impinging upon their society: natural disasters, man-made catastrophes, foreign subjugation, governmental corruption, and the harmful effects of cultural imperialism. Such factors act as catalysts to the formation of millenarian sects. Typically, these have been nonviolent movements. But in some cases, millenarian movements have used violent tactics in revolutionary efforts to transform society.

A direct relationship exists between social upheaval—disaster, catastrophe, or abrupt and significant social change—and millenarianism. Those who foresee an imminent transformation and salvation of society (revolutionary millenarians) often expect that disaster will precede such change and actually prepare the way for it (Barkun 1974).

During the medieval era, millenarian movements emerged as a component of religious opposition in western Europe. Prompted by a growing dissatisfaction with a corrupt and unresponsive church, peasant movements led by charismatic prophets began to appear demanding moral reform (Cohn 1970, 37–52). Revolutionary millenarian movements that erupted between the fourteenth and sixteenth centuries in Western Europe—most notably, the Taborites of Bohemia, which emerged during the Hussite Wars around 1380; the League of the Elect, led by Thomas Muntzer; and the Anabaptists, who ruled Munster from 1532 to 1535—

were profoundly influenced by the possibility of the dawn of an egalitarian Golden Age; they were essentially anarcho-communist in their ideology. In this context, Cohn suggests that they represent the antecedents of twentieth-century totalitarian movements, such as Nazism and Communism, which he theorizes are modern, secularized forms of millenarianism.

The English Civil War (1642–1646) involved elements of millenarianism. During this period apocalyptic expectations were fueled by radical movements such as the Diggers, who also professed an explicitly anarcho-communist ideology manifested in their complete rejection of the institution of private property, and the Fifth Monarchy Men, whose belief in the impending reign of Christ on earth led them to attempt coups against both the Protectorate and the restored monarchy.

Following the Restoration these movements were increasingly viewed as irrational, extremist, and disruptive of the prevailing social order, and they faded into obscurity by the end of the seventeenth century. However, their millenarian beliefs retained an important measure of respectability among the popular religions of England for some time to come (Hill 1972, 77–78, 86–120). The French Revolution produced a groundswell of millenarian faith in both France and England. Prophets in both countries sought to interpret revolutionary events in a biblical context as a clear expression of God's will and anticipated that the consequences would be enormously beneficial to all.

MILLENARIAN REVOLUTION AND THE PROCESS OF DE-COLONIZATION

Michael Adas (1979) has shown that participants in political violence have been stirred by millenarian expectations when confronted by the changes and dislocations engendered by European imperialism, colonization, and cultural conquest of diverse societies in Africa, Asia, and the South Pacific. He argues that traditional religious ritual and apocalyptic myth were utilized in attempts by indigenous peoples to offset European technological superiority, and that the millenarian visions of the prophets of these movements served as catalysts for protests and violence.

In addition, Eric Hobsbawm analyzed millenarian insurgencies in early twentieth-century Mediterranean Europe where capitalism and modernity had recently intruded into peasant society and people were subjected to pervasive government control. He argued that millenarian movements tend to arise in rapidly modernizing societies with the accompanying developing capitalist system and increasing governmental intervention in people's everyday lives. In response, people seek simplicity of life and a new moral order. They come to see themselves as the victims of insidious socioeconomic and political forces that are beyond their control. The abolition of common forest and pasture lands, increased taxes, rapid industrialization, the development of a national market, and the introduction of capitalist legal and social relationships—all had "cataclysmic effects" on these societies. According to Hobsbawm, the participants in the movements he investigated did not grow with or into modern society. Instead, they were "broken into it" (Hobsbawm 1963, 68).

Finally, Michael Barkun claims that social disorders and disasters are the consequences of contact between more complex and less complex cultures, a notion that he labels the "colonial hypothesis." He contends that millenarianism develops in a technologically inferior or colonial society in response to intervention or invasion by a superior foreign power that attempts to impose its cultural values on the people of the colonized society. Subjection to a foreign power is a particularly grievous experience when the subjugated society is profoundly ethnocentric and when its political leader is also a religious leader or, at the least, is perceived as one who is divinely inspired. Perhaps not surprisingly, millenarian expectations tend to emerge as a specific response to the suppression of, or serious interference with, the traditional religious practices of the indigenous peoples by the intervening power. Barkun argues that "the colonial hypothesis, in effect, holds that there is a causal sequence at work: culture contact-social change-mental disturbance-millenarian movements" (Barkun 1974, 34).

In Latin America, the long process of de-colonization and the violence that often accompanied it frequently involved millenarian expectations. Beginning in 1780, the most powerful rebellion to hit the Andean region during the colonial era unfolded in the highlands of Peru, having a profound impact from modern-day Argentina to Colombia. Its immediate goal was to relieve Indians of the extraordinary burdens that had recently been placed on them by the ruling representatives of the Spanish monarchy. Its greater goal was eventually to drive the Europeans out of the region and to restore the Inca emperor (Galindo 1995).

The leader of the rebellion was a native mestizo elite named Tupac Amaru, baptized Jose Gabriel Condorcanqui. Well educated and rather wealthy, he claimed to be a direct descendant of the last Inca ruling family in the sixteenth century. Eventually, he came to fashion himself as the new king of Peru and established a government for the territory that was under his direct control. Such an identity effectively capitalized on a desire for the resurrection and revival of Inca life that was sweeping the region in the late eighteenth century. This millenarian revival among Indian elites was accompanied by the mass of the Indian community yearning for the

Peruvian revolutionary Tupac Amaru II, leader of the rebellion against Spain 1780–1783. (Art Archive/Coll Abric de Vivero Lima/Mireille Vautier)

miraculous return of the Inca to rescue them from the pain of their present conditions. Condorcanqui was able to make use of his lineage to tap into this powerful force. Nonetheless, on April 6, 1781, Condorcanqui and his wife were captured and executed. The Tupac Amaru Rebellion ultimately weakened the hold of the Spanish in the region and contributed in a significant way to Peru's independence in the early years of the nineteenth century (Klaren 2000).

In the mid twentieth century, millenarian movements in colonial societies in Africa and Asia borrowed extensively from the evangelism and messianic imagery of Christianity exported to those regions. Citing examples among the Kikuyu, Maoris, and Bantu, Lanternari identifies how these indigenous peoples "found their sufferings reflected in the biblical history of the Hebrew people." Perhaps just as important, they discovered a "powerful inspiration in both the life and sacrifice of Jesus Christ that could be effectively compared to their own struggle for political independence and promise of salvation" (Lanternari 1965, 243). Revolutions in these colonial societies were frequently characterized by millenarian promise: a hope of spiritual and earthly salvation.

MILLENARIANISM AND REVOLUTION IN CHINA, MEXICO, AND IRAN

The powerful and durable millenarian notion of a chosen people purifying a tyrannical world by destroying the agents of corruption is one that has been a common thread in revolutions in China, Indian Mexico, and Iran.

The pre-modern period in all three of these societies was marked by a durable and pervasive tradition of millenarianism. Although its appearance became most explicit during periods of general social disturbance, millenarianism was a mechanism for bringing about limited social change, lying just below the surface of everyday life even in periods of social stability.

The onset of Western imperialism, including the Spanish conquest of Indian Mexico in the sixteenth century and continuing with foreign intervention in China and Iran in the nineteenth and twentieth centuries, created the most significant challenge and social stress those three societies had faced. The experience was a disaster in each case. Perceived as ineffective, outmoded, and no longer legitimate in the face of the more modern ways of the West, traditional cultural systems went through a significant transformation.

In China, "the most notable of millenarian uprisings occurring" before the modern revolution was the Taiping Rebellion of 1851–1864 (Rinehart 1997, 71). The Manchu dynasty's failure to protect the country from attacks and subjugation by foreign powers, and the economic burden placed on the peasants by the higher taxes and rents meant to raise the funds to pay war indemnities to foreigners, helped lead to this gigantic revolt. The leader was Hung Hsiu-ch'uan of south China's Hakka minority. Hung was "a Christian convert who had been deeply influenced by both the utopian strains of Chinese traditionalism" and the messianic aspects of Christianity (ibid., 72). During an illness he believed that he had experienced a visitation from the Christian God—the Father and His Son, Jesus Christ—and that he was, in fact, the new savior, the younger brother of Jesus. He was to lead a movement to create the kingdom of great peace and equality on earth.

The ideology of the Taiping movement was a mixture of Christian millennialism, Buddhism, Taoism, and aspects of Hakka culture. Millions of poor Chinese peasants were drawn to Hung's call to join the Taipings and create a new heavenly and just society on earth. The Christian church, however, rejected Hung's ideas as heresy, and the Manchu army, with the aid of European mercenaries, destroyed the Taiping Rebellion. But the "similarities of the characteristics of the Chinese Communist movement of the twentieth century to those of the Taiping movement are unmistakable" (ibid., 78). Both movements called for an end to the Confucianist feudalist system, land redistribution to the poor peasants, drastic improvement in the status of women, and collective ownership of resources. And like Hung, Mao was portrayed "as a messiah," the savior of the Chinese people (ibid., 155).

Before the arrival of the Spanish, Mexican Indian culture was characterized by the millenarian tradition of the man-god, Quetzalcoatl, who would some day return "as savior to his people" (ibid., 80–81). That belief later merged with the Christian concept of Christ as God become man to save humankind from sin and lead the way to paradise.

In Mexico, millenarianism among Mexican Indian peasants was a symptom of the divide that existed between the European-oriented culture and economy of the urban areas and the Indian agrarian regions. This chasm had numerous dimensions: white versus dark-skinned peoples, rich versus poor, and the resentments arising from the conflict between a European-centered culture and traditional Indian life. The mix of indigenous and Christian millenarianism provided the Indian peasants with the expectation that someday their long-sought ideal of social justice would come to prevail in Mexican society. Millenarian beliefs were expressed, in particular, in the land-reforming religiosity characterizing the early-nineteenth-century independence movement of Hidalgo and Morelos. In the early twentieth century it was manifested in the Zapatista movement, which, invoking the image of the Virgin of Guadalupe, carried out widespread land reforms in peasant areas without the authorization of the government.

Twelver Shiism, which played a central role in the 1979 Iranian Revolution, possessed a powerful millenarian concept. The adherents of Shia Islam believed that the prophet Muhammad had intended that his cousin Ali, husband of his daughter Fatima, should succeed him as leader of Islam. They also believed that certain male descendants of Ali and Fatima were the real and infallible leaders, or imams, of Islam, until the twelfth and last imam disappeared in A.D. 873. The Shia believe that some day the twelfth imam will return to lead the worldwide Islamic community and establish a true Muslim society on earth characterized by social justice.

Beginning as early as the fourteenth century, numerous millenarian revolts occurred in what is now Iran. Around 1384, for example, a self-proclaimed prophet who claimed to be the twelfth imam, Fadlu'llah Astarabadi, founded the rebel Hurufi sect of Shia Islam. In 1425 rebellion emerged in northeastern Iran when a local elite, Khwaja Ishaq Khatlani, asserted that a young member of his tribe was the returned imam (Arjomand 1984, 75).

The ascendance to power of the Safavid dynasty in Persia in 1501 was accompanied by the establishment of Twelver Shiism as the state religion. Indeed, the founder of the dynasty, Isma'il I, claimed that he was the incarnation of the imam. Millenarian rebellions in Iran were characterized by a constant theme: each was led by a charismatic prophet who perceived that the followers of Muhammad had deviated from the rightful laws of Islam and needed to be brought back to the true path. In this sense, these movements were backward-looking and conservative.

To a large number of Iranians, Ayatollah Khomeini, the central leader of the modern Iranian Revolution of 1978–1979, had a distinctively messianic quality. Many of his followers thought of him in a millenarian context and reportedly discussed intensely whether or not Khomeini was the returned imam. Millions—many believing that Khomeini was divinely inspired—massed in the streets of Tehran to welcome the returning Ayatollah in February 1979 (Rinehart 1997, 141).

Khomeini and certain fellow clerics considered themselves the true interpreters of Islam, worthy of total support and leadership in Iran. To them, Islam should encompass all aspects of society. This view, that their belief system was God's creation and their plan for Iran was God's intention, appealed to many lay Iranians. In particular, it provided poor Iranians with a sense of moral superiority to the man-made cultures and ideologies of the technologically advanced societies. As the shah became progressively identified with foreign interests, the majority of the clergy, with Khomeini at their head, appeared to many Iranians to be the true representatives of Iran's traditional culture and historical identity. Khomeini's preachings were a highly effective reinterpretation of Shia millenarian theology fused with fervent Iranian nationalism and anti-imperialism.

In each of these cases, millenarianism created the potential for a cult to emerge centered on a charismatic person. This figure came to symbolize the aspirations of the people and the need for social transformation and revitalization. He became the leader of a revolutionary movement enjoying tremendous popular support. Indeed, each was perceived by many to possess superhuman, divinely ordained powers to lead his people to salvation through revolution. Mao, Zapata, and Khomeini each benefited from a tradition of apocalyptic beliefs among their peoples and fashioned a millenarian ideology that became widely accepted (ibid., 143)

CONCLUSIONS

Millenarianism is the intellectual mother of all political ideologies. No other set of ideas offers such a compelling message and provides such a powerful tool for influencing the popular mind. It is the definitive articulation of discontent and a powerful unifying force that provides an effective meaning to popular grievances.

The potentially revolutionary role of millenarianism is implicit in the work of the famous Iranian sociologist Ali Shariati, considered by many the second most influential figure of the Iranian Revolution after Ayatollah Khomeini. Shariati, whose writings helped convince many thousands of young Iranians of the revolutionary potential of Shiism, argued that indigenous religions such as Shia Islam possess a revolutionary component that can be used to arouse and energize the people (Abrahamian 1989). He criticized the traditional Marxist indictment that religion functions primarily as a means to control the poor by convincing them that their downtrodden existence is the will of God and that their only hope is to be obedient and achieve happiness in the afterlife.

Shariati claimed, in contrast, that progressive concepts exist within many indigenous religions, and that activists should emphasize and propagate those themes to the religious faithful and, in so doing, mobilize them in a revolutionary effort to combat imperialism and create a better society. Although Shariati died before the revolution, his ideas became manifested, most likely not in the way he would have advocated, in the millenarian-like belief of many Iranians that Ayatollah Khomeini was the long-awaited imam.

Members of millenarian movements, such as Iran's religious revolutionaries, come to believe that ultimate victory against the forces of darkness and injustice will be theirs. In place of despair, they experience a profound hope and sensation of collective identity and purpose. The existence of pervasive millenarian beliefs creates the potential for the acceptance of a charismatic revolutionary leader who has the capacity to tap effectively into relevant cultural traditions and articulate a program of revitalization.

James F. Rinehart

See Also Documentaries of Revolution; Ideology, Propaganda, and Revolution; Iranian Revolution; Mexican Revolution; Taiping Revolution

References and Further Readings
Abrahamian, Ervand. 1989. *The Iranian Mojahedin.* New Haven, CT: Yale University Press.
Adas, Michael. 1979. *Prophets of Rebellion.* Chapel Hill: University of North Carolina Press.
Arjomand, Said Amir. 1984. *The Shadow of God and the Hidden Imam: Religion, Political Order, and Societal Change in Shi'ite Iran from the Beginning to 1890.* Chicago: University of Chicago Press.
Barkun, Michael. 1974. *Disaster and the Millennium.* New Haven, CT: Yale University Press.
Cohn, Norman. 1970. *The Pursuit of the Millennium: Revolutionary Millenarians and Mystical Anarchism of the Middle Ages.* 3rd edition. New York: Oxford University Press.

Galindo, Alberto Flores. 1995. "The Rebellion of Tupac Amaru." Pp. 147–156 in *The Peru Reader: History, Culture, Politics*, edited by Orin Starn, Carlos Ivan Degregori, and Robin Kirk. Durham, NC: Duke University Press.

Hill, Christopher. 1972. *The World Turned Upside Down: Radical Ideas during the English Revolution.* New York: Viking.

Hobsbawm, Eric J. 1963. *Primitive Rebels: Studies in Archaic Forms of Social Movement in the 19th and 20th Centuries.* New York: Praeger.

Klaren, Peter F. 2000. *Peru: Society and Nationhood in the Andes.* New York: Oxford University Press.

Lanternari, Vittorio. 1965. *The Religions of the Oppressed: A Study of Modern Messianic Cults.* New York: Mentor.

Rinehart, James F. 1997. *Revolution and the Millennium: China, Mexico, and Iran.* Westport, CT: Praeger.

Mozambique Revolution

CHRONOLOGY

1956	PIDE (Polícia International e de Defesa do Estado; the Portuguese secret police) established in Mozambique.
1960	In June, Mueda massacre.
1961	In January, the Luanda Angola uprising.
	In March, the revolt in the Baixa de Cassange, Angola.
1962	In June, the formation of Frelimo in Dar es Salaam.
	In September, the first Frelimo Party Congress.
1964	In September, the beginning of the war in Mozambique.
1966	In October, Machel becomes military commander of Frelimo.
1968	Second Party Congress held in Mozambique; Marcello Caetano replaces Salazar as Portuguese prime minister.
1969	In January, defection of Nkavandame.
	In February, the murder of Mondlane.
1970	In May, Machel is elected party leader; Arriaga launches operation "Gordian Knot" in northern Mozambique.
1972	Frelimo attacks south of the Zambesi.
1974	April 25, revolution in Portugal.
	On September 7, Lusaka Accord recognizes Mozambique's independence.
1975	June 25, Mozambique independence.
1977	Third Party Congress; Frelimo declares itself a Marxist-Leninist party.
1980	Mugabe is elected president of Zimbabwe; Renamo moves to South Africa.
1983	Fourth Party Congress changes economic priorities.
1984	Nkomati Accord; Mozambique joins the IMF.
1986	Machel is killed in an air crash in September; Joaquim Chissano becomes prime minister.
1989	Fifth Party Congress dismantles the Marxist state.
1990	Beginning of peace talks in Rome in July.
1992	October, General Peace Agreement.
1994	Elections are won by Frelimo in October.

INTRODUCTION

The Mozambique Revolution began in the early 1960s as a movement to free the country from foreign domination and exploitation. Later its leaders established a one-party state and, while bringing about many improvements in health care and education, they also imposed some unpopular policies that led to widespread armed resistance to the revolutionary Frelimo government. That conflict resulted in tens of thousands of deaths and much destruction to schools, health care facilities, and the economy. Eventually Frelimo abandoned its more extreme policies and permitted the creation of a multiparty democratic political system.

BACKGROUND: CULTURE AND HISTORY

The Portuguese captaincy of Mozambique and Sofala was established in 1506 to exploit the gold and ivory trade of eastern Africa. By the 1530s, Portuguese traders were operating on the Zambesi, and their intervention in African wars in the interior led to the Portuguese acquiring control of land on both sides of the Zambesi River. In the nineteenth century the slave trade dominated the commerce of the region, and the rise of the mining economy in South Africa led to the development of a port in Delagoa Bay that was recognized as Portuguese by French arbitration in 1875. The hectic events of the European competition to control Africa (the "Scramble for Africa") resulted in an agreement between Britain and Portugal in August 1891 establishing the modern frontiers of Mozambique. Unable to administer such a vast territory, the Portuguese divided Mozambique into concession areas that were granted to two chartered companies and five large plantation companies, while the South African Witwatersrand Native Labour Association (WNLA) was granted a monopoly of labor recruitment in the south. During the twentieth century Mozambique developed a successful plantation economy producing copra, sugar, and tea, while rice and raw cotton were produced by peasant farmers under a forced crop-growing scheme introduced by Salazar in the 1930s. Meanwhile, between 200,000 and 300,000 laborers migrated to work in the South African mines and on Rhodesian farms, while earning gold sterling for the Portuguese imperial economy.

During the 1950s the Portuguese encouraged white immigration and began to develop secondary industry around the two major port cities of Beira and Lourenço Marques. At the same time the Portuguese secret police clamped down on all opposition and on any form of African organization. As a result, the only way Africans could express their political ambitions was in exile; political parties were formed in the Rhodesias and Nyasaland and among the small group of intellectuals and professionals receiving their education in Lisbon.

CONTEXT AND PROCESS OF REVOLUTION

The Wars of Liberation in Africa

When rebellion broke out in Angola in 1961 there was still no independence movement in Mozambique, and the Portuguese were pushing ahead with major economic development projects. In 1962, President Julius Nyerere of Tanzania brought together the leaders of three small political groups to form a united front: the Frente de Libertaçao de Moçambique (Frelimo) was established, holding its First Party Congress, later called the Congress of Unity, in September 1962. Eduardo Mondlane, a Mozambican official working for the United Nations and married to a white American, was brought in to lead the party.

Frelimo had strong international backing, but most of its support initially came from the Makonde people in the extreme north of the country. It was the Makonde in Tanzania who had formed the Mozambique African National Union (MANU), the precursor of Frelimo. It was MANU that had undertaken some work in the agricultural cooperatives of northern Mozambique, and it was a MANU demonstration that had been fired on by Portuguese police at Mueda in June 1960. From the start there were deep divisions in Frelimo between the Makonde and the intellectuals, many of them from the south, who made up the party activists. Many Makonde chiefs became party "chairmen" in the Cape Delgado Province, and they, with their leader Lazaro Nkavandame, wanted Frelimo to be a traditional Africanist movement focused on removing the colonial rulers and the oppressive structures of the colonial state. They were little interested in the radical Socialist vision that predominated among the exiled intellectuals.

Fighting had begun in Guinea in 1963, and, under pressure to begin the armed struggle against the Portuguese, Frelimo fighters began to infiltrate the northern provinces and to attack Portuguese targets in September 1964. The party was hardly ready for an armed struggle, but Mondlane feared that, if Frelimo did not take the initiative, a poorly organized rebellion such as had occurred in Angola in the early 1960s might break out at any time, with the same disastrous consequences.

At this stage Frelimo had virtually no presence within the country, and a roundup of suspected dissidents by the Portuguese police in December 1964—which in 1965 was extended to include the writer Luís Honwana and the famous painter Malangatana—destroyed any burgeoning opposition in the country. The exiles who collected in Dar es Salaam became increasingly factious, and the Tanzanian authorities had to deal with violence that broke out from time to time between the rival factions. Moreover, the war made little progress, as the Portuguese, after being taken initially by surprise, easily confined the guerrilla activity to the extreme north and the shores of Lake Malawi. The war in Angola had also nearly petered out, and only the success of Amilcar Cabral's PAIGC (African Party of Independence for Guinea and Cape Verde) in Guinea and the strength of the anti-colonial movement in the United Nations kept the struggle going.

Frelimo Becomes More Effective

The fortunes of Frelimo began to change when Mondlane successfully staged the Second Party Congress at a location inside Mozambique in 1968. That was a significant propaganda victory that also led to a showdown with Nkavandame, who quit the party in January 1969 and defected to the Portuguese. Frelimo was now firmly controlled by the radicals and began to develop a distinctly Socialist rhetoric. However, the party was not able to reap the full benefit of the Congress, as Mondlane was murdered by a parcel bomb in February 1969. Another leadership struggle took place, this time between the military commander, Samora Machel, and the vice president, Uria Simango. It was only in May 1970 that Machel emerged victorious and that the pursuit of the military campaign came to be Frelimo's highest priority.

After the failure of General Kaulza de Arriaga's military offensive in the north in 1970, Frelimo's campaign became rather more effective. A second front was opened in Tete Province that threatened the newly completed Cabora Bassa Dam on the Zambesi, which was the centerpiece of Portuguese development policies. In 1972, for the first time some guerrilla attacks were launched south of the Zambesi. The Portuguese responded by Africanizing their armed forces, creating elite black units that eventually numbered 30,000 and came to constitute half the manpower of the colonial army (*Resenha Historico-Militar Das Campanhas de Africa* 1988, 261). The Portuguese also collected the population in the war zones into protected villages (called *aldeamentos*) and made a bid to win over traditional authorities, particularly in the Muslim areas in the north of the country.

The Portuguese Revolution

From at least 1972 the Portuguese prime minister, Marcello Caetano, had been trying to find a political solution to the African wars, but his efforts had had little success when the end came suddenly on April 25, 1974. A coup carried out by the armed forces in Lisbon sent Caetano into exile and replaced him with a high-profile and charismatic general called António de Spínola. The leaders of the coup, who the previous year had organized the Movimento das Forças Armadas (MFA), had no clear policies for the future of the African colonies but responded to the overwhelming desire of the soldiers in Africa to end the war and to go home. Without waiting for negotiations, the Portuguese army took the initiative into its own hands, refused to continue fighting, and started to fraternize with the guerrillas. The Frelimo leadership seized the opportunity to move units south of the Zambesi and to begin operations in areas where it had previously had

Samora Machel, president of Mozambique (1975–1986). (Hulton Archive/Getty Images)

no presence. At first President Spínola tried to negotiate, offering a lengthy transition period and a position for Mozambique in a Portuguese federation, but Machel refused to grant the Portuguese a cease-fire until full independence had been promised. At that time all the independence movements maintained a common position, refusing to negotiate anything except a direct handover of power to themselves and an immediate recognition of the independence of the colonies.

The leaders of Frelimo feared that unless there was an immediate transfer of power, there would be opportunities for other political movements to organize, and they might lose the fruits of their armed struggle. They knew, for example, that Spínola had encouraged the emergence of a moderate political grouping called Grupo Unido de Moçambique (Mozambique United Group, GUMO), financed by a Portuguese businessman, which he hoped might form the core of a rival political movement. However, on July 27, 1974, after the fall of the Palma Carlos government in Lisbon, the new prime minister, Vasco Gonçalves, an MFA officer, issued Law 7/74 that recognized the right of the colonies to independence. Direct negotiations now took place between Frelimo and the leaders of the MFA behind Spínola's back, and the Lusaka Accord was signed on September 7, 1974. This made provision for a short transition period of nine months, during which time there would be a joint Frelimo-Portuguese government. At the end of that period the Portuguese armed forces would withdraw, and Frelimo would take power. The head of the transitional government was to be Joaquim Chissano, the future president of Mozambique. Not only were there to be no elections, but, in addition, no constitution was agreed before withdrawal, and no provision was made for the future financing and administration of the country.

The Mozambique Revolution Transforms the Country

The most successful achievement of the nine months of transitional government was to arrange for the peaceful evacuation of the Portuguese army. Meanwhile, after a brief attempt by right-wing forces to stage a putsch in the capital, most of the Portuguese left Mozambique, along with many mestizos and Africans who had worked with the regime. Government offices, businesses, and services such as schools and hospitals were left unstaffed, and the need to keep the country running on a day-to-day basis presented Frelimo with an immediate crisis. The only answer was for the state to adopt authoritarian powers and to bring in skilled workers from outside. However, the need to deal with a national emergency is not the sole explanation for the revolutionary policies that were now adopted. Already Machel and his advisers were planning a social and economic revolution to replace what they saw as the corrupt colonial state with a newly regenerated African society. The large numbers of *cooperantes* (volunteers) who came to Mozambique from Eastern Europe, Cuba, and an increasingly sympathetic and liberal Western Europe also brought with them visions of a new society, so that Mozambique briefly became the focus for the political idealism of both East and West. This new country was to be living proof that a just, equal, and progressive society could be created to replace the cruelties, injustices, and inequalities of colonial capitalism.

The new Mozambique had to be built under very difficult circumstances. Its immediate neighbors, South Africa and Rhodesia, were hostile to African aspirations and harbored refugees from the Frelimo regime, while the Cold War forced unwelcome choices on all newly independent colonial states. In 1975, South Africa intervened with armed force in Angola, and in 1976 it sent home most of the Mozambique miners whose remittances had been so important to the colonial economy. In spite of these problems, however, Machel opted to follow the pathway of radical political, social, and economic change.

To achieve the rapid and effective assertion of the authority of the party and the state throughout the country, "dynamizing groups" (*Grupos Dinamizadores,* GDs) of party supporters were dispatched to factories, farms, and businesses to try to restore production. Although the GDs proved to be an effective way of implementing the ideas of the new government, their net effect was disruptive; by 1979 they had all been disbanded.

In 1977, at the Third Party Congress, a Marxist-Leninist constitution was introduced that established the dominance of a vanguard party with a limited membership. All those elected to district and provincial assemblies had to be approved by the party, and delegates to the Popular Assembly (Mozambique's parliament) were nominated by the Central Committee of the party. The constitution proclaimed the primacy of the interests of workers and peasants and adopted the complete lexicon of Marxist rhetoric. As adjuncts to the party organization, a women's organization (Organisação das Mulheres Moçambicanas, OMM) and a youth organization (Organisação da Juventude Moçambicana, OJM) were established, and a system of production councils in large enterprises was put in place instead of trade unions.

Machel adopted a leadership style designed to disarm critics and opponents. His ideas were set out in a series of lengthy published speeches, and from time to time he would initiate campaigns to address matters of concern, such as corruption or bureaucracy. Frelimo adopted the rhetoric of self-criticism and self-examination, and high standards of conduct were demanded from party officials.

Machel, whose ideas were strongly influenced by the Ujama experiment in Tanzania and by the success of the revolution in Cuba, wanted to eradicate all aspects of colonialism. That involved not only removing the Portuguese colonial rulers but also changing the very social structures upon which the colonial state had been founded. Those were identified as racism and class domination, and accusing fingers were pointed at traditional chiefs, owners of private businesses and private property, religious authorities, and people who had served the colonial government. Machel also determined to eliminate the twin evils of educational backwardness and economic underdevelopment. For him ignorance was synonymous with colonial oppression.

To realize these objectives, traditional authorities, polygamists, and those who were associated with the former regime were removed from office and made ineligible to stand for election, while re-education camps were established for those believed to be opponents of the regime. Strong efforts were made to remove the obstacles to the advancement of women. Traditional forms of polygamy and *lobola* (bride-price) were outlawed, and those who practiced them were disenfranchised. Women were encouraged to stand for election and to take up educational opportunities. The regime denounced traditional authorities, who were replaced at the local level by party officials. Traditional ethnic loyalties of the old regime were rejected. As Machel said, "We killed the tribe to give birth to the nation." Traditional religion and medicine were condemned, and the Roman Catholic Church lost its control over marriage and education. Church property was nationalized, and public observance of church festivals was abolished. Machel was dedicated to the idea of modernization. The modern Mozambican would be a citizen, educated in the skills needed by a modern industrialized society and with a mindset guided by scientific rationalism.

Mozambique was also to be rescued from economic underdevelopment. In the 1970s it was believed that countries could use their own resources to achieve self-sustaining growth. This would be achieved by a command economy in which foreign exchange and domestic surplus would be controlled and reinvested by the government to make the country self-sufficient.

The departure of the Portuguese had led to the collapse of industrial production, while after 1976, the South African mines drastically reduced the number of Mozambican migrant workers and hence the flow of hard currency to Mozambique. Tourism also ceased, and the cities were swamped with unemployed. As consumer goods disappeared from the shops and rural stores, the peasant farmers stopped delivering crops and the commercial sector of the economy spiraled into decline. To deal with these problems, Machel adopted a top-down model in which the consumption by ordinary people would be restricted and all available resources would be directed by the government toward industrialization, which was to lead to the modernization not only of the Mozambican economy but also of Mozambican society.

The economic development plan drawn up in 1978 by the National Economic Commission, which had been established at the 1977 Party Congress, made provision for large-scale state investment to be directed to industry and to the state farms that had replaced the old Portuguese *colonatos* (colonies of agricultural smallholders). The state farms were conceived as giant agro-industrial complexes on the East European model. By 1982, 140,000 hectares had been organized as state farms that absorbed 70 percent of agricultural investment, though 80 percent of the population still worked as peasant farmers in the "family farm" sector (Newitt 1995, 549, 551–552). The state farms performed at a very low rate of productivity and consumed a disproportionate part of state investment. While the official economy stagnated, unemployment, inflation, and the lack of consumer goods pushed more

and more people into illegal economic activities, which undermined the ideals and the authority of the state.

The government also devoted a great deal of resources to mass education and health programs focusing on the immunization of the population against smallpox, tetanus, and measles, and on the achievement of basic literacy. In the first six years after independence, infant mortality was cut by 20 percent, while enrollment in primary schools doubled; half a million people, 40 percent of them women, attended adult literacy classes (Isaacman and Isaacman 1983, 139). To achieve this range of ambitious social objectives, Frelimo developed the idea of collectivization. Communal villages or townships would replace the old lineage-based villages in the rural areas. Modeled on Tanzania's Ujama villages (but bearing a close resemblance to the Portuguese *aldeamentos,* many of which were taken over and turned into new-style communal villages), the process of grouping the rural population in large settlements under party control was begun.

The Revolution in Trouble

From the date of independence on June 25, 1975, to the end of the decade, Frelimo enjoyed relatively peaceful conditions at home and the watchful tolerance and even friendship of South Africa. The border with Rhodesia, however, was very disturbed. Machel declared his solidarity with the Zimbabwe African National Union (ZANU) and enforced the closing of the Beira corridor linking Rhodesia to the sea. As a result Mozambique was raided by Rhodesian forces, while, in a more sinister development, the Rhodesian military intelligence began to organize an army of dissidents from among the refugees who had fled from Mozambique after Frelimo took power. These dissidents, who called themselves the Mozambique National Resistance (MNR), also began broadcasts to Mozambique from Rhodesian territory.

In 1979 a settlement was agreed to by which the Rhodesian government would hand over power to an elected majority government. During the negotiations Machel is supposed to have warned Robert Mugabe against taking measures that would lead to the mass exodus of the white population and the subsequent collapse of the economy, as had happened in Mozambique. However, although ZANU took power in 1980 after elections, MNR attacks on Mozambique continued, because the MNR fighters had been airlifted to South Africa and now operated out of the Transvaal under South African control. Over the next three years MNR, now renamed Renamo and led by Afonso Dhlakama, operated almost at will throughout central and southern

Mozambique. It struck at government establishments of all kinds, burning schools and hospitals, killing Frelimo party workers, terrorizing ordinary citizens, interrupting the railways, and making the roads unsafe for all but military convoys. Industrial and agricultural installations of all kinds were systematically destroyed, and a hole was even blown in the Zambesi bridge at Sena. Directed by the South African security forces, Renamo became a weapon in the new Pretoria strategy of "destabilization" designed to combat African nationalism in South Africa by taking the war to its neighbors. The objective of the campaign, insofar as there was one, was to paralyze the neighboring governments and to make them wholly dependent on South Africa. This objective appeared to have been achieved when Machel was forced to meet Botha in 1984 and sign the Nkomati Accord, agreeing to end all support for the African National Congress (ANC).

By the time that Botha and Machel met at Nkomati, Frelimo had already begun to back away from its revolutionary aspirations. Faced with the relentless war waged by Renamo fighters, Frelimo was unable to mount an effective response. Its armed forces were not well-enough equipped to deal with a highly mobile guerrilla force, and the civilian population was uncooperative and sometimes hostile. The Frelimo government began to face the same problems that the Portuguese military had faced a decade earlier. The hostility that Frelimo faced in the countryside took it by surprise, but it is not hard to understand. During the six years of revolutionary change, Frelimo had succeeded in alienating most sectors of the population. Peasant farmers, who made up 80 percent of the population, had seen their standard of living fall and the government neglect their interests; traditional chiefs, those who had worked for the Portuguese, and all sorts of "class enemies" were denounced and disenfranchised; traditional marriage customs and religion were outlawed or despised, while the Roman Catholic Church was alienated by the secularization of the state. Moreover, rightly or wrongly, Frelimo was thought of as being a party of southerners whose location in the capital in the far south meant that it had little understanding of the peoples of the north and their problems. However, by far the worst problem was the communal villages, which proved the most unpopular measure of all and were bitterly resented by the rural population.

By 1983, Mozambique was having to import 30 percent of its basic foodstuffs, and the government was able to survive only by borrowing abroad. Having been refused entry into Comecon (the Council for Mutual Economic Assistance—an international economic association of a number of Communist Party–led nations) in 1981, Machel now had to look for support from Western countries. At the Fourth

Party Conference, held in 1983, economic policy was realigned to recognize the needs of production in the private and peasant farming sectors. In 1984, the year of the Nkomati Accord, Mozambique was admitted as a member of the Lomé Convention and the IMF (International Monetary Fund), while a Private Investment Code was adopted to try to lure overseas investors. Relations with the Vatican were mended, with church property being restored, and the church once again was allowed to run its own schools. Machel also conducted a surprisingly successful diplomatic campaign wooing the Conservative government in Britain and gaining the active support of Zimbabwe and Tanzania, both of which contributed troops to the campaign against Renamo. Pressure was put on Hastings Banda, the president of Malawi, to expel Renamo forces from his territory. However, at this point, Machel's life was brutally cut short. Returning from a meeting of presidents in Lilongwe in September 1986, he was killed when his airplane came down just inside South Africa.

Machel's death made little immediate difference, as the succession passed smoothly to Joaquim Chissano. Moreover the war continued unabated as Renamo forces, expelled from Malawi, now organized themselves from bases inside Mozambique. The year of Machel's death, however, saw the first signs of change in the international situation. Mikhail Gorbachev came to power in the U.S.S.R. and began the process of perestroika, and by 1988 international pressure was mounting on all sides for Frelimo to begin peace negotiations. In 1989, at the Fifth Party Congress, Frelimo announced sweeping changes to Mozambique's constitution, ending the Marxist state and replacing it with a new liberal plural democracy that established individual human rights, allowed the formation of free trade unions, and legalized private property. In 1990, following the election of de Klerk as president of South Africa, South African military support to Renamo finally came to an end, and in July 1990 formal peace talks began in Rome. In October 1992 a General Peace Agreement was signed, and, after two years when the United Nations effectively ruled Mozambique, multiparty elections were held in October 1994. Frelimo's victory in these elections at last established it as a legitimately elected government, but one that had formally abandoned its mission to bring about social and economic revolution.

IMPACTS

The Mozambique Revolution provides an important example of a revolutionary leadership that initially enjoyed wide popular support for the goal of freeing its people from oppressive colonial rule, but adopted revolutionary policies that alienated large sectors of the population. Much of the revolutionary effort involved large-scale grassroots participation. However, once Frelimo had decided to turn itself into a Leninist vanguard party and then proceeded to impose unpopular policies from above, the revolutionary project was imperiled. Frelimo attacks on traditional customs and its attempts to enforce unwanted collectivist economic policies drove significant numbers of people—aided by nearby white minority regimes for their own reasons—to resist the Frelimo government violently. That conflict led to much destruction and the deaths of tens of thousands of people. Only when Frelimo abandoned its more extreme programs for social change and created a multiparty democratic system was the United Nations able to bring relative peace to Mozambique.

PEOPLE AND ORGANIZATIONS

Frelimo (Frente De Libertaçäo de Moçambique, Mozambique Liberation Front)

Dedicated to freeing Mozambique from Portuguese control and later to establishing a Marxist-Leninist political system and a Socialist economy, Frelimo was established in September 1962 and has formed the government of Mozambique continuously since independence.

Machel, Samora (1933–1986)

Samora Machel's father worked a number of contracts on the mines in South Africa before becoming a farmer who became caught up in the forced cotton-growing scheme. Machel attended a Catholic school and trained to become a nurse, one of the only professions open to indigenous Mozambicans. He was appalled at the inadequate medical care provided to Mozambican workers and peasants and joined Frelimo. Machel, after receiving military training in other African countries, became leader of Frelimo's revolutionary army in 1966, party leader in 1970, and then president of Mozambique after independence in 1975. He adopted a very personal style of leadership and advocated a rapid and sweeping social and economic transformation of Mozambique. In the process he antagonized traditional local leaders and much of the population. Economic failures, loss of popular support, and the civil war led Machel and his associates to re-evaluate their policies. Machel was killed in a suspicious airplane crash in 1986 while returning from a meeting of African presidents in Malawi.

Mondlane, Eduardo (1920–1969)

Mondlane was born in 1920. Educated in a Protestant mission school and then at Witwatersrand University, Mondlane obtained a scholarship that enabled him to take a Ph.D. at Northwestern University. He joined the UN Trusteeship Department as a research officer and was chosen as first president of Frelimo in 1962. His greatest success was to hold the Second Party Congress in Mozambique in 1968. He was killed by parcel bomb in 1969.

Movimento das Forças Armadas (Movement of the Armed Forces—MFA)

The MFA, formed within the Portuguese military in 1973, overthrew the authoritarian right-wing government of Portugal in April 1974, leading to Portuguese acceptance of the independence of its former African colonies, including Mozambique.

Renamo (Resistencia Nacional Moçambicana, Mozambique National Resistance)

Originally organized by Rhodesian security agents in 1976 to counter anti-Rhodesian rebels operating from Mozambique, Renamo was later developed by the white South African government into an anti-Frelimo resistance force led by Afonso Dhlakama. In 1994, Renamo ran as a political party in Mozambique's first multiparty elections and finished second to Frelimo.

Malyn Newitt

See Also Angolan Revolution; Colonialism, Anti-Colonialism, and Neo-colonialism; Documentaries of Revolution; Guerrilla Warfare and Revolution; Guinea-Bissau: Revolution and Independence; Population, Economic Development, and Revolution; South African Revolution; Zimbabwean Revolution

References and Further Readings
Abrahamsson, Hans, and A. Nilsson, 1995. *Mozambique: The Troubled Transition.* London: Zed.
Alden, C. 2001. *Mozambique and the Construction of the New African State: From Negotiations to Nation Building.* New York: St. Martin's.
Chabal, Patrick. 2002. *A History of Postcolonial Lusophone Africa.* London: Hurst.
Hall, M., and T. Young. 1997. *Confronting Leviathan: Mozambique since Independence.* London: Hurst.
Isaacman, Allen, and B. Isaacman, 1983. *Mozambique: From Colonialism to Revolution, 1900–1982.* Boulder, CO: Westview.
Kruks, Sonia, and Ben Wisner. 1984. "The State, the Party and the Female Peasantry in Mozambique," *Journal of Southern African Studies* 11: 105–127.
Mittelman, J. 1981. *Underdevelopment and the Transition to Socialism: Mozambique and Tanzania.* New York: Academic.

Munslow, B. 1983. *Mozambique: The Revolution and Its Origins.* London: Longman.

Newitt, Malyn. 1995. *A History of Mozambique.* London: Hurst.

Resenha Historico-Militar das Campanhas de Africa. 1988. Vol. 1: 261. Lisbon: Estado-Maior do Exercito.

Vines, Alex. 1995. *Renamo: From Terrorism to Democracy in Mozambique?* Oxford: James Currey.

Music and Revolution

In order to understand music in relation to revolutionary collective action, one must first briefly review the essential nature and characteristics of music. Music, firstly, is a message-carrying medium or symbol system. Equally important, music, and its unique subspecies, revolutionary music, provides symbolic meanings to collectives or social groups. For social groups music often becomes a "solidarity ritual"—that is, a group ritual in which individuals within a group express their unity, or what makes "them" a "we." Many important thinkers have commented on the nature of music and its importance in society, a few of which are reviewed below.

Plato, in the *Republic,* argued that music and poetry are powerful rhetorical tools, and he speculated that different tunes, depending on the mode (or key), can engender different sensations and promote certain social actions. Marx saw music as a distorted mirror, one that portrays convoluted images masking the true nature of the relations of production, working-class exploitation, and alienation resulting from capitalist society. Many subsequent social scientists, such as Antonio Gramsci and Theodor Adorno, criticized Marx and Marxism for ignoring the complexity of cultural phenomena, including music. For instance, Gramsci (1971) might argue that Marx considered music only in its hegemonic (dominant) form but ignored its antithetic form, manifesting as revolutionary or anti-hegemonic music. Although these theorists offer interesting insights, they ignore the essential elements of music and the diversity of the medium.

A number of queries regarding revolutionary music are worth exploring in more depth. First, how does revolutionary music differ from common forms of music? Second, how does revolutionary music convey its messages? What are the major themes of revolutionary music? Finally, what types of messages in revolutionary music promote a sense of "we"?

In the first place, revolutionary music takes on many forms and can represent many factions during social upheaval. So while one might associate "revolutionary" in the vernacular with radical left movements, the term extends beyond that. With that in mind, revolutionary music is best understood as a form of political discourse between and within competing factions during social upheaval, including, in particular circumstances, socialist, liberal, conservative, fascist, counterrevolutionary, and revolutionary forces. Also, revolutionary music carries clearly intended meanings. Thus, in contrast to the more abstract and metaphorical articulations of meaning in many forms of music, revolutionary songs are less obscure and more rhetorical. Overall, music in the context of a social revolution symbolizes unity, and it defines the struggle and how those involved directly or indirectly should act.

Revolutionary music, in terms of the tune or lyric, frequently conveys unity by referring to pre-existing cultural symbols and combining them in new ways. For example, a revolutionary song might utilize traditional institutions permeating the society prior to the upheaval, such as religious communities, in order to define who is friend and who is foe. The most powerful and widespread theme in revolutionary music is nationalism, a concept that first emerged during the French Revolution. Revolutionary songs will associate the movement with a common heritage, a "brotherhood," or "fatherland," as well as common beliefs, values, and enemies.

In addition to differing themes and symbols, the performance of revolutionary music is unique. Audiences are usually more active participants in revolutionary songs. The border between performer and audience is blurred, as revolutionary songs become a ritual in which all the participants are engaged through the playing of instruments, singing along, or refashioning lyrics. The ritual of performing revolutionary songs together helps convey a message of unity, engenders emotional attachment to the group, expresses revolutionary ideology, and reinforces goals.

To illustrate, the songs sung during the American Revolution were often reminiscent of Puritan hymnals or British folk songs. The tunes made use of instruments, melodies, and styles popular in the culture prior to the revolution. Likewise, the act of the audience's passionate singing of the revolutionary song was highly reminiscent of church activities. The lyrics of the revolutionary songs clearly represent collective unity, as Dr. Joseph Warren conveys in the American Revolutionary song "Free America," written in 1770:

> *Torn from a world of tyrants*
> *Beneath this western sky*
> *We formed a new dominion,*
> *A land of liberty;*
> *The world shall own we're freemen here*
> *And such will ever be,*
> *For love and liberty.* (Warren 1770)

The subjective pronoun "we," or its semantic equivalent in other languages, is a recurring component of the lyrics of "Free America," as it is in many revolutionary songs. "We" is also employed in the first line of "Bonnie Blue Flag," a revolutionary song popular in the South during the American Civil War and eerily similar to "Free America": *"We are a band of brothers, and native to the soil, fighting for our liberty, with treasure, blood, and toil"* (Macarthy 1861). The prevalence of "we" in revolutionary songs illuminates the collective identity theme in revolutionary lyrics.

Other revolutionary songs recall fallen heroes bravely cut down in battle, glorifying those willing to sacrifice all for the movement. In other cases, revolutionary songs will make reference to the enemy and why they are opposed. During the American Civil War the counter-revolutionary Union anthem "Glory! Glory! Hallelujah!" eulogized the martyred John Brown (the "Battle Hymn of the Republic" shared the same melody, but had different lyrics, omitting mention of John Brown). John Brown was a devoutly religious abolitionist who, in 1859, two years before the start of the Civil War, stormed a federal arsenal at Harper's Ferry to arm the slaves and lead a revolt against plantation owners in the South. His attempt failed, ending in his capture and eventual execution, but his spirit lived on, as he became a mythical figure for the Union. The popular refrain of "Glory! Glory! Hallelujah!" begins, *"John Brown's body lies a mould'ring in the grave, his soul is marching on"* (Federal Volunteers 1861 "Music of the American Civil War"). The last verse makes reference to the Confederate president and retribution for slave lynching: *"They will hang Jeff Davis to a tree, as they march along."*

It is also the case, however, that social revolutions can bring about major innovation in musical forms, such as in opera during the French Revolution or the psychedelic music of the late 1960s. Although traditional musical elements are common in revolutionary music, the term "revolution" implies a break with tradition or established social order. In many cases composers may employ new chords, melodies, or instruments to convey this "break with tradition," or to express the freedom and possibilities of a new society. Furthermore, the breakdown of social order and convention could engender an emotional mindset that would encourage innovative compositions. The composers of music during revolutionary upheaval also change, often breaking down class or professional barriers, allowing new perspectives to transform the music. Thus, music in general drastically changes in a culture during a revolution, even if the songs communicate nothing political.

In addition, the lyrical content of popular songs shifts drastically during social upheaval and revolution. Revolutionary lyrics often exhibit more realism, portraying actual and recent historical events in order to produce mythical heroes and events for constructing idealized conceptions of revolutionary action. Revolutionary music, therefore, provides a provocative example of how cultural innovation can coalesce with traditional structures, conventions, and symbols to produce new forms of cultural expression.

Finally, music, although not necessary for a successful social revolution, may function to crystallize the unifying motivation of a revolution. A unifying motivation, such as anti-imperialism, is the ideological impetus of the revolution that transcends traditional social boundaries such as race or class. Because unifying motivation implies a broad coalition, such unity is often difficult to achieve. Consequently, music has played a central role in the construction and dissemination of unifying motivations in many social movements throughout history.

MUSIC DURING THE FRENCH REVOLUTION

The French Revolution witnessed the first large-scale implementation of music for the purpose of conveying political messages and revolutionary propaganda. French revolutionaries successfully made use of national identity and patriotic fervor to combat many of France's powerful neighbors whose leaders were hostile to the democratic and anti-aristocratic messages of the French Revolution. Volunteer armies proudly marched through Paris on their way to war as large crowds passionately sang along with "La Marseillaise":

> *What! These foreign cohorts!*
> *They would make laws in our homes!*
> *What! These mercenary phalanxes*
> *Would cut down our proud warriors (2X).*
> *Good Lord! By chained hands*
> *Our brow would yield under the yoke.*
> *Some vile despots would have themselves be*
> *The masters of our destinies!* (Rouget de Lisle 1792)

"La Marseillaise" was originally entitled "War Song for the Rhine Army" and became the anthem of the French Revolution. Captain Claude-Joseph Rouget de Lisle penned the song for revolutionary armies in April 1792, but it became the battle cry for the Marseillaise (a region of France) Volunteers. "La Marseillaise" was so popular among the French people that it became the French national anthem during the Third Republic (1879). Ironically, "La Marseillaise" was sung during the raising of the French flag in France's imperial colonies, no doubt fodder for anti-imperialist revolutionaries.

During the revolution, both the royalists, who were loyal to the *ancien regime* (monarchy), and the radicals, who wished to abolish the privileged classes, employed music to carry their political messages, because of the speed, low cost, and malleability of the medium. The task of writing most of the revolutionary songs penned during the late eighteenth century fell to commoners and nonprofessional composers. While counter-revolutionary songs were often more formal, professionally composed, and presented in the theaters to more cosmopolitan audiences, many revolutionary and counter-revolutionary songs were street performances. Prior to Robespierre's Reign of Terror, the streets of Paris were alive with the sounds of musical debate between royalists and radicals. Songs were frequently transformed as they were performed at revolutionary gatherings and represented a creative form of political participation. The French people altered the song's lyrics or vocal inflections to produce idiosyncratic and personalized revolutionary messages.

For instance, "Ça Ira," arguably the first "popular" song of the French Revolution, took on many lyrical permutations as the political climate of the revolution changed (Mason 1996). "Ça Ira" was a salient form of political discourse as the streets of Paris echoed with variations, rebuttals, and satires of the song. "Ça Ira" became popular during the 1789 Festival of Federation, when the Three Estates (that is, aristocracy, clergy, and everyone else: merchants, professionals, workers, and peasants) sought to resolve their differences and form a constitutional monarchy. "Ça Ira," meaning "things will work out," was a song of hope and conveyed feelings of unity and reconciliation. An earlier version extols the festival:

> Ah! ça ira, ça ira, ça ira
> We must sing in celebration
> Ah! ça ira, ça ira, ça ira
> All will remember the great festival. (ibid., 44)

Later permutations became radicalized as peasants hungry for bread sang jeeringly on the street corners: *Ça ira, Hang the aristocrats!*" (ibid.). Later performances of the "Ça Ira" occurred at political forums such as the General Assembly, where revolutionaries would drown out opposition speeches with rousing impromptu renditions (ibid., 50).At the same time, royalists altered "Ça Ira" lyrically to mock commoners and were openly hostile to the revolutionaries who sang it.

In summary, the French Revolution illustrates how factions during revolutionary upheaval can effectively employ music as a means of transmitting political propaganda and stirring emotional political sentiments. In this respect, French revolutionary music became the model for musical propaganda, and as the French Revolution spread throughout Europe, so did its democratic and anti-aristocratic spirit transmitted in song.

"COMMUNIST INTERNATIONALE"

The hope of a classless society echoed in the lofty ideals of the French Revolution was quickly squandered as the First Republic was transformed into the Napoleonic empire. Napoléon's military successes did, however, spread the ideology of the revolution throughout the European continent. After his defeat, persisting dissatisfaction with conservative regimes led to further revolutionary uprisings all over Europe and again in France with the rise of the Third Republic. This was the setting for arguably the most popular revolutionary song ever composed, the "Communist Internationale" (or "L'Internationale").

Eugéne Pottier wrote the song's lyrics during the Paris Commune of 1871, where hopes of a democratic working-class government in France were burgeoning. The Paris Commune and its goals were quickly crushed. Nevertheless, "L'Internationale" lived on to embody the hope of ending the exploitation of oppressed peoples everywhere. The song's lyrics electrified the working masses:

> Arise ye workers
> from your slumbers
> Arise ye prisoners of want.
> For reason in revolt now thunders
> And at last ends the age of can't.
> Away with all your superstitions
> Servile masses arise, arise.
> We'll change henceforth the old tradition
> And spurn the dust to win the prize. (Pottier 1871)

The tune, written by Adolphe Degeyter, is bright and brisk with a steady march feel, similar lyrically and musically to "La Marseillaise." Since the advent of "L'Internationale," almost every socialist revolution fueled with the powerful rhetoric of Marxism has adapted the song as its anthem.

"L'Internationale" re-emerged in 1917, during the Bolshevik Revolution in Russia, and eventually became the national anthem of the Soviet Union until the "Hymn of the Soviet Union" replaced it in 1944. This act coincided with the waning of the Soviet Union's commitment to an international Communist revolution.

FASCIST MUSIC

Much like the tumultuous climate that preceded *"La Marseillaise,"* post–World War I Germany was a hotbed of revolutionary activity. Along with similar movments in Italy and Spain, Nazi Fascism represented an extreme right-wing response to the political and social upheaval of post–World War I Europe. The Nazis under the guidance of Joseph

Goebbels created one of the most effective propaganda machines in history, employing nationalism, anti-Communism, anti-Semitism, and racism to seize and solidify power.

The anthem of the Nazi party was the "Horst Wessel's Song." The song tells the story of a party organizer and storm trooper, Horst Wessel, who was allegedly martyred by Communists. The song's chorus strongly expresses anti-Communist rhetoric, announcing: *"Comrades, by the Red Front Reaction* [communists] *killed, are buried, but march with us in image at our side"* (Synder 1997, 164). "Horst Wessel's Song" also couples Nazi symbols with the alleviation of the severe economic conditions that paralyzed German society: *"The Swastika gives hope to our entrenched millions. . . . The day for freedom and bread is at hand"* (ibid.). The strong rhetoric in "Horst Wessel's Song" brings to life the violent political discourse of post-war Germany, and the centrality that the Nazi Party was to have in everyday life.

The shame surrounding the Nazi exploitation of German national pride is still visible today in the "denazified" German national anthem, "Das Lied der Deutschen" ["The Song of the Germans"]. The first stanza of the original version—*"Germany, Germany above all, above anything in the World"* (Hoffmann Von Fallersleben 1841)—has been deleted, because the Nazis misinterpreted the lyric to suggest German superiority above all else. The lyric, originally written in 1841 during the movement for German unification, was meant to signify German unity in place of the divided local fiefdoms and the occupation of foreign powers. In addition to this, it is now illegal to sing the "Horst Wessel's Song" in Germany, a further indication of the post-war "denazification" of music.

THE CULTURAL REVOLUTION IN CHINA

In 1949, China became a Socialist republic under the guidance of the brilliant and charismatic Marxist-Leninist revolutionary Mao Zedong. The initial economic reforms of the Great Leap (1958–1960) were not successful, and the Chinese economy suffered severe setbacks as workers' productivity fell and famines devastated rural areas. Mao speculated that these failures resulted from a lack of cultural adjustment to communal life and from remnants of the cultural values of the supplanted feudal society. He believed that a cultural revolution was necessary to purge the "bourgeoisie ideology" from Chinese art and music in order to produce a permanent "revolutionary consciousness." During the period known as the Cultural Revolution (1966–1968), Chinese opera was greatly transformed, and traditional Chinese operas were replaced with "model operas" (*yangbinxi*) or "revolutionary model operas" (*geming yangbinxi*) (Kraicer 2004).

Jiang Qing, Mao's powerful wife, instituted sweeping reforms and set strict standards for art, music, and drama, ensuring that the new art coincided with revolutionary ideology and Maoist philosophy. These new art forms dealt with contemporary issues, rather than the historical themes pervading traditional Chinese art. Jiang Qing focused particularly on the "model operas" and believed that opera was a key rhetorical tool for transforming Chinese culture. Two themes emerged in the model operas: songs about heroes of the Communist revolution, and songs about heroes who repelled foreign invasions. The most famous examples of model operas include *The Legend of the Red Lantern* [*Hong deng ji*], *Taking Tiger Mountain by Strategy* [*Zhiqu weihushan*], and *Shajiabang*.

The East Is Red, an adaptation of a traditional Chinese folk song and aria in a popular model opera, quickly became the anthem of the Cultural Revolution; it contained many elements that were prominent in other songs of the period. *The East Is Red* became the title song for a model opera which combined traditional folk songs and instruments with Western chromatics, vocal arrangements, and orchestration, using brass and bowed strings (Levine 1995). The music symbolized the desire of China to Westernize technologically but remain culturally and politically distinct and autonomous.

LATIN AMERICAN REVOLUTIONS

Revolutionary movements often use music along with a variety of other tactics outside the mainstream media outlets to construct unity and communicate the unifying motivation behind the fight. That is because counter-revolutionary groups often control these outlets and can make use of greater financial resources to undertake massive propaganda campaigns. Nowhere is this phenomenon more apparent than in Latin America, where revolutionary music greatly impacted social revolutions in Guatemala, Nicaragua, Cuba, El Salvador, and Argentina. In these nations, many people eulogized in song revolutionaries who took up arms against the powerful and exploitive minorities that dominated state and military institutions.

Latin America was under foreign control for hundreds of years after Columbus's voyage in 1492. The Spanish constructed a colonial system centered on the extraction of raw resources such as gold and other valuable metals. This system produced a high concentration of wealth and power in the hands of very few, and an economic system heavily dependent upon slavery. As a result of this power concentration, "high art," including music, was mostly imported from Europe. However, Latin music was unique, with its roots in the lower, exploited classes: the mestizo ("mixed blood") and the Indians. Therefore, Latin American revolutionary music is immediately symbolic of class and racial identity, often referred to in lyric as *el pueblo* ("our people") (Judson 2002, 220–221).

The concept of *el pueblo* transcends national borders, and its ubiquity is a sign of the international spirit of Latin American revolutionary music. For example, El Salvadoran songs make reference to the Cuban Revolution or the Sandinistas in Nicaragua. "Hasta Siembre" ["Until Always"]—a song honoring the Argentinean revolutionary Che Guevara, who played an important role in the Cuban Revolution and also fought for revolution in Africa and South America—is sung throughout Latin America. The lyrics celebrate Che's revolutionary courage beyond Cuba.

> *Your revolutionary love*
> *Leads you to a new undertaking*
> *Where they are awaiting the firmness*
> *Of your liberating arm*
> *We will carry on*
> *As we did along with you*
> *And with Fidel we say to you:*
> *Until Always, Commandante.* (Puebla 2004)

Three factors contribute to the solidarity of *el pueblo* and its manifestation in Latin American revolutionary music. First, like the Thirteen Colonies of North America, the countries of Latin America, with the exception of Brazil, share a common language: Spanish. That has allowed revolutionary ideals to spread rapidly throughout most of Latin America, and also has provided a sense of community. Second, the Catholic Church was a powerful and ubiquitous institution in Latin America, unifying the mestizo population. Hence, religious themes both musically and lyrically abound in Latin American revolutionary songs. Finally, the imperial power of the United States and its economic and political influence in all countries of the region provide a powerful unifying symbol for *el pueblo*. Folk heroes like Che Guevara, Fidel Castro, and Augusto Cèsar Sandino, who stood up to imperialist power, are often lauded in revolutionary songs. Furthermore, the concept in Latin American revolutionary circles of the "dependent bourgeoisie," the elites who benefit from U.S. dominance, is also a prevailing theme in revolutionary lyrics (Judson 2002, 213–215). Nationalism and anti-imperialism are powerful concepts in Latin American revolutionary music, and that music conveys a unique sense of solidarity.

CONCLUSION

Music and its performance represent an essential solidarity ritual for revolutionary movements. Revolutionary songs function to define the motivations of the group and its identity. The songs' lyrics refer to national identity, class, common enemies, a common "fatherland," religious affiliation, and race to define movement participants and the people whose cause the movement advocates. Revolutionary songs, at the same time, must not alienate other potential supporters. In the case of popular revolutions, the songs solidify a connection between the revolutionaries and the vast majority of people who support the revolution. Widespread popular support is essential for revolutionary movements, which often combat well-trained and well-equipped military adversaries. Revolutionary music must balance between inspiring revolutionary combatants and expressing a unifying message that will encourage large-scale support.

The performance of songs in the context of a revolution can evoke strong emotional response among the revolution's participants, especially during violent conflict. Songs are often sung to honor fallen heroes and friends, as well as to remind combatants of what they are fighting for. Thus the performance of revolutionary songs has very often preceded or followed major battles or periods of crisis in order to reinforce commitment to the struggle and remind participants and supporters of the sacrifice necessary to achieve the movement's goals. They also follow great successes, in order to maintain unity and the revolutionary spirit essential for transforming societies once the fighting is over.

Gordon Gauchat

See Also American Revolution; Anarchism, Communism, and Socialism; Chinese Revolution; Cinema of Revolution; Colonialism, Anti-Colonialism, and Neo-Colonialism; Cuban Revolution; Documentaries of Revolution; French Revolution; Ideology, Propaganda, and Revolution; Literature and Modern Revolution; Nazi Revolution: Politics and Racial Hierarchy; Paris Commune of 1871; Russian Revolution of 1917; Salvadoran Revolution; Slave Rebellions in the United States; U.S. Southern Secessionist Rebellion and Civil War

Note Lines from "Ça Ira" reprinted from *Singing the French Revolution,* by Laura Mason. Copyright ©1996 by Cornell University. Used by permission of the publisher, Cornell University Press

References and Further Readings
Adorno, Theodor. 1949. *Philosophy of Modern Music.* New York: Seabury.
_____. 1991. *The Culture Industry: Selected Essays on Mass Culture.* London: Routlege.
Boyd, Malcolm, ed. 1992. *Music and the French Revolution.* New York: Cambridge University Press.
DeFronzo, James. 1996. *Revolutions and Revolutionary Movements.* 2nd edition. Boulder, CO: Westview.
Eyerman, Ron and Andrew Jamison. 1998. *Music and Social Movements: Mobilizing Traditions in the Twentieth Century.* Cambridge: Cambridge University Press.
Gramsci, Antonio. 1971. *Selections from the Prison Notebooks.* London: New Left.
Hoffmann Von Fallersleben, August Heinrich. 1841. "Das Lied der Deutschen," s.v. *Nazi Songs.* Wikipedia,

http://en.wikipedia.org/wiki/Nazi_Songs#Deutschland_Erwache (accessed October 28, 2004).

Judson, Fred. 2002. "Central American Revolutionary Music." Pp. 204–235 in *Marx and Music: Ideas, Practice, Politics,* edited by Regula Burckhardt Qureshi. New York: Routledge.

Klumpenhouwer, Henry. 2002. "Commodity-Form, Disavowal, and Practices of Musical Theory." Pp. 23–41 in *Marx and Music: Ideas, Practice, Politics,* edited by Regula Burckhardt Qureshi. New York: Routledge.

Kraicer, Shelly. 2004. "Beijing Opera, Revolutionary Opera, and Jiang Jie," http://194.21.179.166/cecudine/datahost/fef2004/english/china2004_3.htm (accessed October 17, 2004).

Levine, Wendy. 1995. "The Development of the Beijing Opera during the Cultural Revolution." MBA thesis, University of Colorado at Boulder,

Macarthy, Harry. 1861. "Bonnie Blue Flag": The Music of the American Civil War, http://www.pdmusic.org/civilwar/cws05.txt (accessed October 28, 2004).

Mason, Ann. 1996. *Singing the French Revolution.* Ithaca, NY: Cornell University Press.

"Music of the American Civil War." "Glory! Glory! Hallelujah!" as sung by Federal Volunteers, 1861, http://www.pdmusic.org/civilwar/cws03.txt (accessed October 28, 2004).

Plato. 1995. *The Republic: Book III.* Translated by Desmond Lee. New York: Penguin Classics.

Pottier, Eugéne. 1871. "Internationale": A Little Page on the Internationale, http://www.ifa.hawaii.edu/~yan/int/int.html (accessed October 28, 2004).

Puebla, Carlos. "Hasta siempre comandante Che Guevara." Marxism and Music Archive, http://www.marxists.org/subject/art/music/puebla-carlos/lyrics/hasta-siempre.htm (accessed October 28, 2004).

Rouget de Lisle. 1792. "La Marseillaise": The Marseillaise, http://perso.wanadoo.fr/pierre.gay/EngPages/MarsEN (accessed October 28, 2004).

Synder, Louis. 1997. "Horst Wessel's Song," in *Encyclopedia of the Third Reich.* New York: Marlowe.

Warren, Joseph. 1770. "Free America": Folk Music of England, Scotland, Ireland, Wales, and America, http://www.contemplator.com/america/freeamer.html (accessed October 28, 2004).

N

Nationalism and Revolution

Nationalism is an ideology that typically is manifested through an emotional devotion to a nation-state, or by a people who have a bond of unity from common links such as a sense of shared culture, language, religion, ethnicity, race, history, and geography. It developed in Europe, taking the place of allegiance to local feudal lords and to the political authority of the Roman Catholic Church.

Inspired by the 1648 Treaty of Westphalia's delineation of European nation-states, nationalism spread in eighteenth-century Europe as feudalism and universal loyalty to the church gave way to new secular ideologies of government put forth by the intelligentsia of the Enlightenment. Most scholars credit the late-eighteenth-century French philosopher and writer Jean-Jacques Rousseau as the first to define the ideology and role of nationalism, along with the "general will" of a nation. He called for humanity to avoid feudalism and instead focus on the domestic body politic of one's nation. Rousseau's writings were admired by some elements of the European intelligentsia, especially those like Maximilien Robespierre and Giuseppe Garibaldi, who sought to create a new order through revolution.

The development of nationalism played a key role in shaping modern revolutions. Since the time of the French Revolution, nationalism has been used to both promote and suppress revolutions. French revolutionary Jacobin leaders such as Robespierre were the first to use Rousseau's modern concept of nationalism to support revolution. The famous cry of French revolutionaries for "liberty, equality, fraternity" and the revolutionary anthem "Marche des Marseillaise" were meant to invoke sentiments of nationalism in support of the revolution. Music, poetry, print, icons, and more recently, the electronic media, all have been used to appeal to nationalism to fuel revolution.

Nationalism can strengthen revolutionary movements by stirring up sentiments of national loyalty. Whether motivated by religion, race, or memories of the past, nationalism has the potential to appeal to different social classes, ethnic groups, and rural and urban inhabitants. The psychological power of nationalism can be critical for the survival of initially disorganized or decentralized revolutionary movements, and it can sustain revolutionary momentum in the face of setbacks. Such was the case with the efforts of nineteenth-century Irish revolutionaries, who despite frequent disorganization and repeated failure, successfully maintained their national will to be free from British rule. Furthermore, nationalist solidarity is often a prerequisite for a new revolutionary government to introduce social reform.

There are many different types of nationalism, but those most closely linked to revolutionary movements are integral, exclusionary, risorgimento, unifying, and irredentist (Alter 1994; Brubaker 1996; Kohn 1982). Although some nations and revolutions make use of only one type, others exhibit multiple types of nationalism. For example, during the Algerian Revolution of 1955–1962, Algerians exhibited risorgimento nationalism as they worked to expel the French and unifying nationalism as they sought to pull together revolutionary factions. In some regions of the world certain types of nationalism emerged without being linked to revolution; however, in many cases nationalism can be found to have either a pro-revolutionary role or an anti-revolutionary role.

INTEGRAL NATIONALISM AND REVOLUTION

Integral nationalism asserts a superiority and right to dominate, absorb, or assimilate other nations. Thus, it is often linked to imperialism. Factors such as the assumed economic, political, military, racial, cultural, religious, and linguistic superiority of one's nation and the right to impose colonial or neo-colonial rule (a supposedly independent government in reality serving the interests of the former colonizing power) are typical with this type of nationalism. In many instances integral nationalism may be accompanied by exclusionary nationalism (see below). Nations that have exhibited integral nationalism include Britain, France, Spain, Portugal, Germany, Japan, Belgium, Russia, the United States, and Turkey. Integral nationalism can justify policies of conquering, exploiting, culturally assimilating, and even decimating or annihilating the indigenous people of other societies.

Integral nationalism drove colonial powers to seize control of many lesser-developed parts of the world, including virtually all of Africa. In doing so, the imperialist governments created the conditions that would later give rise to the national liberation movements of risorgimento nationalism (see below). Entering a Third World region, imperialists, such as Leopold of Belgium in the nineteenth century, often devastated the existing social order in establishing control. The imperialist process over time would typically also involve economic and cultural change. The colonizing power would seek to derive available resources from the occupied territory or its people, and attempt to transform aspects of the local economy to benefit the imperialist nation. For example, agriculture might be transformed from growing food crops for local consumption to cultivation of products for the world market, such as cotton plantations in Mozambique under Portuguese control or rubber plantations in Vietnam and Cambodia under the French. Culturally, the colonizing power would generally require the use of its language and propagate acceptance of and appreciation for the culture of the colonizing power. Spreading the use of the language of the imperialist nation would often become the key tool in attempts to assimilate a colonized people, often accompanied by propagation of the imperialist nation's religion—typically first to members of the colony's indigenous elite. For the most part, the previous social order could not be resurrected as a practical means of driving out the imperialist power, nor would the original social order be adequate in the new industrialized world of nation-states after the imperialists left.

By influencing the foreign policy decisions made by those in power in an imperialist state, integral nationalism has had a significant impact on the later development of revolutionary movements. The British, for example, crushed Chinese military resistance to their marketing of opium to the Chinese people in "Opium Wars," beginning in 1839. Later, the burden and plight of millions of Chinese opium addicts would become a significant aspect of anti-imperialist revolutionary ideology in China. The French in the 1920s and 1930s tried to crush Vietnamese movements for independence rather than agree to lose outright political control of their profitable colony. This intransigence eventually contributed to the creation of a Vietnamese revolutionary army, the Viet Minh, which in a costly war violently evicted the French. U.S. integral nationalism may have contributed to its attempts to suppress the Vietnamese Revolution from the mid-1950s through the early 1970s. More recently, Russian integral nationalism might be a major motive for its actions in Chechnya.

In 1898, President McKinley's administration made use of the integral nationalist sentiment, stirred up by the apparently mistaken belief that Spanish forces had blown up the USS *Maine* in Havana harbor, to overthrow Spanish colonial rule in Cuba, Puerto Rico, and the Philippines; the United States held on to the latter two territories granting independence to the Philippines after World War II.

Integral nationalism in the United States had emerged as a powerful ideology during the nineteenth century and apparently played a major role in justifying the westward expansion of the United States and the simultaneous subjugation of Native Americans. U.S. integral nationalism, entering the world stage with the relatively easy U.S. victories in the Spanish American War in 1898, probably contributed to ambitions to dominate Latin America economically and politically and led to numerous U.S. military interventions in Central America and the Caribbean from 1898 to the late twentieth century. For example, U.S. support for the Panamanian secession from Colombia in 1903 enabled the United States to gain access to the Isthmus of Panama and build the Panama Canal under desirable terms, including long-term acquisition of Panamanian territory on either side of the canal. Another example was the U.S.-backed and -assisted overthrow of the democratically elected reform leader of Guatemala, Jacobo Arbenz Guzmán, in 1954. Arbenz's policies were seen as endangering the economic well-being of a major U.S. corporation and might have led to similar political changes detrimental to the profitability of business projects in other Latin American countries if his reforms had succeeded and democracy been preserved in Guatemala.

Massive grassroots opposition to the Vietnam War in the United States, and the failure of U.S. policy there by the mid 1970s, pressured the U.S. government to take a greater interest in its alliances and overall international cooperation. The attacks of September 11, 2001, however, resulted in a drastic increase in sentiments of integral nationalism in the United States. Like the British empire in earlier times, U.S. integral nationalism is now widely viewed as having contributed to invasions and occupations of other countries and to have led to a retrenchment of U.S. military bases around the globe.

EXCLUSIONARY NATIONALISM AND REVOLUTION

Governments that exhibit extreme integral nationalism are sometimes also characterized by exclusionary nationalism, the ideology that ethnic, racial, or religious purity is a necessary aspect of national entity. The result is the expulsion or genocide of segments of the population. Exclusionary nationalism has been used by oppressive regimes that sought to consolidate power by blaming and persecuting disempowered minority groups for social problems and mobilizing popular resentment and action against them. Examples include the Ottoman Turks, accused of killing more than a million Armenians in 1915; Nazi Germans, who murdered 6 million Jews and Gypsies in the Holocaust of the 1930s and 1940s; Hutu extremists in Rwanda, who butchered hundreds of thousands of Tutsis in 1994; and thousands of deaths in campaigns to ethnically cleanse territories in Bosnia in the 1990s. Serbian exclusionary nationalism was used by the Serbian leader Slobodan Milosevic and his followers as a tool to consolidate Serbian power and territorial aggrandizement after the breakup of Yugoslavia in 1993. The international community responded with UN military intervention and war crimes trials of accused perpetrators of genocide.

RISORGIMENTO NATIONALISM AND REVOLUTION

Risorgimento nationalism is an ideology often opposed to the integral nationalism of another country and includes sentiments of liberation and emancipation. Risorgimento nationalism has motivated people to struggle and sacrifice in order to expel, secede from, or resist invasion of an aggressive power. This national-liberation form of nationalism has had a primary role in motivating many revolutionaries to fight to free their peoples from either colonialism or neo-colonialism.

Europe

For nearly two hundred years, risorgimento nationalism has mobilized revolutionary forces in Europe in places such as Russia, Ireland, Italy, Hungary, Germany, Poland, Greece, the Balkans, and Macedonia. The fervor of national liberation led to revolution in the Austrio-Hungarian empire. In the nineteenth century, Hungary and Italy sought to free themselves from Austrian rule. Although the Habsburg dynasty attempted to censor revolutionary dissent, risorgimento nationalistic sentiments became a powerful force for change. This nationalism can be found in the works of the famous Hungarian composer Franz Liszt, who wrote popular music in the 1830s and 1840s designed to inspire sentiments of Hungarian nationalism. Although Liszt was born in Hungary in 1811, he spent most of his life elsewhere. Nevertheless, he retained his national identity and intense loyalty to his nation of birth.

Italian revolutionaries also used music to inspire rebellion against foreign rule. Giuseppe Verdi's musical compositions encouraged Italian nationalism. Indeed, Verdi's politically oriented operas became so popular that the composer became a cultural icon of Italian patriotism. Verdi's music helped to motivate many Italians to support Giuseppe Garabaldi when he arrived to lead Italy to unity and independence in 1860. Ironically, the Italians who fought against Austrian imperialism in the nineteenth century became imperialists themselves as they sought to create their own empire in the twentieth century.

Latin America

Nearly all of Latin America was at one time under the imperial rule of the European powers. Risorgimento nationalism began to motivate revolutions of national liberation in Latin America dating back to the early nineteenth century. Risorgimento nationalism based on racial identity fueled the Haitian Revolution against the French in 1804. In the 1820s, Simon Bolívar summoned the people of Latin America, including whites, mestizos, blacks, and indigenous people, to mobilize and carry out a series of successful revolutions against Spanish domination. In the twentieth century, revolutionaries such as Augusto César Sandino and Ernesto Che Guevara made use of sentiments of risorgimento nationalism against U.S. interventionism and what they viewed as puppet regimes controlled by and serving U.S. interests.

Africa

By the end of the nineteenth century nearly all of Africa had been taken by European powers. During this occupation, European ideas of revolutionary nationalism spread to Africa and combined with African aspirations for freedom to help inspire liberation movements. During World War II, the United States and its European allies made numerous proclamations declaring their war aims to support freedom and democracy. Those ideas were picked up and utilized by African nationalist movements, led by people such as Kwame Nkrumah, Ahmed Sékou Touré; Agostinho Neto, Patrice Lumumba, Nelson Mandela, and many others. Beginning in the 1950s, some European powers peacefully surrendered a number of African territories to indigenous governments. However, Africans in many locales had to resort to violent revolutions to free themselves from imperial rule. These revolutionaries employed sentiments of risorgimento nationalism to gather popular support. For example, during the Algerian Revolution, from 1954 to 1962, the National Liberation Front appealed to Algerian longings for liberation from French rule and from exploitation and discrimination by the French settlers, as later would Angolan and Mozambican revolutionaries in their struggles against Portuguese domination. In Africa today, risorgimento nationalism still motivates opposition to neo-colonialism.

Asia

European concepts of nationalism also spread to Asia and fused with local aspirations for liberation from foreign control to create modern nationalist movements. In the 1940s, after many years of struggle, Mahatma Gandhi led a largely nonviolent movement that succeeded in forcing the British to leave the colony upon which much of Britain's wealth and worldwide dominance had been based. Ho Chi Minh, Vo Nguyen Giap, and other Vietnamese revolutionaries also used risorgimento nationalism to motivate and mobilize initially poorly equipped people to fight a revolution that successfully defeated first the French army and later U.S. military intervention.

UNIFYING NATIONALISM AND REVOLUTION

Frequently a component of risorgimento nationalism but also existing in other contexts, unifying nationalism is a key element of many successful revolutions. In fact, students of revolution have argued that in order for a revolution to have a chance of victory, some unifying factor, such as unifying nationalism, must be present to unite otherwise competing classes in the revolutionary struggle. Unifying nationalism has served to combine different social groups or social classes

with conflicting economic interests in revolutionary alliances against colonial governments or indigenous dictatorial regimes perceived to be serving foreign interests. In China, unifying nationalism in 1911 aided Sun Yat-Sen's National People's Party, the Guo Min Dang, in overthrowing the Qing dynasty, which was viewed as corrupt, incompetent, and incapable of protecting the Chinese people from foreign aggression and exploitation. In Cuba decades later, the widespread belief that the military dictator Fulgencio Batista had become a self-enriching tool of foreign interests helped Fidel Castro and his associates build a powerful and ultimately successful revolutionary coalition. Unifying nationalism also played an essential role in the Iranian Revolution. Iranian secular leftists and religious fundamentalists shared an intense hatred for the monarchal regime of Shah Mohammad Pahlavi that temporarily united them in a revolutionary alliance. Both viewed the shah as a morally corrupting tool of foreign imperialism and economic exploitation whose regime had to be destroyed in order to free the Iranian people. In South Africa, unifying African nationalism served to unite many members of different tribal groups in a revolutionary movement led by the African National Congress that eventually brought about an end to apartheid.

Nationalist unity is often a prerequisite for a new revolutionary government to introduce sweeping social reform. After Castro's Cuban Revolution, the ability of the new government to defeat U.S.-sponsored and -organized intervention at the Bay of Pigs bolstered nationalist support for the revolutionary regime and its radical economic reforms.

Unifying nationalism can also have an at least indirect effect on civil rights movements. Unifying nationalism surged in the United States after the Japanese attack on Pearl Harbor on December 7, 1941, motivating and mobilizing most of the U.S. population to contribute to the war effort. Included were African Americans and women who were temporarily placed into positions previously unavailable to them because of the racist or sexist practices of the time. This experience of minority empowerment helped to inspire new attitudes about civil rights in the United States and the modern Civil Rights Movement, which led to the Civil Rights Act of 1964.

The perceived threat of revolutionary forces, whether foreign or domestic, can also stir up sentiments of unifying nationalism. For example, the granting of dominion status to Canada in 1867 was influenced by the Fenian (Irish-American revolutionaries) invasions of Canada after the U.S. Civil War as part of their strategy to free Ireland from British control. The Fenians also sought to foment a supporting revolution among the Quebecois, the descendants of French settlers. Years after the Fenians' failure, and still facing a threat from Quebecois separatists, the Canadian government agreed to Quebecois demands for autonomy status for Quebec.

Poland provides another major example. After the 1795 third partition of Poland between Russia, Prussia, and Austria, Poland ceased to exist as an independent state. The divided Polish people continued to share a common language and were also bound together by the institution and clergy of the Polish Catholic Church. Nationalist revolutionaries such as Józef Pilsudski secretly worked for Poland's reunification and liberation. During World War I, the three governments that controlled the Polish people all experienced traumatic defeats. Czarist Russia was overthrown in the revolution of 1917, and Germany and the Austro-Hungarian empire were defeated. The victorious Allied leaders at the Paris Peace Conference in 1919 decided to re-create the Polish nation. The Poles quickly became involved in territorial disputes with the new Bolshevik regime in Russia, and Poland was invaded by a large Red Army. Some Bolshevik leaders hoped that Polish workers and peasants would support the Red Army against the Polish upper class and that Poland might then become a conduit through which the Bolshevik Revolution could spread to Germany and western Europe. Instead, the vast majority of Poles united against the threat of foreign invasion and rallied to the defense of their nation. In 1920 near Warsaw the Polish army under Pilsudski defeated the invasion, and not only preserved Polish independence but also played a role in halting the westward expansion of a foreign revolutionary movement, Bolshevism.

IRREDENTIST NATIONALISM AND REVOLUTION

Often associated with unifying nationalism and risorgimento nationalism, irredentist nationalism transcends political borders. Irredentist nationalist movements refer to attempts made by a people sharing a common ethnicity, culture, and history to claim a real or imagined former territorial possession that has fallen under the control of one or more foreign states. The case of Poland, described above, is an example of irredentist nationalism as well as risorgimento and unifying nationalisms.

There are numerous examples of the effects of irredentist nationalism. The "official" Nazi political policy to unite the Germanic Austrians, the Germans of Czechoslovakia, and the Germans of Poland with Germany in a single Reich was a contributing factor to the outbreak of World War II in Europe. Attempts to join all Yugoslavs in one nation helped provoke World War I through the assassination by a Serb of the heir to the Austrian throne. Irredentist nationalism on the part of some component nationalities later contributed to war in Yugoslavia at the end of the twentieth century.

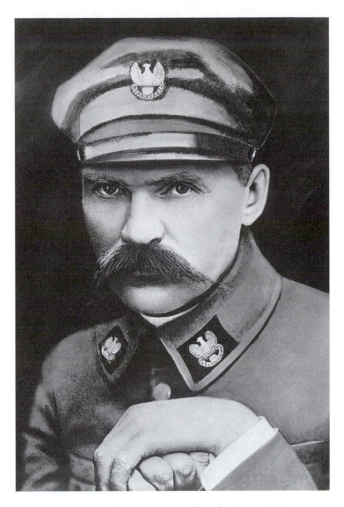

Józef Pilsudski, president (1918–1921) and prime minister (1926–1928, 1930–1935) of Poland. After he led an armed band that stole money from a Russian mail train, he organized an army to pursue his ambition of liberating Poland from Russian control. (Library of Congress)

Irredentist nationalism is also relevant to the Kurdish situation. Many Kurds residing in Iran, Iraq, Turkey, and Syria aspire to unification and the creation of an independent Kurdish state.

CONCLUSION

For more than two hundred years, nationalism has been used by and has inspired revolutionaries, and it has mobilized millions to fight for liberation from foreign domination. In certain forms it has also been an impetus for nations to conquer and exploit the peoples of other lands. Elements of zealous nationalism have been inherent in many of the wars and rev-

olutions of the nineteenth and twentieth centuries. Nationalism has been both a creative and a destructive force in human affairs, and it will quite likely remain a powerful force
for many years to come.

David E. Adleman

See Also Algerian Revolution; Angolan Revolution; Chinese
Revolution; Cinema of Revolution; Colonialism, Anti-
Colonialism, and Neo-Colonialism; Cuban Revolution; French
Revolution; Haitian Independence Revolution; Indian
Independence Movement; Iranian Revolution; Irish Revolution;
Italian Risorgimento; Kurdish Movements; Mozambique
Revolution; Nazi Revolution: Politics and Racial Hierarchy;
Nicaraguan Revolution; Polish Solidarity Movement; South
African Revolution; Spanish American Revolutions of
Independence; Vietnamese Revolution; Yugoslavia: Dissolution

References and Further Readings

Alter, Peter. 1994. *Nationalism* [*Nationalismus*]. 2nd edition.
Translated from the German by Edward Arnold. Frankfurt am
Main: Suhrkamp Verlag.
Brubaker, Rogers. 1996. *Nationalism Reframed.* Boston: Cambridge
University Press.
DeFronzo, James. 1996. *Revolutions and Revolutionary Movements.*
Boulder, CO: Westview.
Galway, James. 1982. *Nationalism and Revolution.* Video recording,
Polytel Film. Produced and directed by Derek Bailey. Princeton,
NJ: Films for the Humanities.
Goldstone, Jack A. 1999. *Who's Who in Political Revolutions.*
Washington, DC: Congressional Quarterly.
Greene, Thomas H. 1990. *Comparative Revolutionary Movements:
Search for Theory and Justice.* Englewood Cliffs, NJ: Prentice-Hall.
Isbister, John. 1991. *Promises Not Kept: The Betrayal of Social Change
in the Third World.* West Hartford, CT: Kumarian.
Jewett, Robert. 2003. *Captain America and the Crusade against Evil:
The Dilemma of Zealous Nationalism.* Grand Rapids, MI: William
B. Eerdmans.
Kohn, Hans. 1982. *Nationalism: Its Meaning and History.* Malabar,
FL: Robert E. Krieger.
Said, Edward W. 1993. *Culture and Imperialism.* New York: Alfred A.
Knopf.

Nazi Revolution: Politics and Racial Hierarchy

CHRONOLOGY

1806   Napoléon dissolves the Holy Roman empire
of the German nation.

1815   Congress of Vienna creates a German Confederation of thirty-nine states under the
presidency of Austria.

1834   The Zollverein (customs union) is created by
Prussia and subsequently joined by several
German states.

1848   Attempted liberal revolutions against authoritarian monarchies in several German
states, including Prussia and Austria. All fail.

1862   Prussian constitutional conflict between the
monarchy and liberals. Otto von Bismarck
appointed minister-president (head of government).

1864   Austria and Prussia victorious in war against
Denmark over Schleswig and Holstein. Prussia gains Schleswig; Austria gains Holstein.

1866   Austro-Prussian Seven Weeks' War, resulting in Austria's loss of Holstein and exclusion from the German Confederation.

1867   Prussia creates the North German Confederation under its leadership.

1870   Franco-Prussian War, in which the south
German states align themselves with Prussia.
Prussia's stunning victory allows Bismarck
to declare King Wilhelm of Prussia the German kaiser (emperor).

1888   Accession of Kaiser Wilhelm II, who is determined to maintain the power of the monarchy. Although there is some liberalization in
the southern states, Prussia retains its authoritarian system. From its inception, the
German empire develops industrially and
economically, especially in Prussia. By 1914
it is the strongest continental European
power and one of the top three industrial
powers in the world.

1914   On August 1, the outbreak of World War I,
by August 4 involves Germany and Austria-
Hungary versus Russia, France, Britain, and
Serbia. Many other powers subsequently en-
ter, including Italy, Turkey, Portugal, and the
United States.

1918   On October 28, naval mutinies break out in
Kiel, and sailors in other ports follow suit.
The unrest spreads to inland towns in the
"German Revolution." This includes an

abortive Communist rising in Berlin in January 1919 and a short-lived Munich Soviet Republic in April 1919.

On November 9, Kaiser Wilhelm II abdicates, bringing the Second Empire to an end. Germany becomes a republic, with a Socialist caretaker government led by Friedrich Ebert.

On November 11, armistice brings World War I to an end.

December 30, founding of the German Communist Party (KPD).

1919 January 5, founding of the Deutsche Arbeiterpartei (German Workers' Party) in Munich, which from February 1920 adopts the name Nationalsozialistische deutsche Arbeiterpartei—National Socialist German Worker's Party (NSDAP, or Nazi Party).

On June 28, German delegation signs the Versailles Treaty, reluctantly accepting significant territorial losses and acknowledging German responsibility for the outbreak of the war, as well as Germany's obligation to pay reparations to the victors.

On August 11, the constitution of the Weimar Republic is adopted.

1920 On February 24, NSDAP's twenty-five-point program is published.

March 13–17 is the Kapp-Lüttwitz putsch (coup) attempt in Berlin.

In March–April, Communist insurrections.

1921 On July 29, Adolf Hitler is elected leader of the NSDAP and invested with absolute authority over it.

1923 On January 11, French and Belgian troops occupy the Ruhr in retaliation for Germany's failure to make a reparations payment. The German government declares passive resistance.

Summer is the height of the crisis of inflation.

On November 9, NSDAP attempts a putsch in Munich, as the prelude to marching on Berlin. The army remains loyal to the republican regime, and the putsch fails ignominiously. Hitler is tried and sentenced to five years in Landsberg Prison, where he dictates the text of *Mein Kampf* [*My Struggle*]. During his time in prison, the NSDAP splits into factions. Hitler decides that, having failed to seize power by illegal means, the party must develop into a formidable political campaigning force so that he can claim power by legal means.

1924 On December 20, Hitler is released from prison.

1925 On February 26, the NSDAP is re-founded under Hitler's unchallenged leadership. The process of building up the party's territorial organization and campaigning capacity begins in earnest.

On April 27, Field Marshal Paul von Hindenburg is elected president of the Weimar Republic for a seven-year term.

1928 Reichstag election gives NSDAP 810,000 votes (2.6 percent), twelve seats.

1929 On October 24, U.S. stock market crash unleashes the Great Depression. Germany is severely affected because U.S. loans to and investment in Germany are suddenly withdrawn. The result is mass unemployment in subsequent years, reaching a peak of 6 million registered unemployed in winter 1932–1933. There are at least 1 million more unemployed in addition.

1930 On September 14, Reichstag election gives NSDAP 6.4 million votes (18.3 percent), 107 seats, as the second largest parliamentary party.

1932 In March–April, two rounds of presidential elections in which Hindenburg is victorious; his closest challenger is Hitler.

The July 31 Reichstag election gives NSDAP 13.75 million votes (37.3 percent), 230 seats, as the largest parliamentary party.

The November 6 Reichstag election gives NSDAP 11.74 million votes (33.1 percent), 196 seats, still as the largest parliamentary party.

1933   On January 30, Hitler is appointed chancellor of Germany with a cabinet of three Nazis and eight others.

On February 27, Reichstag building is set on fire.

On February 28, the Decree for the Protection of People and State suspends some civil rights. KPD banned.

The March 5 Reichstag election gives NSDAP 17.28 million votes (43.9 percent), 288 seats, as the largest parliamentary party, after a campaign of intimidation against other parties.

March 22, Dachau concentration camp opens.

On March 23, the Enabling Law is passed, supported by the Center Party, but opposed by the Sozialdemokratische Partei Deutschlands German Social Democratic Party (SPD), Germany's oldest and largest single party.

In March, the Nazis take over power in the *Länder*.

April 1 is the first official boycott of Jewish-owned shops and businesses.

On April 7, Law for the Restoration of the Professional Civil Service discriminates against political opponents and non-"Aryans," chiefly Jews, in public service.

On April 25, Law to Combat the Surplus in German Schools and Colleges discriminates against Jews by imposing a quota on their numbers.

May 2, Nazi seizure of trade unions' premises and assets.

May 10, creation of the German Labor Front, the largest Nazi mass organization, to embrace "all workers of hand and brain," forcibly replacing the trade unions.

On June 1, the Law to Reduce Unemployment introduces marriage loans to encourage "Aryans" to marry, with the woman giving up work, as one of several measures to combat unemployment.

On June 23, the SPD is forcibly dissolved.

On June 27, the German Nationalist Party dissolves itself.

On July 5, the Center Party dissolves itself.

On July 14, the one-party state is declared.

July 14, a law is passed permitting compulsory sterilization of those deemed to suffer from "hereditary diseases," including "feeble-mindedness."

July 20, Concordat between Hitler's regime and the Vatican is formally signed.

December 5, a decree ordering doctors to report candidates for sterilization.

1934   June 30–July 2, purge of the Sturmabteilungen (SA), the Nazi storm troopers (Brownshirts), in which SA leaders and other targeted individuals are murdered by the Schutzstaffeln (SS), the black-uniformed elite corps of the Nazi Party.

On August 2, President Hindenburg, the only person empowered to dismiss Hitler, dies. Hitler combines the roles of president and chancellor in his person as fuhrer and receives plebiscitary approval of this move.

1935   March–May, reintroduction of conscription/rearmament.

On September 15, Nuremberg Laws deprive non-"Aryans"—chiefly Jews—of German citizenship and civil rights.

On October 18, the Marriage Health Law enacted, prohibiting those with "hereditary diseases" from marrying.

1936   On June 17, Himmler becomes chief of the German police forces.

September 9, promulgation of a Four Year Plan for the economy—with a program of economic self-sufficiency—under Göring's direction.

1938   March 13, *Anschluss*—the annexation of Austria makes it part of the Greater German Reich.

On October 1, Sudetenland annexed under the Munich Agreement.

November 9–10, *Kristallnacht*—massive official pogrom against Jews in Germany, in which hundreds of Jews die and some 30,000 Jews are consigned to concentration camps at Buchenwald, Dachau, and Sachsenhausen, where many perish. Some 7,000 Jewish-owned businesses are destroyed.

In December, Jews are forbidden to own or drive automobiles.

1939   On March 25, Hitler Youth and League of German Girls membership is made compulsory for "Aryan" Germans up to the age of nineteen.

On August 23, the Molotov-Ribbentrop nonaggression pact between the U.S.S.R. and Germany is signed. This enables them to divide Poland between them in September 1939.

On September 1, German armed forces attack Poland. Curfew is imposed on Jews. Jews are permitted to buy food supplies only in designated stores.

September 20, Jews are forbidden to own radio receivers.

In October, Hitler gives the order for the "euthanasia" program to commence.

1940   In February–March, the first deportations of German Jews from Germany begin. Some 1,360 Jews from eastern Germany are deported to the Lublin ghetto in occupied Poland.

In April–June, German armed forces (*Wehrmacht*) score stunning successes in western Europe, occupying Denmark, Norway, The Netherlands, Belgium, Luxembourg, and much of France.

In May in Berlin, Jewish men under fifty-five and Jewish women under fifty are required to register for forced labor.

On May 16, deportation of Roma and Sinti "Gypsies" from Germany to forced labor in occupied Poland begins.

On July 19, Jews are forbidden to own telephones.

1941   In March, all Jews between fifteen and sixty-five years of age are drafted into forced labor.

On June 22, the *Wehrmacht* invades the Soviet Union. By April 1942, the *Einsatzgruppen* (killing squads under SS control) have murdered half a million people in the western U.S.S.R., including virtually its entire Jewish population.

On August 24, the "euthanasia program" is officially terminated, after the deaths of about 120,000 persons and protests by senior churchmen. However, it continues in deep secrecy until virtually the end of the war.

On September 15, all German Jews aged six or over are obliged to wear a yellow star sewn onto their clothes.

In October, deportations of German Jews begin on a regular basis. From March 1942, deportations "to the east," to forced labor in transit camps, and then to extermination camps such as Belzec and Sobibor.

On October 23, Jewish emigration from Germany is prohibited.

1942   On January 20, the Wannsee Conference discusses the details of a "final solution of the Jewish question," by which Jews would be either worked to death or exterminated outright. These processes are already under way.

In February, the first transports of Jews arrive at the extermination center of Belzec, where 600,000 Jews are murdered during 1942.

In March, exterminations begin at Sobibor. By March 1943, 250,000 people, mainly Jews, have been murdered.

On December 16, Himmler gives the order for the deportation of Roma "Gypsies" from eastern Europe to Auschwitz. In August 1943, the "Gypsy" camp there is liquidated. Roma and Sinti are also murdered in other camps.

1943   On February 2, the German Sixth Army surrenders at Stalingrad, undermining the myth of German invincibility and Soviet inferiority. After defeat by the Red Army at the battle of Kursk in July, the *Wehrmacht*'s long retreat in the east begins.

1944   On June 6, Anglo-American landings in Normandy lead to the *Wehrmacht*'s retreat in the west.

In summer, deportations of Jews to extermination centers reach their height. Hungarian Jews are deported to Auschwitz.

On July 20, a plot to kill Hitler with a bomb at Rastenburg fails.

On October 21, the U.S. Army takes Aachen—the start of the invasion of western Germany.

On October 22 the Red Army takes Nemmersdorf, East Prussia—the start of the invasion of eastern Germany.

In October, Auschwitz-Birkenau extermination camp is destroyed on Himmler's orders. The Red Army arrives in Auschwitz in January 1945.

1945   On April 30, Hitler commits suicide in his Berlin bunker.

On May 8, German armed forces surrender to the Allies.

INTRODUCTION

The German Nazi Revolution effected by Adolf Hitler and his henchmen transformed Germany's political system into a one-party dictatorship whose purpose was a racial revolution in Germany and Europe. Its goals included eliminating all domestic opposition; reviving Germany's economy and rebuilding its military, with a view to restoring German pride after defeat in World War I; and purging the "Aryan" German population of both non-"Aryans," such as Jews and "Gypsies," and "hereditarily flawed Aryans." After anticipated German expansion and conquests, Europe's peoples, including those of the western Soviet Union, would be characterized by a racial hierarchy in which "inferior" groups, such as the Slav peoples, would be ruthlessly exploited by the dominant Germans. The racial revolution also involved eugenic policies, including forced sterilization and outright murder to try to cleanse the German "racial body" of "impure" elements, to subjugate the Slav peoples, and to eliminate the Jews of Europe. The Nazi Revolution was destroyed at the end of World War II by the armed forces of Great Britain, the U.S.S.R., and the United States, among others. Through the post-war Nuremberg Trials of former leading Nazi officials, the crimes and atrocities of the Nazi regime were exposed to the world.

BACKGROUND: CULTURE AND HISTORY

The Holy Roman empire of the German nation, which comprised more than three hundred individual states of varying size and sophistication, existed for a thousand years until Napoleon dissolved it in 1806. At the Congress of Vienna in 1815, a German Confederation of thirty-nine states—the most powerful of which were Austria and Prussia—was created under the leadership of Habsburg Austria. Hohenzollern Prussia, however, militarily the strongest German state, emerged as an economic powerhouse, with intensive industrialization facilitated by abundant natural resources. In the 1860s, Prussia, under Otto von Bismarck's political leadership, challenged Austria for dominance in Germany, achieving that as a result of the Seven Weeks' War in 1866, after which Prussia created a North German Confederation. The three southern states, Baden, Württemberg, and Bavaria, aligned themselves with the Prussian-dominated north in the Franco-Prussian War of 1870–1871. As a result of the Prussian victory, Wilhelm I of Prussia was proclaimed kaiser (emperor) of a new German empire, in the Hall of Mirrors at Versailles on January 18, 1871. Bismarck became the first German chancellor (head of government).

The new Germany was a federal Reich (empire), with domestic affairs remaining the responsibility of the individual states. Prussia, by far the largest, remained an authoritarian monarchy with a prominent role for the military in political and social life, three-class voting rights that overwhelmingly favored the landed elites, and censorship of the press and the arts. There was increasing tension between the new urban working class, represented by the SPD (German Social Democratic Party), with its Marxist constitution, and a reactionary, traditional landowner class of Junker (noblemen) whose estates were in the eastern regions. The burgeoning professional and commercial middle classes were generally nationalist and anti-Marxist; they might be conservative or mildly liberal. The substantial peasantry remained broadly conservative and devoutly religious. In both north and south Germany, there were tensions between Evangelicals (Protestants) and Roman Catholics, with the former dominant nationally in a ratio of two to one, although in the south Catholics were in a marked majority. Repressive policies under Bismarck, until 1890, and Kaiser Wilhelm II beyond that, failed to dampen support for the SPD, whose strength increased up to 1914. More liberal monarchies in the southern states and universal manhood suffrage for the Reichstag (national parliament) contrasted with regressive taxation and a thoroughly unrepresentative legislature in Prussia.

Wilhelm II presided over an increasingly bold and risky foreign policy, leaving Germany uncomfortably dependent on its alliance with problem-ridden Habsburg Austria-Hungary while antagonizing Russia and then Britain. The latter two countries, in 1893 and 1904, respectively, both entered ententes with Germany's adversary, France. The Russo-British entente of 1907 completed the anti-German front. When Germany unreservedly backed Austria-Hungary in its quarrel with Serbia in the summer of 1914 and Russia moved to defend Serbia, the alliance system led to first a European and then a world war. Germany's stunning success against Russia by 1917 counted for little when, with the potentially limitless resources of the United States available to the Franco-British side, it became clear in 1918 that Germany could not win on the Western front.

Germany emerged from World War I with massive human, material, and territorial losses. Some 2 million men in the younger adult age groups had been killed, and many more wounded. The unprecedented costs of a long war and an industrial war effort had consumed resources and destroyed the financial system, so that high inflation was endemic by 1918. Although German forces had not been defeated in the field, the peace settlement embodied in the Versailles Treaty of June 28, 1919, treated Germany as a vanquished power that bore responsibility for the outbreak of the war. The treaty's "war guilt" clause, Article 231, and the consequent imposition of reparations to be made by Germany to the victorious powers were a source of resentment against these powers among Germans of most political persuasions.

The outcome of World War I and its aftermath scarred many Germans psychologically. At first, with the failure of Wilhelm II's authoritarian monarchy in World War I, it had seemed that a parliamentary democratic system could succeed in the form of the Weimar Republic. Yet the removal of the old pillars of authority, with the fall of the monarchy, at *Reich* and *Land* (federal state) levels, had far-reaching consequences. Attempted Marxist revolutions in Berlin, Munich, and other major urban centers in 1918–1919, on the model of the Bolshevik Revolution of October 1917, failed dismally. It nevertheless left the law-abiding, God-fearing, property-owning classes utterly on the defensive, especially when the nominally Marxist SPD became the senior partner in government, both at the national level and in the largest *Land*, Prussia. The founding of the German Communist Party (KPD) in late December 1918, along with sporadic attempts at revolution in various urban centers in the years up to 1923, compounded their alarm. There were also small political groups that were anti-Marxist but radical rather than conservative, deriving from a German tradition of racist nationalist mysticism and encouraged by Mussolini's success in Italy. One, the NSDAP (National Socialists—the Nazis), led by Adolf Hitler, tried to emulate Mussolini's alleged "seizure of power" in Italy in 1922 by staging a putsch (coup) in Munich on November 9, 1923, that was an utter fiasco.

In the years following the war, the collapse of the currency—with hyperinflation reaching its peak in the summer of 1923—ruined sections of the middle class and created instability in financial, economic, and political life. Politically, three parties in the "Weimar Coalition"—the SPD, the Roman Catholic Center Party, and the liberal German Democratic Party (DDP)—together commanded 78 percent of the vote in the 1919 elections for the National Assembly. Yet, in the Reichstag election of 1920, their combined share of the vote fell to barely 44 percent. While the SPD was weakened, it remained the strongest parliamentary party until 1932. Although the Center Party's support remained steady and even increased from 1930, the DDP's support collapsed. At the same time, support for the party of traditional Protestant conservatism, the German National People's Party (DNVP), which had been strong in the mid 1920s, diminished, while the German People's Party (DVP), a party of business whose leader, Gustav Stresemann, was foreign minister from 1923 to 1929, withered in the later 1920s. By that time, an increasing number of small special-interest parties had entered the political arena, draining support away from existing parties of the Right and Center.

The absence of the SPD from governing coalitions between 1923 and 1928 and from 1930 meant that governments were composed of five or six different parties whose interests could hardly be reconciled. In 1928–1930, the Social Democrat Hermann Müller was the last chancellor of the Weimar Republic to preside over a coalition commanding a majority of parliamentary votes. His successor, Heinrich Brüning of the Center Party—the only party to figure in every coalition from 1919 to 1932—relied on the president's power to issue decrees in order to govern. After the election that Brüning called on September 14, 1930, the three largest parliamentary parties to emerge from it—the SPD, the NSDAP, and the KPD—remained outside government. There was nothing inevitable about it, but, as it turned out, after little more than a decade, parliamentary democratic government had come to an end in Germany.

Part of the reason for the political instability of the last Weimar years lay in the economic crisis that afflicted not only Germany but also most other countries in the developed world. World War I had disrupted a booming international economy and had taken a heavy toll on its participants. Only the United States emerged without apparent damage, to become the world's economic superpower, lending money on a huge scale to those recovering from the war. Germany received massive amounts of U.S. money, in terms of both loans and investments. The disadvantage of this dependence on the United States became apparent in October 1929, when the U.S. stock market collapsed. U.S. investments and loans were quickly withdrawn, and the German economy contracted rapidly and painfully. As a result, millions of people lost their employment, in both the private and public sectors; in the winter of 1932–1933, there were 6 million registered unemployed and perhaps 2 million more people seeking work.

The Great Depression gave the NSDAP its chance. From being one among many small, radical, anti-Left parties, it shot to prominence as a result of the September 1930 election, becoming the second largest parliamentary party. Some people were attracted by its activist and often violent campaigns against the parties of the Left, in particular its attacks on the KPD. Others welcomed its aggressively nationalist stance and its opposition to reaching an accommodation with the wartime victors. The Nazi ideology of racist mysticism attracted some, but more were drawn to the party by the charismatic figure of the fuhrer (leader), Adolf Hitler, whose oratory and staged rituals were fascinating to many. The economic crisis afforded the Nazis limitless ammunition for attacking the conventional politicians who had, they said, clearly failed the German people. Hitler and his henchmen at central and regional levels offered radical solutions to the crisis, making promises that were not mutually compatible to different interest groups in different locations. The crisis also gave them the opportunity to demonstrate their own approach to the casualties of the crisis, with Nazi activists, men and women, providing practical welfare in the shape of soup

Adolf Hitler at a Nazi Party rally in Nuremberg, Germany, ca. 1928. The economic crisis in Germany that began after World War I, and escalated with the U.S. stock market crash of 1929, created a climate of fear and anger that Hitler and the Nazis skillfully manipulated to gain political clout and power. (National Archives)

kitchens, hostels, and clothing collections for the destitute who had exhausted their meager entitlement to unemployment benefits and crisis relief.

The Nazis aggressively exploited the Depression for their own political ends, and they were rewarded in local, state, and national elections between 1930 and 1932 with a massive increase in support, not least from those who came to accept that, as Nazi propaganda had it, Hitler was their last hope. The Nazis were in a strong position because, during the 1920s, the party's organization had been painstakingly developed at the local level, especially under the leadership of Gregor Strasser as Reich organization leader in the years from 1928 to 1932. Nevertheless, the network of party branches was neither comprehensive nor uniformly spread across the country. Well beyond 1933 there were areas of Germany, especially those with a strong Roman Catholic religious affiliation, that remained obstinately impervious to the Nazi appeal. Yet the NSDAP's organizational structure was much more developed than that of any of the other political parties. The battalions of volunteer workers that it could mobilize for its campaigns convinced the traditional Right that its only chance of regaining the political power it had lost in 1918 was to harness the NSDAP's numerical force in the service of the conservative cause. That seemed more necessary after Hitler made a strong showing against President Hindenburg in the presidential elections of March–April 1932 and after the July 1932 Reichstag election in which the NSDAP emerged as the largest parliamentary party.

Evidence of the aspirations of traditional conservatives could be found in the eagerness of many of them to abandon the democratic system in favor of authoritarianism. The most flagrant example of this was the imposition of authoritarian rule over Prussia, where the Social Democrats had been the leading party of government throughout the Republican period. In the April 1932 election, the ruling coalition of SPD and Center lost its majority in the Prussian *Landtag* (state legislature). While attempts were made to construct a government, this coalition, under the Social Democrats Otto Braun and Carl Severing, remained as caretaker, while the Nazi SA (Sturmabteilungen, or storm troopers), whose proscription had been revoked by the new Reich chancellor, Franz von Papen, went on the rampage. On the pretext of restoring order, on July 20, 1932, Papen obtained a presidential decree for the dismissal of the Braun-Severing government and declared himself Reich commissioner for Prussia. This illegal act removed a government that could have formed a major obstacle to Hitler's consolidation of power in the following year.

The failure of successive chancellors—Brüning, Papen, and Schleicher—to construct coalitions that could command a majority in the Reichstag convinced large numbers of Germans that the parliamentary system was simply not workable; above all, it was not working in time of dire privation for millions of Germans. Yet this did not amount to a vote of confidence in Hitler and the NSDAP. Certainly, from July 1932, the NSDAP attracted more votes than any other party. But the next most popular parties were the SPD and the KPD. Those two Marxist parties, instead of forming an alliance against the Nazis, were hostile to each other for reasons that derived from differences within the SPD before 1914. Hostility also resulted from the way in which an SPD-led government had suppressed attempted revolution in 1918–1919, and from the domination of the KPD by political imperatives set by the Comintern (Communist International organization), which decreed in 1928 that social democratic parties, such as the SPD, must be combated. For large numbers of Christian, propertied Germans, however, it was frightening that two Marxist parties could, between them, command 35 to 40 percent of the votes in the Reichstag. With traditional conservatism, in the form of Papen, Schleicher, and the DNVP, unable to attract more than minimal popular support, the only alternative seemed to be a party that was, in spite of its reputation for rowdiness and crude propaganda, implacably opposed to Marxism in all its forms: the NSDAP.

There certainly were traditional conservatives who feared the radical aspects of the NSDAP. Yet conservatives could not mobilize mass support, and the risk of an authoritarian coup d'état resulting in a bloodbath was high. In January 1933, in the depths of the Depression, the conservatives around President Hindenburg could see no alternative to throwing in their lot with Hitler and his masses of supporters, even if they seemed from election results in and after November 1932 to be less numerous than they had been in the summer of 1932. Hitler had already refused the vice chancellorship in August 1932; his price was and remained the chancellorship, and nothing less. That he was offered on January 30, 1933.

CONTEXT AND PROCESS OF REVOLUTION

The Nazi Revolution had two dimensions: the political and the racial. There was significant social change in the Third Reich, but, contrary to the claims of some historians, there was no social revolution. The capitalist system and the social classes associated with it persisted, even if there were modifications to both. The political revolution created the one-party state, severely curtailed the autonomy of the *Länder*, and instituted a reign of terror against political opponents. This gave the Nazi regime the freedom to introduce measures discriminating against "racial enemies," in particular Jews, and against "Aryans" who did not meet Nazi standards of "value." The cumulative effect of increasingly radical policies of racial engineering amounted to a revolution in which the "worthless" were progressively segregated from the "valuable," deprived of both civil and human rights, and incarcerated or murdered.

The claim to authority of the dictatorial party's leaders was based on neither conventional rank nor lineage, nor on a promise to subvert established social hierarchies. Rather, it was based on an appeal to a racist ideology that exalted the German nation and its "Aryan" people while demonizing non-"Aryans" (especially Jews), castigating foreign countries that had allegedly combined to deny Germany its rights as a major power, and whipping up terror at the specter of Communist forces allegedly poised to strike at Germany from within and without. When Nazi leaders described all Germans as being equal, they were not promising to redistribute assets and status so that social classes would be abolished. Rather, they meant that assets would be redistributed from the "worthless" to the "valuable." That included the seizure of Jewish businesses and property in the "Aryanization" drive, which was intensified from 1938, as well as the withholding of social benefits from individuals and families who, by Nazi criteria, were "worthless." Although party dignitaries at central, regional, and local levels enjoyed enhanced social as well as political status, the Nazi aim was to co-opt rather than to overthrow existing social elites.

While the NSDAP's propaganda sometimes referred to a "seizure of power" (*Machtergreifung*), it also used the more accurate term "takeover of power" (*Machtübernahme*). The means by which the Nazi dictatorship was imposed in the first half of 1933 were audacious and breathtaking; they were, however, also facilitated by both luck and the collaboration of the Nazis' conservative allies. On January 30, 1933, Adolf Hitler, the leader of the largest party in the Reichstag, was appointed chancellor of Germany in the normal constitutional manner by President Hindenburg. Hitler's cabinet consisted of three Nazis—himself, Wilhelm Frick, and Hermann Göring—and eight Nationalists, or nonparty "experts." The first steps toward dictatorship were suggested by non-Nazis at the cabinet meeting on January 31. Vice chancellor von Papen proposed that the Reichstag election called for March 5, to try to obtain a majority for the governing coalition, should be the last of its kind, and that the parliamentary system should not be revived. The finance minister, Graf Lutz Schwerin von Krosigk, proposed that the Reichstag's committees should be dissolved. The Nationalist leader, Alfred Hugenberg, proposed that the deposed Braun government of Prussia should be deprived of its remaining rights. In this cabinet, with a minority of Nazis, there was general agreement to these proposals to dissolve a parliamentary system that was already moribund (Noakes and Pridham 1983, 127–129).

The Nazis' conservative allies only partially comprehended Hitler's ambitions, and they underestimated his quest for total control. They welcomed a return to an authoritarian regime, but they neither willed nor expected a Nazi dictatorship. Hitler's trumpeted hatred of the political Left blinded them to his inherent radicalism, and they failed to understand his determination to extinguish all non-Nazi political and organizational life, including their own. They welcomed the aggressive persecution of left-wing political activists, who were assaulted and incarcerated at will—especially through the uncontrolled local violence perpetrated by the NSDAP's paramilitary wing, the SA—across Germany in the early months of 1933. This reign of terror was given impetus by the burning down of the Reichstag building on February 27, 1933, allegedly as the result of a Communist conspiracy. On the following day, the Presidential Decree for the

Protection of People and State eroded the power of the *Länder* and suspended basic civil rights, including habeas corpus, enabling the governing parties to intimidate opposition politicians and to outlaw the KPD (ibid., 142). In spite of this, the March election gave the Nazi-led coalition only a slender majority, and did not give Hitler the outright NSDAP majority he had sought.

Determined to complete his political revolution, Hitler suspended the Weimar Constitution, initially for four years, through an Enabling Law that the Reichstag passed in the face of opposition from the SPD, alone in its defiance of intimidation by members of the SA and the SS (ibid., 154–162). Hitler's attachment to legal forms was illustrated by his insistence on legislating to renew the Enabling Law for further terms in and after 1937 (Broszat 1981, 84, 94). By July 14, 1933, he was able to effect or demand the dissolution of all opposition parties, including the Nationalists, and to declare the one-party state. The removal of the last remaining obstacle, the Center Party, was part of the price that Pope Pius XI paid for a Concordat with the new regime in July 1933 (Noakes and Pridham 1983, 164–167).

The political revolution continued with the seizure of power in the regions. In March 1933, under orders from the Reich government, the governments of the *Länder* were reconfigured to give NSDAP regional leaders (*Gauleiter*) the leading position of *Reichsstatthalter* (Reich governor) in most of them. In the Prussian provinces, *Gauleiter* and senior SA officers assumed leadership. At *Land* level, too, the one-party state was enforced, enabling *Land* governments to purge their bureaucracies and town halls, with large numbers of mayors replaced by "politically reliable" Nazis. The process was not uniform across the country, with, for example, wholesale purges in Prussia but significant numbers of survivors in office in Württemberg. Yet, even where non-Nazis remained in post, they had no independent political apparatus, which severely limited their room to maneuver.

Hitler's collusion with traditional conservatives aroused opposition within the NSDAP, and especially within the SA, whose leaders believed that they had been cheated of the revolution for which they had fought. The compromise between Hitler, with his closest associates, and the traditional conservative elites meant that NSDAP members did not take over the functions of the state wholesale, and that the SA did not replace or absorb the *Reichswehr*, the German army, restricted to 100,000 men by the Treaty of Versailles. Enough NSDAP functionaries acquired state offices at central, *Land*, or local level to avert a revolt by the party, although most ordinary members received no personal reward. But the SA remained merely the paramilitary wing of the official state party, while the *Reichswehr* remained intact as Germany's defense force. The SA's leaders, especially its chief, Ernst Röhm, repeatedly called for the completion of the revolution, and Hitler, in return, repeatedly warned that "the revolution is over" (ibid., 167–174; 1986, 234–236). Finally, on June 30, 1934, the SA leadership was arrested. On that day and on July 1–2, SA leaders and members, as well as individuals with whom Hitler had a score to settle—including his predecessor as chancellor, Schleicher, and former Nazi organization leader Gregor Strasser—were murdered by SS paramilitaries.

There remained one potential constraint on Hitler's power. President Hindenburg had the formal power to dismiss him. It was Hitler's good fortune that Hindenburg was eighty-five years old in January 1933; on August 2, 1934, he died. The goodwill of the army leadership, achieved by the purge of the SA, now enabled Hitler to merge the offices of chancellor and president in his own person as fuhrer. This completed the political revolution in Nazi Germany. It did not mean that every German became a convinced National Socialist and willingly collaborated with the regime. Throughout the Third Reich there was discontent and, sometimes, obstruction among broad swaths of ordinary people, in town and country. But the revolution had ensured that there was no political alternative, while the ever-growing apparatus of terror and propaganda ensured that dissidence was covert and contained.

The Nazis endeavored to fashion a social order based on "racial value," without disturbing existing distinctions of social class. In theory, those who could not demonstrate their "Aryan" ancestry, through genealogical records, were condemned as "worthless," while some who were "Aryan" were judged to be "of lesser value" because of either an alleged "flaw" in their physical or mental health or a failure to conform to Nazi social and political norms. "Aryans" who were homosexual or prostitutes, men who failed to hold down a regular job, women who were slovenly housekeepers and mothers, people who were in some way disorderly, including those who drank alcohol to excess and women who had several sexual partners, were classed as "asocial," and therefore "worthless."

Initially, although from December 1933 medical doctors had a duty to report those with "hereditary diseases," only some individuals or families were officially classified as "worthless." These included certain applicants for a marriage loan and some of those who had contact with social workers or medical officers. Racial policy was intended to apply to the entire German people, but constraints of personnel and funds ensured that many escaped scrutiny. Nevertheless, those who were identified as "worthless" experienced the full force of the regime's persecutory policies. Patients in state mental asylums were, sometimes literally, starved of resources, while some families with behavioral problems were forced to undergo rigorous "re-education," and some prostitutes and male homosexuals were consigned to concentration camps.

Anti-Semitism and widespread dislike of Roma and Sinti "Gypsies" created a hospitable climate for measures against Jews and "Gypsies." Indeed, there had already been discriminatory legislation against the latter in some *Länder* before 1933. The SA's violence against the political Left in early 1933 included violence against many individual Jews, some of whom were also Socialists or Communists. Hitler's government decreed a national boycott of Jewish shops and businesses, which took place on April 1, 1933, before the one-party state was established. This was followed by the Law for the Restoration of the Professional Civil Service of April 7, 1933, which purged both political enemies and non-"Aryans" from the bureaucracy and the professions, other than those in private practice (Noakes and Pridham 1986, 223–225).

On the day that the one-party state was declared, July 14, the Law for the Prevention of Hereditarily Diseased Offspring introduced "eugenic sterilization" for those with a range of ailments, including schizophrenia, chronic alcoholism, "hereditary deafness," and "hereditary blindness," along with a catchall category, "feeblemindedness" (ibid., 457–458). This reflected a tendency in other developed countries, including Scandinavia and many U.S. states. In Nazi Germany, however, sterilization was forcibly applied to much larger numbers of people and was only the beginning of a revolution in racial and eugenic engineering.

IMPACTS

The political revolution of 1933–1934 effected a rapid and unprecedented centralization of power in Germany in the hands of the Nazi leadership. There could be no legal or constitutional challenge to Hitler's rule, because his government had suspended the constitution; furthermore, the few judges not prepared to work with the regime were removed. The only avenues open to political opponents were conspiratorial activity within Germany or invasion from without. The latter required the support of foreign powers that would not contemplate it until German aggression had involved them in a war. Many SPD and KPD members and sympathizers were rounded up by SA thugs in the early months of 1933. Some were murdered, while others were confined in makeshift concentration camps to await transfer to purpose-built camps such as Dachau and Sachsenhausen. Women prisoners were eventually held at Ravensbrück. During the 1930s and into the war, former SPD and KPD activists conspired against the regime, but the emigration of leading political opponents together with effective infiltration of rebel groups by the secret state police (Gestapo) ensured that overthrow from within remained a vain hope.

Most who abhorred the regime found that its power and terror were sufficient to deter them from challenging it. Complete state control of the press, radio, and the cinema, and all means of cultural production closed off outlets for the expression of dissent. Those who clandestinely printed and distributed opposition literature risked incarceration and torture to extract the names of associates. Those who spread anti-regime propaganda by word of mouth risked denunciation to the authorities by neighbors or workmates, and, again, incarceration and torture. As a result, many artists and writers emigrated in order to enjoy freedom of expression. Those who remained either complied with the regime's prescriptions about cultural expression or withdrew from public exhibition of their work in an "inner migration."

The development in wartime of a broad-based conspiracy of military officers, former regime officials and former trade union leaders, and clergy of both major denominations culminated in the plot to kill Hitler at Rastenburg in East Prussia on July 20, 1944, about six weeks after the D-Day landings by the Allies in France. The failure of this attempted assassination ensured that Hitler's dictatorship would tighten its brutal grip on both the military and civilians, and that Germans would be forced to fight on until the entire country was occupied by enemy armies. The political revolution and its effects meant that only military defeat by a coalition of foreign powers would bring the Nazi regime to an end.

The racial revolution became radicalized in the 1930s and, especially, during the war. The withdrawal of equal civil rights, achieved in the 1860s, through the Nuremberg Laws of September 15, 1935, and consequent decrees (ibid., 535–541), which also applied to Sinti and Roma "Gypsies," was followed by the "Aryanization" of German assets. Jewish-owned businesses and property were seized and redistributed to "Aryans," and especially to NSDAP officials. Jewish cattle dealers were banned from farmers' markets. Jewish adults and schoolchildren endured an infinite number of petty slights and humiliations in their daily lives.

By April 1939, the number of Jews in Germany had been reduced, mainly through emigration, from around 500,000 in 1933 to some 214,000, and from around 720,000 in greater Germany to about 300,000 (Brechtken 2004, 115). Emigration had begun in 1933 and had increased especially after *Kristallnacht* ("the night of broken glass"), the pogrom on November 9 and 10, 1938, that effected a qualitative change in the persecution of German Jews. Nazi thugs destroyed Jewish property, including more than a thousand synagogues, and assaulted Jewish people. Their violence resulted in the death of hundreds of Jews and the incarceration of some 30,000 Jewish men (Benz 2000, 31–32). Those who emigrated were chiefly in the younger age groups; those who remained were mainly the elderly and were more likely to be women than men. The regime became increasingly obsessed with eliminating from German "Aryan" life a diminishing number of Jews. The relatively small numbers of Roma and Sinti "Gypsies" were similarly targeted, with their children, like Jewish children, excluded from "Aryan" schools, and with many families consigned to primitive reservations or concentration camps.

The war changed everything. Germany's victories provided occupied territory in the east, to which Germany's Roma and Sinti were deported in May 1942. In camps on Polish soil, they were subjected to hard labor. The survivors were transported to Auschwitz-Birkenau, where, in August 1943, they were murdered. At least 200,000 European Roma and Sinti were murdered in extermination camps under the authority of Heinrich Himmler's SS in former Poland (ibid., 126–127, 130). The war also made millions of Jews in occupied countries accessible for persecution and murder, in western as well as eastern Europe.

On October 23, 1941, with some 164,000 Jews remaining in Germany, emigration was prohibited; deportations of German Jews "to the East" and probable extermination had already begun. In September 1944 there were barely 15,000 Jews remaining, as well as thousands of *Mischlinge* ("part-Jews") who had experienced some aspects of the persecution of "full Jews" (Benz, Graml, and Weiss 1997, 533, 586–587). Some German Jews were sent to SS concentration camps, including the Theresienstadt ghetto, which ultimately became staging posts for further deportation to death camps such as Treblinka, Majdanek, and, especially, Auschwitz-Birkenau. At first there were mass shootings of Jews, but, increasingly, lives were extinguished either by "annihilation through work" in industrial or extractive businesses associated with concentration camps, or through mass extermination by gas in purpose-built camps. It is estimated that some 6 million European Jews were murdered in the Nazi-ordained Holocaust. These atrocities were carried out under the leadership of Himmler and the SS, at the behest of Hitler and with the compliance of other leading Nazis and government officials. Large numbers of Germans, including *Wehrmacht* (armed forces) soldiers and collaborators in occupied Europe, were directly or indirectly involved in this massive project of state-sponsored dehumanization and murder.

Other aspects of the racial revolution were radicalized. By 1945 some 400,000 individuals had been sterilized, overwhelmingly against their will. That figure does not include those forcibly sterilized after incarceration, including many Jews and Roma and Sinti. Racial policy was given added urgency by the unleashing of Hitler's war in September 1939. The need for hospital accommodation for wounded soldiers, along with the need to house both bombed-out "Aryans" and ethnic German emigrants from eastern Europe—after the

Molotov-Ribbentrop Pact of August 23, 1939, had delineated spheres of interest in eastern Europe between Germany and Soviet Russia—augmented the ideological motive of purging the "Aryan" race of its infirm members. Many patients in mental asylums were removed and murdered in the so-called "euthanasia program." The protests of senior clergymen seemed to halt these murders in 1941; in reality, however, they continued virtually until the end of the war in deepest secrecy.

The racial revolution was seriously undermined by the regime's policy of forcibly bringing into wartime Germany several million foreign workers, mostly Slavs, to try to replace millions of German men conscripted into the *Wehrmacht*. Slavs were, in Nazi terms, "inferior" peoples. Their presence in the German workforce was a source of anxiety to a regime that feared miscegenation. Harsh penalties for sexual relations between foreign men and German women failed to deter some ordinary Germans. Others, especially industrial workers, welcomed their own relative rise in status with the influx of "racial inferiors." By 1944 around 25 percent of the German workforce consisted of foreigners from occupied countries, many of whom were treated brutally (Herbert 1997, 296). The war that had been intended to establish the superiority of the "Aryan" race and the elimination of its racial and political enemies at home and abroad provided the conditions for racial exploitation and murder on a massive scale. In the end, it also extinguished the political system and racial policies of Nazi Germany.

PEOPLE, ORGANIZATIONS, AND NAZI RACIAL CONCEPTS AND POLICIES

"Aryan"

A spurious term (deriving from the Sanskrit *arya*—noble) adopted by Nazi racial theorists for Germans whose antecedents did not include non-Europeans, Jews, Roma and Sinti "Gypsies," Slavs, or Latins. These Germans "of pure blood," allegedly deriving from Nordic ancestors, were described as culturally the most highly developed people, the supreme people. Others to whom Nordic ancestry was ascribed—mostly Scandinavians, Dutch, and Belgian Flemings—were "of related blood" and therefore "racially valuable." The rest were, in varying degrees, "of lesser value" or "worthless," with Jews at the bottom of the racial hierarchy. Jews and Slavs, particularly, were designated "racial enemies" whose aim was to destroy the "Aryan race." A law of April 7, 1933, introduced an "Aryan paragraph" that required public servants to prove that their parents and grand-

parents were "Aryan," on pain of dismissal. The Nuremberg Laws of September 1935 denied German citizenship to non-"Aryans." From 1933, the "Aryanization" of shops and businesses expropriated piecemeal the property of Jews to the benefit of "Aryans."

Center Party

A national political party representing Roman Catholic interests, it was based on existing groups in various German states and founded in 1871 as a counterweight in the new Reichstag to the heavily Protestant political culture of Prussia, the dominant German state. Although loyally monarchist, its leadership accepted the Weimar Constitution. The Center (including after 1918 its Bavarian wing, the BVP) was the only party to figure in every German government from 1919 to 1932. The failure of its last chancellor, Heinrich Brüning (1885–1970) to construct a parliamentary majority led to rule by presidential decree and the end of parliamentary democracy. Mutual hostility between the Center and the NSDAP was mitigated in early 1933 by Hitler's promise to respect Catholic interests, leading the Center to support the Enabling Law on March 23, 1933. In negotiations for a Reich Concordat with the Vatican, signed on July 20, 1933, the pope agreed that the Center should dissolve itself, which it did on July 5, 1933.

Concentration Camps

In Germany, originally ad hoc holding centers created by the SA for incarcerating and assaulting supporters of opposition political parties, especially the KPD and SPD, and Jews after January 30, 1933. Soon purpose-built camps were built, among which was Dachau, near Munich, opened on March 22, 1933, as the "model camp." From 1936, the camp system came under the control of the SS. In the brutal regime of camp life, political and racial "enemies"—as well as social outcasts such as homosexuals, prostitutes, and juvenile delinquents—were disciplined, subjected to forced labor, and, increasingly in wartime, starved. Yet, although many prisoners died in them, camps such as Dachau, Sachsenhausen, Bergen-Belsen, and the women's camp, Ravensbrück, were not extermination centers. These were located in occupied territory in wartime, at places such as Auschwitz-Birkenau, Treblinka, and Majdanek.

Frick, Wilhelm (1877–1946)

Frick participated in Hitler's attempted putsch in 1923. He became the first Nazi to hold ministerial office, as interior and education minister in Thuringia in 1930. He was a member of Hitler's first cabinet in 1933, as Reich minister of the interior, a position he held until 1943. There, he presided over the drafting of much anti-Semitic legislation. Served as Reich protector in Bohemia and Moravia, 1943–1945. Executed at Nuremberg.

Göring, Hermann (1893–1946)

A highly decorated flying ace in World War I, Göring participated in Hitler's attempted putsch in 1923. Member of Hitler's first cabinet, in 1933. In April 1933, Göring became Prussian minister-president and minister of the interior, and exercised Hitler's powers as *Reichsstatthalter* in Prussia. He was commander in chief of the Luftwaffe from 1935, and plenipotentiary for the Four Year Plan for the economy from 1936. Directed the "Aryanization" of Jewish businesses in Germany and the economic exploitation of occupied countries. Committed suicide at Nuremberg.

Himmler, Heinrich (1900–1945)

Himmler participated in Hitler's attempted putsch in 1923. He subscribed obsessively to Nazi racial ideology and worked single-mindedly to implement it in his identity as *Reichsführer-SS* (supreme leader of the black-uniformed paramilitary Schutzstaffeln) from 1929. From June 1936 he was chief of the police forces in all German *Länder,* as well as of the Gestapo (secret state police), which used surveillance, informers, arbitrary arrest, and torture against political opponents and racial "enemies." Himmler presided over the entire apparatus of terror and persecution, including the concentration camps in Germany and elsewhere and the extermination camps in eastern occupied territories. In wartime, he was second only to Hitler in the power that he wielded. Committed suicide in captivity.

Hindenburg, Paul von Beneckendorff and von (1847–1934)

Prussian Junker (nobleman) who, as a career soldier, became field marshal in 1914 and chief of the army's leadership in 1916. In 1925, he was elected president of the Weimar Republic; he was re-elected in 1932, against stiff competition from Adolf Hitler. Strongly influenced by his ultraconservative entourage, including Franz von Papen, chancellor in 1932, he appointed Hitler to the chancellorship on January 30, 1933.

Hitler, Adolf (1889–1945)

An Austrian, a highly decorated soldier in World War I, Hitler became leader of the NSDAP in 1921. Inspired by Mussolini's success in 1922, he launched a March on Berlin on November 9, 1923, at the height of the inflation crisis. It was crushed at its inception in Munich. Hitler was tried and imprisoned; in December 1924 he was prematurely released, and on February 25, 1925, he re-founded the NSDAP as a campaigning force for winning votes to bring him to power. His charismatic appeal won many to the party. With the NSDAP's success in July 1932, he was offered the vice chancellorship, which he refused. His gamble paid off: he became chancellor on January 30, 1933. He presided over a political revolution that, at breathtaking speed, destroyed the parliamentary system and either banned or elicited the dissolution of other parties, as well as trade unions and various professional and social groups. Control of the mass media and creation of a ruthless secret police force ensured that open opposition was virtually impossible. Dictatorial power enabled him, with his supporters, to implement the racial revolution that was his obsession. Excluding Jews from professional, economic, and social life preceded their exclusion from Germany itself, with the destruction of "world Jewry" the aim. Hitler's war delivered Europe's Jews into his hands. He was responsible for the persecution and murder of millions of Jews, as well as countless others including "Gypsies," Slavs, and "Aryans" who were judged to be defective and therefore "worthless." He committed suicide in Berlin.

KPD (German Communist Party)

Party founded on December 30, 1918, by revolutionary Socialists who were former SPD members. Its leaders in Berlin attempted to stage a revolution in 1919 that was suppressed by the SPD-led government. Its revolutionary activity continued sporadically until 1923. Increasingly, its policies reflected the priorities of the Comintern, the Third (Communist) International, founded in Moscow in 1919 as the collective body of international Communist parties and dominated by the Soviet Communist Party. The KPD engaged in street battles and other violence with the NSDAP, and especially the SA. It was the third strongest parliamentary party from 1930 to 1933, and was banned by Hitler's government after the Reichstag fire, on February 28, 1933. Individual Communists and small groups tried to mount underground opposition to Hitler's regime, but most were arrested and incarcerated.

Land (Federal State)

A federal state of the German Reich—for example, Prussia, Bavaria, Schleswig-Holstein. The individual *Länder* had considerable autonomy in domestic affairs under the Second Empire (1871–1918) and, to a lesser extent, during the Weimar Republic. Each had its own *Landtag* (representative assembly). The autonomy of the *Länder* was severely curtailed as a result of the Nazi political revolution in 1933–1934.

NSDAP (National Socialist German Workers' Party—the Nazis)

Founded as the DAP (German Workers' Party) on January 5, 1919, it became the NSDAP in February 1920, adopting a twenty-five-point program. Adolf Hitler joined the DAP in 1919 and became supreme leader (fuhrer) of the NSDAP in 1921. After the attempted putsch in November 1923, the party was banned until February 1925. Then, Hitler, newly released from prison, re-founded it as a political party dedicated to winning sufficient electoral support to form a government that would destroy the parliamentary system. The NSDAP attracted support from all sections of society, through skillful if unscrupulous propaganda. In September 1930 it became the second largest parliamentary party, after the SPD. The Great Depression provided it with the opportunity to exploit people's fears and to engage in practical welfare work. It became the largest parliamentary party in July 1932. After Hitler's assumption of power in January 1933, many leading NSDAP officers, at central, regional, and local levels, acquired state positions, but the NSDAP itself was entrusted with the ideological indoctrination of the population instead of taking over the functions of the state. This could prove dispiriting for party activists in relatively unreceptive areas. Nevertheless, the NSDAP's officers at the local level could exert pressure on citizens to conform, and, with the SA, they took a lead in harassing Jews. They also maintained surveillance and informed on their local populations.

Nuremberg Laws

The Law for the Protection of German Blood and German Honor and the Reich Citizenship Law were announced by Göring at the NSDAP's annual congress at Nuremberg on September 15, 1935. These laws prohibited marriage or sexual relations between Jews and "Aryans," and pronounced that only those "of German or kindred blood" could be citizens. This disqualified Roma and Sinti "Gypsies" as well as Jews. In November 1935, a decree defined a Jew as someone with three Jewish grandparents. Those with one or two Jewish grandparents were *Mischlinge* ("part-Jews"). By the end of 1935, civil rights for Jews had effectively been revoked, paving the way for further discrimination and dispossession.

Reichsstatthalter (Reich Governor)

The office created in March 1933 to facilitate the *Gleichschaltung* (coordination) of the *Länder,* bringing them largely under the control of the Nazi-led Reich government. In most *Länder,* the *Gauleiter* (regional NSDAP leader) became *Reichsstatthalter.* The appointment of *Gauleiter* to these offices was in keeping with the Nazi policy of "personal union" of offices, whereby a party officer took over an equivalent state functionary's post. This linking of party and governmental positions also occurred at lower levels of government. The supreme example of personal union was Hitler, as NSDAP leader and chancellor from January 1933, and as fuhrer (having merged the offices of chancellor and president after the death of Hindenburg) of both party and state from August 1934.

SA (Sturmabteilungen, Storm Divisions, or Storm Troopers)

Founded in 1921 as the brown-shirted paramilitary wing of the NSDAP, the SA had as its main task to provide guards for NSDAP meetings, but it also went on the offensive against other groups, especially the KPD, engaging its members in street battles that in some places amounted to civil war. Ernst Röhm (1887–1934) assumed the SA leadership under Hitler in 1931, at a time when it was becoming a haven for many of the unemployed, providing meals and even accommodation for them. Röhm's ambition was to make the SA Germany's fighting force, by replacing or absorbing the German army of 100,000 men. In 1934, with SA numbers at over 4 million, Hitler moved to purge the SA's leadership, which had refused to heed his warnings that the revolution was over. This he did on June 30–July 2, 1933, using Himmler's SS. Röhm, along with many SA leaders and other targeted individuals, was murdered.

SPD (German Social Democratic Party)

Founded in 1875 as the political representative of German workers, the SPD was declared illegal by Bismarck in 1878.

Emerging from this in 1891, the party adopted a Marxist constitution, built up a formidable grassroots organization, and attracted substantial electoral support. It became the largest parliamentary party in the Weimar Republic, but it had to work in coalitions with liberals and the Catholic Center Party and was out of government from 1923 to 1928. Its last chancellor was Hermann Müller in 1928–1930. The SPD dominated government in Prussia, again in coalition with other parties, where the administration led by Otto Braun and Carl Severing was illegally ousted by chancellor von Papen on July 20, 1932. The SPD alone voted against the Enabling Law on March 23, 1933. It was banned on June 23, 1933. Thereafter, some of its members engaged in generally fruitless opposition activity in Germany, while the leadership went into exile.

SS (Schutzstaffeln—Protective Squads)

The SS was founded in 1925 as Hitler's bodyguard, under the SA's leadership. In 1929, Himmler became *Reichsführer-SS,* determined to mold it into a "racially pure" Nazi elite organization. The SS became independent of the SA after its part in the Röhm purge in 1934. The SS leadership drove Nazi penal and racial policy, spawning diverse agencies concerned with policing, surveillance, and intelligence. In wartime it had its own military wing, the *Waffen-SS.* The SS had authority over the concentration camp system, and it was responsible for exploitation and atrocities within it, as well as for the mass murder in extermination camps of millions of Jews, "Gypsies," Slavs, and others during the war.

Wehrmacht

The German armed forces, army, navy and air force, after the reintroduction of rearmament and conscription by Hitler's government in 1935.

Weimar Republic

The Weimar Republic replaced the discredited monarchy of Kaiser Wilhelm II after defeat in World War I. The Weimar Constitution of 1919 prescribed a parliamentary democratic system with full civil and political rights for all citizens, male and female. The "Weimar coalition" of SPD, Center, and DDP seemed to promise stability, but it was soon undermined. Especially from the later 1920s, the flight to political extremes, accelerated by the Depression, eroded the democratic processes as successive chancellors failed to create a parliamentary majority and ruled by decree. On January 30, 1933, Adolf Hitler was appointed as chancellor of the Weimar Republic, whose constitution he suspended in March 1933.

Jill Stephenson

See Also Democracy, Dictatorship, and Fascism; Documentaries of Revolution; Ethnic and Racial Conflict: From Bargaining to Violence; Human Rights, Morality, Social Justice, and Revolution; Ideology, Propaganda, and Revolution; Italian Fascist Revolution; Japanese New Order Movement; Music and Revolution; Nationalism and Revolution; Terrorism; War and Revolution

References and Further Readings

Aly, Götz. 1999. *"Final Solution": Nazi Population Policy and the Murder of the European Jews.* London: Arnold.

Benz, Wolfgang. 2000. *The Holocaust: A Short History.* London: Profile.

Benz, Wolfgang, Hermann Graml, and Hermann Weiss. 1997. *Enzyklopädie des Nationalsozialismus.* Munich: Deutscher Taschenbuch.

Bessel, Richard, ed. 1987. *Life in the Third Reich.* Oxford: Oxford University Press.

Brechtken, Magnus. 2004. *Die Nationalsozialistische Herrschaft 1933–1939.* Darmstadt, Germany: Wissenschaftliche Buchgesellschaft.

Broszat, Martin. 1981. *The Hitler State. The Foundation and Development of the Internal Structure of the Third Reich.* London: Longman.

Burleigh, Michael. 1994. *Death and Deliverance: "Euthanasia" in Germany 1900–1945.* Cambridge: Cambridge University Press.

Burleigh, Michael, and Wolfgang Wippermann. 1991. *The Racial State: Germany 1933–1945.* Cambridge: Cambridge University Press.

Feuchtwanger, E. J. 1995. *From Weimar to Hitler: Germany, 1918–33.* London: Macmillan.

Fulbrook, Mary, ed. 2001. *20th Century Germany: Politics, Culture and Society.* London: Arnold.

Gellately, Robert. 1990. *The Gestapo and German Society: Enforcing Racial Policy 1933–1945.* Oxford: Clarendon.

———. 2001. *Backing Hitler: Consent and Coercion in Nazi Germany.* New York: Oxford University Press.

Gellately, Robert, and Nathan Stoltzfus, eds. 2001. *Social Outcasts in Nazi Germany.* Princeton, NJ: Princeton University Press.

Heineman, Elizabeth. 1999. *What Difference Does a Husband Make? Women and Marital Status in Nazi and Postwar Germany.* Berkeley: University of California Press.

Herbert, Ulrich. 1997. *Hitler's Foreign Workers.* Cambridge: Cambridge University Press.

Kaplan, Marion A. 1998. *Between Dignity and Despair: Jewish Life in Nazi Germany.* New York: Oxford University Press.

Kershaw, Ian. 1998. *Hitler 1889–1936: Hubris.* London: Allen Lane, Penguin Press.

———. 2000. *Hitler 1936–1945: Nemesis.* London: Allen Lane, Penguin Press.

Nicosia, Francis R., and Jonathan Huener, eds. 2002. *Medicine and Medical Ethics in Nazi Germany: Origins, Practices, Legacies.* New York: Berghahn.

Noakes, Jeremy, and Geoffrey Pridham, eds. 1983. "The Rise to Power." Vol. 1 of *Nazism, 1919–1945: A Documentary Reader.* Exeter, UK: University of Exeter Press.

———, eds. 1986. "State, Economy and Society." Vol. 2 of *Nazism, 1919–1945: A Documentary Reader.* Exeter: University of Exeter Press.

———, eds. 2001. "Foreign Policy, War and Racial Extermination." Vol. 3 of *Nazism, 1919–1945: A Documentary Reader.* Exeter: University of Exeter Press.

Peukert, Detlev J. K. 1987. *Inside Nazi Germany: Conformity, Opposition and Racism in Everyday Life.* London: Batsford.

———. 1992. *The Weimar Republic: The Crisis of Classical Modernity.* New York: Hill and Wang.

Pine, Lisa. 1997. *The Nazi Family, 1933–1945.* Oxford: Berg.

Proctor, Robert N. 1988. *Racial Hygiene: Medicine under the Nazis.* Cambridge, MA: Harvard University Press.

Nicaraguan Revolution

CHRONOLOGY

1522 First Spanish conquistadors arrive; expelled by indigenous resistance led by chiefs Diriangén and Nicarao.

1524 Hernández de Córdoba founds Spanish settlements of Granada and León (later seats of the rival Conservative and Liberal party factions of the elite, respectively).

1821–1823 Central American provinces declare independence from Spain; briefly annex themselves to Mexican empire; then form independent Central American Federation.

1838 Nicaragua becomes an independent republic.

1850 Clayton-Bulwer Treaty signed between United States and Britain, both renouncing rights to monopolize trans-isthmian transit. Britain maintains protectorate on Atlantic "Misquito Coast."

1852 Conservatives and Liberals compromise on Managua as capital city.

1855–1857 U.S. filibusterer William Walker invades at behest of Liberals. Seizes presidency, declares English the official language, institutionalizes slavery. Driven out by coalition of Liberals and Conservatives; later captured in Honduras and executed.

1857–1893 Prolonged Conservative Party rule following defeat of Walker. Indigenous rebellion (against encroachment on traditional lands by rising coffee-growing elite) suppressed in 1881 War of the Comuneros.

1893 Liberal revolt brings authoritarian modernizer José Santos Zelaya to power. Promotes infrastructural and coffee investment; forces British to leave the Misquito Coast, incorporating Atlantic region into national territory in 1894.

1909 U.S.-backed Conservative rebellion ousts Zelaya (after he refuses U.S. terms for canal construction, negotiating options with Britain and Japan). Zelaya's forced exile is followed by fighting between Liberal and Conservative factions.

1912–1925 and 1926–1933 U.S. Marines occupy Nicaragua, propping up pro-U.S. governments and overseeing elections.

1927–1933 Augusto César Sandino, nationalist Liberal Party general, rejects U.S.-sponsored pact; wages guerrilla war against occupying U.S. forces and puppet government. U.S. Marines, unable to capture Sandino, create Nicaraguan National Guard commanded by Anastasio "Tacho" Somoza García and withdraw from Nicaragua.

1934 Following U.S. withdrawal, Sandino comes to Managua for peace talks with Liberal president Juan B. Sacasa and is assassinated by officers of Somoza's National Guard.

1936 Somoza García overthrows Sacasa government and arranges his own "election," inaugurating forty-three-year family dynasty.

1956   Somoza García is assassinated by independent Liberal poet Rigoberto López Pérez. His son Luis Somoza Debayle succeeds him, while his West Point–trained younger son Anastasio "Tachito" Somoza Debayle remains National Guard commander.

1961   Student radicals Carlos Fonseca, Silvio Mayorga, and Tomás Borge—inspired by the Cuban Revolution and rediscovering the nationalist tradition of Sandino—begin organizing FSLN (Sandinista National Liberation Front).

1967   Luis Somoza dies; younger brother Anastasio Somoza Debayle takes power in rigged vote after massacre of marchers protesting the election. Sandinista guerrilla forces are decimated in clashes with National Guard troops in Bocay (1963) and Pancasán (1967), leading FSLN to reassess strategy and re-emphasize political organizing.

1972   An earthquake devastates Managua; Somoza Debayle declares martial law, diverts international relief funds for personal benefit.

1974   Pedro Joaquín Chamorro, editor of Conservative opposition newspaper *La Prensa,* forms Democratic Liberation Union (UDEL), including middle-class and business leaders opposing the Somoza regime. Sandinista commando raid on a party attended by members of the elite results in an exchange of high-level hostages for ransom, prisoner release, and publication of FSLN communiques. Somoza declares state of siege, unleashes widespread repression against opposition.

1975–1977   FSLN splits into three factions, or "tendencies": Proletarian (organizing workers in factories and poor neighborhoods), Prolonged Popular War (building rural base for long-term guerrilla war), and Insurrectional or *Tercerista* ("third way," advocating broad-based coalitions for insurrection).

1976   FSLN founding intellectual Carlos Fonseca is killed in guerrilla combat.

1977   Martial law is lifted. *Los Doce* (Group of Twelve) prominent intellectuals and political figures declare opposition to the regime.

1978   Pedro Joaquín Chamorro, opposition newspaper editor, is assassinated. Escalating demonstrations, and the first of a series of urban popular uprisings. Sandinista and other radical opposition groups form United People's Movement (MPU). Multiclass Broad Opposition Front (FAO) is formed, calling general strikes. Sandinista commando raid on National Palace is led by Edén Pastora, who holds congress hostage, winning political demands. U.S. and Organization of American States (OAS) mediation efforts falter.

1979   Sandinista factions reunite under nine-man National Directorate and launch final offensive. Somoza flees to Miami on July 17, and victorious Sandinista forces enter Managua on July 19, form Government of National Reconstruction. The war killed 40,000–50,000 from 1977 to 1979.

1980   The government forms consultative Council of State, expanded to include more representation of Sandinista "mass organizations" (prompting some conservative politicians to resign from government). Massive literacy crusade is launched.

1981   Reagan administration authorizes covert funding to destabilize Sandinista government, backing former National Guard counter-revolutionary (contra) forces organizing in Honduras. Contra war would leave 30,000 dead and 20,000 wounded by 1989. First agrarian reform law is passed, reflecting mixed economy model.

1982   U.S. House passes Boland Amendment, prohibiting the use of U.S. aid for overthrow of the Nicaraguan government. Following contra attacks, government declares state of emergency.

1984   Sandinista presidential candidate Daniel Ortega wins 67 percent of vote in elections. Seven parties compete but right-wing Nicaraguan Democratic Coordinator (CDN)

boycotts election. The United States denounces elections as unfair, a charge disputed by international observers. CIA directs
mining of Nicaraguan harbors.

1985   The United States initiates a trade embargo
and other economic sanctions. The U.S. Congress approves "humanitarian aid" to contras. Nicaraguan government enacts economic stabilization measures to shore up
floundering economy.

1986   The U.S. Congress approves $100 million in
aid to contras. "Iran-contra" scandal reveals
that Reagan administration illegally diverted
funds from sale of arms to Iran for military
supplies to the contras. World Court rules
U.S. backing of contras violates international
law. New agrarian reform law expands redistribution to individuals and cooperatives.

1987   New constitution is signed after extensive
consultation process. Autonomy is granted
to Atlantic regions. Central American presidents sign Esquipulas II peace accords. Government begins indirect talks with contras.

1988   Government announces direct talks with
contras, lifts five-year state of emergency,
signs provisional cease-fire at Sapoá. Economic reforms are enacted to stem hyperinflation exceeding 33,000 percent.

1989   Regional negotiations lead to government
concessions on news media and electoral
laws. National Opposition Union (UNO)
picks Violeta Chamorro to lead opposition
ticket for 1990 elections, with U.S. backing.
U.S. Congress approves "nonlethal aid" to
keep contras intact pending elections.

1990   Violeta Chamorro, widow of slain editor Pedro Joaquín Chamorro, wins presidency with
55 percent to Daniel Ortega's 41 percent.
Transitional government's efforts at reconciliation are hampered by conflict over reversal of Sandinista property redistribution and
social reforms.

1996   Right-wing populist Arnoldo Alemán, former mayor of Managua, is elected president
on Liberal Party ticket, in Ortega's second
electoral defeat. Arnoldo Alemán's government is marked by corruption, authoritarian
tendencies, and widely criticized Sandinista-
Liberal pacts.

2001   Businessman Enrique Bolaños, wresting
control of the Liberal Party from Alemán
supporters, defeats Ortega in presidential
elections. Former president Alemán subsequently is jailed on corruption charges.
Plight of the poor worsens as economy is
shaken by falling coffee prices.

INTRODUCTION

The Nicaraguan Revolution that brought the Sandinistas to
power in 1979 ended the forty-three-year Somoza family dynasty, and challenged U.S. dominance in its traditional back-
yard. The ideologically eclectic Sandinistas introduced an innovative model of revolutionary government, attempting to
blend political pluralism with radical socioeconomic transformation. They made revolutionary history by stepping
down after losing elections in 1990. The Sandinista experiment, while brief, helped democratize Nicaragua and broke
Cold War–era stereotypes about revolution, influencing subsequent social struggles.

BACKGROUND: CULTURE AND HISTORY

Nicaragua's rebellious past includes resistance organized by
indigenous chiefs Nicarao (the country's namesake) and Diriangén, who expelled the first Spanish invaders in 1522. The
Spanish returned in force in 1524 to establish permanent settlements in the Pacific region in León and Granada under
Hernández de Córdoba (whose name adorns the national currency, the *córdoba*). Britain later established a protectorate on
the Atlantic "Mosquito Coast," (named for the Miskito Indians of the area) appointing an indigenous Miskito "king" and
importing African slaves from Jamaica. Today Nicaragua is 76
percent mestizo, 10 percent white, 11 percent black (English-
speaking Creoles concentrated in the Atlantic region), and 3
percent indigenous (Library of Congress 1993, 1).

The Atlantic Coast remained more sparsely populated
than the centers of power in the Pacific, as well as culturally
distinct and geographically remote. In 1894 an independent
Nicaraguan government under the authoritarian modernizer
José Santos Zelaya forced the British out, incorporating the

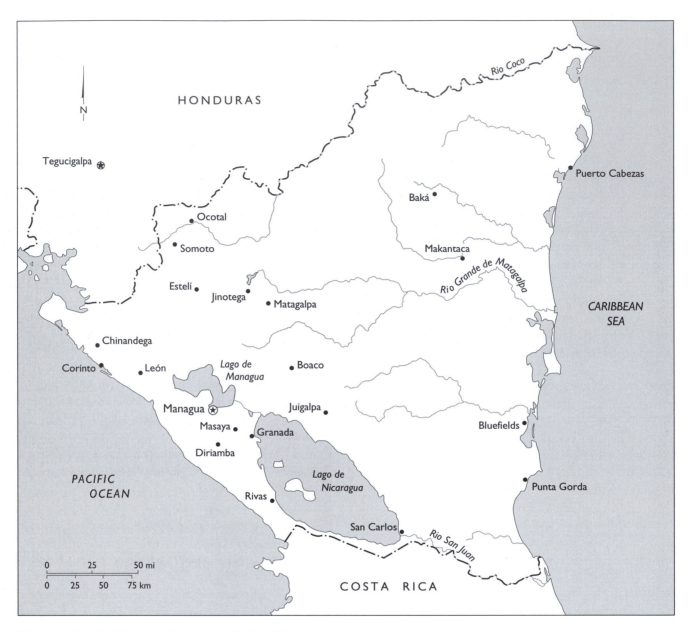

Nicaragua, showing Managua, the capital, and other cities.

region into the national territory. Yet well into the twentieth century, the region's diverse peoples—including Creole, Miskito, and smaller indigenous groups like the Mayagna (Sumo) and Rama—resented control by "the Spanish"— that is, the central government. The Sandinistas belatedly recognized this distinct strand of national history and identity, negotiating a far-reaching regional autonomy in 1987.

Nicaraguan history is marked by anti-imperialist nationalism, and division of elites over how closely to align with powerful external patrons. In 1821 the Central American provinces declared independence from Spain, then briefly annexed themselves to the powerful Mexican empire, before forming an independent Central American Federation in

1823. That was the year of the Monroe Doctrine, the U.S. unilateral declaration of intent to displace European influence from the hemisphere. By the time that Central American unity failed and Nicaragua became an independent republic, in 1838, Spanish influence was waning and British influence rising, with the United States closing in from behind.

With the 1848 California Gold Rush, Cornelius Vanderbilt's Accessory Transit Company profited from shuttling coast-to-coast steamship passengers overland across the Nicaraguan isthmus. U.S. commercial and strategic interests converged around potential canal routes. The United States, as a rising regional power, negotiated the 1850 Clayton-Bulwer Treaty with Britain, in which each agreed not to build a Nicaraguan canal without consulting the other. The Nicaraguan elite of this era were divided between the Conservative Party based in Granada and the Liberal Party based in León. With the rise of coffee as a new source of wealth, the two feuding factions compromised in 1852 on Managua as the capital city. The coffee boom also affected class structure by displacing indigenous communal landholders, and by contributing to the formation of a *burguesía chapiolla* (homespun bourgeoisie) with a less aristocratic, more distinctively Nicaraguan flavor.

In 1855, William Walker, a filibusterer from Tennessee, organized a private expeditionary force that invaded Nicaragua on the side of the Liberals amid ongoing civil conflict. Washington at the time favored the Liberals as allies of convenience against the British-backed Conservatives. Walker succeeded in seizing power, naming himself president, declaring English the official language, welcoming foreign investment, and establishing slavery. A coalition of Liberals and Conservatives, supported by armies of the other Central American republics, drove Walker out in 1857. He attempted a comeback in 1860 but was captured by the British and handed over to the Hondurans, who tried and executed him.

The Walker affair did not end elite factional fighting, but the backlash helped prolong Conservative rule from 1857 to 1893. In the 1881 War of the Comuneros, an indigenous rebellion (against encroachment on communally held land by the rising coffee-grower elite) was suppressed. In 1893, a Liberal revolt brought José Santos Zelaya to power, restarting the dynamic of civil strife and foreign intervention. Zelaya was an authoritarian modernizer, analogous to Mexico's Porfirio Díaz. He centralized state power, promoting investment in modern infrastructure and coffee production for the lucrative export market. His state-building initiatives included incorporating the Atlantic region into national territory by ending the British protectorate, a move supported by the United States. However, when Zelaya's opening to foreign investment meant turning down a U.S. canal proposal and exploring options with Britain and Japan, the United States in 1909 backed a Conservative rebellion that ousted him.

Amid renewed Liberal-Conservative conflict, U.S. Marines occupied Nicaragua from 1912 to 1925 and from 1926 to 1933. U.S. interests included debt collection, protection of investments under the emerging rubric of dollar diplomacy, and blocking any canal construction that might compete with the U.S.-controlled Panama Canal. A corollary interest in local political stability led the U.S. to broker a pact in 1927 in which the Liberals agreed to stop fighting and allow Conservative president Adolfo Díaz to serve out his term, in exchange for U.S. supervision of an election that would presumably return the Liberals to power in 1928. That Pact of Espino Negro was signed by U.S. envoy Henry Stimson and Liberal general José

A guerrilla general, Augusto Sandino fought for social and political reform, as well as independence from U.S. interference in Nicaraguan politics. (Library of Congress)

María Moncada, who was allegedly promised U.S. support for his presidential candidacy. It became a potent symbol of elite pacts that sold out national interests, a recurrent theme in Nicaraguan national history. One maverick Liberal general, Augusto César Sandino, denounced the pact and launched a guerrilla war against the occupying U.S. Marines and the government they propped up.

Sandino, illegitimate son of a landowner from the mountainous Segovias region, was an eccentric but charismatic figure, whose ragtag "Army for the Defense of National Sovereignty" harassed the occupiers and eluded capture for six years. His legendary resistance embarrassed the U.S. Marines, who in 1933 withdrew after creating a Nicaraguan National

Guard under the command of Anastasio "Tacho" Somoza García. Once the Marines had left, Sandino came down from the hills for peace talks with the government in 1934, but he was assassinated by officers of Somoza's National Guard. Somoza then seized power in 1936 and arranged to have himself "elected," beginning the family dynasty. Later in the 1960s, the Sandinista revolutionaries adopted the name of the semi-mythical nationalist hero Sandino.

Somocismo (Somoza rule) was a personalist variant of authoritarianism, sustained by corruption that amassed a family fortune while sharing the spoils with key factions of the elite; repression of opponents through the Somoza-controlled National Guard; and a carefully cultivated, even exaggerated, closeness with the United States. Dynasty founder "Tacho" Somoza was a caudillo (strongman) with a populist flair for gestures of generosity toward the masses, a talent not passed on to his sons. By the time "Tachito" Somoza—known as "the last Marine"—fled to Miami in 1979 to escape the advancing Sandinista forces, the family fortune was estimated at $400 million (Booth 1985, 81).

The Somozas crafted a Liberal Nationalist Party (Partido Liberal Nacionalista, PLN) as an electoral vehicle, changing electoral and constitutional provisions whenever necessary to ensure the election of a Somoza or an occasional interim puppet president. PLN voters received special identification cards, useful for obtaining government jobs and services or avoiding problems with the authorities. Traditional Liberal and Conservative elites were regularly guaranteed shares of lucrative business opportunities and legislative seats. However, independent Liberals and Conservatives periodically engaged in conspiracies and quixotic rebellions, and the independent Liberal poet Rigoberto López Pérez assassinated Tacho Somoza in 1956. Other opposition in the early decades of the dictatorship, including labor organizing by the pro-Moscow Nicaraguan Socialist Party (Partido Socialista Nicaragüense, PSN) and by the centrist Social Christians, met with alternating co-optation and repression.

Tacho was succeeded by elder son Luis, while younger son Anastasio "Tachito" Somoza Debayle held the reins of the National Guard. In the early 1960s, student activists Carlos Fonseca, Silvio Mayorga, and Tomás Borge began organizing what would become the Sandinista National Liberation Front (Frente Sandinista de Liberación Nacional, FSLN). It was Fonseca, the intellectual visionary of the group, whose intense study of Nicaraguan history led to the rediscovery of the legacy of Sandino and the adaptation of that symbol for present purposes. Fonseca broke with the PSN to embrace a more unorthodox Marxism, inspired by the voluntarism of Che Guevara's guerrilla example and the 1959 Cuban Revolution, but deeply rooted in the specific conditions of Nicaraguan history. Small Sandinista rural guerrilla units clashed with the National Guard, and skirmishes in Bocay in 1963 and

Pancasán in 1967 nearly wiped out the nascent revolutionary group. These experiences, and Che Guevara's 1967 death in Bolivia, contributed to the FSLN's shift from *foquismo* (a guerrilla strategy based on tiny "focal points" of exemplary armed action) to mass organizing among the rural and urban poor in the 1970s.

Luis Somoza's death in 1967 generated new political unrest, as a rigged election was being prepared to install Anastasio "Tachito" Somoza. The National Guard opened fire on a demonstration led by Conservative Party activists Fernando Agüero and Pedro Joaquín Chamorro against the planned electoral fraud, killing more than a hundred (Zimmerman 2000, 95). Agüero later signed a 1971 power-sharing agreement with Somoza that entered the Nicaraguan political lexicon as the *Kupia Kumi* (Miskito for pact—literally "one single heart"), reinforcing popular outrage and cynicism about elite pacts.

CONTEXT AND PROCESS OF REVOLUTION

Nicaragua's changing political economy shaped the context for the development of mass opposition to the dictatorship. The Central American economies had been based largely on coffee exports since the mid 1800s, and then banana enclaves in the early twentieth century. The period from the mid 1950s through the mid 1970s, which preceded the outbreak of revolution in Central America, saw an agro-export boom, marked by rapid economic growth but worsening inequalities. New external demand spurred dramatic expansion of export production of cotton, sugar (after the Cuban revolution and U.S. reapportionment of Cuba's sugar quota), and beef cattle for the fast-food market. Nicaraguan cotton production, negligible before the 1950s, overtook coffee exports by 1955. Ten years later Nicaragua was the world's tenth largest cotton exporter, and by 1978, one-third of the rural workforce were landless temporary workers (Dunkerley 1988, 185–192).

Given the rigidities of land ownership and political power in this "agro-export dependency" model, the regional boom was accompanied by growing landlessness and hunger. The elites had little interest in redistributive measures to expand internal demand, since their profits derived from exports. Powerful landowners expanded lucrative export acreage by displacing peasants, who were then conveniently available for low-wage harvest labor. As the economy became more closely tied to world markets, export price fluctuations translated into wage cuts and layoffs backed up by state repression, in a dynamic aptly described as "reactionary despotism" (Baloyra-Herp 1983). Parallel to the agro-export boom, the inauguration of the Central American Common Market in 1960 spawned some industrialization for the regional market, generating diversification of the capitalist class and limited expansion of the middle class and industrial working class. Yet real wages fell, and urban unemployment remained high through the 1970s, partly absorbed by the burgeoning "informal sector" of artisans and the self-employed (Vilas 1986, 97–105). This was the historical setting in which the Sandinistas began broadening their organizing efforts, while the Somoza regime was actually alienating its support base among middle and upper classes.

The 1970s saw the onset of state crisis and division of the elite, two important conditions for the success of revolutionary movements. In 1972 a major earthquake devastated the capital city of Managua. Somoza diverted international relief funds toward businesses of family members and associates, monopolizing lucrative post-earthquake opportunities in sectors such as construction and real estate, often pocketing funds for housing that was never built. Non-Somoza capitalists were outraged at this violation of the unwritten terms of division of the spoils, and they shared with the middle class a growing unease about the ability of such a regime to maintain order. In 1974 those disaffected sectors were grouped into the Democratic Liberation Union (Unión Democrática de Liberación, UDEL) by Conservative activist Pedro Joaquín Chamorro, editor of the opposition newspaper *La Prensa.* Also in 1974, Sandinista commandos staged a daring raid on a Christmas party of the elite at the Managua home of José María "Chema" Castillo, taking hostages who were exchanged for ransom, release of prisoners (including Daniel Ortega), and publication of FSLN communiques. The Chema Castillo raid suddenly boosted the FSLN into the national and international spotlight, and exposed the regime's vulnerability. Somoza responded with a state of siege and a wave of repression, which only widened opposition. Opposition editor Chamorro continued to criticize the corruption and brutality of Somoza rule. Chamorro was assassinated in January 1978, a watershed event that triggered rioting and galvanized ever-widening opposition to the dictatorship.

Meanwhile the Sandinistas were intensifying their grassroots political organizing in the mid 1970s, even in the face of escalating repression under the martial law imposed after the Chema Castillo operation. In the rural parts of the Pacific region (where peasants had been most dramatically uprooted by the cotton and sugar booms), Sandinistas worked with religious organizers inspired by "Liberation Theology," the dissident current of the Latin American Catholic Church that since the 1960s advocated a "preferential option for the poor." These initiatives included lay "Delegates of the Word," and the Center for Agrarian Education and Promotion (Centro de Educación y Promoción Agraria, CEPA), a rural pastoral training program founded by Jesuits in 1969.

Radicalized by these self-help programs, plantation workers in Carazo and Masaya formed Committees of Rural Workers (Comités de Trabajadores del Campo, CTC) in the 1970s to demand better wages and working conditions. The Sandinistas joined the CTC's efforts in a successful 1977 strike at the massive San Antonio sugar plantation. Afterward, the CTCs were grouped into an Association of Rural Workers (Asociación de Trabajadores del Campo, ATC) that spread through the Pacific region. An ATC march and hunger strike in Diriamba in 1978 to protest rural conditions brought National Guard repression, reinforcing ATC collaboration with the Sandinista armed struggle.

Other Sandinista mass organizing in the late 1970s included Workers' Fighting Committees (Comités de Lucha de los Trabajadores, CLT) in factories and working-class barrios. These were regrouped after the 1979 revolutionary victory into the Sandinista Workers' Central (Central Sandinista de los Trabajadores, CST), the main Sandinista urban labor federation. Sandinista organizing among urban workers competed with earlier unions organized by the Socialists mainly in the construction industry; Communists primarily in the textile industry; and the centrist Social Christians in scattered factories. Later competitors included the Maoist Workers' Front (Frente Obrero, FO), which had its own armed wing, the Popular Anti-Somocista Militia (Milicias Populares Anti-Somocistas, MILPAS). In urban as well as rural organizing, Liberation Theology–inspired "Christian base communities" helped raise social and political consciousness, while some radical priests directly aided the Sandinista cause.

The FSLN in 1975 split into three factions or tendencies, mainly over revolutionary strategy, and Carlos Fonseca's 1976 death in combat accentuated the disarray. The FSLN's Proletarian tendency was influenced by orthodox Marxist notions of the working class as the historic agent of revolution, organizing workers later incorporated into the ATC and CST. The "Prolonged Popular War" tendency, influenced by Maoist ideas of a rural base from which to encircle the cities, concentrated on building support among the peasantry for guerrilla operations. The Insurrectional, or *Tercerista* ("third way"), tendency was the most ideologically eclectic and pragmatic, calling for broad-based coalitions and seizing opportunities for insurrectionary action.

The accelerating pace and widening scope of opposition activities in the late 1970s reunited the factions in 1979 for the final push to revolutionary victory, in a strategy ultimately closest to the *Tercerista* position. In 1977, Somoza lifted martial law, partly reflecting U.S. pressure under the newly declared human rights policy of Jimmy Carter. Taking advantage of the space, a Group of Twelve (*Los Doce*) prominent intellectuals and political figures publicly declared their opposition to the regime. Following the 1978 assassination

After the fall of former dictator Anastasio Somoza, Sandinistas arrive in Managua and are greeted by the population. Sandinista leader Daniel Ortega talks to his supporters, July 19, 1979. (Patrick Chauvel/Corbis Sygma)

of Chamorro, a series of popular uprisings erupted that were not actually initiated by the FSLN. The Sandinistas took the opportunity to forge a coalition of radical opposition groups, the United People's Movement (Movimiento Pueblo Unido, MPU). Participation included the Association of Women Confronting the National Problem (Asociación de Mujeres ante la Problemática Nacional, AMPRONAC), a mainly middle- and upper-class women's organization formed in 1977. AMPRONAC was renamed after a fallen woman combatant, the Luisa Amanda Espinoza Nicaraguan Women's Association (Asociación de Mujeres Nicaragüenses Luisa Amanda Espinoza, AMNLAE). Sandinistas also organized for urban insurrection by forming Civil Defense Committees (Comités de Defensa Civil, CDC) at the neighborhood level. These were reorganized after 1979 as the Sandinista Defense Committees (Comités de Defensa Sandinista, CDS).

Pressure on the regime mounted as the Sandinistas joined a multiclass Broad Opposition Front (Frente Amplio Opositor, FAO), which organized general strikes in coordination with the FSLN's armed opposition. In August 1978 a Sandinista com-

mando unit headed by Edén Pastora seized the National Legislative Palace, holding the national congress hostage in a spectacular action that won political demands and captured the public imagination. Participants in the insurrections that finally toppled the regime were mainly urban, including 29 percent students, 22 percent informal sector, 16 percent workers, 16 percent office employees, 7 percent professionals, and 5 percent small merchants and traders, 4.5 percent peasants and farmers, and 0.5 percent others (ibid., 112).

As the insurrectionary momentum was building and the Sandinistas were scrambling to keep up, the international context was also shifting. U.S. foreign policy was in post-Vietnam disarray. Jimmy Carter's mixed signals on human rights weakened Somoza's claims of unconditional U.S. backing, without persuading Somoza himself that the United States was willing to risk letting him go. U.S. efforts to forestall a Sandinista victory through a negotiated outcome (in which Somoza would resign, but key elements of his regime would remain in place) had the unintended consequence of discrediting moderates in the FAO. Other Latin American countries with increasingly independent foreign policies did not share U.S. views of the endgame, and by the time the FSLN began the final offensive of June 1979, the Organization of American States had rejected a U.S. proposal for "peace-keeping" intervention. When Somoza finally fled to Miami on July 17, much of his remaining National Guard disintegrated or surrendered to the FSLN; the victorious Sandinistas entered Managua on July 19, 1979.

IMPACTS

The Sandinista victory, in the same year in which revolutionaries in Iran overthrew another long-standing U.S. client, generated a powerful U.S. backlash that reverberated throughout the last decade of the Cold War. The Nicaraguan revolution helped shatter the myth of invincibility of Cold War autocrats like Somoza, long a staple of U.S. policy. The Carter administration began interrupting aid to Nicaragua's new government, funneling it to anti-Sandinista groups. Candidate Ronald Reagan accused Carter of "losing" Nicaragua and giving away the Panama Canal, and the Reagan Doctrine promised to roll back what was portrayed as an expansionist Soviet "evil empire." The image of "falling dominoes" in Central America fueled a massive escalation of U.S. counter-revolutionary initiatives, focused on militarily preventing revolutionary victories in El Salvador and Guatemala and destabilizing the Sandinista government in Nicaragua. The region became a testing ground for late Cold War U.S. foreign policy.

Almost immediately upon taking office in 1981, the Reagan administration began covertly funding armed counter-revolutionaries (contras), formed initially mainly from former members of Somoza's National Guard. Escalating U.S. hostilities soon became overt, including military exercises in neighboring Honduras that supported the contras, an international financial blockade, CIA operatives mining Nicaraguan harbors in 1984, and a trade embargo in 1985. The contra war from 1980 to 1989 killed about 30,000 Nicaraguans, nearly 1 percent of the population, with damages of $9 billion, equivalent to some thirteen years of export earnings (Walker 2003, 55–56). Economic growth turned negative after the second year of the Sandinista government, and it became difficult to sort out the effects of revolutionary policies from the impact of the contra war. Economic deterioration and the accumulated toll of the war were significant factors in the Sandinista electoral defeat of 1990.

The Nicaraguan Revolution had a mixed impact on revolutionary movements elsewhere in Central America. The Reagan administration's initial rationale for supporting the contras was alleged Sandinista supply of arms to rebels in El Salvador, a grossly exaggerated claim. As U.S. destabilization efforts and contra aid escalated, the Soviet Union supplied arms and some economic credits to the Sandinista government. However, it became evident that the United States was willing to invest far more in counter-revolution in Central America than the Soviets would in aid, even to established revolutionary governments. Nicaragua exemplified the potential for revolutionaries to come to power and resist U.S.-backed armed overthrow. That resistance was complemented by anti-interventionist pressure, within the United States and internationally, and sharpened by revelations of illegal policy—for example, the 1986 "Iran-contra" scandal and World Court ruling against U.S. hostilities toward Nicaragua. Yet the punishing cost of the contra war also reduced the appeal of the Nicaraguan example. By the end of the 1990s, all the Central American revolutions had negotiated ends to the armed conflicts and institutionalized electoral democracy. This was less than the radical socioeconomic transformation many had fought for, but a major political change that revolution brought to the region.

The Sandinista government from 1979 to 1990 had departed from the orthodoxy of twentieth-century revolutions in many important respects. Rejecting the concept of a one-party state, they institutionalized a pluralist multiparty system, holding competitive elections in 1984 (won by Sandinista Daniel Ortega) and 1990; they organized a broadly participatory consultation to write a democratic constitution in 1987. Initially insistent on class-based revolutionary unity, they bent to demands of ethnic minorities in the Atlantic region, passing a historic Autonomy Statute in 1987. Although influenced by Socialist ideals, they maintained a mixed economy, in which the minority state-owned sector coexisted with large private capital, small owners, and cooperatives. The Sandinistas welcomed aid and ideas from a variety of international sources, resisting U.S. attempts to pigeonhole Nicaragua as a Soviet client state.

In each of these innovations, the space for maneuver continually narrowed. The provisional Junta of the Government of National Reconstruction faced an early political test in 1980, when it expanded the composition of the consultative Council of State to reflect the growing strength of the Sandinista-mobilized grassroots "mass organizations." Businessman Alfonso Robelo quit the Junta over that point, leading the opposition Nicaraguan Democratic Movement (Movimiento Democrático Nicaragüense, MDN) before joining the contras in 1982. The numerically small but traditionally influential political and economic elites objected to what the Sandinistas saw as a more inclusive, participatory democracy, and some boycotted the 1984 election. They also objected to FSLN control of Nicaragua's new Sandinista People's Army, which the FSLN viewed as necessary to protect the revolution. The Sandinistas mobilized grass-roots participation in social programs such as national literacy and vaccination campaigns, winning recognition from UNESCO and the World Health Organization. However, top-down relations developed between the FSLN and mass organizations, and critics on the Right saw them as instruments of political control.

Many anti-Somoza capitalists and professionals rejected Sandinista redistributive policies, including ambitious agrarian reform. Disinvestment by uneasy capitalists (and in some cases collaboration with the contras) triggered more property confiscations, in an escalating spiral of tensions between the Sandinista government and the Superior Council of Private Enterprise (Consejo Superior de la Empresa Privada, COSEP). The Sandinistas encouraged small and medium agrarian capitalists to join the alternative National Union of Farmers and Ranchers (Unión Nacional de Agricultores y Ganaderos, UNAG), formed in 1981. UNAG pressured for a second agrarian reform law in 1986, shifting emphasis from state farms to individual titling, in an effort to undercut the appeal of the contras to peasants suspicious of the state.

Tensions with the Catholic Church hierarchy grew, as the Sandinistas appointed Liberation Theology priests to important government posts and enacted radical social policies. Archbishop Miguel Obando y Bravo, a critic of Somoza's human rights record, became a prominent opponent of the Sandinistas. After his 1985 elevation to cardinal, he celebrated Mass with the contra leadership in Miami. Along with Obando and the church hierarchy, the opposition Chamorro family newspaper La Prensa became a symbol of the anti-Sandinista domestic opposition. The Sandinistas periodically restricted the civil liberties of opponents, invoking wartime emergency as opposition groups increasingly aligned themselves with the U.S.-backed contras. The war and U.S. economic embargo drained resources and forced growing reliance on Soviet aid, further inflaming the opposition.

At the end of the 1980s, under the framework of regional Central American peace accords, the Sandinistas signed a cease-fire with the contras and accepted electoral reforms favorable to the opposition. The U.S.-backed National Opposition Union (Unión Nacional Opositora, UNO) coalition ticket, headed by Violeta Chamorro, won the 1990 election in a 55–41 percent upset. The Sandinistas again broke new ground, as the first to win a revolution and then hand over government peacefully after losing elections.

The FSLN's credibility slipped during the post-1990 transition, as some nationalized properties were hastily transferred to party functionaries in the *piñata* (candy grab). The Sandinistas in opposition attempted to defend the revolutionary social gains for the poor, through a strategy of alternating between confrontational mass mobilizations and backroom pacts led by former president Daniel Ortega and his supporters, called *ortodoxos* (the orthodox faction). Former vice president Sergio Ramírez formed a dissident Sandinista Renewal Movement (Movimiento de Renovación Sandinista, MRS), unsuccessfully demanding internal party democratization, greater accountability, and new leadership. The reformist *renovacionistas* failed to build a mass base; meanwhile, the *ortodoxos* were weakened by public cynicism over elite pacts, and by accusations of sexual abuse leveled against Daniel Ortega by his stepdaughter.

Some of the mass organizations first mobilized by the Sandinistas, particularly unions and the women's movement, proved quite resourceful as they established autonomy from the FSLN. Now Sandinista only in their origins, they improvised strategies for confronting neo-liberal economic programs and conservative social policies. While the Sandinista party and leadership's authority receded, the lasting impact of the revolution in Nicaragua was the organizational experience and consciousness it had imparted to its mass participants.

The Sandinista Revolution began democratizing Nicaragua, ending an era when the United States controlled client states by designating autocratic leaders who lacked popular support. The Nicaraguan Revolution also helped to shift the focus of revolution itself, from the seizure of state power to the longer-term process of social transformation. That shift continued with the rise of diverse social movements, confronting not so much the state as transnational capital in the era of globalization.

PEOPLE AND ORGANIZATIONS

Asociación de Mujeres Nicaragüenses Luisa Amanda Espinoza—AMNLAE (Luisa Amanda Espinoza Association of Nicaraguan Women)

Sandinista women's organization, named for the first woman FSLN fighter killed in 1970, AMNLAE was originally the Asociación de Mujeres ante la Problemática Nacional, AMPRONAC (Association of Women Confronting the National Problem). AMPRONAC was a mainly middle- and upper-class women's organization, formed in 1977, that attracted a more radical grassroots base through participation in insurrectionary organizing. After the 1979 Sandinista victory, AMNLAE promoted women's interests, including legislative and constitutional reforms. Feminists criticized the all-male FSLN National Directorate's failure to prioritize women's issues.

Asociación de Trabajadores del Campo—ATC (Association of Rural Workers)

The Sandinista union of agricultural wage workers, formed in 1977, the ATC originated in rural organizing influenced by Liberation Theology, the progressive social doctrine within the Latin American Catholic Church. The ATC remained an important base of organized rural support for the Sandinistas after their 1979 victory.

Central Sandinista de los Trabajadores—CST (Sandinista Workers' Central)

The main Sandinista urban labor union, constituted after the 1979 FSLN victory, CST originated in clandestine organizing in factories and working-class neighborhoods for the insurrection. Unionization soared under the Sandinista government, which favored the Sandinista unions over older rivals. The CST lost credibility as it defended the Sandinista government's increasingly orthodox economic austerity policies in the late 1980s. Most non-Sandinista unions joined with right-wing parties in the UNO alliance that defeated the FSLN in the 1990 election.

Chamorro, Pedro Joaquin (1924–1978)

Conservative Party activist, editor of anti-Somoza newspaper *La Prensa*, assassinated in January 1978. Chamorro was a prominent critic of Somoza and leader of the Democratic Liberation Union (Unión Democrática de Liberación, UDEL), an opposition group of business and professional leaders he co-founded in 1974. His killing highlighted the Somoza regime's ruthlessness, helping galvanize broad multiclass opposition. His widow, Violeta Barrios de Chamorro, led the 1990 UNO coalition ticket to electoral victory.

Chamorro, Violeta Barrios de (Born 1929)

Violeta Barrios de Chamorro was president from 1990 to 1996; widow of *La Prensa* editor and Conservative Party activist Pedro Joaquín Chamorro, whose 1978 assassination highlighted opposition to Somoza by dissident elites. She joined the five-member provisional Junta of the Government of National Reconstruction that replaced the Somoza regime in 1979 but resigned in 1980, later acknowledging disagreement with the Sandinista-dominated government. *La Prensa* was intermittently censored and closed for pro-

contra leanings and for accepting CIA funding. Chamorro won the presidency in 1990 on the U.S.-backed, anti-Sandinista UNO coalition ticket.

Comites de Defensa Sandinista—CDS (Sandinista Defense Committees)

A neighborhood-based Sandinista mass organization; originally Civil Defense Committees (Comités de Defensa Civil, CDC), organized after the September 1978 insurrections by the Sandinista-dominated United People's Movement (Movimiento Pueblo Unido, MPU) to coordinate civilian resistance. After the 1979 Sandinista victory, the CDS sponsored regime-supportive activities, including distribution of rationed basic goods and mobilization for volunteer campaigns.

Consejo Superior de la Empresa Privada—COSEP (Superior Council of Private Enterprise)

A business council, founded as the Superior Council of Private Initiative (COSIP) in 1972, COSEP represented the emerging unity of Nicaraguan capitalists against Somoza; became opponents of Sandinista government.

Contras (Counter-revolutionaries)

U.S.-backed armed irregular forces seeking to overthrow the Sandinista government throughout the 1980s, the contras were initially formed with U.S. assistance under the leadership of former officers of Somoza's National Guard. Later they incorporated leaders from traditional political elites and recruited foot-soldiers among the peasantry of the interior region. Contra human rights abuses intermittently prompted the U.S. Congress to impose aid suspensions, controversially circumvented by the Reagan administration (notably the 1986 Iran-contra scandal).

Fonseca Amador, Carlos (1936–1976)

Intellectual founder of the Sandinista National Liberation Front (Frente Sandinista de Liberación Nacional, FSLN), Fonseca was killed in combat in 1976. A student activist and member of the pro-Moscow Nicaraguan Socialist Party (Partido Socialista Nicaragüense, PSN) in the 1950s, Fonseca broke with the PSN and founded the FSLN, with student leaders Silvio Mayorga and Tomás Borge, around 1961–1962.

Frente Amplio Opositor—FAO (Broad Opposition Front)

A coalition of business and professional groups and intellectuals (UDEL, MDN, and *Los Doce*) formed in May 1978 to oppose the Somoza dictatorship, FAO organized general strikes that helped to destabilize the regime. FAO participated in failed negotiations backed by the United States and the Organization of American States (OAS) in 1979 to persuade Somoza to resign, eclipsed by the successful Sandinista-led insurrections.

Frente Sandinista de Liberacion Nacional—FSLN (Sandinista National Liberation Front)

A leftist group that led an armed uprising overthrowing the Somoza dictatorship in 1979, FSLN established a revolutionary government ratified in the 1984 elections. It then lost the 1990 election and became the main opposition party. Founded in the early 1960s by student activists Carlos Fonseca, Silvio Mayorga, and Tomás Borge, the FSLN forged an eclectic ideological blend of the anti-imperialist nationalism and populism of Nicaraguan folk hero Augusto César Sandino; the voluntarist Marxism (a vision of revolution rooted in the subjective consciousness and will of the participants, not just economic determinism) of Che Guevara; mass participatory democracy; and the social justice philosophy of Liberation Theology, a radical offshoot of Latin American Catholicism. The FSLN shifted from small rural guerrilla cells to grassroots political organizing among peasants and the urban poor in the 1970s, backing urban insurrections that triumphed on July 19, 1979. The revolutionary government espoused political pluralism, a mixed economy, and international non-alignment. They institutionalized a competitive political system through 1984 elections and a new 1987 constitution. The Sandinista government faced unraveling alliances, economic deterioration aggravated by a U.S. embargo, and the devastating contra war. In 1990 they lost elections to the U.S.-backed UNO coalition.

Guardia Nacional (National Guard)

Guardia Nacional was a military and police force of the Somoza dictatorship, formed by U.S. Marines during their 1927–1933 occupation and left under the command of Anastasio Somoza García when they withdrew in 1933. Successive members of the Somoza dynasty used it as their personal instrument of control, until their 1979 revolutionary overthrow.

Los Doce (Group of Twelve)

Twelve prominent intellectuals, professionals, and business leaders composed *Los Doce*, publicly endorsing the Sandinistas in 1977 and joining the Broad Opposition Front (Frente Amplio Opositor, FAO) in 1978. Many took posts in the Sandinista government after 1979, including Vice President Sergio Ramírez.

Movimiento Democratico Nicaragüense—MDN (Nicaraguan Democratic Movement)

Anti-Somoza party of businesspeople and professionals organized by industrialist Alfonso Robelo Callejas in 1978. Robelo joined the five-person governing junta in 1979, resigning in 1980. The MDN functioned as the main opposition party to the Sandinistas until 1982, when Robelo joined armed contras in Costa Rica.

Movimiento Pueblo Unido—MPU (United People's Movement)

A coalition of twenty-two radical student, labor, and other civic and political organizations opposing Somoza rule, MPU came into existence in 1978. The FSLN helped to form the MPU to mobilize support for the war effort.

Obando y Bravo, Miguel (Born 1926)

Archbishop of Nicaragua from 1968, Obando y Bravo was elevated to cardinal in 1985; he shifted from critic of Somoza to prominent opponent of the Sandinista government. His identification with the hard-line anti-Sandinista opposition, including the contras, symbolized the FSLN's rift with the Catholic Church's conservative hierarchy.

Ortega Saavedra, Daniel (Born 1945)

As Sandinista leader, Ortega headed the governing Junta in 1979 and was elected president in 1984. He lost the 1990 election and led the party in opposition. From a middle-class, anti-Somoza family, he joined the FSLN guerrilla forces in 1963 as a university student, spending 1967 to 1974 in prison. Known as a sober and disciplined pragmatist, he coordinated the FSLN National Directorate and then the governing Junta, and was elected president on the Sandinista ticket in 1984. Losing the 1990 election, he made revolutionary history by handing over power through the ballot box, proclaiming in his concession speech that the Sandinistas would "govern from below." However, he resisted appeals from within the party to step aside in favor of fresh leadership, losing elections again in 1996 and 2001.

Pastora Gomez, Eden (Born 1937)

Former Sandinista guerrilla "Commander Zero" who led the spectacular 1978 seizure of the National Legislative Palace, Pastora split with the FSLN in 1982 to lead a Costa Rica–based contra faction, eclipsed by the larger Honduras-based contra group.

Ramírez Mercado, Sergio (Born 1942)

Prominent intellectual in the anti-Somoza movement (including the Group of Twelve, *Los Doce*) in the 1970s, Ramírez was vice president during the Sandinista government. He led a reformist split from Daniel Ortega's orthodox Sandinistas in 1995.

Somoza Debayle, Anastasio (1925–1980)

Anastasio "Tachito" Somoza was the younger son of dynasty founder Anastasio Somoza García. He was president and National Guard chief from 1967 until ousted by the Sandinista Revolution in 1979 (with an interlude from 1972 to 1974 of a puppet president). Running a corrupt and repressive regime, he was nicknamed "the last Marine" for his close ties to the United States, which had created the National Guard. Assassinated in Paraguay by Argentine leftists in 1980.

Somoza Debayle, Luis (1922–1967)

Eldest son of dynasty founder Anastasio Somoza García, he was acting president after his father's 1956 assassination and president from 1957 to 1963. He then ruled through puppet presidents until his death in 1967. Succeeded by younger brother and National Guard commander Anastasio "Tachito" Somoza Debayle.

Somoza García, Anastasio (1896–1956)

Anastasio "Tacho" Somoza was installed by the United States as commander of the National Guard when occupying U.S. Marines withdrew in 1933. He launched a coup in 1936, inaugurating a forty-three-year family dynasty. Power passed to his son Luis Somoza Debayle after his assassination in 1956.

Union Democratica de Liberacion—UDEL (Democratic Liberation Union)

A coalition of businesspeople, professionals, and independent unions formed in 1974 to oppose the Somoza regime, UDEL was co-founded by Conservative newspaper editor Pedro Joaquín Chamorro. It joined the Broad Opposition Front (Frente Amplio Opositor, FAO) after Chamorro's assassination in 1978, participating in general strikes that helped to undermine the Somoza regime.

Union Nacional de Agricultores y Ganaderos—UNAG (National Union of Farmers and Ranchers)

A generally pro-revolution association of small and medium-size farmers and ranchers, UNAG initially grouped with rural workers in the ATC but separated to form its own organization in 1981. More ideologically and socially diverse than the main Sandinista mass organizations, UNAG pushed in the mid-1980s for accelerated redistribution of land to smallholders and cooperatives rather than state enterprises.

Union Nacional Opositora—UNO (National Opposition Union)

A coalition of fourteen small parties formed with U.S. covert and overt assistance for the 1990 elections, UNO successfully ran Violeta Chamorro against Sandinista president Daniel Ortega. The coalition fragmented soon after the election.

Richard Stahler-Sholk

See Also Chilean Socialist Revolution, Counter-Revolution, and the Restoration of Democracy; Cinema of Revolution; Cuban Revolution; Democracy, Dictatorship, and Fascism; Documentaries of Revolution; Guatemalan Democratic Revolution, Counter-Revolution, and the Restoration of Democracy; Guerrilla Warfare and Revolution; Salvadoran Revolution; Student and Youth Movements, Activism and Revolution; Women and Revolution

References and Further Readings
Baloyra-Herp, Enrique A. 1983. "Reactionary Despotism in Central America," *Journal of Latin American Studies* 15 (2): 295–319.
Booth, John A. 1985. *The End and the Beginning: The Nicaraguan Revolution.* 2nd edition. Boulder, CO: Westview.
———. 1991. "The Socioeconomic and Political Roots of National Revolts in Central America," *Latin American Research Review* 26 (1): 33–73.

Close, David. 1998. *Nicaragua: The Chamorro Years.* Boulder, CO: Lynne Rienner.

Close, David, and Deonandan Kalowaite, eds. 2004. *Undoing Democracy: The Politics of Electoral Caudillismo.* Lanham, MD: Lexington.

Dunkerley, James. 1988. *Power in the Isthmus: A Political History of Modern Central America.* New York: Verso.

Gilbert, Dennis. 1990. *Sandinistas: The Party and the Revolution.* Cambridge, UK: Basil Blackwell.

LaFeber, Walter. 1993. *Inevitable Revolutions: The United States in Central America.* 2nd edition. New York: W. W. Norton.

Library of Congress/Federal Research Division. 1993. *Nicaragua: A Country Study.* http://lcweb2.loc.gov/cgi-bin/query/r?frd/cstdy:@field(DOCID+ni0006) (accessed June 22, 2004).

Paige, Jeffery M. 1998. *Coffee and Power: Revolution and the Rise of Democracy in Central America.* Cambridge, MA: Harvard University Press.

Ruchwarger, Gary. 1987. *People in Power: Forging a Grassroots Democracy in Nicaragua.* South Hadley, MA: Bergin and Garvey.

Selbin, Eric. 1998. *Modern Latin American Revolutions.* 2nd edition. Boulder, CO: Westview.

Spalding, Rose J. 1994. *Capitalists and Revolution in Nicaragua: Opposition and Accommodation.* Chapel Hill: University of North Carolina Press.

Vanden, Harry E., and Gary Prevost. 1993. *Democracy and Socialism in Sandinista Nicaragua.* Boulder, CO: Lynne Rienner.

———, eds. 1997. *The Undermining of the Sandinista Revolution.* New York: St. Martin's.

Vilas, Carlos M. 1986. *The Sandinista Revolution.* New York: Monthly Review.

Walker, Thomas W. 1991. *Revolution and Counterrevolution in Nicaragua.* Boulder, CO: Westview.

———, ed. 1997. *Nicaragua without Illusions: Regime Transition and Structural Adjustment in the 1990s.* Wilmington, DE: Scholarly Resources.

———, ed. 2003. *Nicaragua: Living in the Shadow of the Eagle.* 4th ed. Boulder, CO: Westview.

Wickham-Crowley, Timothy P. 1993. *Guerrillas and Revolution in Latin America: A Comparative Study of Insurgents and Regimes since 1956.* Princeton, NJ: Princeton University Press.

Zimmermann, Matilde. 2000. *Sandinista: Carlos Fonseca and the Nicaraguan Revolution.* Durham, NC: Duke University Press.

P

Pakistan Independence and the Partition of India

CHRONOLOGY

1206   First Muslim dynasty, the Slave dynasty, founded in India by a Turk, Qutbuddin Aibak, a slave of the Ghurid dynasty in Afghanistan. Successive dynasties would expand Muslim territory, covering most of northern India.

1526   Zahiruddun Muhammad Babur defeats the then reigning Muslim dynasty, the Lodis, and establishes the Mughal dynasty.

1757   The Battle of Plassey (Pilashi), near Calcutta, ends Mughal rule in the east and establishes the pattern of British expansion in the northwest, eventually to the present border between Pakistan and Afghanistan.

1857   The Sepoy Mutiny by soldiers (sepoys) and others is put down by the British, who become supreme in India. In 1858, the Mughal empire, already greatly weakened, is abolished.

1875   The Muslim Anglo-Oriental College (now Aligarh Muslim University) is founded by Sir Sayyid Ahmed Khan.

1885   The Indian National Congress (now usually known as the Congress Party) is founded in Bombay to represent Indian interests. While mainly Hindu, others, including Muslims, are also members.

1893   The boundary between British territory and Afghanistan, known as the Durand Line, is drawn.

1905   The province of Bengal is divided, the western Hindu majority region retaining the name "Bengal" and the eastern Muslim majority joined with Assam into the province of East Bengal and Assam. The action was reversed in 1911.

1906   A meeting of Muslims in Dhaka, at which Aga Khan III presides, forms the All-India Muslim League to put forward the interests of Muslims, including separate electorates for Muslims and Hindus. A Muslim delegation led by the Aga Khan meets the viceroy, Lord Minto, at Simla.

Mohammed Ali Jinnah joins the Congress. He will leave in 1920. In 1913, he also joins the Muslim League

1909   The Government of India Act of 1909 creates separate electorates for Hindus and Muslims, apportioned on the basis of their population in each province. (Later, separate electorates would be added for other groups.)

1916   Pact agreed at Lucknow calls for Congress and Muslim League to work together for independence and states that the Congress accepts the concept of separate electorates. The key negotiators are Jinnah and Motilal Nehru.

1919   Government of India Act of 1919, which increases participation of Indians in governance.

1930   Muhammad Iqbal, addressing Allahabad session of the Muslim League, proposes that the Muslims of northwestern India should constitute a separate state.

1933   Cambridge student Chaudhury Rahmat Ali suggests that a separate state embracing Iqbal's proposal be named Pakstan (later changed to Pakistan), combining the names of the units to be included: P for Punjab, A for Afghania (the Northwest Frontier Province), K for Kashmir, S for Sindh, and TAN for Balochistan. The name Pakistan can be interpreted to mean "Land of the Pure." Note that Bengal is not included.

1935   Government of India Act of 1935 by the British Parliament greatly increases powers of provincial governments, including providing for cabinet ministers in governments headed by prime ministers (after independence, the title would become chief minister).

1937   Elections are held under the 1935 act with extended constituencies for separate electorate systems. Muslim League does not succeed in forming governments in any of the provinces, all of which or part of which would become part of Pakistan, but does join a coalition in Bengal.

1945–1946   Elections delayed by the war are held. Muslim League carries Muslim seats in Bengal, but fails in western provinces.

1946   British send a cabinet mission to arrange for the transfer of power to India. It proposes a three-tier system: central government and provincial governments, with zonal governments intermediate.

1947   Congress refuses to accept the Cabinet Mission Plan. The viceroy, Lord Mountbatten, decrees the partition of India into India and Pakistan. The provinces of Punjab and Bengal are divided.

On August 14, Pakistan becomes independent, with its capital in Karachi with Jinnah as governor-general (that is, head of state). India becomes independent the following day, with Jawaharlal Nehru as prime minister. Rioting and migration take place, especially in Punjab, as Hindus and Sikhs flee Muslim areas and Muslims flee Sikh and Hindu areas. Substantial movement also occurs between Sindh and Indian territory, while Bengal remains comparatively calm. States ruled by Indian princes are told to merge with either of the new dominions. The maharaja of Jammu and Kashmir, a Muslim-majority state bordering both India and Pakistan, accedes to India. This action culminates in the first Indo-Pakistan War.

INTRODUCTION

Pakistan became an independent state on August 14, 1947, and India became independent the following day, August 15, 1947. Each state became independent from the British empire, and independence required the partition of British India. The partition created a Pakistan that itself was divided, as the Muslim-majority areas of India were located at the eastern and western extremities of united India. The one-day difference in the date of independence is explained by the inability of the viceroy/governor-general, Lord Mountbatten, to be in two places at the same time. With independence, Mountbatten no longer held the title of viceroy (representative of the monarch), although he retained the title of governor-general with respect to India as the head of state. Pakistan named Mohammed Ali Jinnah as governor-general. That title would end in each country when each adopted a republican constitution.

BACKGROUND: CULTURE AND HISTORY

Pakistan's territory was the home of the Indus Valley civilization, centered on such sites as Harappa (in present-day Punjab) and Moenjo Daro (in Sindh). Although much has

British lord Louis Mountbatten (in uniform) officially hands off power to Mohammed Ali Jinnah (to left of Mountbatten), leader of the new nation of Pakistan, on August 14, 1947. Pakistan earned its sovereignty from Great Britian in response to demands for an autonomous Islamic state. The fate of Kashmir, a territory with a Hindu ruler but a primarily Muslim populace, was left unresolved, and became a longstanding source of conflict between India and Pakistan. (Library of Congress)

been learned through archaeology, the written language has not been deciphered. Evidence is clear that trade took place between the Indus Valley and the valleys of the Tigris and Euphrates and of the Nile; there was also trade with apparently less-developed groups in central Asia and perhaps beyond to China.

About 1000 B.C., Indo-European (Aryan) groups moved southward from central Asia, first into what is now Afghanistan and then splitting into two streams and moving into Iran (whose name is derived from "Aryan") and the areas presently in Pakistan and western India. The earlier civilization was overwhelmed. The Aryans brought with them the language Sanskrit, from which the languages of today's Pakistan are derived. (For the history and culture of the former eastern wing of Pakistan, see the entry on the Bangladesh Revolution.)

The people practiced an early version of Hinduism, which would be the dominant religion until the entry of the Muslims. However, there were also movements of Buddhists, and many monuments, such as Taxila and Gandhara, remain, as do some Jain monuments.

The movement of Buddhism from India to China, Tibet, Korea, and Japan passed though northern Pakistan and Afghanistan. The now destroyed Bamian Buddhas in Afghanistan are witness to this. Archaeological research has found remnants of these pre-Islamic cultures. Among the conquerors from the west who entered both Afghanistan and Pakistan was Alexander the Great.

Muslims entered Sindh by sea in 712 and incorporated the area into the Ummayad caliphate, but the major and longer-lasting incursions came from Afghanistan. The so-called Slave dynasty, led by Qutbuddin Aibak, was set up in 1206, although there had been raids before that, especially from the Afghan city of Ghazni.

While governed by a series of dynasties, the Muslims expanded their territories greatly in northern India and to a lesser degree in the south. The strongest and longest-lasting dynasty was the Mughal empire, established by Babur in 1526. This dynasty was the builder of many of the best-known Muslim monuments, including the Taj Mahal in Agra and the fort and central mosque in Lahore.

The British East India Company, from its principal base in Calcutta, began expansion of its territory westward in the north. The battle of Plassey, near Calcutta, in 1757 gained the British control of Bengal, and—by alliance with princes or by conquest—more territory was added. Indian soldiers (called sepoys) serving the British mutinied in 1857. When the conflict concluded with a costly British victory in 1858, the Mughal empire came to an end. Earlier in 1849, following conflict between the British and the Sikh rulers of Punjab, that province was annexed by the British. The Punjab then also included what is today the Northwest Frontier Province; however, the British control of that area was often opposed by the Pathan tribesmen. The effective boundary between that province and Afghanistan was established by the surveying of the Durand Line in 1893, but that line has been disputed by the Afghans. The southern province of Sindh was conquered by the British in 1843. It was part of the Bombay Presidency (province) until 1934. Balochistan was acquired partly by conquest and partly by agreements with tribal leaders. At the time of independence there were several princely states in Pakistan territory, the largest of which was Bahawalpur; probably the best known, however, was Swat. These have been incorporated into Pakistan.

There were demands by Indians for greater participation in the governance of the country, and the Indian National Congress was formed in 1885 to press those demands. The Indian Councils Acts of 1861 and 1892 provided for appointed Indian members of the provincial legislative and executive branches. A demand for the separate representation of Muslims was made by the newly formed Muslim League in 1906 as a prelude to further reforms. These reforms came in the Government of India Act of 1909, under which Indian representatives were elected to legislatures through separate electorates for Muslims (the other electorate was described as "General"). The Congress at first strongly opposed this electoral system, but in 1916 it accepted the system. This agreement at Lucknow was negotiated by Mohammed Ali Jinnah for the League and Motilal Nehru for the Congress.

Another act, that of 1919, expanded the role of Indians by having some of the cabinet seats in the provinces occupied by elected members of the assemblies. That changed with the act of 1935, when all provincial cabinet seats were occupied by elected members and the head of the cabinet was designated the prime minister (this would change to chief minister for each province at independence, as India and Pakistan would each have a prime minister at the center).

The demand for separate electorates did not end the demands of the Muslims. As they saw their secondary position continuing in India, there was some thought that the Muslims should have a separate state encompassing the Muslim majority provinces of India. The suggestion was put forward at the Allahabad session of the Muslim League in 1930 by the poet-philosopher Muhammad Iqbal, who saw the position of Muslims deteriorating. Iqbal's concept was that the northwestern provinces (Punjab, Sindh, Balochistan, and the Frontier) should form the new state. There was no mention of Bengal, also a Muslim majority province. In 1933 a student at Cambridge, Rahmat Ali, proposed a name for this new state if it were to come into being: PAKISTAN. P stood for Punjab, A for Afghania (another name for the Frontier), K for Kashmir, S for Sindh, and TAN for Balochistan. Again, there was no mention of Bengal.

The proposal of a separate state for the Muslim-majority areas became more explicit with the passage of the Lahore Resolution at the 1940 session of the Muslim League. The resolution is often called the Pakistan Resolution, although the word "Pakistan" does not appear. The possibility of two states was present in the phrase "independent Muslim states." The resolution was introduced by a representative of Bengal.

CONTEXT AND PROCESS OF REVOLUTION

The outbreak of World War II and the subsequent entry of Japan on the side of the Axis made India an important base for supply and for manpower. However, while many Indians supported the war effort, others increasingly demanded independence. Gandhi's slogan was "Quit India." To this Jinnah responded "Divide and quit." Gandhi's call for *satyagraha* (nonviolent resistance, practiced to achieve a political goal) greatly hindered the British effort in the war. Opposing Gandhi's movement cost considerably in maintaining law and order.

The British, therefore, concluded that the retention of India would require a commitment of resources to repress the Congress and the Muslim League and their demands that Britain was unlikely to have, even though the demands were in sharp conflict with each other. Developing a method to give independence to India while preferably retaining it as a member of the British Commonwealth became a goal. However, any particular method was certain to be opposed by one of the two groups: the Hindus or the Muslims.

The first in a series of British missions was led by Sir Stafford Cripps in March 1942. Cripps, a leader in the Labour Party, was a minister in Winston Churchill's coalition war cabinet. His visit came just after the Japanese had overrun Southeast Asia, and it was expected that the next Japanese goal would be British territory in Burma and India. (Burma, now Myanmar, had been a part of British India until 1937, when it became a separate colony.) Cripps offered a constituent assembly after the end of the war. The assembly would comprise elected members from the provinces and appointed members from the Indian princely states. The British would accept and implement a constitution framed by the assembly, but with the proviso that any province or princely state could reject the constitution. This proviso made it clear that a unified India was unlikely. Gandhi, who compared the offer to a post-dated check on a failing bank, led the Congress in rejecting the Cripps offer. With few objections, the Congress followed Gandhi's lead. It was nonetheless a step forward, especially as it put the writing of a constitution solely in Indian hands.

The rejection of the Cripps offer was followed by the "Quit India" movement under the leadership of Congress and Gandhi, a nonviolent struggle for the immediate withdrawal of Britain. Gandhi stated that the presence of the British in India was an invitation to Japan to invade. Gandhi, as he had done before, undertook a fast. This did not lead the British to act as Gandhi wished, and he gave up the fast.

In 1943, the British military leader Lord Wavell succeeded Lord Linlithgow as viceroy and governor-general. He was to manage the use of India as a supply base for U.S. and British operations in Burma and China (via the Himalayas "over the hump" route). During 1943, Bengal suffered one of the worst famines on record.

Jinnah and Gandhi met in September 1944. Gandhi tried unsuccessfully to persuade Jinnah that the division of India was wrong. Jinnah held that the division of the country was based on the "two-nation theory," the concept that the differences between Hindus and Muslims were so great that each constituted a separate nation. Gandhi added that if partition took place, the boundaries of what might become Pakistan would have to be determined by a commission approved by the Congress and the League and then further approved by a referendum of the people. The two portions would remain as parts of an Indian federation. Jinnah rejected this idea.

When the war in Europe ended in May 1945, Wavell held a conference in Shimla, the summer capital of British India, beginning on June 25, 1945. A large group attended, including leaders of the Congress and the League, some smaller parties, and the prime ministers of the provinces. Wavell's proposal was an interim central government with all portfolios except that of war held by Indians. There would be an equal number—five—of Muslims and Hindus in the proposed cabinet of eleven members, including the single British minister for war. Jinnah insisted that all five Muslims be named by the Muslim League. Wavell stated that the League could have four of the five, but that a non-League Muslim would fill the fifth. Wavell's reason was that he wished to leave one Muslim seat to be filled by a member of the Punjab-based Unionist Party, a strong foe of Jinnah and the League in that it, as its name indicates, opposed partition. Jinnah and Wavell both stood firm, and the conference ended inconclusively.

Elections to the Central Legislative Assembly and the provincial assemblies were held in 1945 and 1946. These occurred against the background of the Japanese surrender on August 15, 1945, and parliamentary elections in Britain in which the Conservative Party, led by Churchill, was soundly defeated by the Labour Party, led by Clement Attlee. The Indian elections saw the Muslim League form governments in Punjab, Sindh, and Bengal.

In the Frontier the League fell short, and a Congress government was formed. There the League did not win a majority of the Muslim seats, getting only seventeen out of thirty-six.

Attlee appointed Lord Pethwick-Lawrence, a staunch admirer of Gandhi, as minister in charge of Indian affairs. A cabinet mission consisting of Pethwick-Lawrence, Cripps, and A. V. Alexander arrived in India in March 1946 and proposed another plan for Indian independence. This cabinet mission called for a three-tier arrangement, with each tier having specified powers. The provincial governments would look after local affairs as they had under the 1935 act. The central government would perform the duties usually associated with such governments, such as foreign affairs, defense, and currency. The new facet was the creation of zonal governments. It would be up to the zonal governments to decide which powers would be taken from the provincial governments and moved to the zonal governments. Zone B would comprise Punjab, Sindh, and the Frontier (Balochistan did not have a provincial government); Zone C, Bengal and Assam; and Zone A, the remainder of India. There would also be a constituent assembly elected by the provincial assemblies to frame a constitution, with Muslims, Sikhs, and other minorities having representation from each province in proportion to their share of the population. Representatives would also be sent to the assembly by the princely states.

Jinnah and the League accepted this plan; it was rejected, however, by Nehru on behalf of the Congress, although the president of the Congress at the time, Abul Kalam Azad, supported it. Nehru, in a speech, said that the Congress should not be constrained by the plan when framing a constitution.

In his book *India Wins Freedom,* Azad is sharply critical of Nehru. The Pethwick-Lawrence, Cripps, Alexander cabinet mission thus failed.

On August 24, 1946, Wavell formed a new council that initially had only Congress members, but Jinnah soon withdrew his objection and Muslim members were added.

Attlee announced on February 20, 1947, that the British intended to transfer power not later than June 1948. It was also announced that Lord Mountbatten would succeed Wavell. On June 3, 1947, Mountbatten stated that Britain accepted the principle of partition. Only in the Northwest Frontier Province, where a Congress coalition ruled an overwhelmingly Muslim province, was a referendum held. Those who voted supported joining Pakistan by 99 percent.

On August 14, 1947, Pakistan became independent; the next day India became independent. Partition had taken place seventeen years after Iqbal's suggestion and seven years after the Lahore Resolution.

IMPACTS

Violence broke out with the announcement of the partition plan and continued well beyond the dates of independence. Mountbatten had advised the rulers of the princely states to accede to the new states in accordance with their location. Most did.

India and Pakistan became dominions in the British Commonwealth of nations. Therefore the heads of state, Jinnah in Pakistan and Mountbatten in India, held the title of governor-general, as do the heads of state today in such places as Canada and Australia. When each adopted a republican form in their constitutions, the heads of state were titled president, although with a change in the structure of the commonwealth each state has remained a member of the commonwealth.

The partition plan resulted in the division of two provinces: Punjab and Bengal. The province of Sindh, the Northwest Frontier Province, and the territory of Balochistan went to Pakistan in their entirety.

The greatest violence occurred in Punjab. Sikhs and Hindus fled the Pakistani-held western portion of the province to the Indian-held eastern portion, and Muslims fled in reverse order. (In a strange pair of events the president of Pakistan in 2004, Pervez Musharraf, was born in what is now India, and the prime minister of India, Manmohan Singh, was born in what is now Pakistan.) The commercial classes in many key cities of present Pakistan, such as Lahore, were Hindu, and as a result commerce, banking, and industry were disrupted. Sikhs were a major group in the irrigated areas of Punjab. A Sikh group called the Akali Dal asserted its claim to a separate state in the irrigated areas, and that resulted in violence: the claim was rejected. Many Muslims were agriculturists in the portion of Punjab that went to India. Agriculture in both portions of the Punjab took some time to revive.

Punjabi and Frontier Muslims and Punjabi Sikhs were a major component of the pre-independence Indian army, which had been a key element of Allied forces in both world wars. Now the army was being asked to maintain order when members of their own communities were on opposite sides of the conflict. The full extent of the cost of the Punjab rioting cannot be determined. Books by military men and others have described the events, but probably they are expressed best by the Sikh writer Khushwant Singh in his novel *Train to Pakistan* (New York: Grove, 1956). The extent of the movement of non-Muslims from the western wing of Pakistan can be seen in the fact that 97 percent of its population in 2004 was Muslim.

Movement and violence were less in divided Bengal, although not absent. In 2004, the Hindus in the Pakistan section formed 11 percent of the population. However, another aspect of migration to the east was the movement of Urdu speakers, largely from the province of Bihar, but called Biharis regardless of their place of origin. They were greatly outnumbered by the 98 percent of Bangladeshis who speak Bengali.

The division of the waters of the Indus system in the west and the Ganges-Brahmaputra system in the east has proven to be a major topic of dispute. The Indus Waters Treaty of 1960 between Pakistan and India was intended to solve the question by allotting the three eastern rivers (Sutlej, Beas, and Ravi) to India and the three western rivers (Chenab, Jhelum, and Indus) to Pakistan. Nonetheless, there have been frequent disputes over the implementation of the treaty.

As noted, the princely states were advised to accede to India or Pakistan according to their geographic location. One state in India ruled by a Muslim, Junagarh, wished to accede to Pakistan, but that was thwarted by Indian action. The Indians also did not permit the Muslim ruler of Hyderabad to proclaim an independent state.

It is the princely state of Jammu and Kashmir that has been a continuing matter of dispute between Pakistan and India. The ruler was a Hindu, although Muslims were a majority of the population of the state. In 1947, Pakistan-based tribesmen invaded the state, and the ruler appealed to India for aid. India demanded that the ruler accede to India before assistance by Indian troops could begin. The ruler did so. However, the government of India declared that when peace had been restored, a referendum would be held so that the people could determine whether the territory would go to India or Pakistan. That plebiscite has not been held, and Kashmir remains the major point of contention between the two countries; the result has been wars in 1947–1948 and 1965. A third war took place in 1971, when India came to the aid of

Bengalis struggling to establish the independent state of Bangladesh. It was established in 1971, ending the unity of Pakistan as it was in 1947.

PEOPLE AND ORGANIZATIONS

Abdullah, Sheikh Muhammad (1905–1982)

The key political leader of the princely state of Jammu and Kashmir, his party was first the Kashmir Muslim Conference (founded 1931), later renamed the National Conference. Sheikh Muhammad Abdullah opposed accession to Pakistan, but he did not support Maharaja Hari Singh's accession to India. He later supported the concept of a plebiscite to determine the future of the state.

Ahmed Khan, Sir Sayyid (1817–1898)

An Islamic scholar and a government judicial official, Ahmed Khan saw that Muslims were lagging in education and employment opportunities. He founded the Muslim Anglo-Oriental College (now Aligarh Muslim University).

Congress Party. See Indian National Congress

Gandhi, Mohandas Karimchand (1869–1947)

Known as the Mahatma (Great Soul), Gandhi was the leader of the movement for Indian independence, although he did not hold office in the Indian National Congress. He was opposed by the Muslim League on almost all issues, but was also opposed by fundamentalist Hindu groups. A member of a Hindu group assassinated him.

Ghaffar Khan, Khan Abdul (1890–1988)

Founder of the Khudai Khitmatgar (Servants of God) movement in the Northwest Frontier Province that was associated with the Congress, Ghaffar Khan earned the title Frontier Gandhi.

Indian National Congress

Founded in Bombay in 1885, the Indian National Congress developed into the major institution demanding first greater participation of Indians in the governance of India and even-

tually independence. That was achieved in 1947, but to reach it the Congress reluctantly agreed to the partition of India into the new dominions of India and Pakistan.

Iqbal, Allama Sir Muhammad (1877–1938)

A poet and philosopher, Iqbal was also active in politics. As president of the Allahabad session of the Muslim League in 1930, he suggested that if conditions for Muslims did not improve, it might be necessary for the northwestern provinces of India to form a separate state.

Jinnah, Mohammed Ali (1876–1948)

Born in Karachi, Jinnah was a noted lawyer in Bombay. His political experience began with membership in the Indian National Congress, but in 1913 he also joined the Muslim League. He played a key role in the Congress-League agreement, the Lucknow Pact, in 1916, as a result of which the Congress accepted the concept of separate electorates for the Muslims. He left the Congress in 1920 and, except for a time in the 1930s, continued to play a leading role in the Muslim League. His work in the League brought him the title Quaid-i-Azam (Great Leader). He led the League in passing the Lahore Resolution, which stated that if conditions for Muslims did not improve, Muslims would demand separate states (this was later modified to the singular, "state"). At independence on August 14, 1947, he became the governor-general of the new state of Pakistan. He died in office on September 11, 1948.

Khan, Liaqat Ali (1885–1951)

A Muslim political figure from the United Provinces (now Uttar Pradesh), Liaqat was Jinnah's principal lieutenant. At independence he became prime minister of Pakistan, but so long as Jinnah lived, Liaqat was in his shadow. With Jinnah's death in 1948, Liaqat became the principal political figure, but that was to be for a brief period. He was assassinated on October 16, 1951.

Khudai Khitmatgar

A movement in the Northwest Frontier Province that opposed the partition of India, Khudai Khitmatgar was led by Ghaffar Khan. Following the 1946 election, it was able to lead a coalition ministry in the province. Eight days after Pakistan's independence, the ministry was dismissed by Governor-General Jinnah.

Mountbatten, Louis, First Earl (1900–1979)

Mountbatten was viceroy and governor-general of India at the time of independence and partition. Aided by his advisers, he formulated the plan of partition and advised princes to accede to either India or Pakistan, depending primarily on the location of their states. With independence the title of viceroy was abolished, but he remained governor-general of India until June 1948.

Muslim League

Founded in Dhaka in 1906, the Muslim League first moved to demand separate electorates for Muslims in the forthcoming election. The British granted the demand in the Government of India Act, 1909. Although originally opposed, the Congress accepted the concept in 1916. The League gradually came to the position of demanding a separate Muslim state, which was reluctantly granted by the British in 1947, although strongly opposed by the Congress. The party ruled Pakistan much of the time after independence until 1958, when a martial law government was installed under General Muhammad Ayub Khan.

Nazimuddin, Sir Khwaja (1894–1964)

Nazimuddin was a leading member of the Muslim League prior to independence and a rival of Husain Shahid Suhrawardy. He became chief minister of East Bengal (now Bangladesh) after independence. In 1948, he succeeded Jinnah as governor-general upon the latter's death.

Nehru, Jawaharlal (1889–1964)

The son of Motilal Nehru, Jawaharlal Nehru was a lawyer, but he seldom practiced as he became fully involved in the freedom movement. His first major role was in 1929, when he became president of the Congress. He strongly opposed the partition of India but had little choice but to accept it in 1947. He was prime minister of India from 1947 until his death.

Nehru, Motilal (1861–1931)

An attorney, Motilal Nehru and fellow attorney Jinnah worked together to agree on the Lucknow Pact of 1916, under which the Congress accepted the concept of separate electorates. He and Jinnah cooperated often in the Central Leg-

islative Assembly on matters that would increase the Indian role in the governance of India. At that time the idea of a separate state had not been floated.

Suhrawardy, Husain Shahid (1893–1963)

A prominent Muslim Leaguer in Bengal, Suhrawardy became prime minister of Bengal in 1946. With partition, his rival Nazimuddin became chief minister of East Bengal. Suhrawardy left the Muslim League and founded the Awami League in 1949. He served as prime minister of Pakistan from 1956 to 1957.

Unionist Party

Founded in 1923 by Mian Sir Fazli Husain, the Unionist Party set as its goal the protection of the economic interests of all communities (Muslims, Hindus, and Sikhs) in the Punjab. Its peak was reached in the 1937 provincial election, which resulted in a coalition ministry headed by Unionist Sardar Sir Sikander Hayat Khan. His death in 1942 greatly weakened the party; it was soundly defeated in 1946, although it was able to form a ministry with the aid of the Congress and the Sikh party, the Akali Dal. The ministry collapsed in March of 1947.

Craig Baxter

See Also Bangladesh Revolution; Colonialism, Anti-Colonialism, and Neo-Colonialism; Documentaries of Revolution; Ethnic and Racial Conflict: From Bargaining to Violence; Indian Independence Movement; Nationalism and Revolution

References and Further Readings
Ahmad, Syed Nur. 1985. *From Martial Law to Martial Law: Politics in the Punjab, 1919–1958.* Translated from the Urdu by Mahmud Ali, and edited by Craig Baxter. Boulder, CO: Westview.
Allana, Gulam. 1967. *Pakistan Movement: Historical Documents.* Karachi: Paradise Subscription Agency.
Azad, (Maulana) Abul Kalam. 1959. *India Wins Freedom.* Bombay: Orient Longmans.
Bolitho, Hector. 1954. *Jinnah: Creator of Pakistan.* London: John Murray.
Chaudhry, Muhammad Ali. 1988. *The Emergence of Pakistan.* Lahore: Service Book Club.
Gopal, Sarvepalli. 1965. *British Policy in India, 1858–1905.* Cambridge: Cambridge University Press.
Hodson, H. V. 1969. *The Great Divide: Britain, India, Pakistan.* London: Hutchinson.
Jalal, Ayesha. 1985. *The Sole Spokesman—Jinnah, the Muslim League and the Demand for Pakistan.* Cambridge: Cambridge University Press.
Khaliquzzaman, Chaudhury. 1961. *Pathway to Pakistan.* Lahore: Longmans.
Khan, Hamid. 2001. *Constitutional and Political History of Pakistan.* Karachi: Oxford University Press.

Lumby, E. W. R. 1954. *The Transfer of Power in India*. London: Allen and Unwin.

Malik, Hafeez, ed. 1971. *Iqbal: Poet-Philosopher of Pakistan*. New York: Columbia University Press.

———. 1980. *Sir Sayyid Ahmed Khan and Muslim Modernization in India and Pakistan*. New York: Columbia University Press.

Moon, Penderel. 1962. *Divide and Quit*. Berkeley: University of California Press.

Sayeed, Khalid bin. 1968. *Pakistan: The Formative Phase, 1857–1948*. New York: Oxford University Press.

Sherwani, Latif Ahmed. 1969. *Pakistan Resolution to Pakistan*. Karachi: National Publishing House.

Singh, Khushwant. 1981. *Train to Pakistan*. New York: Grove.

Talbot, Ian, and Gurharpal Singh, eds. 1999. *Punjab, Bengal and the Partition of the Subcontinent*. New York: Oxford University Press.

Wolpert, Stanley. 1984. *Jinnah of Pakistan*. New York: Oxford University Press.

———. 1996. *Nehru: A Tryst with Destiny*. New York: Oxford University Press.

Palestinian Movement

CHRONOLOGY

3000–1500 B.C.	The Canaanites inhabit Palestine.
1200–1100	Jews and Philistines conquer the Canaanites and settle in Palestine.
1000	Jews establish Kingdom of Israel and Solomon builds the first Temple in Jerusalem.
927	The Kingdom of Israel splits into two entities: Israel and Judah.
722–140	Assyrians and Babylonians conquer Palestine. Jews revolt and restore their independence until Roman conquest in 63 B.C.
63 B.C.–A.D. 638	Palestine is intermittently under Roman or Byzantine rule. Romans destroy Jerusalem.
638	Palestine comes under Arab-Muslim rule.
661	Palestine becomes a province under the Arab-Islamic Umayyad dynasty.
750	Palestine becomes a province under the Arab-Islamic Abbasid dynasty.
1517	Palestine comes under the rule of the Ottoman empire.
1831	Egypt, under Muhammad Ali, expands its realm into Palestine.
1840	The Ottomans restore their authority over Palestine.
1882–1904	First wave of Jewish immigrants sails to Palestine.
1897	Establishment of the World Zionist Organization; its program to settle Jews in Palestine is launched.
1904–1914	Second wave of immigration of Jewish settlers sails to Palestine.
1911	Founding of the Palestinian newspaper *Filistine* in Jaffa. The paper addresses its readers as "Palestinians," and it warns them about consequences of Zionist colonization.
1913	First Arab Nationalist Congress meets in Paris.
1914	World War I begins.
1915	Sharif Hussein of Mecca and Henry McMahon, the British high commissioner in Egypt, exchange correspondence guaranteeing Arab independence that includes, according to Hussein, the territory of Palestine in return for the Arab revolt against the Ottomans during World War I.
1916	Britain and France secretly sign the Sykes-Picot Agreement, dividing the Ottoman Near East domain (Lebanon, Syria, Jordan, and Iraq) into British- and French-administered zones, with Palestine as an international zone.
1917	The British government issues the Balfour Declaration, pledging British support for the establishment of a national home for the Jewish people in Palestine.
1918	British forces occupy Palestine.

1919   The Palestinians convene their first national congress in Jerusalem, state their opposition to the Balfour Declaration, and demand independence.

1920   The San Remo Conference grants Great Britain a mandate over Palestine. Second and third Palestinian national congresses are held in Damascus and Haifa, electing an executive committee that remains in control of the Palestinian political movement from 1920 to 1935.

1922   The League of Nations endorses a British mandate for Palestine.

1929   Arab-Jewish violence is sparked by a dispute over the Western Wall in Jerusalem. (Arabs claim the wall to be a part of the al-Aqsa Mosque, while Jews claim it as the remaining wall of the ancient Jewish Temple.)

1936   Palestinians revolt in April 1936 against the confiscation of land and increasing Jewish immigration.

1937   The Peel Commission, headed by Lord Robert Peel, investigates violence in Palestine and issues its findings in a report recommending partition of Palestine into a Jewish state and an Arab state, with Jerusalem and Bethlehem placed under the British mandate.

1939   The British government issues the MacDonald White Paper, to limit and restrict Jewish immigration and land purchases in Palestine. Future Jewish immigration is restricted to 75,000 over a five-year period.

1947   Britain decides to leave Palestine and calls on the United Nations to make recommendations. In response, the United Nations convenes its first special session and endorses a resolution to partition Palestine into Jewish and Arab states, with Jerusalem as an international zone under UN jurisdiction.

1948   The mandate over Palestine officially ends, and Israel is established. The Palestinian National Conference meets in Gaza, and an all-Palestine government is established under the leadership of Hajj Amin al-Husayni . The first Arab-Israeli war ends with Israel in possession of a large part of Arab Palestine. Israel now controls 78 percent of Palestine, rather than the 56 percent granted under the UN partition resolution.

1949   Armistice agreements signed to officially end the 1948 war. The United Nations announces the establishment of the UN Relief and Works Agency (UNRWA), to assist Palestinian refugees in the West Bank, Gaza Strip, Jordan, Syria, and Lebanon. The West Bank comes under Jordanian control, while Egypt asserts authority over Gaza.

1952   The Egyptian Revolution begins a trend of Arab revolutionary movements. Egypt's new government under President Gamal Abd al-Naser, commits to Arab unity and the liberation of Palestine.

1956   Suez War (the second Arab-Israeli war). Israel invades and occupies the Gaza Strip and the Sinai Peninsula in preparation for a British invasion of Egypt to reinstate Western control over the Suez Canal.

1957   In Kuwait, Yasser Arafat, among others, founds Fatah (Movement for the Liberation of Palestine).

1964   The Arab League summit in Cairo endorses the creation of the Palestine Liberation Organization (PLO), with three governing branches: the Palestine National Council (PNC), the Central Council, and the Executive Committee. The PNC drafts a National Covenant that calls for armed struggle against Zionism and liberation of Palestine. Ahmed al-Shuqairy becomes the first head of the PLO.

1967   Israel launches an attack that starts the June War. Israel captures East Jerusalem and the West Bank from Jordan, the Gaza Strip and the Sinai Peninsula from Egypt, and the Golan Heights from Syria. Israel annexes East Jerusalem and begins construction of Jewish settlements in East Jerusalem and the West Bank.

The United Nations adopts Security Council Resolution 242, which calls on Israel to withdraw from the territories occupied during the June war in return for peace and secure borders. George Habash forms the Marxist-oriented Popular Front for the Liberation of Palestine (PFLP). Ahmed al-Shuqairy resigns as head of the PLO.

1968   The Battle of Karameh takes place in the village Karameh, east of the Jordan River, in which Palestinian fighters aided by Jordanian army artillery and armor block Israeli forces from entering the East Bank. The Palestinian National Council moves its headquarters to Cairo and modifies the PLO's national charter.

1969   Nayif Hawatmah breaks from the PFLP and forms the Marxist-Leninist Popular Democratic Front for the Liberation of Palestine (PDFLP). In 1975, it officially becomes the Democratic Front for the Liberation of Palestine (DFLP). Yasser Arafat is elected head of the PLO.

1970   PLO-Jordanian power struggle leads to a civil war in Jordan. King Hussein of Jordan launches a full-scale campaign to suppress Palestinian guerrilla groups whose presence in Jordan by the late 1960s constituted a state within a state and challenged the authority of the Jordanian monarch. The fighting ends with Egyptian President Abd al-Naser's mediation and the signing of the Cairo Agreement, which eventually leads the PLO to relocate to Lebanon. The high Palestinian death toll during the time that these events occur results in its being called "Black September" by the Palestinian movement.

1971   The Jordanian army evicts the PLO from Jordan and dismantles its infrastructure. Black September, a Palestinian organization formed after the civil war, claims responsibility for the assassination in Cairo of Wasfi al-Tal, Jordan's prime minister. The PLO moves its offices to Lebanon.

1972   Black September abducts several Israeli athletes at the Munich Olympics. All die, murdered either by Black September members or in a shoot-out during the failed German rescue attempt.

1973   October war breaks out when Egypt and Syria launch a surprise coordinated attack on Israeli forces in the Sinai Peninsula and the Golan Heights.

1974   The Arab Summit in Rabat declares the PLO the sole legitimate representative of the Palestinian people. The PNC accepts the establishment of a Palestinian state in any liberated part of Palestine and discards the option of establishing a secular democratic state in all of Palestine. The UN General Assembly recognizes the PLO as the representative of the Palestinian people and grants it observer status.

1975   UN General Assembly invites the PLO to participate in debates on the Middle East, and endorses a resolution that denotes Zionism as a form of racism and racial discrimination. Civil war breaks out in Lebanon among the PLO, the Syrians, and Lebanese factions.

1978   U.S. president Jimmy Carter, Egyptian president Anwar Sadat, and Israeli prime minister Menachem Begin sign the Camp David Accords. Israel agrees to withdraw from the Sinai in exchange for peace with Egypt and granting the Palestinians "full autonomy" in occupied territories after a transitional period of five years. The PLO rejects the accords and condemns Egypt for separately negotiating peace with Israel.

1982   Israel invades Lebanon and destroys the PLO institutional infrastructure. Lebanese Christian Phalange militia massacres as many as 2,000 Palestinian refugees at Sabra and Shatila camps in Beirut. The Arab states endorse the "Fez Peace Plan," calling for complete Israeli withdrawal from the territories occupied during the 1967 June war and the establishment of a Palestinian state in exchange for Arab recognition of Israel's right to exist. The PLO moves its headquarters from Beirut to Tunis, Tunisia.

1985   The PLO and Jordan sign the Amman Agreement, calling for the establishment of a Palestinian state in the West Bank in confederation with Jordan, with its capital at East Jerusalem.

1987   The first Palestinian *intifada* (uprising) begins in Gaza and spreads to the West Bank. It involves a series of uprisings that include demonstrations, strikes, and rock-throwing attacks on Israeli occupying forces.

1988   Hamas (an acronym for Islamic Resistance Movement) is founded in Gaza. King Hussein renounces claims to the West Bank and relinquishes control to the PLO. The PNC declares creation of a Palestinian state in Gaza and the West Bank, with its capital in East Jerusalem, and asserts readiness to negotiate with Israel based on UN Resolutions 242 and 338. The United States opens channels for diplomatic dialogue with the PLO. The PNC meeting in Algiers declares the State of Palestine as outlined in the 1947 UN Partition Resolution and renounces terrorism.

1989   The PLO Central Council appoints Arafat as the first president of Palestine.

1990   Arafat rejects Hamas's conditions to join the PLO. Hamas requests 40 percent of the Palestinian National Council's seats. The PLO supports Iraq's invasion of Kuwait.

1991   The Arab-Israeli Peace Conference opens in Madrid, with Palestinians involved as members of the Jordanian delegation.

1993   The Norwegian government confirms that fourteen secret rounds of talks were held in Norway between Israeli and Palestinian negotiators. Mahmoud Abbas (Abu Mazen), spokesperson for the PLO Foreign Affairs Department and member of the PLO's Executive Committee, and Israeli foreign minister Shimon Peres sign the Declaration of Principles (DOP), or the Oslo Accords. Arafat and Israeli prime minister Yitzhak Rabin officially sign the accords and shake hands on the lawn of the White House. The PLO establishes the Palestinian Authority (PA) and selects Arafat as its head.

1994   Arafat, Rabin, and Peres are awarded the Nobel Peace Prize.

1995   Arafat and Yitzhak Rabin sign the Palestinian-Israeli Interim Agreement on the West Bank and Gaza Strip (Oslo II) at the White House.

1996   The first national Palestinian election is held in the West Bank and Gaza. Arafat is elected president. The PLO National Charter is amended and the clause for the destruction of Israel removed.

1997   Sheikh Ahmed Yassin, founder of Hamas, is released from Israeli prison and returned to Gaza.

1998   Israel and the PLO sign the Wye River Agreement, negotiated in the United States. It calls for Israel to relinquish control of parts of the West Bank in return for active measures by the PA to curb violence against Israelis.

1999   Israel and the PLO sign the Sharm el-Sheikh Memorandum (known as Wye II).

2000   Israel-Palestinian negotiations at Camp David, Maryland, begin in July. Ariel Sharon makes a controversial visit to the Temple Mount that triggers the second Palestinian *intifada*. The emergence of an offshoot of the Fatah movement, al-Aqsa Martyrs Brigades.

2001   Ariel Sharon promises to nullify the Oslo Accords as he becomes prime minister of Israel.

2002   Israel isolates Arafat and confines him to his Ramallah compound, where he remains until 2004.

2003   Arafat appoints Mahmoud Abbas (Abu Mazen) prime minister of the Palestinian Authority. The Quartet (the U.S., the UN, the European Union, and Russia) introduces the "Road Map" for peace between Palestinians and Israelis. It calls for the creation of a Palestinian state in the West Bank and Gaza side by side with Israel. Mahmoud Abbas resigns. Ahmed Qorei, former speaker of the Palestinian legislative council, succeeds Abbas.

2004	In March, Israel assassinates Sheikh Ahmed Yassin.

In November, Yasser Arafat, long-time leader of the Palestine Liberation Organization and Palestinian Authority president, dies.

2005	In January, former Palestinian prime minister Mahmoud Abbas is elected new Palestinian Authority president.

In August, Israel evacuates Israeli settlers from the Gaza Strip.

2006	On January 25, Hamas wins a majority (74 of 132 seats) in the election for the Palestinian parliament.

INTRODUCTION

The Palestinian national movement emerged with an aim of asserting the Palestinian right to self-determination and statehood. The movement developed and matured over several decades. It began in the 1920s in response to Jewish settlements and British rule in Palestine and resulted in the 1936 Arab Revolt. It continued shortly after the end of the 1948 Arab-Israeli War. At that time, many Palestinians believed that their struggle against Israel was an Arab struggle, and that all Arabs had a responsibility to support them in reasserting their control over the territory. By the 1960s the movement had developed institutionally, when, under the auspices of the Arab League, the Palestine Liberation Organization (PLO) was established. Since then, the PLO has represented the embodiment of the Palestinian national movement on the local, regional, and international scenes. Prior to the 1980s, the movement operated from neighboring Arab countries: Jordan, Syria, Lebanon, and Egypt. In 1987, the first Palestinian *intifada* (uprising), in the West Bank and the Gaza Strip, enabled the movement to consolidate its efforts within the occupied territories, where most of the resistance against Israel emerged. The movement has shifted its strategy vis-à-vis Israel over time. Prior to the 1990s, the majority of Palestinians believed that only through armed struggle could they assert their national rights. Since 1990, the Palestinian leadership has recognized that it can not attain its goals through violence and therefore, it has opted to conduct peace negotiations with Israel. While such negotiations have not, so far, led to the creation of a sovereign Palestinian state, it appears that the Palestinian movement has been convinced that peace is the only workable solution to its conflict with Israel. Overall, the Palestinian movement has contributed to increasing global awareness of the need to protect and advance Palestinian national rights within the framework of creating a sovereign Palestinian state.

BACKGROUND: CULTURE AND HISTORY

The state of Israel currently controls a large part of historical Palestine. The territory is located in western Asia and borders Lebanon on the north, Syria on the northeast, Jordan on the east, Egypt on the southwest, and the Mediterranean Sea on the west. The total surface area of Palestine is approximately 10,800 square miles. Approximately 10 million people inhabit the territory: 5 million Jews and 1 million Arabs reside in Israel; more than 3.5 million Arab Palestinians, along with 350,000 Jewish settlers, inhabit the occupied West Bank, Gaza Strip, and East Jerusalem.

For the Palestinians, the seeds of a strong national identity began in the early 1800s with their struggles against the ruling Ottoman empire, which had controlled the territory since the early 1500s, and against the Egyptians, who ruled the area from 1831 to 1839. These struggles, and latter ones against other outside powers, unified Palestinian Arabs from diverse backgrounds—peasants, urban traders, religious leaders—by pitting them against common enemies.

When Zionist Jews fleeing persecution in Europe and Russia began arriving in Palestine in increasing numbers in the 1880s, the local Arab population gradually resisted them. Before the collapse of the Ottoman empire in 1922, Great Britain had entered into several contradictory commitments concerning Palestine. In a secret agreement in 1916 (the Sykes-Picot Agreement), the Ottoman empire was divided into spheres of control and influence among Britain, France, and Russia. Another agreement, the 1917 Balfour Declaration, endorsed the establishment in Palestine of a national home for the Jewish people without prejudice to the civil and religious rights of existing non-Jewish communities. The British had also promised the Arabs, in the 1915 Hussein-McMahon correspondence, to support their goal for statehood in areas that included, as the Arabs understood, Palestine.

These conflicting pledges and the increasing influx of Jewish immigrants to Palestine were bound to lead to political and economic instability in the area. Although by the end of World War I a few seeds of the future Arab-Israeli conflict had already been implanted, far more serious ones were to take root during the British mandate, from 1922 to 1947. Therefore, when the British, who voiced support for Zionism, won control of the area in 1922, the Palestinians met them with discontent and rejection (Farsoun and Zacharia 1997, 67–68). Arab resistance during the period from 1920 to 1934 was led by a Palestinian-Arab political organization, the Arab

Executive, with a platform calling for condemnation of the mandatory Zionist policy of supporting the Jewish national home based upon the Balfour Declaration; rejection of the principle of mass Jewish immigration; and establishment of a national representative government for Palestine.

In 1922, the League of Nations ratified the British mandate over Palestine, which aimed at preparing the territory for self-determination. Unfortunately, inconsistent British policies were often the root cause of many Arab-Jewish clashes and tension during the 1920s and 1930s. The most important of these clashes resulted from the 1936 Arab Revolt against British policies and the ever-increasing Jewish immigration. When the revolt ended in 1939, the British government decided to limit Jewish immigration to Palestine to 75,000 over five years—and none thereafter, unless it was acceptable to the Arabs. The British government also prohibited future land sales to Jews and promised Palestine independence within ten years, presumably as a bi-national (Arab and Jewish) state.

The Arab Revolt in 1936–1939 was a turning point in Palestinian resistance to the mandate. The Zionist policy of purchasing land and of establishing exclusively Jewish agricultural settlements undermined the interests of small landowners and impoverished peasants, and ultimately contributed to the outbreak of the revolt. In addition, the Jewish community had grown to represent about 30 percent of the total population of Palestine. The trend of the previous three years had been such that the numerical relations in the country could be transformed within a decade (from 1933 to 1935, about 134,000 immigrants had entered Palestine). The threat of that prospect was the immediate cause of the Arab leaders' calling a general strike in April 1936 until the British abolished future immigration. All Palestinian political factions endorsed the strike, and a permanent ten-man executive, the Arab Higher Committee, began to carry it out. The rebellion was widespread and developed in several phases. The first phase was a general strike that lasted until October 1936; the second phase, which lasted intermittently from the fall of 1937 to the spring of 1939, involved violent acts against British and Zionist interests in Palestine. The uprising forced the British government to adopt two controversial policies: the Peel report (calling for partitioning of the land into two states), and the 1939 paper (limiting Jewish immigration) that addressed some Arab concerns. However, Britain also decided to crush the rebellion by declaring the Arab Higher Committee illegal, and it went further to dissolve it, arresting and exiling most of its members. The committee's leader, Hajj Amin al-Husayni, escaped to Beirut. When the revolt ended, approximately 7,000 Palestinians were dead or wounded. The Palestinian nationalist movement had collapsed, and it never fully recovered (Abu-Lughod 1987, 232–235).

After the end of World War II, British policy makers decided that the situation in Palestine was hopeless, and that Arabs and Jews could not coexist in one state. In 1947, Britain informed the United Nations that it would end its mandatory rule. Shortly afterward, a UN Special Commission on Palestine recommended partition of Palestine into two states: one Arab and one Jewish, with Jerusalem under international control. The UN General Assembly endorsed the recommendation on November 29, 1947, as UN Resolution 181.

The Arab states and the Palestinians rejected the UN resolution, feeling that all the land was theirs. The Jews accepted the plan, and on May 14, 1948, they declared the establishment of the state of Israel. Immediately after Israel's declaration of independence, it came under attack by the armies of several Arab states and the Palestinians. What followed was the first major Arab-Israeli war. To the Arabs, the war was a humiliating defeat. It remains a source of bitterness to this day, with the story of how the war drove Palestinians off their lands referred to as al-Nakba (the Catastrophe). Some 700,000 Palestinians, the majority of whom were living in Israel, were forced to leave their homes for the area known as the West Bank, creating the refugee crisis that still exists today.

The immediate results of the 1948 war were astounding: Israel controlled 78 percent of historical Palestine, and the Arab lands set up by the 1948 UN partition were cut in half, down to about 22 percent. Jerusalem emerged divided, with Arabs on the east side of the 1949 armistice line and the Jews on the west. Egypt took control of the Gaza Strip, which came under Egyptian military administrative control, and the West Bank of the Jordan River came under the control of the Jordanian government.

CONTEXT AND PROCESS OF REVOLUTION

Since 1948, the Palestinian movement has faced a number of adverse conditions—the partition of its territory, the exile of a large number of Palestinians, its vulnerability to interference by conflicting Arab governments, and the Arab defeats in the battle over Palestine. Despite such conditions, the movement has been able to rethink and transform its goal over the years: from liberating all of Palestine and refusal to coexist with Israel to liberating parts of Palestine and acceptance of a Palestinian state next to Israel.

There were five key transitions in the development of the Palestinian national movement from 1957 to 2000. Prior to the first transition, in 1957, Palestinians were not well organized or mobilized as a liberation movement with clear goals and objectives. That was due, in part, to the dispersion of so many Palestinians into refugee camps, particularly in the West Bank and Gaza. The emergence of Fatah (the Movement for the Liberation of Palestine) in 1957 enabled the Palestinian movement to define its struggle against Israel by operating alongside, and under the influence of, several Arab nationalist movements, such as the Baath Party in Syria and the Nasserist regime in Egypt. The second transition began in 1967, with the establishment of the PLO. This transition enabled the movement to emphasize its independent armed struggle against Israel through guerrilla warfare. The third transition emerged after the Israeli invasion of Lebanon in 1982, when the movement's leadership and militia groups dispersed and began to rethink their overall strategy. The fourth transition began in 1988, when Arafat, at the PNC meeting in Algiers, declared the independence of Palestine and latently acknowledged that the movement would accept living side by side with Israel along the 1967 borders. This transition enabled the PLO to negotiate with Israel the 1993 Oslo Accords, which allowed Palestinians direct control over territories evacuated by the Israeli army in Gaza and the West Bank. The last transition saw the movement slowly engaged in an inner power struggle that has, since 2000, undermined its essential agenda: Palestinian self-determination.

During the first transition, in 1957, many Palestinians saw their best hope of returning to their homeland in joining progressive and revolutionary Arab regimes (Syria, Egypt, and Iraq) that advocated Arab unity. These regimes were committed to accommodating Palestinian fighters and granting them the necessary resources with which to fight Israel. Yasser Arafat, leader of the Fatah, believed that the struggle to liberate Palestine would lead to Arab unity. He often stated that armed struggle was the only way to defeat Israel. He also believed that strong ties with revolutionary Arab states, particularly those bordering Israel, along with international support, were critically important. The Arab Nationalists' Movement (ANA), an extreme nationalist, Pan-Arab group led by George Habash, believed that Arab unity could maximize and mobilize the necessary resources to defeat Israel. After the 1967 defeat, ANA members joined two more groups and formed the leftist Popular Front for the Liberation of Palestine (PFLP). By 1969 the front had split up, when Nayif Hawatmah, a Palestinian Marxist, formed the Popular Democratic Front for the Liberation of Palestine (PDFLP).

The second transition in the evolution of the Palestinian national movement started in 1964 with the establishment of the PLO. Ahmed Shuqairy was selected chairman of the PLO's executive committee, the organization's top post. The PLO developed a degree of leadership, organization, and mass support quite superior to earlier efforts during and after the British mandate. Over time, Fatah surfaced as the most important group in the PLO. In fact, Fatah members were able to gain a majority in the PLO's legislative body, the Palestine National Council (PNC). In 1969, Arafat became the chairman of the executive committee. In 1971, he became the general commander of the Palestine forces. Arafat's new stature and increasing power proved critical in rallying Palestinians behind the PLO.

In its first decade of existence, the PLO was able to draw international attention to the predicament of the Palestinian people. While some of the organization's operations were unsuccessful, its overall strategy of armed struggle against Israel was critical in the support it gained among a majority of Palestinians and Arabs. However, the outbreak of the June 1967 War proved to be a turning point for the Palestinian movement. The defeat of the Arab armies of Syria, Jordan, and Egypt in the June War left all the land of Palestine, as well as the Egyptian Sinai Peninsula and the Syrian Golan Heights, under Israeli control. The Palestinians recognized that liberating Palestine would require more self-reliance and initiative, rather than relying on the actions or aid of other Arab nations. Hence, in March 1968, Palestinian forces bravely fought an Israeli expeditionary force at the Battle of Karameh on the East Bank of the Jordan River and inflicted heavy causalties on it. The courage and determination of the Palestinian forces in this battle reflected a sharp contrast to the poor performance by the better-trained and -equipped Arab armies in the 1967 War. The PLO's position after Karameh was elevated to one of a vanguard for the anti-imperialists in the Arab world, and it established the Palestinians' claim to being a national liberation organization.

By 1970 the Palestinian movement had established itself in Jordan as a state within a state, with an army, hospitals, social security system, and tax collectors. The apparent weakness of the Jordanian government after the 1967 War enabled a number of Palestinian fighting groups to establish bases there, from which they were able to attack Israeli targets across the River Jordan. Fearing their increasing control of Jordan, King Hussein decided to eradicate many of the Palestinian groups. The crisis was triggered by the hijacking of two international airliners—TWA and KLM—by Palestinian guerrillas who brought them to an airport in Jordan. The hijackings heightened the existing tension between the government and the guerrillas. Armed clashes occurred between them and quickly escalated into a full civil war. The Arab League and President Abd al-Nasser of Egypt mediated and stopped the fighting in September of 1970. The war resulted in the killing or wounding of several thousand Palestinians and the eventual eradication of their bases there. The Jordanian war and later attacks in Lebanon in 1975 and 1982 reduced or eliminated the operational combat capability of the Palestinian movement but did not eliminate its political influence.

Prior to the 1973 Arab-Israeli War, the PLO insisted on achieving the total liberation of Palestine through armed struggle and the establishment of a single secular, democratic state. However, the 1973 October war marked a major shift in Arab political thinking that would eventually affect the Palestinian movement. The successes of the Arab armies of Egypt and Syria in the war strengthened their regimes and enabled them to consider an end to the Arab-Israeli conflict through a negotiated settlement involving U.S. mediation, an option that prior to 1973 had been rejected by the majority of Arab leaders and many sections of Arab society. The Palestinians were in the difficult position of continuing their armed struggle against Israel while their Arab allies were shifting to peaceful negotiations and settlement. As a result, in 1974 the moderate elements of the PNC began considering the establishment of a Palestinian state in those areas to be evacuated by Israel in the future. This implied for the first time, but did not directly state, the concept of coexistence with the state of Israel (Khalidi 1985, 89). However, the idea caused a serious split within the PLO. The smaller and more extremist groups, such as the PFLP, the Arab Liberation Front (ALF), and the Palestine Liberation Front (PLF), withdrew from the PLO's Executive Committee in 1974 in protest. However, none of the Palestinian groups compromised on the key issues that there is a Palestinian people with rights to self-determination and an independent national existence.

In 1974, the Arab Summit in Rabat recognized the PLO as the sole legitimate representative of the Palestinian people, and the United Nations reaffirmed its commitment to an independent sovereign state in Palestine and gave the PLO observer status at the UN. Shortly afterward, Arafat became the first representative of a nongovernmental agency to address the UN General Assembly. These events contributed to the transformation of a liberation movement into a national independence movement ready to make compromises and engage diplomacy as a means to fulfill Palestinian national aspirations.

The Palestinian movement suffered a key setback during the Lebanese civil war in 1975. The war erupted between leftist Muslims (with PLO aid) and conservative Christians. Furthermore, Syria's territorial proximity and historical ties with Lebanon brought it into the conflict, and its army was able to establish a base there while fighting against different Lebanese and PLO factions . When the conflict continued near the Israeli border, it eventually dragged Israel into it. The third transition in the evolution of the Palestinian movement emerged with the 1982 Israeli invasion of Lebanon. The invasion, planned with the aim of destroying the PLO and securing the safety of northern Israel by occupying a part of southern Lebanon, brought the PLO and its leadership under

Yasser Arafat, leader of the Palestine Liberation Organization. (Kern Paul/Corbis Sygma)

siege and ultimately forced it to depart. Arafat, after his departure from Lebanon, established the PLO headquarters in Tunisia.

The expulsion from Lebanon and the tense ties with Syria required that the PLO shift its fighting strategy against Israel by focusing more on the occupied West Bank and Gaza. Arafat gave his organization's support to Palestinians in the West Bank and other territories who began to riot against Israeli occupying forces in what become known as the first *intifada* (uprising) in 1987. The *intifada* provided a resistance blueprint for Palestinian political and social life that is relatively nonviolent. It started as a spontaneous popular revolt among Palestinians, reflecting the frustration, demoralization, and hopelessness that had accumulated over years of Israeli occupation and humiliation. Before the *intifada*, a variety of groups and individuals challenged Arafat's leadership. These included Arab heads of state and such Palestinian formations as the Abu Nidal group, the dissident faction of Fatah under Abu Musa; Ahmed Jibril's Popular Front for the Liberation of Palestine-General Command; and the Palestine National Salvation Front, an umbrella organization opposing Arafat's policies and leadership.

The outbreak of the *intifada* gave Arafat an opportunity to tighten his control over the external leadership of the Palestinian community, a process that had begun in 1987 with a formal reconciliation among the major PLO factions. Arafat used the *intifada* as a vehicle to prevent further organizational splintering while seeking to reaffirm the PLO's status among Palestinians and the world community as the sole legitimate representative of the Palestinian people. This also paved the way to the fourth transition in the development of the Palestinian movement. In 1988, Arafat declared an independent Palestinian state on the West Bank and Gaza and renounced terrorism. He also stated that the PLO supported the right of all parties, including Israel, to live in peace. Arafat's renunciaiton of terrorism was a condition demanded by the United States before the opening of a "diplomatic dialogue" with the PLO.

The *intifada*, coupled with the PLO's acceptance of coexistence with Israel, had a great impact on many Israeli political leaders, forcing them to recognize that the existing relationship between Israel and the Palestinians would have to be re-evaluated. Consequently, the Israeli government and the PLO were eager to pursue a peaceful settlement. However, the PLO's support of Iraq's invasion of Kuwait in 1990, and the ensuing Gulf War to force an Iraqi withdrawal from Kuwait, during which the Iraqi regime of Saddam Hussein launched missile attacks against Israel, resulted in isolating the PLO. This turn of events was detrimental to conducting any peaceful negotiations. Nevertheless, an opportunity to negotiate peace emerged after conclusion of the Gulf War in 1991, when an international peace conference on the Middle East convened in Madrid, Spain. The Palestinians accepted becoming part of a Jordanian delegation to the conference, a precondition imposed by Israel and the United States. While the conference did not bring Israelis and Palestinians closer to a negotiated settlement, it did, however, provide them with an opportunity to exchange views directly and interact for the first time since the creation of Israel in 1948.

In the meantime, a number of Palestinian groups emerged after the *intifada*. Notable among them were Hamas, the Palestinian Islamic Jihad (PIJ), and the al-Aqsa Martyrs Brigades. All were determined to use armed struggle against Israel until all Palestinian territories are liberated. Both Hamas and the PIJ oppose Arafat's PLO and hope to defeat Israel and establish an Islamic Palestinian state. It remains unclear how the PLO and these groups would be able to reconcile their differences and merge as a united front to fulfill what all Palestinians aspire for: a state of their own.

Events in the Middle East took a surprising turn in 1993. An agreement was announced, negotiated secretly in Oslo, Norway, between Palestinian and Israeli negotiators with the mediation of Norway's foreign ministry. In September 1993, Arafat and Israeli prime minister Yitzhak Rabin flew to Washington, D.C., and officially signed the Oslo Accords. These accords called for an end to the *intifada*, the gradual withdrawal of Israeli troops from Gaza and the West Bank, and the creation of the Palestinian Authority as the Palestinian governing body. Following the signing, a long process of negotiation began on the means of transferring power in the occupied lands. A Palestinian National Authority (PA) was established. In 1996 the first Palestinian national election was held, with Arafat elected president of the PA.

The peace process, which had been an on-and-off proceeding since Rabin's assassination by a right-wing Israeli extremist in 1995, broke down by September 2000, when an attempt to reach a negotiated deal through the mediation of President Bill Clinton did not materialize. The fifth and last transition of the Palestinian movement began shortly afterward, when the second *intifada* erupted. It started with Israeli riot police firing rubber bullets at hundreds of Palestinian stone throwers at al-Aqsa Mosque. The violence broke out just moments after the leader of Israel's hard-line opposition, Ariel Sharon, entered the compound. Sharon's victory in Israel's 2001 election exacerbated the situation, brought a halt to the peace process, and increased violence. Moreover, unlike the dovish Labor-led government, the hawkish Sharon-led Likud government was committed to ending negotiations with the PA and maintaining Israeli military occupation of Palestinian lands. Consequently, Palestinians and Israelis have been entangled in a vicious circle of violence that has included Palestinian militant groups carrying out suicide bombing operations inside Israel and lethal Israeli army incursions and helicopter rocket attacks inside heavily populated Palestinian refugee camps, villages, and towns. In all, thousands lost their lives on both sides, and the chances for any peaceful way out without major changes in underlying conditions appeared slim.

On November 11, 2004, Yasser Arafat died. He was succeeded as leader of the PLO and as Palestinian Authority president by Mahmoud Abbas. In August of 2005, the Israeli government proceeded to evacuate Israeli settlers from the Gaza Strip, raising hopes of further progress toward the achievement of an independent Palestinian state. Then on January 25, 2006, Hamas won the Palestinian parliamentary election leading to new concerns about the peace process.

IMPACTS

The Palestinian national movement is a manifestation of decades of struggle to achieve self-determination for all Palestinians. The movement's commitment to armed struggle against Israel in the 1950s and 1960s, while militarily unsuccessful, managed to bring international attention and

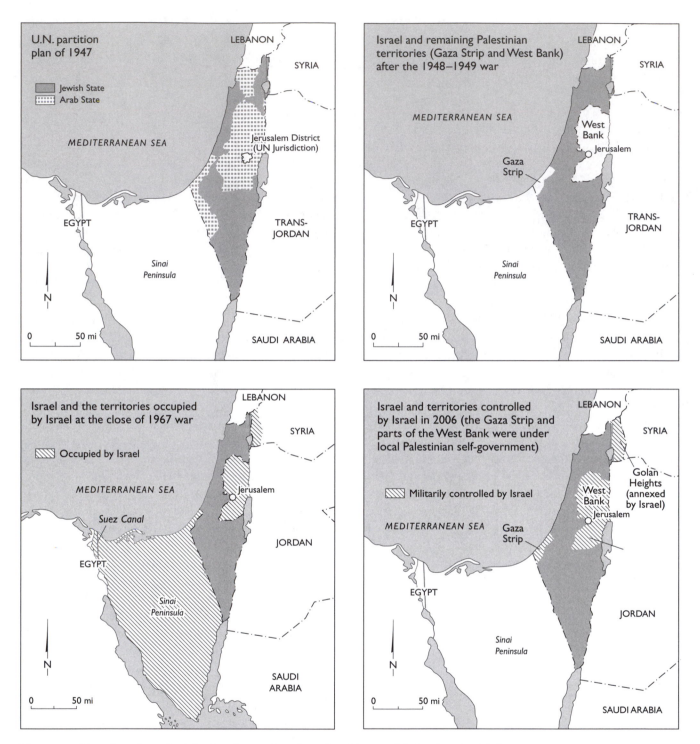

The UN partition plan of 1947 for Palestine, the creation of Israel, and later political and territorial changes.

sympathy to the plight of Palestinians in refugee camps and occupied territories. In addition, the movement's ability to shift its strategy when necessary allowed it to survive and emerge as the sole representative of Palestinian hopes and aspirations, despite Israeli and U.S. policies to undermine it. Furthermore, the movement's decision to accept a two-state solution to end its outstanding issues with the state of Israel is a manifestation of its commitment to peace and co-existence. Although one could argue that the recent acts of violence and terrorism by Palestinian groups proved detrimental to peace and stability in the Middle East, it remains the responsibility of the state of Israel to end the source of this violence, its occupation of Palestinian territories, and accept the inevitable outcome of an independent and sovereign Palestinian state.

PEOPLE AND ORGANIZATIONS

Abbas, Mahmoud (Born 1935)

Also known as Abu Mazen, Abbas was appointed as the first Palestinian prime minister in April 2003. Following a power struggle with Arafat (regarding Abbas having greater control over the security apparatus), Abbas resigned in September 2003. He had been one of the key players in the secret talks that led to the 1993 Oslo Accords and was the former PLO ambassador to Moscow. After the death of Arafat in November 2004, Abbas was elected leader of the Palestine Liberation Organization, and in January 2005, Palestinian Authority president.

al-Aqsa Martyrs Brigades

An armed part of Fatah, the al-Aqsa Martyrs Brigades, during the second *intifada*, targeted Israeli soldiers and settlers in the West Bank and Gaza Strip. There was also a spree of attacks against civilians in Israeli cities.

Arab Higher Committee

The Higher Committee was formed in 1936 with the merger of six Arab political parties: the Palestine Arab Party, the National Defense Party, the Reform Party, the National Bloc Party, the Congress Executive of Nationalist Youth, and the Istiqlal (Independence) Party.

Arafat, Yasser (1929–2004)

Leader of the Palestine Liberation Organization and Palestinian Authority president, Arafat was educated in Cairo, Egypt, where he received an engineering degree. Arafat cofounded the Fatah group in 1957. In 1969, Arafat became the chairman of the PLO's executive committee; in 1971, he became the general commander of the Palestine forces. His name was synonymous with the PLO and with the Palestinian national movement. In January 1996, he overwhelmingly won the Palestinian Authority presidency in the Palestinians' first elections. Israel and others criticized Arafat for a lack of control over extremist Palestinians such as Hamas. Arafat vowed to crack down, and repeatedly expressed sorrow over violent acts by Hamas. In November 2004, Arafat

died and was succeeded as leader of the PLO and as Palestinian Authority president by Mahmoud Abbas.

Fatah

Fatah (the name is a reversed acronym for Harakat Tahrir Filastin, Movement for the Liberation of Palestine) was founded in the late 1950s. It is considered the strongest and most important group within the PLO, with military arm, al-Assifa (Storm).

Habash, George (Born 1925)

A physician turned politician, George Habash founded the left-wing Popular Front for the Liberation of Palestine (PFLP) in 1967. In 1984 he led opposition to Arafat and created a rejectionist front in Damascus, Syria. After 1987, he returned closer to cooperation with the PLO. He resigned after the 1993 Oslo Accords.

Hamas

A grass roots Palestinian organization founded as an outgrowth of the Muslim Brotherhood in the West Bank and Gaza Strip, Hamas was created late in 1987 at the beginning of the first *intifada* (uprising). Hamas is highly regarded by Palestinians for its humanitarian actions, such as building schools and hospitals and helping the community in social and religious ways. The military wing of Hamas, Izzedine al-Quassam, carries out military and suicide bombing operations. The ultimate goal of Hamas is the establishment of a Palestinian Islamic state in all of historical Palestine.

Husayni, Amin al- (1895–1974)

Husayni was a leading notable in Jerusalem who was elected grand mufti of Palestine and president of the Supreme Muslim Council in 1922. He became the recognized leader of the Palestinian national movement that led the Arab revolt against the British and the Jews in 1936. Exiled during World War II, he could not return to Palestine, and remained in exile until his death in 1974 in Beirut.

Intifada (uprising)

Two uprisings of Palestinians against Israeli occupation of the West Bank, Gaza, and East Jerusalem. The first *intifada* began in 1987 and ended with the signing of the Oslo Accords in 1993. The second *intifada*, also called the al-Aqsa *intifada*, began in September 2000 soon after Israeli prime minister Ariel Sharon's controversial visit to the al-Aqsa Mosque. The level of violence escalated from rock throwing and demonstrations during the first uprising to suicide bombings during the second.

Oslo Accords

The 1993 Oslo Accords are the foundation on which peace negotiations between Israel and the Palestinians are based. Officially called the "Declaration of Principles," Israeli and Palestinian delegations negotiated the accords secretly in 1993 in Oslo, Norway, guided by Norwegian foreign minister Johan Jorgen Holst. The declaration lays out the goals to be achieved. Those goals are the complete withdrawal of Israeli troops from the Gaza Strip and the West Bank, and the Palestinians' right to self-rule in those territories. Accompanying the agreement were the "Letters of Mutual Recognition." In signing those letters, Israel officially recognized for the first time the Palestine Liberation Organization as the legitimate representative of the Palestinian people. Moreover, for the first time, the PLO recognized Israel's right to exist, renounced terrorism, rescinded its call for Israel's destruction, and accepted the principle of land for peace.

Palestine Liberation Organization (PLO)

The League of Arab States established the PLO in 1964. It is an umbrella organization for the major Palestinian political groups.

Palestinian National Authority (PA)

The name given to the limited self-rule government of parts of the West Bank and Gaza Strip established under the terms of the 1993 Oslo Accords. In January 1996, Yasser Arafat was elected president of the PA, and eighty-eight others were elected to sit on the Palestinian Legislative Council. Arafat established a cabinet for the PA, which was approved by the legislative council. Several changes were made to reduce the PA's autocratic grip, including reforms of the PA's politics (the position of prime minister was created), finances, and security forces. The authority has been undermined by its inability to control the activities of militant Palestinian organizations such as Hamas, and by the Israeli incursions into Palestinian cities and towns that have done much to destroy the PA.

Yassin, Ahmed (1937–2004)

Ahmed Yassin founded the Islamic Center and University of Gaza in 1973. Spiritual leader and founder of Hamas, he was detained by the Israelis in 1989 and released several years later. Israel assassinated him in March 2004.

Ahmed H. Ibrahim

See Also Cinema of Revolution; Colonialism, Anti-Colonialism, and Neo-Colonialism; Documentaries of Revolution; Guerrilla Warfare and Revolution; Islamic Fundamentalist Revolutionary Movement; Literature and Modern Revolution; Nationalism and Revolution; Terrorism; Transnational Revolutionary Movements; Zionist Revolution and the State of Israel.

References and Further Readings
Abu-Lughod, Ibrahim, ed. 1987. *Transformation of Palestine*. Evanston, IL: Northwestern University Press.
Aburish, Said. 1998. *Arafat: From Defender to Dictator*. New York: Bloomsbury.
Brown, Nathan J. 2003. *Palestinian Politics after the Oslo Accords: Resuming Arab Palestine*. Berkeley: University of California Press.
Carey, Roane, ed. 2001. *The New Intifada*. London: Verso.
Cobban, Helena. 1984. *The Palestine Liberation Organization: People, Power, and Politics*. New York: Cambridge University Press.
Farsoun, Samih K., with Christina E. Zacharia. 1997. *Palestine and the Palestinians*. Boulder, CO: Westview.
Ganim, Asad. 2001. *The Palestinian Regime: A Partial Democracy*. Portland, OR: Sussex Academic.
Harub, Khalid. 2000. *Hamas: Political Thought and Practice*. Washington, DC: Institute for Palestine Studies.
Hunter, Robert. 1993. The *Palestinian Uprising: A War by Other Means*. Berkeley: University of California Press.
Khalidi, Rashid. 1985. "The Palestinian Dilemma: PLO Policy after Lebanon," *Journal of Palestine Studies* 15 (1): 88–103.
———. 1997. *Palestinian Identity: The Construction of Modern National Consciousness*. New York: Columbia University Press.
Nassar, Jamal R. 1993. *The Palestine Liberation Organization: From Armed Struggle to the Declaration of Independence*. New York: Praeger.
Said, Edward. 1991. "Reflection on Twenty Years of Palestinian History," *Journal of Palestine Studies* 20 (4): 5–22.
———. 1994. *The Politics of Dispossession: The Struggle for Palestinian Self-Determination*. New York: Random House.
Smith, Charles D. 2004. *Palestine and the Arab-Israeli Conflict: A History with Documents*. Boston: Bedford/St. Martin's.
Tamari, Salim. 1991. "The Palestinian Movement in Transition: Historical Reversals and the Uprising," *Journal of Palestine Studies* 20 (2): 57–70.
———. 2003. "No Obvious Destination," *Al-Ahram Weekly* 656 (September): 18–24.

Paris Commune of 1871

CHRONOLOGY

1848	In December, Louis-Napoléon Bonaparte is elected president of the Second Republic.
1852	Louis-Napoléon Bonaparte is proclaimed Emperor Napoléon III.
1870	July, the outbreak of the Franco-Prussian War.

1870 — On September 1, a French army is defeated at the Battle of Sedan and surrenders on September 2, with Napoléon III taken prisoner.

On September 4, a bloodless republican revolution in Paris ousts Emperor Napoléon III.

September 19–20, Paris is encircled and besieged by German troops.

1871 — On January 28, armistice is signed.

February 8, the election of National Assembly is held.

On March 17, the army is ordered to seize hundreds of National Guard cannon.

On March 21, the National Assembly at Versailles rejects compromise with Paris revolutionaries.

March 25–31, short-lived Communes at Lyon, Marseille, Saint-Etienne, Toulouse, Narbonne, Limoges (April 4–5), and Bordeaux (April 17).

On March 26, election of Paris Commune.

On March 29, formation of executive commission.

On April 2, fighting begins.

April 28–May 1, establishment of Committee of Public Safety.

May 21–28 "Bloody Week."

INTRODUCTION

The Paris Commune of March, April, and May 1871 was one of the largest urban insurrections in European history. Most Parisian voters elected a commune or city government committed to protecting the new republic from a restoration of monarchic rule and pursuing economic policies beneficial to Parisian workers and small businesses. The Commune was perceived as a threat to the propertied classes and to Christianity by the more conservative National Assembly, which, in May, ordered the regular army to attack the Parisian National Guard and other armed resistors. In the civil war that followed, thousands were killed or executed in the French capital. Despite the destruction of the Commune and the deaths of many of its supporters, it inspired many later revolutionaries, bequeathing to them the famous revolutionary song *The Internationale*. Also, it convinced Lenin and others that more centrally organized revolutionary leadership and greater repressive measures toward counter-revolutionaries were necessary if future revolutions were to avoid the fate of the Paris Commune.

BACKGROUND: CULTURE AND HISTORY

In February 1848, revolution in Paris was followed by the establishment of a Second Republic and the election by "universal" (that is, male) suffrage of a constituent assembly dominated by conservatives and moderate republicans from the provinces, and determined to re-establish social "order." Their hopes for far-reaching social reform disappointed, in June Parisian revolutionaries once again resorted to insurrection; they were crushed by military force. In December, Louis-Napoléon Bonaparte, nephew of the first emperor, was elected president of the republic; determined to remain in power, he launched a well-prepared coup d'état on December 2–3, 1851. While retaining male suffrage, he established an authoritarian regime with extremely weak parliamentary institutions and elections subject to administrative interference. A year later, and sanctioned by a plebiscite, he was proclaimed emperor. His regime would be authoritarian and populist.

Eager to modernize France, Napoléon III and his prefect, Baron Georges-Eugène Haussmann, were determined to create a modern capital that would enhance the regime's reputation. They presided over an unprecedented renewal of the city's physical fabric and social geography. As well as enhancing the appearance of central Paris, the construction of broad boulevards was intended both to reduce traffic congestion and facilitate military/police control of the city. Slum clearance would both improve public hygiene and push the poor into peripheral areas more distant from the center of government. In spite of substantial electoral support, particularly from an increasingly prosperous rural population, criticism of the emperor's personal rule mounted in the 1860s. Unlike his predecessors, however, Napoléon was prepared to adapt and engage in the difficult process of regime liberalization, once again legitimizing the process by means of a plebiscite, in May 1870.

Throughout the Second Empire, Parisian voters had overwhelmingly supported moderate republican opponents of the regime. Although incomes were growing, many small businessmen and especially workers appear to have been more conscious of rising prices and rents and of the increasing social segregation resulting from urban renewal. The city's economy was still dominated by small-scale manufacturing and construction, and both entrepreneurs and skilled workers felt threatened by changes in the structure of manufacturing and commercial activity that were perceived to endanger their livelihoods and social status. There was widespread resentment of a regime perceived to be exclusively serving the interests of "idle" and "parasitic" speculators, "capitalists," and a "reactionary" Roman Catholic Church, while taxing the "poor" to finance its grandiose building projects, "bloated" bureaucracy, and military adventures. As political debate revived in the late 1860s, proposals for political and social reform were commonly discussed.

Regime liberalization, designed to reinforce mass support, also revitalized opposition. In the hothouse atmosphere of the newly legalized public and electoral meetings held in 1868–1869, a variety of Socialist and revolutionary speakers boldly anticipated the destruction of the imperial state and the "exploitative" capitalist society it protected. They also squabbled frequently about the details of the new society they planned to create—and particularly over whether it should be mutualist (with the workers' cooperative as the basic unit) or collectivist (and based on state ownership of property), as well as whether administration should be decentralized or centralist in the Jacobin tradition. According to the old revolutionary Louis-Auguste Blanqui, the bureaucracy and army should be suppressed and the "black army" of priests expelled (Price 2004, 375). The moderate republicans who had crushed the June insurrection in 1848 and seemed prepared to wait indefinitely for electoral success were regarded with similar contempt. Although they made a great deal of noise, amplified by the conservative press, which deliberately sought to stimulate social fear among "respectable" citizens, at this stage the revolutionaries were probably relatively few in number. It would take the Franco-Prussian War to create an at least potentially revolutionary situation.

Welcomed with patriotic fervor, the emperor's decision in July 1870 to risk war was intended to re-establish a power balance upset by the Prussian victory over Austria in 1866. Military catastrophe, however, destroyed the regime's legitimacy. News of the capitulation of the emperor and a major army at Sedan in eastern France was followed by the bloodless Parisian revolution of September 4, 1870. The capital's moderate republican deputies established a Government of National Defense, legitimized by popular acclaim. They were determined to secure victory as well as to prevent a revolutionary takeover in the city. Intensely patriotic themselves, and glorifying the *levee en masse* of the 1790s, the leading figures on the Left, including Blanqui, Varlin, Vallès, Malon, and Vaillant, demanded mass mobilization. The vigilance committees they formed to promote the war effort sent delegates as early as September 11 to a Central Committee of the Twenty Arrondissements (the twenty districts of Paris), intended to coordinate their activities. Furthermore, in a "red poster" they promoted such immediate measures as food rationing, and additionally the future establishment of a social and democratic republic, greater autonomy for Paris by means of the establishment of an elected Paris Commune—a further reference to the institutions of the 1790s—the abolition of poverty, and, following a victory that would allow Paris to offer leadership to the struggling masses throughout the world, the establishment of a "universal republic."

On September 19, as the advancing German forces finally enveloped the city and its surrounding forts, Parisians enrolled in the National Guard. Military commanders, while launching occasional poorly organized sorties to satisfy these impatient citizen-soldiers, generally felt compelled to wait for the arrival of relieving forces. In the meantime the guardsmen, members of units of neighbors with elected officers and noncommissioned officers, trained, paraded, socialized, and bonded together. In gaining the right to bear arms they had achieved a long-standing democratic objective. Nevertheless, they constantly complained about what they perceived to be the "treason" of the generals and the iniquities of the social system. The incoherent administration of food distribution and of poor relief in the besieged city, widespread undernourishment as well as the onset of winter and intense cold, increased their anger. Economic collapse, which ensured that the only resource for many families was National Guard pay, set off a process of mass pauperization and growing demoralization that intensified popular hostility toward the better off and those suspected of hoarding and profiteering from the sale of scarce resources. Calls for the establishment of a Paris Commune, of a popular government that

Members of the Paris Commune of 1871. (Alinari Archives/Corbis)

might somehow transform their situation, were also increasingly heard.

In spite of their efforts to rebuild the army, the Government of National Defense was finally forced to admit defeat and, on January 28, 1871, was accorded an armistice by the Prussian chancellor, Bismarck. Although welcoming the opportunity to reprovision the city, patriots were dismayed by the agreement to surrender their forts to the enemy. The armistice further provided for national elections on February 8, essentially to determine whether the war should continue, as republican candidates demanded, or end, as their primarily monarchist and clerical opponents wished. Parisian republicans would dismiss the election of a monarchist majority as the vote of the same "ignorant" rural population that had previously supported Napoléon III. The city's voters had themselves largely favored mainstream radical republicans rather than the revolutionary Left or the more conservative moderate republicans that had dominated the Government of National Defense and who were now reappointed

by the new National Assembly to a government headed by the conservative, former July Monarchy minister Adolphe Thiers as chief of the Executive Power.

The decisions taken by Thiers, his ministers, and conservative deputies would rapidly exacerbate the already tense situation in Paris. The peace treaty ratified on March 1 ceded the province of Alsace and much of Lorraine. The concession of a German victory parade through central Paris on March 1 was regarded as a massive humiliation by the city's defenders. Subsequent decisions, designed to restore "normality" as rapidly as possible, included ending the moratorium on commercial bills introduced during the siege. Although payments were to be phased over three months, it was widely believed that immediate payment was required, and many small businessmen felt threatened with imminent bankruptcy. The prospect of paying rent arrears and the ending of payment for service in the National Guard were additional threats. The republic, which Parisians had fought to defend, and with it their aspirations for democratic and social reform, was also menaced by the clear determination of monarchist deputies to secure the throne for the Bourbon pretender, the Comte de Chambord.

The decision to enhance the assembly's security by meeting in Versailles appeared to be the symbolic representation of this objective, and for Parisians additionally represented the "decapitalization" of their city. The National Assembly was determined to assert its legitimate authority. Most of its members, republicans as well as monarchists, shared a widely held fear of the revolutionary potential of the capital city. The widely publicized verbal violence of the political clubs during the empire and the siege had increased their anxiety. Their concerns were intensified by stereotyped views of a Parisian working class mired in crime and vice. There appeared to be a growing threat from the "dangerous classes" not simply to the possession of private property and to social status but also to the decencies of family life and Christian civilization.

CONTEXT AND PROCESS OF REVOLUTION

On March 18, 1871, regular French troops were ordered to seize the 300 to 400 cannon parked by National Guards on the heights of Montmartre, as a first step in restoring the state's monopoly of armed force. They were rapidly surrounded by thousands of local National Guards together with their womenfolk and children. Military discipline collapsed. Members of the crowd executed two senior officers. In response, Thiers ordered a general withdrawal by the authorities and army, adopting a tactic he had proposed to King Louis-Philippe during the February 1848 revolution—namely, removing demoralized military units to allow for their reorganization and reinforcement, followed by the establishment of a cordon around disaffected areas and the eventual crushing of the insurrection by overwhelming military force. Into the power vacuum created by this retreat stepped an unofficial body, the Central Committee of the Republican Federation of the Paris National Guard—originally established at mass meetings in February to promote a *guerre à outrance* (all-out war) against the Prussians—to defend the republic and oppose their own disarmament. The members of the committee established themselves in the city hall, the seat of the Paris Commune in 1792.

It was still generally assumed that a negotiated settlement was possible. Certainly there was little desire within the city to risk a repetition of the civil war fought in June 1848. The Central Committee, supported by the city's deputies and arrondissement mayors, agreed to hold elections on March 26. It had been widely held for some time that democratization by means of the election of a city council (the Paris Commune) was necessary in order to replace the imperial system of authoritarian prefectoral control. However, the elections revealed a substantial radicalization of the electorate. Furthermore, many conservative and moderate republican voters had left Paris for more comfortable surroundings at the end of the Prussian siege. Others, hostile to both revolution and monarchy, chose to abstain in these elections. While in 1869 only 6,000 voters had supported revolutionary candidates, now that figure had risen to 190,000; only 40,000 voted for their opponents (Tombs 1999, 70). Revolutionaries inspired by the myths and memories of 1792 and 1848 and determined to promote the establishment of a more egalitarian republic thus dominated the Commune, proclaimed on March 28. This result ensured that, more than ever, the National Assembly would be unwilling to contemplate a workable compromise. From this point the Paris Commune was doomed. In spite of the establishment of short-lived communes in the provinces, the city was isolated. A second siege began that was to be far more destructive than the first. With the German forces still occupying the northern and eastern approaches to the city as interested spectators, a vicious civil war began. Sharing the universal conservative fear of "red revolution," Bismarck sanctioned the rapid transport of the former French imperial army from its prisoner-of-war camps in Germany to join in the battle.

Within the city, the establishment of the Commune initially encouraged a tremendous sense of expectancy among its supporters. The "people" again took possession of the city center, from which many had previously been excluded by Haussmann's clearances. A sense of *fête* (festival) prevailed briefly, during which everything appeared possible. A new social order seemed to be in the making, in which poor people could openly express their contempt for the "idle rich," employers, landlords, shopkeepers—all those "bloodsuckers" guilty of fattening themselves at the workers' expense—as well as for the policemen and the priests, who had repeatedly humiliated them, and all the "reactionaries" associated both with the imperial regime and the "betrayal" of 1848. An entry in the Goncourt journal for March 19 records the disgust and fear of middle-class citizens still marooned in a city in which the "vile multitude" appeared to have assumed control, "at the sight of their stupid, abject faces, in which triumph and intoxication created a sort of dissolute radiance" (Baldick 1962, 184).

Determining the aspirations of rank-and-file communards who wrote very little is difficult. However, information on debates in political clubs and even on the streets suggests an overwhelming commitment to defense of the republic as the only legitimate form of government. That was a principle superior even to universal suffrage. The "enlightened" citizens of Paris were duty bound to defend this potential fount of "progress" and of social reform against the monarchists and "ignorant" peasants. Suspicious of "bourgeois" politicians of whatever political stripe, many workers supported the establishment of some form of direct democracy, allowing the "people" to elect their representatives and officials and recall those who failed to respect their mandates. Public funding for the establishment of producers' cooperatives would allow them to escape from exploitation and provide the means for an affirmation of the dignity of labor (Price 2004, 358).

The elected members of the Commune had more pressing concerns. Faced with the practical problems of waging war, they had little time to discuss social reform. Nevertheless, as well as introducing service in the National Guard for all able-bodied men, measures such as the cancellation of rent arrears from the beginning of the war, the suspension of sales from the municipal pawnshop (March 29), and provision for the phased repayment of commercial bills over three years (April 14) were intended to relieve pressure on the living standards of workers and the lower-middle classes. Proclamation of the separation of church and state pointed toward a longer-term agenda. The Declaration to the French People, published by the Commune on April 19, and largely drafted by Pierre Denis and Charles Delescluze, represented an eclectic compromise between ideas that had come to be associated with Proudhon, including direct democracy and producers' cooperatives and the Jacobin, Blanquist tradition of centralized, revolutionary authority. It was remarkable for its similarities with Gambetta's radical republican program of 1869, focusing on political reform as the engine of subsequent social reform, combining a promise of communal autonomy with "consolidation of the Republic," and promising "the end of the old governmental, priest-ridden world, of militarism, of bureaucracy, exploitation, speculation, monopolies, privileges, to which the proletariat owes its enslavement" (Price 1972, 76).

In spite of this ringing statement of principle and a deteriorating military situation, divisions of principle and personality remained evident within the Commune, within the Executive Commission set up to enforce its decrees, and between these and the Central Committee of the National Guard. The establishment on May 1 of a Committee of Public Safety reflected a common tendency to look back to 1793 for inspiration and an increasingly desperate desire to establish effective authority. Even then Delescluze, the old Jacobin, anxious not to alienate moderates, insisted paradoxically that the intention was "to ally moderation to energy," to adopt "revolutionary means" but also "to observe the forms, to respect the law and public opinion" (ibid., 81). Within the city things went on as normal. Much of the city administration continued with its usual activities, maintaining roads, collecting the *octroi* (municipal toll) and the tobacco tax. Orders for military equipment were put out to tender, and businesses, large and small, desperate for work, put in their bids. The privately owned Bank of France continued to function under only loose supervision by François Jourde, the Commune's delegate. Even the decrees handing over abandoned workshops to workers' cooperatives, described by Marx as a "step to Socialism," was intended as a temporary measure and certainly not a threat to the private ownership of property.

The rights of employers were slightly diminished when fines in the workplace were abandoned and night work in bakeries banned (April 20)—the latter a measure described by Marx's correspondent Leo Fränkel as "the only truly Socialist decree that the Commune has passed." Even those measures were described as illegitimate interference in relations between employers and workers by some members of the Commune (ibid., 79). It was easier to agree on the need to introduce free, compulsory, and secular education. The enlightenment of the masses required higher levels of school attendance and the exclusion of "obscurantist" and reactionary members of the church's teaching orders. Proudhon had previously justified his own abandonment of Christian Socialism by insisting that: "For as long as men bow before altars, mankind will remain damned, the slave of kings and priests" (Vincent 1984, 105). Youthful Blanquists in particular tended toward a virulent anti-clericalism, vandalizing churches, arresting priests, and spreading rumors concerning their sexual depravity.

On April 2, fighting began in the western suburbs, always a weak point in the defense because of the hostility toward the Commune of their largely middle-class residents, as well as the reluctance of National Guards from other districts to accept deployment outside their neighborhoods. The communards were rapidly disabused of their belief in the "invincibility of the people" in a struggle against supposedly poorly motivated regular troops. A *sortie torrentielle* (mass attack) launched by 30,000 to 40,000 men on April 3 rapidly collapsed. The participants were undisciplined and poorly led. There was little else they could do except wait for an attack from Versailles. Certainly serious efforts were made by a hard core of men with military experience to improve the organization and supply of the Commune's armed forces, and to make full use of the city's existing fortifications. Photographs of National Guard units seem to reveal a continuing sense of pride and solidarity. It must have been difficult to accept that their revolution was on the brink of failure and that only a renewed appeal for negotiation or else a humiliating surrender could save them from complete catastrophe. However, any remaining optimism would prove impossible to sustain.

On the night of May 21–22, Versailles forces succeeded in entering the city. Their assault heralded the beginning of what would come to be known as "bloody week." The Commune's military delegate, Delescluze, called for a mass uprising, but many demoralized guards simply went home. The more committed, 10,000 to 20,000 in all, who were dispersed throughout the central, northern, and eastern parts of the city, began to construct some 900 barricades (Tombs 1999, 166), both to obstruct the movement of troops and to protect their own neighborhoods. Some of these were massive structures, designed to control access to major squares and boulevards, but most were smaller, blocking side streets. The army, which already in 1848 had carefully reviewed its street-fighting tactics, bombarded and outflanked these obstacles. Their defenders fought bravely or fled to escape the retribution to which Versailles forces were clearly committed. Major buildings in the city center were set on fire either by artillery, or by communards in a desperate effort to delay the advancing troops. The last desperate battles were fought in eastern Paris, in the working-class streets of Belleville, Ménil-montant, and Popincourt. The brutality of the military repression reflected conservative fear of social revolution, the sense—as the moderate republican minister Jules Favre put it—that "June 1848, March 1871" represented "the same struggle." Contempt and hatred for the "vile multitude" was barely restrained. The Goncourt brothers were not alone in expressing the hope that "the bleeding had been done thoroughly" and that "killing the rebellious part of the population" would "postpone the next revolution by a whole generation" (Price 1971, 345).

That atrocities were occurring on both sides was only too apparent. The bloodletting would contribute to the creation of potent myths. In the closing stages of the conflict, hostages, arrested initially in response to the Versailles execution of prisoners on April 3, were shot as news spread of the mass killings by troops. The wealthy had not been targeted. Instead, policemen and 120 priests, symbols of political reaction, had been incarcerated. They included Mgr. Darboy, archbishop of Paris, who with twenty-three other priests now met his death, largely at the hands of out-of-control Blanquist police officials of the Commune. The slaughter engaged in by government forces, led by generals determined to defend Christian civilization against "barbarism," was far greater in scale, more systematic, and officially countenanced. The Versailles forces lost some 3,500 men killed and wounded. Communard casualties can only be guessed at. More than 15,000 were arrested during the conflict. At least 10,000 were shot on suspicion of involvement and thousands more following cursory courts-martial. Subsequently, following numerous and usually anonymous denunciations, 40,000 others were arrested; 12,500 of them were brought to trial and 10,000 found guilty. At this stage few were executed, but 4,000 were expelled from France, to endure lengthy sentences in the penal colony in New Caledonia (Tombs 1999, 171, 180). The more fortunate sought exile, particularly in Britain and Switzerland.

IMPACTS

In sum, the Parisian population was politicized over decades through participation in major political events and in the debates, which continually resurfaced in the capital city. Workplace and cafe sociability, the political clubs of the late 1860s, and the experience of service in the National Guard during two sieges had reinforced their sense of both community and class. Those who were prepared to risk their lives, in the last desperate stages of the Commune, were caught up perhaps in circumstances from which escape was difficult. They were inspired by a sense of loyalty to comrades and hatred of an enemy determined to employ the most brutal violence to restore monarchy and to preserve an oppressive social system, and whose success would destroy their own dreams of democracy and a republic in which they and their families would enjoy better working and living conditions, educational opportunities, and the respect due to those whose labor was the source of all wealth.

Robert Tombs described the Paris Commune as "the biggest popular insurrection in modern European history" (ibid., 12). Its primary causes were the particular circumstances created by war and defeat, and particularly incompetent government crisis management, which created a political vacuum into which stepped militants already radicalized by their experience of an authoritarian empire and military defeat and able to circumvent the state's normal monopoly of armed force. In *The Civil War in France,* in deliberately exaggerated terms, and in what was a political manifesto designed to support and glorify a movement he assumed was doomed, Marx described the Commune as "the political form" for "the emancipation of the proletariat." As Jacques Rougerie pointed out, it was also "the culmination and end of the French revolutionary saga" (1995, 241).

Although the conservative triumph would soon be memorialized by the construction of the basilica of Sacré Coeur in expiation of the sins that had led God to punish France so severely, the expected Bourbon restoration would not occur. The conservative republic, which had so effectively crushed the Commune, would be widely accepted as the regime that divided French citizens the least. The Third Republic would, particularly from the 1880s, prove more effective at institutionalizing protest than its predecessors. Even as the Socialist Left recovered from its losses, and in spite of its often-revolutionary rhetoric, there was little desire to repeat such an experience. Lenin and Trotsky would, of course, reach different conclusions, insisting that the evident willingness of the bourgeoisie to massacre its enemies demanded the creation of a vengeful revolutionary dictatorship.

Until the centenary celebrations in 1971, most historians adopted a sympathetic, Marxist-inspired view of the Commune. Subsequently, narratives based on class have been challenged by a concern with community, political culture, and gender. Much of this has represented an attempt to impose schematic analytical frameworks, inspired by cultural or feminist theory, on a complicated social movement. Much more valuable has been research using the arrest statistics, interrogation records, and accounts of discussions at public meetings, inspired largely by the pioneering work of Rougerie (ibid.), and taking its most developed form so far in Tomb's general study *The Paris Commune of 1871* (1999). That work, together with his *War against Paris 1871* (1981), also provides an invaluable case study of the crucial importance of military power in the internal politics of nineteenth-century France.

PEOPLE AND ORGANIZATIONS

Committee of the Republican Federation of the Paris National Guard

This was an unofficial body set up on February 15 to coordinate the activity of the National Guard battalions.

Communards

Who were the Communards? Clearly, there were varying degrees of commitment. Moreover, professional categorization is not easy. The members of the Commune council were essentially from the lower-middle class of skilled workers, and men who had previously established reputations as journalists or militants in the trade unions and Workers International. The registers listing the large numbers arrested offer a glimpse at their backgrounds, although the value of this information is reduced by the police tendency to arrest the "usual suspects." If there was a typical insurgent, he was relatively young (twenty to forty years of age), married, and a skilled metalworker, cabinetmaker, or representative of a myriad of other luxury trades, or else a building worker. There were also significant numbers of the *bourgeoisie populaire*—small businessmen, including many of the cafe owners who played such a key role in popular sociability, and clerks, as well as unskilled laborers. This was not the drunken criminal horde of conservative legend—although some 20 percent had criminal records listing a host of minor offenses. Nor was this the "proletariat" of Marxist legend, unless the word is employed in the contemporary sense to include (almost) all of those who work for wages. In spite of the involvement of workers from modern engineering plants, the profile of those arrested is similar to that of participants in the February revolution and June insurrection in 1848, and not entirely dissimilar from that of the *sans-culottes* of the 1790s. Thus the fundamental lines of social antagonism can be drawn between *peuple* and *bourgeoisie*.

Government of National Defense

The Government of National Defense was established following the collapse of the Second Empire on September 4, 1870, and made up of moderate republican Parisian deputies, presided over by General Trochu, the military governor of the city.

Paris Commune

The original Paris Commune was the government of Paris during the French Revolution, made up of representatives of the Paris sections and radicalized following the insurrection of August 10, 1792. It provided inspiration for the revolutionaries who supported the Paris Commune or city government of Paris during the spring of 1871.

Thiers, Louis Adolphe (1797–1877)

A former interior minister during the July Monarchy, Thiers was elected chief executive by the newly elected National Assembly, meeting on February 12, 1871, at Bordeaux. He presided over the suppression of the Paris Commune.

Women and the Paris Commune

Some 1,000 of those arrested were women, mainly employed in the clothing trades, as laundry women or cleaners, or gaining a desperate living as prostitutes. The heroic commitment of such emblematic figures as Louise Michel or Paule Minck to improving women's conditions has recently attracted considerable interest. However, contemporaries on both sides generally saw female engagement in public life as contrary to the natural order. For conservatives, the mythical figure of the arsonist, the *pétroleuse*, and of all those women who fought on the barricades was a loathsome symbol of subversion. In practice, relatively few women took an active part in the fighting, and then mostly in traditional female roles as *cantinières*, offering sustenance to male fighters, or as nurses. Initially, at least, many encouraged their menfolk in the struggle for a better world. Similarly, female participation in public debate was discouraged by male communards as well as by their own sense of propriety. The influence exerted by the Union des Femmes was far more limited than women's historians would wish.

Roger Price

See Also Anarchism, Communism, and Socialism; Documentaries of Revolution; European Revolutions of 1848; French Revolution; Inequality, Class, and Revolution; Music and Revolution; Russian Revolution of 1917; War and Revolution

References and Further Readings
Baldick, Robert, ed. 1962. *Pages from the Goncourt Journal.* Oxford: Oxford University Press.
Eichner, Carolyn. 2004. *Women in the Paris Commune.* Bloomington: Indiana University Press.
Price, Roger. 1971. "Conservative Reactions to Social Disorder: The Paris Commune of 1871," *Journal of European Studies* 1: 341–352.
———. 1972. "Ideology and Motivation in the Paris Commune of 1871," *Historical Journal* 15: 75–86.
———. 2004. *People and Politics in France, 1848–70.* New York: Cambridge University Press.
Rougerie, Jacques. 1995. *Paris insurgé: La Commune de 1871.* Paris: Gallimard.
Shafer, David. 2005. *The Paris Commune.* New York: Palgrave Macmillan.
Tombs, Robert. 1981. *The War against Paris.* New York: Cambridge University Press.
———. 1999. *The Paris Commune, 1871.* London: Longman.
Vincent, Steven. 1984. *Pierre-Joseph Proudhon and the Rise of French Republican Socialism.* Oxford: Oxford University Press.

Peruvian Shining Path

CHRONOLOGY

1200	Legendary leaders Manco Capac and Mama Ocllo establish Inca empire.
1438	Pachacuti Inca begins imperial Inca expansion out of Cuzco valley.
1493	Huayna Capac takes over the Inca empire and eventually expands it to its greatest size.
1532	Spanish conquistador Francisco Pizarro defeats Atahualpa at Cajamarca; begins Spanish rule of Peru.
1572	Spanish capture and execute Tupac Amaru, the last Inca ruler.
1780	Tupac Amaru II uprising sweeps across Peruvian highlands.
1824	Peru gains its independence from Spanish rule.
1894	Marxist intellectual José Carlos Mariátegui is born.
1928	Mariátegui publishes *Seven Interpretive Essays on Peruvian Reality;* founds Peruvian Socialist Party and seeks to affiliate it with the Communist International.
1930	Mariátegui dies; the Peruvian Socialist Party becomes the Peruvian Communist Party.
1934	Shining Path leader Abimael Guzmán is born.
1959	Hugo Blanco begins to organize peasants in La Convención Valley.
1962	Guzmán begins to teach philosophy at the University of Huamanga.
1963	Police capture and imprison Hugo Blanco.
1964	The Peruvian Communist Party splits into pro-Moscow and pro-Chinese factions.
1965	Failure of Luis de la Puente Uceda's guerrilla *foco* (armed revolutionary group); Guzmán travels to China.
1968	General Juan Velasco Alvarado's Revolutionary Government of the Armed Forces assumes control of the Peruvian government.
1969	Promulgation of Agrarian Reform Law.
1970	Population shifts take Peru from a predominantly rural, highland, indigenous society to a majority urban, coastal, and mestizo one; Guzmán forms the Communist Party of Peru—Shining Path.
1976	*Rondas campesinas* (rural patrols) are established in the northern highlands to address civil and criminal problems.

1979   The Central Committee of the Peruvian Communist Party—Shining Path decides to prepare for armed struggle.

1980   Fernando Belaúnde Terry wins Peru's first presidential elections in seventeen years; the Shining Path launches the armed phase of its "People's War."

1981   Peruvian government declares terrorism to be a special crime.

1982   Death of Shining Path leader Edith Lagos; Ayacucho is placed under a state of emergency.

1983   Peruvian government creates *rondas campesinas* (rural patrols) in the southern highlands to fight the Shining Path.

1984   Founding of the Tupac Amaru Revolutionary Movement (MRTA).

1985   Alán García wins Peruvian presidency.

1986   Shining Path inmates riot in Lima prisons; military kills 287.

1990   Shining Path calls for an "armed strike" in Lima; Alberto Fujimori wins the presidency in Peru and subsequently implements economic austerity measures ("Fujishock").

1992   The Shining Path executes popular leader María Elena Moyano; Fujimori assumes dictatorial rule ("Fujicoup"). Shining Path battles police at Lima's Canto Grande prison, resulting in the deaths of about fifty inmates; Shining Path detonates car bombs in the wealthy Lima suburb of Miraflores; Guzmán is captured and sentenced to life imprisonment.

1993   Guzmán calls for an end to armed struggle and offers to negotiate with the Peruvian government.

1995   Peru grants amnesty for members of the police and military implicated in human rights abuses since 1980.

1999   The government captures Oscar Ramírez Durand, alias Feliciano, the highest-ranking Shining Path leader still at large after Guzmán's capture.

2000   Fujimori falls from power and goes into exile in Japan.

2001   Alejandro Toledo is elected president of Peru.

2003   Peruvian government releases the final report of the Truth and Reconciliation Commission, examining political violence between 1980 and 2000.

INTRODUCTION

On May 17, 1980, on the eve of Peru's first presidential election in seventeen years, an armed group stole ballot boxes and voting lists in the highland town of Chuschi and burned them in the central plaza. The Shining Path guerrilla group pointed to this as the beginning of the armed phase of their "People's War" against the Peruvian government. This seemingly innocuous beginning in many ways represents the contradictions inherent in the Shining Path's rise to one of the largest and most bloody guerrilla movements in Latin America. This initial action went virtually unreported in the press, and in its first year almost no one paid any attention to the embryonic group. However, it quickly grew into one of the world's best known guerrilla movements.

While Peru was moving away from a military dictatorship and toward a civilian democracy, the Shining Path mounted a violent revolution. Revolutionary movements in Latin America tend to emphasize an open and voluntarist flavor of Marxism, but the Shining Path imposed an authoritarian and dogmatic ideology. It became a mass movement, but it was based on a secretive cell structure that showed little interest in advertising its ideology or goals to the public in general. It emerged among an ethnically Quechua indigenous group but espoused an orthodox Marxist class analysis. The Shining Path became noted for the attraction of women to its ranks, but one of its most noted victims was community leader María Elena Moyano. It presented an idealized vision of rural society even while Peru was quickly becoming an increasingly urban country.

Since the capture of its leader, Abimael Guzmán Reynoso, in 1992, the Shining Path has collapsed and become merely a shadow of its former self. Although small armed bands continue to stage attacks in the Peruvian highlands, the Shining

Path's eventual victory is no longer the assured event that it once seemed to be. The contradictions inherent in the Shining Path, however, continue to grab people's interest. Since the 1980s, a sizable body of literature has grown up around the group. How did the Shining Path emerge, and why did it take the direction that it did?

BACKGROUND: CULTURE AND HISTORY

The Shining Path emerged out of a situation of crushing poverty and racist oppression in which indigenous peoples, who made up a majority of the Peruvian population, lived. These Quechua Indians were the descendants of the Inca empire, which ruled over Peru from about 1200 to 1532. (While "Inca" has been the traditional spelling, many Quechua linguists now say that "Inka" is a more accurate rendering.) Emerging out of its legendary founders Manco Capac and Mama Ocllo, the Incas saw themselves as great civilizers who brought agriculture, learning, and order in the face of chaos. Through the use of promises, threats, and force, the Incas spread their superior language (Quechua) and religion (sun worship) across the Andes. When the eleventh Inca, Huayna Capac (1493–1527), died, the empire broke into a civil war between two of his sons, Huascar and Atahualpa.

Shortly after Atahualpa's victory over his brother, he encountered the Spanish conquistador Francisco Pizarro at the northern Peruvian city of Cajamarca, on November 16, 1532. Finding the two hundred Spanish explorers more of a curiosity than a significant threat to the battle-hardened Inca troops, Atahualpa was shocked at the invaders' attack in the face of what he assumed was a shared tradition of unarmed diplomatic meetings. In what could be seen as foreshadowing the collapse of the Shining Path 460 years later, the Inca troops accepted the defeat, capture, and execution of their leader as representative of their own fate. While subsequently the Inca empire no longer existed in its previous glory, a fractional group retreated in an attempt to re-create an Inca empire in exile. For forty years that group continued to harass Spanish attempts to assume rule of the empire, until the eventual capture and execution of Tupac Amaru in 1572. While Inca leaders like Tupac Amaru became important symbols of indigenous resistance in Peru, they never entered into the Shining Path's pantheon of heroes, the group preferring to focus instead on traditional Marxist and Western figures.

Under Spanish colonial rule, Peru became divided into two parts: the Republic of the Spanish and the Republic of the Indians. A large rural, marginalized indigenous population remained isolated from urban politics and economy. This cre-

ated the context for one of the largest indigenous uprisings in the Americas. In 1780, a local leader named José Gabriel Condorcanqui took the name of the last Inca ruler, Tupac Amaru, as he called for the expulsion of the Spanish and the re-establishment of an independent Inca empire. Initial victories led to growing support for his movement that quickly spread like wildfire throughout the Andes. Although he nearly succeeded in evicting the Spanish, six months later royal officials captured and executed the rebel. The Tupac Amaru II uprising, however, irrevocably altered social relations in the Andes. His mobilization of rural populations and challenge to Spanish colonial power eventually led to Peruvian independence, in 1824. This uprising further established the name Tupac Amaru as a symbol of indigenous resistance.

By the twentieth century, Peru had one of the most unequal and archaic land tenure and labor systems in Latin America. The majority of the population was still rural and indigenous, removed from a small urban elite that defined the country's economic, political, and cultural life. Ayacucho, where the Shining Path first emerged, was one of the poorest, most remote, most rural, and most indigenous parts of Peru. Evictions from traditional landholdings and a growing sense of hopelessness drove a migration from the highlands to plantations on the coast, and from rural areas into impoverished urban neighborhoods (euphemistically called *pueblos jóvenes* or *new towns*) surrounding the capital city of Lima. By the 1970s, a majority of the population had left their indigenous roots and was in the process of assimilating into an urban, Catholic, Spanish-speaking dominant culture. The Shining Path drew on the rising expectations of disinherited populations in both rural and urban areas for its base of support.

CONTEXT AND PROCESS OF REVOLUTION

José Carlos Mariátegui

In 1970, Abimael Guzmán, then a philosophy professor at the University of Huamanga in the highland town of Ayacucho, broke from the mainline Communist Party and announced his intention to push forward *por el sendero luminoso de José Carlos Mariátegui,* by the shining path of José Carlos Mariátegui. He formed a group with this name that he later changed to Partido Comunista del Perú—Sendero Luminoso (Communist Party of Peru—Shining Path) and finally shortened in common parlance to simply Sendero Luminoso, or the Shining Path.

Mariátegui (1894–1930) is traditionally seen as the founder of Peru's Communist Party and is claimed as a symbolic leading figure of virtually the entire Peruvian Left, with different groups often accusing others of misinterpreting his philosophy and legacy. In 1926, Mariátegui founded the avant-garde journal *Amauta,* which provided a vanguard voice for the revolution. He also published the book *Seven Interpretive Essays on Peruvian Reality* (1928), which became a fundamental work on Latin American Marxism. In addition to his writings, he founded the Peruvian Socialist Party (PSP) and sought its integration into the Communist International. Unfortunately, Mariátegui died in 1930, before he could work out in practice all of the implications of his theories. His followers changed the name of his party to the Peruvian Communist Party (PCP) and took it in a more doctrinaire direction.

Mariátegui's unique approach to Marxist theory becomes particularly apparent when examining his critique of Peru's land tenure system and the role of rural indigenous peoples in a revolutionary movement. Unlike orthodox Marxism, which looked to an urban working-class vanguard to lead a revolution and believed that a traditional peasantry was reactionary, Mariátegui understood that in Latin America in the early twentieth century there was a very small urban proletariat. In Peru, 80 percent of the population was rural and indigenous, and a Marxist critique must focus on improving their marginalized and impoverished condition. He argued that the rural populations could develop a revolutionary consciousness, and advocated an "Indo-American" Socialism based on the ancient communal values of the Incan empire. Rather than moving through set stages of history, Mariátegui argued, the indigenous peasantry in the Andes could advance directly to the advanced stage of a Communist society. Guzmán drew on these ideas as he forged the ideology that drove the Shining Path.

1960s Peasant Movements

Peruvian governmental attempts to reform the archaic land tenure system that Mariátegui described largely met with failure. Unfulfilled promises led in the 1960s to peasant land invasions and an increasingly militant guerrilla movement. Hugo Blanco, a peasant organizer in La Convención Valley north of Cuzco in the Peruvian highlands, was one of the most charismatic and effective leaders. Under the slogan "Land or Death," he organized a revolutionary mass movement that slowly moved toward guerrilla warfare. The peasants, however, lacked training in armed insurrection, and Blanco proved to be more effective as a peasant organizer than a guerrilla fighter. At the same time, and under the influence of the Cuban Revolution, Luis de la Puente Uceda attempted to establish a guerrilla *foco* with the goal of triggering a mass uprising. Before it could gain much traction, the military wiped out the guerrilla group. While Blanco's movement had organized peasants in desperate need of guerrilla support, de

la Puente's guerrillas failed because of lack of support from an organized peasantry. The military also quickly defeated a third group, Héctor Béjar's Ejército de Liberación Nacional (Army of National Liberation, ELN), which had splintered from the Peruvian Communist Party. Much of the leadership of these movements emerged from urban political movements that lacked strong ties with rural activists or a good understanding of local traditions and customs. These failures effectively ended any guerrilla activity in Peru until the emergence of the Shining Path fifteen years later.

In October 1968, when General Juan Velasco Alvarado took over the government, many observers initially assumed that this was just another in the long series of palace coups that have plagued Peru's history. Velasco, however, quickly implemented deep-seated reforms that proposed a third way of national development, between capitalism and socialism. His Revolutionary Government of the Armed Forces implemented sweeping reforms, including an extensive agrarian reform law (appropriately named the Plan of Tupac Amaru), designed to do away with unjust social and economic structures. While this reform ended serfdom and increased rural wages and the quality of life, the slow-moving reform, with its centralized planning, resulted in its limited effectiveness. An ultimate goal of removing threats from guerrilla movements by undercutting their social base, however, was largely successful.

A 1978 constituent assembly paved a return to civilian government. For the first time in Peru's history, illiterates had the right to vote in these elections—effectively extending citizenship rights to indigenous peoples. The new civilian government undid many of Velasco's reforms. Among the actions it took was the privatizing of agricultural land that had been converted into cooperatives, and restoring the free market system. These neo-liberal policies led to a decline in living standards, growing unemployment, and an increase in social protest. It was out of this context that the Shining Path emerged, its leaders condemning the limited reforms of Velasco's military government while at the same time feeding off peasant frustrations at a failure to receive the benefits the government had promised.

Emergence of the Shining Path

Guzmán formed the Peruvian Communist Party—Shining Path out of a split between pro-Moscow and pro-China wings of the party. Rather than joining either wing, he excelled in building a new party, using internal purges to build a single party line while at the same time cultivating a cult of personality around himself. Initially he relied on Mariátegui's analysis of Peru in the 1920s, emphasizing issues of land tenure, imperialism, and the role of the proletariat. Under the nom de guerre of Presidente Gonzalo, Guzmán began to develop his own "Gonzalo thought," which positioned the Shining Path as the "fourth sword" of Marxism after Marx, Lenin, and Mao. At the university, Guzmán had trained teachers who upon returning to their rural communities formed the cadre of the Shining Path. Free education (which the 1968 military government had eliminated) became a more important demand for these activists than land.

Rather than joining leftist coalitions that participated in massive national strikes that pushed Peru toward a civilian government, the Shining Path decided in a 1979 Central Committee meeting to prepare for an armed struggle. On April 19, 1980, the guerrillas graduated the first class of combatants from their newly formed military school and announced the ILA, *inicio de la lucha armada*, or initiation of the armed struggle. Like John Brown, the violent opponent of slavery before the U.S. Civil War who wanted to "purge this land with blood," the Shining Path promised to pay "the quota" of blood necessary to transform society. While early actions were initially concentrated around Ayacucho, their activities eventually extended throughout the highlands and to the capital city of Lima on the coast.

The Shining Path's "People's War" began in 1980 with symbolic actions such as hanging dogs from lamp posts and blowing up electrical towers. The dogs apparently represented the notion of "running dogs of capitalism," meaning people who served the interests of exploiting capitalists. They gained support for their emphasis on popular justice and moral behavior, including holding "people's trials" that often ended in the execution of abusive property owners, police officers, and other unpopular figures. Much of their support came from rural students and schoolteachers who found their social mobility blocked because of racial prejudice and economic stagnation. The Shining Path emerged partly as the result of its isolated provincial context, and partly as a logical outcome of a situation in which, faced with no legal routes for bringing about social change, activists turned to violence. The uprising did not emerge so much out of a situation of poverty and misery in the rural highlands as a failure of reforms over the previous two decades to meet the rising expectations that those reforms had encouraged. Furthermore, the guerrilla movement did not emerge automatically as a result of objective conditions. It was very deliberately designed and inaugurated by a central leadership. At the height of its activities, it had 10,000 to 12,000 people under arms and could draw on the collaboration of a civilian base perhaps ten times that size. Guerrilla activity extended to all but two of Peru's twenty-five departments (provinces), although, except for select communities, the Shining Path never controlled much territory.

At first, President Fernando Belaúnde Terry used the police forces to respond to the Shining Path's threat, but with the police unable to suppress the uprising in 1982, he placed Ayacucho under a state of emergency and sent in the military. Most significant were the *sinchis,* a counter-insurgency unit named after the Quechua word for "powerful" and trained by U.S. special forces. The military could not distinguish between the guerrillas and other rural residents and so engaged in severe repression of civilian populations, including rapes, tortures, disappearances, and massacres. Even some persons in the military acknowledged that the large majority of the people they arrested or killed probably had nothing to do with the guerrilla insurgency. Of the several thousand people killed from 1982 to 1985, it is likely that no more than a few hundred were combatants. Throughout the course of this conflict, while the Shining Path's human rights violations were more severe than those of any other insurgent group in Latin America, military abuses were yet more extreme and more of a problem. Many observers note, however, that fundamentally the Shining Path's struggle was a political one. Military responses only tended to force peasants into joining the Shining Path, because there did not appear to be any other alternative. It appeared, and was largely true, that the mestizo, urban, coastal government in Lima cared little about the rural, indigenous realities in the highlands. The colonial division of "two Perus" remained very much a reality.

In spite of the Shining Path's having been organized principally among a rural Quechua indigenous population, many observers noted the seeming lack of an Andean context for the Shining Path insurgency. The guerrillas rejected race and ethnicity as tools of analysis, adhering instead to the orthodox Marxist dogma of class warfare. While emerging out of deep divisions between the two Perus, ideologically and religiously it was rooted in the Western tradition. Even the leader's nom de guerre was that of a Spanish conquistador (Gonzalo Pizarro). The Shining Path could be seen as a messianic or millenarian movement, but seemingly without roots in the rich history of Tupac Amaru and other indigenous revolts. Its leaders did not desire to return to an Incan empire from the past, but rather to move forward into a utopian Communist future.

The Shining Path imposed a top-down leadership style, rejecting major participation by the masses in decision making, in favor of the domination by the party elite. This authoritarian approach resulted in a strong hierarchy in which leaders were depicted as teachers from an external urban and mestizo world, whereas the masses were students from a rural indigenous realm. The intention, observers claimed, was not to empower the masses; the Shining Path wanted to herd, not lead. Such tight centralization of power brought several advantages that allowed the organization to flourish. It eliminated the divisive ideological and personal tendencies that had ripped the 1960s guerrilla movements apart. A vertical hierarchy and carefully designed autonomous cell structure provided for efficient actions and for tight security that proved very difficult for the government to penetrate. These strengths, however, were also weaknesses. Its authoritarian nature and failure to empower the people at the grassroots level alienated potential supporters and ultimately limited its strength.

Interestingly, as Carol Andreas (1991) notes, the Shining Path provided a special appeal to women, and many of their leaders were women. The feminine attraction to the movement dates from the beginnings of the Shining Path. In a 1975 essay, leader Abimael Guzmán explained this appeal to women by pointing out that Mariátegui had argued that an analysis of society must begin at its base with a study of the role of women and family structures. Women have traditionally played a significant role in public and political life in the Andes, and perhaps 35 percent of the Shining Path's leaders were women (Castro 1994, 219). Part of the appeal of the organization was that it provided adherents with a faith and identity, as well as providing women with a protected space in which they knew that they would not face humiliation or discrimination for being poor, Indian, and female. The Shining Path also drew on the desire of people for progress, as well as their personal ambitions for power and a place in a new and emerging society. Furthermore, it provided an opportunity and mechanism for settling scores in a traditional society, including challenging the abuse from husbands, fathers, and other male-dominated authority structures. It also constituted a challenge to leftist political parties and mass organizations that mouthed women's rights but largely failed to do anything to follow through. In this way, the Shining Path became an effective vehicle for women to counter the forces that oppressed them. Also, as Andras noted, women were often willing to risk more when in an oppressive society, since they had less to lose.

At first the Shining Path gained a certain amount of sympathy, both within Peru and internationally, because of its apparent idealism and stance in behalf of the marginalized and impoverished rural masses. Locally, the promise of social mobility appeared to attract poor but aspiring peasants and students to the guerrilla ranks as they sought to position themselves more favorably in a new emerging order. As the guerrilla group grew larger, its brutal tactics and dogmatic philosophy became more apparent. It made what others would see as serious tactical mistakes, including imposing control over agricultural harvesting and commerce, placing young people in control of communities in which elders traditionally had assumed leadership roles, and executing violators of social norms rather than using lesser and more appropriate punishments. All of this was part of imposing a rigid vertical control. As Orin Starn (1999) has described in his book *Nightwatch,* rural communities began to approach

the military to ask for arms to protect themselves from guerrilla attacks. The resulting vigilant groups, known as *rondas campesinas* (rural patrols), began cooperating with the military and were largely responsible for the decline in the Shining Path's presence in the highlands. Communities that refused to join the *rondas* found themselves squeezed between the guerrillas and the military, under suspicion from both of collaboration with the other.

In that context, the victory of Alán García in the 1985 elections appeared to present a fresh alternative. García, from the center-left American Popular Revolutionary Party (APRA) party, had campaigned on a populist, reformist program that defended Velasco's agrarian and industrial reforms while rejecting Belaúnde's free market policies. Initial economic gains led to very high approval ratings, but then increasing problems—including cleavages between the indigenous rural highlands and the more prosperous mestizo urban coast—led to growing tension. Human rights groups also condemned the excesses of his repressive security forces attempting to end the Shining Path insurgency. From the beginning, the Shining Path attacked the García government for pursing reformist rather than revolutionary goals. A military attack on Shining Path cellblocks in three Lima jails that killed hundreds of inmates in 1986 appeared to mark a turning point in García's strategy. Furthermore, the growing war made leftist activists from his APRA party targets for the guerrillas, which in turn led to an increase in military atrocities. García's popular support plummeted, and he left office as one of the most disliked politicians in Peru's history. By the late 1980s, Peru led the world in disappearances and security force massacres, arguably forcing peasants into the arms of the Shining Path.

Many of the Shining Path's most virulent attacks were reserved for social movements that they criticized for being part of a reformist and revisionist Left. They denounced leftist politicians as part of the old order, and insisted that everyone follow their line. As a result, the Shining Path became divorced from growth on the Left, and remained disconnected from other popular organizations including political parties, labor unions, and neighborhood associations. The Shining Path's ideological rigidity and refusal to enter into alliances with other groups were perhaps its greatest weaknesses. Representative of the Shining Path's rejection of other social movements was the execution of María Elena Moyano in Villa El Salvador in 1992. She had organized community soup kitchens and called for an end both to Shining Path's violence and to government repression. The guerrilla leadership accused her of following a reformist line rather than seeking a radical change in society. Blowing up her body with dynamite in front of her family was not intended to eliminate a competitor so much as to intimidate and place fear in those who might challenge the Shining Path's dominance. These ideological conflicts and the Shining Path's drive to exercise

Women who fled the violence of the Shining Path insurgency use a textile style called "arpillera" to depict their lives "yesterday" in the conflictive zone of Ayacucho and "today" in a poor settlement near Lima. (Photo by Marc Becker)

absolute control over the revolution led to a weakening of grassroots social movements and leftist political parties.

The Shining Path pursued a Maoist strategy of prolonged popular war that included laying siege to the city from the countryside, eventually bringing its war to poor shantytowns on Lima's periphery. By the early 1990s, car bombings of TV stations, military barracks, and banks; assaults on trucks; and the dynamiting of power lines had a real effect on the urban population. The Shining Path responded to an attack on its militants in Lima's Canto Grande high-security prison that killed about fifty of its followers with a bombing campaign against middle- and upper-class targets in the Lima suburb of Miraflores that further polarized an already tense situation. By 1992, the government had brought about half of the country under emergency rule. About 25,000 people had been killed in the conflict, most of them noncombatants. The war displaced about 250,000 peasants, and resulted in $24 billion in property damage. It appeared that, militarily, the Shining

Path could not take power, and that the government was incapable of destroying the movement. Nevertheless, given the Shining Path's ruthless dedication to the pursuit of its goal, eventual victory—even if it took a generation or a hundred years—seemed inevitable, to at least some observers.

IMPACTS

The inability of Alán García's government to solve persistent problems effectively brought an end to Peru's traditional political parties and led to the victory of Alberto Fujimori, an obscure agronomist and son of poor Japanese immigrants, in the 1990 election. Fujimori ran as a political outsider and populist who promised to address people's basic needs. Once in office, he implemented severe neo-liberal austerity measures known as "Fujishock," which removed consumer price subsidies and privatized public enterprises in an attempt to attract foreign capital. Facing frustration over political debates with congress, on April 5, 1992, he suspended the constitution and took dictatorial powers it what was called the "Fujicoup." His main goals were to end corruption and the Shining Path insurgency. At first he seemed to achieve neither objective.

On September 12, 1992, Fujimori scored a major victory with the capture of Abimael Guzmán and nineteen other Shining Path leaders, as well as key organizational records. The broadcast of pictures of Guzmán in a striped convict suit and in a tiger cage did much to collapse the aura around him. The Shining Path had been built as a cult of personality, but with its leader gone the movement was now decapitated. The tightly centralized control that had made the Shining Path so powerful now proved to be its undoing. More than anything else, Guzmán's arrest gave Fujimori a significant boost in public support. The situation in Peru had become increasingly desperate, and the country experienced a collective sigh of relief over the end of the war.

After the 1992 coup, Fujimori put in place a series of draconian anti-terrorist laws that sharply curtailed an accused person's right to a legal defense and fair trial. Anonymous military tribunals and other judicial abuses with 97 percent conviction rates not only helped collapse the Shining Path's support structures but also resulted in the imprisonment of many innocent people. Fujimori's amnesty program encouraged guerrillas to turn in their weapons and provide intelligence on the organization, which further eroded their significance as a military force. Fujimori's increased executive power and support for having defeated the Shining Path made possible his re-election in 1995. By 2000, however, abuses of power and corruption scandals led to Fujimori's fall from grace, resulting in his resignation and exile to Japan.

From jail, Guzmán called for an end to the armed struggle in 1993 and negotiated a peace agreement with the government. Most of his followers laid down their arms, but nevertheless, even after Guzmán's capture, Shining Path splinter groups, known as the *Sendero Rojo* (Red Path), continued to simmer. These small groups sought to continue the armed struggle, but they ceased to be a significant political threat to the Peruvian state. Nevertheless, it appeared that a low-level guerrilla war might drag on in isolated areas of Peru for years. In June 2003, guerrillas staged a large-scale attack against a gas pipeline that seemed to signal a re-emergence of the Shining Path.

In the aftermath of the war, Peru established a Truth and Reconciliation Commission to investigate wartime abuses. It discovered that, in keeping with the racial and social divisions in Peru, many of the abuses in rural areas had never been reported to the government. The commission discovered that more than 69,000 people had died in the conflict,

twice the highest previously reported number, most of them civilians, with a disproportionate number of rural and indigenous victims. It reported many acts of sexual violence during the conflict, with more than 80 percent of the crimes committed by government forces (Remón 2003, 4). A generous amnesty program permitted members of the security forces implicated in human rights abuses to escape punishment. Critics complained that the government was paying little attention to the commission's recommendations, such as paying reparations to victims of violence. After Alejandro Toledo was elected president in 2001, Peru continued to be governed in an authoritarian manner. Poverty, alienation, and the government's inability to address social issues meant that Peru faced conditions similar to those that had originally led to the Shining Path insurgency. Little had been resolved.

PEOPLE AND ORGANIZATIONS

Fujimori, Alberto (Born 1938)

Born in Lima in 1938, the son of Japanese immigrants, Fujimori was an agronomist; in the 1980s, he served as a dean at the Agrarian National University. In 1989, Fujimori founded the political party Cambio 90 and presented himself as an outsider candidate in the following year's presidential election. Through populist rhetoric he defeated the apparent frontrunner, writer Mario Vargas Llosa. Once in power, he implemented neo-liberal economic reforms and in 1992 closed down the congress and judiciary, assuming dictatorial powers. That same year he captured Shining Path leader Abimael Guzmán, effectively ending the guerrilla insurgency. While these victories won him temporary popular support, he achieved his successes through repressive measures and abuses of power that proved to be his eventual undoing. As more abuses and violations of human rights came out into the open, he was forced to resign in 2000 and went into exile in Japan.

García, Alán (Born 1949)

The president of Peru from 1985 to 1990, García initially appeared to present a new, refreshing, and youthful face to Peruvian politics. Elected as the candidate of the center-left American Popular Revolutionary Alliance Party (APRA), at thirty-five years of age he was the youngest president in Peru's history. A collapsing economy and failure to solve the Shining Path guerrilla insurgency, however, led to a rapid fall in his popularity, and he left office as one of the country's most disliked politicians.

Guzmán Abimael (Born 1934)

A philosophy professor at the National University of San Cristobal de Huamanga in the highland town of Ayacucho, Guzmán provided the defining ideology for the Shining Path, and effectively was the glue that held the group together. Under the nom de guerre of Presidente Gonzalo, he developed an "Andean Maoism" that was to be a beacon of world revolution.

Lagos, Edith (1963–1982)

A nineteen-year-old Shining Path leader who led a 1982 attack on a prison in Ayacucho where captured guerrillas were held. Police forces subsequently captured, tortured, and executed Lagos. Her funeral procession attracted 30,000 people, about half the population of Ayacucho, and represented a high point in the Shining Path's popularity. Lagos had joined the Shining Path at the age of sixteen; she represented the frustrated aspirations of highland peasants as well as the central role of women in the guerrilla struggle.

Maríategui, José Carlos (1894–1930)

Born on July 14, 1894, Mariátegui grew up on the outskirts of Lima. Because of a lack of financial resources and the need to support his family, he acquired only an eighth-grade education. Mariátegui entered the field of journalism and used it as a vehicle for expressing his political views. In 1924, Mariátegui lost his right leg, and he spent the rest of his life confined to a wheelchair. In spite of his failing health, Mariátegui increased the intensity of his efforts to organize a social revolution in Peru. His *Seven Interpretive Essays on Peruvian Reality* presented a brilliant analysis of Peruvian problems from a Marxist point of view. Mariátegui founded the Peruvian Socialist Party (PSP) in 1928 and served as its first secretary general. In 1929 the PSP launched the General Confederation of Peruvian Workers (CGTP), a Marxist-oriented trade union federation, as an effort by the party to organize the working class. Although the political party and labor confederation that he had helped to launch flourished, Mariátegui's health failed, and he died on April 16, 1930.

Movimiento Revolucionario Tupac Amaru (MRTA—Tupac Amaru Revolutionary Movement)

In 1984, radical-left organizations founded the Tupac Amaru Revolutionary Movement (MRTA). While never as large or effective as the Shining Path, some activists saw them as a more moderate organization that stressed the importance of working together with social organizations, including trade unions, worker and student groups, and peasants. The MRTA was most noted for a daring commando raid on the Japanese ambassador's residence in Lima on December 17, 1996. The raiders held seventy-two hostages for four months, until the military attacked the house and killed the MRTA guerrillas. Rather than collaborating with the MRTA, the Shining Path saw them as competitors and would occasionally attack their guerrilla positions.

Moyano, María Elena (1958–1992)

In February 1992, the Shining Path executed Moyano one day after she had organized a march in the poor Lima shantytown of Villa El Salvador, denouncing the Shining Path's violence. She had organized community soup kitchens and was head of the neighborhood *Vaso de Leche* ("glass of milk") program, which provided breakfast to impoverished children. The Shining Path attempted to use intimidation to eliminate social movements separate from their control.

Partido Comunista del Perú—Sendero Luminoso (Communist Party of Peru—Shining Path)

Commonly known as the Shining Path, this is a clandestine political organization founded by philosophy professor Abimael Guzmán in 1970 in the Peruvian highland city of Ayacucho. It launched the military phase of its "people's war" in 1980. Over the next twelve years it grew in strength until the time of the capture of Guzmán in 1992, which effectively brought the guerrilla insurgency to an end.

Rondas Campesinas

These were rural self-defense patrols that peasants first organized in the 1970s in northern Peru to stop cattle rustling. With the emergence of the Shining Path guerrilla movement, communities used this same structure to defend themselves from the insurgents' coercion and violence. The military found them to be an effective mechanism for creating "strategic hamlets" in their fight against the Shining Path. The government began to impose this type of social organization in other parts of Peru, arming peasants and forcing them to fight against the guerrillas.

Marc Becker

See Also Anarchism, Communism, and Socialism; Documentaries of Revolution: Guerrilla Warfare and Revolution

References and Further Readings

Andreas, Carol. 1991. "Women at War," *NACLA Report on the Americas* 24 (4) (December 1990–January 1991): 20–27, 38–39.

Béjar, Héctor. 1970. *Peru 1965: Notes on a Guerrilla Experience.* New York: Monthly Review.

Blanco, Hugo. 1972. *Land or Death: The Peasant Struggle in Peru.* New York: Pathfinder.

Castro, Daniel. 1994. "'War Is Our Daily Life': Women's Participation in Sendero Luminoso." Pp. 219–225 in *Confronting Change, Challenging Tradition: Women in Latin American History,* edited by Gertrude Matyoka Yeager. Wilmington, DE: Scholarly Resources.

Central Committee, Communist Party of Peru. 1985. "On the Shining Path of Mariátegui," *A World to Win* 2 (April): 46–51.

Degregori, Carlos Iván. 1990. *Ayacucho, 1969–1979 el surgimiento de Sendero Luminoso.* Lima: Instituto de Estudios Peruanos.

———. 1991. "A Dwarf Star," *NACLA Report on the Americas* 24 (4) (December 1990–January 1991): 10–16, 38.

———. 1997. "After the Fall of Abimael Guzmán: The Limits of Sendero Luminoso." Pp. 179–191 in *The Peruvian Labyrinth: Polity, Society, Economy,* edited by Maxwell A. Cameron and Philip Mauceri. University Park: Pennsylvania State University Press.

Gorriti Ellenbogen, Gustavo. 1999. *The Shining Path: A History of the Millenarian War in Peru.* Chapel Hill: University of North Carolina Press.

Guzmán, Abimael. 1975. *El marxismo, Mariátegui y el movimiento feminino.* Lima: Editorial Pedagógica Asencios.

Mariátegui, José Carlos. 1971. *Seven Interpretive Essays on Peruvian Reality.* Austin: University of Texas Press.

Moyano, María Elena. 2000. *The Autobiography of María Elena Moyano: The Life and Death of a Peruvian Activist.* Gainesville: University Press of Florida.

Palmer, David Scott, ed. 1994. *Shining Path of Peru.* 2nd edition. New York: St. Martin's.

Poole, Deborah, and Gerardo Rénique. 1992. *Peru: Time of Fear.* New York: Monthly Review.

Remón, Cecilia. 2003. "Never Let It Happen Again," *Latinamerica Press* 35 (18) (September 10): 3–4.

Starn, Orin. 1999. *Nightwatch: The Politics of Protest in the Andes.* Durham, NC: Duke University Press.

Stern, Peter A. 1995. *Sendero Luminoso: An Annotated Bibliography of the Shining Path Guerrilla Movement, 1980–1993.* SALALM Secretariat, General Library, University of New Mexico, Albuquerque.

Stern, Steve J., ed. 1998. *Shining and Other Paths: War and Society in Peru, 1980–1995.* Durham, NC: Duke University Press.

Philippine Huks and the New People's Army

CHRONOLOGY

1521–1571	Ferdinand Magellan reaches the islands now called the Philippines and claims them for the Spanish Crown. Spanish settlements founded; capital established in Manila.
1600s–1830s	Spanish rule the colony through governors-general, friar orders, and soldiers. Natives are appointed heads of villages and towns. Friars convert most to Catholicism. Occasional rural revolts by millenarian movements.
1834	Philippine ports are opened to world trade. Nascent Filipino bourgeoisie starts being educated in Europe.
1872	Spanish retaliate to Filipino soldiers' mutiny by garroting three native priests. Execution strengthens proto-nationalist sentiment.
1872–1882	Reformists lobby for Philippines to be made province of Spain, but assimilation is rejected by Spain.
1887	Banned anti-Spanish novel by Jose Rizal, *Noli Me Tangere,* becomes an underground sensation.
1892	Rizal founds *La Liga Filipina,* political and economic reform group; he is arrested days later. Andres Bonifacio founds revolutionary secret society, the Katipunan.
1896–1897	Katipunan launches revolution; ensuing crackdown results in many deaths, arrests, and deportations. Although not directly involved, Rizal is executed by colonial authorities. Bonifacio is executed by fellow Katipuñeros. Aguinaldo agrees to truce; goes into exile.
1898	Spain and United States at war; Spanish fleet is sunk in Manila Bay; Aguinaldo resumes revolution with promise of support from U.S. forces; lays siege to Manila. United States and Spain sign Treaty of Paris, handing Philippines to the U.S.; Spanish surrender to Americans.
1899	In January, revolutionaries found Malolos Republic.
	In February, fighting breaks out between Filipino and U.S. soldiers; bloody war follows.

1901–1930   Aguinaldo is captured on March 23, 1901. President Roosevelt declares end of war on July 4, 1902.

United States rules Philippines through appointed governors; establishes Philippine Assembly of Filipinos elected by partial suffrage.

1930–1932   Partido Komunista ng Pilipinas (PKP) is founded in Manila; Socialist Party of the Philippines is founded in rural Luzon. PKP is banned a year later.

1934–1935   U.S. Congress promises independence in ten years. Manuel Quezon is elected president of the Philippine Commonwealth.

1938   Socialist and Communist parties merge into a new PKP.

1942–1943   Japanese army invades Manila; after show of resistance, General Douglas MacArthur departs. PKP founds Hukbalahap, headed by Luis Taruc; President Quezon leaves for United States. Japanese establish puppet Philippine republic.

1944–1945   Quezon dies in the United States. MacArthur returns to Philippines; Japanese defeated in battle for Manila; MacArthur arrests and disarms Huk guerrillas.

1946–1950   Manuel Roxas becomes president of independent Philippines. Democratic Alliance wins seats in national congress but is not permitted to take them up. PKP reorganizes Hukbalahap into an army of national liberation and takes up armed struggle against government. Roxas declares the PKP illegal, appoints Ramon Magsaysay defense secretary.

1950–1954   Senior PKP leaders are arrested. Magsaysay is elected president; PKP splits, Taruc surrenders, insurgency fades.

1969   PKP breakaway group founds new Communist Party of the Philippines (CPP). Former Huk armed group becomes New People's Army. President Ferdinand

Marcos wins re-election but faces criticism from both radical nationalists and elite factions opposed to growing corruption.

1970–1972   Protests by students and workers increase. Marcos declares martial law. On September 22, Congress is shut down, along with news media. Subversive organizations are declared illegal; thousands arrested.

1975–1981   CPP-NPA builds guerrilla fronts in rural areas; cadres in urban areas build mass organizations. Movement becomes most important opposition to regime. Marcos's elite political rival, Benigno Aquino, is released from jail for medical treatment in the United States. Marcos suspends martial law but retains dictatorial powers. Radical and elite opposition boycotts national election, which Marcos wins through fraud.

1983–1985   Aquino returns to Philippines; is assassinated at Manila airport. Conservative opponents of Marcos regime start joining radicals in street protests; capital flight out of Philippines increases pressure on Marcos.

1985–1986   Marcos calls election; widow of Aquino declares candidacy for president. In February, both Aquino and Marcos declare victory; combination of military mutiny and mass protest forces Marcos to flee. Aquino is sworn in as president.

1987–1992   Aquino government restores formal democracy, but is subjected to several coup attempts. CPP-NPA enters into peace negotiations that eventually fail. Internal disagreements over strategy under new political conditions lead to CPP splits.

INTRODUCTION

The armed revolutions launched by the "old" and "new" Communist parties of the Philippines, in 1946 and 1969, respectively, were two separate but linked processes. Neither was ultimately successful, but both attempts were inspired and sustained by the effects of the mass poverty and inequality that still characterize Filipino society. While the

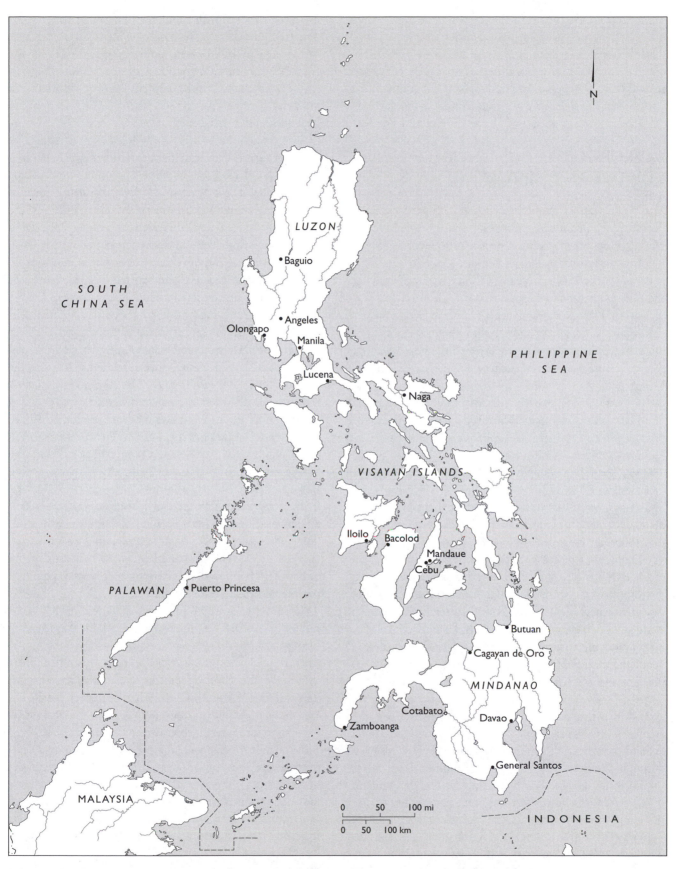

Republic of the Philippines showing the major islands of Luzon and Mindanao and large cities, including Manila.

Communists have thus far failed to win state power, they have contributed to the growth of a vibrant civil society contesting elite monopoly of power, and directly spawned several post-Communist organizations that strive peacefully for radical social change for the poor majority. The Communist Party's New People's Army remains a threat to the state.

BACKGROUND: CULTURE AND HISTORY

The population of the Philippines is around 80 million people, of whom 83 percent are Catholic, 9 percent Protestant, and 5 percent Muslim. The two official languages are Filipino (based on Tagalog) and English. Around 90 percent of the population speaks Tagalog/Filipino or one of twelve of the 171 indigenous languages.

The Philippines is a republican democracy with a bicameral congress, led by a president who is both titular and political head with strong powers. It remains a relatively poor country whose wealth is concentrated in few hands; literacy is high, but so are unemployment, underemployment, and the percentage of people who live below the official poverty line. Every year, an estimated 700,000 people leave the Philippines to work overseas; in 2003, more than 7 million overseas Filipino workers remitted more than U.S.$7.6 billion (Bangko Sentral ng Pilipinas 2004).

Colonized by Spain at the end of the sixteenth century, the Philippines was the first country in Asia to fight a war for independence against a European colonial power. Until the mid 1800s, the main economic activity was the Manila-Acapulco galleon trade, but when the Philippines was opened up to trade with other countries, a capitalist economy began to develop. A Filipino elite of large landowners and agricultural exporters emerged but was frustrated by remaining Spanish trade and other economic restrictions, lack of political representation, and treatment as social inferiors. Educated in Spain and aware of political changes taking place in Europe in the nineteenth century, this elite formed organizations to try to win reforms from the colonial power.

Following Spain's failure to meet their demands, the emergent bourgeoisie joined with others, including workers and peasants, in a militant association calling for freedom for Filipinos. The Katipunan, founded by Andres Bonifacio, a petit-bourgeois inspired by the traditions of rural revolt, launched the revolution in 1896. After military setbacks, internal divisions (including the execution of Bonifacio by Emilio Aguinaldo's faction), and exile, the revolutionaries waged war again in 1898 with a promise of support from the United States, then at war with Spain. The revolutionaries had all but routed the Spanish when they inaugurated Asia's first democratic republic in January 1899.

However, in a deal with Spain, the Philippines was handed over to the Americans, who, having betrayed the republicans, fought a brutal war of suppression against them; the country became a colony once again. Both of the Communist-led rebellions of the twentieth century claimed to be pursuing the successful conclusion to the revolution launched by the Katipunan.

U.S. colonial authorities suppressed radical nationalist sentiment and encouraged the veneration of Jose Rizal, a reformer who had not joined the revolution but nevertheless was executed by the Spanish. Under a regime of so-called benevolent assimilation the Americans set out to "tutor" the Filipinos and create a nation in their own image that would one day be ready for self-government. Residual anti-colonial sentiment among Filipino elites evaporated as they took up positions in new local and national government structures, and participated in a growing economy. A series of treaties and agreements giving favorable U.S. market access to Filipino exporters, especially of primary products such as sugar, and giving the United States stable military bases in the Pacific, became known as the "special relations" between the United States and the Philippines. Unlike in post-war Japan, the United States never implemented a land reform program in the Philippines; large haciendas were left intact, land grabbing became common, and thus ownership became even more concentrated in elite hands. From the early 1900s to the outbreak of World War II, the percentage of farmers who were tenants increased from around 16 percent to 35 percent; in the rice-growing provinces of central Luzon, the percentage was much higher (Putzel 1992, 55). Moreover, the population of those provinces nearly doubled in the same period (Kerkvliet 1977, 17–18). Land reform was a major demand of both the Huk and CPP-NPA movements, and remains a central political issue today.

In 1930, the Partido Komunista ng Pilipinas (PKP, Communist Party of the Philippines) was established by Crisanto Evangelista, on the strength of already organized urban workers, who were numerically dominant in both membership and leadership. Around the same time, the Socialist Party (SP) was formed by Pedro Abad Santos, one of the few from the landowning class ever to speak in the interests of the rural poor, who were the constituents of the SP. In 1938 the PKP and the SP merged, creating a party now dominated numerically by poor peasants but dominated by intellectuals in its leadership. Although the new PKP built up mass followings among both workers and peasants in Manila and central Luzon, its social base remained unrepresented in state political structures. Mainstream Filipino political parties have always been divided by clan affiliations and personal loyalties rather than ideology, and they are almost completely dominated by the wealthiest, most powerful families. Only in recent years, with some changes to the electoral system, has this control of power begun to be challenged, albeit in a limited way (Hutchcroft and Rocamora 2003).

In December 1941, the Japanese invaded the Philippines. After a few months of fighting on Bataan Peninsula and Corregidor Island, General Douglas MacArthur, commander of the U.S. Armed Forces in the Far East (USAFFE), retreated, and President Quezon and his party were secretly evacuated, to form the Commonwealth government in exile. The ensuing Japanese occupation sparked a war of resistance by USAFFE units left behind, and by bands of guerrilla fighters, the largest of which was the Hukbo ng Bayan Laban sa Hapon (People's Army Against the Japanese: the Hukbalahap, or Huks for short). While the Huks and others resisted, the elites mostly decided upon pragmatic collaboration. Jose Laurel was made the president of the "independent" Second Republic, established in October 1943 (Agoncillo and Alfonso 1967, 465). When the Japanese were defeated and the Commonwealth government returned—with Sergio Osmeña at its head after Quezon's death in exile—Laurel was interned, but along with other high-level collaborators was granted amnesty in 1947 (Steinberg 1967, 162).

CONTEXT AND PROCESS OF REVOLUTION

The Hukbalahap was established by the merged Socialist and Communist parties in line with the anti-Fascist popular front policy of the Third Communist International. It became "the largest, strongest and most ferocious" resistance force in Luzon (Nemenzo 1984, 72). In addition to attacking Japanese, the Hukbalahap also formed clandestine village government structures, staffed by locals, called the Barrio ["village"] United Defense Corps (BUDC). The BUDC recruited fighters, collected supplies for Huk units, adjudicated disputes, and organized the collection, distribution, and price control of rice that was kept hidden from the Japanese and from landlords, many of whom had fled the provinces for Manila. After liberation, however, the landowners returned, expecting farm relations to revert to their pre-war state, and to recoup wartime losses (Kerkvliet 1977, 119–120).

While elite collaborators went unpunished, Huk fighters immediately met suspicion and violent discrimination. Seeing the Hukbalahap as a political threat, MacArthur's Counter Intelligence Corps and USAFFE units disarmed many Huks; he refused recognition as legitimate anti-Japanese guerrillas to all but one Huk unit (rendering them ineligible for U.S. veterans' benefits); broke up BUDC structures; and arrested a number of leaders, including Commander-in-Chief Luis Taruc (Lachica 1971, 116–117). Nevertheless, the PKP and its mass organizations tried to play a peaceful role in post-war politics.

In July 1945 the PKP initiated the formation of the Democratic Alliance (DA), a coalition united around demands for immediate independence for the Philippines, removal of collaborators from positions of influence, economic reforms, civil liberties, and support for all former guerrilla fighters (Steinberg 1967, 139–140). When national independence was promised for July 1946, the DA put up candidates in the coming election. Although their preferred presidential candidate, Osmeña, lost to the more pro-U.S. Manuel Roxas, six of the DA won lower house seats, including Taruc and Jesus Lava, a PKP leader. However, the congress refused to allow the winners to take their seats. This was one factor—another was the growth of private armies raised by landowners—that led to the Hukbalahap disinterring its guns and taking up armed struggle against the Philippine government.

In March 1948, President Roxas declared the Hukbalahap illegal and ordered the military police (and later, the Philippine constabulary) to defeat them. After Roxas's death and some Huk military victories, his successor, Elpidio Quirino, invited the PKP to peace negotiations, but they failed. Subsequently, the PKP reorganized the Hukbalahap into the Hukbong Mapagpalaya ng Bayan (People's Liberation Army, HMB, or Huks). In January 1950, on the basis of PKP leader Jose Lava's analysis that there was a "revolutionary situation" in the country, the armed struggle was intensified with a view to taking power in two years (Nemenzo 1984, 73). By the end of the year, Huk numbers were reportedly up to almost 13,000 armed fighters, and around 50,000 PKP members and active supporters. But the PKP/HMB now faced an ambitious and popular secretary of defense, Ramon Magsaysay, who, with the support of the Joint U.S. Military Assistance Group, used the reorganized Philippine army to fight the guerrillas while the CIA assisted with anti-Communist "psychological warfare" (Schirmer and Shalom 1987, 115–116). While the PKP neglected political organizing to focus on military actions, Magsaysay adopted tactics of "attraction," including talk of land reform and an amnesty and resettlement program, to undermine support for the rebels.

In late 1950, Jesus Lava and other senior PKP members were captured along with numerous party documents. Consequently, the Huks endured even greater losses, and the PKP began to split over the escalated military strategy. Taruc and others who had never been convinced that there was a revolutionary situation (and certainly not outside Luzon) either left or were expelled from the PKP. In 1954, Taruc surrendered to President Magsaysay, compounding Huk demoralization. By the end of that year, the rebellion was substantially over.

In 1957, the Anti-Subversion Law declared that membership in the PKP or its "mass organizations" would attract severe penalties, so for the next few years the PKP kept a low profile, even encouraging its members to surrender and take

Luis Taruc (holding newspaper), rebel leader of the Huks in the Philippines, poses with other other peasant militants in an undated photograph. (AFP/Getty Images)

up amnesty offers (Nemenzo 1984, 74). When world events and the state of the nation began to politicize a new generation of young Filipinos, the PKP was only just beginning to revitalize itself.

THE NEW COMMUNIST PARTY AND THE NEW PEOPLE'S ARMY

In 1962, a young scholar and activist, Jose Maria Sison, was invited to join the PKP. A new wave of nationalism was rising, especially on university campuses. Believing the PKP ideologically and organizationally incapable of leading the new generation of anti-imperialists, Sison wrote a report of the party's failures, especially under the leadership of the Lava brothers, and urged it to rebuild on the basis of revolutionary "Mao Tse Tung Thought." The report was rejected, and some months later, Sison was out of the party; he

says he resigned, but the PKP claims he was expelled (Weekley 2001, 25–26).

In December 1969, Sison and twelve others "re-established" the Communist Party of the Philippines (CPP) to pursue "genuine national democracy" against the forces of "imperialism, feudalism and bureaucrat capitalism." They would do so via Mao's strategy of "protracted people's war," in which they would "encircle the cities from the countryside" (ibid.). A small band of Huk fighters still active in central Luzon, led by Bernabe Buscayno (aka Kumander Dante), agreed to join the CPP, and in March 1969, the New People's Army (NPA) was officially established. Later, the CPP founded the National Democratic Front (NDF) to assemble broad popular support for the revolution, but it was never as successful as either the CPP or the NPA: the insistence that members be committed to the primacy of armed struggle kept non-Communist allies away.

While the CPP-NPA was emerging, President Ferdinand Marcos was preparing for re-election. The cost of the 1969 election contributed to an economic crisis that forced Marcos to ask for U.S. and International Monetary Fund assistance. Austerity measures followed, and Marcos began to face opposition from radicals and moderates alike demanding the closure of the U.S. bases and an end to Filipino involvement in the Vietnam War, constitutional reforms, improved wages and working conditions, and land reform. The population had grown; also, it was younger, more literate, and more urbanized, and unemployment was high. These factors combined with international developments—the war in Vietnam, the Cultural Revolution in China, the militant student movements across Europe and the United States—to generate what was known as the "parliament of the streets" (Nemenzo 1984, 83).

Despite growing criticism of his rule from so many sides, and a constitutional bar, Marcos was determined to serve a third term as president. Citing the combined threats of Communism and the Muslim insurgency in the south, Marcos declared martial law on December 23, 1972. All "subversive" organizations were banned; thousands were arrested, including Marcos's chief political rival, Senator Benigno Aquino; congress was suspended; the news media was shut down; and many businesses owned by Marcos's rivals were taken over and given to his cronies.

The CPP had anticipated martial law and was better prepared than most organizations to deal with it. Members immediately went underground, and many fled to the countryside. The party's primary task was to create guerrilla fronts in rural areas, and by 1976 fifteen fronts had been established across the country; twenty years later, there were fifty-nine. The NPA gained favor among peasants for activities such as punishing and frightening off their enemies, and helping them to increase their harvest shares (Chapman 1988, 127–129). Although the urban working class (proletariat) is officially the vanguard of the revolution, the peasantry, or rural masses, always provided the greatest number of CPP members, followed by urban workers, then students and other intellectuals. By the end of the decade the CPP claimed 30,000 members, and the NPA numbered up to 24,000 regulars and part-timers, not all of whom were CPP members (Weekley 2001, 92). This was achieved without real assistance from external sources, and also despite the arrests in 1977 of many leading cadres, including Sison, who remained a prisoner until 1987.

Partly because there was no other substantial organized opposition force, many thousands of people supported what became known as the "national democratic movement"—that is, the collection of groups associated with the aims of the CPP-NPA, but not all of whose members were also CPP members. Although Marcos had implemented a land reform program (albeit a very limited one), and momentarily re-established order, the revolutionary movement grew. During his

dictatorship, human rights abuses increased; corruption grew to dramatic proportions, particularly by the ruling family and its cronies; the economy shrank while national debt skyrocketed; and non-Communist opposition was weak. The leading position of the national democratic movement began to be challenged only when Aquino, who had been living in exile in the United States since 1980, returned to the Philippines and was assassinated at the airport by elements within the regime. That was the final straw for those elites not aligned with Marcos; they began to join the radicals in street protests.

Beset by personal illness and a flight of capital, and stripped of political legitimacy, Marcos called another election, for February 1986. The CPP announced that the national democratic movement would boycott the election, although the elite and non-Communist opposition had agreed to support Aquino's widow, Corazon, to run against him. When the unofficial election watchdog declared Aquino the winner but Marcos refused to step down, a combination of a mutiny by reform elements of the AFP (Armed Forces of the Philippines) and popular protest—referred to as the "People Power" revolution—finally forced him to flee in a U.S. aircraft to Hawaii, where he died in 1989.

Aquino's ascendancy spelled the end of the CPP's leadership of Left opposition in the Philippines. The decision to boycott the election left it isolated from former associates and with less political bargaining power vis-à-vis the new government than it might have had otherwise. Internal disagreements about the relevance of the protracted people's war strategy in the new circumstances developed into serious divisions, and in 1992, the CPP-NPA-NDF began to split. While Communist guerrillas remain a potent force among disenfranchised rural populations and a thorn in the side of government, the armed struggle is no longer fought by a united party, but rather by several different groups of Communists, who are also fighting each other. Thousands of former Communists turned away from armed struggle, and many took up active roles in the legal political arena.

IMPACTS

Neither the Huks of the late 1940s–early 1950s, nor the CPP-NPA guerrillas and activists of the 1970s–1980s succeeded in overthrowing the Philippine state. However, they enduringly politicized the problems of unequal social relations between the rich and powerful, and the poor and weak. The Huk rebellion left a legacy of militant action among the peasantry of central Luzon that later Communists built upon. While political power, land ownership, and national wealth remained highly concentrated in elite hands, Communists contested the prevailing economic and political order, keeping alive a discourse of opposition.

During the Marcos era, CPP-NPA cadres brought to the world's attention the human rights abuses of martial law, and by being the first, most consistent, and most militant of the dictator's opponents, laid the groundwork for the People Power uprising, even if they did not participate in it directly. Communist cadres established hundreds of unions and political groups among workers and the urban poor, which continue to lobby for improved lives for the majority of Filipinos. They established the first national federation of independent trade unions, which remains a substantial player in the trade union movement. Inasmuch as the party viewed the peasantry as the main force in the armed struggle and therefore too important to be involved in reform politics, no similar peasant/rural worker organization was built.

The CPP-NPA was also responsible for some serious abuses of its own cadres in the 1980s, including the deaths of hundreds of suspected spies (Weekley 2001, 102–103). Only now are these purges being discussed openly, and those affected are debating how the mistakes should be acknowledged and atoned for.

The CPP-NPA was crucial to the development of a large, sophisticated network of mass organizations, giving the Philippines one of the world's liveliest civil society sectors. Not only was the CPP responsible for breaking the political silence imposed by martial law, thereby showing that a regime is not unassailable, but, in addition, it has provided a great deal of the analytical, organizational, and leadership skills, and political experience, of this civil society. Cadres who left the CPP in the 1990s have provided the non-government organization sector with many of its most able leaders.

After the downfall of the dictatorship, Aquino came under a great deal of pressure from this politicized civil society not simply to restore pre–martial law political structures but also to improve the opportunities of the poor to partake in political and economic life. One of the legacies of her rule that has the potential to do so is the Local Government Code, which devolves some financial power to local governments and increases the potential for nontraditional political actors to participate in decisionmaking (Hutchcroft and Rocamora 2003, 279). Nongovernmental organizations and small political groups are now focusing on trying to effect change at the local government level.

The other main legacy of the Aquino government that may increase participation by marginalized social classes is the party-list system. This system reserves up to 20 percent of congressional seats to be elected according to a preferential system for small parties that are supposed to speak for the marginalized and underrepresented. (The reserved seats were first put aside by Marcos, who filled them by appointment.) For every 2 percent of the vote received, a party gains one seat, but no party may gain more than three seats. While the system is extremely limited, it has given Left and other nontraditional organizations in the Philippines their first real chance to participate in national electoral politics. In the 2004 elections, left-wing groups collectively received nearly 30 percent of the party-list vote, winning ten of the twenty-four party-list seats. Groups closely linked to the CPP won six of those seats, even though the party has long eschewed pursuit of its goals through electoral participation, and still does not see elections as a significant arena for political struggle.

PEOPLE AND ORGANIZATIONS

Abad Santos, Pedro (1857–1945)

Coming from a wealthy Luzon landowning family, Abad Santos founded the Socialist Party to fight for the rights of the poor agricultural workers of Luzon. He studied some Marxist texts, and the Socialist Party was the first rural organization that both followed a specific program and was prepared to use violent means to achieve its goals.

Aquino, Benigno, Jr. (1932–1983)

Born into a wealthy political family, "Ninoy" Aquino was a mayor by age twenty-two, then provincial governor, and elected senator in 1967. He was arrested and imprisoned by Marcos, who saw him as his main political rival. He was allowed to fly to the United States for medical treatment in 1980. Upon returning to the Philippines in August 1983, he was shot dead at the airport by an unidentified assassin.

Aquino, Corazon (Born 1933)

"Cory" Aquino is also from a wealthy family; she entered politics in her own right after the assassination of her husband, Benigno. Persuaded to run against Marcos in the 1986 election, she campaigned to wide popular acclaim. When Marcos refused to acknowledge defeat, she led a mass protest to support a military mutiny, whose leaders had agreed to recognize her claim to the presidency. She is remembered for restoring formal democratic rule, although she achieved little else.

Armed Forces of the Philippines (AFP)

The Philippine army, navy (including Coast Guard and Marine Corps), and air force. Used to fight the CPP-NPA as well as the Moro National Liberation Front (MNLF). From a total of some 60,000 personnel in 1972, the AFP was expanded to 155,000 by 1985; the percentage of the national budget that went to the AFP more than doubled during the same period.

Buscayno, Bernabe (Born 1943), also known as Ka, or Kumander Dante

Son of a poor tenant farmer who had fought in both the Hukbalahap and the HMB, Buscayno was recruited into the Huks at a young age. A full-time revolutionary by age twenty-one, he rose to district commander but became disillusioned by his leader's corruption. He joined his band of guerrillas to the newly formed CPP in 1969, in return for representation on the Central Committee; he served as head of the New People's Army until 1986.

Communist Party of the Philippines (CPP)

The CPP was established, or re-established, in 1969 by a breakaway group from the old PKP that adopted a Maoist revolutionary strategy of surrounding the cities from the countryside with a people's army (the NPA). It grew rapidly across the country during the Marcos martial law years to become a major threat to state power by the mid 1980s. Since the ascendancy of civilian government in 1986, its presence has waned but not disappeared.

Democratic Alliance

A short-lived coalition of radicals and liberals established in 1946 to contest the elections for the first Philippine congress. Members included the PKP and the Civil Liberties Union of the Philippines. Six of its members won seats in the lower house, but they were refused permission to take up their positions by a government fearful of their radical stances.

Hukbo ng Bayan Laban sa Hapon (People's Army Against the Japanese—the Hukbalahap)

Established by the PKP in 1942 to resist the Japanese occupation, the Hukbalahap was led by Luis Taruc, member of the PKP (formerly of the Socialist Party). They fought the Japanese, punished collaborators, and set up local political structures to govern poor rural communities. They were reputed to be the boldest and fiercest of the guerrilla groups during World War II.

Hukbong Mapagpalaya ng Bayan (People's Liberation Army—HMB)

Formerly the Hukbalahap, which was reorganized in 1948 following the PKP decision to take up arms against the Philippine government. The HMB rebellion was beaten by a combination of its own strategic mistakes (chiefly, a focus on military means to the detriment of political activity) during a bloody war to suppress them, and the popularity of the defense secretary, then president, Ramon Magsaysay.

Lava Brothers Vincente (1894–1949), Jose (1912–2000), and Jesus (1914–2003)

The Lava brothers were highly educated men who successively headed the PKP from 1942 to 1964. Jose Lava is held responsible for the failed "quick military victory strategy" of 1948–1954 that was premised on the belief that a revolutionary situation existed in the country.

MacArthur, Douglas (1880–1964)

General MacArthur was military adviser to President Quezon and later commander in chief of the U.S. Armed Forces in the Far East. He fled the country after the Japanese invasion, declaring, "I shall return." He returned for the liberation in 1945 and helped to restore pre-war political arrangements.

Magsaysay, Ramon (1907–1957)

Secretary of defense under presidents Roxas then Quirino, 1950–1953, Magsaysay was responsible for defeating the Huk Rebellion. Known as "the Huk killer," he was a popular politician, one of the first in the Philippines to describe himself as a man of the people. He won the 1953 presidential election but died in an airplane accident in 1957.

Marcos, Ferdinand E. (1917–1989)

Born in northern Luzon and trained as a lawyer, Marcos was first elected to the lower house in 1949, then to the senate in 1959. He became president in 1965, won re-election in 1969, and declared martial law in 1972 in order to remain in office. Under his rule, thousands were killed, tortured, or imprisoned; businesses were sequestered and distributed to his cronies; the national debt increased vastly; and the Marcos family corruptly accumulated millions of dollars. He was overthrown in 1986 through the People Power uprising.

National Democratic Movement

This term is used to describe the collective groups and activists of the martial law and post–martial law period who supported the aims of the CPP for "genuine national democracy," but not all of whom were members of the CPP, NDF, or NPA. National democrats, or "nat dems," distinguished themselves from social democrats and liberal democrats.

New People's Army (NPA)

The NPA is the military wing of the Communist Party of the Philippines, established in 1969 from the remnants of a former Huk guerrilla group of Tarlac and Luzon, led by Bernabe Buscayno. In line with a Maoist revolutionary strategy, the NPA is made up chiefly of peasants and rural workers; it is both a military and a political force in the countryside, and is supported by "the people." At its height in the mid 1980s, the NPA numbered around 24,000 fighters and had established guerrilla fronts in nearly every province.

Partido Komunista ng Pilipinas

The first Communist party established in the Philippines, in 1930, with advice and assistance from the Communist International, local Chinese Communists in the Philippines, and the Communist Party of the United States. Its members were predominantly workers until it merged with the Socialist Party in 1938. The PKP went into decline after the Huk Rebellion was defeated in the early 1950s, and was later marginalized by the new CPP, established by breakaway members in 1969.

Quezon, Manuel (1878–1944)

Quezon fought in the 1896 Revolution and later entered politics. The top political figure for decades, Quezon became the president of the Philippine Commonwealth in 1935 but fled the country when the Japanese invaded, forming the government in exile. He died in the United States of tuberculosis.

Taruc, Luis (1913–2005)

Taruc came from a peasant family in central Luzon. He joined the Socialist Party, later merged with the PKP, and was appointed military head of the Hukbalahap. He was one of the

Democratic Alliance candidates elected to the congress in 1946 but who were not permitted to take up their seats. In 1954, he surrendered to President Magsaysay and was imprisoned. After his release, he continued to lobby for the rights of Hukbalahap war veterans.

Kathleen Weekley

See Also Guerrilla Warfare and Revolution; Philippine Independence Revolution and Wars; Philippine Muslim Separatist Rebellions; Philippines: The 'People Power' Revolution of 1986; War and Revolution

References and Further Readings
Agoncillo, Teodoro, and Oscar Alfonso. 1967. *History of the Filipino People.* Quezon City: Malaya.
Bangko Sentral ng Pilipinas. 2004. "Overseas Workers' Remittances by Country and by Type of Worker." http://www.bsp.gov.ph/statistics/sefi/ofw.htm (accessed January 10, 2004).
Chapman, William. 1988. *Inside the Philippine Revolution: The New People's Army and Its Struggle for Power.* London: I. B. Tauris.
Cullather, Nick. 1994. *Illusions of Influence: The Political Economy of United States–Philippines Relations, 1942–1960.* Stanford, CA: Stanford University Press.
Hutchcroft, Paul, and Joel Rocamora. 2003. "Strong Demands and Weak Institutions: The Origins of the Democratic Deficit in the Philippines." *Journal of East Asian Studies* 3: 259–292.
Kerkvliet, Benedict. 1977. *The Huk Rebellion: A Study of Peasant Revolt in the Philippines.* Berkeley: University of California Press.
Lachica, Eduardo. 1971. *Huk. Philippine Agrarian Society in Revolt.* Manila: Solidaridad.
Nemenzo, Francisco. 1984. "Rectification Process in the Philippine Communist Movement." Pp. 71–105 in *Armed Communist Movements in Southeast Asia,* edited by Joo-Jock Lim and S. Vani. Singapore: Institute of Southeast Asian Studies.
Putzel, James. 1992. *A Captive Land: The Politics of Agrarian Reform in the Philippines.* Quezon City: Ateneo University Press.
Schirmer, Daniel B., and Stephen Rosskamm Shalom, eds. 1987. *The Philippines Reader: A History of Colonialism, Neocolonialism, Dictatorship, and Resistance.* Boston: Southend.
Steinberg, David J. 1967. Philippine Collaboration in World War II. Ann Arbor, MI: University of Michigan Press.
Weekley, Kathleen. 2001. *The Communist Party of the Philippines 1968–1993: A Story of Its Theory and Practice.* Quezon City: University of the Philippines Press.

Philippine Independence Revolution and Wars

CHRONOLOGY

1570   Founding of Manila. The first galleon of silver and gold to exchange for Chinese goods arrives the following year. The profitable annual exchange continues until 1815 and shapes the economic and religious life of the colony.

1840s and 1850s	Opening of the country to commercial export agriculture and the rise of the colony's Chinese mestizos and elite Filipinos.
1872	Spanish friars use a January mutiny of Filipino soldiers at the Cavite Province naval yard on Manila Bay to charge three prominent native priests with sedition. The arrest, trial, and execution of Frs. Jose Burgos, Mariano Gomez, and Jacinto Zamora outrage Filipinos and inspire a new generation of nationalist youth.
1880s and 1890s	Filipinos and Filipino-Chinese mestizos studying in Europe begin a "Propaganda" Movement seeking reforms. The most prominent member is Dr. Jose Rizal. Their newspaper, *La Solidaridad* (1889–1895), filters back to the Philippines and shapes opinion.
1887	Rizal publishes his novel *Noli Me Tangere* (Latin for "Touch Me Not"), satirizing Spanish rule, attitudes, and greed. The book clarifies the colonial relationship and creates a national consciousness.
1887–1892	The government sides with the monastic orders versus Filipino tenants who claim that the friars usurped their lands to create large haciendas. The tenants are turned out by Spanish troops. Rizal's family is among the ejected.
1891	Rizal's second novel, *El Filibusterismo* [*The Subversive*], considers violence, but ultimately opts for a reformist approach.
1892	In July, Rizal returns to the Philippines and founds a reform movement, La Liga Filipina. He is arrested days later and the Liga dies. Liga member Andres Bonifacio forms a secret society, the Katipunan, dedicated to violent revolution.
1892–1896	The Katipunan grows rapidly to tens of thousands of members in Manila and neighboring provinces. It also has a women's branch and newspaper.
1896	On August 19, a member reveals the Katipunan's existence to a friar, and the government soon begins a roundup of members.
	On August 26 at Balintawak, north of Manila, Bonifacio rallies his supporters, tears apart his tax *cedula* (a symbol of vassalage), and calls for independence.
	On August 30 at the battle of San Juan del Monte, the revolution starts with Spanish defenders repelling a rebel attack.
	On August 31 in Kawit, Cavite, Katipunan member Emilio Aguinaldo begins the revolution in his province.
	On November 11, Aguinaldo's forces defeat regular Spanish troops.
	In December, Bonifacio's forces suffer a number of defeats in Manila. He retreats to Cavite and joins Aguinaldo.
	On December 30, Rizal is executed on Manila's fashionable promenade, the Luneta. His death is a colossal Spanish blunder. Filipinos who previously did not support violence now commit themselves to the struggle.
1897	February–April, Spain launches a number of successful military advances into Cavite.
	On March 22, a stormy meeting in Tejeros, Cavite, results in Aguinaldo assuming leadership of the revolution. After an engagement with Aguinaldo's forces, Bonifacio and his brothers are captured and tried for sedition. Aguinaldo signs the death warrant and Bonifacio is executed on May 10.
	In June, Aguinaldo and his government and army relocate to the mountains of Biaknabato in Bulacan Province north of the capital.
	On November 1, Declaration of the Republic of Biaknabato and the promulgation of its constitution.
	December 14–15, Governor Fernando Primo de Rivera's negotiations result in the Pact of Biaknabato. Aguinaldo and his principal

supporters accept exile in exchange for cash payments. Aguinaldo and twenty-five others sail for Hong Kong on the 27th; the money is used to purchase weapons.

1898   January–April in the Philippines, neither Spain nor the rebels keep their promises. Rebels who turned in their weapons are persecuted, while other rebels continue the insurgency, awaiting Aguinaldo's return.

On April 25, the United States declares war on Spain.

On May 1, Commodore George Dewey's squadron enters Manila Bay and destroys the Spanish fleet. Dewey's demands for the surrender of Manila are rebuffed. He turns to Filipino rebels for support.

On May 19, Aguinaldo arrives on the USS *McCulloch,* which Dewey dispatched to Hong Kong for him.

On May 24, Aguinaldo declares a dictatorial government to serve until independence can be won. He calls his people to arms. By the end of June, only isolated outposts on Luzon are still in Spanish hands. Manila's Fort Santiago is virtually surrounded.

On June 12, Aguinaldo declares the Philippines independent. His Declaration of Independence is based on the U.S. document. A new national flag is unfurled, and a new national anthem played. On the 18th, he issues a decree creating local and provincial governments.

On August 13, commanders of newly arrived U.S. troops and Spanish authorities conclude a secret agreement for a phony battle for Manila. The one-day battle gives the citadel to the United States, and Filipino soldiers are denied access. Relations between Aguinaldo's government and the United States deteriorate.

September 15: a constitutional congress of eighty-five representatives begins deliberations in Malolos, Bulacan, that conclude in late November. The new constitution creates a government with three branches, separates church and state, and guarantees basic freedoms.

On December 10, the Treaty of Paris awards the Philippines to the United States.

1899   On January 4, General Elwell Otis releases President William McKinley's proclamation of "benevolent assimilation." The next day, Aguinaldo issues a counter-proclamation, vigorously rejecting U.S. rule.

January 11–28, talks between General Otis and Aguinaldo's emissaries fail to reach an understanding.

On January 23, in Malolos, the Philippine Republic is proclaimed and President Emilio Aguinaldo inaugurated. The new government founds official newspapers and creates a school system, office of finance, departments of the army and navy, and sends diplomats to the United States, Europe, and Japan.

On February 2, another U.S. expedition to Cebu takes that island's capital as well.

On February 4, Private Robert Grayson shoots and kills a Filipino soldier at the bridge at San Juan del Monte, sparking the Philippine-American War.

February 5–March 31, U.S. troops repulse Filipino attacks in the heart of Manila, secure the city, and push north to capture Malolos. Aguinaldo retreats north to San Fernando, Pampanga.

On February 6, in reaction to reports of the outbreak of fighting, the U.S. Senate approves the Treaty of Paris and the acquisition of the Philippines.

On February 11, a U.S. expedition to Iloilo takes that Visayan island's capital.

On March 4, troops under General James F. Smith occupy Bacolod, Negros Occidental, with little opposition.

April 1–5, a further U.S. offensive northward results in the taking of San Fernando. Aguinaldo relocates to San Isidro, Nueva Ecija Province.

On April 2, the (Jacob G.) Schurman Philippine Commission appointed by McKinley to secure U.S. rule begins deliberations.

In April, U.S. forces complete the capture of Laguna Province, south of Manila.

May 19–August 20, General John C. Bates secures the Muslim archipelago west of Mindanao in the south by concluding a treaty with Sultan Jamalul Kiram II.

In October, U.S. forces take San Isidro; Aguinaldo retreats farther north.

On November 12, from his new headquarters in Bayambang, Pangasinan Province, Aguinaldo disbands the regular army and institutes guerrilla warfare. He creates a number of military zones under local commanders.

November 13–late December, Aguinaldo leaves Bayambang and retreats through northwest Luzon and the island's central Cordillera mountain range to Palanan, Isabela Province, in the remote northeast. His location remains secret throughout 1900 as he directs national resistance.

1900 In January, the islands of Samar, Leyte, Marinduque, and Masbate are secured by two separate U.S. expeditions. However, fighting on the first two islands continues until 1902.

January 20–March 27, another U.S. expedition secures the Bicol region, the long arm of Luzon that extends to the southeast. The local general, Vito Belarmino, continues resistance for another year.

In May, U.S. forces occupy the islands of Palawan and Calamianes.

On June 3, the Second Philippine Commission arrived, under William H. Taft, with legislative authority to create the colonial government.

On December 23, Dr. T. H. Pardo de Tavera founds the Federalista Party, used to attract Filipinos away from the revolution. Members are given positions in the new U.S. government.

1901 On January 7, fifty-seven "irreconcilable" Philippine rebels who refuse to take the oath of loyalty to the United States are exiled to Guam.

On January 8, a courier carrying messages from Aguinaldo is captured, revealing his location. General Arthur Funston initiates a plan to capture the rebel leader. He, four officers, and a contingent of loyal Philippine troops travel to Isabela.

On March 2, the (Senator John C.) Spooner Amendment to the army's annual appropriation's bill mandates civil government for the Philippines. Taft is proclaimed the first civil governor on July 4.

On March 23, Funston's contingent reaches Aguinaldo's camp. The Filipino soldiers pretend to be rebel reinforcements bringing captured Americans to Aguinaldo. Once in his presence, the U.S.-led party overpowers the rebel leader's guards, and Funston places Aguinaldo under arrest.

On April 1, Aguinaldo arrives in Manila and is received by General Arthur MacArthur. He takes the oath of allegiance to the United States. He later calls on his countrymen to cease fighting and accept U.S. rule. Many officers and men comply, but a significant number continue fighting, especially Vicente Lukban in Samar and Miguel Malvar in Batangas.

On August 23, the USS *Thomas* transport ship arrives with 540 young American teachers who teach English and help create a national school system.

On September 14, Vice President Theodore Roosevelt assumes the presidency after McKinley's assassination.

On September 28, General Lukban's troops surprise a U.S. contingent in Balangiga;

forty-eight defenders are killed, and only three escape.

1902   On February 27, General Vicente Lukban is captured.

On April 16, General Miguel Malvar is captured.

In May, Taft visits Rome for an audience with Pope Leo XIII regarding the U.S. purchase of friar lands. They are purchased in 1903 and resold to Filipino tenants on easy terms.

On July 4, President Theodore Roosevelt proclaims the Philippines pacified and an end to fighting with the rebel government. Thereafter, resistance by recalcitrant Filipino rebels is regarded as banditry.

INTRODUCTION

Philippine nationalists launched Asia's first anti-colonial revolution at the end of the nineteenth century. The movement was started by native Filipino and Chinese mestizo elites who challenged Spanish religious and secular rule that had dominated the country since 1570. The nationalist movement began as a reform effort led by Dr. Jose Rizal, but, because of Spanish intransigence, it evolved into a revolution led initially by Andres Bonifacio. His successor, Emilio Aguinaldo, fought Spain to a stalemate in 1896–1897; shortly afterward, the Spanish-American War of 1898 brought U.S. intervention. Despite declaring their independence and establishing a constitutional government, Filipino aspirations were crushed by the U.S. imperialist era's impulse for colonial possessions. The Philippine government's new army was unable to defend the country against the U.S. military assault (1899–1902) and inducements offered to captured revolutionary leaders to join the new colonial government. Tragically, the revolution was replaced by a colonial partnership based on dependency, the legacy which lingered even after independence in 1946.

BACKGROUND: CULTURE AND HISTORY

For more than two centuries, Spain's primary interest in the Philippines was as a transit point in an immensely profitable galleon trade with China. From 1571, a year after Manila's founding, until 1815, ships laden with silver and gold set out from Mexico for the journey to Manila, where the precious metals were exchanged for Chinese goods delivered by merchants from south China. The profit from the annual galleon's arrival was so great that it supported Manila's Spanish community and the colonial budget while enriching Madrid. From its earliest days, the capital hosted a substantial community of immigrant Chinese merchants, but their movements were severely circumscribed to Manila, where they were forced to live in specific areas of the city. These immigrants frequently married local women, and they and their progeny provided badly needed entrepreneurial skills. Meanwhile, the remainder of the archipelago was retained for political and strategic reasons and administered by a small number of Spanish civil and military officials, while Spanish missionary priests, the "friars," interacted with the local population. In a tight symbiotic relationship, the government subsidized the work of the friars, who, in turn, acted as local government overseers. This relationship suited Spanish needs while making the friars immensely powerful.

By the latter decades of the 1700s the arrival of free trader British merchants cut into Spain's dominance of the China market, while Chinese demand for silver dropped off considerably. Even before the galleon trade was officially ended, Spanish governor-generals in Manila made efforts to develop profitable export crops, and gradually the country's ports were opened to foreign merchants. In a further effort to keep the colony profitable, old restrictions were lifted for the colony's half-caste Chinese "mestizo" population, and they moved into the countryside in search of profitable ventures for international markets. By the 1840s and 1850s the country had begun to export substantial amounts of sugar, coffee, and hemp, largely as a result of efforts by this Chinese mestizo group and their local elite Filipino partners.

These economic developments laid the basis for the rise of a new elite who chafed under colonial restrictions and began to challenge Spain's suzerainty. The challenge was led by the sons of this new elite group and took two forms: entry into the priesthood, which posed an alternative to the Spanish friars, and a political critique directed by young students enrolled in Spanish and European universities. However, nationalism was sparked by a January 1872 failed mutiny by Filipino soldiers in the Cavite naval facility, south of Manila. In an effort to reverse Filipino gains in the priesthood, Spanish friars mounted specious charges of rebellion against three prominent Filipino priests, Frs. Jose Burgos, Mariano Gomez, and Jacinto Zamora. The priests were given a mock trial and garroted. That the Spaniards had so callously mistreated these respected Filipino priests outraged indigenous sensibilities and heightened antagonisms between the friars and the native priesthood.

The events of 1872 also reshaped the collective outlook of Filipinos studying in Europe. There, they discovered strong anti-clerical and liberal political movements that emerged in the wake of the Enlightenment. In the 1880s, the young students began to agitate for changes at home in what became known as the Propaganda Movement. The students consorted with sympathetic Europeans, gave numerous public speeches, and founded a newspaper, *La Solidaridad,* in 1889. Among the activist students, Dr. Jose Rizal stood out in his critical analysis of colonialism, as seen in his 1887 novel *Noli Me Tangere* [*Touch Me Not*]. Rizal's masterful expose of Spanish foibles, greed, and racism clarified the colonial relationship as nothing had previously. The novel reflected contemporaneous Philippine events in which tenants on friar haciendas were brutally evicted by government troops for attempting to establish their true ownership of the property. One of the tenant families was Rizal's. Copies of his novel and the group's newspaper were smuggled into the country and created a national consciousness. Rizal's second novel, *El Filibusterismo* [*The Subversive*], considered, but ultimately rejected, violent revolution, but that would not spare Rizal. In July 1892, Rizal returned to the Philippines and founded a reform society, La Liga Filipina, only to be arrested days later.

In the face of Spanish intolerance, a Liga member, Andres Bonifacio, immediately founded a new organization, the Katipunan, dedicated to violent revolution. Katipunan members soon built a secret society featuring blood oaths, passwords such as "Gomburza" (for the martyred priests Gomez, Burgos, and Zamora), a newspaper, and a women's auxiliary, while collecting arms for an uprising. After developing a leadership core, the Katipunan grew rapidly to tens of thousands of members and spread to provinces surrounding Manila.

A writer, physician, and patriot, Jose Rizal was perhaps the first Asian nationalist. His writing revealed the injustices he saw in the Philippines and so angered colonial officials that they banned his work and severely persecuted him. (Library of Congress)

CONTEXT AND PROCESS OF REVOLUTION

The Revolution Begins: Rising Up against Spain

The Katipunan's existence was betrayed to Spanish authorities on August 19, 1896, and arrests soon followed, nearly netting the society's leaders. Forced to begin the revolutionary struggle before enough arms had been collected, Bonifacio gathered his forces on the 26th at Balintawak, north of Manila, where he called for independence and in an act of symbolic defiance ripped his *cedula* tax card. Four days later, a contingent of Katipuneros unsuccessfully attacked Spanish troops in San Juan del Monte, starting the Philippine Revolution.

The following day, Emilio Aguinaldo of Kawit, Cavite, and fellow Katipunan members took the town and began the revolution in their province; other towns quickly joined. The revolution also spread to other provinces around Manila with Katipunan chapters, while Spain's governor, Ramon Blanco, seemed unable to respond. Only in Manila, where the Iberian defenders were entrenched, did Bonifacio suffer defeat in a series of engagements. Then, on November 11, Aguinaldo and his troops distinguished themselves by defeating Spanish regular troops sent to win back the province. By December, with the battle going badly in Manila, Bonifacio and his followers retreated to Cavite, where they were warmly welcomed.

On December 30, a Spanish firing squad ended the life of Dr. Jose Rizal. The reformer had been on his way to Cuba to serve in the Spanish army when he was intercepted and returned to Manila. If Manila's new governor, Camilo de Polavieja, thought that executing Rizal would end the revolution, he was mistaken. Now, even Filipinos who previously advocated moderation and reform supported armed struggle. Still, in early February 1897, a determined Spanish General Polavieja led an offensive into Cavite, where he overcame stiff resistance and achieved results by early March. Meanwhile, his offensive contributed to increasing tensions between Bonifacio and his hosts that broke out at a stormy March 22 meeting in Tejeros, Cavite. At the assembly, the Katipunan was formally abolished and a new revolutionary government formed; Bonifacio was given only a minor position, while Aguinaldo and his supporters gained dominance. Bonifacio rejected the results, stormed out of the meeting, and days later his group was attacked by Aguinaldo's men, resulting in Bonifacio's capture. He was charged with sedition, tried, and found guilty. After some hesitation, Aguinaldo signed his rival's death warrant, and the Katipunan's founder was executed on May 10.

By June, increasing Spanish pressure induced Aguinaldo to relocate his army and government to the relative safety of the mountainous area of Biaknabato in Bulacan Province, north of Manila, after an extended march around Manila that was completed by early July. The rebels resumed the offensive in September, while working on a constitution they completed by November 1. Meanwhile, Spain's new governor, Fernando Primo de Rivera, chose to confront the rebellion with diplomacy rather than arms. Aguinaldo also realized that a stalemate with Spain was unacceptable, and he was receptive to negotiations. As early as August a series of exchanges were begun, with Manila lawyer Pedro A. Paterno acting as intermediary; by mid December they succeeded, with the signing of the Pact of Biaknabato. Under the agreement, Aguinaldo and his advisers agreed to voluntary exile in Hong Kong in exchange for a series of cash payments, while individual fighters would be compensated for surrendered weapons.

On December 27, Aguinaldo and his men left for Hong Kong but did not give up the struggle. Upon reaching the British colony, the exiles formed the Hong Kong Junta, a reorganized revolutionary government, and deposited the Spanish money in a bank account for purchasing weapons. Meanwhile, local rebel commanders back home continued armed resistance around the country. Especially notable was the leadership of General Francisco Makabulos, who established a provisional revolutionary government based on a new constitution that he wrote. At the same time the Spaniards were just as unfaithful to the agreement, persecuting former rebels and failing to distribute all of the promised payments. As Filipino rebels and Spanish colonial leaders maneuvered for advantage, events in Cuba and the United States soon reached the Asian archipelago, overwhelming both sides.

Temporary Filipino-American Alliance and Fatal Antagonisms

Throughout 1897 and 1898, U.S. legislators and the general public became preoccupied with events in Spanish Cuba. Powerful agrarian interests supported Cuban rebels, and imperialist leaders in Congress and the military were eager to make the United States a world power. On February 25, ten days after the battleship *Maine* was blown apart in Havana, Commodore George Dewey's Asiatic Squadron was ordered to proceed to Hong Kong in anticipation of future conflict. After receiving word of the April 25 U.S. declaration of war, Dewey set sail for Spain's Asian outpost, reaching Manila Bay on May 1. The battle was over shortly after noon, with the total destruction of Spain's fleet, but Dewey had no troops with which to attack Manila's citadel, Fort Santiago. Under these circumstances, U.S. and Filipino interests coincided.

Dewey sent the USS *McCulloch* to fetch Aguinaldo in Hong Kong; he returned to Manila on the 19th. Anticipating U.S. help in gaining independence, Aguinaldo accommodated U.S. requests, even while announcing the creation of a dictatorial government on the 24th to rule until independence. He also called on his people to rise up, and by late June all but a few outposts on Luzon were in rebel hands; Manila was surrounded and her water supply cut off. Earlier, on June 12, Aguinaldo had issued a Philippine Declaration of Independence, a new national flag was unfurled, and a new anthem played. On the 18th, he issued a decree creating local and provincial governments for the new Filipino regime.

Concurrently, U.S. forces arrived in ever greater numbers, significantly altering the power relationship. Spanish defenders soon made contact with U.S. commanders requesting that the United States take the capital after a brief phony battle. Spanish military officers feared a court-martial if there was no resistance, and the Iberian community within the walled city feared the prospect of Filipino forces breaching the gates. On August 13, Dewey's shipboard cannons fired at Fort Santiago but seemed to aim mysteriously high, while on the ground, Spanish military officers pulled back quickly from one defensive position after another. Meanwhile, as they advanced, the U.S. force of 11,000 men kept the much larger Filipino army from entering the city. By late afternoon, the U.S. flag appeared over the ramparts. Aguinaldo soon learned of the Spanish-U.S. duplicity, and Filipino relations with the United States markedly deteriorated over the following months. Native forces openly demonstrated their antipathy, and both sides constructed fortifications directed at the other.

Within this poisoned context, Aguinaldo struggled to avoid the outbreak of hostilities, at least until his forces were better prepared—even as he raced to increase the legitimacy of his rule. On September 15, an eighty-five-member constitutional convention assembled in Malolos, Bulacan, and by late November they produced a model for a representative government of three branches that guaranteed basic individual freedoms. Especially contentious issues included a provision for the separation of church and state and limits on the effective powers of the chief executive. This latter point kept Aguinaldo from accepting the document until some changes were made. In the meantime, on December 10, the signing of the Treaty of Paris between Spain and the United States undercut Philippine sovereignty by giving the islands to the United States. Then, on January 4, 1899, Commanding General Elwell Otis released President William McKinley's December 21 "benevolent assimilation" proclamation, describing his plan for U.S. rule. Aguinaldo responded the following day, rejecting the idea of either assimilation or U.S. benevolence as the relationship deteriorated further. Otis and his staff then held six meetings with Aguinaldo's representatives, but neither side was willing to concede any of its demands. Finally, on January 23 in Malolos, the Philippine Republic was proclaimed and Aguinaldo was sworn into office as the first president. In the next few days, the new president moved rapidly to create his government, founding official newspapers, a school system, an office of finance, and departments of the navy and army. A number of diplomats were also sent to Japan, Europe, and the United States in the hope of gaining official diplomatic recognition.

The Philippine-American War

The long-delayed conflict erupted on the evening of February 4, when a U.S. soldier shot and killed a Filipino sentry at a bridge in the suburb of San Juan del Monte. This shooting was used as a justification for a U.S. assault that quickly followed while many of Aguinaldo's officers were in Malolos attending a dance. Still, in the United States the hostilities were portrayed as Filipino treachery, and, interestingly, the news reached Congress just as the Senate was taking up passage of the Treaty of Paris. That treaty, which many "anti-imperialists" had condemned, passed easily now in a show of jingoistic nationalism.

Until late March, and despite having a force of some 24,000 men, the United States was hard pressed to quell a well-coordinated attack on Manila that resulted in the destruction of substantial portions of the city. However, a U.S. army column was able to push north against poorly armed and trained Filipino troops. The offensive was very successful and even captured Malolos, forcing Aguinaldo and his fledgling government to retreat to San Fernando, Pampanga. Concurrent U.S. expeditions to the central Visayan Islands saw the capture of the capitals of Iloilo and Cebu islands, and of Bacolod, the capital of Negros Occidental. Meanwhile, in April the newly arrived Philippine Commission under Jacob G. Schurman attempted to reach out to Filipinos and gained the collaboration of some very wealthy mestizos who wished to avoid war.

The remainder of 1899 saw more U.S. advances to the southern islands, including the Sulu archipelago of the Muslim peoples and drives both north and south of Manila. Aguinaldo's government was driven from one capital to another until finally reaching Bayambang, Pangasinan. Before abandoning that place, too, Aguinaldo disbanded the regular army and instituted guerrilla warfare under a number of local commanders responsible for their respective military zones. After almost ten months of fighting a superior army, Aguinaldo's switch to guerrilla warfare, coupled with knowledge of the terrain and the people, gave his forces an advantage. He then embarked on an extended retreat through some of the northwest provinces of Luzon, across the steep mountains of the central Cordillera range, and down to the eastern side of Luzon to the remote Cagayan valley. There, he finally located in the even more remote town of Palanan, Isabela, in which he set up a secret shadow government from which he oversaw the fighting. Throughout 1900 and into the first quarter of 1901, his location remained a secret from pursuing Americans.

The switch to guerrilla tactics profoundly changed the character of the war. Although the U.S. advance continued to add further territory, the war raged with undiminished intensity. For example, the capital of Samar Island was secured in January, but fighting continued and culminated on September 28, 1901, when forces under General Vicente Lukban attacked a U.S. contingent in Balangiga, killing forty-eight and wounding twenty-two; only three escaped unharmed. In retaliation, General Jake Smith told his men to make Samar "a howling wilderness" and to "kill everyone over ten" (Sexton 1939, 276). Later, Smith was disciplined severely by a court-martial, but not before Samar's civilians felt his wrath. More broadly, methods of interrogation such as the "water cure," which forced water into the body and then out by jumping on the belly, became a well-known practice. For their part, Filipinos staged numerous raids and ambushes and were so successful that the invaders were always on guard.

Ultimately, Philippine guerrilla warfare was countered by a combination of measures that included a relentless military pursuit of the enemy. In 1900 and 1901 an ever-increasing number of Aguinaldo's advisers and military commanders fell into U.S. hands. In extreme cases in which popular support was very high, the civilian population was "concentrated" in heavily guarded encampments in which thousands died of dehydration and a variety of diseases. The most egregious example was in Batangas Province, where statistics show a severe population decrease. In addition to practicing brutality, the United States attempted to attract key revolutionary leaders. In early June 1900, the Second Philippine Commission under William H. Taft arrived and immediately began creating a civilian government that would include Filipinos. On December 23, 1900, Dr. T. H. Pardo de Tavera, an early convert of the Schurman

Commission, formed the Federalista Party, whose members actively solicited the surrender of their former comrades. U.S. officials did not run the party, but newly surrendered "insurgents" were often given substantial positions in the colonial government.

The turning point in the conflict came in the first quarter of 1901, when the alternate policies of repression and attraction achieved results. On January 7, some fifty-seven prominent "irreconcilable" Philippine nationalists who refused to take an oath of loyalty to the United States were sent to Guam, where they would remain in exile for years. The following day, a courier carrying Aguinaldo's personal correspondence fell into U.S. hands, thereby revealing his whereabouts. Brigadier General Frederick Funston then proposed a risky plan to pose as a U.S. prisoner who would be taken to Aguinaldo by pro-American scouts, who would then overpower and arrest the Philippine leader. Funston's party secretly left Manila on a ship that brought them to within a few days' march from Palanan. On March 23, after encountering and joining Aguinaldo's personal guards, the trap was sprung as planned. Aguinaldo's men surrendered rather than risking the life of their leader, and Aguinaldo was brought back to Manila, where he swore allegiance to the United States in April and urged his followers to follow his example.

Meanwhile the expansion of the civil government continued, with support from the passage of the Spooner Amendment to the army's annual appropriations bill in 1901, shifting authority from the military to a civilian government. In the Philippines, members of the Taft Commission established provincial governments on Luzon in February, and islands in the south by early March. Taft and his daughter Alice charmed local leaders and rapidly won friends for U.S. colonialism. The dualistic pacification strategy continued with the formation of the Philippine Constabulary in July 1901. Although they were under U.S. officers, Filipino units of 150 men per province were critical in keeping the peace and reducing charges of U.S. atrocities. Then, on August 23, the USS *Thomas,* a transport ship, arrived carrying 540 young U.S. teachers. Assigned in pacified areas to teach English and assist in developing a national school system, the "Thomasites" made a significant psychological impact.

As more and more guerrilla leaders heeded Aguinaldo's call, the conflict diminished rapidly throughout most of the archipelago in 1901 and the early months of 1902. Only a few diehards, such as Lukban and Miguel Malvar, continued the struggle until their capture in February and April 1902. In May 1902, Taft made a diplomatic visit to the Vatican, where he met with Pope Leo XIII over the issue of friar lands. Although negotiations were difficult and contentious, the church realized the necessity of divesting it-self of those properties, which had cost them so much ill will. Eventually, an agreement was made to sell the lands to the United States, for resale to Philippine tenants. Finally, on July 4, President Theodore Roosevelt announced Philippine pacification, bringing the formal conflict to an end. A few "irreconcilable" revolutionaries continued the struggle, such as Teodoro Sandiko, who was arrested and hanged in 1907, and Artemio Ricarte, who went into exile to Hong Kong and then Japan. But most former revolutionaries accommodated themselves to cooperation with the United States, which held out the prospect of eventual independence after an indeterminate period of tutelage in democracy.

IMPACTS

Overwhelming U.S. military might crushed the fragile Philippine Republic, which had begun to build a solid nationalist foundation for a modern state. Over the course of the campaign the United States committed more than 126,000 men to the battle, of whom 4,234 died, while the U.S. Treasury spent more than $600,000,000 to support 2,811 engagements. But the Filipinos suffered more. At least 16,000 Filipino soldiers died in action, while an estimated 200,000 civilians perished because of famine and pestilence (Campomanes 2002, 138–139). The monetary losses that the Philippine economy incurred are difficult to calculate, but statistics do not show an appreciable upturn in the nation's economy until 1909, which indicates the severity of the conflict. In the long run, the U.S. military offensive and programs to win the population worked too well. The first decades of the century are often referred to as the "era of suppressed nationalism," and Philippine political leaders too often assumed the viability of a continued dependence on the United States. After gaining independence in 1946, the ultimate consequence of the crushing of the spirit of the Propaganda Movement, the sacrifice of the Katipuneros, and the work of the Malolos Republic was a challenge that Filipinos have had to face.

PEOPLE AND ORGANIZATIONS

Aguinaldo, Emilio (1869–1964)

Aguinaldo joined the Katipunan in 1895 and assumed leadership of the revolution from rival Andres Bonifacio. As president of the Malolos Republic he created an independent government crushed by the 1899–1901 U.S. assault. Captured in March 1901, he took the oath of loyalty to the United States and retired.

Bonifacio, Andres (1863–1897)

Bonifacio was a member of the Liga Filipina and founder of the Katipunan. Although respected for his fiery nationalism, he was politically sidelined by Aguinaldo and later executed for sedition.

Dewey, Commodore George (1837–1917)

Dewey was commander of the U.S. naval contingent that destroyed Spain's fleet in Manila. He remained to secure the U.S. claim to the archipelago and provide artillery support for the city's eventual capture by the U.S. army.

Federalista Party (1900–1905)

The Federalista was created by T. H. Pardo de Tavera. The party advocated U.S. statehood for the Philippines and elicited the surrender of revolutionary leaders who were then given positions in the new U.S. colonial government.

Katipunan (1892–1897)

The Katipunan was a revolutionary secret society founded by Andres Bonifacio days after Rizal's arrest. The society advocated the violent overthrow of Spanish rule and grew rapidly. Its discovery in August 1896 resulted in the start of the revolution. The society was abolished at the Tejeros convention in March 1897 but persisted informally.

La Liga Filipina (1892)

La Liga Filipina was a Manila reformist party formed by Jose Rizal in July 1892. Rizal's arrest days later ended the party and efforts seeking reform from the Spanish colonizers.

Otis, Elwell (1856–1928)

Otis was a commander of U.S. troops at the outbreak of war with the Philippine government. Although a cautious commander, his troops achieved an important series of victories while he attempted to negotiate with rebel leaders.

Propaganda Movement (ca. 1884–1895)

The Propaganda Movement refers to the activities of Filipino students in Europe who bridged the gap between modern liberal ideals of the Enlightenment and their own country, in the process creating Asia's first nationalist revolution.

Rizal, Jose (1861–1896)

Rizal was a most prominent member of the Propaganda Movement whose essays in the newspaper *La Solidaridad* and his two novels, *Noli Me Tangere* and *El Filibusterismo*, created a national consciousness in the Philippines. A reformer, not a revolutionary, his party in Manila, La Liga Filipina, was suppressed immediately, and he was executed in December 1896 when armed revolution erupted.

Taft, William Howard (1857–1930)

Taft was the head of the Second Philippine Commission, starting in June 1900, and first civil governor, in July 4, 1901. He courted Philippine leaders, introduced local governments, and settled the contentious friar land issue. Later, as U.S. secretary of war, he continued to monitor Philippine affairs.

Paul A. Rodell

See Also Colonialism, Anti-Colonialism, and Neo-Colonialism; Guerilla Warfare and Revolution; Nationalism and Revolution; Philippine Huks and the New People's Army; Philippine Muslim Separatist Rebellions; Philippines: The 'People Power' Revolution of 1986

References and Further Readings

Bain, David Haward. 1984. *Sitting in Darkness: Americans in the Philippines.* New York: Houghton Mifflin.

Blount, James H. 1913. *American Occupation of the Philippines: 1898–1912.* New York: G. P. Putnam's Sons.

Campomanes, Oscar V. 2002. "Casualty Figures of the American Soldier and the Other." Pp. 134–162 in *Vestiges of War: The Philippine-American War and the Aftermath of an Imperial Dream, 1899–1999,* edited by Angel Velasco Shaw and Luis H. Francia. New York: New York University Press.

Corpuz, Onofre D. 2002. *Saga and Triumph: The Filipino Revolution against Spain.* Quezon City: Cavite Historical Society and the University of the Philippines Press.

Escalante, Rene R. 2002. *The American Friar Lands Policy, 1898–1916.* Manila: De la Salle University Press.

Ileto, Reynaldo C. 1997. *Pasyon and Revolution: Popular Movements in the Philippines, 1840–1910.* Quezon City: Ateneo de Manila University Press.

Karnow, Stanley. 1990. *In Our Image: America's Empire in the Philippines.* New York: Ballantine.

May, Glenn A. 1991. *Battle for Batangas: A Philippine Province at War.* New Haven, CT: Yale University Press.

Miller, Stuart. 1984. *Benevolent Assimilation: The American Conquest of the Philippines, 1899–1903.* New Haven, CT: Yale University Press.

Schirmer, Daniel, and Stephen R. Shalom, eds. 1987. *The Philippines Reader*. Boston: South End.

Sexton, William T. 1939. *Soldiers in the Sun*. Harrisburg, PA: Military Service Publishing.

Shaw, Angel Velasco, and Luis H. Francia, eds. 2002. *Vestiges of War: The Philippine American War and the Aftermath of an Imperial Dream, 1899–1999*. New York: New York University Press.

Tan, Samuel K. 2002. *The Filipino-American War, 1899–1913*. Quezon City: University of the Philippines Press.

Philippine Muslim Separatist Rebellions

CHRONOLOGY

ca. 1380	Arab missionary-scholar Mukdum arrives in the Sulu archipelago and begins to spread the faith.
ca. 1450	Abubaker of Palembang, Sumatra, marries the daughter of a local rajah and founds the sultanate of Sulu with Islam as the state religion.
1450–1570	Rapid spread of Islam through much of the Philippines, first to the northern and western regions of Mindanao Island, and from there as far north as Manila Bay by 1570.
1565–1898	During its lengthy colonial occupation, Spain sends many hundreds of missionary priests to convert Filipinos to Christianity. They are critical in reversing the Islamic conversion process, except for the Sulu archipelago and Mindanao.
1570–1571	Spanish explorer Miguel Legazpi moves from Cebu to Manila. Rajah Soliman, a local ruler, attacks the Spaniards, who return fire, routing his forces. Legazpi then concludes a treaty with Soliman, granting Spain present-day Manila.
1578, 1579	Spain sends expeditions to Jolo and Mindanao. Both forces are met by fierce resistance. In 1596, a large colonization effort is repulsed by Mindanao's Muslims.
1635–1663	In April 1635, a Spanish-Christian Filipino military force secures the coastal town of Zamboanga and begins construction of a fort in that strategic location. In 1637, the colonial governor leads large-scale attacks on the Muslims of Lake Lanao, Mindanao. These actions spark clashes lasting decades and result in the Muslim recapture of Zamboanga.
1718–1731	Spain reoccupies Zamboanga and begins futile military expeditions that conclude in 1731. A number of forts are constructed in the southern islands, and watchtowers in Christian Filipino towns throughout the country, to guard against frequent Muslim raids.
1848–1851	The introduction of three steam warships that are faster than Muslim sailing ships. After a series of raids on his strongholds, the sultan of Sulu sues for peace.
1876–1898	Despite the 1851 treaty, conflict soon resumes; major Spanish assaults are made on Jolo (1876), Cotabato (1886, 1891, and 1898), and Lanao (1895).
1899	U.S. troops occupy Jolo and Zamboanga. On August 20, Brigadier General John C. Bates and Sultan Jamalul Kiram II of Sulu sign a treaty to prevent fighting. In October, the U.S. Military District of Mindanao, Jolo, and Palawan is created, and U.S. forces occupy the areas.
1903	In June, the civilian Moro Province is created.
1904	In March, U.S. president Theodore Roosevelt abrogates the Bates Treaty.
1906	In March, the battle of Bud Dajo at an extinct volcano near Jolo; 600 Muslim warriors, women, and children are killed by U.S. troops who fire from the rim of the volcano into the mass of people huddled below.
1912–1946	Government efforts to populate Mindanao with settlers from Christian areas begins. Expanded role for Filipinos in the colonial bu-

reaucracy brings Philippine Christians into positions of authority in Muslim areas. Meanwhile, the government co-opts elite Muslims with rewarding positions, while little is done for the majority of the Muslim people.

1913	Battle of Mt. Bagsak. Another 300 Muslims are slain in an engagement similar to the 1906 slaughter.
1962	President Diosdado Macapagal renews the 1922 Philippine claim to the territory of neighboring Sabah.
1968	In March, the Jabidah Massacre of young army recruits from Sulu being trained to wrest Sabah from neighboring Malaysia. Testimony from the sole survivor creates an international incident and inflames long-buried Muslim resentment.
	In May, Governor Datu Udtog Matalam of Cotabato Province announces the formation of the Muslim Independence Movement. Congressman Rashid Lucman sends ninety-two young Muslims for guerrilla warfare training in Malaysia. Included in this group are Nur Misuari and others who will found the Moro National Liberation Front (MNLF).
1972	In October, in response to President Ferdinand Marcos's September 21 declaration of martial law, the MNLF attacks army units in Jolo, sparking regional armed rebellion. The MNLF grows rapidly and soon has the Philippine military stalemated.
1976–1977	Marcos is anxious for peace, and Misuari agrees to drop independence demands for autonomy. An agreement is signed in December, but Marcos soon reneges on his commitments. Salamat Hashim criticizes Misuari and leads an unsuccessful power grab in December 1977.
1984	In March, Hashim founds the Moro Islamic Liberation Front (MILF) based on religious tenets.
1986	In January, the People Power revolution ousts Marcos and catapults Corazon Aquino

to power. Misuari and Hashim look forward to negotiations with the Aquino government.

1987	Abdurajak Janjalani quits the MNLF and goes to Libya to study Islam. He later fights in Afghanistan and returns in 1990 and founds the radical Muslim group Abu Sayyaf.
1988	Muhammad Jamal Khalifa, brother-in-law of Osama bin Laden, creates business and charity fronts.
1989	In August, the government unilaterally creates the Autonomous Region of Muslim Mindanao (ARMM) and holds elections despite objections from Misuari and Hashim, who protest the size of the region and being cut out of the process. Fighting renews.
1992–1996	President Fidel Ramos holds talks with both mainstream Muslim organizations. In September 1996 an agreement is reached, but Ramos modifies key points. Misuari loses credibility and the MILF grows.
1994	With Abdurajak Janjalani's support, Ramzi Ahmed Yousef sets up a small al-Qaeda cell in Manila and plans bombings that include blowing up eleven airliners over the Pacific. The cell is exposed when a fire starts in his apartment while he is making bombs.
1995	In April, the Abu Sayyaf group joins an MNLF rogue faction in a bloody raid on Ipil, Zamboanga del Sur, and gains national attention.
1996	The MNLF and the government sign a peace creating the Autonomous Region of Muslim Mindanao. Fathur Rohman al-Ghozi, of the radical Indonesian Islamic group the Jemaah Islamiyah (JI), arrives in the Philippines to work inside the MILF's Camp Abubakar at a separate site for JI training. A full schedule of training begins in 1997. Salamat Hashim permits the MILF-JI linkage because of his friendship with JI cofounder Abdullah Sungkar.
1996–1997	In July 1997, the government agrees to make forty-four MILF camps "zones of peace and development" that are off-limits to government troops.

1999	In October, frustrated with the slow pace of peace negotiations with the MILF, President Joseph Estrada sets a December deadline for progress.
2000	In January, Estrada orders military action. By July the army overruns Camp Abubakar, among many other MILF strongholds.

In March, the Abu Sayyaf kidnaps one priest, twenty-two teachers, and twenty-seven students from four schools on Basilan Island. Two teachers are beheaded, and three others and the priest die during the final rescue on May 3.

In April, the Abu Sayyaf attack a diving resort in Sipadan, Malaysia, taking a number of tourists hostage. Many are European; they are held for months until many millions of U.S. dollars are paid in ransom.

In December, al-Ghozi as well as al-Qaeda and MILF operatives conduct a multiple target bombing attack in Metro Manila on the 30th. Thirty-two people are killed and almost 200 wounded.

2001   In May, Abu Sayyaf raid the Dos Palmas resort, Palawan Island, taking twenty hostages, including three Americans. Three nurses and an orderly are taken from a Basilan Island hospital. One American is beheaded; another dies during the rescue, on June 7, 2002.

In November, President Gloria Macapagal-Arroyo joins the U.S.-led "War on Terror" during a White House visit. U.S. military assistance and advisers arrive.

On November 19, Nur Misuari leads an unsuccessful revolt in Jolo that is intended to disrupt a plebiscite on the political configuration and leadership of the ARMM. Earlier, Misuari had been ousted as MNLF chair and removed as chair of the Southern Philippine Council for Peace and Development. Misuari attempts to flee to Malaysia; he is captured and returned to the Philippines, where he is arrested for insurrection and jailed.

2003   February–May, President Macapagal orders a military advance into the MNLF's Buliok

Complex in North Cotabato. A series of bombings strike at Mindanao's power grid. Davao City's airport and wharf are bombed, and attacks are made on civilians in towns in Lanao del Norte and Zamboanga del Norte.

On July 10, Fathur al-Ghozi of the Jemaah Islamiyah and two Abu Sayyaf members escape from a high security prison in the police constabulary headquarters in Manila. After a national manhunt, al-Ghozi is gunned down in October at a police checkpoint in North Cotabato Province.

On July 13, MILF leader Salamat Hashim dies of heart failure. He is succeeded by Al Haj Murad, the organization's military chief.

In July, the MILF signs a cease-fire agreement with the government.

February 7–15, armed attack on the city of Jolo by a force of 800 that includes elements from both the Abu Sayyaf and the MNLF.

On February 14, a coordinated national Valentine's Day bombing attack occurs on the Manila suburb of Makati and the Mindanao cities of Davao and General Santos. The bombings are the combined effort of radical members of the Abu Sayyaf, the MILF, and Jemaah Islamiyah.

2004   Abu Sayyaf bombs *Super Ferry 14* in Manila Bay on February 27. The ship sinks with the loss of more than 100 passengers.

In March, raids in Metro net a six-man Abu Sayyaf team and 80 pounds of explosives.

2005   On April 16, peace talks between the MILF and the Republic of the Philippines begin in Malaysia.

INTRODUCTION

When the Spanish began to colonize the Philippines in the late sixteenth century, they brought hundreds of priests in a largely successful effort to stop the spread of Islam and Christianize the people. In several areas, however, commitment to Islam remained strong. Muslims, suffering deprivation of resources and political and economic discrimination, eventually responded first with the creation of the Moro National Liberation Front and then the Moro Islamic Liberation Front.

Later, Islamic radicals created Abu Sayyaf and established ties with organizations linked with al-Qaeda. After the September 11, 2001, al-Qaeda terrorist attacks on New York and Washington, D.C., U.S. and Philippine forces pursued the radicals, while more moderate Muslims continued negotiations with the Philippine government to resolve grievances.

BACKGROUND: CULTURE AND HISTORY

Islam was first introduced by Arab merchants and a few missionary scholars who arrived in the late fourteenth century. The entry point was that area known as the Sulu archipelago, the southwestern peninsula that juts off the island of Mindanao, and the chain of islands that includes Jolo and Basilan as well as Sulu. As scholars, the new arrivals had enough prestige to compel the local people to listen to their message of a single god that was more powerful than the multiple spirits and natural phenomena that the people had always worshipped. They also married into the families of the local rulers, further increasing their prestige and enhancing the spread of the new faith. From this beginning, the religion spread rapidly through Mindanao and some of the central islands called the Visayas and even reached the region of present-day Manila. When the Spaniards arrived in the late 1500s, the local rulers referred to themselves with Islamic titles such as sultan, datu, and rajah.

The Spaniards assisted their priests in converting the local population. Since Spain itself had only recently finished the long process of reconquering the Iberian Peninsula and expelling Muslims, the Spaniards were anxious to reverse the Islamic advance they encountered in Asia. The Spanish crown liberally supported the missionary activities of many hundreds of Catholic priests, and the "friars" achieved remarkable success in limiting Islam's spread. Nonetheless, people in areas in the south, where Islam had first made converts, remained true to their faith, part of their identity that differentiated them from the rest of the archipelago's population under Spain's control. Over time, five distinct groups of Muslims emerged: the Badjaos, who live almost their entire lives on their boats; the fierce warrior Tausugs of the Sulu archipelago; the Samal, who reside on the long Zamboanga peninsula of Mindanao; the Maranao, who live around Lake Lanao in the northern part of Mindanao; and the Maguindanao, who populate the southwestern half of that large island.

Despite ruling the Philippines for more than three hundred years, Spain's control of the Muslim south was weak until the introduction of steam-powered patrol boats during the mid nineteenth century. Before then, fast-moving Muslim sailing boats easily outran the heavy Spanish ships. Although Spain built a fort in the port of Zamboanga in 1635, and mounted military raids against Muslim strongholds, they did not subdue the independent Muslims. Rather, Muslims made frequent raids on Christian villages in search of captives for Southeast Asia's lucrative slave trade. Missionary priests attempted to protect their communities by using church bell towers as lookouts for Muslim raiders and, then, linking their churches into a coastal signaling system that would warn local residents and neighboring towns of approaching danger.

By the second half of the nineteenth century, a combination of Spain's improved naval capabilities and political intervention in succession disputes in the Sulu and Maguindanao sultanates resulted in a decline in Muslim power, though resistance continued until the end of Spain's colonial reign. When the United States entered, Brigadier General John C. Bates signed a treaty with Sultan Jamalul Kiram II of Sulu on August 20, 1899, that was never ratified by the U.S. Congress. It included reference to U.S. "sovereignty" in the English version, but not in the translated copy. In October the military district of Mindanao was created, leading to the occupation of Jolo and Palawan islands and other Muslim territories despite armed opposition by the Maranao. Military rule was replaced in June 1903 with the creation of the civilian Moro Province. That led to further resistance to U.S. domination by fighters in Sulu and a three-year guerrilla war by Muslim forces loyal to Datu Uto of Cotabato. In March 1904, Theodore Roosevelt unilaterally abrogated the Bates Treaty, further intensifying Muslim bitterness. In March 1906 an uprising resulted in the slaughter of more than 600 men, women, and children at Bud Dajo, an extinct volcano on Sulu Island, but the carnage did not curb Muslim resistance. A second massacre killed hundreds of Muslims in June 1913 at Bud Bagsak in Jolo Island, after which open conflict virtually ceased.

Although peace returned to Muslim territories, many thousands of Christian settlers were introduced to Mindanao, thanks to resettlement programs. Before World War II, almost 97,000 hectares of Cotabato Province in southwestern Mindanao was occupied by the settlers. U.S. corporations, such as Del Monte and B.F. Goodrich, held thousands of hectares in Basilan Island, and in Bukidnon Province in northern Mindanao as well as Cotabato. The U.S. government introduced Christian Filipino civil servants to Muslim territories who controlled local offices of the national government and co-opted traditional Muslim leaders with appointments to colonial posts, thus depriving the region of leaders who might otherwise have continued resistance to the new regime.

According to the 1948 census, Mindanao's 933,101 Muslims constituted only 32 percent of the island's population. It had been 76 percent in 1903. In the 1950s and 1960s the Muslim percentage deteriorated even more rapidly, as new large-scale resettlement programs introduced many more thousands of Christian Filipinos. By 1970 the island's 1,669,708 Muslims made up only 21 percent of Mindanao's population. Much of the best land was held by the settlers and corporate owners. Most of the region's development investments and government services went to the Christian population, so that today the majority Muslim provinces are among the poorest and most backward in the country.

CONTEXT AND PROCESS OF REVOLUTION

Jabidah—The Spark that Ignites Separatism

The spark that ignited long-standing grievances was a 1968 massacre of young Tausug men who had been recruited into an ultra-secret Philippine army unit code-named Jabidah. The covert government plan was to launch a phony rebellion in Sabah, which was then being incorporated into the neighboring country of Malaysia. The Philippines had first claimed Sabah in 1922, and the "rebellion" by the Tausug recruits was to be a pretext for Philippine military intervention to preempt Malaysia. In December 1967, the recruits were brought to a remote section of Corregidor Island at the mouth of Manila Bay for military instruction. The program soon deteriorated for reasons that are still murky, and many of the trainees unsuccessfully attempted to petition President Ferdinand E. Marcos about their grievances. They were then transferred out to regular military camps. On March 18, two batches of twelve men each were ordered to prepare their personal effects and told that they would be flown home. Rather than being put on an airplane, however, all the recruits except one were massacred. Jibin Arulas escaped to the sea despite being wounded and was later picked up by fishermen who brought him to their provincial governor. The resulting scandal led to an inconclusive congressional investigation and an international incident with Malaysia's prime minister Tunku Abdul Rahman. Yet, more important than the political controversies, Jabidah completely alienated Philippine Muslims from the government and its programs promoting ethnic accommodation. Instead, a new Islamic thinking emerged regarding an independent Bangsamoro (Muslim nation) people. This psychological turn provided the critical rationale for all subsequent separatist movements.

Only a few months after Jabidah, a Muslim governor formed an independence movement, while a Muslim congressman sent a batch of ninety-two young Muslim men for training with the Royal Malaysian Special Forces. Once they returned home, they established training camps in Sulu and Mindanao that by 1971 had trained an estimated 30,000 others in weapons and guerrilla tactics. Soon armed Christian gangs called *Ilagas* (rats) appeared in response to the increased Islamic militancy and perpetrated attacks on Muslim civilians, often with the support of Christian politicians. The spread of lawlessness soon embroiled the Philippine Armed Forces (AFP), and the resulting conflict in Mindanao became one of the justifications that President Marcos used to declare martial law on September 21, 1972.

Evolution of the Struggle: Misuari's MNLF to Hashim's MILF

One of that first batch of young Muslims to go to Malaysia for training was Nur Misuari, an ethnic Tausug who was a student and later professor at the University of the Philippines. Although he initially allied with the traditional Muslim leadership, he and his fellow trainees broke from those early mentors and formed the Moro National Liberation Front (MNLF). After the declaration of martial law, fierce fighting broke out in Jolo that resulted in the virtual destruction of the city as a result of a withering counterattack by government aircraft and artillery. Despite its loss in Jolo, the MNLF gained in prestige, spreading throughout the Muslim region. By 1975 some sixty battalions of the Philippine Armed Forces were fighting in Mindanao, and the war costs were threatening to undermine the country's economy. Even though the MNLF had achieved a strategic stalemate with government forces, Misuari realized that he could not gain an independent Muslim republic. The situation dictated that Marcos and Misuari reach a political accommodation. Talks were held under the auspices of the Organization of Islamic Conferences (OIC) and were hosted by Libya's President Mu'ammar al-Qadhafi. The resulting agreement, signed in Tripoli in December 1976, offered the creation of an autonomous regional government for thirteen Muslim provinces. Although the agreement seemed to lay the foundation for an end to conflict, Marcos soon undercut it by creating his own regional government and appointing all of its leaders.

This betrayal of the Tripoli agreement resulted in a loss of credibility for Misuari and dealt a blow to the MNLF from which it could not recover. The MNLF had been a secular, rather than an Islamic, movement that broke from the control of traditional Muslim leaders and transcended earlier ethnic divisions. Once Misuari's leadership was called into question, traditional leaders such as Sultan Rashid Lucman and Senator Salipada Pendatun tried to reassert their earlier dominance; in December 1977 an internal rival, Salamat Hashim, led an unsuccessful attempt to take over the MNLF. Although Misuari retained control, the departure of Hashim and a number of other leaders further weakened the organization. After years of leading a separate MNLF faction, on March 1984, Hashim declared the founding of a new organization, the Moro Islamic Liberation Front, whose very name signified a more radical religious turn in the Philippine Muslim struggle. Since Hashim was an *ustadz* (Islamic teacher) with a degree from the Institute of Islamic Research, al-Azhar University, Cairo, his MILF gave greater weight to religious considerations and Islamic imam (religious leaders), and *alim* (Islamic scholars) played prominent roles in the organization.

Ethnic divisions also re-emerged after 1977, with Hashim's MILF being largely identified with Muslims from Maguindanao Province who were linked with Maranaos from the Lake Lanao area in a delicate alliance. Meanwhile, Misuari's remaining MNLF base was made up of fellow Tausugs from the Sulu archipelago. Later, a more radical organization, the Abu Sayyaf, was founded by another Tausug from Sulu, Abdurajak Janjalani. In addition to rival ethnicities, all Muslim organizations have been plagued by internal divisions wherein strong local leaders act independently of the main organization. These independent groups have sometimes been referred to as "Lost Commands," and they have been known to turn to banditry. Even the small Abu Sayyaf group may have had as many as five rival factions at one time. The MILF, especially, has had increasing difficulty controlling the action of some of its more radical local leaders, some of whom have given protection to Indonesian Islamic militants of the al-Qaeda–linked Jamaah Islamiyah, pursued by Philippine authorities. To cite a recent example, in June 2003 the MILF admitted that some of its troops under a local commander were responsible for a massacre of civilians in the town of Siocon, Zamboanga del Norte Province, that it did not order and, in fact, strongly condemned.

Until the mid 1990s, the MILF was still obscured by Misuari's MNLF, which the government and the outside world continued to see as the primary independence movement. The MILF's strategy was to portray itself as a moderate organization and win OIC recognition in place of the MNLF. Nonetheless, Hashim's armed force had reached an estimated 8,000 to 15,000 fighters by 1999 and was led by commanders who were trained in Libya and Palestine or had combat experience in Afghanistan. Before falling from power in 1986, Marcos attempted to undercut Misuari further by entering into peace negotiations with Hashim's group. By 1986 the situation in Muslim Mindanao had reached a deadlock, with neither of the Muslim organizations strong enough

to threaten the government, while Manila could not end the virtual state of rebellion.

The dynamic began to change with the January 1986 People Power Revolution, in which the Filipino people rose up in days of peaceful massive civil disobedience. As the military shifted its allegiance to an initial band of mutineers, the end of the Marcos regime was certain; Corazon Aquino, the wife of his former political adversary, Benigno Aquino, assumed the presidency. Both Misuari and Hashim were delighted with this turn of events and agreed to reconcile and enter into joint negotiations with the new Aquino government. The truce did not last, however, because in September, Aquino made a private visit to Misuari, her clear recognition of who would still represent the country's Muslim population. Early the next year the MILF leaders began a three-day offensive in a belated attempt to assert their position as the true representatives of the Muslim people. The talks did not prosper, however, as the government insisted on implementing the autonomy provisions of its new constitution without negotiating terms with the MNLF or any other Muslim group. On August 1, 1989, the Philippine Congress passed legislation creating the Autonomous Region of Muslim Mindanao (ARMM); in a November plebiscite, only four provinces voted to join the new body, which was officially inaugurated in November 1990 over objections from both Misuari and Hashim.

Aquino's successor, former general Fidel Ramos, came into office in May 1992. His administration held concurrent negotiations with the MNLF in Tripoli and the MILF in the Philippines. After four and a half years, an amnesty commission was formed and a cease-fire declared. Unfortunately, a number of Mindanao's Christian politicians and key leaders in the Philippine senate modified and delayed the final peace agreement, and Ramos issued an executive order that further modified the September 1996 agreement on a number of important points. As a result the new ARMM was as limited as its predecessor, and it never received sufficient resources from the national government. Misuari was appointed governor, but his inability as an administrator and concessions he had to make to prominent Muslim families created a bloated ARMM bureaucracy that failed to deliver basic social services or alleviate the region's poverty. As well, since only a fraction of the former MNLF rebels were incorporated into the country's military, many disgruntled MNLF members joined the MILF.

As a consequence of the flawed 1996 agreement and the weak ARMM, the MILF emerged as the greater hope for the majority of Philippine Muslims. In contrast to Misuari and the MNLF, Salamat Hashim enjoyed a respectable reputation as an Islamic scholar, and his inner circle was composed of honest, competent, and dedicated men. As well, the MILF's increasingly formidable fighting force gave promise of success. Hashim engaged the AFP in a series of "pocket wars" in 1996–1997, even while conducting peace negotiations. That strategy appeared to work, and in July 1997 the Ramos government agreed to a general cessation of hostilities that included recognizing forty-four MILF camps as "zones of peace and development" in which the AFP would not interfere.

Meanwhile, Misuari's end as a leader came in 2001, the first year of Gloria Macapagal-Arroyo's presidency. Misuari had very little social or economic progress to show for having been ARMM governor and concurrent chair of the Southern Philippine Council for Peace and Development (SPCPD). A number of his MNLF council members were growing impatient with his leadership. In late April, the council decided to remove him from his MNLF chairmanship. The president took advantage of the internal MNLF dissatisfaction with Misuari to remove him as SPCPD chair. Then, in August, the president announced a Mindanao plebiscite to be held in late November that would determine the political composition of the ARMM and its elected leadership, including its governor. Perhaps sensing a move to replace him, Misuari led a boycott protest and even refused to run for re-election. A week before the plebiscite, Misuari led the MNLF in an ill-planned revolt in Jolo that failed to stop the voting. He attempted to flee to Malaysia, but authorities there placed him under arrest and deported him to Manila for trial.

The Odyssey of the Abu Sayyaf

While the MNLF-dominated ARMM plodded along, events in the Sulu were heating up with the emergence of Abu Sayyaf. The original organization was created by a young radical Tausug from Sulu, Abdurajak Janjalani, who quit the MNLF in 1987. Janjalani studied Islam's ultra-conservative Wahabism in Libya and fought with the Mujahidin in Afghanistan. In 1990, he returned to the Philippines and with fellow radical Muslims founded the core of what became the Abu Sayyaf. Key to Janjalani's rise was his relationship with Osama bin Laden's brother-in-law Muhammad Jamal Khalifa, who recruited the young man to his radical Islamist ideology. Khalifa had married a Filipina and set up a rattan import-export business as a cover to funnel money to al-Qaeda through established Islamic charities. He also recruited volunteers such as Janjalani to fight in Afghanistan. During his time in Afghanistan, Janjalani had met another important al-Qaeda agent, Ramzi Ahmed Yousef, who came to the Philippines in 1991–1992 with two other agents to instruct the Abu Sayyaf group in the use of explosives. The new radical group first gained national notoriety when it participated in a bloody raid on the town of Ipil in Zamboanga del Sur in 1995.

Earlier, in the fall of 1994, Yousef and three other al-Qaeda agents established themselves in Manila and began terrorist operations, the best known code-named Oplan Bojinka. This plan was to bomb eleven airliners over the Pacific simultaneously. A test bomb was exploded on a Philippine Airlines flight to Japan, killing a Japanese passenger. An apartment fire exposed this small al-Qaeda cell and scattered its accomplices.

In December 1998, Janjalani and two other Abu Sayyaf members were killed in a gun battle with police on Basilan, after which his younger brother, Khaddafy, and Aldam Tilao, aka Abu Sabaya, succeeded him. With his death the Abu Sayyaf seemed to lose any claim that it was an Islamic religious group, and its leaders shifted entirely to criminality for personal profit. In 2000, Abu Sayyaf raiders kidnapped a group of twenty-one people from a Malaysian resort. The incident was resolved successfully by an estimated $10 million to $25 million ransom paid by the Libyan government. Earlier, another Abu Sayyaf group had kidnapped twenty-seven elementary and high school students, along with twenty-one teachers and a Catholic priest, resulting in the deaths of five teachers and the priest.

The ransom money seemed to encourage the Abu Sayyaf's new bandit tendency, and in May 2001 it kidnapped three Americans, including a Christian missionary couple, from a Philippine resort. This time, however, the Abu Sayyaf group was pursued by the Philippine military, who scoured the island of Basilan, where the hostages were taken. Attempts to elicit ransom money met with resistance, leading to the beheading of one of the Americans, a businessman from California. After the September 11 attack on New York's Twin Towers, the Philippine drama became linked with the U.S. president George W. Bush's "War on Terrorism." U.S. troops were dispatched in early 2002 to assist Philippine forces. On June 7, 2002, a Philippine contingent ambushed the kidnappers. In the firefight that followed, the missionary husband was killed and the wife injured. U.S. support played a critical role in helping the Philippine military to deal a number of setbacks to the Abu Sayyaf, including the death of Abu Sabaya. With the group's numbers reduced some of the remaining forces adopted a low profile, while others, including Khaddafy Janjalani, scattered to new areas, including the Maguindanao region of western Mindanao. Over the longer term, however, increased military pressure and the failure to elicit more ransom money seemed to return the group to its original Islamic mission of fostering *jihad* in the Philippines.

In 2002 and 2003, it seemed that elimination of Abu Sayyaf was only a matter of time as counterinsurgency measures chalked up one success after another, including the arrest of some principal leaders such as Ghalib Andang, alias Commander Robot. That illusion was shattered on February 27,

Abu Sayyaf leaders Khaddafy Janjalani (second from left) and Radulan Sahiron (third from left) sit with fellow Abu Sayyaf rebels inside their jungle hideout somewhere in the area of Sulu Province in the southern Philippines on July 16, 2000. (AP/Wide World Photos)

2004, when the passenger ship *Super Ferry 14* suffered a huge explosion as it sailed out of Manila Bay, sinking quickly with the loss of more than 100 people. Abu Sayyaf leader, Khaddafy Janjalani, and the group's spokesperson, Abu Soliman, claimed responsibility. A month later, some careless boasting by the bomber led authorities to break up a six-person Abu Sayyaf cell in Manila. Analysts soon noted the return of the group to its long-deceased founder's vision of *jihad,* as caches of explosives were discovered and undetonated bombs defused. In addition, the Abu Sayyaf terrorist threat seemed to have expanded to include new linkages with the Jemaah Islamiyah and disaffected radical members of both the MNLF and the MILF. In the second week of February 2005, a combined Abu Sayyaf-MNLF force of almost 800 men staged a brief uprising in Jolo. Then, on Valentine's Day, a combined group of Jemaah Islamiyah, Abu Sayyaf, and MILF members detonated a near simultaneous series of bombings in the Manila suburb of Makati and the Mindanao cities of Davao and General Santos. Although the Abu Sayyaf promises to re-

main deadly, terrorism undertaken simply for its own sake only alienates both Muslims and Christians. Without a positive political agenda, the Abu Sayyaf may continue to survive but remain a fringe extremist organization.

IMPACTS

MILF and Jemaah Islamiyah—Breaking Ties and Pursuing Peace

While the Abu Sayyaf never really broke its links with al-Qaeda, the relationship between Osama bin Laden's organization and the MILF appeared to be quite different. Al-Qaeda made important links with the MILF in the mid 1990s through Khalifa's original companies and via international phone calls between al-Qaeda's Abu Zubayadah and key MILF officials. An important additional relationship linked the Indonesian organization Jemaah Islamiyah with the MILF through their two leaders: the MILF's Salamat Hashim and his friend Abdullah Sungkar, who was a cofounder of the Jemaah Islamiyah along with Abu Bakar Ba'asyir of the radical Islamic school, the Pesantren al-Mukmin. In 1995, as a consequence of that link, the Indonesian group was granted permission to establish training facilities in MILF's main Camp Abubakar in Mindanao. One of the Jemaah Islamiyah agents assigned to set up the camps and serve as a trainer was the Afghan veteran Fathur Rohman al-Ghozi, originally from Madiun, East Java.

This close relationship between the MILF and the Indonesian group was disrupted by President Joseph Estrada, who had succeeded Ramos in 1998. Estrada demanded that the negotiation process with the MILF accelerate so as to deliver a final agreement by December 1999 or risk a renewed government offensive. In early 2000, Estrada ordered the military into action, and by July a number of MILF strongholds, including Camp Abubakar, had fallen to the Philippine military's assault. The offensive scattered MILF forces and destroyed their credibility as a fighting force that could resist the government military. In December, in an apparent response to the offensive, al-Ghozi and Riduan Isamuddin, alias Hambali, al-Qaeda's representative for Southeast Asia, along with the support of an MILF "special operations group" headed by Saifullah Yunos, set off a wave of bomb attacks in Metro Manila on the city's light rail transit system, in shopping malls, and in various other locations, killing more than thirty people. Philippine authorities knew of al-Ghozi's role in the bombings and began hunting for him. The elusive Jemaah Islamiyah operative was eventually arrested in January 2002. He led authorities to some 21 tons of explosives that, he claimed, were to be used in suicide attacks on Western embassies and other targets in Singapore.

Meanwhile, in a series of political and corruption scandals, Estrada was ousted by a second People Power uprising in January 2001 that brought his vice president, Gloria Macapagal-Arroyo, into office. The MILF then returned to the negotiating table. Despite some progress, President Macapagal-Arroyo showed that she, too, could take a hard line, and in February 2003 she ordered a brief offensive against the MILF's new headquarters in the provinces of North Cotabato and Maguindanao. This offensive further demonstrated the MILF's military weakness and resulted in losses of men and material and disruption of MILF administrative and logistical capabilities. The MILF's feeble response was a series of bombings in March that struck power lines in Mindanao, the airport, and the public wharf in the city of Davao, killing innocent civilians. This turned out to be counterproductive and elicited a sharp rebuke from the international Islamic community.

Three other events occurred in July 2003 that, in retrospect, had a significant impact on the MILF and its relationship with the Jemaah Islamiyah. The first was the MILF's signing of a cease-fire agreement, with the government with the possibility that it might lead the way to the resumption of peace talks. More dramatically, on the 10th, al-Ghozi and two Abu Sayyaf inmates made a bold nighttime escape from a high-security jail in the Manila headquarters of the national police constabulary. The escape sparked a national manhunt that finally ended in mid October when al-Ghozi was gunned down at a police checkpoint in North Cotabato Province. It soon became known that individual MILF commanders had given the Indonesian refuge. With increased U.S. military support going to the AFP as part of the U.S. "War on Terrorism," the cost of being associated with the al-Qaeda–linked Jemaah Islamiyah was becoming too high for Philippine Muslim secessionists.

Also in July, the MILF lost its founder, Salamat Hashim, who suffered a fatal heart attack, dealing a profound blow to the MILF's leadership and prestige. The MILF's vice chair for military affairs, Al Haj Murad Ebrahim, emerged as its new leader. Chairman Murad was widely perceived as more moderate than Hashim. Being a civil engineer, as opposed to an Islamic scholar, the new MILF leader was thought to be more open to constructive engagement with Manila. In fact, the MILF led by Murad took a number of steps to distance itself from the Jemaah Islamiyah and reach a long-term agreement with the government.

While many remained skeptical, by mid 2004 government and MILF forces had combined to free kidnap victims. More important, senior government military officials noted publicly that the MILF had acknowledged the need to purge its ranks of extremists. By August the MILF announced that it had driven fifteen to twenty Jemaah Islamiyah members from the Mt. Kararao region of Lanao del Sur, where they had established a terrorist training camp. The government responded quickly and on the 26th dropped all charges against 138 MILF leaders for their alleged role in the March 2003 bombings in Davao. Conjecture about an imminent resumption of long-adjourned peace talks became the topic of Manila coffee shop gossip as peace monitors from the OIC arrived in Mindanao, and Malaysia extended an offer to serve as host.

Despite the optimism, MILF leaders conceded that they anticipated long and difficult discussions, since the talks would include complex issues. High on the agenda was a comprehensive political settlement that might affect existing structures such as the ARMM, and the question of the "ancestral domain" of the Muslim people that had been lost to Christian settlers. That latter point included more than simple farmland, encompassing the control of Mindanao's natural resources. A number of logistical considerations and some outbreaks of violence in Mindanao delayed the start of the talks, but they convened in the Malaysian capital of Kuala Lumpur on April 16, 2005; early reports indicated that substantial progress was being made. The world may hope that perhaps this twentieth-century conflict will have a satisfactory resolution.

PEOPLE AND ORGANIZATIONS

Abu Sayyaf

Abu Sayyaf, a radical rebel group, was created by Abdurajak Janjalani. Linked to al-Qaeda, its members carried out kidnappings, murders, and bombings in a terrorist form of *jihad*.

al-Ghozi, Fathur Rohman (1971–2003)

Al-Ghozi, originally from East Java, was one of the Jemaah Islamiyah agents sent to the Philippines to train JI members at MILF camps. Believed to have organized bombings, he was captured, escaped, and then was killed by Philippine government forces.

Autonomous Region of Muslim Mindanao (ARMM)

The ARMM, dominated by the MNLF, was created by the Philippine government in 1989 in an attempt to satisfy Muslim demands for autonomy.

Hashim, Salamat (1942–2003)

Salamat Hashim was an *ustadz* (Islamic teacher) with a degree from the Institute of Islamic Research, al-Azhar University, Cairo, who founded the Moro Islamic Liberation Front (MILF) in 1984.

Janjalani, Abdurajak (1953–1998)

Janjalani, a young radical Tausug from Sulu who quit the MNLF in 1987, studied Islam's ultra-conservative Wahabism in Libya and fought with the Mujahidin in Afghanistan. In 1990 he returned to the Philippines and, with fellow radical Muslims, founded the core of what became the Abu Sayyaf. He died in a shootout with police on Basilan Island.

Jemaah Islamiyah (JI)

The JI is an al-Qaeda–linked Indonesian radical Islamic group that established ties with Abu Sayyaf and the MILF.

Misuari, Nur (Born 1940)

Nur Misuari, an ethnic Tausug, was a student and later professor at the University of the Philippines. He and his fellow trainees broke from traditional Islamic leaders to form the Moro National Liberation Front (MNLF). He led a failed uprising in 2001 after being removed as MNLF head.

Moro Islamic Liberation Front (MILF)

This Philippine Muslim organization, founded by Salamat Hashim, adopted a more Islamic agenda than Misuari's MNLF. Some members of the MILF, a rival to the MNLF, worked with Abu Sayyaf and the al-Qaeda–affiliated Jemaah Islamiyah of Indonesia.

Moro National Liberation Front (MNLF)

The MNLF was created by Nur Misuari to fight for the interests of the Philippine Muslim peoples. By the mid 1970s it had achieved a military stalemate with Philippine government forces and entered into negotiations to achieve autonomy for Muslim provinces. Betrayal or undermining of agreements by Philippine officials led to renewed fighting. The MNLF came to dominate the ARMM, which the Philippine government created in 1989 to satisfy Muslim demands for autonomy. Other Islamic groups—the MILF and the more radical Abu Sayyaf—competed for the support of Philippine Muslims and continued a violent struggle.

Murad Ebrahim, Al Haj (Born 1949)

Murad succeeded Salamat Hashim as MILF head. More moderate than Hashim, Murad increased cooperation with the government, including the resumption of peace negotiations.

Paul A. Rodell

See Also Documentaries of Revolution; Ethnic and Racial Conflict: From Bargaining to Violence; Islamic Fundamentalist Revolutionary Movement; Philippine Huks and the New People's Army; Philippine Independence Revolution and Wars; Philippines: The 'People Power' Revolution of 1986; Terrorism

References and Further Readings

Abuza, Zachary. 2003. *Militant Islam in Southeast Asia: Crucible of Terror.* Boulder, CO: Lynne Rienner.

Barreveld, Dirk J. 2001. *Terrorism in the Philippines: The Bloody Trail of Abu Sayyaf, Bin Laden's East Asian Connection.* San Jose, CA: Writers Club.

Buendia, Rizal G. 2004. "The GRP-MILF Peace Talks, Quo Vadia?" Pp. 205–221 in *Southeast Asian Affairs 2004*, edited by Daljit Singh and Chin Kin Wah. Singapore: Institute of Southeast Asian Studies.

Burnham, Gracia, with Dean Merrill. 2003. *In the Presence of My Enemies,* Wheaton, IL: Tyndale House.

Gaerlan, Kristina, and Mara Stankovitch, eds. 2000. *Rebels, Warlords and Ulama: A Reader on Muslim Separatism and the War in Southern Philippines.* Quezon City, Philippines: Institute for Popular Democracy.

Gunaratna, Rohan. 2002. *Inside Al-Qaeda: Global Network of Terror.* New York: Berkley.

International Crisis Group. 2004. "Southern Philippines Backgrounder: Terrorism and the Peace Process." ICG, Singapore/Brussels, Asia Report 80 (July 13). http://www.crisisgroup.org/home/index.cfm?id=2863&l=1.

Kiefer, Thomas M. 1986. *The Tausug: Violence and Law in a Philippine Moslem Society.* Long Grove, IL: Waveland.

Majul, Cesar Adib. 1999. *Muslims in the Philippines.* Quezon City, Philippines: University of the Philippines Press.

McKenna, Thomas M. 1998. *Muslim Rulers and Rebels: Everyday Politics and Armed Struggle in the Southern Philippines.* Berkeley: University of California Press.

Ressa, Maria A. 2003. *Seeds of Terror: An Eyewitness Account of Al Qaeda's Newest Center of Operations in Southeast Asia.* New York: Free Press.

Rodell, Paul A. 2002. "The Philippines: Gloria in Excelsis." Pp. 215–236 in *Southeast Asian Affairs,* edited by Daljit Singh and Anthony L. Smith. Singapore: Institute of Southeast Asian Studies.

———. 2004. "The Philippines: Playing Out Long Conflicts." Pp. 187–204 in *Southeast Asian Affairs 2004,* edited by Daljit Singh and Chin Kin Wah. Singapore: Institute of Southeast Asian Studies.

———. 2005. "The Philippines and the Challenge of International Terrorism." Pp. 122–142 in *International Terrorism and Transnational Violence in Southeast Asia: Challenge to States and Regional Stability,* edited by Paul Smith. Armonk, NY: M. E. Sharpe.

Vitug, Marites D., and Glenda M. Gloria. 2000. *Under the Crescent Moon: Rebellion in Mindanao.* Quezon City, Philippines: Ateneo Center for Social Policy and Public Affairs and the Institute for Popular Democracy.

Warren, James F. 1981. *The Sulu Zone, 1768–1898: The Dynamics of External Trade, Slavery, and Ethnicity in the Transformation of a Southeast Asian Maritime State.* Singapore: Singapore University Press.

Philippines: The 'People Power' Revolution of 1986

CHRONOLOGY

Pre-1565 Pre-Hispanic Philippines consists of societies in transition from primitive to feudal. Northern and central Philippines (Luzon and Visayas) are still in the pre-feudal state. Southern Philippines (Mindanao) attained a more advanced political and social organization with the establishment of the sultanates of Sulu and Maguindanao in the fifteenth and sixteenth centuries.

1565–1898 Spain colonizes and Christianizes much of the archipelago. Despite a series of wars spanning three centuries—the "Moro Wars"—Spain fails to subjugate the *moros* (Muslims) in Mindanao. The Spanish colonialists mobilize the colonized and Christianized *indios* to fight the *moros,* thus laying the roots of the Christian-Muslim conflict in Mindanao. Filipinos stage many revolts against abuses or harsh policies of the colonial government, but, before 1896, these are mainly local in nature.

1896–1898 Filipinos wage a struggle for national liberation from Spain, the Philippine Revolution of 1896–1898. Taking advantage of the Spanish-American War, the Filipino revolutionary forces liberate almost all of the colonized Philippines. The United States, however, has imperial ambitions. After "defeating" the Spanish armada in a mock battle at Manila Bay, U.S. troops enter Manila. In the Treaty of Paris of 1898, Spain cedes the Philippines to the United States.

1899–1942 The first Philippine republic is inaugurated in January 1899. Shortly afterward, however, the Filipino-American War (1899–1902) breaks out. In Luzon alone, possibly as many as 600,000 Filipinos die of starvation and disease. After subduing the Christian areas, the Americans turn their guns on the Muslims and vanquish them in a fiercely fought Moro-American War (1901–1916). The United States introduces secular public education and U.S.-style electoral politics in its new colony.

1941–1945 In World War II, Japan attacks and then invades and occupies the Philippines.

1945–1946 U.S. troops and Filipino freedom fighters drive out the Japanese. A year later, the United States grants independence to the Philippines.

1946–1952 The Huk rebellion breaks out in Central Luzon after government troops and the armed men of powerful landlords repress peasants seeking to reform the land tenancy system.

1965   Senator Ferdinand Marcos defeats President Diosdado Macapagal in hotly contested general elections.

1968–1969   Tensions start to build up in the southern Philippines after the "Jabidah massacre"—the murder of at least twenty-three Muslim army recruits in Corregidor—and the establishment of the Muslim Independence Movement by a prominent Muslim politician. Young Muslim nationalists secretly set up the Moro National Liberation Front (MNLF) and prepare for an armed struggle for secession. Meanwhile, young leftist radicals establish the Maoist Communist Party of the Philippines (CPP). A few months later, the CPP sets up the New People's Army (NPA) and launches a revolutionary war to overthrow the government.

1969   Marcos wins a second presidential term in elections marred by violence.

1970   In Manila, student protests end in street battles between police and leftist activists. Some demonstrators are killed.

1970–1972   In Mindanao, land disputes between Christians and Muslims escalate. Powerful political figures on both sides build their own private armies. Killings ensue.

1971   Unidentified men throw grenades at an opposition rally in Plaza Miranda, killing nine persons. Blaming the Communists, Marcos suspends the writ of habeas corpus and throws some leftists into jail.

1972   Citing threats to the republic from the Communists, Muslim secessionists, and "rightists," Marcos declares martial law on September 21. The military imprisons leading elite oppositionists, including Senator Benigno Aquino, and thousands of activists. Muslims rise up in arms in Marawi City. The MNLF becomes the leading force of the secessionist struggle.

1973–1976   Full-scale war ensues between the Armed Forces of the Philippines (AFP) and the MNLF in Mindanao-Sulu. Tens of thousands are killed. Marcos holds a series of "citizens' assemblies" or "referenda," beginning with one for the "ratification" of a new constitution to try to legitimize his authoritarian rule.

1974–1977   Despite the repression, mass movements of workers, urban poor, and students revive, with radical leftists taking the lead.

1976   The government and the MNLF sign a peace pact—the Tripoli Agreement—that provides for regional autonomy for Muslims.

1977   The Tripoli Agreement collapses after Marcos's unilateral actions to "implement" it. The MNLF returns to the battlefield.

1978   In line with his program of "normalization," Marcos calls for elections for a provisional parliament, the Interim National Assembly (IBP). The traditional elite opposition participates in the elections; the radical Left (except in Manila) boycotts them. Marcos's New Society Movement (KBL) rigs the polls, but some oppositionists manage to win in certain regions.

1979   Hoping to inspire the people to rise up, a small anti-Marcos group burns some buildings owned by Marcos and his cronies.

1980   Pro-Marcos candidates dominate local elections, which the Left boycotts. Some anti-Marcos politicians win. Aquino is allowed to leave for the United States for heart surgery. A new insurrectionary group composed of some elite oppositionists and social democrats sets off bombs in Metro Manila, but the military soon rounds up the members of the April 6 Liberation Movement.

1981   Marcos "lifts" martial law but authoritarian rule continues. He calls for a presidential election. Prodded by the radical Left, the traditional opposition also boycotts it.

1981–1983   The NPA stages a series of guerrilla offensives in Mindanao, Negros, and elsewhere.

1983   Aquino and an unidentified man are shot and killed at the Manila International Airport upon Aquino's return from exile. The government claims that the other man, later identified as Rolando Galman, purportedly a hired gunman with links to the Communists, had killed Aquino, and that soldiers had then gunned down the assailant. Few believe the story. Massive anti-dictatorship protests erupt throughout the country.

1984   Marcos calls for elections for the "regular" National Assembly (BP). The radical Left fails to sway the bulk of the elite opposition to boycott the elections. Marcos's KBL dominates the BP, but the opposition significantly increases the number of its seats.

1984–1985   General strikes (*welgang bayan*) spearheaded by the radical Left paralyze large parts of Mindanao, Negros, and Bataan, but prove unsuccessful in Manila.

1985   A group of officers with links to Defense Minister Juan Ponce Enrile set up the Reform the AFP Movement (RAM), ostensibly to work for military reforms. In early November, Marcos announces a snap presidential election, to be held in February 1986. The elite opposition unites behind the candidacy of Aquino's widow, Corazon. The radical Left again campaigns for a boycott.

1986   Marcos rigs the election anew, but numerous irregularities are exposed. After the BP proclaims Marcos the winner, Cory Aquino calls for a campaign of civil disobedience. Amid the turmoil, General Fabian Ver, the AFP chief, unearths a RAM coup plot and starts to arrest those involved. Enrile and RAM members hole themselves up in Camp Aguinaldo. Lieutenant General Fidel Ramos, the AFP deputy chief, joins them. Over the radio, Cardinal Jaime Sin calls on the people to support the military rebels. Tens of thousands flock to Epifanio de los Santos Avenue (EDSA), in front of Camps Aguinaldo and Crame. Marcos orders government troops to attack rebel positions, but the crowds at EDSA block the way. Whole units of soldiers soon defect to the rebel side. After four days of "People Power" at EDSA, Marcos flees Manila and eventually ends up in Hawaii. Inaugurated as the new president, Aquino forms a revolutionary government.

1986–1989   Marcos loyalists or RAM stage seven major coup attempts. With the firm backing of AFP chief (later defense secretary) Ramos, Aquino survives them all.

1987   A new constitution is overwhelmingly ratified in a plebiscite.

2001   Once again, People Power ousts a corrupt president. In January, massive protests drive President Joseph Estrada, who has been implicated in an illegal gambling racket, out of office. The nonviolent popular uprising becomes known as "People Power II," or "EDSA II."

INTRODUCTION

In February 1986, a massive outpouring of popular protest— "People Power"—toppled the corrupt dictator Ferdinand Marcos, who had imposed authoritarian rule in September 1972. The Philippine People Power Revolution had a "demonstration effect" on transitions to democracy in Asia, and the term "People Power" itself has become a buzzword in "democratic revolutions" all over the world. People Power continues to have great resonance in the Philippines, as poor and marginalized classes and communities fight for popular empowerment and social justice in a land dominated by an increasingly predatory oligarchic elite.

BACKGROUND: CULTURE AND HISTORY

Prior to Marcos's imposition of martial law in September 1972, the Philippines had been reputed to be one of a small number of developing countries with a deeply rooted democratic tradition. After fighting for independence from Spain in the Philippine Revolution of 1896–1898, Filipinos established a republic in January of 1899—a short-lived one, but nonetheless the very first in Asia. The United States, which took over the former Spanish colony, introduced Filipinos to U.S.-style electoral politics. In 1935, the United States established the Philippine Commonwealth, headed by a president elected by Filipinos, a prelude to granting full self-rule. The republic that emerged after independence in 1946 featured a presidential system patterned after that of the United States.

In the 1950s and 1960s, Filipinos enjoyed civil and political liberties and had perhaps the freest press in Asia. Elections were held regularly.

Somewhat hidden by the formal democratic processes and structures, however, were deep social cleavages—class, ethnic, intra-elite, and the like—that were growing worse. In the Philippines an elite few control much of the country's wealth and power, while millions wallow in poverty. Large slum communities stand in stark contrast to high-walled plush villages of the affluent nearby. Many political scientists characterized the Philippine political system from 1946 to 1972 as a period of elite rule, or "elite democracy." The Philippine politico-economic elite is well entrenched. The Spanish and U.S. colonial regimes had nurtured the members of the Filipino elite, providing them with positions in the colonial government, in which they learned the ways of patronage and clientelism (Paredes 1988). A few years after independence, tensions between rich landlords and poor, landless peasants came to a head in the Huk Rebellion, in which the Partido Komunista ng Pilipinas (PKP) played a prominent role. The government crushed the rebellion, but by the late 1960s, class tensions had built up again. Amid the growing unrest, a new Maoist-oriented Communist Party of the Philippines (CPP) emerged and launched a "people's war" to overthrow the government.

The most contentious ethnic divide in Philippine society has been that between Christians and Muslims in Mindanao, southern Philippines. This has roots in the three centuries of Moro wars, during the Spanish colonial period, which stunted the development of Muslim areas. Policies of subsequent regimes worsened the Muslims' plight. Encouraged by the U.S. colonial regime and later by the Philippine government, thousands of Christian families from northern and central Philippines transmigrated to Mindanao. Many Muslims were displaced from their homelands. The Muslims' resentment deepened with the government's policy of "national integration," which tended to denigrate their religion and culture. In the late 1960s and early 1970s, Mindanao simmered. A powerful Muslim politician organized the Muslim Independence Movement (later renamed Mindanao Independence Movement). As land disputes worsened, paramilitary units of Christian and Muslim warlords terrorized Muslim and Christian communities, respectively.

From 1946 to 1972, members of the Philippine elite competed for positions in government, largely through the country's two main political parties. According to Landé (1965), the two parties were nonideological organizations structured mainly by networks of patron-client and other personal relationships that were multiclass and multiethnic in character. By the late 1960s, however, it became clear that intra-elite competition no longer conformed to this benign and integrative patron-client model. In the pursuit of political and

economic power, factions of the elite had been increasingly resorting to corruption, fraud, and violence, or the proverbial "guns, goons, and gold." In 1969, Ferdinand Marcos won re-election to the presidency, defeating Senator Sergio Osmena, Jr., who candidly admitted that he had been "outgunned, outgooned, and outgold." The 1971 congressional elections registered a record 534 violent incidents and 905 deaths (Linantud 1998, 301).

Constitutionally barred from seeking a third term, Marcos declared martial law on September 21, 1972, to perpetuate himself in power. To justify his action, he exaggerated the armed threat posed to the Philippine Republic by the Communists, and also cited threats from Muslim secessionists and "rightists." Marcos suspended the congress and ruled by decree. Suppressing civil and political rights, he cracked down on all opposition, including that from the elite, putting thousands in detention. Among those he imprisoned was Senator Benigno Aquino, his foremost political opponent. Marcos vowed to break the political and economic dominance of the "oligarchs" (read: the traditional elite opposition) and to bring about national development through a more unified and disciplined "new society." He sought to gain legitimacy for his "constitutional authoritarianism" initially through supreme court rulings and controlled "referenda." The United States, which acquiesced to the imposition of martial law, gave Marcos increased economic and military assistance. In 1978, the dictator, ever mindful about legitimacy, embarked on a process of "normalization," by restoring elections and a legislature—a unicameral Interim National Assembly (IBP), in lieu of a bicameral congress. These were, of course, less than democratic. In 1981, he "lifted" martial law, but not in essence.

Instead of containing the threats from Communists and Muslim secessionists, Marcos's authoritarian rule increased them. Muslim secessionists rose up and engaged government troops in a full-scale war in Mindanao that claimed tens of thousands of lives and forced hundreds of thousands to flee their homes. The government and the Moro National Liberation Front (MNLF) signed a peace agreement in Tripoli, Libya, in December 1976 that provided for regional Muslim autonomy. Disagreements on its implementation, however, led to resumption of hostilities. By then, however, the MNLF had split and somewhat weakened. Government forces, nonetheless, got no respite, as the Maoist insurgency expanded rapidly in the late 1970s and early 1980s. The CPP's New People's Army (NPA), which had established guerrilla zones in all regions, carried out bold actions. In urban centers, radical activists aligned with the CPP organized anti-dictatorship rallies of workers, urban poor, students, and others. The moderate Left, the social democrats, undertook their own protest activities. Marcos's authoritarian regime committed numerous human rights abuses—summary killings, torture, and so forth—against suspected political dissenters. These, however, served to increase rather than cow opposition to the regime.

Backed by the International Monetary Fund and the World Bank, Marcos had embarked on an ambitious program of export-oriented industrialization. Failing to draw enough investors, however, the effort generated too few manufactured exports. By the end of the 1970s, the economy was in serious straits. GNP growth slowed. The country's foreign debt ballooned. Worse, while millions of Filipinos continued to live in poverty, the avaricious dictator, together with his wife, Imelda, and cronies, plundered the country's resources and amassed and flaunted their wealth.

"Normalization" provided the traditional elite opposition with opportunity to revitalize and contest the IBP elections. In Metro Manila, elite oppositionists led by Aquino (then still in detention) forged an alliance with moderate and radical leftists, and competed against Marcos's KBL, headed by his wife, Imelda. In obviously rigged polls, Imelda's lineup completely shut out Aquino's ticket. In certain regions, however, the opposition managed some wins. Two years later, despite continuing less-than-democratic conditions, some oppositionists won in local elections. With pressure from the radical Left, the traditional opposition largely boycotted the 1981 presidential election, which saw Marcos trouncing a relatively unknown stooge.

CONTEXT AND PROCESS OF REVOLUTION

The assassination of former senator Aquino in August 1983 triggered a massive outpouring of anti-dictatorship protest throughout the country. In Metro Manila, 2 million participated in the funeral march. In other major urban centers, tens of thousands took to the streets. Many Filipinos who had not been politically involved before joined rallies and marches. "Cause-oriented groups" mushroomed. In the immediate aftermath of the assassination, the coalition Justice for Aquino, Justice for All (JAJA) coordinated the protest actions, bringing together a broad range of forces opposed to the dictatorship: traditional elite opposition; radical and moderate leftists; sectoral organizations (labor, urban poor, peasants, students, women, artists, and so forth); church groups; business groups; Muslim groups; and the like.

The radical Left and the traditional elite opposition competed for leadership of the burgeoning anti-dictatorship movement. After years of painstaking work under great repression, the radical Left had built an extensive network of underground as well as open, legal "mass organizations" and had become the biggest and most militant organized force fighting the dictatorship. However, it had basic weaknesses.

Many Filipinos viewed the CPP's alternative—"national democracy"—as nothing more than a one-party dictatorship. Moreover, the CPP leadership remained fixated on a military victory in the long term and refused to shift to an electoral or insurrectionary strategy. Although the NPA had stepped up its tactical offensives, the guerrilla army remained puny compared with that of the AFP. The elite opposition was fractious, with more than a dozen competing for its leadership and aspiring to become the country's next president. But it drew the support of the church hierarchy, the business sector, and the middle class. The United States, fearing a Communist takeover if the Marcos regime suddenly collapsed, showed sympathy to the elite opposition.

Hoping to relegitimize and stabilize his regime, Marcos proceeded with further liberalization, calling for elections for the "regular" National Assembly (BP) in 1984. The radical Left sought to thwart Marcos's scheme and to polarize Philippine society through a boycott of the elections. Many in the elite opposition, however, favored participation, seeing it as a means to further weaken the dictatorship. The Congress of Filipino Citizens (KOMPIL) brought advocates of both boycott and participation together and worked out a compromise "boycott unless" tactic: boycott unless Marcos acceded to certain demands. The dictator succeeded in splitting the opposition, however, by shrewdly granting a few concessions on voting procedures and temporarily lifting some repressive decrees. The radical Left, together with some nationalists in the elite opposition, went ahead with boycott; the bulk of the elite opposition participated in the elections. Marcos's KBL retained a huge majority in parliament, but the opposition substantially increased the number of its seats.

With a presidential election looming, the elite opposition, prodded by anti-Marcos businessmen and professionals, tried to organize itself. The election was slated for 1987, but many suspected that Marcos could move it to an earlier date to take advantage of opposition disunity. Two major initiatives for selecting a common opposition candidate arose: the National Unification Committee (NUC) set up by Assemblyman Salvador Laurel, the leader of the largest opposition party in parliament, the United Nationalist Democratic Opposition (UNIDO); and the Convenors' Group (CG), consisting of Senator Aquino's widow, Corazon, former senator Lorenzo Tañada, and businessman Jaime Ongpin. The pro–United States and anti-Communist NUC basically served as a mechanism for Laurel's presidential bid. The CG was more nationalist (for example, being opposed to U.S. bases) and favored a broad unity of opposition forces, including the radical Left. The presidential aspirants who agreed to the CG selection process distrusted Laurel, who had run under Marcos's ticket in 1978. They gravitated toward backing Cory Aquino, who had both moral stature and a traditional political base. She herself, however, was reluctant to run. In April 1985, the NUC and CG agreed to put up a single presidential candidate. Meanwhile, a group of military officers known as the Reform the AFP Movement (RAM) began to engage in protest activities and held meetings with the elite opposition. While outwardly working for military reform, RAM, which was linked to Defense Secretary Juan Ponce Enrile, secretly planned to stage a coup.

The CPP, bent on overthrowing the Philippine Republic, was not interested in contesting "bourgeois elections." Girding for a "strategic stalemate" in a few years, the radical Left spearheaded a series of *welgang bayan* (general strikes), that paralyzed large parts of Mindanao, Negros, and Bataan. The radicals tried to build a broad anti-dictatorship front under their leadership called the New Patriotic Alliance (BAYAN). But reacting to the radicals' moves to control BAYAN, many elite opposition figures, together with social democrats and independent leftists, withdrew from the alliance at its founding.

In late October, even as Laurel continued to build his electoral network, Aquino announced that she would run if a million signatures could be gathered in support of her candidacy. With the opposition in seeming disarray, Marcos announced in November 1985 that a snap presidential election would be held in February 1986 and that he would run for re-election.

Feverish negotiations ensued among the factions of the elite opposition. Laurel at first refused to give way. Aquino's candidacy, however, drew wide popular support—she quickly got the million signatures. Anti-Marcos businessmen swung to Aquino. Cardinal Jaime Sin, the archbishop of Manila, interceded between Aquino and Laurel. Finally, at the eleventh hour, Laurel relented, in exchange for certain political concessions for UNIDO. The elite opposition reached unity on an Aquino-Laurel ticket. The radical Left, however, maintained that the election would be nothing more than "a noisy and empty political battle" between factions of the ruling classes. The CPP called for a boycott and directed its cadres in legal organizations to implement the boycott policy. Many of the radicals' moderate allies still in BAYAN deserted it.

Aquino's campaign rallies drew huge crowds, much larger than those of her opponent. Marcos paid particular attention to securing the support of the local government machinery. As expected, Marcos rigged the elections. However, he did not make a good job of it. The National Citizens' Movement for Free Elections (NAMFREL), which monitored the elections, exposed numerous cases of electoral disenfranchisement, fraud, and intimidation. Two days after the election, thirty computer operators at the headquarters of the Commission of Elections walked off their jobs, charging manipulation of the count. The official count showed that Marcos was winning; NAMFREL's independent count put Aquino in the lead. The BP, however, declared Marcos the winner.

Aquino called for a campaign of peaceful civil disobedience. Catholic bishops immediately endorsed it. With Marcos's position fast deteriorating, other political forces—the radical Left and RAM—sought to take advantage of the situation. Marginalized by their electoral boycott, the radicals prepared a nationwide *welgang bayan,* through which they hoped to regain leadership of the anti-dictatorship movement. BAYAN leaders made overtures to Aquino and other elite opposition figures, arguing that civil disobedience would fizzle out and that the struggle had to be stepped up to a new level. Meanwhile, Enrile and RAM, who had discontinued their plan to stage a coup in December 1985 because of the snap election, now planned to strike in late February.

Uncovering the coup plot, General Fabian Ver, the AFP chief of staff, began to round up those involved. Enrile and most RAM members evaded arrest and barricaded themselves into Camp Aguinaldo; Lieutenant General Fidel Ramos, the AFP deputy chief, joined them. In a press conference, the military rebels called on the people to support them, but no support came. Later, however, Cardinal Sin, speaking on Radio Veritas, called on civilians to protect the rebels.

Tens and then hundreds of thousands gathered at the Epifanio de los Santos Avenue (EDSA), in front of Camps Aguinaldo and Crame. When Marcos and Ver ordered AFP soldiers to attack the rebels, huge crowds blocked the tanks and refused to budge. The loyalists could not get to the rebels without causing a massacre. Soon there were mass defections of Marcos's troops. Images of People Power, flashing in the international news media, completely shattered the last shreds of Marcos's legitimacy. After advising Marcos, the United States arranged for him to be flown first to Clark Air Base and eventually, against his will, to Hawaii. People Power had toppled a corrupt dictator.

IMPACTS

The Philippine People Power Revolution of 1986 has been held up as one of the shining beacons of democratization throughout the world. "As the first democratic transition in Asia during the so-called third wave of democratization," writes Thompson (1995, 1), "the Philippine transition had a 'demonstration effect' on the region. In successful struggles for political change in Pakistan, South Korea, and Taiwan— as well as in failed movements for democracy in Burma and China—both democratic oppositionists and authoritarian regimes were aware of the parallels between their own experience and that of the Philippines." The term "People Power" itself has become part of the lexicon of democratization and "democratic revolutions" an international buzzword for "a peaceful, spontaneous popular revolt that topples an unbending dictatorship" (Thompson 2004, 18).

Thanksgiving mass to celebrate the fall of the Ferdinand Marcos regime in the Philippines following the February 1986 elections that brought Corazon Aquino to the presidency with her "People Power" campaign. (David H. Wells/Corbis)

Since the 1986 revolution, however, democracy has not fared all that well in the Philippines. Early on, Wurfel (1988, 274) observed that "the change in leadership does not seem to have brought more fundamental alterations in the political system." Other political scientists have tended to qualify the country's democracy with a variety of depreciatory adjectives. Bello and Gershman (1990) and Timberman (1991), among many others, characterize it as a return to "elite democracy." Others describe it as an oligarchic democracy, or a "weak state," captured by powerful political families. Indeed, one cannot truly speak of "rule of the people" when the country is dominated by powerful politico-economic clans who resort to patronage, or to "guns, goons, and gold" to maintain their wealth and power. After 1986, the gap between the rich and the poor, instead of narrowing, became larger. The Philippines is now regarded as the most elite-dominated nation in Southeast Asia. Furthermore, restoration of democracy did not help much in economic development. The Philippines so lags behind its neighbors that it has been dubbed the "sick man of Asia."

Over the past decade or so, corruption in the Philippines has reached such staggering proportions that political scientists have come up with even more damning characterizations of Philippine politics. According to Hutchcroft (1998), the country's elite, not just Marcos and his cronies, is patrimonial. He describes the Philippines as having a "patrimonial oligarchic state," as being a weak state preyed upon and plundered by a powerful oligarchy. The predatory elite, which takes advantage of, and extracts privilege from, a largely incoherent bureaucracy, has greatly hindered the country's development. Sidel (1999) depicts "bossism" as a common phenomenon in the Philippines, describing how bosses achieve political and economic domination in their respective areas through patronage and corruption, and through violence and coercive pressures. Many Filipinos now perceive Philippine politics as so dirty that they refer to most politicians as *trapos*. Short for "traditional politician," *trapo* ordinarily means an old rag that is used to wipe dirt and that ends up all grimy and greasy.

In the Philippines, the term "People Power" continues to be very much in use, but its meaning has gone beyond simply the popular struggle for the restoration of democracy. It now has more to do with popular empowerment and social justice and with the deepening of democracy. The Philippines has become a "contested democracy," in which the elite and the *trapos* strive to maintain a formal democracy with "free and fair" elections that they can easily manipulate and dominate, and in which large sections of the poor and marginalized classes, sectors, and ethnic communities, and some sections of the middle and upper classes as well, work and fight for a more participatory and egalitarian democracy. The process of the deepening of democracy has taken on the character of a struggle of "democracy from below" versus "elite democracy" (Quimpo 2005).

In January 2001, it would have seemed that the popular movement against oligarchic rule had scored a spectacular victory with the ouster of the corrupt "boss"-president Joseph Estrada, through another awesome display of People Power at EDSA. That came to be called "People Power II," or "EDSA II." In her inaugural speech, President Gloria Macapagal-Arroyo stressed the need to outgrow "our traditional brand of politics based on patronage and personality" and to promote a politics of reform. But it was quickly back to *trapo* politics; Arroyo, the daughter of a former president, picked a cabinet composed mostly of members of powerful political families. Less than four months after People Power II, pro-Estrada forces countered with their own show of force and even tried to depict this as People Power III. EDSA III was to a significant extent a protest against elite politics. Most of the "great unwashed" who gathered at EDSA in support of the deposed Estrada and later attacked Malacañang Palace came from the poorest of the poor and harbored deep resentment against the rich. In the end, however, they fell victim to the populist appeals of pro-Estrada politicians.

Some new parties with close links to social movements and NGOs, as well as some reform-oriented politicians in traditional parties, have been espousing a more participatory "new politics" to counter *trapo* politics. In their efforts to help deepen democracy, however, they have had to contend not just with the *trapos* but also with the extreme Left. The Philippines continues to be beset by problems with Maoist insurgents and Muslim rebels. Ultra-rightist elements within the military, however, constitute a more immediate threat. Over the last few years, they have again become very active in plotting coups.

PEOPLE AND ORGANIZATIONS

Aquino, Benigno, Jr. (1932–1983)

A member of a powerful political clan in Tarlac Province, Benigno "Ninoy" Aquino, Jr., emerged as Marcos's foremost political opponent after the latter was re-elected president in 1969. After a brief stint as a newspaper reporter, Aquino entered politics, becoming the country's youngest mayor, provincial governor, and senator at the time he assumed those posts. Very much threatened by the charismatic, articulate, and politically skillful Aquino, Marcos had him arrested and imprisoned immediately after declaring martial law. In 1978, when Marcos called for elections for the interim parliament (IBP), Aquino, still in prison, headed the opposition ticket in metropolitan Manila. After seven and a half years in prison, Ninoy was allowed to leave for the United States to undergo a triple bypass operation. Marcos did not want Aquino to return, hoping that long exile would eventually make him politically irrelevant. While in prison and in the United States, however, Aquino maintained strong links not just with the traditional elite opposition but also with urban insurrectionary groups such as the April 6 Liberation Movement. Despite the risk of being imprisoned again or even killed, Aquino returned to the Philippines in August 1983. Upon his arrival at the Manila International Airport, government soldiers shot him to death.

Aquino, Corazon Cojuangco (Born 1933)

The widow of the assassinated Senator Aquino, Corazon "Cory" Aquino, was the central figure of the People Power revolution of 1986. The daughter of another powerful politico-economic clan in Tarlac, the Cojuangcos, the convent school–bred Cory largely kept away from public life when Ninoy was still alive, content to play the role of housewife and mother. After Ninoy's assassination in 1983, the small and unassuming Cory was suddenly thrust into the political limelight. On account not only of her being Ninoy's widow but also of her moral stature and her acceptability to both the traditional elite opposition and the "cause-oriented" groups, she became a rallying figure of the broad anti-dictatorship movement. When Marcos called for a snap presidential election, the opposition (except for the radical Left) united behind Cory's candidacy. As expected, Marcos stole the elections. Protest actions, however, brought about a chain of events that culminated in the People Power uprising at EDSA.

Bagong Alyansang Alyansang Makabayan (BAYAN—New Nationalist Alliance)

Initiated by the radical Left, BAYAN was envisaged as a broad anti-dictatorship coalition in which the Left would play a leading role. Because of the radicals' blatant maneuvers to control the coalition, however, the social democrats and many anti-Marcos politicians withdrew from it right at its founding congress in 1985. BAYAN's boycott of the 1986 snap election isolated the radicals from the rest of the anti-dictatorship movement even further.

Communist Party of the Philippines (CPP)

Fixated on armed struggle, the CPP called for a boycott of the 1986 snap election and directed its cadres and activists in open, legal Left organizations to implement the boycott policy. A Maoist party set up in 1968, the CPP has been waging a "protracted people's war" to overthrow the government and to establish a "national democracy" patterned after China's "people's democracy" under Mao.

Diokno, Jose (1922–1987)

A much-respected nationalist and civil libertarian, former senator Diokno was the anti-Marcos politician most identified with the "parliament of the streets." Arrested immediately after the declaration of martial law, he was detained for two years. Diokno worked closely with the radical Left in the 1970s and early 1980s, even as he differed with their vision of a one-party state and their strategy of armed struggle.

Enrile, Juan Ponce (Born 1924)

A long-time close associate of Marcos, Enrile became very rich through holdings in the coconut, logging, and timber industries. But he aspired to become the country's ruler. In early 1985, Enrile already worked closely with RAM in plotting a coup. The holing-up of Defense Minister Enrile and other coup plotters at Camp Aguinaldo provided the occasion for the mobilization of "People Power" in 1986.

Justice for Aquino, Justice for All (JAJA)

Established soon after the Aquino assassination, JAJA brought together anti-dictatorship forces from different classes, sectors, regions, and political affiliations (Left to Right), and coordinated their actions, starting with the Aquino funeral march. The coalition's name reflected the strong influence of the radical Left, which insisted on broadening the demand for justice to include all victims of Marcos's political repression. JAJA faded away as factions of the traditional elite opposition and the Left jockeyed to build and lead new coalitions.

Kilusang Bagong Lipunan (KBL—New Society Movement)

Founded in 1978, the KBL was Marcos's political party.

Laurel, Salvador (1928–2004)

Leader of UNIDO, Assemblyman "Doy" Laurel stood as the opposition's vice presidential candidate in 1986. When Marcos declared martial law in 1972, Laurel, then a senator, kept silent. Running on Marcos's ticket in 1978, he won a seat in the interim parliament. He turned against Marcos in 1979, but it took some time for other anti-Marcos politicians to regard him as part of the opposition.

Marcos, Ferdinand (1917–1989)

In power for twenty years, Ferdinand Marcos was the corrupt dictator that the People Power Revolution toppled in 1986. Ferdinand was the son of a prominent lawyer-politician in Ilocos Norte. At twenty-one, while finishing his law studies, he was convicted for the murder of his father's political opponent. Despite the murder conviction, he still managed to take—and top—the national bar exams. Taking over his own defense, the young lawyer succeeded in getting the supreme court to overturn his conviction. In 1949, Marcos was elected congressman, the country's youngest ever at that time. After three terms as congressman and one term as senator, he ran for president in 1965, defeating President Diosdado Macapagal; he ran again in 1969, defeating Senator Sergio Osmeña, Jr. Constitutionally barred from seeking a third term, Marcos declared martial law and dissolved the congress in September 1972; he had a new constitution "ratified" through "citizens' assemblies" in early 1973. Suppressing all opposition, Marcos's authoritarian regime committed numerous violations of human rights—summary executions, torture, and the like. Starting in 1978, Marcos pursued a program of "normalization," with controlled elections and parliament, then the "lifting" of martial law. Massive protests after the Aquino assassination forced Marcos to liberalize further and eventually to call for the fateful snap presidential election of 1986. Transparency International has rated Marcos as the world's second most corrupt leader (after Indonesia's Suharto), amassing U.S.$5 billion to $10 billion while in power (http://www.guardian.co.uk/print/0%2C3858%2C4888689–103547%2C00.html).

Marcos, Imeda Romualdez (Born 1929)

The dictator's wife, Imelda Romualdez Marcos, perhaps as infamous as her husband, is particularly notorious for her extravagance and ostentation. Although the Romualdezes were a powerful political clan in Leyte Province, Imelda's family constituted the poor side of it. The young Imelda, beautiful and charming, was crowned Miss Manila. After a whirlwind courtship, Ferdinand married Imelda in 1954. An indefatigable campaigner for her husband, Imelda helped to attract big crowds with her beauty and singing. She charmed national and local politicians, as well as foreign dignitaries. Soon she came to have political ambitions of her own. By the early 1970s, Imelda was already being bruited about as Marcos's probable successor, even though she had not held any significant governmental post. During the early years of martial law, Marcos often sent his wife on special diplomatic assignments abroad. In 1978, Imelda topped the list of winning candidates in metropolitan Manila in fraudulent elections for the interim parliament. Marcos appointed her Metro Manila governor and later the minister of human settlements. Imelda was so much a partner of Ferdinand in politics and plunder that Marcos's authoritarian rule has at times been referred to as the "conjugal dictatorship."

National Movement for Free Elections (NAMFREL)

A revival of a citizens' watchdog organization of the 1950s, NAMFREL monitored the 1986 snap election and conducted its own count, parallel to that of the official count. NAMFREL played a crucial role in exposing election irregularities at the local and national levels, which undermined the credibility of Marcos's claimed electoral victory.

New People's Army (NPA)

The NPA, the guerrilla army of the CPP, began as a ragtag group in 1969 but grew into a nationwide force under martial law. After the Aquino assassination, the NPA intensified its guerrilla actions in preparation for the attainment of a "strategic stalemate" with government forces.

Ramos, Fidel (Born 1928)

Lieutenant General Ramos, the AFP deputy chief of staff, joined Enrile and RAM at Camp Aguinaldo after the discovery of the Enrile-RAM coup plot. A West Point graduate, Ramos belonged to a family of distinguished diplomats. Unlike others around Marcos, Ramos did not enrich himself. Nonetheless, his record was also tainted; he headed the Philippine Constabulary, the branch of the AFP

that committed the most human rights abuses. Both Ver and Ramos were relatives of Marcos, but Marcos trusted Ver more and thus chose him over Ramos as AFP chief of staff in 1981.

Reform the Armed Forces of the Philippines (RAM)

Composed mostly of young military officers, RAM was the group involved in the February 1986 coup plot that General Ver uncovered. RAM, whose core consisted of the class of 1970 and 1971 graduates of the Philippine Military Academy, first came out into the open in early 1985 with protests against corruption in the military. Advocacy for military reforms served at least in part as a smokescreen for the plotting of a coup.

Sin, Jaime (Born 1928)

Like others in the Catholic Church hierarchy, Cardinal Jaime Sin, the archbishop of Manila, had adopted a stance of critical collaboration toward Marcos's authoritarian rule. In the early 1980s, Sin turned more critical, especially of governmental human rights abuses. After the Aquino assassination, Sin became openly sympathetic to the opposition and often helped settle differences between anti-Marcos politicians. By urging the people to converge in front of Camp Aguinaldo in support of Enrile, Ramos, and the RAM rebels, Cardinal Sin, in effect, issued the crucial rallying call for People Power.

Tañada, Lorenzo (1898–1992)

A feisty nationalist, former senator Tañada was the "grand old man" of the opposition. Because of his independence, integrity, and age (ergo, no more presidential ambitions), Tañada was the only politician included in the Convenors' Group, tasked to pick a presidential candidate of the opposition. Tañada acceded to serve as the chair of the leftist BAYAN even when many other anti-Marcos politicians had deserted it. He went "on leave," however, when the Left opted to boycott the 1986 snap election.

United Democratic Organization (UNIDO)

Certain factions of the elite opposition, including that of former Senator Aquino, set up the UNIDO (later renamed United Nationalist Democratic Organization) in an attempt to unite the opposition. Some politicians with close links to the "cause-oriented groups," however, refused to join it. After the Aquino assassination, Laurel gained ascendancy in UNIDO.

Ver, Fabian (1920–1998)

General Ver, the AFP chief of staff, is widely believed to have been one of the chief perpetrators of the assassination of Aquino. A cousin of Marcos, Ver first served him as his chauffeur and bodyguard, then as head of the palace security force. After the imposition of martial law, Marcos appointed Ver the head of the elite Presidential Security Command. As AFP chief of staff, Ver set up the Regional Unified Commands, encroaching upon the powers of both Enrile and Ramos.

Nathan Gilbert Quimpo

See Also Armed Forces, Revolution, and Counter-Revolution; Democracy, Dictatorship, and Fascism; Documentaries of Revolution; Philippine Huks and the New People's Army; Philippine Independence Revolution and Wars; Philippine Muslim Separatist Rebellions

References and Further Readings
Anderson, Benedict. 1998. *The Spectre of Comparisons: Nationalism, Southeast Asia and the World.* London: Verso.
Bello, Walden, and John Gershman. 1990. "Democratization and Stabilization in the Philippines," *Critical Sociology* 17 (1): 35–56.
Bello, Walden, David Kinley, and Elaine Elinson. 1982. *Development Debacle: The World Bank in the Philippines.* San Francisco: Institute for Food and Development Policy and Philippine Solidarity Network.
Bonner, Raymond. 1987. *Waltzing with a Dictator: The Marcoses and the Making of American Policy.* New York: Times Books.
Franco, Jennifer. 2001. *Elections and Democratization in the Philippines.* New York: Routledge.
Hawes, Gary. 1987. *The Philippine State and the Marcos Regime: The Politics of Export.* Ithaca, NY: Cornell University. http://www.guardian.co.uk/print/0%2C3858%2C4888689–103547%2C00.html (accessed December 12, 2004).
Hutchcroft, Paul. 1998. *Booty Capitalism: The Politics of Banking in the Philippines,* Ithaca, NY: Cornell University.
Javate-de Dios, Aurora, Petronilo Daroy, and Lorna Kalaw-Tirol, eds. 1988. *Dictatorship and Revolution: Roots of People's Power.* Metro Manila: Conspectus Foundation.
Karnow, Stanley. 1989. *In Our Image: America's Empire in the Philippines.* New York: Random House.
Landé, Carl. 1965. *Leaders, Factions and Parties: The Structure of Philippine Politics.* New Haven, CT: Yale University.
Linantud, John. 1998. "Whither Guns, Goons, and Gold? The Decline of Factional Election Violence in the Philippines," *Contemporary Southeast Asia* 20 (3): 298–318.
Paredes, Ruby, ed. 1988. *Philippine Colonial Democracy.* New Haven, CT: Yale University Southeast Asia Studies.
Quimpo, Nathan. 2005. "Oligarchic Patrimonialism, Bossism, Electoral Clientelism and Contested Democracy in the Philippines," *Comparative Politics* 37 (2) (January): 229-250.
Sidel, John. 1999. *Capital, Coercion, and Crime: Bossism in the Philippines,* Stanford, CA: Stanford University Press.
Thompson, Mark. 1995. *The Anti-Marcos Struggle: Personalistic Rule and Democratic Transition in the Philippines.* New Haven, CT: Yale University.
———. 2004. *Democratic Revolutions: Asia and Eastern Europe.* London: Routledge.
Timberman, David. 1991. *A Changeless Land.* New York: M. E. Sharpe.
Wurfel, David. 1988. *Filipino Politics: Development and Decay.* Ithaca, NY: Cornell University.

Polish Solidarity Movement

CHRONOLOGY

966	Baptism of Prince Mieszko I; coming of Christianity to Poland; founding of Polish statehood.
1386	The dynastic union between the Kingdom of Poland and the Grand Duchy of Lithuania.
1569	The establishment of the Polish-Lithuanian Commonwealth. An elective monarchy, the commonwealth is an ethnically heterogeneous state ruled by a Polonized gentry.
1772	The first partition of Poland, among Russia, Prussia, and Austria.
1791	Constitution of May Third.
1793	The second partition of Poland, between Russia and Prussia.
1794	The failed Kosciuszko Uprising against Russia.
1795	The third partition of Poland, between Russia, Prussia, and Austria; the end of the Polish state.
1815	The Congress in Vienna establishes a Kingdom of Poland, also known as the Congress Kingdom, a rump Polish state under the rule of Russia.

1830   The November Uprising against Russia.

1863   The January Uprising against Russia; the disappearance of the Congress Kingdom; the abolition of peasant serfdom in the Russian partition.

1918   The collapse of the partitioning powers in the wake of World War I; the rebirth of the Polish state.

1939   Ribbentrop-Molotov Pact between Nazi Germany and the Soviet Union; the German and Soviet invasions of Poland; the beginning of World War II.

1944   Creation of a Polish Liberation Committee in the U.S.S.R.; failed Warsaw Uprising against Germans; introduction of Communist control in liberated areas.

1945   Soviet liberation of Poland from Nazi forces; Yalta Conference. Great Britain and the United States agree to Soviet territorial and political gains in Poland.

1947   Rigged national elections give victory to the Communists; introduction of Communist dictatorship to Poland under Soviet control.

1948   Unification of the Socialist and Communist parties into the Polish United Workers' Party (PZPR); purge of Wladyslaw Gomulka, a Communist leader advocating the "Polish road to Socialism"; beginning of Stalinism in Poland.

1956   Nikita Khrushchev's secret speech denouncing Stalin's crimes; beginning of de-Stalinization in Poland; Workers' revolt in Poznan. Gomulka returns to power in October.

1966   Celebrations of the Millennium of Christianity and Polish statehood.

1968   Student protests in Poland; anti-Semitic campaign; defeat of revisionist opposition within the Communist Party.

1970   Workers' protests in response to food price rises. The army and police massacre protesters in the cities of Gdansk, Gdynia, and Szczecin on the Baltic coast. Edward Gierek replaces Gomulka as party leader.

1976   Workers' protests precipitated by food price increases. Violent clashes in Radom and Ursus. Repression against workers leads to the establishment of the Committee for the Defense of Workers, an organization of dissident intellectuals. Beginnings of the new opposition against the Communist regime.

1978   Election of Cardinal Karol Wojtyla, archbishop of Krakow, as Pope John Paul II.

1979   The pope's visit to Poland causes spiritual revival of millions and undermines the prestige of the Communist Party.

1980   July Strikes caused by food price increases.

         In August, strike begins in the Lenin Shipyard in Gdansk. Lech Walesa assumes the leadership of the Interfactory Strike Committee (MKS). On August 31, the MKS signs the agreement with the government that permits independent free trade unions. Similar agreements are signed in Szczecin and Jastrzebie.

         In September, Stanislaw Kania replaces Gierek as party leader. New trade unions form the National Coordinating Commission, which submits the application for legal registration of the Independent Self-Governing Trade Union "Solidarity" (NSZZ, "Solidarnosc").

         In October, general warning strike. Registration crisis begins.

         In November, the supreme court registers Solidarity.

         In December, the U.S. government reports the concentration of Soviet forces alongside Poland's borders; Warsaw Pact summit in Moscow.

1981   In January, peasants' occupation strike begins to demand the registration of Rural Solidarity.

In February, General Wojciech Jaruzelski becomes prime minister. Jaruzelski appeals for ninety days without strikes. End of peasants' occupation strike.

In March, three Solidarity activists are brutally beaten by police in Bydgoszcz. Solidarity threatens a general strike.

In May, registration of Rural Solidarity. Pope John Paul II is critically wounded in an assassination attempt. Death of Cardinal Stefan Wyszynski, primate of Poland since 1947.

In August, food shortages and price increases; wildcat strikes and public protests. A deadlock in negotiations arises between Solidarity and the government.

In September, the first National Solidarity Congress opens in Gdansk.

In October, Solidarity congress ends with Lech Walesa's re-election as chairman. At the plenary session of the Central Committee of the PZPR, Jaruzelski replaces Kania as party leader. The government prepares a crackdown on Solidarity.

In November, military operational groups are sent into the cities; student strikes throughout Poland.

On December 13, General Jaruzelski imposes martial law. The Military Council for National Salvation (WRON) takes over the functions of the government. Thousands of Solidarity activists are arrested and interned. The military and security forces seal off the country.

On December 16, security forces kill nine miners at the Wujek coal mine. By the end of December, occupation strikes are crushed.

1982   In April, formation of Solidarity's underground Provisional Coordinating Commission (TKK).

In October, new law on trade unions dissolves Solidarity.

1983   In June, Pope visits Poland for the second time.

In July, martial law is lifted.

In October, Lech Walesa receives Nobel Peace Prize.

1984   In June, Solidarity organizes a boycott of local government elections. General amnesty.

In October, abduction and assassination of the Reverend Jerzy Popieluszko, Solidarity's chaplain, by a group of security police officers.

1985   In March, Mikhail Gorbachev becomes general secretary of the Communist Party of the Soviet Union.

1986   In September, amnesty for political prisoners is declared. Formation of Solidarity's Provisional Council.

1987   In June, Pope visits Poland for the third time.

In November, Lech Walesa forms Solidarity's new National Executive Commission. The government loses referendum on "second stage of economic reform."

1988   In February, food price rises.

In April–May, strikes spread throughout Poland.

In August, there is a second wave of strikes in major industrial centers; calls for re-legalization of Solidarity. Discussions between Solidarity's representatives and government officials begin.

In November, there is a televised debate between Lech Walesa and chairman of the pro-government trade unions, Alfred Miodowicz.

In December, Walesa forms Citizens' Committee, an advisory board to the chairman of Solidarity.

1989   In January, the Central Committee of the PZPR agrees to re-legalize Solidarity.

In February, the Roundtable Talks begin.

Roundtable Talks conclude in April. The agreement foresees that 35 percent of the seats in the Sejm (lower house) and 100 percent of the seats in the Senate will be contested in parliamentary elections in June. Solidarity is re-legalized.

On June 4, Solidarity wins 35 percent of the seats in the Sejm and 99 out of 100 seats in the Senate.

In August, Tadeusz Mazowiecki, a Solidarity activist, is appointed prime minister.

In September, formation of a coalition government.

In December, Parliament passes economic reforms, commonly known as the "Balcerowicz plan," paving the way for a transformation to market economy.

1990   In January, the Balcerowicz plan is introduced. Self-dissolution of the Communist Party.

In June, Solidarity splits into a number of parties.

In December, Lech Walesa is elected president of Poland.

1991   In October, the first fully free parliamentary elections are held. Fragmented parliament.

1993   In September, Post-Communist Alliance of the Democratic Left wins parliamentary elections and forms government.

1995   In November, Aleksander Kwasniewski, leader of the Alliance of the Democratic Left, defeats Lech Walesa in presidential elections.

1997   In September, coalition of post-Solidarity parties wins parliamentary elections and forms a center-right government.

1999   In March, Poland joins NATO.

2000   In November, Aleksander Kwasniewski is re-elected president.

2001   In September, Alliance of the Democratic Left wins parliamentary elections. Defeat of post-Solidarity parties.

2004   May 1, Poland joins the European Union.

2005   April 2, Pope John Paul II (Karol Wojtyla) dies.

INTRODUCTION

Created in 1980, the Polish Solidarity Movement started the process of dismantling Communism in Eastern Europe. Conceived as the first independent trade union in the Soviet Bloc, Solidarity was a genuine mass movement with a membership of 10 million at the peak of its popularity in 1981. By challenging the monopoly of the one-party state in Poland and the Communist system at large, Solidarity reintroduced the concept of civil society and paved the way for the 1989 revolutions that abolished Communism and reintegrated formerly Communist states with the rest of the democratic world.

BACKGROUND: CULTURE AND HISTORY

The origins of the Polish state date back to the tenth century A.D., when Prince Mieszko I from the Piast dynasty was baptized in the Latin Christian rite. In 1383 the Polish kingdom formed a dynastic union with the Grand Duchy of Lithuania. Under the rule of the Jagiello dynasty, the Polish-Lithuanian state acquired the position of a regional power, with its borders stretching from the Baltic Sea to the Black Sea, and extending eastward to what is now western Russia. During the sixteenth century, the Polish-Lithuanian Commonwealth developed a "noble democracy," in which supreme power lay with a parliament dominated by the nobility. The monarchy became an elective institution with the nobles appointing Polish kings in public assemblies. In contrast to other countries in continental Europe, in which absolutism brought into existence a strong and centralized state, Poland had a weak central government. The peasantry was enserfed, while the middle class remained weak and often unassimilated. Only the nobility enjoyed full citizen rights.

Following a series of wars against Sweden, Russia, and Turkey in the seventeenth and eighteenth centuries, the commonwealth grew extremely weak. All attempts to reform the state failed because of the opposition of the gentry, which guarded its liberties. The advancement of the Enlightenment led to a major effort to modernize the Polish state, the liberal Constitution of May 3, 1791. However, democratic reforms failed as a consequence of the Russian invasion of Poland and the opposition of the great magnates. The commonwealth fell victim to its powerful and aggressive neighbors, Russia, Prussia, and Austria, which carved up the Polish lands in the partitions of 1772, 1793, and 1795.

Although Poland disappeared from the map of Europe, the Poles continued to struggle for the resurrection of their state. During the Napoleonic Wars, Polish patriots fought alongside French armies against the partitioning powers. Subjected to the oppressive rule of Lutheran Prussia and Orthodox Russia, the Poles came to identify national identity with Roman Catholicism. Polish nationalism also developed cultural-political messianism, a strong belief that through its suffering Poland would eventually redeem Europe. As the impoverished and degraded nobility began migrating to urban centers, it formed the intelligentsia, a socially and politically distinctive group of the educated members of society who viewed their destiny as the preservation of patriotic culture and the enlightenment of the peasant masses. By the end of the nineteenth century, the intelligentsia had established a network of educating institutions and mobilized various forms of socio-political activism, which embodied the development of civil society. The advance of modern nationalism brought into existence two political currents devoted to conflicting visions of the Polish nation: the nationalist National Democratic movement led by Roman Dmowski, and the progressive and tolerant Polish Socialist Party (PPS). Under the leadership of Józef Pilsudski, the PPS subordinated Socialist ideology to the struggle for national independence. Altogether, during 123 years of dependency, the Poles developed a strong sense of national identity consisting of the following traits: fervent patriotism, distrust of Russia and Germany, ardent Catholicism, belief in Poland's historical mission, and the tradition of grassroots activism.

The collapse of the partitioning powers in the wake of World War I led to the rebirth of sovereign Poland, also known as the Second Republic. The new Polish state that emerged from the Versailles peace conference and Riga peace treaty ending the 1920 Polish-Soviet War, in which Polish forces defeated the Bolshevik-led Red Army, was a large country inhabited by some 27 million people, one-third of whom were non-Polish (Crampton 1994, 41). The largest minorities included Ukrainians, Jews, Belorussians, and Germans. Composed of former Austro-Hungarian, German, and Russian territories, the new country faced the daunting tasks of territorial, ethnic, socio-political, and economic adjustments. As a result of bitter border disputes with neighbors, German and Soviet attempts to win back territories lost to Poland, and lack of a coherent foreign policy after two decades of its existence, Poland was no nearer to securing its frontiers than in 1918. The Second Republic was particularly unsuccessful in its policy toward national minorities. The ill treatment of the Ukrainian and Belorussian minorities and widespread and virulent anti-Semitism in public life antagonized Ukrainians, Belorussians, and Jews. Following a brief period of inefficient parliamentary rule, Pilsudski in 1926 launched a military coup d'état, establishing authoritarian rule.

Yet despite all of its failures, the Second Republic proved conspicuously immune to the ideological currents of Nazism and Communism. In September 1939, Poland was the first country to offer armed resistance to Hitler. The Nazi-Soviet pact of August 1939 foresaw the partition of the Polish state between Germany and the Soviet Union. After the defeat of Poland in September 1939, the Nazis and the Soviets introduced a ruthless occupation, killing 6 million Polish citizens, including 3 million Jews. Altogether, 22 percent of the Polish population of 1939 perished in the war (ibid., 196). Polish statehood continued in the form of the government in exile in London, while Polish troops fought alongside the Allies. In occupied Poland, the resistance movement was led by the Home Army (AK), loyal to the government in exile. As Soviet armies advanced into Polish lands in 1944, Stalin created a Communist-dominated provisional government, the so-called Polish Liberation Committee, which claimed to be the only existing Polish regime. The AK tried to prevent a Communist takeover by launching a series of offensives against the Germans before or at the time of the arrival of the Red Army. The biggest military strike took place in Warsaw, where the Poles launched an uprising against the Nazis in August 1944. The Germans crushed the revolt with savage brutality, killing some 200,000 civilians (Korbonski 1981, 200) and burning the city to the ground, while the Soviets stood on the right bank of the Vistula and refused to help the rebels.

For the Soviets and their Polish agents, the Communists from the Polish Workers' Party (PPR), the tragedy of Warsaw paved the way for the domination of the country. The historical anti-Communist elite vanished from the scene, while AK military units were either destroyed by the Germans or hunted down by the Soviet NKVD (secret police) and Communist political police. Hundreds of thousands of Polish patriots were deported to the Soviet Union or sentenced to long prison terms by the new regime. Some fell victim to judicial murders. Anti-Communist guerrillas resisted Polish and Soviet security forces until 1947, and in some rural areas even until the 1950s. At the Yalta conference in February 1945 and at Potsdam in July, the Allied leaders agreed to revise Polish borders by ceding Poland's eastern territories to the Soviet Union and moving its western frontiers westward to the Oder and Neisse rivers. As a result, Poland experienced huge population transfers: the expulsion of the Germans corresponded with the influx of the Poles from the east. After border changes, the nearly total destruction of Polish Jewry by the Nazis, and the fact that the Ukrainian and Belorussian minorities stayed in the Soviet-annexed territories, Poland became an ethnically homogenous state.

Territorial adjustments went in parallel with political transition to Communist rule. According to the Yalta agreement, the country's future government was to be formed after free and unfettered elections. Although the Communists were forced to recognize the political opposition, they did not intend to give up their power. In the rigged elections of 1947, they defeated the agrarian Polish Peasant Party through the combination of terror, fraud, and intimidation. Other political parties, especially the Polish Socialist Party, were gradually dominated and subdued by Communist stooges and sympathizers. In December 1948, the PPR and PPS merged into a new Communist party, the Polish United Workers' Party (PZPR), which launched the full Sovietization of Poland. The socio-political and economic system, which took hold of eastern Europe in the late 1940s, contained the essential features of a totalitarian state: one-party dictatorship, total control over society exercised through ideological mobilization and coercion, the command economy, and the creation of a ruling class recruited from among beneficiaries of the system. Finally, individual Communist parties had to answer to the Soviet leadership. It must be stressed, however, that Polish Communism failed to reach the most extreme form. The Stalinist show trials that left a strong imprint on Czechoslovakia and Hungary bypassed Poland, since its rulers could not afford the weakening of the party. More important, the Polish Communists did not succeed in conquering two important vestiges of civil society—private farming and the Roman Catholic Church. The main beneficiaries of a land reform launched by the Communist-led provisional government in 1944, peasant masses also formed the backbone of the Polish labor force used by the Stalinist regime for giant industrialization projects. Although many peasants moved to growing cities and new industrial centers, they also preserved their traditional habits and customs, including ardent Catholicism. In ethnically homogenous Poland, Catholicism became the main pillar of national identity, especially against the Communists brought to power by a foreign and atheist power. Under the charismatic and energetic leadership of Cardinal Stefan Wyszynski, the church separated itself from the secular Communist regime and offered to the Poles an alternative community, a repository of traditional values and patriotic spirit. As a result, by the mid 1950s, Poland was a tightly controlled but still not an Orwellian state.

Stalinism lasted in Poland until 1956. Its advent and collapse were tied to the political fortunes of one man, Wladyslaw Gomulka. A Communist leader in occupied Poland during World War II, Gomulka displayed less ideological orthodoxy and more flexibility than his comrades who had spent the war in the Soviet Union. He defended the "Polish road to Socialism," proposing that Polish Communism should acknowledge the historical traditions of the Polish nation and socio-economic conditions, rather than blindly copying the Soviet system. Gomulka, for example, opposed the speedy collectivization of agriculture and favored working relations with the church, instead of persecution of it. He also detested the omnipresence of Soviet advisers and disputed the degree of Soviet control over national Communist parties. Gomulka's views and stubbornness caused his purge from the Communist leadership during the early days of Stalinism in 1948. He was back, however, in 1956, when the Polish party faced a huge legitimacy crisis after Stalin's death and subsequent liberalization and the denunciation of Stalin's crimes. Widespread discontent among intellectuals and reform-minded party members over the slow progress of de-Stalinization, as well as the bloody workers' uprising in Poznan in June 1956, set off a major political crisis. Although the Poznan revolt was crushed, the regime was forced to liberalize the political system, by introducing amnesty for political prisoners, lifting censorship, and allowing the popular movement for democratization of Socialism. To pacify Polish society, the Communist Party designated Gomulka as its chairman in October, against the objections of Soviet leaders who flew to Warsaw in order to prevent Gomulka's re-election. After dramatic talks conducted under the threat of military invasion, Gomulka won the Soviets' trust, reassuring them that his accession to power would ease political tension and restore control over a pro-reform movement. The majority of the Poles viewed the retreat of the Soviets as a great patriotic victory and perceived Gomulka as a national hero.

After the initial period of political-economic reforms and greater artistic freedom, Gomulka consolidated the party's authority and gradually retreated from democratization. By the mid 1960s, Gomulka's regime had grown authoritarian, ideologically conservative, and economically incompetent. While aiming to legitimize and reinforce its flagging rule, the regime employed Polish nationalism—namely, the glorification of the national past, aggressive Germanophobia, and anti-Semitism. One of the outcomes of these developments was the "Polonization" of the Communist Party, culminating in the 1967–1968 purge of Jewish members. In March 1968, the government took advantage of the student protests against intensifying censorship to discredit the opposition as agents of West Germany and Israel. The ensuing anti-Semitic campaign led to the exodus of 13,000 Polish Jews (Stola 2000, 213), cultural pogrom, and the defeat of the reformist faction within the party. The combined effect of an anti-Semitic frenzy in Poland and the suppression of the "Prague Spring" in Czechoslovakia deprived the Communists of the last vestiges of intellectual support for their ideology and proved that Communism could not democratize itself.

CONTEXT AND PROCESS OF REVOLUTION

The Gomulka leadership survived for only two more years. Although the ossified economic system did not produce enough consumer goods and failed to improve living conditions, the regime succeeded in keeping the population calm by preserving low food prices for a decade. However, by 1970 it had become clear that the continuing price freeze only aggravated the economic distortions. The government announced a food price increase of up to 30 percent (Paczkowski 1998, 387), without warning, in December 1970, less than two weeks before Christmas. Social protests paralyzed the coastal cities of Gdansk, Gdynia, and Szczecin, where thousands of shipyard workers went on strike and marched on local party buildings. In response, the government ordered in army and police units that fired at workers, killing tens of protesters and wounding hundreds. Although the army crushed the workers' revolt, it failed to liquidate strikes and work stoppages. Moreover, Gomulka's tactic of violent confrontation alarmed the Soviets and several members of the PZPR party leadership. In late December the Polish Politburo sacked Gomulka and elected Edward Gierek as party leader.

Gierek proved capable of pacifying social unrest by means other than violence. First, he won over the striking workers in direct negotiations, showing humility and frankness. Second, the new government withdrew the price increases and used Soviet loans to stabilize wages. Unlike Gomulka, Gierek was not an ideology-driven zealot but a pragmatic politician. Having spent twenty years of his life in France and Belgium, Gierek had little in common with old Polish Communists who had undergone their political initiation in Soviet party schools or pre-war jails. Gierek knew that Communist ideology and coercion could not legitimize the party state. Instead, he believed that prosperity was the key to winning compliance. Gierek based his broad strategy on raising standards of living, providing consumer goods, and showing greater tolerance in intellectual, cultural, and religious domains. He increased wages and implemented an investment boom through Western loans. However, the misguided investment policy rivaled the incompetent management of party bureaucrats and government officials. Loans from Western banks went to obsolete heavy industries, while imported technologies failed to produce exportable products that were necessary to pay back foreign debts. A trade deficit developed as the government did not adjust prices to increasing wages.

By 1975 economic growth rates had begun to drop, and Gierek's ambitious program of building a modern Poland was running out of steam. By the summer of 1976, Gierek and his associates could no longer bury their heads in the sand. Gierek resorted to the same solution that had been reached by Gomulka six years before: in June 1976, the government announced a general food price increase of from 30 percent to 70 percent (Berend 1996, 255). Strikes and social protests erupted in several cities. In Radom, southeast of Warsaw, protestors besieged and burned local party headquarters, clashed with police, and looted stores. Although the security forces did not use firearms, they put down the riots with the utmost brutality. Hundreds of workers were tried and sentenced to prison terms or fines, while others were fired, blacklisted, and condemned as "hooligan elements" at the party-organized rallies. But ultimately the government capitulated, rescinding the price increases.

As in 1970, the Polish workers succeeded in blocking the unpopular actions of the Communist government. In addition, the Radom riots and their brutal suppression sparked a significant political initiative that eventually produced an alternative to one-party rule—the dissident movement. Acting in response to the workers' trials, a group of Warsaw intellectuals formed a committee in July of 1976 to offer legal advice to the prosecuted and support their families. In September, they adopted the name of the Committee for the Defense of Workers (KOR). The group included former Marxist revisionists, veterans of the 1968 student protests, members of the pre-war Socialist Party, and anti-Nazi and anti-Communist resisters.

KOR presented itself ostensibly not as a political but as a social movement aspiring to establish an independent public sphere. The initial task of helping the arrested workers soon broadened into other activities: the promotion of human rights, underground publishing, independent education, and the activation of free trade unions. The expansion of KOR's goals was reflected by the modification of its name: in September 1977 the organization renamed itself the Committee for Social Self-Defense KOR (KSS KOR). In its efforts to defend human liberties, KOR relied on the Helsinki Accords on peace, security, and civil rights, signed by the Polish government in 1975, as well as the provisions of the Polish constitution. Members of KOR publicly revealed their names and addresses. This formula of openness and emphasis on legality demonstrated that people could pursue the goal of self-determination without any official intermediaries. As Gierek struggled to secure more loans, he chose not to antagonize Western leaders by brutalizing the dissidents. It is also evident that he did not consider KOR a dangerous threat but rather a "safety vent," relieving intellectuals' criticism without any serious consequences.

Contrary to Gierek's opinion, KOR did not disappear but served as the nucleus of the democratic opposition in Poland, and it influenced dissident groups in other countries—for example, Charter 77 in Czechoslovakia. Throughout the rest of the 1970s the Polish opposition swelled into several organizations of different political persuasions, hundreds of participants, and thousands of sympathizers. KOR members and supporters made forays into the working class and helped to organize the Free Trade Unions of the Coast in Gdansk, notable as the site of the workers' revolt of 1970. One of the leading activists in the new organization was a young electrician and veteran of the 1970 strike, Lech Walesa. In September 1979 the representatives of the Free Trade Unions announced the Charter of Workers' Rights, listing such demands as the right to strike, free independent trade unions, and just wages, to name a few.

By the end of the 1970s, Poland became the strongest center of opposition to Communist authoritarianism in the Soviet Bloc. However, the alliance between the intelligentsia and the working class that began to materialize under the tutelage of KOR encompassed only a tiny fraction of the Polish population. The development of civil society could not take place without the support of the Polish Catholic Church. The situation was complicated by the fact that Marxist-oriented intellectuals—the driving force of the revisionist opposition, the student protests of 1968, and, to a large extent, KOR—were staunchly anti-clerical. Yet, in the mid 1970s, they understood that the church was the strongest autonomous institution that existed in Poland. These developments were seconded by the growing outspokenness of Polish church leaders about human and civil rights. In his response to the repression of workers in 1976, Cardinal Wyszynski declared that it was the duty of the church to defend the workers against government repression. Reverend Jan Zieja, a Catholic priest, was among the founding members of KOR, and Cardinal Karol Wojtyla, archbishop of Krakow, met with the group's leadership in November 1976.

In the late 1970s, the church and the non-Communist Left from KOR were overcoming mutual resentment and joining forces in the struggle against a totalitarian state. From then on, the democratic opposition found protection, benevolent neutrality, and at times active support in the Polish church. The major boost to this trend was the naming of Cardinal Wojtyla as Pope John Paul II in October 1978, the first Slavic and Polish pontiff in history, as well as a church leader from a Communist country. Wojtyla's election caused widespread euphoria in his native country. Shortly after his election, the pope expressed his wish to visit Poland. John Paul II arrived in Warsaw in June 1979. The impact of the papal visit on the Polish people can hardly be overestimated. For the Poles, it was an experience of redemption, moral renewal, and spiritual reawakening. The pope delivered dozens of sermons in six cities, attracting millions of people. His Mass in Warsaw saw a crowd of 1 million, while the pontifical Mass in Krakow was attended by 2.5 to 3 million laymen (Kubik 1994, 139). The pope's eloquent and articulate language contrasted with party propaganda. Departing for Rome, he urged the Poles to "have the courage to go the way no one has followed before" (Luxmore and Babiuch 1999, 139). By transforming the Polish public, the papal visit of 1979 paved the way for a great political and moral revolution that was to sweep Poland within a year.

While the new opposition provided revolutionary cadres and the church offered spiritual mobilization, it was the economic crisis caused by the Gierek regime that started the political upheaval of 1980. The beginnings of the Solidarity Revolution bore a striking resemblance to the 1970 and 1976 workers' revolts. Between 1975 and 1979, Poland's foreign debt rose from $8 billion to $23 billion (Paczkowski 1998, 404). In response, the government decided to increase exports and cut down food supplies for the domestic market. In the summer of 1980, it began adjusting prices for inflation and increasing the share of meat sold in the commercial stores for much higher prices. Predictably, the prices of meat skyrocketed. The first work stoppages took place in July. In the second half of July the workers' demands broadened, adding to the demand for pay increases the call for the reform of family subsidies, the reduction of police and military benefits such as high family allowances and pensions, work-free Saturdays, and free trade unions. New strikes continued to erupt across the country. The opposition played an important role by regularly informing and updating Western mass media—especially those radio stations that, like Radio Free Europe, the BBC, and the Voice of America, broadcast in Polish. The population was thus aware of the massive wave of protests.

The breakthrough came on August 14, when the Lenin Shipyard in Gdansk, the site of the 1970 workers' protests, went on strike in defense of a free trade-union activist, Anna Walentynowicz, who had been sacked by the management five days earlier. Under the energetic leadership of Lech Walesa, who was coached by a KOR activist, Bogdan Borusewicz, the strike took on a political character. The initial demands were reinstatement of Anna Walentynowicz and Walesa (he was fired in 1976); wage increases of 2,000 zloty; guarantees of no reprisals; family benefits on a par with those of the police; and erection of a monument to the workers killed in 1970 (Garton Ash 1983, 43).

Born in a peasant family in 1943, Walesa left home as a teenager to become an electrician. At the age of twenty-four, he moved to Gdansk and took a job at the Lenin Shipyard. He was a member of the strike committee in 1970. Disillusioned with the Gierek regime, Walesa engaged himself in various acts of political defiance, including vehement criticism of the state-sponsored trade unions, democratic agitation, and calls for the commemoration of the fallen shipyard workers; he lost his job in 1976. In 1978 he joined the Founding Committee of the Free Trade Unions. By 1980, Walesa was a well-known member of the opposition in Gdansk and popular figure among local workers (Walesa 1987).

On August 16 the management accepted the demands, and Walesa ended the strike. However, the representatives of other enterprises from the region that went on strike in solidarity with the Lenin Shipyard convinced him to continue the strike. On the night of August 16 and 17, Walesa and delegates of twenty other strike committees formed the Interfactory Strike Committee (MKS). By August 18, some 156 factories had joined the MKS (Paczkowski 1998, 462). The Interfactory Strike Committee produced a list of twenty-one demands, including the creation of free trade unions independent of the party, the right to strike, guarantees of the freedom of expression, release of political prisoners, and specific economic demands (Garton Ash 1983, 46–48). Analogous demands were formulated by the second MKS in Szczecin. The Gdansk strike attracted Western journalists and TV crews. By the end of August the wave of political strikes encompassed the whole country. Party leaders ultimately agreed on a peaceful settlement. On August 31, Communist Politburo member Mieczyslaw Jagielski and Walesa ceremoniously signed the Gdansk agreement. In the Gdansk and Szczecin accords, along with one other signed in Jastrzebie on September 3, the Communist regime conceded most of the strikers' demands, including the right to set up free and self-governing trade unions. On September 5, Stanislaw Kania, an experienced high party official, replaced Gierek as the first secretary. Moscow viewed the August accords as a temporary compromise and expected the Polish Communist Party to regain control over the country gradually and dismantle the new popular movement (Paczkowski 1998, 473).

During the first half of September, mushrooming new trade unions attracted 3 million members (Garton Ash 1983, 80). On September 17, delegates of thirty-five Interfactory Strike Committees and several opposition activists met in Gdansk to decide whether they should create one national organization or continue as autonomous unions. The talks ended in a compromise. The National Coordinating Commission (KKP) was set up under the chairmanship of Walesa, and the creation of the national federation of unions, the Independent Self-Governing Trade Union "Solidarity," was announced. In late September the KKP submitted the application for legal registration of Solidarity to the Warsaw Provincial Court. Fearing that the new organization would have enough strength to challenge the party, the regime blocked the process of registration. In retaliation, Solidarity

launched a one-hour general warning strike that halted the entire country. The government yielded. In a compromise between government and union negotiators, the legalization of Solidarity was agreed in return for acceptance of the leading role of the party in the state. On November 10, the court officially registered Solidarity as a legal entity.

For the first time in its history, the Communist government was forced to permit the existence of a nationwide movement outside its control. Professional associations, one after another, pledged allegiance to Solidarity. Peasants, students, and even members of the police force applied for registration of their own autonomous associations. The creation of Solidarity also sparked an unprecedented wave of social activism, grassroots initiatives, and pluralist discourse. By the end of 1980, Solidarity had 9 million members. To quote historian Gale Stokes, "Solidarity sought a partnership with the government, or even a kind of tripartite agreement, with the church as the third entity" (Stokes 1993, 39). In this configuration the party held political power, guaranteeing to Moscow that Poland would not break away from the Soviet Bloc; Solidarity managed nonpolitical activities, whereas the church mediated between the two partners. In addition, the Poles still held vivid memories of the Soviet invasions of Hungary in 1956 and of Czechoslovakia in 1968, understanding that calls for a greater degree of freedom could provoke the Soviets.

However, the partnership between Solidarity and the Communist Party was incompatible with the nature of the system, since it threatened the party's monopoly on power. Having tasted victory, revolutionized masses would inevitably push for political concessions, while the Communist regime had no intentions of diminishing its dominance. The confrontation between the government and Solidarity was inevitable.

On January 2, 1981, a peasants' occupation strike began in southeastern Poland under the demand of registering Rural Solidarity, the farmers' independent association. Although the farmers won an important victory in the form of a law guaranteeing the inviolability of private land ownership, the creation of Rural Solidarity was put off.

General Wojciech Jaruzelski was appointed prime minister in February. A professional soldier with strong patriotic credentials—he had fought in World War II—Jaruzelski was widely perceived as an energetic, competent, and uncorrupted leader standing above party politics. As minister of defense he commanded the army, the bulwark of national pride and an extremely popular institution in society. However, he was a devoted Communist, fanatically loyal to the Soviet Union.

Jaruzelski began under a promising sign by calling for ninety days without strikes and a national consensus in face of the grave economic crisis. Solidarity respected the general's appeal and called off strikes. In early March, Jaruzelski met Walesa to discuss the situation in the country. However, the truce between the government and Solidarity was broken in the same month when police officers brutally assaulted and beat three Solidarity activists who had gone to a meeting of the local government council in Bydgoszcz demanding the legalization of Rural Solidarity. Solidarity condemned the incident and demanded the punishment of those guilty of the police violence. Although the regime finally permitted the legalization of Rural Solidarity, it grew intransigently hostile toward the opposition. At the end of March, General Jaruzelski approved the set of guidelines for the implementation of a state of war, strengthening those forces within the party that sought to destroy Solidarity by force.

During the following months Solidarity underwent increasing radicalization, gradually giving up the nonpolitical and self-limiting character of its revolution. The legal press organ of Solidarity, the weekly *Tygodnik Solidarnosc,* launched in April, openly discussed the plans for political and social reforms, including the union's possible role in future parliamentary elections. The self-confidence of the union grew when Andrzej Wajda's *Man of Iron,* a film epic about the birth of Solidarity, won the Palme d'Or at Cannes in May. But in the same month a feeling of anxiety swept the country after the assassination attempt on the pope's life and the death of Cardinal Wyszynski almost robbed Poland of its two spiritual leaders. The moderating influence of the church on Solidarity substantially weakened. This was especially unfortunate at a time of acute economic crisis. Price increases and the introduction of monthly rations for food and consumer products caused social protest, including hunger marches and spontaneous strikes.

During the fall of 1981 a climate of political confrontation dominated the Polish political discourse. The program adopted by Solidarity during its first national congress in September and October demanded the "Self-Governing Republic," a pluralist state in which citizens were to take political, social, and cultural matters into their own hands. The delegates, who gathered in Gdansk at a time of joint military maneuvers in Poland by the Warsaw Pact nations, also issued a "Message to the Working People of Eastern Europe," calling for the creation of free trade unions and closer contacts between democratic-minded groups from the Soviet Bloc (Garton Ash 1983, 221–222).

The party perceived the calls from Gdansk as a declaration of war. Subjected to harsh criticism for his alleged indecisiveness, Kania resigned in October. He was replaced by Jaruzelski. By then, the general held the three most important offices in the country: first secretary, prime minister, and minister of defense. On December 5, 1981, the Politburo finally agreed to implement martial law. On the night of December 12 and 13, General Jaruzelski gave the order. Some

100,000 military and police troops supported by 4,000 tanks and armored vehicles took total control of the country, arrested thousands of Solidarity activists and sympathizers, including most of the union's leaders, cut off communications, and isolated urban centers. The functions of the government were taken over by the Military Council for National Salvation, headed by Jaruzelski, suspending civil rights, placing enterprises under military control, and creating special military courts. All political and social associations, Solidarity included, were suspended and their assets put under the government's control. From a military point of view, the introduction of martial law was a formidable success achieved against little resistance. Solidarity was defeated, and some 5,000 of its members were sent to detention camps. Those union leaders who escaped the arrest called upon society to abstain from violent resistance to avoid more casualties. In October 1982 the government officially dissolved Solidarity and confiscated its property.

However, Jaruzelski's martial law was a Pyrrhic victory, as it proved that the rule of the party could be saved only by naked force. In that respect, the brutal suppression of Solidarity proved the political and moral bankruptcy of the Communist regime, which always claimed to represent and act on behalf of the working class. Martial law was condemned by the democratic world. The economic sanctions imposed by the United States on the Jaruzelski regime only aggravated the economic crisis in the country. Within a few years, the restoration of economic ties with the West became the top priority of Polish politicians. The sixteen months of the Solidarity movement had completely transformed Polish society and politics by activating civil society and forming a socio-political alternative to the party state. Solidarity was banned and humiliated, but only momentarily defeated.

IMPACTS

The success of martial law did not result in the restoration of pre-1980 conditions. The regime lacked the economic strength and political legitimacy to appease society and eliminate the opposition, which continued its activities underground under the command of those leaders who, like Zbigniew Bujak, had escaped detention in December 1981. Set up in April 1982, a clandestine Provisional Coordinating Commission (TKK) pursued the twin goals of self-governing republic and democratization of the system. This involved a pattern of political struggle in Poland between two active minorities, the party and the opposition, confronting each other in face of the silent majority. In an attempt to prove that the political situation was under control, Jaruzelski began releasing detainees, including Walesa, dissolved the WRON, and lifted martial law in July of 1983. The permission granted to the pope to visit the country in the same year showed the regime's self-confidence. But in October 1983 the government found itself in an embarrassing position when Walesa received the Nobel Peace Prize.

Far more devastating for Jaruzelski was the abduction and subsequent murder of the Reverend Jerzy Popieluszko, a well-known supporter of Solidarity and outspoken critic of the regime, by a group of security police officers in October of 1984. The crime galvanized both Polish and foreign public opinion. But Jaruzelski's resolution of the affair was truly surprising: the assassins were arrested, tried, and sentenced to long prison terms.

Since 1982, Jaruzelski had sought to normalize the situation in the country by expanding the channels of "permissible pluralism" while simultaneously persecuting Solidarity. In 1984 the government launched a labor alternative to Solidarity, the National Trade Union Accord (OPZZ), formally independent of the Communist Party. Two years later, the regime granted a complete amnesty to political prisoners. Following the accession of Mikhail Gorbachev to power in the Soviet Union and the launching of socio-political reforms, commonly known as perestroika, Jaruzelski acquired the reputation of Gorbachev's most ardent supporter in Eastern Europe. However, the success of Jaruzelski's strategy of normalization relied on two conditions: the total compliance of society and successful economic recovery. Both goals turned out to be illusory.

Although by the mid 1980s most Poles were abstaining from opposition activities, the underground Solidarity still commanded the loyalty of a significant part of the intelligentsia and the workers. But Solidarity no longer held a monopoly on opposition activities as new organizations came into being: pacifists, nationalists, environmental activists, anarchists, and art groups. While some of these collaborated with Solidarity, others considered the union ossified, and pursued more radical goals, or chose different means of political action. Neither the underground Solidarity nor the new opposition milieus had enough power to dismantle the party regime, but together they possessed a potential for mobilizing and directing public protests under favorable conditions. Such an opportunity materialized in 1987–1988, when the government decided to implement harsh economic measures by increasing prices and production levels.

Jaruzelski pursued the contradictory goals of implementing market mechanisms, such as the expansion of private business and opening foreign trade to global markets, and preserving central planning and the power of party apparatus. These economic reforms were to be accompanied by political liberalization—not including, however, the legalization of Solidarity. In November 1987, the government conducted a referendum, asking for society's approval of austerity policies and democratization. Solidarity under-

stood that the success of the referendum would legitimize the regime, and it called for a boycott of the vote. As a result the referendum did not receive the requisite quorum, and the government was forced to admit defeat. Nevertheless, substantial price rises were introduced, leading to the outbreaks of strikes in April and May 1988 and then in August of the same year. These strikes were led by the young and radicalized workers who often had not participated in the old Solidarity of 1980–1981. Walesa and other union leaders joined and took command of the strikes.

Late in August, General Czeslaw Kiszczak, minister of internal affairs, met Walesa and invited Solidarity to roundtable negotiations in return for ending the strikes. The offer was accepted, and preliminary talks, through the mediation of the church, began in September. These meetings were soon suspended because of the opposition of party hard-liners and a new reformist prime minister, Rakowski, who attempted to absorb the opposition into closely controlled perestroika without official recognition of Solidarity as a political partner. The breakthrough came in November, when in a televised debate, Walesa defeated Alfred Miodowicz, chairman of the OPZZ and one of the leading opponents of dialogue with Solidarity. A month later Walesa established the Citizens' Committee, an advisory board that also served as a shadow cabinet and the cadre of candidates for future parliamentary elections. In January 1989, Jaruzelski, Kiszczak, and Prime Minister Rakowski coerced the Central Committee into agreeing to the legalization of Solidarity.

The minimalist approach to negotiations that began in February 1989 was registration of Solidarity in return for the endorsement of the system and acquisition of Western economic aid; the maximal goal was the introduction of limited democracy (Elster 1996, 5, 41). The final agreement, signed on April 5, 1989, provided for the re-legalization of Solidarity; partially free parliamentary elections in which the Solidarity-led opposition was allowed to contest 35 percent of the seats in the Sejm and 100 percent in the Senate; introduction of a presidency; and a number of socio-economic reforms (ibid., 56–57). However, in the June elections of 1989, Solidarity won all freely contested seats in the lower chamber and all but one of the seats in the Senate. The party had no choice but to accept its defeat after Gorbachev made it clear that the Soviets would not intervene in Poland. The new parliament elected Jaruzelski president by a slim majority, so as not to upset the Soviets and to preserve the political equilibrium. Walesa negotiated with the pro-Communist satellite parties to create a Solidarity-led cabinet. On August 24, Tadeusz Mazowiecki became the first non-Communist prime minister in Eastern Europe since the 1940s.

The victory of Solidarity had enormous consequences for Eastern Europe. Along with democratic reforms in Hungary, which in the summer of 1989 opened its border with the West, thus triggering the exodus of East German refugees, the peaceful collapse of the Polish Communist regime sparked the other 1989 revolutions. At the beginning of that year, Poland was the only nation in the region that had the mass, well-organized, and preexisting opposition to challenge and subsequently force the Communists into a dialogue—and that was the result of the Polish Revolution of 1980. Solidarity was an icebreaker. Poland developed a pioneering democratic movement that encompassed the whole of society and forged peaceful resistance to the Communist state. In practical terms, the Polish Roundtable Talks set the precedent for the negotiated abolition of Communism throughout the Soviet Bloc; in Hungary, Czechoslovakia, the German Democratic Republic, and Bulgaria, though it should be noted that Roundtable Talks in those countries aimed at larger changes. Having taken the lead, Poland was a political laboratory testing the limits of pluralistic reforms and, last but not least, the Soviet willingness to permit changes. Conversely, the success of Solidarity greatly enhanced the bargaining position of the opposition elsewhere. Finally, ingredients of Solidarity's approach—such as the emphasis on civil society, the strategy of nonviolent struggle, and grassroots activism—had a major effect on the nations of Eastern Europe and beyond.

After the collapse of Communism, Solidarity underwent political fragmentation and bitter factional struggles. The pluralistic character of the movement, which was its major asset during the struggle against the regime in the 1980s, turned out to be the reason for its demise under democracy. Mazowiecki's grand coalition government had enough prestige and power to introduce necessary reforms, making possible a transformation to a market economy. However, in the face of free elections held in other post-Communist countries, the political contract based on the coexistence with the Communists became anachronistic. Together with members of his closest entourage, Walesa called for the acceleration of political changes and made a bid for the presidency. Following Jaruzelski's decision to step down as president, the Sejm (parliament) scheduled presidential elections for November 1990, and Walesa won. The national, fully democratic elections that took place in October 1991 produced a fragmented parliament in which a large number of post-Solidarity parties competed against each other.

Poland was the first country in the former Soviet Bloc to adopt economic shock therapy and redirect its economy on a Western, liberal model. It was also the first to experience the side effects of the changes: unemployment, cuts in welfare spending, and a growing sense of insecurity among large strata of society. In 1993 post-Solidarity politicians, who had implemented and oversaw the transition to a market economy, paid the price as voters brought the post-Communist Alliance of the Democratic Left, which included many former

Lech Walesa served as the president of Poland from 1990 to 1995. In fighting for workers' rights in Poland, Walesa led the Solidarity movement that for a time unified the democratic desires of the entire nation. (Embassy of Poland)

Communists, to power. Ironically, it was an increasingly radicalized and discontented Solidarity, by then again a trade union, that brought down the government, making possible national elections that were won by former Communists. Two years later, in the presidential elections of 1995, Walesa lost to the leader of the Alliance, Aleksander Kwasniewski. Ironically, the victory of a former Communist over the icon of Solidarity signaled the successful conclusion of transition to democracy. During the 1990s and the first years of the new millennium, most of the Polish political leaders, notwithstanding their political past, contributed to integrate Poland with international democratic institutions: NATO in 1998 and the European Union in 2004. Solidarity continued as a trade union. It served as the builder of the right-center coalition Electoral Action "Solidarity" (AWS), which defeated the Alliance of the Democratic Left in the 1997 national elections. However, four years later, the Alliance of the Democratic Left won again.

PEOPLE AND ORGANIZATIONS

Alliance of the Democratic Left

A post-Communist coalition of leftist political parties that includes many former Communists.

Citizens' Committee

The Citizens' Committee was created as an advisory board to Lech Walesa in December 1989. Members of the committee formed Solidarity's shadow cabinet, cadres of negotiators in the Roundtable Talks, and the bulk of candidates in the 1989 national elections.

Committee for the Defense of Workers (KOR)

This was the opposition group set up by dissident intellectuals in 1976. Known by its Polish abbreviation, KOR, the committee was set up in response to the workers' protests against price rises in June 1976. It offered legal counseling and financial aid to the arrested and fired workers and their families. This initial task soon broadened into the promotion of civil society by monitoring human rights' abuses, engaging in underground publishing, and activating independent trade unions. KOR was the first organization of the democratic opposition in Poland, and it provided political strategy and future cadres for the Solidarity Movement. In 1977, it renamed itself the Committee for Social Self-Defense "KOR" (KSS KOR).

Gierek, Edward (1913–2001)

Edward Gierek was party leader from 1970 until 1980. Between 1923 and 1948, in France and Belgium, he was a member of the Belgian and French Communist parties. Gierek joined the Polish Communist Party in 1946. He was the author of the program of rapid modernization of Poland in the 1970s that, as a result of misguided investment and credit policy, led to the economic crisis and the birth of Solidarity. In 1980 he was replaced as first secretary by Stanislaw Kania and retired. He was expelled from the Communist Party in 1981.

Interfactory Strike Committee (MKS)

MKS was a network of striking factories in August 1980. In September 1980, delegates of interfactory committees set up the Independent Self-Governing Trade Union, "Solidarity."

Jaruzelski, Wojciech (Born 1923)

Wojciech Jaruzelski, a professional soldier and Communist politician, fought in the Soviet-commanded Polish armed forces in World War II. In 1968 he was appointed minister of defense, and from 1981 to 1990, first secretary of the Polish United Workers' Party. Prime minister from 1981 to 1984, he introduced martial law in 1981. He sanctioned the Roundtable Talks and agreed to re-legalize Solidarity in 1989. In 1989–1990, he served as president of Poland. Questioned about the introduction of martial law, Jaruzelski consistently claimed that his main concern was the threat of Soviet military intervention.

Kuron, Jacek (1934–2004)

Jacek Kuron was an opposition activist, democratic politician, and historian. From 1953 to 1964, he was a member of the Communist Party. In the 1960s, however, he became one of the first dissidents. In 1965, Kuron, with Karol Modzelewski, announced the "Open Letter to the Party," criticizing Communist rule from left-wing positions. As a result he was incarcerated, spending nine years in Communist jails. Kuron, as cofounder of KOR and a leading theoretician of the new opposition in the 1970s, was interned and jailed under martial law. He was elected to parliament in 1989 and served as minister of labor in two Solidarity governments. Kuron's contributions to the collapse of Communism in Eastern Europe were on a par with those of Walesa and Vaclav Havel.

Mazowiecki, Tadeusz (Born 1927)

Catholic activist, Solidarity leader, and politician, in the 1950s and 1960s Mazowiecki was the editor of Catholic periodicals. From 1961 to 1971, he was a member of parliament. After 1976, Mazowiecki cooperated with the democratic opposition and in 1980 was Solidarity's intellectual adviser. Interned under martial law. In the 1980s, Mazowiecki was one of the leading Solidarity activists. From 1989 to 2001 he served as a member of parliament and in 1989–1990 was prime minister of Poland. In 1990, Mazowiecki ran against Walesa in the presidential elections.

National Coordinating Commission (KKP)

In 1980–1981, the KKP was Solidarity's supreme body coordinating the union's activities on a national level.

National Trade Union Accord (OPZZ)

The official trade unions set up in 1982 to counterbalance underground Solidarity, OPZZ participated in the Roundtable Talks in 1989.

Pilsudski, Józef (1867–1935)

Józef Pilsudski, politician and soldier, in the 1890s and 1900s was leader of the Polish Socialist Party. In World War I he was commander of the Polish Legions, military units fighting alongside the Central powers against Russia. Pilsudski was one of the founding fathers of independent Poland in 1918, and in 1920 marshal of Poland. He led Polish forces to victory in the 1920 Polish-Soviet War. Organizer of a military coup in 1926, from 1926 to 1935 he was leader of the Polish state.

Polish United Workers' Party (PZPR)

The PZPR, the Polish Communist Party, was created in 1948 after the fusion of the Communist Polish Workers' Party and the Polish Socialist Party. From 1948 to 1989, it was the ruling party in Poland. The PZPR dissolved itself in 1990.

Popieluszko, Jerzy (1947–1984)

Jerzy Popieluszko, Catholic priest and Solidarity supporter, in 1984 was abducted and brutally murdered by a group of security police officers. The crime galvanized Polish society, forcing the Communist regime to try to convict Popieluszko's assassins in 1985.

Temporary Coordinating Commission (TKK)

Created in 1982, the TKK was the main organ of underground Solidarity under martial law.

Walesa, Lech (Born 1943)

A trade union activist and politician, Walesa was leader and first chairman of Solidarity. In 1967, he was employed as an electrician in the Lenin Shipyard in Gdansk. A participant in the 1970 workers' strike in Gdansk, in 1976 Walesa was fired from the Lenin Shipyard for opposition activities. Walesa was active in the Free Trade Unions and a leader of the strike in the Lenin Shipyard in August 1980. From 1980 to 1990, he served as chairman of Solidarity. Under martial law, he was interned. Laureate of the Nobel Peace Prize in 1983, from 1990 to 1995, Walesa was president of Poland.

Wojtyla, Karol (1920–2005)

Karol Wojtyla, a Roman Catholic Church leader, was ordained a priest in 1946. In 1958, he was named auxiliary bishop of Krakow. From 1964 to 1978 he was archbishop of Krakow, and in 1967 he was nominated cardinal. Wojtyla was an advocate for a more open and intellectual Catholicism. A sympathizer with and protector of dissidents, Wojtyla was elected Pope John Paul II in 1978. Wojtyla's election as pope and his visit to Poland in 1979 had an enormous impact on the spiritual and moral renewal of Polish society, paving the way for the birth of Solidarity.

Mikolaj Kunicki

See Also Cinema of Revolution; Democracy, Dictatorship, and Fascism; Documentaries of Revolution; East European Revolutions of 1989; Elites, Intellectuals, and Revolutionary Leadership; Nationalism and Revolution; Russian Revolution of 1991 and the Dissolution of the U.S.S.R.; Student and Youth Movements, Activism and Revolution.

References and Further Readings
Berend, Ivan T. 1996. *Central and Eastern Europe, 1944–1993: Detour from the Periphery to the Periphery.* Cambridge: Cambridge University Press.
Crampton, R. J. 1994. *Eastern Europe in the Twentieth Century.* London: Routledge.
Elster, Jon, ed. 1996. *The Roundtable Talks and the Breakdown of Communism.* Chicago: University of Chicago Press.
Garton Ash, Timothy. 1983. *The Polish Revolution: Solidarity 1980–1982.* London: GrantaBooks.
Kenney, Padraic. 2002. *A Carnival of Revolution: Central Europe 1989.* Princeton, NJ: Princeton University Press.
Korbonski, Stefan. 1981. *The Polish Underground State: A Guide to the Underground, 1939-1945.* New York: Hippocrene Books.
Kubik, Jan. 1994. *The Powers of Symbol against the Symbols of Power: The Rise of Solidarity and the Fall of State Socialism in Poland.* University Park: Pennsylvania University Press.
Laba, Roman. 1991. The *Roots of Solidarity.* Princeton, NJ: Princeton University Press.
Lipski, Jan Józef. 1984. *KOR: A History of the Workers' Defense Committee in Poland.* Berkeley: University of California Press.
Luxmore, Jonathan, and Jolanta Babiuch. 1999. *The Vatican and the Red Flag.* London: Goeffrey Chapman.
Michnik, Adam. 1993. *The Church and the Left.* Translated from Polish by David Ost. Chicago: University of Chicago Press.
Ost, David. 1990. *Solidarity: The Politics of Anti-Politics: Opposition and Reform in Poland since 1968.* Philadelphia: Temple University Press.
Paczkowski, Andrzej. 1998. *Pól wieku dziejów Polski [Half a Century of Poland's History].* Warsaw: PWN.

Stokes, Gale. 1993. *The Walls Came Tumbling Down: The Collapse of Communism in Eastern Europe.* New York: Oxford University Press.

Stola, Dariusz. 2000. *Kampania antysyjonistyczna w Polsce 1967–1968* [*The Anti-Zionist Campaign in Poland 1967–1968*]. Warsaw: ISP PAN.

Touraine, Alain, et al. 1983. *Solidarity: Analysis of a Social Movement: Poland 1980–1981.* Translated from the French by David Denby. Cambridge: Cambridge University Press.

Walesa, Lech. 1987. *A Path of Hope.* London: Collins/Harvill.

Population, Economic Development, and Revolution

The human population has grown dramatically in the past century, from 1.6 billion people in 1900 to more than 6 billion in 2006. Since 1950 alone, 3.5 billion people have been added to the planet, with the vast majority of that increase occurring in low-income countries. Worldwide population growth rates peaked in the late 1960s at around 2 percent a year, but the current rate of 1.2 percent still represents a net addition of 77 million people per year (UN Population Division 2001, 5).

This enormous expansion in human numbers has had important implications for both economic development and the prospects for revolution and rebellion. Revolution and rebellion, in turn, have affected both population levels and economic prospects.

POPULATION GROWTH AND ECONOMIC DEVELOPMENT

The relationship between population growth and economic development is complex and controversial. Over the years, two contending scholarly approaches have emerged with widely divergent positions on the relationship: neo-Malthusianism and neoclassical economics.

Neo-Malthusians work broadly within the intellectual tradition of the Reverend Thomas Malthus, whose famous 1798 treatise, *An Essay on the Principles of Population,* argued that exponential population growth would eventually outstrip the ability of land to provide for human needs. In the contemporary period, neo-Malthusians, such as Paul Ehrlich and Allen Kelley, argue that, under certain conditions, rapid population growth can perpetuate poverty and retard economic growth, especially in low-income countries. According to this view, as the size of the labor force expands faster than the economy can accommodate, wages will decline and un- and under-employment will increase. In rural areas of the developing world, where millions of individuals remain dependent on agriculture for their daily survival and land is often distributed unequally, rapid population growth contributes to the subdivision of agricultural plots and landlessness, forcing individuals to migrate to areas that are less suitable for growing crops or raising livestock. By their nature, marginal lands—including steep slopes, forests, semi-arid regions, and coastal areas—are incapable of supporting dense populations and are prone to environmental degradation. A vicious cycle may ensue whereby the over-exploitation of natural resources driven by poverty and population growth contributes to the degradation of croplands, pastures, forests, water resources, and fisheries that, in turn, worsens poverty. To escape this downward spiral, many individuals have left rural areas altogether and moved to cities in search of employment, partially explaining the explosive rates of urbanization experienced throughout the developing world in recent decades. However, neo-Malthusians emphasize that the living conditions for new city residents are often little better than those they left behind, because migrants frequently cluster in urban slums with little access to adequate housing, education, health care, sanitation, or other basic services.

Beyond the issue of poverty, neo-Malthusians argue that rapid population growth can undermine the overall prospects for economic development. As populations swell, it can lower the ratio of capital to labor (an effect called "capital shallowing"), undermining per capita productivity and making countries less competitive. Rapid population growth can also contribute to higher dependency ratios and make it more difficult for families to educate and pass on capital to children. Higher dependency ratios also encourage families to shift more of their financial resources toward consumption. In the aggregate, this can erode domestic savings, reduce a country's ability to finance needed investments, and increase reliance on foreign loans. Finally, the environmental degradation exacerbated by population growth may also jeopardize economic development by eroding the resource base upon which many low-income countries ultimately depend.

Scholars working within the tradition of neoclassical economics, such as Ester Boserup and Julian Simon, have long criticized neo-Malthusian accounts as overly pessimistic. In terms of the connection between population growth, environmental degradation, and poverty, neoclassical economists argue that markets, governments, and other social institutions usually adjust in ways that head off the most significant problems. Indeed, demand-induced increases in the price of critical natural resources brought about by population expansion are argued to produce incentives for individuals, firms, and governments to develop less expensive substitutes, more efficient means of extraction, and methods of conservation. More generally, neoclassical economists claim that population growth generates many positive economic effects, including economies of scale; larger, younger, and more dynamic labor forces; and induced innovation and technological change—all of which tends to balance out the negative effects of capital shallowing, higher dependency ratios, and environmental degradation. Neoclassical economists also argue that government policies are ultimately much more important than population growth in determining prospects for economic development.

After centuries of debate, it has become clear that population growth is not universally detrimental to the economy. Indeed, a major challenge to the economic vitality of industrialized countries in the contemporary period is an emerging *shortage* of young workers stemming from low fertility rates, aging, and restrictive immigration policies. It is also clear that the effects of markets and institutions can easily trump the effects of population growth. Nevertheless, in low-income countries with sluggish economies, scarce or costly natural resources, poorly defined property rights, or otherwise dysfunctional markets, and with government policies biased against labor (typically the most abundant factor of production), rapid population growth can undermine economic productivity and create substantial challenges to development. Moreover, while economic development is certainly possible in the context of rapid population growth, the prospects for economic advancement hinge decisively on the initial level of development and the adoption of appropriate economic strategies. Unfortunately, governments in many low-income countries have historically adopted important substitution strategies and other policies that have encouraged capital-intensive industries that underutilize abundant supplies of labor. Many governments have also adopted policies—such as high taxes on farm inputs and outputs—that are ill suited for labor-intensive agricultural sectors, and policies have often overemphasized urban areas at the expense of rural development. Consequently, government strategies have often been incompatible with the promotion of economic development in the context of rapid population growth; given these policies, population growth has often had a negative effect.

There appears to be growing empirical support for this conclusion. For decades, studies failed to find a strong correlation between population growth and economic output. However, a recent study by Allen Kelley and Robert Schmidt (2001) that disaggregates population growth into several components (that is, population size and density, as well as changes in mortality and fertility, labor force size, and youth dependency ratios) strongly suggests that the net effect of rapid population growth on economic progress in low-income countries has been negative, at least since the 1980s. Other studies suggest that rapid reductions in fertility levels in some low- and middle-income countries in recent decades have created a "demographic bonus" that has accelerated economic development. In countries in which fertility rates have fallen toward the replacement level (approximately two children per woman), the number of working-age adults per child has increased. This has raised household savings, helped families to invest more in each child, increased the number of taxable adults per dependent, and reduced burdens on public education and other expensive government services—all factors that encourage development.

IMPLICATIONS FOR REVOLUTION AND REBELLION

Of all the possible causes of revolution and rebellion, none have received more attention than economic ones. Indeed, among the first modern theorists of revolution, Karl Marx placed the contradictions and conflicts produced by capitalist development at the center of his account of inevitable upheaval. In recent decades, scholars of revolution and rebellion have pointed to economic grievances and state failure brought about by fiscal crises and economic collapse as fundamental drivers of turmoil. To the extent that population growth contributes to underdevelopment and economic distress, therefore, demographic pressures are a potentially important contributor to political instability.

One group of scholars argues that population growth and related economic stresses are linked to revolution and rebellion via the logic of relative deprivation. This argument builds on Ted Gurr's classic work on rebellion, *Why Men Rebel* (1970). It starts from the premise that individual grievances will mount as living standards and social status fall below peoples' expectations. If these grievances are sufficiently widespread, frustration can turn to aggression and revolt, targeted at those seen as responsible for their plight. Demographic changes such as rapid urbanization and large youth cohorts (or "youth bulges" in the population age structure), for example, have often been associated with periods of rising grievances among slum residents and unemployed youth, resulting in riots and support for insurgent groups. Societies that have large proportions of teenagers and young adults in their populations, usually the result of previous rapid population increase, are more prone to the development of rebellions or revolutionary movements, because, among other things, young people typically are not yet bound by the responsibilities of supporting families and are often more receptive to new concepts, including revolutionary ideas.

Some social scientists have pointed to the ways in which demographic and environmental pressures interact to produce relative deprivation and conflict. Norman Myers (1993), for example, has argued that rapid population growth and environmental degradation in many developing countries have worsened poverty, exacerbated competition for jobs, and contributed to scarcities of vital natural resources, especially land, encouraging individuals to take up arms against their neighbors and governments.

Others, however, contend that relative deprivation alone is a poor predictor of upheaval. The world's poor are not constantly engaged in organized violence, strongly suggesting that poverty and a sense of injustice are not sufficient to lead people to rebel against their governments or fight with each other. Some note that the relative deprivation claim fails to acknowledge that individuals contemplating organized violence face significant collective action problems. At the individual level, the risks to one's life and property inherent in intergroup or anti-state violence generate high potential costs, and the choice to forgo wages and peaceful exchange with others creates large opportunity costs. In terms of benefits, each individual's contribution, in and of itself, has very little impact on the prospects for success, and the benefits to be accrued from joining a violent social movement are frequently "public," or collective, in nature (that is, they are nonrival and nonexcludable). This can create powerful incentives for individuals to "free-ride" on the efforts of others that, in the aggregate, work against the formation of organized conflict groups. Moreover, although the relative deprivation argument seeks to explain a political outcome, it is curiously apolitical. In particular, it fails to recognize that the prospects for violence are substantially shaped and shoved by the strength of the state. Because strong, capable, and cohesive states are typically able to provide relief to aggrieved individuals, co-opt opposition leaders, and use force to deter or repress violence before it escalates, grievances alone rarely lead to revolutions and rebellions.

Building on this last claim, several scholars analyzing the linkages among population growth, economic development, and violent political instability have followed Theda Skocpol's (1979) famous invitation to "bring the state back in." In particular, studies by Jack Goldstone (1991), Thomas Homer-Dixon (1999), and Colin Kahl (2006) argue that revolutions, rebellions, and other forms of civil strife are most likely when the economic strains produced by population growth simultaneously increase grievances among mass and elite groups *and* cripple state institutions, thereby expanding the "political space" for violence to occur. These authors have linked demographic change to state weakness in a number of ways. Rapid population growth may produce substantial fiscal strains on governments by increasing demands from suffering mass and elite groups for costly investments and corrective measures. Population growth and related natural resource scarcities can also undermine crucial sectors of the economy and reduce revenue flows to the state. Reduction in state revenue, in turn, may result in the deterioration of a government's coercive capacity if it experiences difficulty in paying, feeding, or arming its soldiers. Finally, population pressures have sometimes produced competition among elites for shrinking government revenue, civil service positions, and the like, undermining regime cohesion and legitimacy.

The connection between demographic variables and economic conditions, on the one hand, and revolution and rebellion, on the other, has received substantial empirical support. Goldstone's important study of early modern revolutions (1991) suggests a strong correlation and causal relationship between rapid population expansion and revolutions in England, France, China, and elsewhere. A series of cases by Homer-Dixon (1999) and Kahl (forthcoming) have demonstrated that the synergy of rapid population growth, environmental stress, economic troubles, and state crises has contributed to contemporary bloodshed in Chiapas (Mexico), Israel's occupied territories, the Philippines, Kenya, Rwanda, and many other low-income countries.

Furthermore, a growing body of cross-national statistical analyses has reinforced these case study findings. In one well-known report, Goldstone, Gurr, Barbara Harff, and other members of the State Failure Task Force (2000), a group of academics commissioned by the U.S. government to analyze the origins of rebellion, ethnic war, genocide, and adverse regime change, found that population size, population density, and infant mortality were all significantly correlated with episodes of violence. Another study, by Richard Cincotta, Robert Engleman, and Daniele Anastasion (2003), suggests that countries at earlier stages of the "demographic transition" (when birth rates and death rates are both high), as well as those with large numbers of young adults and rapid rates of urbanization, have been much more prone to violence since the 1970s.

THE EFFECTS OF REVOLUTION AND REBELLION ON POPULATION GROWTH AND ECONOMIC DEVELOPMENT

It is important to recognize that the causal connections among population growth, economic development, and revolution and rebellion run in both directions. That is, violent conflict within countries can have a substantial effect on population levels and on the prospects for economic development. The demographic implications of revolution and rebellion can be substantial. Most obviously, revolutions and rebellions have adversely affected mortality rates by producing large numbers of casualties. Indeed, tens of millions have died as a direct result of civil wars since 1945. Internal strife has also been a major contributor to starvation and disease spread, including the HIV/AIDS pandemic and malaria, leading to millions of additional deaths, especially in sub-Saharan Africa.

Societal upheavals can also affect fertility. Historically, revolutionary regimes have often taken dramatic steps to restructure every aspect of social life, affecting population levels by altering reproductive choices. Revolutionary regimes in Romania and Iran, for example, encouraged rapid increases in fertility by restricting access to birth control. In China, by contrast, the regime imposed a draconian "one child" policy, causing the number of births per couple to decline rapidly in the 1980s. Altered fertility levels have also been the unintentional by-product of revolutionary change. The turmoil and uncertainty stemming from the collapse of the Soviet Union in 1991, for example, produced a drop in both marriage and birth rates and a dramatic increase in death rates, especially for men, resulting from factors such as a significant decline in medical services and a surge in health problems, including those related to high levels of alcoholism. Russia's 1992 population of 148.7 million people declined by about 5 million by 2002, and in that latter year its death rate exceeded its birth rate by approximately 70 percent (Powell 2002, 344).

Finally, revolutionary violence and rebellions have been shown to dramatically affect a country's economic prospects. A recent report by Paul Collier and his associates at the World Bank (2003), for example, provides compelling evidence that civil wars devastate essential infrastructure, erode social trust, encourage human and capital flight, and divert precious financial resources toward military spending. Furthermore, Collier et al. note that the negative economic consequences rarely stay contained within the afflicted country. Episodes of violent turmoil often undermine trade, threaten the reputation of entire regions in the eyes of investors, and produce large numbers of refugees that spill across borders, producing significant socioeconomic and health problems in neighboring countries.

In short, an accumulating set of historical, political, and social analyses indicate that revolutions and rebellions are partly the products of population and economic factors, and that revolutions or post-conflict policies often have significant effects on population characteristics and economic development.

Colin H. Kahl

See Also Chinese Revolution; Ethnic and Racial Conflict; French Revolution; Inequality, Class, and Revolution; Russian Revolution of 1991 and the Dissolution of the U.S.S.R.; Theories of Revolution

References and Further Reading

Boserup, Ester. 1965. *The Conditions of Agricultural Growth.* Chicago: Aldine.

Cincotta, Richard P., Robert Engleman, and Daniele Anastasion. 2003. *The Security Demographic: Population and Civil Conflict after the Cold War.* Washington, DC: Population Action International.

Collier, Paul, et al. 2003. *Breaking the Conflict Trap: Civil War and Development Policy.* Washington, DC: World Bank and Oxford University Press.

Ehrlich, Paul R., and Anne H. Ehrlich. 1990. *The Population Explosion.* New York: Touchstone/ Simon and Schuster.

Goldstone, Jack A. 1991. *Revolution and Rebellion in the Early Modern World.* Berkeley: University of California Press.

Goldstone, Jack A., et al. 2000. *State Failure Task Force Report: Phase III Findings.* McLean, VA: Science Applications International.

Gurr, Ted Robert. 1970. *Why Men Rebel.* Princeton, NJ: Princeton University Press.

Homer-Dixon, Thomas F. 1999. *Environment, Scarcity, and Violence.* Princeton, NJ: Princeton University Press.

Kahl, Colin. 2006. *States, Scarcity, and Civil Strife in the Developing World.* Princeton, NJ: Princeton University Press.

Kelley, Allen C., and Robert M. Schmidt. 2001. "Economic and Demographic Change: A Synthesis of Models, Findings, and Perspectives." Pp. 67–105 in *Population Matters: Demographic Change, Economic Growth, and Poverty in Developing Countries,* edited by Nancy Birdsall, Allen C. Kelley, and Steven W. Sinding. Oxford: Oxford University Press.

Malthus, Thomas. 1985 [1798]. *An Essay on the Principles of Population.* New York: Penguin.

Myers, Norman. 1993. *Ultimate Security: The Environmental Basis of Political Stability.* New York: W. W. Norton.

Powell, David E. 2002. "Death as a Way of Life: Russia's Demographic Decline," *Current History, 101* (October): 344–348.

Simon, Julian L. 1981. *The Ultimate Resource.* Princeton, NJ: Princeton University Press.

Skocpol, Theda. 1979. *States and Social Revolutions.* Cambridge: Cambridge University Press.

UN Population Division. 2001. *Population, Environment, and Development: The Concise Report.* New York: UNPD.

Index

Editor Biography

James V. DeFronzo of the Sociology Department at the University of Connecticut has taught over 7,000 students in his revolutions course and over 9,000 students in his criminology course and is preparing the third edition of his textbook on revolutions, *Revolutions and Revolutionary Movements.* He has written dozens of research articles published in various academic journals dealing with topics such as criminology, social policy related to crime, demography, gender issues, teaching, and social stratification. Born in New Britain, Connecticut, he received a B.A. in Sociology from Fairfield University, Connecticut, and attended graduate school at Indiana University on a federal quantitative methodology fellowship and later on a research assistantship. He taught for three years in the Sociology Department at Indiana University-Purdue University at Fort Wayne, Indiana, and also taught as an adjunct instructor at Indiana University in Bloomington. He completed his Ph. D. the year after he began teaching at the University of Connecticut at Storrs. His teaching experience at Indiana University or the University of Connecticut includes Introductory Sociology, Social Problems, Social Psychology, Social Conflict, Criminology, Methods of Social Research, Social Stratification, and Revolutionary Movements Around the World. He is a member of the American Sociological Association and the American Society of Criminology. His writing and research interests include social movements, criminology, general sociology, social problems and political and historical sociology and developing textbooks for several of these areas.